BOOMERS

How We Changed The World

Vol.1 1946-1980

A Generational Biography:
Baby Boomers; Those Born From 1946-1964

Richard Jordan

Alford Press, LLC

Boomers: How We Changed The World. Vol.1 1946-1980.
A Generational Biography: Baby Boomers; Those Born From 1946-1964.

Copyright © 2010 by R. A. Jordan
ISBN-13: 978-0-615-34032-6

Alford Press, LLC

First Edition: 2010

The Alford Press name and logo are trademarks.
For information see:
Boomers: How We Changed The World, at AlfordPress.com
Any suggestions, ideas, corrections, things you would like to see added or removed can also be addressed at AlfordPress.com

Library of Congress Cataloging–in–Publication data is on file.
Jordan, Richard 1948-

Boomers: How We Changed The World Vol.1 1946-1980/ Richard Jordan   1st ed.
A Generational Biography: Baby Boomers; Those Born From 1946-1964.
Warning and Disclaimer:
Every effort has been made to make this book as accurate as possible, but no warranty or fitness is implied. The information provided is just one person's opinion. The information is provided on an "as is" basis.

Cover by *Oikey1*

Printed in the United States of America
Worldwide Distribution

To Judith, my wife, whose love and support

make it all possible and worthwhile.

Introduction

This book is about YOU, the Boomers. The years from 1946 through 1980 Volume 1, and 1981 through 2010 Volume 2. You lived it. Sometimes you enjoyed it and sometimes you just got through it, but does anyone really understand what we went through?

Did you ever try to talk to your grandchildren about the **Vietnam War**? Do they understand that while the **"Easy Bake Oven"** was the hottest toy for the 1963 Christmas season, **31 million people were starving to death in China**?

Annual Average Domestic Crude Oil Price was $2.91 a barrel.

Gallon Gasoline: 30 cents

1 oz Gold: $35.25

1oz of Silver: $1.29

Minimum Wage: $1.18/ hr

Average Cost of a New Home: $19,300

Inflation Rate: 1.24%

GDP was only: $468.71 Billions of Dollars

"The Great Leap Forward" was responsible for 31 million to 33 million deaths in China due to starvation and famine which remained mostly unknown to the western world until 1980.

The **University of Alabama** desegregated after Gov. George Wallace stepped aside when confronted by **federally deployed National Guard troops** on June 11.

Civil rights leader Medgar Evers is assassinated, June 12.

Martin Luther King's "I Have A Dream" speech, August 28.

South Vietnam President Ngo Dinh Diem was assassinated, November 2.

President John F. Kennedy is assassinated in Dallas, Texas, November 22.

Jack Ruby Shoots Lee Harvey Oswald, November 24, on Live TV.

This is the summer of 1963. Did you even remember that all of this was going on while you were in front of the TV watching **"Petticoat Junction"** or **"The Fugitive"** which both premiered?

There is no way to explain all of this to your grandchildren and sometimes even your children just do not understand what the world was like for Boomers growing up. Give them a copy of this book and they will get a small glimpse into your world. This is in no way an attempt to document even 50% of what we lived through. It is more like looking at a photo album of the past. There are many quick moments of time captured that will jog your memory and give you a place to begin more research if you so choose. And that is all this is, just like looking through a photo album of your past.

If you look through the data it is obvious how the citizens of the United States of America fought for honor, decency, high moral values and against all of the warnings we started to slide ever so slowly down that path to where we are today. What so many of us do not remember is how long and hard we fought.

This book will mean something different to every person who reads it because we are all different with a common ground. Our intention is to take you back in time and allow you to feel exactly what it was like. This book should make you laugh and cry, feel anger and remorse. It should pierce your heart and soul. The language has not been sanitized, it is as it was. Deal with it.

Disclaimer: Yup, Boomers need all the help we can get. Although the author has done his best to insure accuracy of the data, **this book makes no claim for accuracy.** It is to be used as a beginning point to jar your memory and help explain, **"Who We Are".** So before you go and "bet-the-farm" based on information found in this book you are warned to thoroughly check the information as everything in this book should be considered opinion. All information in this book can be referenced online or at your local library.

If we left out something we apologize. There was no way everything could be included so this is a starting point for both you and your family. It has been an incredible journey, and **"We're Not Done Yet!"**

Richard Jordan and friends, January 2010

BOOMERS

Just what kind of a world did we inherit?

1946

The baby boom begins: 1946-1964.

Cost of the Average House: $4,800	
Median Family Income: $2,170	**Minimum Wage:** 40 cents/ hr **Average Hourly Wage:** $1.00
Gallon of Milk: 70 cents	**Gallon Gasoline:** 21 cents
New Car: **Chevrolet Fleetmaster:** $1,280 **Willys Station Wagon:** $1,560	**Pepsi:** 24 cents/six 12 oz bottles **Loaf of Bread:** 10 cents **First-class Stamp:** 3 cents

Unemployment Rate: 3.9% Nine million people have been transferred from the military into civilian life. This raises the rate from 1.9 to 3.9%. The **Employment rate** reaches levels not seen again until Carter and Reagan.

Only 9 cents buying power in 1946 = **$1.00 in 2008.**
In 1946 what cost our parents 9 cents to purchase
now costs us $1.00 in 2008. Where did the $0.91 go?

Movies: "It's a Wonderful Life," "The Best Years of Our Lives," "My Darling Clementine," "The Blue Dahlia," "Great Expectations," "Henry V," "Duel in the Sun," "The Big Sleep," "Notorious," "The Postman Always Rings Twice," "The Razor's Edge," "The Yearling." "Boom in the Moon" starring Buster Keaton. "A Night in Casablanca" with the Marx Brothers. "Song of the South" by Walt Disney. "The Time of Their Lives", starring Bud Abbott and Lou Costello. "Chick Carter, Detective," "King of the

Forest Rangers," "The Phantom Rider," "Daughter of Don Q."

Broadway: "Annie Get Your Gun," "Show Boat," "Call Me Mister."

TV: "Hourglass" the first hour-long musical variety show, airs. "Faraway Hills" becomes the first TV soap opera. The first church service is telecast, "Grace Episcopal Church," in New York. "Gillette Cavalcade of Sports." "Muffin the Mule," "Play the Game," "Let's Rhumba," "Tom and Jerry," "The Looney Tunes Show."

Music: Frank Sinatra, "Five Minutes More." Nat King Cole, "Sentimental reasons." Vaughn Monroe, "Let it Snow! Let it Snow! Let it Snow!" Perry Como, "Prisoner of Love." Jo Stafford, "Fools Rush In." Bing Crosby and The Jesters, "Sioux City Sue." Spike Jones, "Hawaiian War Chant." Perry Como, "Winter Wonderland." Bob Wills, "New Spanish Two step." Merle Travis, "Divorce Me C.O.D." Lionel Hampton, "Hey-Ba-Ba-Re-Bop."

Deaths: W.C. Fields, Gertrude Stein, H.G. Wells. In April 1945, Franklin Delano Roosevelt had been President of the United States for a little over a dozen years. He led the nation through the Great Depression and World War II, but the journey had taken a physical toll. Franklin Roosevelt died on April 12 and Vice President Harry S. Truman became President.

President: Harry S. Truman (D) Baptist; vetoes 250/ 12 overrides

Vice President: None
(From April 12, 1945 the vice presidency remained vacant until 1949)

House: D-242; R-191

Senate: 79th Congress (1945-1947) Majority Party: Democrat (57 seats) Minority Party: Republican (38 seats) Other Parties: 1 Progressive Total Seats: 96.

Federal Debt: $269.42 billion or 121 % of the GDP

Consumer Price Index CPI-U (1982 Base of 100): 46.00

GDP: $222.3 billion	**Inflation Rate:** 8.43%

Dow Jones: 212.50 (May 29)/ 171.47 (Oct.-01)

Prime Rate: 1.75%

Average Home Mortgage Rate: 4.75%

1 oz Gold: $38.25	**1oz of Silver:** $0.92

President Franklin Roosevelt ended the right of all American citizens to surrender paper dollars for gold and to own gold bullion in 1933. Americans were forced to surrender their gold to the government at a set price or face fines and jail.

Average Monthly S.S. Benefits Paid: $26 / month
The first S.S. payment: Ernest Ackerman got a payment for 17 cents in January 1937. This was a one-time, lump-sum pay-out, which was the only form of benefits paid during the start-up period
January 1937-December 1939.

Federal Debt: $269,422,099,173.26

Federal Deficit: $15.9 billion dollars

Defense Spending: $53.33 billion	**Interest Spending:** $3.87 billion
Health Care Spending: $320 million	**Pensions Spending:** $590 million
Welfare Spending: $650 million	**Education Spending:** $500 million
Transportation Spending: $1.28 billion	**Misc. Other Spending:** $4.19 billion
Protection Spending: $70 million	**Total Government Spending:** $66.53 billion

% of GDP that goes towards just the interest payment: 1.7%

U.S. Population: 141,389,000	**World Population:** 3,276,816,764
U.S. Birth Rate: 3,411,000	**U.S. Abortions:** 819

U.S. Homicide Rate: 6.4 / 100,000 population

Annual Average Domestic Crude Oil Prices:
$1.63 / barrel, $17.66 (2007 adjusted)

1946

Oil:

1938 – Oil is discovered in **Kuwait** by British Petroleum (BP).

1938 – **Mexico** expropriates foreign-owned shares in the Oil Industry when the state-run co. **PEMEX** takes over.

February 14, 1945 – **President Roosevelt** and **King Abdul Aziz** of the Kingdom of Saudi Arabia make an agreement of military protection in exchange for oil.

1945 – **The German and Japanese military machines run out of oil.** Germany and Japan are defeated and their societies reach near collapse, World War II ends. The war involved the mobilization of over **100 million military personnel,** making it the most widespread war in history. Over sixty million people were killed and over half were civilians, making it the deadliest conflict in human history.

1930's – Libya. Geologists did not think Libya had worthwhile oil deposits and no oil discoveries were made under the Italian administration.

1930-1946 – Saudi Arabia. Beginning in the 1930s, **ARAMCO,** including **Standard Oil of California,** and other firms, discovered huge quantities of petroleum. Saudi Arabia has about one third of the world reserves which is the world's single largest repository of petroleum. Most of the oil is close to the surface making production inexpensive. They also have the world's largest developed reserve pumping capacity which allows them to control prices by adjusting the supply with very little effort. A world shortage in oil is countered by simply pumping more oil.

The discovery of oil transformed the kingdom and gave it, and the entire Gulf Region extraordinary strategic importance. The Saud family rule as absolute monarchs, oil revenues contribute to their personal fortunes and have never helped to develop the standard of living of the general population. Poor management and a high birthrate have left Saudi Arabia a relatively poor country. About 67% of adult males and 56% of females are literate. Infant mortality is approximately 49 per thousand and the annual per capita income is close to $7,100 in 2001.

Abbreviation for Crude Barrels (BBL). In the early 1860's, when oil production began, there was no standard container for oil, so oil and petroleum products were stored and transported in barrels of all different shapes and sizes (beer barrels, fish barrels, molasses barrels, turpentine barrels, etc.). By the early 1870's, the 42-gallon barrel had been adopted as the standard for oil trade. This was 2 gallons per barrel more than the 40-gallon standard used by many other industries at the time. The extra 2 gallons was to allow for loss and leaking during transport as most barrels were made of wood. Standard Oil began manufacturing 42-gallon barrels that were blue to be used for transporting petroleum. **The use of a blue barrel, abbreviated "bbl," guaranteed a buyer that this was a 42-gallon barrel**.

Major News:

February 1945 – Yalta Conference. Winston Churchill declares **"an iron curtain"** has descended across Europe and this is considered by many to be the symbolic beginning of the **Cold War.**

April 1945 – The Allies capture Berlin in April and achieve victory in Europe.

August 6, 1945 – The **United States** first uses an **atomic bomb** in war. **"Little Boy,"** a 4 ½ ton uranium bomb, was dropped on Hiroshima August 6, 1945 from a B-29 bomber named the **Enola Gay.** The bomber's primary target was the **city of Hiroshima** which had a civilian population of almost 300,000 and was an important military center, containing about 43,000 soldiers. At approximately 8:15 a.m. the bomb was dropped and within seconds, 66,000 people were killed and 69,000 injured by a 10-kiloton atomic explosion. This was the equivalent explosive power to what 2,000 B-29s can carry on a single mission.

The area of total vaporization from the atomic bomb blast measured one half mile in diameter with total destruction one mile in diameter, and severe blast damage as much as two miles in diameter. Within a diameter of two and a half miles, everything flammable burned. **President Truman** warned that if **Japan** still refused to surrender unconditionally, as demanded by the **Potsdam Declaration** of July 26, the United States would attack additional targets with equally devastating results. Two days later, on August 8, the **Soviet Union** declared war on Japan and attacked Japanese forces in

Manchuria, ending American hopes that the war would end before Russian entry into the Pacific theater.

August 9, 1945 – The plutonium bomb, nicknamed **"Fat Man,"** could not be dropped at its primary target of **Kokura, Japan,** which contained a massive collection of war industries adjacent to the city. So many things went wrong that the aircraft, with an **armed atomic bomb** and only enough fuel to return to its secondary airfield, flew to its secondary target, the city of **Nagasaki.** At 11:02 a.m., at an altitude of 1,650 feet, Fat Man **exploded** over Nagasaki. The explosion affected a 43 square mile area and the yield of the explosion was later estimated at 21 kilotons. This is 40 percent greater than that of the **Hiroshima bomb.** It has been estimated that 40,000 people died initially, with 60,000 more injured. Over sixty million people were killed during WWII; this bomb effectively ends the war.

August 8, 1945 – Russia Declares War on Japan.

August 14, 1945 – Japan surrenders and World War II ends.

1946 – Atomic Weapons. The first of 23 nuclear explosions by the United States is detonated in the area of the Bikini atoll.

January 1, 1946 – First Boomers. At one minute after midnight Kathleen Casey Wilkins is born, the first of nearly 80 million baby boomers, beginning a generation that results in unprecedented school population growth and massive social change. **They will change the world as we know it for the next 100 years.**

January 1946 – Lucky Luciano is pardoned, released from jail, and deported to Sicily by New York Governor **Thomas Dewey.** This is part of an arrangement for Luciano in return for providing intelligence during World War II and leads to a long term Mafia, U.S. government relationship.

January 24, 1946 – The first meeting of the **United Nations General Assembly** occurs after its founding on October 24, 1945, by fifty-one nations, including the Security Council nations of China, France, the Soviet Union, the United Kingdom, and the United States. These actions lead to the disbanding of the League of Nations on April 18, when its mission is transferred to the U.N.

April 1, 1946 – Four hundred thousand mine workers go on strike, with other industries following their lead.

July, 1946 – A conference is held by the **National Crime Syndicate in Atlantic City, New Jersey.**

July 4, 1946 – The island nation of the **Philippines** is given its independence by the **United States.** This ends four hundred and twenty-five years of dominance by the west. **Spain** ruled the Philippines for 333 years. In 1898, during the Spanish-American war, a German squadron arrived in Manila and declared that if the United States did not seize the Philippines as a colonial possession, **Germany** would. The United States defined its territorial mission as one of tutelage, preparing the Philippines for eventual independence and stayed.

December 22, 1946 – A conference held in **Havana, Cuba,** is attended by syndicate leaders including **Meyer Lansky** and **Lucky Luciano.** The rivalry between Luciano and **Vito Genovese** is discussed, as well as discussions on the matter of **Benjamin Siegel,** following the losses of the Las Vegas casino **The Flamingo.**

Civil Rights Movement:

August 1945 – Ebony magazine's first issue comes off the press.

February 26, 1946 – Columbia, Tennessee Race Riot. Like other outbreaks of violence in the South in the immediate postwar era, the incident involves military veterans who are unwilling to accept prevailing racial norms upon returning to their hometowns.

1946 – The Women's Political Council, an organization for black women and later the initiator of the Montgomery bus boycott in 1955, is founded by Mary Fair Burks after Montgomery, Alabama's **League of Women Voters** refuses to accept black members. Members included Mary Fair Burks, Jo Ann Robinson, Irene West, and Uretta Adair. The **WPC** was the first group to officially call for a boycott of the bus system during the Montgomery Bus Boycott.

July 4, 1944-April 1, 1946 – On the morning of July 4, 1944, **Primus E. King,** an African American duly registered to vote in Georgia, tried to cast a ballot at the Muscogee County Courthouse in Columbus in the Democratic Party's primary election. Shortly after entering the courthouse, King was roughly turned away by a police officer who escorted him back out to the street. The U. S. Supreme Court, in the case of Primus King vs. State of Georgia, declares the "white primary" to be unconstitutional. This removed a significant legal barrier to black voting in the state. Primus King's almost two-year-long struggle against the white primary, paid for by more than $10,000 dollars raised by the Columbus chapter of the National Association of Colored People **(NAACP),** finally eliminated the legal barriers that had stood in the way of black Georgians' right to cast ballots in state and local elections.

I walked on up there to the lawyer's office and the lawyer said to me: "Primus, do you really want to sue the Democratic Primary Party? Do you know what you're doing?" I told him, yes sir, I know."

"I don't know why, but I started crying. The Judge asked me if I wanted the right to vote or the $5,000. **I told him I wanted the right to vote for me and my people."**

1944-1946 – Irene Morgan vs. Commonwealth of Virginia, the **Supreme Court bans segregation** in interstate bus travel. In 1944, the 27-year-old Baltimore-born African-American was arrested and jailed in Virginia **for refusing to give up her seat on an interstate Greyhound bus** to a white person. In a 1946 landmark decision, the Supreme Court rules 7–1 on June 3 that a Virginia law requiring segregated seating on interstate buses is an unconstitutional burden on interstate commerce.

August 6, 1946 – **The Atlanta Constitution** publishes a letter to the editor from 17 year old **Martin Luther King, Jr.** stating that black people "are entitled to the basic rights and opportunities of American citizens." In September he begins his junior year at Morehouse; his courses include Shakespeare, the Bible, American Literature,

Intermediate French, Contemporary Social Trends, Social Anthropology, and a seminar in Sociology.

August 1946 – Elmore vs. Rice. South Carolina. George Elmore tries to vote in the August Democratic primary, is refused, and becomes plaintiff in a suit filed by the **NAACP.** The next year he wins his case against the all-white primary. His action ended one of the most egregious charades, the transformation of primaries into "private clubs," devised by Southern politicians to deny blacks the right to vote that had been guaranteed to them decades earlier. What compelled Elmore, a Columbia businessman who owned a five-and-dime, liquor stores and moonlighted as a taxi driver and photographer, to risk his livelihood and challenge a system that had elected every Governor, State House representative and congressman since 1900 remains unclear.

December 5, 1946 – In response to a wave of violence against **African-Americans** in the South, **President Truman** appoints a presidential committee on civil rights on December 5.

1946 – The Civil Rights Section of the Justice Department gains its **first successful prosecution against a lyncher**. Florida constable Tom Crews is sentenced to a $1,000 fine and one year in prison for civil rights violations in the killing of an African-American farm worker.

1946 – Moore's Ford Bridge Murders. A mob of white men shoot and kill two young African-American couples near Moore's Ford Bridge in Walton County, Georgia, sixty miles east of Atlanta. This **lynching of the four young sharecroppers**, one a World War II veteran, shocks the nation and is a key factor in President Harry Truman's making civil rights a priority. Georgia Governor Ellis Arnall offered a reward of $10,000 for information. After the FBI interviewed nearly 3,000 people in their six-month investigation, 100 subpoenas were issued. Very little physical evidence was found. The investigation received little cooperation, no one confessed, no one was indicted for the crime, and the FBI was unable to prosecute. It was the **last mass lynching.**

The Moore's Ford Bridge case was reopened in 1992 when a witness, Clinton

Adams, testified to the FBI on events he had seen as a 10-year-old child. This was given major coverage by the *Atlanta Constitution,* and five years later, by other newspapers.

In 1997, a biracial **Moore's Ford Bridge Memorial Committee** was formed to recognize these deaths and work for racial reconciliation. Among other activities, they restored cemeteries where victims were buried, had tombstones erected, and have established education scholarships in memory of the people who died.

In 2001 then-Governor Roy Barnes reopened the investigation with the Georgia Bureau of Investigation. In June 2008, as part of the continuing investigation, the Georgia Bureau of Investigation dug up a back yard at a home in Walton County, Georgia near the Gratis community and collected material they believed related to the infamous racial crime. The murders are still unsolved.

Women's Movement:

1945 – Charity Edna Adams completes her tour of service in Europe after winning the highest rank in the army of any African-American woman, Lt. Colonel, and serving as a Battalion Commander in the European Theater of Operations. Nearly fifty years later, after a lifetime of public service in voluntary and charitable organizations, she is named by the Smithsonian as one of the **top 100 women** in Black History.

July 7, 1946 – Mother Maria Frances Cabrini (1850-1917) is canonized by **Pope Pius XII.** She is the first U.S. citizen to become a saint.

Popular Culture:

1946 – The U.S. Department of Agriculture launched its **Hemp for Victory program**, encouraging farmers to plant hemp by giving out seeds and granting draft deferments to those who would stay home and grow hemp. By 1943 American farmers registered in the program harvested 375,000 acres of hemp. Typically, Hemp contains below 0.3% THC, while **Cannabis** grown for **marijuana** can contain anywhere from 6 or 7% to 20% or even more.

November 1945 – Slinky. With a $500 loan, Richard James designed a coiling machine and produced four hundred units of the Slinky in November 1945. Richard and Betty James, through an arrangement with **Gimbels Department Store** in Philadelphia, were granted permission to set up an inclined plane in the toy department and demonstrate the spring's battery-less "walking" abilities. The toy was a hit, and the first 400 units were sold within 90 minutes. Over 300,000,000 Slinkys have been sold.

1943 – The Motion Picture Association of America withdraws its seal of approval for **Howard Hughes's movie "The Outlaw"** after he refuses to submit film ads to the MPAA for approval.

Business / Technology:

1946 – Lucky Luciano, considered the father of modern organized crime and the mastermind of the massive postwar expansion of the international **heroin trade,** is deported after serving a 10-year prison term.

In 1936, **Lucky Luciano,** the boss of **Mafia drug** and **prostitution rackets** in New York City, was finally convicted as a result of Thomas Dewey's prosecution and sentenced to thirty to fifty years in prison. Then in 1942, during WWII the U.S. Office of Naval Intelligence made a secret deal with Luciano while he was still in prison to have New York waterfront workers watch for enemy agents and activity.

Luciano's Mafia connections in Italy and Sicily were used to furnish intelligence for U.S. forces. Lucky put the word out to cooperate and overnight dockworkers, fishermen and mobsters cooperated with Naval Intelligence.

Albert Anastasia, controlled the docks, and promised there would not be any dockworker strikes as U.S. military intelligence agencies used Luciano's Mafia connections to gather information on communist influence in resistance groups and local governments both during and also after WWII. Because Luciano cooperated, he was allowed to run his crime empire from his jail cell. The prison authorities even allowed him to have a private chef, co-defendant Dave Betillo, who cooked for him in a small kitchen set aside for this purpose.

Luciano was released in 1946, after he promised to leave the U.S. After his deportation **he lived in Cuba and ran a world wide heroin cartel.** The U.S.

government then forced his return to Italy where he died of natural causes some years later.

February 1946 – The public gets its first glimpse of the **ENIAC, a computing machine** built by John Mauchly and J. Presper Eckert.

April 1946 – **Strikes.** Workers in **packinghouses** nation-wide go on strike. A strike by **400,000** mineworkers in the U.S. begins. **U.S. troops seized railroads and coal mines** the following month to prevent them from shutting down operations.

July 5, 1946 – **The Lanham Act**, which lays the groundwork for all future trademark legislation, **defines a trademark** as "any word, name, symbol, device, or any combination thereof adopted by a manufacturer or merchants to identify goods and distinguish them from those manufactured or sold by others."

1946 – **The first bank card, named "Charge-It,"** is introduced by John Biggins, a banker in Brooklyn, according to MasterCard. When someone used the card, Biggins' bank paid it and then billed the customer. The banker collected on both ends and grinned.

August 1945 – **The Cost of the Manhattan Project** through August 1945 is $2 billion. In August, 1939, Albert Einstein and several other scientists told President Franklin D. Roosevelt of efforts in **Nazi Germany** to purify uranium-235, which could be used to build an atomic bomb and in June, 1941, the United States Government began "The Manhattan Project." The Manhattan Project was committed to expediting research that would produce a viable atomic bomb.

Estimates of other WWII costs include: **All bombs, mines and grenades,** $3.1 billion. Small arms materiel, not including ammunition, $2.4 billion. All tanks, $6.4 billion. All **field artillery, $3.4 billion.** The total cost to the United States for World War II was **more than $1 trillion dollars.**

October 4, 1946 – **Strikes. The U.S. Navy seizes oil refineries** in order to break a 20-state strike. Most of the labor conflict is caused by the no strike pledge that many labor unions agreed to during WWII. No other year, saw so many strikes, and such a large percentage of people on strike, or so many industries affected by strikes, as 1946.

There were strikes during WWII, but they were localized and almost none of them were over wages. In 1946 the overwhelming majority of strikes are over disciplinary and management issues. Never before had labor unions flexed so much muscle and this is also the beginning of labor's long-term downfall.

December 26, 1946 – Bugsy Siegel opens the **Flamingo Hotel** in **Las Vegas** at a cost of **$6 million.** Siegel and partners Moe Sedway, Gus Greenbaum and Meyer Lansky invested $1 million in the new property. Later when Siegel took over the final phases of construction he convinced more of his underworld associates to invest in the Flamingo. The problem was Siegel had no experience in construction or design, causing costs to mount from constant changes and gouging from construction firms and suppliers. Some of his suppliers delivered materials, stole them back again at night, and then resold them the next day. Siegel actually bought some of the same materials twice. Finally Bugsy lost patience with the rising costs, and his notorious outbursts unnerved his construction foreman. Reputedly, Siegel told him, **"Don't worry, we only kill each other."** A year after the official groundbreaking, the resort had produced no revenue and drained the resources of his mob investors. Meyer Lansky charged, at a major mob meeting in Cuba, that either Siegel or his girlfriend **Virginia Hill** was skimming from the resort's building budget. It did not help matters when Virginia Hill went to Switzerland with $2.5 million dollars.

Finance:

1944 – United States. Income is running at $183 billion dollars, yet $103 billion dollars is being spent on World War II. This is thirty times the spending rate during World War I. and the American taxpayer is picking up 55% of the total allied cost of the war which has been estimated at more than $1 trillion dollars.

July 1946 – International Monetary Fund. In Bretton Woods, New Hampshire, the **International Monetary Fund** (IMF), and the **World Bank** are approved with full United States participation. The principal architects of the Bretton Woods system, and the IMF, are **Harry Dexter White** and **John Maynard Keynes.** Harry Dexter White, who died in 1946, was identified as **a Soviet spy** whose code name was,

"Jurist," on October 16, 1950, in an FBI memo. Also, John Maynard Keynes was a British citizen. These two bodies broadened powers of a worldwide power base the National Banking Act of 1864 and the Federal Reserve Act of 1913 had established **over** the United States.

The **International Monetary Fund** and the **World Bank** created a **banking cartel** comprising the world's privately owned central banks, which gradually assumed the power to dictate credit policies to the banks of all nations. The IMF has also been given the authority to issue a world fiat money called, "Special Drawing Rights," or SDR's and member nations are pressured into making their currencies fully exchangeable for SDR's. The IMF is controlled by its board of governors who are either the heads of different central banks or the heads of the various national treasury departments who are dominated by their central banks. Because of the way votes are taken within the IMF, the United States and the United Kingdom (the Federal Reserve and the Bank of England), really control everything. See euro-med.dk /?p=6118 for in-depth information.

1945 – The second "League Of Nations," now renamed the **"United Nations,"** is approved.

1946 – The Bank of England is nationalized. The Treasury acquired all the shares in the Bank of England, and they are held in trust by the Treasury Solicitor. However, the government has no money to pay for the shares, so instead of receiving money for their shares, the shareholders are issued government stocks. The state now receives the operating profits of the bank and the government has to pay interest on the new stocks it has issued to pay for the shares. So, even though the Bank of England is now state-owned, the fact is that the British money supply is once again almost entirely in private hands, with 97% of it being in the form of interest bearing loans of one sort or another, created by private commercial banks. As a result of this, the bank is largely controlled and run by those from the world of commercial banking and conventional economics. The Bank of England is called a central bank but is now essentially a regulatory body that supports and oversees the existing system. It is sometimes referred to as "the lender of last resort," in so far as one of its functions as the bankers' bank is to support any bank or financial institution that gets into difficulties and suffers a run on its liquid assets. Interestingly, in these circumstances, it is not obliged to disclose details of any such measures, the reason being so as to avoid a crisis in confidence. see Richard Greaves at prosperityuk.com for in-depth information on Money.

Books:

1946 – Dr. Benjamin Spock. "The Common Sense Book of Baby & Child Care." One of the biggest best-sellers of all time, by 1998 it had sold more than 50 million copies and been translated into 39 languages. His ideas about childcare influenced several generations of parents.

1946 – The U.S. publication of "Animal Farm." **George Orwell.**

1945 – "A Tree Grows in Brooklyn," a novel by **Betty Smith**. It is a "coming-of-age" story of its main character, Francie Nolan, and her Austrian/ Irish-American family struggling against poverty in Williamsburg, Brooklyn, New York City. The novel, first published in 1943, is set in the first and second decades of the 20th century. The book is an immense success, a nationwide best-seller that was distributed to servicemen overseas. It was adapted into a popular motion picture in 1945.

TV:

1940 – The first televised hockey and basketball games. The first televised sporting event was a college baseball game between Columbia and Princeton in 1939, covered by one camera providing a point of view along the third base line.

1946 – Seven thousand television sets are sold in the U.S. during 1946.

June 19 1946 – Close to 150,000 viewers tune in to watch the first televised **heavyweight title fight** between **Joe Louis and Billy Conn.** So few homes have TV this is watched in taverns with TV sets. It was suggested to Louis that Conn might outpoint him because of his hand and foot speed. In a line that would be long-remembered, **Louis replied: "He can run, but he can't hide."**

1946

Radio:

1946 – Nat King Cole becomes the first African American to have a radio variety show.

1946 – "The Great Gildersleeve" 5th season. *Stories for Children, Told in His Own Way by the Great Gildersleeve,* was released on 78 rpm record albums in 1945 and was Capitol's first-ever such release for children. With orchestral accompaniment, it featured "Puss in Boots," "Rumpelstiltskin," and "Jack and the Beanstalk."

Sports:

June 6, 1946 – The Basketball Association of America is founded. It will be known as the National Basketball Association (NBA) in 1949 after its merger with the rival National Basketball League.

Music:

1945 – Miles Davis (19) recorded with **Charlie Parker** (25) for the first time.

1946 – Twenty-one year old **Bill Haley's** professional musical career begins as a member of **The Down Homers.** His earliest known recordings are made during a Down Homers radio performance, but will not be released until 2006.

Natural Disasters:

1946 – Hilo, Hawaii. A Tsunami is triggered by an earthquake in the Aleutian Islands killing 159 people.

1946 – An F4 tornado hits Windsor, Ontario. The tornado touched down in Michigan in the U.S. and crossed over into Canada narrowly missing Windsor Airport. Some homes were lifted off their foundations. Four-hundred homes were damaged or destroyed. Another violent tornado will hit one half mile away in 1974.

1946 – Vancouver Island. A 7.3 magnitude earthquake strikes. Two people are killed.

Man vs. Man / Wars:

1940-1945 – Seeking guarantees of Vietnamese independence**, Ho Chi Minh** returned to southern China to meet with American and French representatives. After receiving no encouragement, Ho Chi Minh returned to Vietnam in 1941to lead the Việt Minh independence movement. With support from the **United States Office of Strategic Services,** he had led many successful military operations against the **Vichy French** and **Japanese occupation** of Vietnam during World War II.

It has been said that during WWII Ho carried a copy of the **American Declaration of Independence** and could quote freely from it. The proclamation of Independence of the Democratic Republic of Vietnam borrowed much from the French and American declarations. On September 2, 1945, after the August Revolution and Emperor Bao Dai's abdication, Ho Chi Minh read the Declaration of Independence of Vietnam, under the name of the **Democratic Republic of Vietnam.** His government was not recognized by any country and he repeatedly petitioned **American President Harry Truman** for support for **Vietnamese independence,** but Truman never responded.

As soon as Ho Chi Minh traveled outside of Vietnam, his subordinates imprisoned 25,000 non-communist nationalists and forced 6,000 others to flee. Hundreds of political opponents were killed, all rival political parties were banned and local governments were purged to minimize opposition.

In September 1945, General Sir Douglas Gracey led 20,000 troops of the 20th Indian Division to occupy Saigon. Guerilla war developed between rival Vietnamese factions and French forces and British commander, General Gracey, declared martial law. When the Viet Minh leaders called for a general strike in late September 1945, a **force of 200,000 Chinese Nationalists** arrived in Hanoi and Ho Chi Minh made an arrangement with their general, Lu Han, to dissolve the Communist Party and to hold an election which would bring about a coalition government.

1945 – Philippines. MacArthur liberates Manila. Sergio Osmeña, the second President of the Commonwealth of the Philippines, establishes a government.

1946

July 4, 1946 – **Philippines**. The Philippines become an independent nation. Manuel Roxas Acuña is elected the first president with 54% of the vote.

March 11, 1946 – Former Auschwitz Commandant Rudolf Hoess, posing as a farm worker is arrested by the British. He testifies at Nuremberg, is tried in Warsaw, is found guilty and hanged at Auschwitz, April 16, 1947, near Crematory I. "History will mark me as the greatest mass murderer of all time," Hoess writes while in prison, along with his memoirs about Auschwitz.

April 28, 1945 – Mussolini is captured and executed by partisans as he attempts to flee to Switzerland.

October 16, 1946 – Hermann Wilhelm Göring commits suicide with a potassium cyanide capsule, the night before he is to be hanged. During his imprisonment, a now repentant Hans Frank states, "A thousand years will pass and the guilt of Germany will not be erased." Hans Frank and the others were hanged. The bodies of Göring and the other executed Nazi leaders were cremated with the ashes then scattered into a local river.

December 9, 1946 – Twenty-three former SS doctors and scientists go on trial before a U.S. Military Tribunal at **Nuremberg.** Sixteen are found guilty; seven are hanged.

World War II, 1939-1945 – France was conquered by Germany.

World War II, 1941-1945 – Europe was liberated by the Allies (the British Empire, the Union of Soviet Socialist Republics, and the United States of America were known as "The Big Three" and China Poland and France, were considered major allies. VS. Germany, Italy, Japan, Hungary.
Finland fought the Soviet Union.
Iraq – Iraq was fighting The United Kingdom. In 1940 Anti-British leaders in Iraq side with the Axis powers (Germany, Italy, and Japan), in the early part of World War II. 1941 – **Britain defeats Iraq** and pro-Axis leaders flee.1943 - Iraq declares war on the Axis countries.1945 - Iraq becomes a charter member of the Arab League. **Thailand** was a formal ally of Japan.

Countries also involved were: **Romania, Bulgaria,Yugoslavia, Manchuria, Mengjiang (Inner Mongolia), Burma, Philippines, China, India, Vietnam, Cambodia, Laos, Montenegro, Slovakia, Serbia, Albania, Croatia, Greece, Pindus and Macedonia, France, Denmark, Spain.** In all, 61 countries with 1.7 billion people, three-fourths of the world's population, took part in WWII. A rough consensus has been reached on the total cost of the war. The human cost is estimated at 60 million dead, 27 million in the military and 33 million civilians. The cost in dollars to the U.S. has been estimated at over $1 trillion. The amount of money spent has been estimated at more than $3.3 trillion, which makes World War II more expensive than all other wars combined.

Just some of the Individual extermination camps during WWII. The first figure is the estimated number of men women and children killed at the camp. These were mostly all civilians; men and women, brothers and sisters, aunts and uncles, whole families were very commonly murdered and whole neighborhoods were slaughtered as a regular practice. These were people just like you and me. They laughed and cried, they loved and were loved. And they were tortured, slaughtered, killed in slave labor and the bodies tossed or bulldozed into large pits.

1,500,000-2,500,000 people were killed. The **Auschwitz** extermination camp was operated by **Nazi-Germany** and located in Oświęcim, Poland, 1940-1945.
   Rudolf Hoess, Commandant of Auschwitz: Testimony at Nuremburg, 1946.
   2) I have been constantly associated with the administration of concentration camps since 1934, serving at Dachau until 1938; then as Adjutant in Sachsenhausen from 1938 to 1 May, 1940, when I was appointed Commandant of Auschwitz. I commanded Auschwitz until 1 December, 1943, and estimate that at least 2,500,000 victims were executed and exterminated there by gassing and burning, and at least another half million succumbed to starvation and disease, making a total dead of about 3,000,000. This figure represents about 70% or 80% of all persons sent to Auschwitz as prisoners, the remainder having been selected and used for slave labor in the concentration camp industries. Included among the executed and burnt were approximately 20,000 Russian prisoners of war (previously screened out of Prisoner of War cages by the Gestapo) who were delivered at Auschwitz in Wehrmacht transports operated by regular Wehrmacht officers and men. The remainder of the

total number of victims included about 100,000 German Jews, and great numbers of citizens (*mostly* Jewish) from Holland, France, Belgium, Poland, Hungary, Czechoslovakia, Greece, or other countries. We executed about 400,000 Hungarian Jews alone at Auschwitz in the summer of 1944. Mass executions by gassing commenced during the summer 1941 and continued until fall 1944. I personally supervised executions at Auschwitz until the first of December 1943 and know by reason of my continued duties in the Inspectorate of Concentration Camps WVHA2 that these mass executions continued as stated above. All mass executions by gassing took place under the direct order, supervision and responsibility of RSHA.31 received all orders for carrying out these mass executions directly from RSHA.

6) The "final solution" of the Jewish question meant the complete extermination of all Jews in Europe. I was ordered to establish extermination facilities at Auschwitz in June 1941. At that time there were already in the general government three other extermination camps; BELZEK, TREBLINKA and WOLZEK. These camps were under the Einsatzkommando of the Security Police and SD. I visited Treblinka to find out how they carried out their exterminations. The Camp Commandant at Treblinka told me that he had liquidated 80,000 in the course of one half year. He was principally concerned with liquidating all the Jews from the Warsaw Ghetto. He used monoxide gas and I did not think that his methods were very efficient. So when I set up the extermination building at Auschwitz, l used Cyclon B, which was a crystallized Prussic Acid which we dropped into the death chamber from a small opening. It took from 3 to 15 minutes to kill the people in the death chamber depending upon climatic conditions. We knew when the people were dead because their screaming stopped. We usually waited about one-half hour before we opened the doors and removed the bodies. After the bodies were removed our special commandos took off the rings and extracted the gold from the teeth of the corpses.

7) Another improvement we made over Treblinka was that we built our gas chambers to accommodate 2,000 people at one time, whereas at Treblinka their 10 gas chambers only accommodated 200 people each. The way we selected our victims was as follows: we had two SS doctors on duty at Auschwitz to examine the incoming transports of prisoners. The prisoners would be marched by one of the doctors who would make spot decisions as they walked by. Those who were fit for work were sent into the Camp. Others were sent immediately to the extermination plants. Children of

tender years were invariably exterminated since by reason of their youth they were unable to work. Still another improvement we made over Treblinka was that at Treblinka the victims almost always knew that they were to be exterminated and at Auschwitz we endeavored to fool the victims into thinking that they were to go through a delousing process. Of course, frequently they realized our true intentions and we sometimes had riots and difficulties due to that fact. Very frequently women would hide their children under the clothes but of course when we found them we would send the children in to be exterminated. We were required to carry out these exterminations in secrecy but of course the foul and nauseating stench from the continuous burning of bodies permeated the entire area and all of the people living in the surrounding communities knew that exterminations were going on at Auschwitz.

8) We received from time to time special prisoners from the local Gestapo office. The SS doctors killed such prisoners by injections of benzene. Doctors had orders to write ordinary death certificates and could put down any reason at all for the cause of death.

9) From time to time we conducted medical experiments on women inmates, including sterilization and experiments relating to cancer. Most of the people who died under these experiments had been already condemned to death by the Gestapo

I understand English as it is written above. The above statements are true; this declaration is made by me voluntarily and without compulsion; after reading over the statement, **I have signed and executed the same at Nurnberg, Germany** on the fifth day of April 1946.**Rudolf Franz Ferdinand Hoess,** "Affidavit, 5 April 1946," in *Trial of the Major War Criminals Before the International Tribunal, Nuremberg,* 14 *November* 19451 *October* 1946 (Nuremberg: Secretariat of the International Military Tribunal, 1949), Doc. 3868PS, vol. 33, 27579.

1,000,000-1,400,000 people were killed. The **Treblinka** extermination camp was operated by **Nazi Germany** and located in Treblinka, Poland, 1942-1943.

480,000-600,000 people were killed. The **Belzec** extermination camp was operated by **Nazi Germany** and located in Belzec Poland, 1942-1943.

350,000 people were killed. The **Majdanek** extermination camp was operated by **Nazi Germany** and located in Lublin Poland, 1942-1944.

300,000 people were killed. The **Chelmno** extermination camp was operated by **Nazi Germany** and located in Chelmno Poland, 1941-1943.

260,000 people were killed. The **Sobibór** extermination camp was operated by **Nazi Germany** and located in Sobibor Poland, 1942-1943.

55,000 people were killed. The **Neuengamme** concentration camp was operated by **Nazi Germany** and located near Hamburg, Germany, 1938-1945.

53,000-840,000 people were killed. The **Jasenovac** extermination camp was operated by **NDH Ustaše Nazi regime in Croatia.** Jasenovac was a complex of five sub-camps spread over 93 sq mi on the banks of the Sava River. The largest camp was at Jasenovac. The complex also included large grounds at Donja Gradina directly across the Sava River, **a camp for children** in Sisak to the northwest, and **a women's camp** in Stara Gradiška to the southeast. On the night of August 29, 1942, the prison guards made bets among themselves as to who could liquidate the largest number of inmates. One of the guards, Petar Brzica, boasted of cutting the throats of about 1,360 new arrivals with a butcher knife that became known as *srbosjek* ("Serb-cutter"). Other participants who confessed to participating in the bet included Ante Zrinusic, who killed some 600 inmates, and Mile Friganovic, who gave a detailed and consistent report of the incident. Friganovic admitted to having killed some 1,100 inmates. He specifically recounted his torture of an old man named Vukasin; he attempted to compel the man to bless Ante Pavelic, which the old man refused to do, although Friganovic cut off his ears, nose and tongue after each refusal. Ultimately, he cut out the old man's eyes, tore out his heart, and slashed his throat. This incident was witnessed by Dr. Nikola Nikolic. The Jasenovac Memorial Area maintains a list of names and estimates total deaths at 85,000 to 100,000 men, women and children.

September 2, 1945 – Japan formally surrenders on the deck of the **U.S. battleship Missouri,** ending World War II. Japan begins the process of returning to China all the territories it had colonized, including Taiwan, called Formosa, which it had acquired in 1895 after the first Sino-Japanese war.

1946 – Bolivian Popular Revolt. Major Gualberto Villarroel López became President after he overthrew the Peñaranda regime in 1943. Villarroel is overthrown in 1946. He had been unable to organize popular support and faced opposition from conservative groups and increasing political terrorism that included the murders of the government's opponents.

1945-1946 – Burmese Rebellion. During World War II, Burma became a major frontline in the Southeast Asian Theatre. The British administration collapsed ahead of the advancing Japanese troops, jails and asylums were opened and Rangoon was deserted except for the many Anglo-Burmese and Indians who remained at their posts. Known as "The Trek," a stream of some 300,000 refugees fled across the jungles into India, while 30,000 people died in the attempt. Initially the Japanese-led Burma Campaign succeeded and the British were expelled from most of Burma. The British counter-attacked using troops of the British Indian Army and by July 1945, the British had retaken the country. Many Burmese fought initially for the Japanese, while some Burmese, mostly from the ethnic minorities, fought with the British in Burma.

1946-1949 – Chinese Civil War. After the Japanese surrender, Communist Chinese forces occupied much of previously Japanese-occupied north China. **Fifty-three thousand American marines occupied Peking** and many strategic north Chinese centers. As civil war resumed General George C. Marshall's attempt to mediate resulted in a temporary truce.

1946-1954 – France vs. Vietnam. The First Indochina War is between the military forces of France and the Democratic Republic of Vietnam (DRV), led by **Ho Chi Minh.** The DRV's goal is to independence for Vietnam.

   Before WWII, the French government bought opium in Afghanistan and India, and stored it in Hanoi. When they could no longer import opium during the war, they encouraged local poppy-growing for the Chinese, the Vietnamese and French smokers in the colony. The Lao themselves never smoked much opium, neither did the Cambodians.

   The French tried to deal directly with the opium growers but ended up buying some 40 tons of opium a year from a new class of middle-men in Laos. Cambodia was too flat, hot and humid to grow its own opium and the mountains of northern Laos and northwestern Tongkin (northern Vietnam) took over from India and the Middle East as the main supplier of opium to consumers all over **French Indochina.**

1944-1947 – Greek Civil War. British forces became involved in the early stages of the Greek Civil War when they liberated Greece from German occupation toward the end of 1944.

1946 – Haitian Military Coup. Haitian President Elie Lescot established a tyrannical and corrupt dictatorship. The U.S. provided military and economic aid in exchange for supporting the Allies in World War II. After declaring war on the Axis powers in 1941, Lescot suspended the constitution and assumed "emergency powers" and in 1944 he extended his presidential term from five years to seven. Political opponents were arbitrarily arrested and foreign assets appropriated for his family's control. After the war he attempted to end the opposition press sparking student demonstrations. In 1946 President Lescot fled to the U.S. when Major Paul Eugene Magloire brought a military coup against his government. Dumarsais Estime is made President but is forcibly removed from office by Magloire in 1950 when he tries to extend his rule for an indefinite period.

1946 – India. Strikes, and **Riots.** The newly elected Labour government in Britain conceded it must leave India, but wanted to do so gradually. In August 1946 the **Muslim League,** frustrated by the negotiations, launches "Direct Action Day" which unleashed an unprecedented wave of communal riots. Events were the most bloody in Calcutta where **10,000 people were killed in a day.** The governor of Bengal, who did not lift a finger to stop the killing, described how the streets were "littered with corpses. I can honestly say that parts of the city...were as bad as anything I saw when I was with the Guards on the Somme." A leading League figure in Sindh declared that anyone opposing the demand for Pakistan "shall be destroyed and exterminated." The Calcutta killings are followed by communal riots and killings in east Bengal, Bihar and the United Provinces and then the whole of the Punjab is engulfed from March 1947 onwards.

　　The strikes of 1946 surpassed all previous records. There were police strikes in April, threats of an all-India rail strike continued throughout the summer, a post strike in July, and a one day strike in support of the postal workers in Calcutta. The empire was literally crumbling, from August 1946 onwards. In November the cabinet agreed that the army would not be capable of crushing a mass revolt and the British decided to leave. The descendants of the original Raj that had sowed divisions so cunningly now declared solemnly that **partition was the only way** to end communal violence.

1945 – The Iraqi Army and the British RAF put down the **Kurdish Revolt** of 1945 which lasted from August 10 to October, led by **Mullah Mustafa Barzani,** who escaped into Iran. Mullah Mustafa Barzani was a major player until his death March 3, 1979 in Georgetown Hospital in Washington, DC.

1939-1945 – The Irish Republic remains neutral in World War II while **Northern Ireland** becomes an important Allied sea and air base.

1946 – Korean Occupation Rebellion. Once the United States occupation force chose to bolster the status quo and resist radical reform of colonial legacies, it immediately ran into opposition from the majority of South Koreans. The United States Army Military Government in Korea, from 1945-1948, spent most of its first year suppressing the many "people's committees" that had emerged in the provinces. This action provoked a massive rebellion in the fall of 1946.

The three-year occupation by the United States, following the liberation of Korea from Japan, was characterized by uncertainty and confusion. United States policymakers had little understanding of the strategic value of South Korea and no clear policy. The intensification of the confrontation between the United States and the Soviet Union, and the polarization of Korean politics between left and right added to the instability. The United States had maintained diplomatic ties with the Choson Dynasty between 1882 and 1905, but Korea is a remote country known only to a small number of missionaries and adventurous businessmen, and is not considered to be of any great strategic interest.

1945-1946 – Kurdish Mahabad Republic. In 1946 Mala Mustafa Barzani emerged as the President of the short-lived **Kurdish Mahabad Republic,** which had been established with **Soviet aid** in northwestern Iran. After the Soviet forces withdrew in

1947, the republic collapsed, and Barzani took refuge in Soviet Azerbaijan, where he remained until he was allowed to return to Iraq after that country's 1958 revolution.

1945-1948 – The Palestinian Mandate is a **League of Nations** Mandate formally approved by the League of Nations in June 1922, based on a draft by the principal Allied and associated powers after the First World War. The mandate also formalized **British rule in Palestine,** which began during the First World War. The mandate finished in 1948, and the period 1920 to 1948 is also referred to as the "**British Mandate.**" The term also refers to the territory in the Middle East including the modern territories of **Israel, Jordan,** and the **West Bank** and **Gaza Strip.**

1946 – Paraguayan Coup 1946. As the country moves towards a more democratic regime there is a failed coup attempt.

July 4, 1946 – The Philippines, which had been ceded to the U.S. by Spain at the end of the Spanish-American War, becomes an independent republic with numerous strings attached. The U.S. retains sovereignty over dozens of military bases, and independence is linked to legislation passed by the U.S. Congress and designed to insure that the Philippines will remain an economic ward of the United States.

Filipino nationalists were never happy about the annual July 4 holiday with its bands and parades, and in 1962 they prevailed upon **President Diosdado Macapagal** to change the date. Dr. Samuel Tan of the National Historical Institute says Macapagal was trying to boost his own standing with the nationalists and was "looking for something to rally people that were associated with our revolutionary identity, rather than our colonial identity." July 4 was briefly retained as a national holiday and renamed "Philippine-American Friendship Day." Macapagal moved the date to June 12, which commemorates the declaration of independence of Filipino revolutionaries who in 1898 proclaimed their freedom from Spain.

1945-1954 – Philippines. Huk Rebellion. At the end of World War II, most rural areas, particularly in Central Luzon, were ready to explode politically. Tensions grew as landlords who had fled to urban areas during the fighting returned to the villages in late 1945, demanding back rent, and employing military police and their own armed militias to enforce these demands. Food and other goods were in short supply. The majority of elite landowners had supported the Japanese while the tenants had joined the guerilla resistance. Now armed and having combat experience, guerrilla veterans and those close to them are not as willing to be intimidated by landlords as they had been before 1942.

1946 – Portuguese Military Coup. António de Oliveira Salazar, Prime Minister and de facto dictator of Portugal, crushes opposition and isolates Portugal from the world community. Salazar survives an attempted military coup.

1945-1991 – The Cold War. USA & NATO Belgium, the Netherlands, Luxembourg, France and the United Kingdom (1948) & United States, Canada, Portugal, Italy, Norway, Denmark and Iceland. (1949) & Greece and Turkey (1952) vs. Soviet Union.

1945 – AD Coup in Venezuela. On October 18, the AD (Acción Democrática), in conjunction with junior military officers suddenly overthrow President Medina Angarita. After the coup, **Rómulo Betancourt** named a seven-man governing junta consisting of four members of AD, two military officers, and one independent. AD then controlled the government, and the UPM (Unión Patriótica Militar) controlled the military. All officers with ranks above major before the 1945 rebellion were forced to retire. Political reform was the first item on the junta's agenda.

September 26, 1945 – Vietnam. Lt. Colonel Peter A. Dewey, an employee of the **CIA**'s precursor agency, the **Office of Strategic Services,** is shot and killed on his way to the Saigon airport, becoming the **first American casualty of the Vietnam War.**

1946 – Vietnam. Following a breakdown in negotiations, **Ho Chi Minh's Vietminh** forces begin a war to liberate themselves from their colonial ruler, France.

1945 – Yugoslavia. After World War II, the monarchy became a communist republic under **Prime Minister Tito,** now called the **Federal People's Republic of Yugoslavia.** It was composed of six republics: **Serbia, Croatia, Bosnia** and **Herzegovina, Macedonia, Slovenia,** and **Montenegro**, as well as two provinces, **Kosovo** and **Vojvodina.** The **Yugoslav Front** of World War II, also known as the **Yugoslav**

1946

People's Liberation War was fought in occupied Yugoslavia during World War II between the Yugoslav resistance forces, primarily the Yugoslav Partisans, and the Axis powers. Two guerrilla armies: The communist-led Yugoslav Partisans and the royalist Chetnik movement began fighting each other after a short period of cooperation.

1947

The Oldest Boomer is 1 year old.

Cost of the Average House: $5,900	
Apartment: 3 rooms, furnished, $20/ week	
Median Family Income: $3,000	**Minimum Wage:** 40 cents/ hr
Gallon of Milk: 79 cents	**Gallon Gasoline:** 23 cents
New Car: Buick Roadmaster, Convertible: $2,651	**Loaf of Bread:** 13 cents
	First-class Stamp: 3 cents
Plymouth P15 Club Coupe: $1,445	**Idaho Potatoes:** 5 cents/ lb

Unemployment Rate: 5.9% Another 2.8 million were transferred out of the military into civilian life. This raised the rate from 1.9 to 3.9% in 1946 and this rate held in 1947.

11 cents buying power in 1947 **= $1.00 in 2008.**
In 1947 what cost our parents 11 cents to purchase
now costs us $1.00 in 2008.

Movies: "Gentleman's Agreement," "The Bishop's Wife," "Crossfire," "Great Expectations," "Miracle on 34th Street," "The Farmer's Daughter," "The Egg and I," "The Bachelor and the Bobby-Soxer," "Life With Father," "Road to Rio," "Forever Amber," "The Ghost and Mrs. Muir," "The Secret Life of Walter Mitty," "Buck Privates Come Home" & "The Wistful Widow of Wagon Gap," starring Bud Abbott and Lou Costello. "Son of Zorro," "Jesse James Rides Again," "Jack Armstrong."

Broadway: "Brigadoon," "Finian's Rainbow," "Street Scene," "A Streetcar Named Desire."

TV: "Howdy Doody." "Kukla, Fran and Ollie" which premiered as the hour-long *Junior Jamboree*. "Meet the Press." The Louis-Walcott fight is viewed by 1,000,000 people. The first telecast of a World Series game:

NY Yankees vs. Brooklyn Dodgers. Harry Truman becomes the first President to make an address to the public on TV from the White House. The Groucho Marx quiz show, "You Bet Your Life." "Kraft Television Theater," "Mary Kay and Johnny."

Music: Ted Weems, "Heartaches." Perry Como, "Chi-Baba, Chi-Baba." James Basket, "Zip-a-Dee-Doo-Dah." Guy Lombardo, "Frankie And Johnny." The Andrews Sisters, "Anything You Can Do." Frank Sinatra, "Always." Dinah Shore, "The Lonesome Road." Hoagy Carmichael, "Huggin' And Chalkin'." Louis Jordan, "Ain't Nobody Here But Us Chickens." Tex Williams Western Caravan, "Smoke, Smoke, Smoke, That Cigarette."

President: Harry S. Truman (D) Baptist; vetoes 250/ 12 overrides

Vice President: None
(From April 12, 1945 the vice presidency remained vacant until 1949)

House: D-188; R-246

Senate: 80th Congress (1947-1949) Majority Party: Republican (51 seats) Minority Party: Democrat (45 seats) Other Parties: 0 Total Seats: 96

Federal Debt: $258.29 billion or 106 % of the GDP

Consumer Price Index CPI-U (1982 Base of 100): 22.30

GDP: $244.2 billion	**Inflation Rate:** 14.65%

Dow Jones: 183.81 (08-01) / 171.91 (May 1)

Prime Rate: 1.75% (12-01)	**Average Home Mortgage Rate:** 4.80%
1 oz Gold: $43.00	**1oz of Silver:** $0.91

Average Monthly S.S. Benefits Paid: $27 / month

Federal Debt: $258,286,383,108.67

Federal Deficit: ($4.0 billion dollar surplus)

Defense Spending: $22.83 billion	**Interest Spending:** $4.09 billion

Health Care Spending: $510 million	**Pensions Spending:** $670 million
Welfare Spending: $850 billion	**Education Spending:** $1.63 billion
Transportation Spending: $1.09 billion	**Misc. Other Spending:** $3.82 billion
Protection Spending: $80 million	**Total Government Spending:** $41.40 billion
% of GDP that goes towards just the interest payment: 1.68%	
U.S. Population: 144,126,000	
U.S. Birth Rate: 3,817,000	**U.S. Abortions:** 749
U.S. Homicide Rate: 6.1/ 100,000 population	
Annual Average Domestic Crude Oil Prices: $2.16 / barrel, $20.75 (2007 adjusted)	

Oil:

1947 – After World War II, it is obvious the world is going to need a lot more oil than **Socal** and **Texaco** in **Saudi Arabia** can provide so the U.S. Government stepped in and people got rich.

The U.S. government encouraged companies to find and develop more oil and **Exxon, Chevron and Mobil** (Socony-Vacuum) joined in.

Everyone understood **Saudi Arabia** was going to be rich and the U.S. promoted new incentives; a 50/50 split of oil profits between the companies doing the work and the countries where the oil was located. At the time most of these countries were extremely poor and this worked out to everyone's advantage.

1947 – To match the **American assets in Saudi Arabia**, the British developed a vast oil industry in **Iran.** At this time it is the biggest single foreign asset of Great Britain.

1947

1947 – **Alberta, Canada.** Early fur traders described oil bubbling out of the ground or seeping out of the sand on riverbanks. The discovery at **Leduc** triggers an oil boom.

1947 – **Kerr-McGee Corp.** drills the world's first commercial oil well out of sight of land in the Gulf of Mexico, the Keramac 16, and strikes oil in October 1947. Kermac 16 is drilled in just 20 feet of water.

In 2006 the Jack 2 well will be drilled at a depth of 20,000 feet in the Gulf of Mexico at a cost of $100 million and may increase America's oil reserves by 50%. This is both good news and bad news. Because the cost is so high the oil industry has embraced Globalism and the London based BP is in 2006 the largest oil producer in America! In 2005 they produced over 15% of all U.S. crude output. In 2006 energy companies from **Japan, Italy, Brazil, Australia, Britain, France,** and **Canada** are actively prospecting for oil in the **United States Gulf of Mexico.**

Major News:

January 2, 1947 – Mahatma Gandhi begins a march for peace in East-Bengali.

January 25, 1947 – Al Capone dies of a cerebral hemorrhage at his Miami, Florida estate as a result of advanced syphilis.

March 1947 – President Truman declares an active role in the **Greek Civil War**.

March 15, 1947 – The Truman Doctrine is passed by the U.S. Congress, granting $400 million in aid to Greece and Turkey to battle Communist terrorism. President Harry S. Truman implements the act on May 22.

April 2, 1947 – The United Nations Security Council unanimously approves the trusteeship of Pacific Islands formerly controlled by Japan to the United States.

April 15, 1947 – Jackie Robinson breaks Major League Baseball's barrier against black players when he debuts at first base for **Branch Rickey's Brooklyn Dodgers.**

April 25, 1947 – Theodore Roosevelt National Park is established by President Harry Truman along the Little Missouri River and scenic badlands of North Dakota.

June 5, 1947 – The "Marshall Plan" is announced. Two years after the end of World War II, the U.S. booms while Europe still teeters on the brink of chaos. Europeans face rationing for basics like bread. In Great Britain, fishing fleets are kept in port for lack of fuel. In Germany, the economy seems to slide toward subsistence farming and a life style similar to the middle Ages. The threat of starvation and Communism have a heavy hold over Western Europe, so Secretary of State George C. Marshall proposes aid to European nations for war recovery. This is known as the Marshall Plan, and leads to Congressional approval of $12 billion dollars in foreign aid over the next four years.

   As the U.S. pours $12 billion worth of economic support and technical expertise into Europe (over $120 billion in 2010 dollars) the aid gives Europe an immediate boost, spurring new investment and pulling the Continent out of its slump.

   The Marshall Plan's secondary, or maybe main purpose, is to rebuild Europe in such a way that no **Communists** could ever win an election. To this end, the **CIA** played a major role in administering the Marshall Plan.

1947 – The Dead Sea Scrolls are first discovered in a cave. Consisting of roughly 850-870 documents, including texts from the Hebrew Bible, the Dead Sea Scrolls are discovered between 1947 and 1956 in eleven caves in and around the Wadi Qumran near the ruins of the ancient settlement of Khirbet Qumran, on the northwest shore of the Dead Sea. The texts are of great religious and historical significance, as they include some of the only known surviving copies of Biblical documents made before 100 C.E., and preserve evidence of considerable diversity of belief and practice within late Second Temple Judaism. They are written in Hebrew, Aramaic and Greek, mostly on parchment, but with some written on papyrus. These manuscripts generally date between 150 BCE to 70 CE. Unfortunately those who found the scrolls were often paid "by the piece" and they often tore parts of the scrolls into more pieces to increase their profits.

June 20, 1947 – Mobster Benjamin Siegel is killed by an unidentified gunman at the Beverly Hills, California home of girlfriend Virginia Hill. Siegel had built the

Flamingo Hotel and casino in **Las Vegas** using millions of dollars in of **mafia money**. When the project failed to make a profit, the enraged mobsters ordered Siegel's execution because they thought he was skimming money.

June 20, 1947 – President Harry S. Truman vetoes the Taft-Hartley Labor Act which would have curbed strikes, only to be overridden by Congress on June 23.

July 1947 – The "Exodus 1947" left France, for Palestine with over 4,500 Jewish men, women, and children, all displaced persons or survivors of the Holocaust. Even before the ship reached Palestine's territorial waters, British destroyers surrounded it. A struggle followed in which a Jewish crew member and two passengers were killed while others suffered bullet wounds and injuries. **British Foreign Secretary Ernest Bevin** orders the illegal immigrant ship, the *Exodus 1947,* to be sent back to Europe.

Civil Rights Movement:

1947 – In the case of **Everson vs. Board of Education**, the U.S. Supreme Court rules by a 5-4 vote that a New Jersey law that allows reimbursements of transportation costs to parents of children who ride public transportation to school, even if their children attended Catholic schools, does **NOT** violate the Establishment Clause of the First Amendment.

March 12, 1947 – Martin Luther King, Jr. is elected chair of the membership committee of the Atlanta **NAACP Youth Council** in a meeting on the Morehouse College campus. **He is 18 years old.**

April 9, 1947 – The Committee on Racial Equality (**CORE**) and the Fellowship of Reconciliation (FOR) send sixteen black and white **"Freedom Riders"** through the South to test compliance with the Supreme Courts June 3, 1946 decision in Irene Morgan vs. Commonwealth of Virginia. Called the **"Journey of Reconciliation,"** the integrated group activists ride interstate buses in **Virginia, Kentucky, Tennessee,** and **North Carolina.** The members are arrested several times. In North Carolina two young black men are found guilty of violating the state's **Jim Crow bus statute** and are sentenced to thirty days on a chain gang. The Judge then made it clear he found the behavior of the white men even more objectionable when he sentenced two young white Jewish men, at the same time, to ninety days on the chain gang for the same offense.

April 15, 1947 – Jackie Robinson plays his first game for the **Brooklyn Dodgers** becoming the first African-American player in major league baseball since the 1880s. In 1947, Brooklyn Dodgers president Branch Rickey approached Jackie about joining the team. The Major Leagues had not had an African-American player since 1889, when baseball became segregated. Jackie agreed and when he first wore a Brooklyn Dodger uniform, he pioneered the integration of professional athletics in America. By breaking the color barrier in baseball, the nation's preeminent sport, he courageously challenged the deeply rooted custom of racial segregation in both the North and the South.

July 1947 – NAACP President James Hinton asks the Reverend J.A. DeLaine to find someone willing to help challenge public school transportation in South Carolina. Reverend DeLaine's friend, Levi Pearson, the father of three school age children, files a petition with the public schools in Clarendon County, asking that his children and other Negro schoolchildren be provided a school bus so that black children wouldn't have to walk up to 10 miles to school.

In retaliation for that public request, Reverend DeLaine's **home and church were burned.** This begins the case that evolves into **Briggs vs. Elliot,** which will eventually be joined with **Brown vs. Board of Education.**

Pearson will lose the initial case and become President of the local NAACP. He is denied credit and local businessmen refuse to buy the timber he cuts to make a living. Henry and Eliza Briggs are both fired from their jobs. And **Brown vs. Board of Education** will not be settled until 1954.

July 1947 – Four months after **Jackie Robinson** breaks the color barrier in the **National League, Larry Doby** is signed for the **Cleveland Indians,** and is the first black ballplayer in the **American League.** Doby later becomes the first African-American to hit a home run in an All-Star game, and in 1978 he was the second

African American to be hired as a major league manager. **Frank Robinson** was first African American to be hired as a major league manager in 1975.

December 1947 – To Secure These Rights. The commission, appointed by President Harry S. Truman was charged with: (1) examining the condition of civil rights in the United States, (2) producing a written report of their findings, and (3) submitting recommendations on improving civil rights in the United States. In December 1947, the committee produced a 178-page report entitled *To Secure These Rights: The Report of the President's Committee on Civil Rights.* In the report, it proposed to improve the existing civil rights laws; to establish a permanent Civil Rights Commission, Joint Congressional Committee on Civil Rights, and a Civil Rights Division in the Department of Justice; **to make lynching a federal crime;** to establish a permanent Fair Employment Practices Commission, with enforcement powers; to abolish poll taxes; end segregation in the armed forces; secure voting rights, and abolish segregation in interstate transport.

Southern Senators and Congressmen continued to block such legislation. United States Lynching 1900 to 1950 - Whites: 195, Blacks: 1,791, Total: 1,986.

Popular Culture:

July 1947 – Alien Spacecraft and Crew. On June 21, 1947, an airplane pilot named Kenneth Arnold spotted what he described as crescent shaped craft over Mt. Rainier in the State of Washington, launching the modern UFO era. Shortly thereafter something mysterious crashed in **Area 51**near Roswell, New Mexico. The United States military claims debris from an experimental high-altitude surveillance balloon was recovered in Area 51. Many UFO proponents maintain that a **crashed alien spacecraft containing alien bodies was recovered,** the military engaged in a cover-up, and the extraterrestrials' bodies and their spacecraft are stored at Area 51.

It is still unresolved in 2010.

January 15, 1947 – The "Black Dahlia" murder case. Elizabeth Short, a 22-year-old wannabe actress is found murdered on January 15, when a passerby spots her **nude body in a vacant lot near Hollywood.** Her bruised, beaten body has been cut in half.

The name **"Black Dahlia"** evolved from her black hair and black attire. Some say she was named the Black Dahlia before her murder, others say the name was applied by journalists to sensationalize the crime. There have been well over 50 people that have "confessed" to the crime and yet according to the LAPD, the case goes unsolved.

1947 – **Teenagers** became a recognized force in the forties. With men off to war, teenage boys and girls find employment readily available and have money to spend. With fathers away and mothers at work, another new phenomenon surfaces: the **juvenile delinquent.**

1947 – **U.S. House Un-American Activities Committee,** an investigative committee of the United States House of Representatives, attacks the entertainment industry. They are tracking down suspected communists in positions of influence.

1947 – **TV Censorship.** NBC cuts to dead air when Fred Allen tells a joke about NBC Vice Presidents.

October 1947 – Levittown opens in October. Levittown gets its name from its builder, the firm of Levitt & Sons, Inc., which built it as a planned community between 1947 and 1951. Levittown was the first truly **mass-produced suburb** and is widely regarded as the archetype for postwar suburbs throughout the country.

1947 – **CIA. The Central Intelligence Agency** is established. The National Security Act of 1947 establishes the CIA. The National Security Act charged the **CIA** with coordinating the nation's intelligence activities and correlating, evaluating and disseminating intelligence affecting national security.

Business / Technology:

1947 – **Two million** radios can receive FM broadcasts.

1947 – Seven U.S. East Coast **TV stations begin regular programming**.

1947 – An estimated 4.74 billion movie theater tickets are sold this year in the U.S. and Canada. This is the peak year for theater attendance.

1947

1947 – The Polaroid Land Camera produces instant B&W photographs. Edwin Land's Polaroid camera prints pictures in a minute.

1947 – Dennis Gabor, a Hungarian engineer in England, invents **holography**.

1947 – The AK-47 assault rifle is developed for motorized infantry and later adopted for service with the Soviet Army in 1949. This is the first true assault rifle and, due to its durability, low production cost and ease of use, the weapon and its numerous variants remain the most widely used assault rifles in the world through 2010. The flag of Mozambique was adopted on May 1, 1983. It includes the image of an AK-47 and is the only national flag in the world to feature such a modern Assault rifle.

1947 – X-1 supersonic aircraft. This is a joint NACA-U.S. Army Air Forces/ U.S. Air Force supersonic research project and the first aircraft to exceed the speed of sound in controlled, level flight. The Army Air Force became frustrated with the slow pace of the testing under Bell Aircraft Corporation and took the contract to fly the X-1-2 from Bell and put it in the hands of NACA for testing. On October 14th, the X-1-2 piloted by Air Force Captain **Charles "Chuck" Yeager,** was dropped from the modified bomb bay of a Boeing B-50 Superfortress and began flight #50 in the program. On that flight, the aircraft became the first manned aircraft to achieve supersonic flight, reaching a recorded speed of Mach 1.06 (807.2 mph).

1947 – The first recorded rock and roll song. Roy Brown, **"Good Rocking Tonight."**

1947 – The Raytheon Company's **microwave oven hits the market at** 5 1/2 feet tall, weighing over 750 pounds, and costing about $5,000. The first unit is placed in a Boston restaurant for testing.

During World War II, two scientists invented the magnetron, a tube that produces microwaves. Installing magnetrons in Britain's radar system, the microwaves were able to spot Nazi warplanes on their way to bomb the British Isles. The idea of using microwave energy to cook food was accidentally discovered by Percy LeBaron Spencer of the Raytheon Company when he found that radar waves had melted a candy bar in his pocket. Percy never confirmed rumors that anything else had melted.

1947 – The first environmental law of the 20th century is passed. **The Federal Insecticide, Fungicide and Rodenticide Act** requires companies to register pesticides used in interstate commerce.

Finance:

1947 – The television rights for the 1947 World Series are sold for $65,000 while the radio rights go for $175,000.

July 15, 1947 – The Office of International Finance is created within the Treasury Department.

July 1947 – *Foreign Affairs*. **Military-Industrial Complex.** After WWII, Americans begin to understand **Joseph Stalin** has a lot in common with **Adolf Hitler.** In March 1947 the Truman Doctrine announced the commitment to resist Soviet expansionism anywhere in the world. President Truman declared that it must be a policy of the United States to **support free peoples who are resisting attempted subjugation** by armed minorities or by outside pressures.

George Kennan, writing anonymously in *Foreign Affairs* magazine offers a plan that ultimately will become the U.S. blueprint for the Cold War. Kennan argues that the United States should pursue a policy in which Soviet moves are "contained by the adroit and vigilant application of counter-force." Proceeding from the assumption that America has limited resources with which to wage such a policy, Kennan prioritized the areas of vital U.S. interests, Western Europe, Germany, and Japan, and argued that outside these select areas the nation should not over-commit itself.

1947 – The transistor, invented at Bell Labs by three scientists, will replace vacuum tubes. Today in 2009 we use TFT, or Thin Film Transistor Technology for the ultimate LCD display. Also called **Flat Panel Displays,** a typical 17-inch TFT flat screen monitor has about 1.3 million pixels and 1.3 million transistors. Try that with vacuum tubes.

1947 – A 1947 Wheat Penny is worth about 7 cents in 2010. They contain 95% copper and the melt value is about $0.021237

1947

Books:

1947 – Mickey Spillane publishes his first detective novel, "**I The Jury**," which he wrote in 19 days in an effort to boost his income so that he and his wife could buy a summerhouse. "**I, The Jury**" sold six and a half million copies in the United States alone. More than 225 million copies of his books have sold internationally and he wrote seven of the top 15 all-time bestselling fiction titles in America. Spillane started as a writer for comic books while working as a salesman in Gimbel's Department Store basement in 1940 when he was 22.

1947 – James Michener's writing career starts with "**Tales of the South Pacific.**" Michener wrote that he did not know who his parents were or exactly when or where he was born. He was raised a Quaker by an adoptive mother, Mabel Michener, in Doylestown, Bucks County, Pennsylvania. His novels sold an estimated 75 million copies worldwide and he gave away a great deal of the money he earned, contributing more than $100 million to universities, libraries, museums, and other charitable causes. In October 1997, Michener ended the daily dialysis treatment that had kept him alive for four years. He soon died of kidney failure at the age of 90.

1947 – "Tarzan and the Foreign Legion," Edgar Rice Burroughs.

1947 – "Anne Frank: The Diary of a Young Girl," by Doubleday & Company, is published. It is the personal diary of a Jewish girl who was born in the city of Frankfurt am Main in Weimar Germany, and who lived most of her life in or near Amsterdam, in the Netherlands. She gained international fame posthumously following the publication of her diary which documents her experiences hiding during the German occupation of the Netherlands in World War II. She died in early March 1945 at age 15.

1947 – French publisher Jean-Jacques Pauvert published the works of the **Marquis de Sade,** and then proceeded to fight a protracted legal battle in which it was ruled in 1958 that four of Sade's works, *120 Days of Sodom, The New Justine, Juliette* and

Philosophy in the Boudoir, would continue to be suppressed. By the late 1960's *Justine* will be legally available on film.

1947 – "Dark Carnival," **Ray Bradbury's first published book** is a collection of short stories that will not be reprinted until 2001.

TV:

1947 – **Color TV. The "Howdy Doody" show with Buffalo Bob Smith** is one of the first to recognize the potential of television to market products to kids. Some of its sponsors are Welch's Grape Jelly, Wonder Bread, and Colgate. Howdy Doody is the first regular network series in color. The audience of kids is called the **Peanut Gallery** and there is a huge waiting list for tickets to the show. Some of the shows other characters are the seltzer wielding clown, **Clarabell**, **Chief Thunderthud**, **Princess Summerfall Winterspring,** and the evil and cantankerous **Phineas T. Bluster**. Throughout the show's run Clarabell never spoke, except once, on the last show he said, "Good-bye kids."

November 18, 1947 – The first couple to share the same bed on American television was Mary Kay and Johnny, in an episode of the **"Mary Kay and Johnny" show** which aired on November 18, 1947 on the DuMont network. This live domestic-comedy was also the very first network situation comedy. It revolved around young New York newlyweds Mary Kay and Johnny Stearns. She was pretty, pert, and something of a screwball, while he was more serious and always getting her out of various dilemmas. Johnny worked in a bank, but the setting for the action was usually the couple's apartment in Greenwich Village.

1947 – **The first televised World Series game,** New York Yankees vs. the Brooklyn Dodgers, is broadcast to an amazing-3.9 million viewers, mostly in bars with TV.

1947 – **When NBC televised** the World Series, heavyweight fights, and the Army-Navy football game, the sales of television sets just soared. By 1948 there were 190,000 TV sets in the U.S.

1947

Radio:

1947 – **Allen Funt** begins his foolery with **Candid Microphone** on ABC radio.

1947 – "**Lassie**", and "**Sgt. Preston of the Yukon,**" two radio shows for kids.

Sports:

1947 – **Jackie Robinson** joins the **Brooklyn Dodgers,** desegregating baseball. Jackie Robinson, a 28-year-old African-American ballplayer and war veteran, is brought up from the minor leagues to play for the Brooklyn Dodgers. The nation was divided at first. Many whites and nearly all blacks applauded the move and said it was long overdue. A large number of whites, including many major league baseball players, did not want Jackie Robinson in an all white league.

1947 – The zoom lens covers **baseball's World Series** for TV.

Music:

Patti Page, Frankie Laine, Kay Star, George Jones, Perry Como, Frank Sinatra, Dinah Shore, The Andrews Sisters, The Harmonicats, The Ink Spots, Danny Kaye, Guy Lombardo, Glen Miller, Kay Kaiser, Arthur Godfrey, Vic Damone, Ted Weems, Woody Herman, and Bing Crosby. The first Al Jolson album is released.

Natural Disasters:

September 4-21, 1947 – A Hurricane moving through southeast Florida., Louisiana, Mississippi, and Alabama kills 51 people.

April 9, 1947 – **The deadliest tornado in Oklahoma history** tears through Woodward, Oklahoma, killing 107 people and destroying 100 city blocks.

April 16-18, 1947 – **Texas City, Texas.** Most of the city is destroyed by a fire and subsequent **explosion on the French freighter** *Grandcamp*, which is carrying a cargo of ammonium nitrate, Fertilizer. At least 516 people are killed and over 3,000 people are injured. All firemen and practically all spectators on the pier were killed along with many employees at the Monsanto Chemical Company and throughout the dock area. As of April 29, 1947, 433 bodies had been recovered and approximately 135 people who were known to have been on the dock are still missing. Over 2,000 people, many were school children 6,000 feet from the explosion, suffered injuries from flying glass fragments and debris.

The cargo ship ***Grandcamp*** was being loaded on April 16, when a fire was detected in the hold. Two thousand and six hundred tons of tons of ammonium nitrate sacks were already onboard. The captain closed the hold and started pumping pressurized steam into the area in an attempt to put out the fire. One hour later, the ship exploded, killing several hundred people and setting fire to another vessel, the *High Flyer*, which was moored 800 feet away and contained 1,050 tons of sulfur and 960 tons of ammonium nitrate. The *Grandcamp* explosion also created a powerful earth shock that knocked two small planes flying at 1,500 feet out of the sky.

November 1947 – A Chinese troopship evacuating Nationalist troops from Manchuria sinks off Yingkou killing an estimated 6,000 people.

1946-1947 – Ukraine and Russia. Famine in the Soviet Union kills between 1,500,000 and 2,000,000 people as a cumulative effect of the consequences of collectivization, war damage, government social policy and mismanagement of grain reserves.

October 16, 1947 – Fairbanks, Alaska. An earthquake registering 7.2 strikes Fairbanks.

Man vs. Man / Wars:

Assassinated – July 1947. Burma. Aung San. Political rivals assassinate Aung San and several cabinet members. Aung San is 32 and considered a Burmese Hero who fought for independence. In February he signed the Panglong accord with the leaders of ethnic nationalities, who agreed to work with the Burmese for Independence. In April, his party, the Anti-Fascist People's Freedom League, won a landslide election

victory, setting the scene for the writing of Burma's Constitution. The nation felt a gentle euphoria because they had a leader they loved and trusted, and Independence was just around the corner. **In July he is assassinated.**

January 23, 1947 – Representative Andrew J. May (D-Kentucky) is **indicted** on charges of conspiracy to defraud the U.S. government by accepting bribes. He allegedly received money for using his influence with the War Department to promote the interests of a munitions company. He is **convicted** on July 7, 1949, serves 9 months of an 8-24 month sentence, and is paroled September 18, 1950. Andrew May continued to retain influence in Democratic Party politics and **President Truman** decided to grant Andrew May a full pardon in 1952.

September 15, 1947 – Twenty-one former Nazi S.S. Einsatz leaders go on trial before a **U.S. Military Tribunal in Nuremberg.** Fourteen are sentenced to death, however only the four group commanders are executed. The other death sentences are commuted.

1947 – Ecuadorian Military Coup. Ecuador's President Jose Maria Velasco Ibarra is forcibly removed from office by a military coup because of corruption, mismanagement, and high inflation. Colonel Carlos Mancheno assumes power.

August 15, 1947 – India and Pakistan. Indian Annexation of Junagadh. The British ruled the Indian subcontinent for nearly 200 years-from 1756 to 1947. The British government found that the stand of the Muslim League on separation and that of the Congress on the territorial unity of India were irreconcilable. The British government then decided on partition and on August 15, 1947, transferred power divided between both India and Pakistan.

1947-1948 – India vs. Pakistan First Kashmir War. Both nations gained independence from Britain simultaneously in 1947. Between 600,000 and **900,000 people died** due to the rioting and dislocation associated with partition.

May 27-June 15, 1947 – Kurdish Campaign. The Soviets drop their support for the Kurds in Iran and the Shah of Iran invades the Mahabad Republic. The Shah orders members of the Kurdistan government, including Qazi Mohammad, to be arrested and executed. After returning to Iraq from the failed Mahabad Republic, Iraqi government arrests and executions caused Mustafa Barzani and 496 followers to begin a fighting retreat from the Barzan region in northern Iraq through Turkey and into Iran in an attempt to reach the Soviet Union. They reached the U.S.S.R. on June 15, 1947, followed by the Iranian Army.

1947 – Palestine. While the UN Special Commission on Palestine was visiting Palestine, in July 1947, Jewish and Zionist delegations met with the committee; the Arab Higher Committee boycotted the meetings. September 1947, one month after Partition of India, UNSCOP **recommended partition in Palestine.**

March-August 1947 – Paraguayan Civil War. By the end of the rebellion in August, a single party, one that had been out of power since 1904, had almost total control in Paraguay. The fighting simplified politics by eliminating all parties except the Colorado party and by reducing the size of the army. Nearly four-fifths of the officer corps had joined the rebels and this meant fewer individuals were now in a position to compete for power. Still, the Colorado party split into rival factions trying to gain and hold absolute power.

1947-1948 – Madagascar Revolt. The Malagasy Uprising is an attempted revolution against the French rule by nationalists on the island of Madagascar. Although the rebels gain control of one third of the island, the revolt is crushed by Paul Ramadier's Socialist government and the French are able to restore order after reinforcements arrive from France. The group of leaders responsible for the uprising, which came to be referred to as the Revolt of 1947, has never been identified conclusively. The French outlawed the MDRM while its leadership consistently maintained its innocence.

French military courts charged 77 officials of the MDRM even though most of them had little to do with the revolt. Twenty of them apparently had something to do with it and were executed. Other trials produced, by one report, some 5,000 to 6,000 convictions, and penalties ranged from brief imprisonment to death. **Upwards of 35,000 men, women and children are killed** during the revolt.

1947-1948 – Pakistani Annexation of Kalat. In 1940 **the Muslim League** formally endorsed the **partitioning** of **British India** and the **creation** of **Pakistan.** The India Independence Act left the Princes theoretically free to join with either India or Pakistan. The khan of Kalat in Balochistan declared independence on August 15, 1947, but offered to negotiate a special relationship with Pakistan. Other tribal chiefs also expressed their preference for a separate identity. Newly formed **Pakistan** took military action and brought them into **agreement by force** in 1948.

April 4, 1947 – Poland. After WWII ended, ethnic cleansing crimes were still being committed in Poland until 1949, and sporadic fighting continued until 1956. Vice-Minister of Defense General Karol Swierczewski was involved in the persecution of the independence movement in Poland, and signed many death sentences, while he established a communist regime.

The Ukrainian Insurrection Army ambush and execute Vice-Minister of Defense General Karol Swierczewski on April 4.

April 16, 1947 – Poland. Rudolph Hoess is **executed** at **Auschwitz.** The former camp commandant is hanged near the site of the #1 crematorium. Rudolf Hoess, the Commandant at **Auschwitz,** and the man who knew more than almost anyone about how **Nazi Germany** implemented the **Final Solution** was captured by the British after the war, tried, and sentenced to death. He was ordered to write his autobiography in the weeks between his trial and his execution, which fittingly took place in Auschwitz itself. Hoess apparently enjoyed the task, and the most careful checking by researchers showed he took great pains to tell the truth. The result is a vivid and unforgettable picture of the 20th century's defining and most horrific event. *Royalties from this book go to the fund to help the few survivors of Auschwitz.* ISBN-10: 1842120247

July 1947 – Poland. A joint Soviet, Czech and Polish military exercise annihilates the last remnants of Stefan Bandera's Ukrainian Insurrection Army in the Bieszczady Mountains.

1945-1947 – Expulsion of Germans from East Europe. Over 1,250,000 people died from Poland. Over 245,000 people died from Czechoslovakia. **Between 2,100,000 and 3,000,000 people died** including over 1,000,000 Germans who died fleeing while the war was still raging.

1947-1948 – Sino-Mongolian Border Clashes. The Mongolian-Chinese border in the Altai Mountain region is unclear. The Soviets had developed gold and tungsten mines in areas the Chinese considered part of Xinjiang, China. Kazakh rebels opposed to the Chinese regime had declared their autonomy in 1944, probably with Soviet encouragement. When China reestablished control over Xinjiang in 1946, some of the Kazakh leaders defected to China and others did not.

November 1947 – Thailand. Thai Coup d'état Group. In 1946 **King Rama VIII** was found dead in his bed at the palace, a bullet wound through his head. Although the official account attributed the King's death to an accident, Prime Minister Pridi Phanomyong's prestige suffered permanent damage as rumors implicated him in the death. He was forced to resign and leave the country. In November 1947, the so-called Coup d'Etat Group, led by two retired generals and backed by Phibun Songkhram, seized power from the civilian government. This is the same Phibun Songkhram who was one of the 114 members of the Promoters, the group that launched the coup on June 24, 1932 that changed the government to a constitutional monarchy.

February 28, 1947 – Taiwan. "2–28 Incident." Monopoly bureau officials in Taiwan beat up a woman they suspect of selling cigarettes on the black market and shoot a passerby who tries to intervene. The incident, which is known as the **"2–28 Incident,"** ignites an island–wide revolt and thousands of angry citizens, pour out into the streets. The protesters are met by China's Nationalist forces, called the Kuomintang, or KMT, on March 8. **Upwards of 20,000 people are brutally slaughtered** in the confrontation.

1948

The Oldest Boomer is 2 years old.

Cost of the Average House: $11,500 ($7,700-$13,500)	
"Mr. Blandings Builds His Dream House," cost = $30,000	
Median Family Income: $3,200	**Minimum Wage:** 40 cents/ hr
Gallon of Milk: 87 cents **Loaf of Bread:** 14 cents	**Gallon Gasoline:** 26 cents **Coffee:** 42 cents/ lb
New Car: Nash: $1,478 **Plymouth Deluxe, 4 door sedan:** $1,554	**Cantaloupe:** 23 cents **Fresh Chickens:** 55 cents/ lb **Kellogg's Corn Flakes:** 35 cents/2 **Perch Fillets:** 35 cents/ lb
Unemployment Rate: 3.8%-3.5%-4.0%	**First-class Stamp:** 3 cents

12 cents buying power in 1948 **= $1.00 in 2008.**
In 1948 what cost our parents 12 cents to purchase
now costs us $1.00 in 2008.

Movies: "The Road to Rio," "Easter Parade," "Hamlet," "Johnny Belinda," "The Red Shoes," "The Snake Pit," "The Treasure of the Sierra Madre," "The Bicycle Thief," "Red River," "The Three Musketeers," "Call Northside 777," "Mr. Blandings Builds His Dream House," "Rope," "Abbott and Costello Meet Frankenstein". "Superman," "Tex Granger," "Congo Bill," "G-Men Never Forget."

Broadway: "South Pacific," "Kiss Me Kate."

TV: "Break the Bank," "Perry Como Show," "I Remember Mama," "Johnny Belinda," "Barney Black, Police Reporter," "The Snake Pit," "Arthur Godfrey's Talent Scouts," "Superman". The "Texaco Star Theater" made its debut on NBC-TV with Milton Berle hosting. "Ted Mack's Original

Amateur Hour," "NBC News," "CBS News," "Our Miss Brooks." Mark Goodson's first game show, "Winner Take All" premieres. "Toast of the Town," with Ed Sullivan, premieres, with guests Dean Martin and Jerry Lewis. "Candid Microphone." Premieres and is renamed "Candid Camera" in 1949.

Music: "I'm Looking Over a Four Leaf Clover," "Buttons and Bows," "All I Want For Christmas is my Two Front Teeth," "Bumble Boogie." Wynonie Harris, "Good Rockin' Tonight. Eddy Arnold, "Bouquet Of Roses." Kay Kyser, "Woody Woodpecker Song." Pee Wee Hunt, "Twelfth Street Rag." Vaughn Monroe, "Red Roses For A Blue Lady." Doris Day, "It's Magic." The Mills Brothers, "Gloria."

Deaths: D.W. Griffith, Babe Ruth, Orville Wright.

President: Harry S. Truman (D) Baptist; vetoes 250/ 12 overrides

Vice President: None
(From April 12, 1945 the vice presidency remained vacant until 1949.)

House: D-188; R-246

Senate: 80th Congress (1947-1949) Majority Party: Republican (51 seats) Minority Party: Democrat (45 seats) Other Parties: 0
Total Seats: 96

Federal Debt: $252.29 billion or 94 % of the GDP

Consumer Price Index CPI-U (1982 Base of 100): 24.10

GDP: $269.2 billion	**Inflation Rate:** 7.74%

Dow Jones: 191.18 (06-01)/ 168.14 (03-01)

Prime Rate: 2.00% (08-01)	**Average Home Mortgage Rate:** 4.91%
1 oz Gold: $42.00	**1oz of Silver:** $0.91

Average Monthly S.S. Benefits Paid: $25 / month

Federal Debt: $252,292,246,512.99

Federal Deficit: ($11.8 billion dollar surplus)

Defense Spending: $19.75 billion	**Interest Spending:** $4.32 billion
Health Care Spending: $710 million	**Pensions Spending:** $760 million
Welfare Spending: $1.06 billion	**Education Spending:** $2.76 billion
Transportation Spending: $900 million	**Misc. Other Spending:** $3.44 billion
Protection Spending: $80 million	**Total Government Spending:** $35.59 billion

% of GDP that goes towards just the interest payment: 1.61%

U.S. Population: 146,631,000

U.S. Birth Rate: 3,637,000	**U.S. Abortions:** 16

U.S. Homicide Rate: 5.9/ 100,000 population

Annual Average Domestic Crude Oil Prices:
$2.77 / barrel, $24.76 (2007 adjusted)

Oil:

1948 – The United States becomes a net importer of oil for the first time. Chevron, Exxon, Gulf, Mobil and Texaco, British (British Petroleum), Dutch (Shell) and one French CFP, are the major oil companies. The countries owning the oil reserves are scattered across the world and include **Indonesia, Iran, Iraq, Kuwait, Saudi Arabia** and **Venezuela.** The oil companies extract the oil and control the supply and profits while American policy makers express concern over both corporate trust violations and national security concerns.

U.S. dependence on foreign oil is seen as a security risk in 1948 and it only represents **10% of supply.** The five American oil companies are allowed and actually encouraged to create a monopoly in conjunction with the three foreign firms. This monopoly will be very successful for the next twenty-three years.

According to data from the Energy Information Administration for crude oil field production in the U.S., our current July, 2008, annual domestic production of about 1.873 billion barrels of crude oil or 5.132 million barrels per day, **is about exactly the same** as oil production in 1948.

1948 – Ghawar, the world's largest oil field, is discovered in eastern Saudi Arabia. Ghawar is so large that its production accounts for about 60% of all Saudi Arabian oil and will remain the region's crown jewel. Production begins in 1950 and reaches a peak of 5.7 million barrels per day in 1981. By 2008 it is down to 5 million barrels a day and in decline. **It is a little known fact that the mid east is running out of oil at a much greater rate than anyone cares to admit.** If it were openly known, the Countries status in OPEC would decline and the oil and gas stocks would also lose so much value that it just is not in anyone's best interest to make this information widely known.

"We have about 50% of the world's wealth but only 6.3% of its population . . . Our real task in the coming period is to devise a pattern of relationships which will permit us to maintain this position of disparity without positive detriment to our national security." George F. Kennan, U.S. State Dept, 1948.

1948 – Crude Oil prices rang between $2.77 and $3.00 a barrel from 1948 through the end of the 1960s. The price of oil rose from $2.77 in 1948 to about $3.00 in 1957. This apparent price increase just kept up with inflation. Oil sold for $3.00 a barrel in 1959 and $3.30 a barrel in 1969. ($25.20 a barrel in 1979, $18.33 in 1989, $16.56 in 1999, and $91.50 in 2008 and then down to $43.10 in early 2009.

Major News:

January 30, 1948 – Indian pacifist and leader **Mahatma Gandhi** is **assassinated**, shot at point-blank range by Nathuram Godse, an activist of the Hindu Mahasabha. Since 1934, there were five unsuccessful attempts to kill Gandhi.

May 14, 1948 – The State of Israel is established. When the British officially withdraw on May 14, the Jewish National Council proclaims the State of Israel and U.S. recognition comes within hours. **The next day,** Arab forces from Egypt, Jordan,

Syria, Lebanon, and Iraq invade the new nation. The U.S. had been the first to recognize Israel, as President Truman had hoped and wanted. The Soviet Union followed suit three days later.

1948 – Hollywood Ten. The House Un-American Activities Committee interviewed 41 people working in Hollywood. All were "friendly witnesses," attended voluntarily and were members of the anti-Communist Motion Picture Alliance for the Preservation of American Ideals. They included producer **Jack L. Warner,** novelist **Ayn Rand,** and actors **Gary Cooper, Robert Montgomery, Ronald Reagan** (then President of the Screen Actors Guild), **Robert Taylor,** and **Adolphe Menjou.** Their testimony portrayed a Hollywood virtually at the mercy of militant Communists whose orders came directly from Moscow and they accused nineteen people of holding left-wing views. Of the nineteen, a group of **writers, producers** and **directors,** were then called as witnesses in the **House Committee's Investigation of Un-American Activities.**

When the ten refused to disclose if they were or were not **Communists** they were **jailed** for contempt of Congress. Known as the Hollywood Ten, they **claimed that the 1st Amendment** of the United States Constitution **gave them the right** to do this. The House Un-American Activities Committee and the courts disagreed. All were found guilty of contempt of congress and **each was sentenced to between six and twelve months in prison.** Many people were "blackballed" from Hollywood, lost their jobs and forfeited their careers.

In 1951, HUAC launched new hearings. Witnesses were called, and more than 300 uncooperative witnesses were blacklisted by the movie industry.

April 30, 1948 – The Organization of American States is founded by twenty-one nations to provide a mutual security pact after World War II. Founding nations are Argentina, Bolivia, Brazil, Chile, Columbia, Costa Rica, Cuba, Dominican Republic, Ecuador, El Salvador, Guatemala, Haiti, Honduras, Mexico, Nicaragua, Panama, Paraguay, Peru, the United States, Uruguay, and Venezuela.

June 24, 1948 – The Berlin Blockade begins. The Soviet Union begins its land blockade of the Allied sectors of Berlin, Germany. In response to the **Soviet blockade** of land routes into **West Berlin,** the **United States** and **Great Britain** began a massive airlift of food, water, and medicine to the citizens of West Berlin. Supplies from British and American planes sustain the more than 2 million people in West Berlin for close to 12 months until both blockades are lifted on September 30, 1949.

July 26, 1948 – Executive Order 9981, **ending segregation in the United States military** is signed into effect by **President Harry S. Truman**.

November 2, 1948 – President Harry S. Truman rallies from behind, capturing his first presidential election from the supposed winner Thomas E. Dewey, the Governor of New York. Headlines in national newspapers had already announced a Dewey victory, only to be proven wrong. Truman won the Electoral College vote with 303 to Dewey's 189, with **Strom Thurmond,** running as the States' Rights candidate, receiving 39 Electoral votes. **Truman won the election with less than 50% of the popular votes**, with additional candidate, Henry Wallace, siphoning off over one million votes in the four man race.

December 15, 1948 – Alger Hiss, a former State Department official, is indicted December 15 for perjury, after denying he had passed secret documents to **Whittaker Chambers** to forward to a **Communist spy ring.** He will be convicted of the conspiracy on January 21, 1950 and receive a five year jail sentence.

Civil Rights Movement:

March 30, 1948 – A. Philip Randolph, representing the *Committee Against Jim Crow* in Military Service and Training, testifies to the Senate Armed Services Committee that **African-Americans would refuse to serve in the armed forces** if a proposed new draft law does not forbid segregation. **Randolph** warned President Truman at a White House meeting on March 22 that he would lead a civil disobedience campaign against the draft unless the armed forces were integrated.

June 8, 1948 – Martin Luther King, Jr. at the age of 19 is ordained and appointed assistant pastor at Ebenezer Baptist Church in Atlanta.

July 13, 1948 – The platform committee at the **Democratic National Convention rejects** a recommendation put forward by **Mayor Hubert H. Humphrey** of Minneapolis calling for **abolition of segregation** in the armed forces. President Truman and his advisors support and the platform committee approve a moderate platform plank on civil rights intended to placate the South.

July 14, 1948 – The Democratic National Convention adopts a liberal platform plank on civil rights causing a split in the party. On July 17, **Southern "Dixiecrats"** hold a States' Rights convention and nominate **Governor Strom Thurmond** of South Carolina for President. Thurmond, who served as Governor of South Carolina and as a United States Senator, temporarily leaves the **Democratic Party in protest** over the **civil rights plank** in the national platform and runs for President under the State's Rights or Dixiecrat banner, carrying South Carolina in the Electoral College.

July 26, 1948 – **President Truman** issues two executive orders on July 26, 9980, establishing a **Fair Employment Board** to promote nondiscriminatory employment practices in the federal civil service, and 9981, which **begins desegregation of the armed services.** Although African Americans had participated in every major U.S. war, it was not until after World War II that the U.S. armed forces were integrated and it will not be until September 30, 1954 that the last all-black military unit is abolished.

September 14, 1948 – **Martin Luther King, Jr.** receives his Bachelor of Arts degree in sociology from Morehouse College. He skipped ninth and twelfth grade, and entered Morehouse College at age fifteen without formally graduating from high school. In 1948, he graduated from Morehouse with a Bachelor of Arts degree in sociology, and enrolled in Crozer Theological Seminary in Chester, Pennsylvania, where he graduated with a Bachelor of Divinity degree in 1951.

May 3, 1948 – **In "Shelley vs. Kraemer,"** the Supreme Court rules 6–0 on May 3 that judicial enforcement of **racially restrictive property covenants** is a violation of the equal protection clause of the Fourteenth Amendment.

1948

October 1, 1948 – The California Supreme Court voids the law banning interracial marriages. **Miscegenation laws** were laws that banned **interracial marriage** and sometimes interracial sex between members of two different **races**. In the United States, interracial marriage, cohabitation and sex have been termed "miscegenation" since 1863. In North America, laws against interracial marriage and interracial sex existed and were enforced in the **Thirteen Colonies** from the late seventeenth century onwards, and subsequently in several **U.S. States** and **U.S. territories** until 1967.

December 10, 1948 – The General Assembly of the United Nations adopted and proclaimed the **"Universal Declaration of Human Rights."**

Popular Culture:

1948 – U.S. Supreme Court ruling, McCollum vs. Board of Education. The court finds **religious instruction in public schools** to be a violation of the establishment clause and therefore **unconstitutional.**

1948 – The development of **antibiotics** in the 1940s made most of the severe venereal diseases of the time curable, namely **gonorrhea and syphilis.**

1948 – Lyndon Johnson. It has been well established by both conservative and liberal historians that Lyndon Johnson's election to the Senate in 1948 was won by massive **voter fraud.** Known as **"Landslide Lyndon,"** he was "elected" by only 87 votes. His challenger, Coke Stevenson challenged his election and presented credible evidence that hundreds of votes for Johnson had been faked. Johnson, however, was successful in blocking Stevenson's effort by the clever use of court injunctions. It was later discovered that votes had been cast at the last minute in alphabetical order.

June 24, 1948 – Harry S. Truman signs the **Selective Service Act**, creating the **first peacetime draft in the U.S.**

1948 – Andrew Wyeth, "Christina's World," one of the best-known American paintings of the middle 20th century.

1948 – DeBeers, "A diamond is forever." N.W. Ayer & Son.

1948 – Springmaid sheets, "A buck well spent." In-house.

1948 – I was born in 1948. The **cost of the average house** in the United States was **$11,500** and the **average median family income was $3,200** a year. **Minimum wage was 40 cents an hour.** A loaf of **bread was 14 cents** and a **gallon of milk was 87 cents**. A brand **new car was $1,230** and **gasoline (real gasoline) was 26 cents** a gallon. The United States was the number one oil producer in the world, producing most of the world's total supply. **The dollar had just pushed the British pound aside** as the number one currency in the world. **WWII** was over and we had won. The United States was busy helping rebuild European economies. NBC was celebrating its eighth year as a major TV station and **only one in ten Americans had seen a television up to this point**. I was a baby and like a lot of you, we were not very well off but never seemed to notice. We played, ate, had friends, laughed and cried. We walked to school and ran home on occasion to avoid the school yard bullies. Sometimes we did not make it all the way home and had our share of growing up. Everyday, normal stuff. If we did something wrong at school or in our neighborhood, we first received a punishment at their hands and then again at home. "Wait until your father gets home!" was still the most dreaded statement when we were eight or nine years old. Boomers are still children for many more years.
    This is the world we inherited.

1948 – The game of **Scrabble** is introduced by James Brunot. **Alfred Mosher Butts**, an out-of-work architect from Poughkeepsie, New York, invented the game first called LEXIKO and later called CRISS-CROSS-WORDS. Established game manufacturers were unanimous in rejecting Butts' invention for commercial development.

1948 – McDonald's. Richard McDonald said few people realize he's the namesake of 12,141 fast-food restaurants, not a clown called Ronald. The 82-year-old McDonald used to brace himself for celebrations honoring Ray Kroc as the "father of fast food" since Kroc bought his first **McDonald's restaurant** from McDonald and his brother, Maurice "Mac."

1948

The McDonald brothers were fast-food firsts when their restaurant opened in 1948 in San Bernardino, California. Roy Kroc was selling them milkshake machines at the time. In 1954, fifty-two year old milk-shake machine salesman Raymond Kroc became the franchising manager for the McDonald brothers.

Kroc went on to become the founder and builder of McDonald's Corporation. In 1961, Ray Kroc purchased the company from the brothers. The agreement was for the McDonald brothers to receive $2.7 million for the chain and to continue to receive an overriding royalty of 1.9%. 1998 total sales were $36 billion for McDonald's versus $10.3 billion for Burger King. In 2007 McDonald's operated over 31,000 restaurants worldwide, employing more than 1.5 million people.

1948 – Comic Book, Abbott and Costello (1948 St. John) #14, cover price 10 cents / sells for $11.52 in February 2009.

Business / Technology:

1948 – About two dozen different TV set models are on sale, ranging from Pilot's 3" set at $100, to DuMont's 20" set at $2,495 (that is very roughly $25,000 in 2009). Televisions are now found in over 340,000 homes, up from just 5,000 households three years earlier. After the manufacturing freeze imposed during WWII was lifted, sales rose from .5% of U.S. households in 1946 to 56% of U.S. households in 1954. By 1962 90% of all U.S. households had at least one Television set.

1948 – European nations import quotas on foreign films hit Hollywood.

1948 – Leo Fender invents the electric guitar.

1948 – French ink maker Marcel Bich introduces the Bic ballpoint pen.

1948 – TV signals are re-broadcast across nine states via airplane.

1948 – CATV, Community Antenna Television, the forerunner to cable TV. CATV provides television to consumers via radio frequency signals transmitted to televisions through fixed optical fibers or coaxial cables.

1948 – Western Union manufactures 50,000 Deskfax machines for **fax** transmission.

1948 – Freddie William's team develops the **Manchester Mark 1 computer.** In 1946 Freddie William was appointed as head of the Electrical Engineering Department of the University of Manchester. There, with Tom Kilburn he pioneered the first stored-program digital computer. He is particularly well known for the invention of the Williams-Kilburn tube, an early memory device, and the Manchester Mark 1 computer.

1948 – IBM's Selective Sequence Electronic Calculator computed scientific data in a public display near the company's Manhattan headquarters. Before its decommissioning in 1952, the SSEC produced the moon-position tables used for plotting the course of the 1969 Apollo flight to the moon.

1948 – Columbia Records introduced the **33 1/3 LP** Long Playing Record. Made in the U.S. of vinyl it played at 33 1/3 rpm offering an unprecedented 25 minutes of music per side, compared to the four minutes per side of the standard 78 rpm record.

April 20, 1948 – Labor leader Walter Reuther is shot and seriously wounded by would-be assassins. As a prominent figure in the **anti-Communist** left, he was a founder of the **Americans for Democratic Action** in 1947. He became President of the CIO in 1952.

May 10, 1948 – President Truman orders the army to operate the Nations Railroads, to prevent a nationwide rail strike.

1948-1951 – The Foreign Assistance Act, Marshall Plan, agreed to provide more than $13 billion in aid to war torn Europe between 1948 and 1951.

1948 – The UN creates the **World Health Organization.**

Finance:

1948-July 2009 – Official figures for June 2009 released today show large falls in both the **Consumer Prices Index (CPI)** and the **Retail Prices Index (RPI).** The figures raise the very real specter of deflation with the RPI heading into negative territory not seen since records began in 1948. At 1.8% CPI has fallen below the government's 2% inflation target for the first time since September 2007.

Books:

1948 – Author Jack Kerouac introduces the phrase "**Beat Generation.**"

1948 – Charlie Brown, Lucy, and the other "**Peanuts**" begin as "**Li'l Folks.**"

1948 – "Sexual Behavior in the Human Male," Alfred Charles Kinsey.

1948 – Norbert Wiener published "**Cybernetics,**" a major influence on later research into artificial intelligence.

TV:

1948 – Perry Como has his first television Christmas Special.

1948 – Professional wrestling makes its television TV debut.

Radio:

1948 – Ted Mack's "Original Amateur Hour."

1948 – Two radio sitcoms: **"Our Miss Brooks"** and Lucille Ball's **"My Favorite Husband."**

Sports:

1948 – The Summer Olympics are held in London, England. Alice Coachman becomes the first African American woman to win an Olympic Gold Medal when she wins the high jump competition.

1948 – **The Winter Olympics** are held in St. Moritz, Switzerland.

January 29, 1948 – Commissioner Happy Chandler fines the Yankees, Cubs, and Phillies $500 each for signing high school players.

1948 – Dick Button wins his first **Olympics gold.** He landed the **double axel jump** in practice for the first time the day before and decided to put it in his free skate. He also landed it and at nineteen becomes the youngest man to win the Olympic gold in figure skating. Dick Button went on to win the **1948 World Championships.**

Natural Disasters:

1948 – Instances of **Polio**, infantile paralysis**,** increased around the world. **When diphtheria and pertussis vaccines were introduced** in the 1940s, cases of paralytic poliomyelitis skyrocketed. Several studies have shown that the injections increased susceptibility to polio.

   When national immunization campaigns were initiated in the 1950s, the number of reported cases of polio following mass inoculations with the killed-virus vaccine was significantly greater than before mass inoculations, and may have more than doubled in the U.S. as a whole. U.S. government studies also link increases in cancer and a possible link to AIDS. Source: U.S. Government statistics.

June, 1948 – Flooding in Foochow, China kills 3,500 people.

October 5, 1948 – Earthquake, Soviet Union. More than **110,000 people are killed** when a 7.3 magnitude earthquake shakes the area around Ashgabat in Turkmenistan (Soviet Union). A 2007 report by the State News Agency of Turkmenistan says up to 176,000 people are killed.

Man vs. Man / Wars:

New figures now show the total estimated human loss of life caused by World War II (1939-1945) was roughly 72 million people making it the deadliest and most destructive war in human history. The civilian toll was around 47 million, including

20 million deaths due to war-related famine and disease. The military toll was about 25 million, including the deaths of about 4 million prisoners of war in captivity.

Assassinated – Bogotá, Colombia. Presidential candidate Jorge Eliécer Gaitán is assassinated midday in downtown Bogota on April 9. An angry mob immediately seized and killed the assassin. This set off a riot where 3,000 to 5,000 people were killed, thousands more were injured, and a large portion of downtown Bogotá was destroyed. The aftershock of Gaitan's murder continued through the countryside and triggered a period in the history of Colombia known as *La Violencia* that lasted until 1958. A culture of violence.

Assassinated – Egypt. Nukrashi Pasha, Prime Minister of Egypt, is assassinated by the **Muslim Brotherhood.**

Assassinated – Yemen. February 17, 1948. **Yahya Muhammad Hamidaddin** (or **Imam Yahya**) died during an unsuccessful coup attempt and was succeeded by his son Imam AhmadAhmad bin Yahya. The Assassin was known as Alqardaei who was from the Bani Murad tribe. The plot lead by Abdullah Alwazir was supported by the British, and the **Muslim Brotherhood** lead by Hassan Banna in Cairo. They also targeted his son Seif Ul Islam Ahmad in Taiz, yet that attempt failed.

Assassinated – Gandhi. January 30, 1948. Hindu extremist Nathuram Godse assassinates **Political and Spiritual Leader Mohandas Karamchand Gandhi** also known as **Mahatma Gandhi**, age 78.

Gandhi first employed non-violent **civil disobedience** as an expatriate lawyer in **South Africa**, in the resident Indian community's struggle for civil rights. **World War II** broke out in 1939 when **Nazi Germany** invaded **Poland** and initially, Gandhi had favored offering non-violent moral support to the British effort. Later Gandhi and his supporters made it clear they would not support the war effort unless India was granted immediate independence. Thousands of freedom fighters were killed or injured by police gunfire, and hundreds of thousands were arrested. Gandhi and the entire Congress Working Committee were arrested in **Bombay** by the British on August 9, 1942. His 50-year old secretary Mahadev Desai died of a heart attack **6 days**

later and his wife Kasturba died after 18 months imprisonment on February 22, 1944. Six weeks later Gandhi suffered a severe malaria attack. He was released before the end of the war on May 6, 1944 because of his failing health, necessary surgery and the Raj did not want him to die in prison. Gandhi was assassinated January 30, 1948.

November 8, 1948 – Representative J. Parnell Thomas (R-New Jersey) is **indicted** on conspiracy to defraud the U.S. government, payroll padding, and receiving salary kickbacks. Thomas, **chairman of the House Committee on Un-American Activities,** padded his congressional payroll and took kickbacks from his staff. He is convicted on November 30, 1949, sentenced to 6-18 months, and paroled on September 18, 1950. He is then pardoned on December 24, 1950.

April 16, 1948 – Robert Henry Best is **convicted** of **treason** and **serves a life sentence**. When Germany declared war on the United States in December, 1941, Robert Best was arrested along with other U.S. reporters for deportation, but was allowed to remain in Vienna with his fiancée Erna Maurer, an Austrian reporter for the Associated Press. Best was one of two dozen Americans recruited at various times to broadcast to the United States from Berlin. He was hired in March, 1942, by the German Foreign Office radio division which was a **Nazi propaganda** machine created by **Joseph Goebbels.** Best began broadcasting Nazi propaganda from Germany and his broadcasts were anti-Semitic and anti-Roosevelt, even though many of his former friends in Austria were Jewish. Best's broadcasts became so strident that his Nazi supervisors took him off the air on July 14, 1942.

1948-1949 – Communist Purge in Albania. After 1946 the United States and the United Kingdom began implementing an elaborate covert plan to overthrow **Albania's communist regime** by backing anticommunist and royalist forces within the country. The pro-Yugoslav faction had decisive political power in Albania well into 1948. At a party plenum in February and March, the communist leadership voted to merge the Albanian and Yugoslav economies and militaries. In September 1948, the Soviet Union stepped in and anti-Titoist purges in Albania bring about the liquidation of fourteen members of the party's thirty-one-person Central Committee. Thirty-two of the 109 People's Assembly deputies are also executed. Overall, the party purged about 25 percent of its membership. By 1949 the United States and British intelligence organizations were working with **King Zog** and the **mountain men** of his personal guard.

1948 – British Guiana. Enmore Shootings. Throughout Guyana, the social conditions are deplorable. The *Ten Year Planning Report* of 1948 shows that 25 percent of all school children suffer from nutritional deficiencies. The infant mortality rate is as high as 86 per 1,000, as compared with 32 per 1,000 in the United Kingdom. The sugar industry continues to dominate the economic and social life of the country and 20% of the people are housed on the plantations in slum conditions that date back to the days of slavery.

On June 16, police opened fire on a group of strikers at Plantation Enmore, killing five people and wounding 14 others. The Enmore shootings focused discontent and helped Cheddi and Janet Jagan move the PAC (Political Affairs Committee) into national prominence.

January 4, 1948-present (Myanmar) – Burma Revolt. Burma gained its Independence on January 4 and the nation became an independent republic, named the **Union of Burma.** Unlike most other former British colonies and overseas territories, it did not become a member of the **Commonwealth.** Since 1948 this has been a long and complex civil war involving several different uprisings and rebellions.

March 12-April 24, 1948 – Costa Rican Civil War. Rebel army commander **José Figueres** rose up against the government of President **Teodoro Picado**, which it quickly defeated. More than 2,000 people were killed during the five weeks. After the war, José Figueres ruled for a year and a half as head of a provisional government **junta** which abolished the military and oversaw the election of the Assembly that produced the new Costa Rican Constitution of 1949.

1947-1948 – Czechoslovakia. During the summer of 1947, the Communists began a campaign of political agitation and intrigue that gave them complete control of the government by February, 1948.

The Communists in Czechoslovakia fear Soviet intervention and stage a coup. The communist-controlled Ministry of Interior deploys police regiments to sensitive areas and equips a workers' militia. On March 10, the moderate foreign minister of the government, Jan Masaryk, is found dead in an apparent suicide, although the suspicious circumstances surrounding his death have led some to believe that it was a political assassination. Czechoslovakia becomes a Soviet-style state.

1948 – El Salvador. Salvadoran Military Revolt. The **coffee barons'** direct control of the Presidency ultimately came to an end as a consequence of the **Great Depression,** which began in 1929. A coup installed **General Maximiliano Hernández Martínez** as President in December 1931 and initiated a succession of **military governments** that controlled the country through 1979.

   A military coup by young army officers installed a junta headed by **Major Oscar Osorio** in 1948. Osorio launched a variety of reform projects, such as the development of hydroelectric facilities and urban housing projects. He also extended **collective bargaining** rights to urban workers, but, for the most part, the reforms served to encourage economic growth and to benefit the **middle class**. He served until 1956.

1948 – India. When the British relinquish control the 562 independent princely states were given the option to join with either India or Pakistan. India insisted that Hyderabad join India and more than a year after India had gained its independence, Hyderabad was invaded. On September 17, the Nizam signed an Instrument of Accession to the Union of India and Hyderabad was successfully annexed by India.

January to May 1948 – Iraqi. The al-Wathbah Uprising. Iraqi leftists vs. Iraqi government. The movement is sparked by the students and it later spreads to the workers and to the peasants that occupied the land in many parts of the country. Several huge demonstrations take place with tens of thousands on the streets. On January 27 the police shoot and kill 300 to 400 people, but this does not stop the protesters. The Prime Minister is forced to flee to Britain and a new government is formed.

May 1948-1949 – Israeli War of Independence, 8,000 people died. Israel: 3,000, Egypt: 2,000, Syria: 1,000, Jordan: 1,000, Iraq: 500, Lebanon: 500.

   One day before the termination of the **British Mandate of Palestine,** on May 14,

1948

1948, **David Ben-Gurion** declared the independence of the state of **Israel**, and the 1948 Palestine war entered its second phase, Arab forces from **Egypt, Jordan, Syria, Lebanon,** and **Iraq** invaded the new nation the following day.

1948-1949 – Korean Guerrilla War. On August 15th, 1945, **Japan surrendered** ending the Pacific War, but **10 days later Korea was divided into North and South Korea.** The United States took control of surrendering Japanese soldiers south of the 38th Parallel while the Soviet Union took control of the north. The United Nations called for elections in 1947 but the North Koreans refused. The United States turned its authority over to South Korea (the Republic of Korea) in 1948 and left a small group of military advisors.

The communist Democratic People's Republic in the north begins its war with the south in an attempt to control all of Korea under a communist government backed by the Soviet Union. President Syngman Rhee's southern regime, gaining sovereignty in 1948, suppressed all leftist political activity, put down a guerrilla uprising and held up to 30,000 political prisoners by the time communist North Korea invaded on June 25, 1950.

October 1948 – South Korea. Ysu Rebellion in U.S. Occupied Korea 1948. A communist-led revolt of army regiments in the southern part of Korea consumed much of the army's attention and resources. A massive purge in the aftermath of that revolt weakened the entire military establishment. Given South Korea's precarious future and the communist victory in China, the United States was not eager to provide support, and by June 29, 1949, United States occupation forces had been withdrawn except for a handful of military advisers.

1948-present – Lebanon. Israeli-Palestinian Conflict. As a member of the Arab League, Lebanon declared war on Israel in 1948 but took little part in the conflict.

1947-1948 – Madagascar Revolt. In 1946, the island of Madagascar became a French overseas territory, prompting the establishment of its first formal political party, called the Mouvement Democratique de la Renovation Malagache (MDRM), whose objective was independence for Madagascar. In less than a year, Malagasy nationalist tribesmen rose in revolt in the island's eastern areas. After receiving reinforcements, resident French soldiers were able to contain the revolt, but not before much bloodshed occurred. The French admit to 11,505 known dead. Unofficial totals go up to **80,000 dead.**

1948-1960 – Malaya. Malayan Emergency. A guerrilla war for independence fought between **British Commonwealth armed forces** and the **Malayan National Liberation Army.** The withdrawal of **Japan** at the end of **World War II** left the Malayan economy disrupted. The British administration was attempting to repair Malaya's economy quickly, especially as revenue from Malaya's tin and rubber industries was important to Britain's own post-war recovery. As a result, protesters were dealt with harshly, by measures including arrests and deportations. In turn, protesters became increasingly militant.

1948 – Palestine. Deir Yasin Massacre. The **Deir Yassin massacre** refers to the **killing of between 107 and 120 Palestinian unarmed civilian villagers**, the estimate generally accepted by scholars, during and possibly after the battle at the village of Deir Yassin near Jerusalem in the British Mandate of Palestine by Jewish Zionist guerrilla fighters between April 9, and April 11. It occurred while Jewish Yishuv forces fought to break the siege of Jerusalem. The killings were condemned by the leadership of the **Haganah**, the Jewish community's main paramilitary force, and by the area's **two chief rabbis**. It had been agreed during planning meetings that the residents be expelled and the troops were specifically ordered not to kill women, children, or prisoners.

1948 – Paraguayan unsuccessful Military Coup. Warring elements within the Colorado Party members took part in coup attempts in 1948 and 1949, and **Alfredo Stroessner Matiauda** was a main player in each attempt. At one point, he was forced to flee to Brazil to escape reprisal for his role in an unsuccessful revolt. He was back in the country within a few months, however, after taking part in a successful coup in 1949.

1948 – Peru. Military Coup. Manuel Arturo Odría Amoretti led a successful military coup and took over the government. A thriving economy allowed him to indulge in expensive but crowd-pleasing social policies. At the same time, however, **civil rights** were severely restricted and **corruption** was rampant throughout his régime.

1948 – The National Party of the Dutch Afrikaners began the policy of **apartheid in South Africa.** With the enactment of apartheid laws in 1948, racial discrimination is institutionalized. Race laws touch every aspect of social life, including a prohibition of marriage between non-whites and whites, and the sanctioning of "white-only" jobs.

1948 – Sri Lanka gained its Independence from Great Britain.

1948-1965 – Taiwan, Republic of China. Sino-Taiwanese War. After the defeat of **Japan** during **World War II**, Taiwan surrendered to the **Allies**, with Republic of China troops accepting the surrender of the Japanese garrison. Military administration of the ROC extended over Taiwan, which led to widespread unrest and increasing tensions between Taiwanese seeking independence and mainlanders.

The arrest of a cigarette vendor and the shooting of a bystander on February 28, 1947, triggered island-wide unrest, which was then suppressed with military force. The administration declared **martial law** in 1948. As many as **28,000 civilians were killed.**

1948 – Venezuelan Reactionary Coup. President Romulo Gallegos, Venezuela's first democratically elected leader is overthrown within eight months of his election in a **military coup** led by Marcos Perez Jimenez, who forms a government with backing from the armed forces and the U.S. In 1945, Pérez Jiménez participated in a coup that helped install **left wing Democratic Action party** founder, Rómulo Betancourt, as President of the Revolutionary Government Junta.

Pérez Jiménez and Lt. Colonel Carlos Delgado Chalbaud were not pleased with cuts in pay and the lack of modern equipment in the military so they staged another coup in 1948. Betancourt and Gallegos were exiled, political parties were suppressed, and the Communist Party was once again banished by the Military Junta. The Military Junta changed its name to a Government Junta, and reorganized itself with Pérez Jiménez pulling the string of puppet President, Germán Suárez Flamerich. In

1952, Pérez Jiménez was "elected" President. During his tenure, Venezuela was transformed into one of the most modern nations in Latin America.

1948 – Vietnam. By 1948, three years after the **Saigon Commune uprising**, the U.S. State Department recognized quite clearly that the Viet Minh, the anti-French resistance led by Ho Chi Minh, was the national movement of Vietnam. But the Viet Minh did not cede control to the local oligarchy. It favored independent development and ignored the interests of foreign investors.

1949

The Oldest Boomer is 3 years old.

Median Family Income: $3,100	**Minimum Wage:** 40 cents/ hr
Gallon of Milk: 82cents	**Gallon Gasoline:** 27 cents
New Car: Buick Special: $1,945 **Ford Custom:** $1,472	**Loaf of Bread:** 14 cents **Ivory Soap:** 27 cents /2 bars
Unemployment Rate: 4.3%-7.9%-6.6%	**Pepsi-Cola:** 22 cents/ 6 bottles **First-class Stamp:** 3 cents

11 cents buying power in 1949 = **$1.00 in 2008.**
In 1949 what cost our parents 11 cents to purchase
now costs us $1.00 in 2008.

Movies: "The Third Man," "Gun Crazy," "All The King's Men," "Battleground," "The Heiress," "A Letter to Three Wives," "Twelve O'clock High," "White Heat," "The Further Adventures of Ma and Pa Kettle." "Abbott and Costello Meet the Killer, Boris Karloff." "The Adventures of Ichabod and Mr. Toad." "Africa Screams," starring Bud Abbott and Lou Costello. "Adventures of Sir Galahad," "Batman and Robin."

Broadway: "South Pacific," "Death of a Salesman."

TV: "The Lone Ranger" premiered. Bozo the Clown made his TV debut on "Bozo's Circus." "Arthur Godfrey and His Friends," "I Remember Mama," "The Life of Riley," "Hopalong Cassidy," "Easy Aces," "Ripley's Believe It or Not," "Voice of Firestone," The Presidential inauguration is televised. "These Are My Children," soap opera. The first detective series "Martin Kane, Private Eye" premieres. The first science fiction series "Captain Video and His Video Rangers" premieres. The Three Stooges short films first aired.

Music: Dinah Shore, "Buttons and Bows." Perry Como, "Some Enchanted Evening." Frankie Laine, "Mule Train." Vaughn Monroe, "Ghost Riders In The Sky." Gene Autry, "Rudolph the Red-Nosed Reindeer." Buddy Holley

cut a demo of Hank Snow's "My Two-Timin' Woman" on a home tape recorder, his first known recording. Paul Williams, "Hucklebuck." Eddy Arnold, "Don't Rob Another Man's Castle." Dinah Shore & Buddy Clark, "Baby, It's Cold Outside." Fats Domino, "The Fat Man."

Deaths: Charles Ponzi, the con artist built a pyramid of investors by paying very high returns from the cash inflows from new investors. There is no creation of real value; early investors profit from the gullibility of later investors.

President: Harry S. Truman (D) Baptist; vetoes 250/ 12 overrides.

Vice President: Alben W. Barkley (D) Methodist

House: D-263 ; R-171

Senate: 81st Congress (1949-1951) Majority Party: Democrat (54 seats) Minority Party: Republican (42 seats) Other Parties: 0 Total Seats: 96

Federal Debt: $252.77 billion or 95 % of the GDP

Consumer Price Index CPI-U (1982 Base of 100): 23.80

GDP: $267.3 billion	**Inflation Rate:** -0.95%

Dow Jones: 191.23 (11-01)/168.08 (07-01)

Prime Rate: 2.00%	**Average Home Mortgage Rate:** 4.93%
1 oz Gold: $49.50	**1oz of Silver:** $0.91

Average Monthly S.S. Benefits Paid: $25 / month

Federal Debt: $252,770,359,860.33

Federal Deficit: ($0.6 billion dollar surplus)

Defense Spending: $21.99 billion	**Interest Spending:** $4.36 billion
Health Care Spending: $830 million	**Pensions Spending:** $880 million
Welfare Spending: $1.34 billion	**Education Spending:** $2.80 billion

Transportation Spending: $1.01 billion	Misc. Other Spending: $5.02 billion
Protection Spending: $80 million	Total Government Spending: $40.20 billion
% of GDP that goes towards just the interest payment: 1.63%	
U.S. Population: 149,188,000	
U.S. Birth Rate: 3,649,000	U.S. Abortions: 675
U.S. Homicide Rate: 5.4/ 100,000 population	
Annual Average Domestic Crude Oil Prices: $2.77 / barrel, $24.99 (2007 adjusted)	

Oil:

1949 – The U.S. and Latin America provide Europe's oil until the end of the 1940s.

1949 – First offshore heavy lift barge (150 tons - McDermott).

1949 – First offshore submersible barge (Breton Sound 20 - Hayward).

Major News:

March 2, 1949 – Captain James Gallagher lands the **B-50 Lucky Lady II** in Texas after completing the first around-the-world non-stop airplane flight. It was refueled four times in flight.

March 31, 1949 – Newfoundland becomes **Canada**'s tenth province.

April 4, 1949 – NATO, the North American Treaty Organization, is formed by the United States, Canada, and ten Western European nations (Belgium, Denmark, France, Iceland, Italy, Luxembourg, Netherlands, Norway, Portugal, and the United Kingdom). The treaty stated that any attack against one nation would be considered an attack against them all.

1949

May 11, 1949 – Israel is admitted to the United Nations.

May 12, 1949 – The Berlin Blockade ends.

September, 1949 – Mao Zedong, a Communist, takes control of China as major combat in the Chinese civil war ends. The Communist Party of China is in control of mainland China, and **Chiang Kai-shek** and the Kuomintang (KMT) retreat to Taiwan. The Mao regime proclaims the People's Republic of China on October 1, 1949, with Beijing as the new capital and Zhou Enlai as Premier. Mao Zedong begins a total overhaul of the land ownership system, and extensive land reforms.

August 29, 1949 – Nuclear Arms Race. The Soviets explode their first atomic bomb. The USSR successfully detonates its first atomic bomb at Semipalatinsk in Kazakhstan on August 29. **It is a *copy* of the Fat Man bomb** and has a yield of 21 kilotons. This marks the beginning of the nuclear arms race that will last more than forty years.

October 14, 1949 – Eleven leaders of the **U.S. Communist Party** are **convicted** October 14, of advocating the violent overthrow of the U.S. government and are **sentenced to prison**. The Supreme Court will uphold the convictions on June 4, 1951.

October 26, 1949 – President Truman signs legislation raising the **federal minimum wage** from 40¢ an hour to 75¢ on October 26.

1949 – A Supreme Court decision splits movie studios from theater chains.

1949 – Hollywood studios begin to produce television programs.

Civil Rights Movement:

1949 – The Truman Administration proposes legislation to make **lynching a federal crime,** create a new Fair Employment Practices Commission (FEPC), abolish poll taxes in national elections, and end segregation in interstate transportation, but none of the bills are brought to a vote in the Senate.

November 1949 – Harry Briggs is the first name on a list of more than a hundred petitioners in a test case filed with Clarendon County, South Carolina by the state **NAACP** that goes beyond the earlier request for equal transportation by asking for total educational equality. Modjeska Montieth Simpkins writes the petition. Briggs and others in the case, including **Reverend J.A. DeLaine**, who is a school principal, are **fired from their jobs**. The case is filed in federal court in 1950.

1949 – The Peekskill Riots are **anti-communist riots,** with anti-black and anti-Semitic undertones, that take place at Van Cortlandtville, Westchester County, New York in 1949. The catalyst for the rioting is an announced concert by black **singer Paul Robeson**, who was well known for his **strong pro-trade union stance on civil rights** and his out spoken beliefs in international socialism and anti-colonialist movements. The concert, organized as a benefit for the Civil Rights Congress, was scheduled to take place on August 27 in Lakeland Acres, just north of Peekskill.

June 1949 – Wesley Brown becomes the **first African American to graduate from** the **Naval Academy** at Annapolis.

Women's Movement:

July 8, 1949 – Vietta M. Bates became the **first enlisted woman sworn into the WAC** as part of the regular U.S. Army. Women are no longer limited to medical roles.

1949 – Eugenie Anderson is sent to Denmark as the first woman Ambassador from the United States.

Popular Culture:

1949 – Network TV is **established** in the U.S.

1949 – Arthur Miller's Pulitzer Prize play, **"Death of a Salesman."**

1949 – The War Department is renamed the Department of Defense. The War Department existed from 1789 until September 18, 1947, when it was renamed as the

Department of the Army, and became part of the new, joint National Military Establishment. In 1949 it was renamed to the Department of Defense, which the Department of the Army is part of today.

1949 – The United States has **98 television stations**.

1949 – **Beatnik.** In the late Forties, a generation of crazy, illuminated **hipsters** suddenly rose up and began roaming America, bumming and hitchhiking everywhere. Among the authors voicing this generation are **Jack Kerouac** and **Allen Ginsberg.** The Beatnik was hip and cool, daddy-o.

1949 – **Milton Berle** hosts the first telethon.

1949 – **Silly Putty** was originally created by accident during research into potential rubber substitutes for use by the United States in World War II. Ruth Fallgatter, owner of the Block Shop toy store in New Haven contracted marketing consultant Peter Hodgson to produce her toy catalog including a written description of bouncing putty offered in a clear plastic case for $2. When the new catalog was released Bouncing Putty outsold every item in the catalog except one, a box of hexagonal **Crayola crayons** which sell for 50 cents. Despite this success, Fallgatter declines further interest in marketing it.

Without missing a beat Peter Hodgson **borrows $147** to buy a batch of the putty and packs one ounce portions into plastic eggs selling for $1 each. He renames it Silly Putty and in August a *New Yorker* writer discovers **Silly Putty at a Doubleday bookstore** and writes a story about it for the *Talk of the Town* Section. Hodgson received over 250,000 orders for Silly Putty in three days. In 1957 Hodgson produced the first televised commercial for Silly Putty, which aired during the **Howdy Doody Show** and **Captain Kangaroo.** Over 300,000,000 Silly Putty eggs have been sold since 1950.

1949 – **Maidenform**, "I dreamed I went shopping in my Maidenform bra." Norman, Craig & Kunnel.

Business / Technology:

1949 – Whirlwind at MIT is the **first real-time computer.** Development of the Whirlwind computer began in 1945, and the system was first demonstrated on April 20th, 1951.

1949 – The Manchester Mark I computer functions as a complete system using the Williams tube for memory. Memory size: 128 + 1024 40-digit words. Components: **1,300 vacuum tubes.** It is as large as a medium size room.

1949 – RCA offers the 45 rpm record. Columbia has the 33 1/3 rpm LP.

1949 – The AT&T phone combines a ringer, handset and volume control.

1949 – The Freedom of Association and Protection of the Right to Organize Convention, 1949, one of the two primary labor conventions of the International Labor Organization ILO, came into force on July 4. By 2001 over 150 countries have ratified this Convention.

1949 – The British **EDSAC computer** stores programs in memory and then switches programs.

Finance:

1949 – After many years of misery through the depression and World War II, postwar prosperity is starting to get underway.

Books:

1949 – Edwin Sutherland publishes the first edition of **"White-Collar Crime"** in which he details the criminal behaviors of the 70 largest U.S. corporations at the time. He does not mention the names of the corporations out of apparent fear of reprisal.

1949 – Nelson Algren's novel of drug addiction, **"The Man with the Golden Arm."**

1949

1949 – "The Sheltering Sky," Paul Bowles.

1949 – George Orwell, **"Nineteen Eighty Four."**

1949 – Harold Robbins, "The Dream Merchants." The book is a "rags-to-riches" story of a penniless young man who goes to Hollywood and builds a great film studio.

TV:

1949 – The first TV daytime soap opera, **"These Are My Children,"** is broadcast.

1949 – Bozo the Clown makes his TV debut on **"Bozo's Circus."**

Radio:

1949 – Radio is the lifeline for Americans in the 1940's, providing news, music and entertainment, much like television today. Programming includes soap operas, quiz shows, children's hours, mystery stories, fine drama, and sports. **Kate Smith** and **Arthur Godfrey** are popular radio hosts. The government relies heavily on radio for propaganda. Like the movies, radio faded in popularity as television became prominent. Many of the most popular radio shows continued on in television, including **Red Skelton, Abbott and Costello, Jack Benny, Bob Hope,** and **Truth or Consequences.**

1949 – "Dragnet" starts on **NBC radio.**

1949 – Businessman Jesse Blanton, Sr. establishes **WERD-AM, the first black owned radio station.** It begins broadcasting in Atlanta on October 3.

Sports:

1949 – The **Basketball Association of America** and the **National Basketball League** merge to form the **National Basketball Association (NBA).**

1949 – Joe DiMaggio of the **NY Yankees** becomes the 1st $100,000/ year baseball player.

January 1949 – The New York Giants sign their first black players: **Negro Leaguers** outfielder **Monte Irvin** and pitcher **Ford Smith.** Monte Irvin will star for the Giants, but Ford Smith does not make it to the major leagues.

Music:

1949 – Mitch Miller begins his career as one of the 20th century's most successful record producers at Mercury. The Karaoke style and bouncing ball come later.

1949 – Bing Crosby's smooth voice made him one of the most popular singers, along with **Frank Sinatra, Dinah Shore, Kate Smith** and **Perry Como.** Be-Bop and Rhythm and Blues grew out of the big band era toward the end of the decade even though these were distinctly black sounds, epitomized by **Charlie Parker, Dizzie Gillespie, Thelonious Monk, Billy Holiday, Ella Fitzgerald** and **Woody Herman.**

1949 – The song **"Rudolph the Red-Nosed Reindeer"** began life as a poem handed to shoppers at the Montgomery Ward department store chain in 1939. It was recorded in 1949 by **Gene Autry** after **Perry Como** turned it down.

Natural Disasters:

January 2-4, 1949 – Winter Storm. Nebraska, Wyoming, South Dakota, Utah, Colorado, and Nevada. One in a series of winter storms between January 1, and February 22. Although only 12 to 30 inches of snow fell, fierce winds of up to 72 mph created drifts as high as 30 ft. Tens of thousands of cattle and sheep died.

September 2, 1949 – China. Fire on the Chongqing (Chungking) waterfront **kills 1,700 people.**

December 5, 1949 – Korea. A typhoon strikes the fishing fleet off the coast of Korea and several thousand men are reported dead.

1949

1949 – U.S. Nationwide. Polio kills 2,720 people, and 42,173 cases are reported.

1949 – Khait earthquake, Tajikistan. **18,000 people died.**

April 13, 1949 – Earthquake. Olympia, Washington. **Property damage** estimated at upwards of **$25 million** is caused by a magnitude 7.0 earthquake near Olympia, Washington. There are eight deaths and many people are injured.

1949 – The Landes region wildfire in France kills 230 people.

August 17, 1949 – Turkey. A 7.1 magnitude earthquake strikes Turkey on the North Anatolian Fault.

August 22, 1949 – British Columbia, Canada. An 8.1 earthquake hits the Queen Charlotte Islands, in British Columbia, Canada.

Man vs. Man / Wars:

October 7, 1949 – Tokyo Rose, Iva Toguri D'Aquino, who broadcast as "Orphan Ann," the femme fatale of Japanese war broadcasts, is sentenced to ten years in prison. She will be paroled in 1956 and pardoned in 1977. **Tokio Rose** was a generic name given by Allied forces in the South Pacific during World War II to any of approximately a dozen English-speaking female broadcasters of Japanese propaganda.

March 8, 1949 – Mildred Gillars, "Axis Sally," is **convicted of treason** on March 8. She serves 12 years of a 10 to 30 year prison sentence.

1949 – George Koval is mustered out of the Red Army as a lowly private. In 2002 he will be recognized as the **Soviet spy Delmar.** In November 2007, **Russian President Vladimir Putin** will posthumously award Koval a gold star marking him as a Hero of the Russian Federation and publicly name him as Delmar.

George Koval was born in the U.S. and then immigrated to the Soviet Union with his family when he was 19. He finished some of his schooling, married, became a Soviet citizen, joined the Soviet Main Intelligence Directorate, and then returned to the U.S. where he was drafted and ends up working on the Manhattan Project in 1944 by day and stealing secrets for the Soviets with alarming speed. The first Soviet atomic bomb detonation is on August 29, 1949, and the plutonium is "prepared to the 'recipe' provided by military intelligence agent Delmar." **The Soviet atomic bomb is a *copy* of the Fat Man bomb.**

1949 – Bolivia. MNR Coup Attempt in Bolivia. The Nationalist Revolutionary Movement's attempt to gain power is unsuccessful. Its 1949 coup attempt failed, although with the support of the workers and some military officers it succeeded in gaining control of most major cities except La Paz.

April 18, 1949 – Britain recognizes the independence of the **Republic of Ireland** as it withdraws from the British Commonwealth. **Northern Ireland** remains a part of the United Kingdom while Ireland becomes a full republic and the British government gives new constitutional guarantees to the Northern Ireland Parliament at Stormont.

The province's Catholic minority welcomes the British troops sent to Northern Ireland in response to an upsurge in sectarian violence and the **Provisional IRA** break away from the **Official IRA,** which is criticized for failing to protect Catholic enclaves.

October 1, 1949 – Chinese Civil War. KMT vs. Communists. On January 21, 1949, Kuomintang forces suffer massive losses against Mao's Red Guard. In the early morning of December 10, 1949, Red Guard troops lay siege to Chengdu, the last KMT-occupied city in mainland China, and **Chiang Kai-shek** retreats from the mainland to Taiwan (Formosa) the same day. The People's Republic of China was established on October 1, 1949, with its national capitol at Beijing and **Mao Zedong, Chairman Mao,** was China's leader from 1949 until his death in 1976. The 1945-1949, Chinese civil war death toll is around 2,500,000 people.

1949 – China. In 1949 crude death rates were probably higher than 30 per 1,000, and the average life expectancy was only 32 years. The Chinese Civil War, 1945 to 1949 is responsible for **25,000 people killed due to famine,** and **Democide by Communists killed 2,323,000 people.** The term Democide is a term coined by political scientist R. J. Rummel and means the killing of a person in cold blood, or causing the death of a person through reckless and wanton disregard for their life. Thus, a government incarcerating people in a prison under such deadly conditions that they die in a few years is murder by the state. Democide by Guomindang, the Nationalist Party of China, killed 2,645,000 people. 1,200,000 people were killed in battle.

1943-1949 – The Greek Civil War, is fought between the Greek governmental army, backed by Britain and the USA, and the Democratic Army of Greece, the military branch of the Greek Communist Party; **55,000 to 60,000 people died.**

1947-1949 – India-Pakistan. The conflict for **Kashmir.** In 1949 a UN Peacekeeping mission arrived and has remained as observers ever since. India and Pakistan concluded a formal cease fire agreement January 1, 1949 but the conflict will still be going strong in 2010.

December 27, 1949 – Indonesia. Queen Juliana of the Netherlands granted sovereignty to Indonesia. In 1945, after the Japanese had been defeated, the Netherlands-Indies was given back to the Netherlands. In August 1945, however, the Indonesian nationalist **Sukarno** proclaimed the **Republic of Indonesia.** This eventually led to a 4 year long war between the nationalists and the Dutch army. In 1949 the Dutch came under heavy international pressure and gave independence to Indonesia. This formally happened on December 27 1949. This is also the reason why internationally the Indonesian independence is registered on that date, and not, as the Indonesians do, on August 17, 1945.

July 20, 1949 – Israel's 19 month war of independence ends with a ceasefire agreement with **Syria.** According to Israel's Foreign Ministry, **6,373 people**, or nearly 1 percent of the Jewish population, **were killed** during Israel's War of Independence.

June 29, 1949 – Korea. The United States withdraws its troops from Korea. North Korea will invade South Korea in 1950.

1948-1949 – North Korea. South Korea. Between 1946 and 1949 at least 10,000 North Korean youths were taken to the Soviet Union for military training. A draft was instituted, and in 1949 two divisions, 40,000 troops, of the former Korean Volunteer

Army in China, who had trained under the Chinese communists, and had participated in the Chinese civil war returned to North Korea. Although it continued to provide modest military aid to the south, the U.S. withdrew its occupation forces, leaving behind a 500-man Military Advisory Group by June 1949. Fighting between South and North Korea began on May 4, and as many as 5,000 guerrillas trained in North Korea were infiltrated into the mountainous areas of eastern and southern South Korea by the winter of 1949.

1949 – Taiwan. Mao Zedong stresses the importance of eventual unification with Taiwan under a principle of "One China," which will be foundation for the Chinese government's policy on Taiwan for the next 50 years.

1949 – Thai Naval Revolt. When leaders of an anti-Phibun army group were arrested in October 1948, the supporters of former Prime Ministers Pridi and Khuang in the Navy and the Marines were not arrested. In February 1949, a revolt instigated by Pridi supporters in the Marines and Navy is suppressed after three days of fighting.

1949 – Vietnam. Former Vietnamese emperor Bao Dai enters into the Elysée Agreement with the French, committing both sides to oppose **Ho Chi Minh.**

1950

The Oldest Boomer is 4 years old.

Cost of the Average House: In 1950, the average home is about 983square feet and sells for $11,000. Average cost was $10.30/sf.

Median Family Income: $3,300	**Minimum Wage:** 75cents/ hr **Average Hourly Wage:** $1.44
Hourly Wage Mfg: $1.59	**Hourly Wage Gov:** $1.45

Gallon Gasoline: 27 cents

New Car: Cadillac: $3,654 **Dodge Wayfarer 3 passenger Coupe:** $1,611	**Potatoes:** 35 cents/ 5 pounds **Sliced bacon:** 35 cents/ pound
Unemployment Rate: 6.5%-5.5%-4.3%	**First-class Stamp:** 3 cents

11 cents buying power in 1950 = **$1.00 in 2008.**
In 1950 what cost our parents 11 cents to purchase
now costs us $1.00 in 2008.

Movies: "Sunset Boulevard," "All About Eve," "Born Yesterday," "The Third Man," "King Solomon's Mines," "Harvey," "Cinderella," "Cheaper by the Dozen," "Father of the Bride," "Broken Arrow," "The Asphalt Jungle," "Ma and Pa Kettle Go to Town." "Abbott and Costello in the Foreign Legion." "Atom Man vs. Superman," "Flying Disc Man from Mars."

Broadway: "Guys and Dolls," "Peter Pan," "Brigadoon," "Carousel" London. "Call Me Madam."

TV: Saturday morning children's programming begins. "The Colgate Comedy Hour, "Your Hit Parade," "The Jack Benny Show," "George Burns and Gracie Allen Show," "What's My Line," "Cisco Kid," "Gene Autry," "Truth or Consequences," "You Asked For It," "You Bet Your Life,"

"Dangerous Assignment." Sid Caesar and Imogene Coca, "Your Show of Shows." "Beat the Clock."

Music: Joe Liggins, "Pink Champagne." Hank Snow, "I'm Movin' On." Hank Williams, "Long Gone Lonesome Blues." Dominoes, "Sixty Minute Man." Nat King Cole, "Mona Lisa." Red Foley, "Chattanoogie Shoe Shine Boy." Gene Autry, "Peter Cottontail."

Deaths: Al Jolson, George Orwell, George Bernard Shaw.

President: Harry S. Truman (D) Baptist; vetoes 250/ 12 overrides

Vice President: Alben W. Barkley (D) Methodist

House: D-263 ; R-171

Senate: 81st Congress (1949-1951) Majority Party: Democrat (54 seats) Minority Party: Republican (42 seats) Other Parties: 0 Total Seats: 96

Federal Debt: $257.36 billion or 88 % of the GDP

Consumer Price Index CPI-U (1982 Base of 100): 24.10

GDP: $293.8 billion	**Inflation Rate:** 1.09%

Dow Jones: 228.89 (12-01) / 196.81 (01-13)

Prime Rate: 2.25% (09-22)	**Average Home Mortgage Rate:** 4.95%
1 oz Gold: $40.25	**1oz of Silver:** $0.91

Average Monthly S.S. Benefits Paid: $29 / month

Federal Debt: $257,357,352,351.04

Federal Deficit: $3.1 billion dollars

Defense Spending: $24.24 billion	**Interest Spending:** $4.40 billion
Health Care Spending: $960 million	**Pensions Spending:** $990 million
Welfare Spending: $1.62 billion	**Education Spending:** $2.84 billion

Transportation Spending: $1.12 billion	**Misc. Other Spending:** $6.61 billion
Protection Spending: $90 million	**Total Government Spending:** $44.80 billion
% of GDP that goes towards just the interest payment: 1.50%	
U.S. Population: 151,325,798	**World Population:** 2,555,078,074
U.S. Birth Rate: 3,632,000	**U.S. Abortions:** 7
U.S. Homicide Rate: 5.3/ 100,000 population	
Annual Average Domestic Crude Oil Prices: $2.77 / barrel, $24.74 (2007 adjusted)	

Oil:

1950 – During the Korean War, oil prices did not increase.

1950 – The 754 mile long (1,214 km) **Trans-Arabian Pipeline** is completed, linking Eastern Province oil fields in **Saudi Arabia** to **Lebanon and the Mediterranean.**

1950 – The government of **Saudi Arabia is granted a 50% share of AramCo** oil profits.

Major News:

January 14, 1950 – **The United States** recalls all consular officials from China after the seizure of the American Consul General offices in Peking. Four Chinese Communist officials and their police escort take possession of the office of U.S. Consul General O. Edmund Clubb. They had warned Clubb last week and it proceeded businesslike and very cool on both sides. No one was arrested and Consul General Clubb moved many of his papers into his residence next door without interference.

1950

January 17, 1950 – Masked bandits rob the **Brink's, Inc.,** Boston express office, of $1.2 million in cash and another $1.5 million in checks and securities. This is the largest robbery in the U.S. up to this time. The case was not solved until 1956 when one of the robbers who had been in and out of prison started talking. He was not happy with his share of the loot and was a bit upset that the others had tried more than once to have him killed. Eight people were found guilty and all were sentenced to life imprisonment.

January 21, 1950 – Alger Hiss is convicted of perjury after denying he had given secret documents to **Whittaker Chambers** who had given them to a Communist spy ring.

January 31, 1950 – President Harry S. Truman orders development of the hydrogen bomb, in response to the detonation of the Soviet Union's first atomic bomb in 1949.

February 9, 1950 – Senator Joseph McCarthy begins his **anti-Communist crusade.** United States Senator Joe McCarthy has accused more than 200 staff in the State Department of being members of the Communist Party. He made the startling allegation in a public speech in Wheeling, West Virginia, saying the State Department was infested with communists and brandished a sheet of paper which purportedly contained the traitors' names. **The Era of McCarthyism begins.**

February 12, 1950 – Albert Einstein warns that nuclear war could lead to mutual destruction.

February 13, 1950 – The U.S. Army begins to deploy anti-aircraft cannons to protect nuclear stations and military targets.

February 13, 1950 – The U.S. Air Force loses a Convair B-36 bomber that carries an Mk-4 atomic bomb off the west coast of Canada, and produces the world's first Broken Arrow.

April 24, 1950 – Jordan formally annexes the West Bank.

April 27, 1950 – Apartheid. In South Africa, the Group Areas Act is passed, formally segregating the races.

May 9, 1950 – EU. European Union. Robert Schuman proposes what comes to be known as the **Schuman Plan.** A proposal drafted by Jean Monnet and put forward by the French Foreign Minister Robert Schuman to pool European coal and steel. The plan will go into effect in 1952 giving France, Germany, Italy, Belgium, Holland, and Luxembourg a voice within the newly formed European Coal and Steel Community. This is the forerunner of the European Union.

May 26, 1950 – The Senate Special Committee to Investigate Organized Crime in Interstate Commerce, opens hearings in Miami, Florida. What becomes known as the Kefauver Committee holds hearings in major cities throughout the country until August 17, 1951.

September 25, William Drury, a former acting police captain in Chicago, and Marvin Bas, attorney for the Republican nominee for Cook County Sheriff, are shot to death at separate locations in Chicago. Police believe the **two men were murdered** due to information they provided the Kefauver Committee on organized crime activities in Chicago. Chicago mobsters Paul Ricca and Louis Campagna are held for questioning in the murder, but due to lack of evidence are never formally charged.

June 25, 1950 – The Korean War begins when 135,000 North Korean Communist forces, backed with Soviet weapons, invade South Korea. The UN asks for troops to restore peace and on June 27, U.S. President Harry S. Truman orders American military forces to aid in the defense of South Korea.

June 27, 1950 – President Harry S. Truman deploys the **7th Fleet** to waters off **Taiwan** to prevent the spread of the conflict in Korea to other Far East countries.

June 28, 1950 – North Korean forces capture Seoul.

June 1950 – President Truman orders the Air Force and Navy to Korea on June 27, and approves ground forces and air strikes against **North Korea** June 30.

1950

June 1950 – The U.S. sends **35 military advisers** to **South Vietnam on** June 27, and agrees to aid the anti-Communist government.

August 27, 1950 – The Army seized all U.S. railroads on August 27, on President Truman's order to prevent a general strike. The Army used only 46 officers, one sergeant, and eight civilian clerks. They stayed in the background without interfering with operations unless necessary, to maintain uninterrupted rail service. The railroads were returned to their owners in **1952.**

September 1950 – U.S. forces landed at Inchon September 15. UN forces took Pyongyang on October 20, reaching the Chinese border November 20. On November 26, China sends troops across the border.

November 1, 1950 – Two Puerto Rican nationalists, Oscar Collazo and Griselio Torresola, **attempt to assassinate President Truman.** They arrived in Washington D.C. the day before from the Bronx in New York City, where they were active in the Puerto Rican Nationalist Party. They thought the assassination would call attention to Puerto Rico and advance the cause of Puerto Rican independence.

November 10, 1950 – A U.S. Air Force B-50 Superfortress bomber, experiencing an in-flight emergency, **jettisons and detonates a Mark 4 nuclear bomb** over Quebec, Canada. The bomb had not been fitted with its plutonium core.

The operation was a practice run to see if the B36 - Peacemaker bombers could handle the sub zero freezing weather required of a nuclear strike on the Soviet Union because the B36 was known to have cold weather issues with its engines. The temperature is minus 40 degrees centigrade at takeoff and three hours into the flight three engines start flaming and are shut down. With only three engines operational the plane does not have enough power and the crew decides to abandon the aircraft and bail out. There is enough evidence to believe that the plane crashed over an unpopulated area of British Columbia after all but the captain had bailed out. There is also supporting evidence that the bomb was never detonated but instead went missing. Armed or unarmed?

November 26, 1950 – United Nations forces retreat south toward the 38th parallel when Chinese Communist forces open a counteroffensive in the Korean War. This action halted any thought of a quick resolution to the conflict.

November 29, 1950 – The National Council of the Churches of Christ in the USA is founded.

November 30, 1950 – Douglas MacArthur threatens to use nuclear weapons in Korea.

December 8, 1950 – The U.S. bans shipments to Communist **China** and to Asiatic ports trading with China.

Civil Rights Movement:

November 11, 1950 – The Mattachine Society, the first national gay rights organization, is formed by Harry Hay, in Los Angeles, California. The Mattachine Society is considered by many to be the beginning of the gay rights movement.

1950 – W.E.B. DuBois served as chairman of the Peace Information Center and ran for the U.S. Senate on the American Labor party ticket in New York. In 1950-1951 Du Bois was tried and acquitted as an agent of a foreign power **in one of the most ludicrous actions ever taken by the American government.**

1950 – The NAACP decides to make its legal strategy a full-scale attack on educational segregation.

February 23, 1950 – The Atlanta branch of the **NAACP votes** to support a lawsuit filed by **Reverend Martin Luther King, Sr.**, a Baptist minister, and advocate for social justice, seeking to win equal pay for black teachers.

June 5, 1950 – The Supreme Court issues three **important anti-segregation decisions.** Sweatt vs. Painter was a U.S. Supreme Court case that successfully challenged the "separate but equal" doctrine of racial segregation established by the 1896 case Plessy vs. Ferguson. The Court orders the **University of Texas School of**

1950

Law to admit black students because a law school founded for blacks could not be equal to the established and prestigious white law school. In McLaurin vs. Oklahoma segregation is abolished in school classrooms, libraries, and cafeterias because "such restrictions impair and inhibit the ability to study, engage in discussions and exchange views, with other students, and, in general, to learn his profession." And Henderson vs. United States the Court rules that segregated seating on railroad dining cars denies the equal access to public accommodations guaranteed by the Interstate Commerce Act.

June 12, 1950 – Martin Luther King Jr., Walter R. McCall, Pearl E. Smith, and Doris Wilson are refused service by Ernest Nichols at Mary's Cafe in Maple Shade, New Jersey. Ernest Nichols fires a gun into the air when they persist in their request for service.

September 22, 1950 – Ralph Bunche becomes the first African American recipient of a Nobel Peace Prize. Dr. Ralph E. Bunche, Principal Director of the Department of Trusteeship and Information from Non-Self-Governing Territories at the United Nations is awarded the Nobel Peace Prize for his mediation of the Palestine conflict.

1950 – U.S. Census U.S. population: 150,520,798, Black population: 15,044,937 (10%)

Women's Movement:

May 1, 1950 – Gwendolyn Brooks of Chicago becomes the first African American to receive a Pulitzer Prize. She wins the prize in Poetry.

December 12, 1950 – Paula Ackerman becomes the first woman in the United States to serve a congregation as a Rabbi.

Popular Culture:

1950 – The 1950 U.S. census determined the resident population of the United States to be 150,520,798, an increase of 14.5 percent over the 132,164,569 persons counted during the 1940 Census.

1950 – Beatniks are part of a sub-culture in the 1950s and early 1960s that subscribe to an anti-materialistic lifestyle. Finger-snapping is Far Out. These were cool cats. I mean they were far out daddy-o! You dig?

1950 – Clowns. An endless stream of clowns emerge from a very small car, in what is the traditional circus-clown-car routine. This routine originates in 1950 under the big top of the **Cole Brothers Circus.** German "Master Clown" Otto Griebling, who later went on to star in the **Ringling Brothers and Barnum & Bailey Circus,** is credited with inventing it.

October 2, 1950 – Charles Schulz introduces the **"Peanuts"** comic strip when it is published in 7 U.S. newspapers.

1950 – Chevrolet, "See the USA in your Chevrolet." Campbell-Ewald.

1950 – Gene Autry says: "Sunbeam is MY Favorite Bread!"

1950 – Hamm's beer, "From the Land of Sky Blue Waters." Campbell-Mithun.

1950 – Brylcreem, "A little dab'll do ya." Kenyon & Eckhardt.

1950 – Elizabeth Taylor weds Conrad Hilton Jr. in her first marriage.

September 4, 1950 – The comic strip "**Beetle Bailey**" is created by **Mort Walker.**

1950 – The **Billy Graham** Evangelistic Association begins.

1950 – More than **3 billion tickets** are sold at U.S. movie theaters, down from the peak of 4.7 billion in 1947.

Business / Technology:

September 22, 1950 – The **first nonstop transatlantic jet flight** takes just 10 hours and 1 minute.

1950

1950 – Party lines make up 75 percent of all U.S. telephone lines. People shared a telephone line with their neighbors, so when you "picked up" if you heard them talking it was considered polite to say "sorry" and hang up for awhile.

1950 – Kodaks Colorama is exhibited at Grand Central station. It is considered breathtaking at 18 feet wide x 60 feet high.

1950 – The Flow-Matic, the first English language data-processing compiler.

1950 – CBS broadcasts in **color** to 25 television sets.

1950 – The FCC adopts the CBS color TV standard and then **changes its mind** three years later.

1950 – DJIA. After the Korean War began in June the market dropped 13 percent in a month.

1950 – The first **Xerox** machine is produced.

1950 – The first **self-service elevator** is installed by **Otis Elevator** in Dallas and elevator operators see their jobs being replaced by **high tech.**

1950 – The **first successful kidney transplant** takes place at Loyola University.

1950 – Engineering Research Associates of Minneapolis builds the ERA 1101, the first commercially produced **computer.** It holds 1 million bits on its magnetic drum, the earliest magnetic storage devices. Drums eventually stored as many as 4,000 words and retrieved any one of them in as little as five-thousandths of a second. The company's first customer is the **U.S. Navy.**

Finance:

January 2, 1950 – A report by the United States Dept. of Commerce shows that for the period July 1, 1945 to September 30, 1949, the **United States spent almost**

twenty-five billion dollars on foreign aid. Military spending for the same years has been one third of the yearly budget.

July 19, 1950 – President Truman calls for partial mobilization after **North Korea** crosses the 38th parallel and also asks Congress for ten billion dollars for the military. President Truman gets fifty-seven billion dollars for defense for 1951.

1940-1950 – Every nation involved in World War II greatly multiplied their debt. Between 1940 and 1950, U.S. Federal Debt went from 43 billion dollars to 257 billion dollars, a 598% increase. During that same period Japanese debt increased by 1,348%, French debt increased by 583%, and Canadian debt increased by 417%.

February 7, 1950 – James Paul Warburg appearing before the Senate on February 7, states, **"We shall have World Government, whether or not we like it.** The only question is whether World Government will be achieved by conquest or consent." This is when the central bankers got to work on their plan for global government which starts with a three step plan to centralize the economic systems of the entire world. These steps are: **1) Central Bank domination** of national economies worldwide. **2) Centralized regional economies** through super-states such as the European Union, and regional trade unions such as NAFTA. **3) Centralize the World Economy** through a World Central Bank, common world money, and ending national independence through the abolition of all tariffs by treaties like GATT. For some real fun take a deep breath and check out http://euro-med.dk/?p=3226

August 27, 1950 – President Truman orders the U.S. Army to seize control of all major U.S. railroads from the 194 owning companies, to prevent a general strike. The U.S. is dependent on its railroads as they are the country's most important means of transportation. The railroads are not returned to their owners for two years.

Books:

1950 – David Riesman, **"The Lonely Crowd."**

1950 – **"The Wall,"** John Hersey.

1950

1950 – Betty Crocker's Picture Cookbook. Women are homemakers, cakes have at least two layers and salad is iceberg lettuce. Betty Croker is invited into American homes and she stays for a long time.

1950 – Ray Bradbury, **"The Martian Chronicles."**

1950 – James A. Michener, "Return to Paradise."

1950 – Gayelord Hauser, **"Look Younger, Live Longer."**

TV:

1950 – The television networks knuckle under to Red Channels and **blacklist** "subversives."

1950 – Estes Kefauver's Senate hearings on harmful media influences begin.

1950 – "Your Show of Shows" debuts on TV.

September 7, 1950 – The game show **"Truth or Consequences"** debuts on television.

Radio:

1950 – The Soviet Union starts jamming foreign radio broadcasts.

1950 – Many popular **soap operas** and prime-time radio shows shift to television.

Sports:

1950 – Tennis. U.S. National Championships. **Althea Gibson** appeared at the U.S. Championships and this is considered one of the top moments in **Black Tennis History**. Gibson, 23 years old, broke the color barrier when she entered the U.S. Championships, becoming the first African-American to be allowed to enter, forever changing the sport.

Music:

1950 – "Cool jazz" develops from bebop.

Natural Disasters:

June 1, 1950 – Volcano Mauna Loa in Hawaii starts erupting.

August 15, 1950 – India, an 8.6 magnitude earthquake affects 30,000 square miles in Assam. 1,500 people are killed and 5,000,000 are left homeless.

November 25 to 27, 1950 – The Eastern U.S. "Storm of the Century" generates heavy snow and hurricane-force winds across 22 states claiming 383 lives. Damages are estimated at $70 million.

December 3, 1950 – Mt. Etna erupts in Sicily.

Man vs. Man / Wars:

Assassination – Venezuela. Carlos Delgado Chalbaud, chairman of the military junta of Venezuela is **killed** while in office. He was kidnapped and assassinated by a group led by Rafael Simón Urbina and his nephew Domingo Urbina; his kidnapping took place in Caracas.

Assassination attempt – Two Puerto Rican pro-independence activists, Oscar Collazo and Griselio Torresola, attempt to assassinate **U.S. President Harry S. Truman** on November 1. The deadly battle lasted no more than 40 seconds and 30 rounds were fired. One White House police officer was killed, Torresola is dead, and Coffelt is dying. **President Truman was not harmed.**

1950 – Representative Walter E. Brehm (R-Ohio) is **indicted** on December 20, for accepting illegal campaign contributions. Brehm accepted cash contributions from two clerks in his office. He was **found guilty** of getting $1,000 from Clerk Emma Craven, but not guilty of taking money from a 74-year-old clerk in his Washington office. He was **convicted** on April 30, 1951 and sentenced to 5-15 months in prison. The sentence is suspended and he is fined $5,000.

1950-1952 – Albania. The communists turned the war of liberation into a civil war, and then committed crimes and used terror against their own people. The Albanian Communists were supported by Yugoslavia, on the condition that Albania would return Kosovo to Serbia after the war. After taking over the country, the Albanian communists launched a tremendous terror campaign, shooting intellectuals and arresting thousands of innocent people.

    The U.S. and British governments were determined to remove the communist government in Albania and assisted guerrilla units entering Albania in 1950 and 1952, but Albanian security forces killed or captured all of them. Soviet double agent, **Kim Philby,** working as a liaison officer between the British intelligence service and the United States Central Intelligence Agency, leaked details of the infiltration plan to Moscow, and the security breach claimed the lives of about 300 infiltrators.

1950-1972 – Burma. Chinese KMT Invasion. KMT, Chinese soldiers retreat across the Chinese-Burma border to escape the advancing Chinese Communist armies of **Mao Zedong.** In 1950 the U.S. Defense Department assisted the French in Indochina and the CIA began regrouping remnants of the defeated KMT army in the Burmese Shan States for a future invasion of southern China. The Kuomintang (KMT) National People's Party was not successful in its military operations; however it succeeded in monopolizing and expanding the Shan States' **opium trade** in what came to be known as the **Golden Triangle.** The Kuomintang army increased the opium production 1,000%, almost 1/3 of the world supply, and ruled the area until 1972.

1950-1958 – China. Chinese Communist Terror. Mao Zedong, Chairman Mao, himself claimed that a total of 700,000 people were executed during the years 1949-1953. Mao got this number from a report submitted by Xu Zirong, Deputy Public Security Minister, which stated 712,000 counter revolutionaries were executed, 1,290,000 were imprisoned, and another 1,200,000 were subjected to control.

1950 – China. Tibet. Communist Chinese forces invade Tibet. Tibet enjoyed de facto sovereignty from 1913 when they claimed independence from China until the Chinese invasion of 1950-1951. The Chinese Communist government led by Mao Zedong invaded the Tibetan area of Chamdo, defeating sporadic resistance from the Tibetan army. In 1951 a "Seventeen Point Agreement" affirms China's sovereignty over Tibet. Rebellion against the Chinese occupation resulted in tens of thousands of Tibetans killed and the 14th Dalai Lama and other government principals fleeing into exile in India. The Central Tibetan Administration states that the number of Tibetans that have died of starvation, violence, or other indirect causes since 1950 is approximately 1.2 million. It is closer to 300,000-400,000 which is no small number of human lives needlessly lost.

1950 – Indochina War, France, U.S. VietNam. The First Indochina War 1946-1950 was a draw. The French with overwhelming superiority in weapons could take and hold any particular area it really wanted while the Viet Minh recruited locally from a large population and always had more soldiers.

The United States decision to provide military assistance to France and the Associated States of Indochina was reached informally in March and announced on May 8. The U.S. wanted to avoid direct involvement in a colonial war, and knew that France's political and military situation in Indochina was deteriorating. The Joint Chiefs would go no further than to say that prompt delivery of the aid would do no more than create the **"possibility of success."**

1945-1950 – Indonesia. Indonesian War of Independence. Indonesia vs. Dutch. One of the largest revolutions of the twentieth century, the struggle lasted for over four years and involved sporadic but bloody armed conflict, internal Indonesian political and communal upheavals, and two major international diplomatic interventions. Dutch forces were too weak to prevail over the inexperienced but determined Indonesians, but strong enough to resist being expelled. Estimates of Indonesian deaths in fighting range from 55,000 to 100,000 and civilian casualties exceeded 35,000 and may have been as high as 100,000. Tens of thousands of Chinese and Eurasians were killed or left homeless and 7 million people were displaced on Java and Sumatra.

1950

1950-1953 – Korean War. USA, Britain, France, Turkey & the UN Army vs. North Korea and China. CIA China station officer Douglas Mackiernan received Chinese and North Korean intelligence, predicting the summer invasion of the South. He and a team of local CIA mercenaries then escaped the Chinese in a months-long horse trek across the Himalaya Mountains. Mackiernan was killed within miles of Lhasa city, but his team delivered the intelligence to headquarters. Thirteen days later, the North Korean People's Army crossed the 38th-parallel border and invaded South Korea.

More than 70 percent of all North Korean troops are deployed in areas along the 38th parallel within the first few months of 1950. By summer, North Korean forces number between 175,000 and 200,000 troops split into ten infantry divisions, one tank division, and one air force division. They are equipped with over 200 fighter planes and 280 tanks. The Soviet Union is supplying the North Korean forces with everything they need in preparation to fight the ill-equipped South Korean army of less than 100,000 men with few tanks and combat airplanes. The south lacked heavy artillery and did not have troops trained to use modern equipment. South Korea called up their police force of 45,000 officers. The USA, Britain, France, Turkey & the UN Army came to South Korea's defense with the entire country now fighting for its life. Then in October China joins the war on North Korea's side.

Before a cease-fire agreement is signed on July 27, 1953, four million people died and one third of all homes were destroyed. The armistice ended the fighting, but Korea has remained divided and there is always the possibility of a new war at any time.

1948-1960 – Malaya. Guerrilla war for independence. In 1950 the British send the Special Air Service Regiment, disbanded after WWII to Malaya, augmented by Rhodesia and New Zealand. The following year helicopters enable the British to insert troops deep into the jungle. The terrorism will last twelve years. The terrorists killed 3,000 civilians, 1,350 policeman, 128 Malayan and over 500 British and Gurka soldiers. Some 12,000 communists took part in active operations. Of these 6,710 were killed, 1,290 were captured, and 2,996 surrendered.

1950-1951 – Nepal Congress Rebellion. Many Nepalese in exile had actively taken part in the Indian Independence struggle and wanted to liberate Nepal as well. King Tribhuvan fled from his "palace prison" in 1950, to newly independent India, touching off an armed revolt against the Rana administration. The revolt caused constitutional change and a cabinet was introduced, forcing the Prime Minister of the Rana family, to share power in Nepal. In 1951 the country is opened to foreign visitors and by 1965 **Kathmandu** was a favorite destination of many hippies.

1950 – Puerto Rico. Nationalist Uprising. Puerto Rico seeks independence with revolts and uprisings in various towns. The United States declares martial law in Puerto Rico and sends the Puerto Rico National Guard to the various towns involved in the nationalist uprisings. In Utuado, a group of 32 nationalists fought against the local police. The group which was reduced to 9 men surrendered to the National Guard later on in the day. They were marched into town and taken behind the police station where, without a trial, they were machined gunned. Four of the nationalists died, and five survived.

1950 – South Africa. Apartheid. In 1950, the Population Registration Act required that all South Africans be racially classified into one of three categories: white, black (African), or colored (of mixed decent). The colored category included major subgroups of Indians and Asians. Classification into these categories was based on appearance, social acceptance, and descent. For example, a white person was defined as "in appearance obviously a white person or generally accepted as a white person." A person could not be considered white if one of his or her parents were non-white. The determination that a person was "obviously white" would take into account "his habits, education, and speech and deportment and demeanor." A black person would be of, or accepted as a member of an African tribe or race, and a colored person is one that is not black or white. The Department of Home Affairs was responsible for the classification of the citizenry. Non-compliance with the race laws were dealt with harshly. All blacks were required to carry "pass books" containing fingerprints, photo and information on access to non-black areas.

August 10, 1950 – Vietnam. The First shipload of U.S. arms aid to pro-French Vietnam arrives. In May, **President Harry S. Truman** authorized a modest program of economic and military aid to the French, who were fighting to retain control of their Indochina colony, **including Laos and Cambodia as well as Vietnam.**

When the **Japanese invaders** were pulling out of **French Indochina** after WWII, **France** announced its plans for an alliance of Indochina within the French union which would allow these new "states" to form their own governments. **Cambodia** and **Laos** accepted the federation without question. **The Vietnamese Nationalists** demanded that the French grant complete independence to Annam, Cochin China and Tonkin as Vietnam. The French agreed to recognize Vietnam as a free state within the French Union but **Ho Chi Minh** and the **communist Vietminh** refused the terms. The Vietminh begin their attack on the French. China and then the Soviet Union back Ho Chi Minh and the U.S. sends aid and advisors to assist the French. This will result in 2,500,000 to 5,000,000 people killed through 1975 during the Vietnam conflict. The U.S. never officially declared war.

1951

The Oldest Boomer is 5 years old.

Median Family Income: $3,700	**Minimum Wage:** 75cents/ hr
Gallon Gasoline: 27 cents	
New Car: Oldsmobile: $2,558 **Desoto:** $4,278	
Unemployment Rate: 3.7%-3.2%-3.1%	**First-class Stamp:** 3 cents

12 cents buying power in 1951 **= $1.00 in 2008.**
In 1951 what cost our parents 12 cents to purchase
now costs us $1.00 in 2008.

Movies: "The African Queen," "A Streetcar Named Desire," "An American in Paris," "Decision Before Dawn," "A Place in the Sun," "Strangers on a Train," "Quo Vadis?" "Alice in Wonderland," "Show Boat," "The Enforcer," "Ma and Pa Kettle Back on the Farm." "Abbott and Costello Meet the Invisible Man." Ronald Reagan starred with a chimpanzee in "Bedtime for Bonzo." "A Christmas Carol," "The Day the Earth Stood Still."

Broadway: "The King and I," "The Mikado," "A Tree Grows in Brooklyn," "Paint Your Wagon."

TV: "I Love Lucy," "Amos 'N' Andy," "See It Now," new with Edward R Murrow. "The Dinah Shore Show," "Ernie in Kovaksland," Ernie Kovacs. "The Red Skelton Show." "Sky King," "Roy Rogers," "Dragnet," "Search for Tomorrow," "NFL Football," "Hallmark Hall of Fame," "Love of Life." Smilin' Ed McConnell and his Buster Brown Gang.

Music: Ruth Brown, "Teardrops From My Eyes." Joe Turner, "Chains Of Love." Hank Williams, "Cold, Cold Heart." Eddy Arnold, "I Wanna Play House With You."

President: Harry S. Truman (D) Baptist; vetoes 250/ 12 overrides

Vice President: Alben W. Barkley (D) Methodist

House: D-235 ; R-199

Senate: 82nd Congress (1951-1953) Majority Party: Democrat (49 seats) Minority Party: Republican (47 seats) Other Parties: 0 Total Seats: 96

Federal Debt: $255.22 billion or 75 % of the GDP

Consumer Price Index CPI-U (1982 Base of 100): 26.00

GDP: $339.3 billion	**Inflation Rate:** 7.88%

Dow Jones: 272.56 (10-01)/ 232 January

Prime Rate: 3.00% (12-19)	**Average Home Mortgage Rate:** 4.93%
1 oz Gold: $40.00	**1oz of Silver:** $0.89

Federal Debt: $255,221,976,814.93

Federal Deficit: ($6.1 billion dollar surplus)

Defense Spending: $29.22 billion	**Interest Spending:** $4.22 billion
Health Care Spending: $970 million	**Pensions Spending:** $1.77 billion
Welfare Spending: $1.57 billion	**Education Spending:** $2.20 billion
Transportation Spending: $1.13 billion	**Misc. Other Spending:** $5.43 billion
Protection Spending: $100 million	**Total Government Spending:** $48.94 billion

% of GDP that goes towards just the interest payment: 1.24%

U.S. Population: 154,287,000	**World Population:** 2,592,861,684
U.S. Birth Rate: 3,820,000	**U.S. Abortions:** 649

U.S. Homicide Rate: 4.9/ 100,000 population

Annual Average Domestic Crude Oil Prices: $2.77 / barrel, $22.93 (2007 adjusted)

Oil:

March 1951 – Iran nationalizes the oil industry. Iran, is denied the 50-50 profit share arrangement similar to what the Saudis received last year, and nationalizes the Anglo Iranian Oil Company. As a result Iranian oil is boycotted from 1951 through 1953.

Iran's first comprehensive agricultural and industrial Development Plan was to be financed from oil revenues and the oil issue figured prominently in elections for the Iranian Parliament. The nationalists in the new Iranian Parliament were determined to renegotiate the Anglo Iranian Oil Company agreement and in November the Iranian Parliament rejected a draft agreement in which the AIOC had offered the government slightly improved terms. These terms did not include the fifty-fifty profit-sharing provision that was part of other new Persian Gulf oil concessions. Because the British are so set against the 50/50 deal in 1951, the Iranians simply nationalize the oil industry and the British are now cut out. Nationalism is rising in the Middle East, and the balance of oil power is just beginning to shift.

1951 – Kentucky. Drilling activity increased considerably in Kentucky, resulting in a record of more than 11 million barrels of oil produced. Several significant discoveries are made which indicate promising possibilities for a large area in the southwestern part of the state.

April 4, 1951 – Oil is discovered in **North Dakota.** There is no shortage of oil in the U.S. and gasoline is available everywhere which means there is no market. The Bakken Oil Formation, which covers **North Dakota** and portions of **Montana** and **South Dakota,** is believed to have 175 to 500 billion barrels of recoverable oil and will not be "discovered" until much later.

Major News:

January 12, 1951 – The Federal Civil Defense Administration is established.

February 27, 1951 – The 22nd Amendment to the U.S. Constitution, limiting the number of terms a President may serve, is ratified.

1951

February 28, 1951 – The preliminary report from the **Senator Estes Kefauver investigation** that began on May 11, 1950 into organized crime is issued. The report states organized crime collects more than **$20 billion per year** from gambling. A lot of the gambling money is generated in **Arkansas** and controlled by the mob.

March 29, 1951 – **Julius Rosenberg, his wife, Ethel, and Morton Sobell are found guilty** of conspiracy to commit wartime espionage for passing atomic secrets to the Russians. The Rosenberg's **are sentenced to death for treason** and are executed June 19, 1953. Morton Sobell is sentenced to 30 years in prison and released in 1969.

April 11, 1951 – **General Douglas MacArthur** is removed from his command in **Korea** as commander of United Nations and U.S. forces, by **President Truman,** for public statements calling for an attack on mainland China unless Communist forces laid down their arms in Korea.

April 18, 1951 – **European Union. The Treaty of Paris** creates the **European Coal and Steel Community** (ECSC). Six countries, Belgium, France, Germany, Italy, Luxembourg, and the Netherlands, sign the Treaty. The ECSC created a common market for coal and steel to lessen the chance of a future war. The headline of the delegation's first bulletin read **"Towards a Federal Government of Europe."** It is the beginning of what will become the European Union.

May 29, 1951 – **Charles F. Blair** flying a North American P51 Mustang makes the first solo flight across the North Pole.

June 4, 1951 – **"Dennis vs. United States."** The Supreme Court upholds **the Smith Act of 1940** and rejects a challenge to the law by **eleven Communist Party leaders convicted** of conspiring to teach and advocate the violent overthrow of the government. In 1940 the Smith Act was passed. The Act made it a crime to advocate the violent overthrow of the government, to distribute any material that teaches or advocates such, or to belong to a group with such an aim.

July 1951 – Korea. Cease-fire talks begin and last two years while the fighting ends on July 27, 1953.

July 16, 1951 – The United States Secret Service. Congress enacts legislation that permanently authorizes Secret Service protection of the President, his immediate family, the President-elect, and the Vice President, if he wishes. (Public Law - 82-79).

September 1, 1951 – The U.S., Australia, and New Zealand sign the **ANZZUS** mutual security pact.

September 4, 1951 – The First transcontinental telecast occurs with the broadcast of President Truman's speech at the Japanese Peace Treaty Conference in San Francisco. The treaty is signed on September 8, 1951, by the U.S., Japan, and forty-seven other nations.

December 12, 1951 – Richard Buckminster Fuller patents the **Geodesic Dome.** The dome building, under his design, will be utilized in many futuristic constructions, particularly by Fuller in world exhibitions, such as his famous United States Pavilion at the Montreal World's Fair in 1967.

Civil Rights Movement:

May 8, 1951 – Martin Luther King Jr., graduates from **Crozer Theological Seminary** with a Bachelor of Divinity degree and delivers the valedictory address at commencement. Crozer Theological Seminary is a multi-denominational religious institution located near Chester, PA in Upland. The school serves the Baptist Church, training seminarians for the entry into the Baptist ministry.

May 24, 1951 – A mob of 3,500 whites attempt to prevent a black family from moving into a Cicero, Illinois apartment. Illinois **Governor Adlai Stevenson calls out the Illinois National Guard** to protect the family and restore order.

May 24, 1951 – The U.S. Supreme Court rules racial segregation in District of Columbia restaurants is **unconstitutional.**

1951

September 13, 1951 – Martin Luther King Jr., begins his graduate studies in systematic theology at **Boston University**.

1951 – Richmond, Virginia. Martinsville Seven. In 1949, in Martinsville, VA, seven black men were arrested for the rape of Ruby Stroud Floyd, a 32-year-old married white woman. All seven men signed written confessions within thirty hours of the alleged crime and within one week all seven men were convicted and sentenced to death. In 1951 the seven black men are executed in the Virginia state electric chair. Beginning at ten A.M. Friday three of the men were electrocuted, one every ten minutes. On Monday morning the remaining four men were electrocuted. This is supposedly the first time the death penalty is given for the crime of rape in Virginia. **Thurgood Marshall,** later to become the first black Supreme Court judge and then head of the NAACP's Legal Defense Fund, helped represent them. **Communist Russia** and **China** sent telegrams to the **White House** asking the U.S. to spare their lives but then President Truman refused to grant clemency. Around the world, they became known as the Martinsville Seven.

December 25, 1951 – Harry T. Moore, an **NAACP** leader who campaigned against police brutality and led voter registration drives, is killed and his wife, Harriette Moore, a schoolteacher, dies from wounds received when their home in Mims, Florida, is bombed on Christmas day.

1951 – The Governor of South Carolina, James Byrnes supports a three cent sales tax for education, mainly to improve African-American schools in hopes of avoiding integration. Byrnes is thought to be a strong progressive voice for moderate Negro rights as he understands the South can no longer continue with its entrenched segregationist policies. Afraid Congress will impose sweeping civil rights legislation on the South, he decides to at least make some changes and pours state money into improving Black schools, buying new textbooks and new buses, and hiring more teachers. **Governor James Byrnes** also wanted to remove the power of the **Ku Klux Klan** and pushed a law through the legislature that prohibited adults from wearing a mask in public on any day other than Halloween.

1951 – Elizabeth Gurley Flynn is a **Labor leader, activist,** and in 1920 a founding member of the **American Civil Liberties Union.** In July 1948, twelve leaders of the Communist Party were arrested and accused of violating the Smith Act by advocating the overthrow of the U.S. government by force and violence. Elizabeth Flynn started protesting for their release and in 1951 Flynn was arrested for conspiracy to overthrow the United States government, under the Smith Act of 1940. She was convicted in 1953 and served her prison term in Alderson Prison, West Virginia, from January 1955 to May 1957. In 1961, she was elected National Chairman of the **Communist Party,** making her the first woman to head that organization. She remained chairman of the party until her death. Flynn died while in **Moscow** in 1964 of a heart ailment and was given a state funeral in Red Square.

Popular Culture:

1951 – The film "One Summer of Happiness" starring Ulla Jacobsson and Folke Sundquist depicted scenes that were at the time considered too sexual, but by today's standards would be fairly mild.

1951 – The Motion Pictures Production Code specifically prohibits films dealing with abortion or narcotics.

1951 – The Planned Parenthood Federation of America runs **200 birth control clinics. Margaret Sanger** has been successful in fighting legal restrictions on contraceptives, and birth control has gained wide acceptance in America.

1951 – Campus Crusade for Christ is founded by Bill and Vonette Bright at UCLA.

1951 – The Radio program "My Favorite Husband" moves to TV as **"I Love Lucy."**

1951 – British film censors add an **X rating.**

1951 – Grace Hopper discovers the **first computer bug**, a real moth.

1951 – Miss World debuts as a new beauty competition.

1951

1951 – One and a half million TV sets are now in the U.S.; this is ten times more than just one year ago.

1951 – The Durham-Humphrey Amendment establishes more specific guidelines for prescription drugs. The bill requires any drug that is habit forming or potentially harmful to be dispensed under the supervision of a health practitioner as a prescription drug, and must carry the statement, "Caution: Federal law prohibits dispensing without prescription."

1951 – U.S. tycoon Al Hubbard tries **LSD** and starts promoting its recreational use. He has been called the "Johnny Appleseed of LSD"'" and the first person to emphasize LSD's potential as a visionary or transcendental drug.

1951 – Cinerama will briefly dazzle with a wide, curved screen and three projectors.

1951 – The Boggs Amendment to the Harrison Narcotic Act adds mandatory minimum and maximum prison sentences for **narcotic violations.** The government sees the potential dangers and attempts to legislate a solution to the problem.

1951 – Hathaway Shirts, "The man in the Hathaway shirt." Hewitt, Ogilvy, Benson & Mather.

Business / Technology:

1951 – Color television is introduced in the U.S. as Color TV sets go on sale.

April 20, 1951 – The Whirlwind computer is operational. It is the first computer to operate in "real time" and uses an oscilloscope screen to display text and graphics. This is a real breakthrough from the older mechanical computer models and leads directly to the United States Air Force's Semi Automatic Ground Environment (SAGE) system and indirectly to almost all business computers and minicomputers in the 1960s. Whirlwind uses core memory for RAM, another first. The Whirlwind computer has been in development since 1946. The machine was continually enhanced, eventually using 12,000 vacuum tubes, 20,000 diodes and occupying 3,300 square feet on two floors of an MIT campus building. It is a 16-bit parallel, single-address, binary computer.

1951 – CBS presents 4 hours of color TV, but only CBS executives and engineers have color TV sets.

1951 – Direct Distance Dialing, without an operator for long distance, begins in New Jersey. Americans can dial long distance calls directly instead of needing an operator.

1951 – Still cameras get built-in flash units.

1951 – Bing Crosby's company tests videotape recording. Bing Crosby Enterprises mounts the first successful demonstration of black and white magnetic video recording, an experimental 12-head VTR running at 100 ips.

1951 – Univac, Universal Automatic Computer, the first business computer to handle both numeric and alphabetic data, is introduced. Univac is the first mass-produced **computer.**

1951 – The first nuclear power plant is built by the U.S. Atomic Energy Commission.

1951 – The first Tupperware Home Party was held in 1948 and by 1951 the Tupperware Home Demonstration system was working so well that all Tupperware products were taken off store shelves to be distributed through the Home Party System.

July 18, 1951 – The Right to Organize and Collective Bargaining Convention, one of the two primary labor conventions of the ILO, entered into force on July 18, 1951 Adopted on July 1, 1949 by the General Conference of the International Labor Organization at its thirty-second session. By 2001, 154 Nations will ratify this convention.

1951 – First Credit Card in wide spread use. Diners Club and American Express launch their charge cards in the U.S., the first "cardboard money." **In 1951, Diners**

1951

Club issued the first widely used credit card to 200 customers who could use it at 27 restaurants in New York. By 1951 Diners Club had over 20,000 members.

Finance:

January 24, 1951 – The Office of Price Stabilization is created.

April 30, 1951 – President Truman gets fifty-seven billion dollars for defense.

May 24, 1951– **Switzerland** enters into a tax treaty with the **U.S.** agreeing to exchange information only in criminal cases involving **"tax fraud."**

1951 – **Military spending** in most years since the Korean War will drive the **U.S.** balance-of-payments deficit until in 2010 **China's central bank** will be the largest holder of U.S. Government and other dollar securities. This will place China in the uncomfortable position of being the largest financier of U.S. military adventurism, including U.S. attempts to encircle China and Russia militarily.

In 1951 we see the emergence of this Global economy begin to sprout everywhere. The main flaw embedded in our own economy is rising debt in excess of the ability to pay while simultaneously avoiding taxation, thereby receiving an actual fiscal subsidy. And the beat goes on . . .

Books:

1951 – **"The Catcher in the Rye."** J.D. Salinger

1951 – Herman Wouk's novel, **"The Caine Mutiny."**

1951 – **Truman Capote**'s novel, "The Grass Harp."

1951 – **"Pogo,"** Walt Kelly.

1951 – "From Here to Eternity," **James Jones**.

1951 – **"The Illustrated Man,"** Ray Bradbury.

1951 – "Prelude to Space," **Arthur C. Clarke.** Pre-Sputnik and amazingly prophetic.

TV:

1951 – In the first broadcast of **Edward R. Murrow's "See It Now"** series, Murrow shows the **split-screen image of the Golden Gate and Brooklyn bridges** and tells viewers it is the first time to see the Atlantic and Pacific oceans simultaneously.

1951 – **The Whirlwind computer** from the lab at **MIT** debuted on Edward R. Murrow's "See It Now" television series.

1951 – **"Out There,"** one of the more interesting science fiction programs only lasted for 12 episodes.

1951 – Smilin' Ed McConnell and his **Buster Brown Gang - PLUNK YOUR MAGIC TWANGER, FROGGY !** - and good old Buster Brown shoes.

Radio:

1951 – **Disk jockey Alan Freed** introduces the term **rock 'n' roll**. In an effort to introduce rhythm and blues to a broader white audience, which is hesitant to embrace "black music," disc jockey Alan Freed uses the term rock 'n' roll to describe R&B.

Sports:

October 3, 1951 – In baseball, the **"Shot Heard 'Round the World"** is the term given to the walk-off home run hit by New York Giants outfielder Bobby Thomson off Brooklyn Dodgers pitcher Ralph Branca at the Polo Grounds to win the National League pennant. As a result of the "shot" (baseball slang for "home run" or any hard-hit ball), the Giants won the game 5-4, defeating the Dodgers in their pennant playoff series, two games to one. This may be the most famous case of sign-stealing in baseball.

1951

1951 – Two co-captains of **Manhattan College's 1949-1950 men's basketball team** are **arrested** and charged with bribery and conspiracy in a point-fixing scandal. Ultimately, **32 players from seven colleges** will admit to accepting bribes to fix 86 games in 17 states from 1947-1950. Seven of the players had been on the **CCNY team** that swept the NCAA and NIT championships in 1950.

CCNY is the only team in men's college basketball history to win both the NIT and the NCAA Tournament in the same year, 1950. Because seven CCNY basketball players were arrested for taking money from gamblers to affect the outcome of games this accomplishment will always have questions related to its validity. The scandal led to the decline of CCNY from a national powerhouse in Division I basketball to a member of Division III and damaged the national profile of college basketball in general.

1951 – **Betty Chapman** becomes the first black professional player for the **Admiral Music Maids of the National Girls Baseball League** out of Chicago.

January 14, 1951 – **The National Football League** has its first Pro Bowl Game.

Natural Disasters:

1951 – **Avalanche.** An avalanche in the Swiss-Austrian Alps kills over 265 people.

August 6-7, 1951 – **Flooding** in Manchuria kills over 4,800 people.

1951 – **Tornado.** Comoros, Congo. The Comoro Tornado kills over 500 people.

January 15, 1951 – **A Volcano** in Mount Lamington, New Guinea, kills 3,000 to 5,000 people.

July 1951 - **Kansas and Missouri. The great flood of 1951** covers 2 million acres, damages or destroys 45,000 homes, leaves $2.1 billion in damage and kills 28 people.

August 21, 1951 – A 6.9 magnitude Earthquake strikes Kona, Hawaii.

1951 – A 6.8 magnitude earthquake strikes the North Anatolian Fault in Turkey.

Man vs. Man / Wars:

Assassinated – Abdullah I, King of Jordan. While he is visiting Al Aqsa Mosque in Jerusalem, **King Abdullah** is shot dead by a **Palestinian** from the Husseini clan. The assassin was afraid King Abdulla would make a separate peace with Israel.

Abdullah I was the ruler of Transjordan and its successor state, Jordan, from 1921 to 1951, first as Emir under a British Mandate from 1921 to 1946, then as King of an independent nation from 1946 until his assassination. Abdullah was in Jerusalem to give a eulogy at a funeral and for a prearranged meeting with Reuven Shiloah and Moshe Sasson. The King was shot while attending Friday prayers at the Dome of the Rock in the company of his grandson, **Prince Hussein** who was at his side and was also shot. A medal that had been pinned to Hussein's chest at his grandfather's insistence **deflected the bullet and saved his life.**

Assassinated – July 16, 1951. Riad Bey al-Solh, a former Prime Minister of Lebanon, is assassinated in Amman, where rumors are circulating that Lebanon and Jordan are discussing a joint separate peace with Israel. The assassin passed through heavy security to get to his target.

Assassinated – Liaquat Ali Khan, Prime Minister of Pakistan. Liaquat Ali Khan was a Pakistani politician who became the first Prime Minister of Pakistan and Defense Minister. He was also the first Finance Minister of India. On October 16, 1951, Liaquat had been scheduled to make an important announcement in a public meeting of the Muslim City League at Municipal Park, Rawalpindi. Liaquat was shot twice in the chest during that meeting by a man sitting in the audience only fifteen yards away. It was reported that the police immediately killed the assassin, who was later identified as Saad Akbar Babrak, an Afghan from the same Zadran tribe as Pacha Khan Zadran.

Assassinated – Ali Razmara, Prime Minister of Iran. On March 7, 1951, Razmara is assassinated outside the Soltaneh Mosque by a member of the Fedaeyān-e Eslām, an extremist religious organization with close ties to the traditional merchant class and the clergy. Within a short time, Mohammad Mosaddeq is elected Prime Minister, and nationalizes the country's oil industry.

1951 – Argentina. Argentine Revolt. During the Fourth Attempt in 9 Years to Oust Dictator **President Peron,** Troops loyal to **Peron** claimed Saturday to have crushed two major rebel strongholds in predawn battles and said a strong force was at the gates of a third. The tide thus appeared to be swinging sharply to the side of Argentina's strongman in the bloodiest rebellion he has faced in nine years of power. The key areas reportedly seized by the loyalist forces are the naval base at Rio Santiago in southern Argentina and the army post it Curuzu-Cuatia in Entre Rios Province about 325 miles north of Buenos Aires. There is no accurate estimate of casualties in the bitter fighting but the toll is expected to far outstrip the 300 to 400 dead and 1,000 wounded in the June 16 upheaval. The largest announced death count was at Eva Peron, the Capital of Buenos Aires Province, where 80 policemen were reported killed.

Argentina became a virtual **dictatorship** under President Juan Domingo Peron who was assisted in the government by his wife Eva, or **Evita.** In 1951, the country's economy was headed for disaster, with decreasing export trade, climbing inflation, and striking railway workers, firemen, and engineers. Peron declared Martial Law to break the strikes claiming they were instigated by "foreign agitators." After "La Prensa," Argentina's largest independent newspaper, criticized his government, Peron suspended publication which caused riots. The papers publisher flees the country and Peron seizes the newspaper.

A few Army Generals lead an unsuccessful coup in September after Peron attempted to have his wife Evita nominated as Vice President. They were outraged by the idea of Evita becoming commander of armed forces. Peron remains in control.

1951 – Pakistan. Rawalpindi Conspiracy. Major General Akbar Khan, along with other armed forces officers meet to plan a military coup. This is the first of many conspiracies in the armed forces of Pakistan to overthrow the civilian government.

May 1951 – Panama Vice Presidential Coup. Panamanian President Arnulfo Arias is deposed by coup and is succeeded by Vice President Alcibiades Arosmena. Former

President de la Guardia returns from exile and begins to challenge the government. In May there is a run on the Federal Trust Company savings bank, which is subsequently closed and when former President de la Guardia protests the closing, he is arrested. On May 10 Colonel Remón turns against President Arnulfo Arias, who is then overthrown, and Vice President Alcibíades Arosemena assumes power the following day. Colonel Remón will win the Presidential election of 1952 only to be assassinated in January 1955.

1951 – South Africa. Apartheid. In 1951, the Bantu Authorities Act established a basis for ethnic government in African reserves, known as "homelands."' These homelands are independent states to which each African is assigned by the government according to the record of origin, which was frequently inaccurate. All political rights, including voting, held by an African were restricted to the designated homeland. The idea was that they would be citizens of the homeland, losing their citizenship in South Africa and any right of involvement with the South African Parliament which held complete control.

From 1976 to 1981, four of these homelands were created, **denationalizing 9,000,000 South Africans.** The homeland administrations refused the nominal independence, maintaining pressure for political rights within the country as a whole. Nevertheless, Africans living in the homelands needed passports to enter South Africa. They were made aliens in their own country.

June 1951 – Thailand. Thai Naval Revolt. In June 1951, marine and navy troops again rebelled and abducted **Phibun Songkhram.** The revolt, which was put down by loyal army and air force units, resulted in a serious cutback of naval strength and a **purge of senior naval officers.** Leading Admirals are arrested, the central and eastern provinces previously occupied by the navy are re-assigned to army command, and entire battalions of marines are disbanded. The air force assumes control over the navy's air section, and the naval headquarters are moved from the capital to the eastern seaboard. Nothing remained of the navy's political power and the Thai army now has control of the country.

In August and October 1951 the powerful police chief, **Phao Siyanon,** traveled to Switzerland to persuade the young King Bhumibol to accept a constitution more amenable to the military. When the King did not agree the "Coup Group" decide to proceed without his approval and in November they stage yet another coup. **Phao Siyanon** gains the most from the coup due to his own appointment as Deputy Minister of the Interior, giving him effective control over this politically powerful ministry and allowing him to ruthlessly eliminate parliamentary opposition. His police force expanded quickly and became a second army consisting of 43,000 officers. **Phao is deeply involved in the opium trade,** amassing great wealth that allows him to more easily bribe and pay off those he can not eliminate.

1951 – Vietnam. U.S. military aid amounted to more than $500 million by 1951.

1952

The Oldest Boomer is 6 years old.

Median Family Income: $3,900	**Minimum Wage:** 75 cents/ hr
Gallon Gasoline: 28 cents	**Loaf of Bread:** 12 cents
New Car: Austin A40: $1,895 **Dodge Diplomat Hardtop:** $2,602	**Pork and Beans:** 25 cents/ 3 cans **Grapefruit:** 25 cents/ 6
Unemployment Rate: 3.2%-3.0%-2.7%	**First-class Stamp:** 3 cents

12 cents buying power in 1952 **= $1.00 in 2008.**
In 1952 what cost our parents 12 cents to purchase
now costs us $1.00 in 2008.

Movies: "Singin' in the Rain," "High Noon," "The Greatest Show on Earth," "The Bad and the Beautiful," "Moulin Rouge," "Ivanhoe," "The Quiet Man," "The Snows of Kilimanjaro," "Hans Christian Andersen," "Viva Zapata," "The Jazz Singer," "Ma and Pa Kettle at the Fair." "This is Cinerama," filmed for curved screen Cinerama. "Abbott and Costello Meet Captain Kidd." "Bela Lugosi Meets a Brooklyn Gorilla." "Jumping Jacks," starring Dean Martin and Jerry Lewis. "The Black Castle" starring Stephen McNally, Boris Karloff, and Lon Chaney Jr.

Broadway: "Pal Joey," "Pirates of Penzance," "Wish You Were Here," "The Mousetrap."

TV: "The Adventures of Ozzie and Harriet," "The Adventures of Superman," "Ding Dong School," "Dragnet," "Arthur Godfrey and His Friends," "The Ernie Kovacs Show," "The Honeymooners," The Jackie Gleason Show. "This is Your Life," "Annie Oakley," "Death Valley Days." An Atomic bomb test in Nevada is shown on live television. "American Bandstand," "Guiding Light."

Music: Arthur Freed, "Singin' In the Rain." Jimmy Boyd, "I Saw Mommy Kissing Santa Claus." Patti Page, "I Went To Your Wedding." Percy Faith &

his Orchestra, "Delicado." Kay Starr, "Wheel of Fortune." Vera Lynn, "Auf Wiederseh'n Sweetheart." Jo Stafford, "You Belong to Me." Franki Laine, "High Noon, Do Not Forsake Me." Eddie Fisher, "Anytime." The Mills Brothers, "The Glow-Worm." Doris Day, "A Guy Is a Guy." Rosemary Clooney, "Half As Much." Les Paul and Mary Ford, "Tiger Rag." Nat King Cole, "Unforgettable." Johnnie Ray, "Walkin' My Baby Back Home." Louis Armstrong, "A Kiss to Build a Dream On."

Deaths: Curly Howard.

President: Harry S. Truman (D) Baptist; vetoes 250/ 12 overrides

Vice President: Alben W. Barkley (D) Methodist

House: D-235 ; R-199

Senate: 82nd Congress (1951-1953) Majority Party: Democrat (49 seats) Minority Party: Republican (47 seats) Other Parties: 0 Total Seats: 96

Federal Debt: $259.11 billion or 72 % of the GDP

Consumer Price Index CPI-U (1982 Base of 100): 26.50

GDP: $358.3 billion	**Inflation Rate:** 2.29%

Dow Jones: 283.70 (12-01)/ 256.35 (05-01)

Average Home Mortgage Rate: 5.03%

1 oz Gold: $38.70	**1oz of Silver:** $0.85

Federal Debt: $259,105,178,785.43

Federal Deficit: $1.5 billion dollars

Defense Spending: $51.69 billion	**Interest Spending:** $4.26 billion
Health Care Spending: $1.01 billion	**Pensions Spending:** $2.28 billion
Welfare Spending: $1.51 billion	**Education Spending:** $1.72 billion
Transportation Spending: $1.34 billion	**Misc. Other Spending:** $5.09 billion

Protection Spending: $140 million	Total Government Spending: $71.57 billion
% of GDP that goes towards just the interest payment: 1.19%	
U.S. Population: 156,954,000	World Population: 2,634,919,408
U.S. Birth Rate: 3,913,000	U.S. Abortions: 551
U.S. Homicide Rate: 5.2/ 100,000 population	
Annual Average Domestic Crude Oil Prices: $2.77 / barrel, $22.41 (2007 adjusted)	

Oil:

1949-1952 – The Federal Trade Commission (FTC) orders an **investigation** into the activities of the **world's major oil companies**. After a three year examination the FTC releases a 400 page report **in 1952** titled **"The International Petroleum Cartel."** The report revels the seven major oil companies control all principle oil-producing areas outside of the United States. They divide world markets, share pipelines and tankers, and keep prices artificially high **overcharging consumers untold billions of dollars**. Harry Truman's government sets out to correct the situation but surrenders to the oil companies a few years later.

1952 – Kentucky. Drilling activity increased slightly in 1952 and resulted in a new record of more than 11½ million barrels of oil produced.

1952 – Iranian President Mohammad Mosaddeq nationalized the Anglo-Iranian Oil Company in 1951 to ensure that more oil profits remain in Iran but the British are not at all happy. Mosaddeq was *TIME* magazine's **Man of the Year** for 1951. President Harry Truman threw the British representatives out of his office when they suggested a coup to overthrow the Iranian government while stating, "We don't overthrow governments; the United States has never done this before, and we're not going to start now."

When Eisenhower is elected in November 1952 the British try a different approach and tell him President Mossaddeq is going to take Iran towards Communism. They lied and knew it, **Eisenhower is duped** and a coup in Iran is organized.

1952 – **Dwight D. Eisenhower** received considerable funds from **Texas oilmen** in the 1952 presidential elections. Soon after being elected, Eisenhower stopped a grand jury investigation into the **"International Petroleum Cartel"** citing reasons of "national security". President Eisenhower owed the oil industry for their support.

Major News:

February 6, 1952 – George VI of England dies and his daughter becomes Queen Elizabeth II.

April 8, 1952 – President Truman authorizes the **seizure of United States steel mills** in order to avert a strike, but his action is ruled illegal by the U.S. Supreme Court.
    The **strike** by the United Steelworkers of America against U.S. Steel and nine other steelmakers was set to begin April 9, but President Harry S. Truman nationalized the American steel industry hours before the workers walked out. On June 2, the U.S. Supreme Court decided he lacked that authority.

May 26, 1952 – A Peace contract between West Germany, U.S., Great Britain, and France is signed May 26.

May 1952 – A conference is held by the **National Crime Syndicate** in the Florida Keys.

May 27, 1952 – European Union. Belgium, France, Germany, Italy, Luxembourg, and the Netherlands sign the **European Defense Community Treaty** in Paris.

July 25, 1952 – Puerto Rico becomes a U.S. commonwealth.

September 23, 1952 – Vice Presidential candidate **Richard Nixon**, gives his **"Checkers" speech.** The **Checkers speech** is an address made by United States Senator and Republican Vice Presidential candidate Richard Nixon on television and radio on September 23. **Senator Nixon** had been accused of improprieties relating to a fund established by his backers to reimburse him for his political expenses. With his place on the Republican ticket in doubt, Nixon flies to Los Angeles and delivers a half hour television address in which he defends himself, attacks his opponents, and urges Americans to contact the Republican National Committee to tell it whether or not he should remain on the ticket. During the speech, he stated that regardless of what anyone said, he intended to keep one gift, a black-and-white dog which was named **Checkers** by the Nixon children, thus giving the address its popular name.

October 1952 – Great Britain announces its development of **atomic weapons.**

November 1, 1952 – Some 43 nuclear tests were fired at Enewetak from 1948 to 1958. The **first hydrogen bomb test, code-named Ivy Mike,** was in late 1952 as part of Operation Ivy, and **vaporized the island of Elugelab.** This test included the use of B-17 Flying Fortress drones to fly through the radioactive cloud for the purpose of testing onboard samples.

In 2000, the Marshall Islands Nuclear Claims Tribunal awarded in excess of $340 million to the people of Enewetak for loss of use, hardship, medical difficulties and further nuclear cleanup. This award does not include the approximately $6 million annually budgeted by the U.S. for education and health programs in the Marshall Islands.

November 1952 – General Dwight D. Eisenhower, a newcomer to politics, but popular due to his role in winning World War II as European commander, gains an easy victory over Democratic challenger Adlai E. Stevenson. The Electoral College vote is 442 to 89.

December 2, 1952 – President-elect Dwight Eisenhower follows through with his campaign promise to visit Korea.

Civil Rights Movement:

1952 – The Tuskegee Institute reports **no lynching in the United States for the first time in 71 years** of tabulation.

1952

June 27, 1952 – **The United States Customs Service** is charged with enforcing provisions of the **Immigration and Naturalization Act** as the last racial and ethnic barriers to naturalization are removed.

November 1952 – **Ruby McCollum**, an African-American woman, goes on trial at the Suwanee County Courthouse in Live Oak, Florida for the **murder** on August 3, of Dr. C. LeRoy Adams, a white physician and state Senator who was the father of her youngest child. During the trial the prosecution claimed that a dispute over a medical bill was the motive for the murder and successfully challenged attempts by the defense to present testimony regarding the personal relationship between McCollum and Adams. McCollum was **found guilty and sentenced to death**, but her conviction was **overturned** by the Florida Supreme Court because of a procedural error made by the trial judge. In September 1954 she was found unfit to be retried due to insanity and was confined in a mental hospital until her release in 1976. Among the journalists who covered her trial was Zora Neale Hurston, who wrote about the case for the "Pittsburgh Courier" (October 1952–April 1953) and whose reporting was extensively quoted by William Bradford Huie in his book "Ruby McCollum" (1956).

1952 – **Malcolm X** becomes a minister of the **Nation of Islam**. Over the next several years his influence increases until he is one of the two most powerful members of the Black Muslims (the other was its leader, Elijah Muhammad). A Black Nationalist and separatist movement, the Nation of Islam contends that only blacks can resolve the problems of blacks.

December 9–11, 1952 – The Supreme Court hears arguments in the school desegregation case **"Brown vs. Board of Education of Topeka."**

Popular Culture:

1952 – The National Association of Broadcasters writes a code of **ethics.**

1952 – **Mr. Potato Head** is advertised on Television.

1952 – **3-D movies** are a big hit as the audiences duck.

1952 – *Mad magazine* an American humor magazine is founded by Editor Harvey Kurtzman and publisher William Gaines.

1952 – **The Eisenhower-Stevenson Presidential race** sharply increases political commercials.

1952 – **Sony sells a miniature transistor radio.**

1952 – **Richard Nixon**'s **"Checkers speech"** on TV saves his Vice Presidential candidacy. Politicians are learning how to apply "spin" to any situation.

1952 – **An Atomic bomb** test in Nevada is shown on live television.

1952 – There are now television sets in about 19 million U.S. homes.

1952 – **PEZ expands their sales by bringing the product to the United States.** To make their product more appealing to Americans they place heads on the dispensers and market them to children.

1952 – **Lucille Ball, while pregnant**, plays a pregnant character on TV, but can't say "pregnancy" because of the censors.

1952 – **Timex, "Takes a licking and keeps on ticking."** W.B. Doner & Co & predecessor agencies.

1952 – **Anacin, "Fast, fast, fast relief."** Ted Bates & Co.

1952 – **Ruling that motion pictures are protected** by the 1st Amendment to the Constitution, the Supreme Court **overturns a New York court's ban** on the showing of **"The Miracle,"** which was accused of being sacrilegious. The Supreme Court gives movies First Amendment **free speech protection.**

1952 – Public Law 550, the **Veterans Readjustment Assistance Act** of 1952, modifies the G.I. Bill for veterans of the Korean War.

1952

Business / Technology:

April 8, 1952 – Unions felt that during World War II the National War Labor Board had unfairly held wages below the level of inflation while doing little to rein in corporate profits. **The Seizure of nation's steel mills** is ordered by President Truman to avert a strike. This was ruled illegal by Supreme Court June 2, 1952.

1952 – **Grace Hopper** develops the first computer compiler.

1952 – **Acrylic splints** are used as a form of **penile implant** to help impotent men regain the ability to penetrate during intercourse.

1952 – The **IBM 726** is one of the first practical high-speed magnetic tape systems for electronic digital computers. It rents for $850 a month.

1952 – The huge **Electronic Delay Storage Automatic Calculator** (EDSAC) **computer** is programmed to play tic-tac-toe. EDSAC is a British computer the size of a small room. It has 3,000 vacuum valves arranged on 12 racks and uses tubes filled with mercury for memory. **EDSAC can carry out 650 instructions per second.** In 2009 the Intel core i7 extreme 965EE handles 76,383 million instructions per second (MIPS) at 3.2 GHz.

 1952 – Claude Shannon uses an **electric mouse** and maze to prove **computers can learn**.

Finance:

For the first eighteen years after WW II, Truman (1945-1953), Eisenhower (1953-1961) and Kennedy (1961-1963) all worked vigorously to keep spending under control. Of the seven years Truman was in office, the **national debt** came down in four. In 1946-1947, with a Republican Congress for his first two years in office he brought down spending. The following year, with a Democratic Congress he reduced what was commonly called the "War Debt" again. Two of the eight years Eisenhower served as President saw debt reduction during the years when Democrats were in charge of Congress, 1956-1957.

January 21, 1952 - The President's **budget** calls for expenditures of eighty-five billion four hundred and forty-four million dollars for the coming fiscal year. Slightly over three fourths of the budget is to be spent on **national security**.

Books:

1952 – **The Revised Standard Version of the Bible** is published.

1952 – **Hemingway**, "The Old Man and the Sea."

1952 –"East of Eden," **John Steinbeck.**

1952 – **"Charlotte's Web,"** E. B. White.

1952 – Ralph Ellison, **"Invisible Man."**

1952 – **"Fahrenheit 451,"** Ray Bradbury.

1952 – **"Martha Quest,"** Doris Lessing.

TV:

1952 – **Univac projects the winner** of the Presidential election on CBS.

1952 – **Fifty-six million people** watch Richard **Nixon's "Checker's speech"** on TV.

1952 – Starting in Akron, Ohio, **Rex Humbard** is one of the first evangelists to build a ministry that incorporates radio and television programming.

1952 – **TV Censorship. While Lucile Ball is pregnant** during an entire season of **"I Love Lucy,"** the actual word "pregnant" isn't allowed on air. Instead, the show uses phrases that seem equally informative but, somehow, less fraught with sin, such as "with child," "having a baby," and "expecting."

1952 – The first political ads are broadcast when Democrats buy a 30 minute slot for Presidential candidate, Adlai Stevenson. **Stevenson is bombarded with hate mail** for interfering with the regularly scheduled broadcast of *I Love Lucy.*

Radio:

March 21, 1952 – First reported Rock and Roll riot breaks out at Alan Freed's **Moondog Coronation Ball** in Cleveland, Ohio. Teenage excitement is blamed for the frenzy.

October 7, 1952 – The First edition of **Bob Horn's Bandstand** is broadcast as a local show from station WFIL-TV in Philadelphia, Pennsylvania. It is later renamed American Bandstand and syndicated.

1952 – Ralph Edward's **"This Is Your Life"** moves from radio to television.

Sports:

1952 – World Series. The New York Yankees win 4 games to 3 over the **Brooklyn Dodgers.**

February 14, 1952 – The 1952 Winter Olympics games open in Helsinki, Finland with thirty nations taking part. During these games, **the first triple jump** in figure skating history is performed by **Dick Button,** who wins one of four gold medals by U.S. athletes.

Natural Disasters:

1952 – Polio kills 3,300 people nationwide out of 57,628 reported cases.

March 21-22, 1952 – South-central U.S. A tornado plows through the South-central United States killing 343 people.

July 1952 – California. The towns of Tehacapi and Arvin are hit by the July Kern County earthquake. Twelve people die, many are injured, and there is $60 million in property damage.

December 5, 1952 – A dense smoke-filled fog shrouds **London** and brings the city to a standstill for four days. A Ministry of Health report estimated that **4,075 more people died** than would have been expected under normal conditions. Some estimate the number of smoke related deaths to be double this number or even triple this number.

November 4, 1952 – Kamchatka, Russia. A 9.0 magnitude earthquake hits. The **Kamchatka earthquake** occurs off the coast of the Kamchatka Peninsula in Russia causing a tsunami. A series of **tsunami** resulted, causing destruction and loss of life around the Kamchatka peninsula and the Kuril Islands. Hawaii was also struck, with estimated damages of up to $1million and livestock losses, but no human casualties were recorded. Japan reported no casualties or damage. The tsunami reached as far as Alaska, Chile, and New Zealand.

Man vs. Man / Wars:

1952 – Bolivia. April Revolution. In 1951 a military coup in Bolivia disposed President elect Victor Paz Estenssoro, soon after his election. The coup provoked a popular armed revolt which became known as the **April Revolution of 1952.** The military is subsequently defeated and Paz Estenssoro is restored to power. The MNR will introduce universal adult suffrage, carry out a sweeping land reform program, promote rural education, and nationalize the country's largest tin mines.

March 10, 1952 – Cuba. Second Batista Coup. Three months before the elections and almost twenty years after the "Revolt of the Sergeants," **former President Batista**, with army backing, stages a coup and seizes power. He ousted outgoing President Carlos Prío Socarrás, cancelled the elections and assumed control of the government as "provisional President." Shortly after taking power by force the United States government recognized his regime. Batista ruled as **the nation's dictator**. He was backed by labor unions, communists, and at first the U.S., but the United States soon imposed an embargo on the government and recalled their ambassador, weakening the government's mandate. Batista became increasingly unpopular among the public and his support was limited to communists. Even communists began to pull their long-term support from Batista in mid-1958.

Labor unions and the Mafia backed Batista until the very end when he was ousted on January 1, 1959, by guerrillas led by **Fidel Castro.**

October 1952-1955 – Buraimi Oasis Dispute. British forces intervened on behalf of Muscat and Oman against Saudi Arabian forces that had taken the disputed Buraimi Oasis.

1951-1952 – Egypt vs. British. Anglo-Egyptian War of 1951-1952. Egyptian guerrillas, aided by the government carry out a campaign against British forces stationed at the Suez Canal and against other symbols of Britain and the West.

On January 25, 1952, The British attack an Egyptian police barracks when its occupants refuse to surrender to British troops. Fifty Egyptians are killed and 100 wounded. The incident leads directly to **"Black Saturday,"** January 26, 1952, which begins with a mutiny by police in Cairo in protest against the death of their colleagues. Concurrently, groups of people in Cairo go on a rampage attacking British property and other symbols of the West. By the end of the day, 750 establishments valued at £50 million have been burned or destroyed. Thirty persons are killed, including eleven British and other foreigners and hundreds are injured.

On July 23, 1952, **King Farouk of Egypt** is ousted by a military coup and the conflict comes to an end with the eventual withdrawal of **British troops.**

1952-1959 – Cyprus. Enosis Campaign in Cyprus. The British took control of the island in 1878. In 1952 the self-determination movement forces led by **Colonel George Gravas** and encouraged by the island's **Greek Orthodox Archbishop Makarios III** began a guerrilla war for union with **Greece** against **British** occupying forces, together with terrorist attacks on the island's **Turkish** minority.

1952-present – India. Naga Rebellion. The Naga ethnic group seeks independence from India. A third of the 3-million-strong tribe live in neighboring Manipur, mostly in its hills, and two other northeastern states. The Naga rebellion is India's oldest insurgency, a 60-year revolt in which tens of thousands were killed in Nagaland before a truce was declared in 1997. Negotiations with New Delhi have made little progress since then.

1952-1956 – Kenya. The Mau-Mau War is a militant African nationalist movement among the Kikuyu people of Kenya. The **Mau Mau** advocate violent resistance to British domination in Kenya. In October 1952, after a campaign of sabotage and assassination attributed to Mau Mau terrorists, the British Kenya government declared a state of emergency and began four years of military operations against Kikuyu rebels. By the end of 1956, more than 11,000 rebels were killed in the fighting, along with about 100 Europeans and 2,000 African loyalists. More than 20,000 other Kikuyu were put into detention camps, where intensive efforts were made to change their political views. Despite these government actions, Kikuyu resistance spearheaded the Kenya independence movement, and Jomo Kenyatta, who had been jailed as a **Mau Mau** leader in 1953, became Prime Minister of an independent Kenya 10 years later.

October 20, 1952 – Mau Mau killings of European cattle and the execution of a Kikuyu Chief loyal to the British cause a state of emergency to be declared and an order sent out for the arrest of 183 people. Kenyatta is one of those arrested and, after a trial, is imprisoned for seven years for masterminding Mau Mau. While fearful whites collect guns to protect their lives and property, the first Kikuyu murder of a white settler occurs a week after the emergency when the settler was hacked to death with a machete-like tool. Some thirteen thousand people and untold animals will be killed in the Mau Mau anticolonial struggle, most of them Kikuyus.

June 1952 – Lebanon. Maronite Coup in Lebanon. In June 1952 an organization called the Social National Front is formed by nine deputies led by Kamal Jumblatt, head of the Progressive Socialist Party; Camille Shamun, former ambassador to Britain, Emile Bustani, a self-made millionaire businessman, and other prominent people. This front dedicated itself to radical reform, demanding that the authorities end sectarianism and eradicate all abuses in the governmental system. The SNF founders were encouraged by people claiming to be dissatisfied with the favoritism and corruption thriving under the Khuri regime, and on September 23, 1952 after the election of Camille Chamoun as President, Lebanon formed closer ties with the West.

1952-1955 – Thailand. Thai Anti-Chinese Campaign. The government appoints the "upper half" of members of the new unicameral assembly. Most appointees are from the very wealthiest class. On the other hand, the communist Party of Thailand, realizing the lack of capable cadres, begins sending students for Marxist-Leninist education to China and North Vietnam. Communism is officially banned in Thailand. General elections in February for members of the "lower" half" of the assembly are held. And military backed candidates win by large margins. Problems will continue with the communist representatives, including the Malayan Communist Party (CPM), through 2008.

1952 – Tunisia. Textile Workers' Strike in Egypt. Textile workers are an organized political force and a sign of industrial modernity. **Gamal Abdel Nasser** seizes power and is widely supported by both workers and peasants.

Over 10,000 workers at the Misr mills in Kafr al-Dawwar believe Nasser will allow them to renew their campaign for representative trade unions. The 3,000 workers at the Beida Dyers mill won this demand after a brief strike on August 9 and at Misr Fine Spinning and Weaving there was a company controlled union.

Large demonstrations of workers trying to reform the union set fire to the building and destroy machinery. The army is called in to end the strike and fires on the demonstrators, killing five people and injuring many more. As the workers clash with the police 545 demonstrators are arrested. Two demonstrators are quickly sentenced at a military tribunal and executed on September 7. The government had no intention of encouraging a popular revolution that it could not control. Most of the textile industry was and remains nationalized.

1952-1957 – Venezuela. Venezuela one of the world's largest producers of oil has a brutal dictatorship, controlled by Gen. Marcos Pérez Jiménez and his Security Police boss, Pedro Estrada. His virulent anti-Communism and his tolerant attitude toward foreign oil companies, however, gained him the backing of the United States.

Pedro Estrada, described by historian Hubert Herring "as vicious a man hunter as Hitler ever employed," headed the vast National Security Police network that rounded up any opposition, including military officers, unable to escape. Hundreds, if not thousands, were brutally tortured or simply murdered at the notorious Guasina Island concentration camp in the Orinoco jungle region.

1953

The Oldest Boomer is 7 years old.

Median Family Income: $4,200	**Minimum Wage:** 75cents/ hr
Gallon Gasoline: 29 cents	**Potatoes:** 10 lb/ 35 cents
New Car: Chevrolet Corvette: $3,498	**Hudson Jet:** $1,858
Unemployment Rate: 2.9%-2.5%-4.5%	**First-class Stamp:** 3 cents

12 cents buying power in 1953 = **$1.00 in 2008.**
In 1953 what cost our parents 12 cents to purchase
now costs us $1.00 in 2008.

Movies: "From Here to Eternity," "Shane," "Roman Holiday," "Julius Caesar," "The Robe," "Peter Pan," "House of Wax," "Gentlemen Prefer Blondes," "How to Marry a Millionaire," "Call Me Madam," "It Came from Outer Space," "Niagara," "Ma and Pa Kettle on Vacation." "Abbott and Costello Go to Mars" & "Abbott and Costello Meet Dr. Jekyll and Mr. Hyde." "The Moon Is Blue," was the first U.S. movie to use the words "pregnant" and "virgin." "Scared Stiff," starring Dean Martin & Jerry Lewis.

Broadway: "Kismet," "Danny Kaye-revue." "Jose Greco-revue," "Can-Can." "Comedy in Music," Victor Borge.

TV: "Make Room for Daddy," The Danny Thomas Show. "Topper". Forty-four million viewers tune in to "I Love Lucy" for a baby's birth. "Romper Room." "Winky Dink and You." "Robin Hood," "The George Jessel Show," "Philip Morris Playhouse."

Music: "The Band Wagon," Arthur Schwartz and Howard Deitz. Bill Haley & His Comets record their first rock hit, "Crazy Man Crazy." Fats Domino, "Goin' Home." "Kitty Wells, "It Wasn't God Who Made Honky Tonk Angels." Patti Page, "The Doggie In The Window." Tony Bennett, "Rags To Riches." Perry Como, "Don't Let The Stars Get In Your Eyes." Les Paul and Mary Ford, "Bye Bye Blues." Big Mama Thornton, "Hound Dog." Dean Martin, "That's Amore." Frank Sinatra, "Three Coins In The Fountain."

"Your Cheatin' Heart," recorded by Hank Williams and also recorded by Joni James, and then by Frankie Laine. Ray Charles, "Mess Around." Fats Domino, "Please Don't Leave Me."

President: Dwight D. Eisenhower (R) Presbyterian; vetoes 181/ 2 overrides

Vice President: : Richard M. Nixon (R) Quaker

House: D-213 ; R-221

Senate: 83rd Congress (1953-1955) Majority Party: Republican (48 seats) Minority Party: Democrat (47 seats) Other Parties: 1 Independent Total Seats: 96

Federal Debt: $266.07 billion or 70 % of the GDP

Consumer Price Index CPI-U (1982 Base of 100): 26.70

GDP: $379.4 billion	**Inflation Rate:** 0.82%

Dow Jones: 284.0 (Dec.)/ 265.68 (10-01)

Prime Rate: 3.25% (04-27)	**Average Home Mortgage Rate:** 5.09%
1 oz Gold: $35.50	**1oz of Silver:** $0.85

Federal Debt: $266,071,061,638.57

Federal Deficit: $6.5 billion dollars

Defense Spending: $56.94 billion	**Interest Spending:** $4.86 billion
Health Care Spending: $960 million	**Pensions Spending:** $3.09 billion
Welfare Spending: $1.81 billion	**Education Spending:** $1.24 billion
Transportation Spending: $1.63 billion	**Misc. Other Spending:** $6.80 billion
Protection Spending: $120 million	**Total Government Spending:** $79.99 billion

% of GDP that goes towards just the interest payment: 1.28%	
U.S. Population: 159,565,000	**World Population:** 2,680,253,696
U.S. Birth Rate: 3,965,000	**U.S. Abortions:** 490
U.S. Homicide Rate: 4.8/ 100,000 population	
Annual Average Domestic Crude Oil Prices: $2.92 / barrel, $23.40 (2007 adjusted)	

Oil:

1953 – Iran. The United States and Britain support a successful coup d'état against the democratically elected government of Mohammed Mossadeq in Iran following his nationalizing Iranian oil resources. The boycott on Iranian oil is lifted and the Shah takes over control of Iranian politics.

In 1951, Prime Minister Mossadeq nationalized the oil industry which Britain controlled up to this point. Mossadeq argued that Iran should begin profiting from its oil reserves which had been exclusively controlled by the Anglo-Iranian Oil Company later named British Petroleum (BP). The **CIA** and the **British** helped to undermine Mossadeq's government through bribery, libel, and planned riots. Agents posing as communists threatened religious leaders until Mossadeq is overthrown and sentenced to three years in prison followed by house arrest for life. Three hundred people died in firefights in the streets of Tehran.

Major News:

January 13, 1953 – Josip Broz Tito becomes President of Yugoslavia. He was the Marshal (1943–1980), Prime Minster (1945–1953), and President (1953–1980) of the Socialist Federal Republic of Yugoslavia. Tito's policies encouraged separatist and nationalist tendencies among rival republics, which helped to sow the seeds for bloody civil war in the 1990s, some ten years after his death.

1953

January 20, 1953 – Thirteen communist leaders, including Elizabeth Gurley Flynn, **are convicted** of conspiracy charges by a Federal jury in New York. Although they had done nothing overt, the government accused them of conspiring to organize as the Communist Party and to publish and teach the principles of Marxism-Leninism. The government then charged this was the same as advocating the overthrow of the government of the United States by force.

The Communist Party of the United States had grown since the 1930s until it had over 75,000 members in 1941. At the end of World War II, the Soviet Union installed repressive Communist puppet régimes across Central and Eastern Europe and the Communist Party in America was seen as a real threat.

Elizabeth Gurley Flynn and her codefendants were fined and imprisoned. The Supreme Court would reaffirm constitutional protections regarding free speech and self-incrimination while raising the requirement of "intent"" to a level that made it difficult for prosecutors to show a Communist Party member had a criminal purpose in 1957 putting an end to the communist trials under the 1940 Smith Act, although it remains on the books.

January 20, 1953 – General Dwight D. Eisenhower is inaugurated President of United States.

March 5, 1953 – Joseph Stalin dies. In 1939, the Soviet Union under Stalin signed a non-aggression pact with Nazi Germany, followed by a Soviet invasion of Poland, Finland, the Baltics, Bessarabia and northern Bukovina. When Germany violated the pact in 1941, the Soviet Union joined the Allies to play a lead role in the Axis defeat. After WWII Stalin installed communist governments in most of Eastern Europe, forming the Eastern bloc, behind what was referred to as an **"Iron Curtain"** of Soviet rule. This launched the long period of antagonism known as the **Cold War.**

1953 – Joseph Stalin. Soviet Union. After the Soviet Union broke apart evidence from the Soviet archives stated in the official records that under Stalin 800,000 prisoners were executed for political or criminal offenses. There were 1.7 million deaths in the Gulags (labor camps) and some 390,000 people died during the kulak forced resettlement. Three million people's deaths are officially recorded and there were many more people killed under Joseph Stalin's regime.

April 1953 – Dag Hammarskjöld begins his term as the second Secretary-General of the United Nations. He served from April 1953 until his death in a plane crash in September 1961. He is the only person to have been awarded the **Nobel Peace Prize** posthumously.

June 17, 1953 – East Berliners rise against Communist rule but are quickly held under control by troops and tanks. East Berlin is still battered from the war that ended eight years ago and consumer goods are still in short supply. Electricity is rationed and homes are often dark at night.

The government is making the transition to communism by taking control of private farms and regulating private business into insolvency where they are then taken over by the communist government. Over 130,000 citizens flee the country in the first four months of 1953. In June with the announcement of a 10% production quota increase, coupled with a cut in pay for those unable to reach this goal, workers of the Hospital Friedrichshain call for a general strike. This in turn encourages various demonstrations and thousands of construction workers go on strike. The protesters swelled to over 40,000 the next day. Soviet troops were called in to put down what had become a worker uprising in which government buildings were sacked. In total, around 16 Soviet divisions with 20,000 soldiers as well as 8,000 soldiers from the German **National People's Army** are called into service. Protests quickly spread to 500 other cities and villages. According to the West German government, 383 people are killed in the unrest, including 106 who were executed under martial law. Over 1,800 people are injured, 5,100 people are arrested, and 1,200 people are sentenced to imprisonment.

Construction begins August 13, 1961, on the **Berlin Wall,** to keep people from leaving. From 1961-1989, when the wall comes down, there will be 98 confirmed killings of people **trying to escape East Berlin.**

June 18, 1953 – King Farouk **was removed** with a coup d'état **in 1952. In 1953 the Egyptian Republic was declared**, with General Muhammad Naguib as the first

President of the Republic. Naguib was forced to resign in 1954 by **Jamal Abdel Nasser**, the real architect of the 1952 movement, and was later put under house arrest.

June 19, 1953 – Julius Rosenberg and Ethel Rosenberg are executed in the **Sing Sing Prison electric chair** in Ossining, New York, for betraying nuclear secrets to the Soviet Union. Seven different appeals are denied by the Supreme Court of the United States, and pleas for executive clemency are dismissed by President Harry Truman. Ethel Rosenberg became the first woman executed in the United States since Mary Surratt was hanged in 1865 for her alleged role in the assassination of Abraham Lincoln.

July 1953 – The Korean War truce. Armistice is signed July 27, 1953. Technically, the Korean War never ended. In 2010, the U.S. still has troops stationed in South Korea.

August 20, 1953 – Moscow announces the explosion of a hydrogen bomb. The first Soviet test of a hydrogen bomb, nicknamed "Joe 4," is on August 12. It was not considered a "true" fusion bomb. Through sources in the Manhattan project, notably Klaus Fuchs, Soviet intelligence obtained important information on the progress of the U.S. atomic bomb effort. Stolen U.S. atomic weapons secrets were shown to the head of the Soviet atomic project, Igor Kurchatov, and had a significant impact on the direction of his own team's research. Scholar Alexei Kojevnikov has estimated, based on newly released Soviet documents, that the primary way in which the espionage may have sped up the Soviet project was that it allowed Khariton to avoid dangerous tests to determine the size of the critical mass, called **"tickling the dragon's tail"** in the U.S. The Soviets first atomic bomb, "Joe 1," was almost a duplicate of the American "Fat Man" bomb.

October 5, 1953 – California Governor **Earl Warren** is sworn in as the 14th **Chief Justice** of U.S. Supreme Court.

Civil Rights Movement:

1953 – Atlanta and New Orleans recently opened golf courses for Negroes.

February 1953 – The Baltimore chapter of the Congress of Racial Equality (**CORE**) begins **lunch counter sit-ins** in February. They convince two of Baltimore's downtown department stores to desegregate their lunch counters.

January 1953 – Baton Rouge, LA. Bus fares are raised 50%, from 10 to 15 cents and in early February, Black community leader **Reverend Jemison** complains to the City Council about Blacks having to stand in the overcrowded rear section while "white" seats are empty. The City Council adopts Ordinance 222 which changes **segregated seating** so that Blacks fill up the seats from the rear forward and whites fill the bus from front to back on a first-come, first-served basis. Under this plan, if a bus is filled with Blacks they can occupy the front seats, but they cannot sit on a seat next to a white, or sit in any seat that is in front of a white.

December 31, 1953 – Hulan Edwin Jack becomes the **first African American Borough President of Manhattan**. At the time he is the highest ranking black elected official in the nation. A high school dropout he eventually went to work for the Peerless Paper Box Company Inc., in New York City where he began as a janitor but eventually rose to become one of the firm's Vice Presidents. Hulan Jack served as Manhattan Borough President for nearly two terms. His second term was marred by a 1960 Grand Jury indictment for bribery and conspiracy to obstruct justice. He was also charged with three violations of the New York City Charter. Hulan Jack was convicted of the charges and resigned his position as Borough President, effectively ending his political career.

1953 – In Seattle, Negroes are now free to play on all public golf courses, but they still may not take part in tournaments played on the same courses. In Chicago, where they play on public courses without restriction, the number of Negro golfers has gone up from 25, a few years ago, to more than 2,000. In New York there are no restrictions on public courses, and Negroes do play in tournaments.

Women's Movement:

1953 – *Playboy* **Magazine. An American men's magazine, is founded in Chicago, Illinois** by Hugh Hefner and his associates with **Marilyn Monroe** stretched out on the cover. Circulation hit the 800,000 mark by the end of 1956, thus surpassing that of the formerly most widely read men's magazine, *Esquire.* In 1964 *Playboy* was selling two-million copies a month, and by 1968, five-million.

1953 – Jerrie Cobb is the first woman in the U.S. to undergo astronaut testing. **NASA,** however, cancels the women's program in 1963 and it is not until 1983 that an American woman gets sent into space.

Popular Culture:

1953 – "*TV Guide,*" the initial press run of "*TV Guide*" is 1.5 million copies.

1953 – Speedy Gonzales, born 1953.

1953 – Life Expectancy in the United States is 68.8 years.

1953 – "The Moon Is Blue" uses the word **"virgin,"** which leads to picket lines.

1953 – Baseball cards, 1953 Topps, Satchel Paige, VG. Book-$600.00 Sale-$200. (02/2009)

1953 – Piltdown Man is determined to be **a hoax** after close observation uncovers it is the jaw of an ape and a human skull.

1953 – Bazooka Joe first appears on Topps comics.

October 30, 1953 – The Cold War continues in earnest when President Dwight D. Eisenhower approves a top secret document stating that the **U.S. nuclear arsenal** must be expanded to combat the communist threat around the world.

Business / Technology:

April 1953 – James Watson and Francis Crick reveal the structure of **DNA** and publish their discovery of the molecular model. The sentence **"This structure has**

novel features which are of considerable biological interest" may be one of science's most famous understatements. It appeared in April 1953 in the scientific paper where Watson and Crick presented the structure of the DNA-helix, the molecule that carries genetic information from one generation to another.

1953 – **Remington-Rand** builds a high speed computer printer.

1953 – **Color TV** sets cost $1,157 which are still way too expensive for most people.

1953 – **Hollywood** hopes wide-screen **Cinemascope** will counteract TV.

1953 – **Magnetic core memory** is installed in the Whirlwind computer.

1953 – **Transistor Radio** - There are numerous claimants to the title of the first company to produce practical transistor radios, often incorrectly attributed to Sony (originally Tokyo Tsushin Kogyo). Texas Instruments had demonstrated all-transistor AM radios as early as 1952, but their performance was well below that of equivalent vacuum tube models. The **Regency TR-1** put on sale in November 1954 was the first practical transistor radio made in any significant numbers.

1953 – **The pre-recorded reel-to-reel tape** at 7 1/2 ips goes on sale.

1953 – Community Antenna Television. **CATV system** uses microwave to bring in distant signals.

Finance:

August 19, 1953 – The United States **CIA** assists in the overthrow of the government in **Iran,** and returns the Shah Mohammad Reza Pahlavi to the throne.

July 9, 1953 – **The Bureau of Internal Revenue** was renamed the Internal Revenue Service.

1953-2010 – Fort Knox Gold. Most Americans still believe that all U.S. gold is still at Fort Knox. In **1953 President Eisenhower orders the last known audit of Fort**

Knox ever held. Fort Knox contained 701.8 million ounces of gold, an incredible 70% of all the gold in the world. How much remains? No one knows. Federal law requires an annual physical audit of Fort Knox gold but the Treasury has consistently refused to conduct one.

What happened to **America's gold** at Fort Knox? Rumors have surfaced since 1971 that all of the gold was removed when the dollar was "freed" from the gold standard, and the Federal Reserve placed American gold with the Bank of England. Once the gold was gone from Fort Knox, President Nixon closed the gold window by repealing Roosevelt's Gold Reserve Act of 1934, finally making it legal once again for Americans to buy gold." An audit may shed some light on answering some basic questions: How much gold, if any, is in Fort Knox? Where is the balance of the 701.8 million ounces?

It has been reported **the Federal Reserve Bank of New York maintains a vault that lies 86 feet below sea level.** Currently, it is reputedly the **largest gold repository in the world**, more than Fort Knox. The gold is owned by many foreign nations, central banks and international organizations. The Federal Reserve Bank does not own the gold but serves as guardian of the precious metal, which it protects at no charge as a gesture of good will to other nations. Since there is only so much gold in the entire world it seems unlikely it can be in two places at the same time. So where is it? It still should belong to the American people unless it was sold while we were asleep. themoneymasters.com -the *Money Masters* DVD and *Money as Debt* DVD's are both available here. Everyone interested in money should view these, and then make up your own mind.

Books:

1953 – James Baldwin's first novel, "Go Tell It on the Mountain."

1953 – Ray Bradbury, **"Fahrenheit 451."** A novel of censorship and fascism.

1953 – The Kinsey Reports, "Sexual Behavior of the Human Female." The research astounded the general public and was immediately controversial and sensational. The findings caused shock and outrage, both because they challenged conventional beliefs about sexuality and because they discussed subjects that had previously been taboo.

TV:

1953 – **Walt Disney**'s True Life Adventures: "Bear Country, The Living Desert.".

February 18, 1953 – Lucille Ball and Desi Arnaz sign an 8 million dollar contract to continue the **"I Love Lucy"** show through 1955.

December 24, 1953 – The television show **"Dragnet"** becomes the first network sponsored TV show.

1953 – "Romper Room" premiers.

Sports:

May 29, 1953 – Mt. Everest. The first summit of **Mt. Everest** is accomplished by **Edmund Hillary** of New Zealand and **Tenzing Norgay** of Nepal. Neither will ever acknowledge which of them was technically the first.

1953 – World Series. In a rematch of the 1952 Series the Yankees won in six games for their fifth straight title. New York Yankees vs. Brooklyn Dodgers (4-2).

1953 – Kansas City mobster Joseph Benintende is sentenced to 4–7 years in prison after being convicted for his role in the **NCAA point shaving** scandal. Seven CCNY players are given suspended sentences, five LIU players are given suspended sentences, four Bradley players are acquitted and three are given suspended sentences. One LIU player is sentenced to serve 1 year in prison. One CCNY player is sentenced to 6 months in prison. All other players were allowed to walk. Mobsters and former players involved served jail time.

1953 – Toni Stone becomes the first female player in the Negro Leagues when she takes over second base for the **Indianapolis Clowns,** replacing a young man who had just been called up to the **Boston Braves.** The young man was **Henry Aaron,** who is the all time major league leader in home runs. Stone was a good player (she once got a hit off Satchel Paige), although she was shunned by the other members of the team who liked her, but didn't believe baseball was a place for women.

Music:

1953 – Elvis Presley records for the first time.

1953 – Eddie Fisher becomes **"The Coca-Cola Kid"** on the TV show *Coke Time*, at a salary of one million dollars a year.

January 1, 1953 – Hank Williams is on his way to play a New Year's Day show in Canton, Ohio. He **died** sometime after midnight in the back seat of his Cadillac. He was 29 years old.

1953 – "Crazy Man, Crazy," recorded by Bill Haley & His Comets, becomes the first rock and roll single to make the **"Billboard"** national American musical charts.

Natural Disasters:

January 31-February 5, 1953 – Flooding in Northwestern Europe. A storm followed by floods **devastates the North Sea coastal areas.** The flooding and the storm combine to create a major natural disaster which affects the coastlines of the Netherlands, England, Belgium, Denmark and France. A high spring tide and the severe windstorm caused a storm tide in combination with a tidal surge. The resulting waves overwhelm sea defenses causing extensive damage. Officially, **1,835 people are killed** in the Netherlands, 307 are killed in the United Kingdom, and 28 are killed in West Flanders, Belgium. **The ferry "MV Princess Victoria"** is lost at sea in the North Channel east of Belfast with 133 deaths, many fishing trawlers sank and 230 people were killed on watercraft along Northern European coasts as well as in deeper waters of the North Sea.

May 11, 1953 – The Waco, Texas tornado outbreak affects the central United States from May 9-May 11. An F5 tornado strikes Waco, Texas, killing 144 people.

June 8, 1953 – Flint, Michigan. Less than a month after the Waco tornado, another F5 monster ripped through portions of greater Flint, Michigan killing 116 people and injuring 844 along a 27-mile path. Named the Flint-Beecher tornado it is rated as the ninth deadliest twister ever recorded in the United States. This tornado was one of ten that hit southeast Michigan and northwest Ohio that afternoon and evening. The others cause a total of 26 deaths and 449 injuries with damage stretching from **Alpena, Michigan,** on the western shore of Lake Huron, to **Cleveland, Ohio.**

June 9, 1953 – Worcester, Massachusetts. The Flint-Worcester Tornadoes are two tornadoes, one occurring in Flint, Michigan on June 8, the other in Worcester, Massachusetts on June 9. These tornadoes are among the deadliest in United States history and were caused by the same storm system as it moved eastward. It was debated in the U.S. Congress whether the June 4, **atomic bomb testing** in the upper atmosphere had caused both of the tornadoes. Congress demanded a response from the government but meteorologists quickly claimed there was no cause and effect. The Worcester storm is responsible for the deaths of 94 people.

In total, 1953 reported 422 tornadoes resulting in 519 deaths. June contributed 111 tornadoes and 244 deaths to that figure.

1953 – Love Canal. Niagara Falls, N.Y. Love Canal, a neighborhood in Niagara Falls, New York, becomes the subject of national and international attention, controversy, and eventual environmental notoriety following the discovery of **21,000 tons of toxic waste** buried beneath the entire neighborhood. This will be marked as one of the most appalling environmental tragedies in American history that began in the early 1890s when William T. Love thought that by digging a short canal between the upper and lower Niagara Rivers, power could be generated cheaply to fuel the industry and homes of his would-be model city. As William Love dug his canal, Congress passed a regulation in which water was not to be removed from the Niagara River because they wanted to preserve the Niagara Falls. This along with the panic of 1893 and **Nikola Tesla's** discovery of how to economically transmit electricity over great distances by means of an alternating current stopped the project. William Love was barely able to begin digging the canal and build a few streets and homes before his money ran out. In the 1920s the seeds of a genuine nightmare were planted when the canal was turned into a municipal and industrial chemical dumpsite. By the 1940s, Hooker

Chemical Company founded by Elon Hooker was granted permission by the Niagara Power and Development Company to dump its wastes in the Love Canal. In 1942 Hooker Chemical Company added 21,000 tons of chemicals such as "caustics, alkaline, fatty acids and chlorinated hydrocarbons from the manufacturing of dyes, perfumes, solvents for rubber and synthetic resins."

In 1953, the Hooker Chemical Company, then the owners and operators of the property, covered the canal with dirt and sold it to the city for one dollar. In the late 1950s, about 100 homes and a school were built at the site. Then in 1978 after a heavy rainfall, chemicals, fifty gallon drums, and assorted waste floated to the surface of streets and backyards. Trees turned black and died. And this was just the beginning.

August 8-August 12, 1953 – Kefalonia, Greece. A 7.2 magnitude earthquake kills 476 people. Kefalonia is just to the east of a major tectonic fault and this disaster causes huge destruction in all areas except the North. Damage is estimated to run into tens of millions of dollars, but the real damage to the local economy occurs when residents leave the island. An estimated 100,000 of the population of 125,000 leave the island soon after the earthquake with no plans to return.

Man vs. Man / Wars:

June 25, 1950-July 27, 1953 – Korean War. U.S. sources state that the number of American and Korean deaths was 36,940 people and Chinese deaths ranged from 400,000 to 1,500,000 people. The North Korean battle dead estimates were close to 520,000 people killed. South Korean civilian estimated deaths were close to 425,000 people killed. Total civilian deaths were between 2,000,000 to 3,000,000 people killed. **These were PEOPLE-men women and children, families, friends that had lives, things to do and places to go.** Regarding their own casualties, Chinese sources said "the Chinese People's Volunteers suffered 148,000 deaths altogether (among which 114,000 died in combat, incidents, and **winterkill, (how nice and generic)**; 21,000 died after being hospitalized and 13,000 died from diseases; 380,000 were wounded and 29,000 missing, including 21,400 POWs (of whom 14,000 were sent to Taiwan, 7,110 were repatriated)." This same source concluded with these numbers for North Korean casualties, "the Korean People's Army had 290,000 casualties and 90,000

POWs; there were a large number of civilian deaths in the northern part of Korea, but no accurate figures were available. During the Korean War approximately 2 million eight hundred thousand men women and children were killed or died as a result of this political action. Two million eight hundred thousand people killed is a huge price to pay. Who actually won and what did they win?

June 17, 1953 – Representative Ernest K. Bramblett (R-California) **is indicted** for making false statements about congressional payroll kickbacks. Bramblett put the wife of the House Clerk on his congressional office payroll for 16 months. Though she did not work for Bramblett, she kicked back to her "employer" at the rate of $3,300 a year. Ernest K. Bramblett is convicted on February 2, 1954. He is fined $5,000 and sentenced to 2-4 months in prison, but the sentence is suspended on June 15, 1955.

1953 – Iran. The Iranian coup of 1953 is one of the first known successful replacements of a foreign government by the CIA. **After nationalizing** the **oil** industry **Iranian Prime Minister** Mohammed Mossaddegh is overthrown in a coup orchestrated by the **CIA** and **British intelligence.** This sets the stage for the **Islamic revolution in 1979**, and for a generation of anti-American hatred in one of the Middle East's most powerful countries. British intelligence along with the CIA planned and initiated the coup due to their shared interest in maintaining control of **Iranian oil.**

1953 – Guyana. British forces remove Guyana's elected Prime Minister, Cheddi Jagan, head of the left-oriented People's Progressive Party. The Guiana Industrial Workers Union went on strike in support of the Labor Relations Act and the workers in the sugar industry. Since 1948, the GIWU had been calling "recognition" strikes and was closely aligned with the ruling party. Those opposing the strike said the GIWU was seeking to gain control over the colony's economic and social life and this gave the British an excuse for their military intervention.

On October 9, 1953, London suspended the colony's constitution and, under pretext of quelling disturbances, sent in troops. When British troops land in Guyana they are amazed to find no signs of revolt. There is total peace throughout the country, and a cricket match between Guyana and Trinidad is being played in Georgetown. The PPP Government has been in office for only 133 days and is overthrown by a combination of British emergency orders and heavily armed British troops.

1953 – Colombia. Colombian Military Coup. Colombia's commander in Chief Gustavo Rojas Pinilla, supported by both Liberals and Conservatives, seizes power by coup and rules as a dictator from 1953 to 1957.

The violence between the Liberals and the conservatives emerged again in 1953. Riots known as the Bogotazo, lasted from 1948 mid 1950 in which more than 300,000 people were killed, making it the deadliest conflict in the Americas after the U.S. Civil War and Mexican Revolution. Order was restored by the 1953 military coup of General Rojas Pinilla and he enjoyed considerable popular support, due largely to his success in reducing "La Violencia." When he did not restore democratic rule, he was overthrown by the military in 1957 with the backing of both political parties, and a provisional government was installed.

1953 – Cuba. 26th of July Movement. Castro wants to be rid of Batista through an armed uprising. On July 26, at age 26, Castro led 160 fellow revolutionaries in an attack against the Moncada army barracks in Santiago de Cuba. They captured weapons, supplies and started encouraging the civilian population to rally to their cause. All of their objectives failed. Government troops killed or captured most of his force. Castro received a fifteen-year prison sentence and Raul, his younger brother, received a thirteen-year sentence.

1953 – East Berlin Uprising. The 1953 uprising was a pivotal event in the Cold War and one of the first serious disorders to occur in the "workers' paradise." The spontaneous uprising against communist rule in East Germany is limited to the major industrial centers and does not engage the population in the rest of the country in the same way rebellions in Hungary, Czechoslovakia, or Poland were able to.

The west feared reunification of Germany. Foreign Office minister of state, Selwyn Lloyd, told Winston Churchill in a memo on June 22 that the allies felt "a divided Germany is safer at present. But none of us dare say so in public because of the impact on public opinion in Germany." Red Army tanks are brought in and the Soviet military commander declared a state of emergency.

1953 – Indonesia. Aceh Rebellion. Ache is located on the northern tip of the island of Sumatra. The Aceh war against the Dutch was fought from 1873 until 1942. During World War II, Japanese troops occupied Aceh and in 1945 when WWII ended, civil war broke out between rival warlords. Aceh was incorporated into Indonesia in 1950, as the province of North Sumatra, but there was local resistance to Indonesian rule.

In 1953, Tengku daud Beureuh, military Governor of Achin before its annexation, led a rebellion against the Indonesian government of **President Sukarno.** They attacked police and army posts, in an attempt to obtain more weapons for a full-scale rebellion. Scattered guerrilla fighting continued until a cease-fire was arranged in March 1959, when Aceh was giving it a greater degree of autonomy from the central government.

Aceh was the closest point of land to the epicenter of the massive **2004 Indian Ocean earthquake,** which triggered a **tsunami** that devastated much of the western coast of the region, including part of the capital of Banda Aceh. Over 170,000 persons were killed or missing, and approximately 500,000 people were left homeless. This event helped trigger the peace agreement between the government of Indonesia and the Free Aceh Movement. Aceh has substantial natural resources, including coal, oil and gas and the fight for control continues through 2010.

1953-1975 – The Laotian Civil War is an internal fight between the Communist Pathet Lao and the Royal Lao Government in which both receive heavy external support for a proxy war from the global Cold War superpowers. The fighting in Laos includes participation by the **North Vietnamese, American, Thai,** and **South Vietnamese military** forces fighting directly and through proxies for control over the Laotian Panhandle. The North Vietnamese Army uses the panhandle as the Ho Chi Minh Trail supply corridor and staging area for offensives into South Vietnam. The other area of conflict is the northern Plaine des Jarres. In April, 1953, the Viet Minh invade northeastern Laos with 40,000 troops commanded by General Vo Nguyen Giap and Souphanouvong joins them with a token force of 2,000 Pathet Lao. Their objective is the capture of the Royal Capital of Luang Prabang and the Plaine des Jarres. They are opposed by 10,000 Lao troops and 3,000 French regulars. When the French airlift in battalions of Foreign Legionnaires and Moroccans the Vietnamese invasion is stalled.

1953

1953-1956 – Morocco vs. France. Moroccan War of Independence. France's exile of the highly respected **Sultan Mohammed V** to Madagascar in 1953 and his replacement by the unpopular Mohammed Ben Aarafa, whose reign was perceived as illegitimate, sparks opposition to the French both from nationalists and those who saw the Sultan as a religious leader. Two years later, faced with a united Moroccan demand for the Sultan's return, rising violence in Morocco, and the deteriorating situation in Algeria, the French government brought Mohammed V back to Morocco. The negotiations that led to Moroccan independence began the following year.

1953 – South Africa. In 1953, the Public Safety Act and the Criminal Law Amendment Act are passed, which empowers the government to declare stringent states of emergency and increase penalties for protesting against or supporting the repeal of a law. The penalties included fines, imprisonment and whippings.

1953-1954 – Syria. Druse Uprising. In July 1953, Syrians approve a new constitution making Syria a Presidential Republic with **Shishakli as President.** The resulting Chamber of Deputies is filled with ALM deputies, the other parties having boycotted the election. Signs that Shishakli's regime would collapse appear at the end of 1953 with **student strikes** and the circulation of unusually virulent pamphlets urging rebellion. The major political parties, meeting at Homs in September, **agree to overthrow Shishakli,** however trouble developed among the Druse, and Shishakli declared martial law. It will take until February 25, 1954 for the army, infiltrated by Shishakli's opponents, to stage **Syria's fourth coup** and restore the 1949 government.

1954

The Oldest Boomer is 8 years old.

Median Family Income: $4,200	**Minimum Wage:** 75cents/ hr
Gallon Gasoline: 29 cents	

New Car: Nash Metropolitan Convertible: $1,469
Packard Clipper: $2,624

Unemployment Rate: 4.9%-6.1%-5.0%	**First-class Stamp:** 3 cents

12 cents buying power in 1954 **= $1.00 in 2008.**
In 1954 what cost our parents 12 cents to purchase
now costs us $1.00 in 2008.

Movies: "White Christmas," "20,000 Leagues Under the Sea," "Rear Window," "The Caine Mutiny," "Three Coins in the Fountain," "A Star is Born," "On the Waterfront," "The Country Girl," "Dial M for Murder," "Godzilla," "Seven Brides for Seven Brothers," "Young at Heart," "Ma and Pa Kettle at Home."

Broadway: "Golden Apple," "Pajama Game," "By the Beautiful Sea." "The Boy Friend," London.

TV: "Father Knows Best," "People Are Funny," "The George Gobel Show," "Lassie," "Captain Midnight," "Annie Oakley," "Davy Crockett," "The Little Rascals." "The Adventures of Rin Tin Tin," "Face the Nation," "Disney," "NBA Basketball." Regular color TV broadcasts begin in the U.S. The McCarthy hearings are televised. "The Tonight Show," hosted by Steve Allen.

Music: Cha-cha-cha, an offshoot of the mambo, is popular. The Drifters, "Honey Love." Hank Snow, "I Don't Hurt Anymore." Doris Day, "Secret Love." Joe Turner, "Shake, Rattle And Roll." The Midnighters, "Work With Me, Annie." Eddie Fisher, "Oh My Papa." Muddy Waters, "I'm Your Hoochie Coochie Man." The Spaniels, "Goodnight Sweetheart

Goodnight." The Crew-Cuts, "Sh-Boom." The Mills Brothers, "You're Nobody Till Somebody Loves You." Elvis Presley, "That's All Right." The Chordettes, "Mr. Sandman." Penguins, "Earth Angel."

President: Dwight D. Eisenhower (R) Presbyterian; vetoes 181/ 2 overrides

Vice President: Richard M. Nixon (R) Quaker

House: D-213 ; R-221

Senate: 83rd Congress (1953-1955) Majority Party: Republican (48 seats) Minority Party: Democrat (47 seats) Other Parties: 1 Independent Total Seats: 96

Federal Debt: $271.26 billion or 71 % of the GDP

Consumer Price Index CPI-U (1982 Base of 100): 26.90

GDP: $380.4 billion	Inflation Rate: 0.32%

Dow Jones: 401.97 (12-01)/ 289 (January)

Prime Rate: 3.00% (03-17)	**Average Home Mortgage Rate:** 5.15%
1 oz Gold: $35.25	**1oz of Silver:** $0.86

Federal Debt: $271,259,599,108.46

Federal Deficit: $1.2 billion dollars

Defense Spending: $52.83 billion	**Interest Spending:** $4.98 billion
Health Care Spending: $960 million	**Pensions Spending:** $3.69 billion
Welfare Spending: $1.95 billion	**Education Spending:** $1.12 billion
Transportation Spending: $1.42 billion	**Misc. Other Spending:** $8.28 billion
Protection Spending: $120 million	**Total Government Spending:** $77.69 billion

% of GDP that goes towards just the interest payment: 1.31%	
U.S. Population: 162,391,000	**World Population:** 2,728,222,066
U.S. Birth Rate: 4,078,000	**U.S. Abortions:** 440
U.S. Homicide Rate: 4.8/ 100,000 population	
Annual Average Domestic Crude Oil Prices: $2.99 / barrel, $23.92 (2007 adjusted)	

Oil:

1954 – Takula Oil Field and the Greater Takula Area, Cabinda, Angola. The earliest indications that Cabinda was a potentially rich oil province were oil seeps and asphalt ic outcrops in the onshore areas. These encouraging signs led to the formation of **Gulf Oil Corporation's** first geologic field parties to the Portuguese colony of Cabinda.

1954 – President Eisenhower announces **"Atoms for Peace,"** a program to convert part of the military nuclear program for civilian electrical generation. This should theoretically cut back on the use of oil.

1954 – Paul Douglas begins making speeches in the **Senate** about the need for tax reforms in order to **eliminate special privileges** such as the oil depletion allowance. Douglas attempted to join the very powerful Finance Committee. He held seniority priority and should have been given one of the two available seats on the committee. **Senator Lyndon Johnson** had to apply considerable pressure on Harry Byrd, the chairman of the Finance Committee, to stop this from happening. Johnson owed "big oil."

1954 – Coup d'état in Egypt. Gamal Abdel **Nasser** assumes the Presidency. In July, **Israeli Defense Minister** Pinhas Lavon instigates commando operations in Egypt in an attempt to depose Nasser, but this fails when **Israeli frogmen** are captured as they come ashore in Alexandria. Some of the other attacks are directed against U.S.

interests in an effort to drive a wedge between Egypt and America. On October 26, an assassination attempt against Nasser fails and in December six members of the **Muslim Brotherhood** are hanged for their alleged roles in the plot.

Major News:

January 21, 1954 – "Nautilus," the first atomic-powered submarine, is launched from Groton, Connecticut.

March 1954 – The KGB is established in the Soviet Union. It is similar in some ways to the U.S. Central Intelligence Agency (CIA) and British MI-6. Under Communist Party control, it became the world's largest secret police and espionage organization, with seven directorates including foreign operations, internal political control, military counter-intelligence, surveillance, and border guards.

March 1, 1954 – H-Bomb. The largest U.S. nuclear explosion to date, "Castle Bravo" at 15 Megatons. The largest dry fuel thermonuclear hydrogen bomb device ever exploded by the United States cuts a crater about one mile wide in the Pacific archipelago of Bikini with a fireball close to four miles wide. The U.S. H–bomb was 1,200 times larger than the bomb dropped on Hiroshima because of a miscalculation by the Los Alamos scientists. The intended size was supposed to be in the range of 5 million tons of TNT, but "Castle Bravo" yielded 15 megatons vaporizing islands with temperatures hitting 99,000 degrees Fahrenheit, and shaking islands up to 120 miles away. The mushroom cloud rose 62 miles over the South Pacific and radioactive fallout reached Australia and Japan. Residents of Rongelap Atoll, about 100 miles east of Bikini, first heard the explosion and within minutes the ground began to shake. Within a few hours the colorful ash–like powder began to drop on the people.

In 2008 the area above the crater remains contaminated and unfit for humans while the area within the crater yields fantastic coral reefs with 12 inch thick tree size trunks. The reefs reach a height of 27 feet. Forty–two species of fish that were in the area prior to the blast now appear to be missing but there are plenty of fish.

September 12th, 2009 – The Rongelap Atoll is one of the 29 atolls and 5 islands in the central Pacific region that make up the Republic of the Marshall Islands (RMI).

The land area of Rongelap Atoll consists of 61 islets with a combined area of approximately 3 square miles. The lagoon covers 388 square miles. In the near future, the first families will settle in their new homes and begin the job of rebuilding their community.

March 1, 1954 – Five members of the U.S. Congress are wounded in the House of Representatives by four Puerto Rican independence supporters who fired at random from a spectators' gallery.

March 23, 1954 – The Soviet Union grants sovereignty to East Germany.

March-May 1954 – French army is defeated by the Vietnamese at Dien Bien Phu.

April 22 - June 17, 1954 – Army vs. McCarthy inquiry. A Senate subcommittee report blames both sides. At the televised Army-McCarthy hearings, before a Senate subcommittee, Army officials accuse Senator Joseph McCarthy (R - Wisconsin) of seeking preferential treatment for a draftee, and McCarthy accuses the Army of hindering the probe of Communist infiltration into the Army.

July 1954 – The Geneva Conference in July determined that hostilities are to cease immediately and formerly French Indochina is to be partitioned into four fully independent states: **the Kingdoms of Laos, Cambodia,** the **Republic of South Vietnam** and **communist North Vietnam.**

July 1954 – Vietnam is split at the 17th parallel.

September 6, 1954 – President Eisenhower launches the world **atomic pool** without the Soviet Union.

1954 – SEATO. The Southeast Asia Treaty Organization, formed by defense pact, is signed in Manila September 8, 1954 by the U.S., Britain, France, Australia, New Zealand, Philippines, Pakistan, and Thailand.

November 1954 – Dr. Jonas Salk starts inoculating children against polio.

1954

December 2, 1954 – Condemnation of Senator McCarthy. The U.S. Senate voted 67-22, to condemn Joseph McCarthy for contempt of a Senate subcommittee, abuse of members, and insults to Senate colleagues during Army investigations.

December 8, 1954 – European Union. The Council of Ministers of the Council of Europe adopts as it emblem, the blue flag hosting 12 golden stars.

Civil Rights Movement:

March 7, 1954 – Martin Luther King, Jr. delivers a trial sermon, **"The Three Dimensions of a Complete Life,"** at Dexter Avenue Baptist Church in Montgomery, Alabama.

May 17, 1954 – Brown vs. Board of Education ends "separate but equal" school segregation. The Supreme Court rules against **separate education** for **blacks** and **whites**, unanimously banning racial segregation in public schools.

"Brown vs. Board of Education" is actually a combination of five cases from different parts of the country and is an historic first step in the long journey toward equality in U.S. education. Chief Justice Earl Warren, writing for the court, declares that the "separate but equal" doctrine has no place in public education and requests further argument concerning implementation. From the time the 14th Amendment was ratified in 1868, it was challenged. And the "Plessy vs. Ferguson" decision introduced the "separate but equal" standard that legalized segregation until the Brown decision in 1954.

1954 – Following the Supreme Court's order that public schools be desegregated in "Brown vs. Board of Education" and other cases, including "Briggs vs. Elliot,"

On the night of Oct. 10, 1955, night-riders fired shots at the DeLaine home, and DeLaine fired back, but only, he said, to mark the vehicle the assailants were using. The Reverend DeLaine and his family are forced to leave **South Carolina** because he is now facing charges of assault and battery with intent to kill stemming from his defense of his home against white night-riders angered by his civil rights activities. **Within weeks Reverend J.A. DeLaine's** Church and home are burned and his life is threatened. The DeLaine home burned to the ground under mysterious circumstances, as local firefighters watched, saying it was not in their jurisdiction because it was just outside the city limits.

Reverend DeLaine then spends the rest of his working life in New York where he founds a new Church. When he retired, he moved to Charlotte, North Carolina.

Forty-five years after the alleged crime and twenty-five years after his death the Reverend J.A. DeLaine was cleared of all charges.

May 17, 1954 – By a unanimous vote, the **Dexter Avenue Baptist Church** calls Martin Luther King, Jr. to its pastorate which he begins in September. Martin Luther King, Jr. is 25 years old.

July 11, 1954 – The First White Citizens Council meeting is held in Indianola, Mississippi. The **White Citizens' Council** (**WCC**) was an American white supremacist organization with about 15,000 members, mostly in the South. The group was well known for its opposition to racial integration in the South and was lead by St. Louis attorney Gordon Lee Baum. Its issues involved the protection of European-American heritage from those of other ethnicities.

The successor organization to the "White Citizens' Council" is the **"Council of Conservative Citizens"** an American far-right political organization that supports a large variety of conservative causes in addition to white nationalism and white separatism.

September 1, 1954 – Malcolm X, formerly **Malcolm Little,** becomes a minister of the Nation of Islam's Harlem Temple No. 7.

October 27, 1954 – Benjamin Oliver Davis, Jr. becomes the first black Air Force General. He also becomes the first African American to command an airbase.

October 30, 1954 – The Department of Defense announces on October 30 that the armed forces have been fully **desegregated.**

1954 – The School year begins with the integration of 150 formerly segregated school districts in eight states while many other school districts remain segregated.

1954

Popular Culture:

1954 – McDonald's, the largest fast-food chain in the world. In 1954 **milkshake-mixer salesman Ray Kroc** is fascinated by the McDonald's restaurant popularity. Others who had visited the restaurant and come away inspired were James McLamore, founder of **Burger King**, and Glen Bell, founder of **Taco Bell**. After seeing the restaurant in operation, Kroc at first wanted to sell them a lot more milkshake mixers and then he sensed something bigger, much bigger. He approached the McDonald brothers, who have already begun franchising, with a proposition to let him franchise McDonald's restaurants outside the company's home base of California and Arizona, with himself as the first franchisee. Kroc understood that the American public no longer had time to "dine", they just eat and run. Ray Kroc has an obsession with Quality, Service, Cleanliness and Value. He sold a simple, casual and identifiable restaurant with friendly service, low prices, and no waiting.

1954 – Burger King's first restaurant is opened in Miami, Florida by James McLamore and David Edgerton.
　　Howard Johnson's restaurant is one of the leaders with 400 restaurants in 32 states. About 10% are company-owned turnpike restaurants that are extremely profitable. The rest are franchises, many of which will serve over 1.5 million people a year at their peak. This chain and others really begin to grow as America becomes more mobile.

1954 – Wimpy is the brand name of a chain of fast-food hamburger restaurants based in the United Kingdom. **"Wimpy Bar"** was established at the Lyons Corner House in Coventry Street, London. Originally the bar was a special fast-food section within the more traditional Corner House restaurants, but the success soon led to the establishment of separate Wimpy restaurants serving only hamburger based meals. The Wimpy name was inspired by the character of **J. Wellington Wimpy** from the **Popeye cartoons** created by Elzie Crisler Segar.

1954 – The Supreme Court let stand a lower court ruling, Tudor vs. Board of Education against the **distribution of Bibles** by outside groups like the **Gideons.** By refusing to review it, they affirmed a lower court, ruling the practice of allowing **volunteers** to distribute free copies of the **Gideon Bible** at public schools was a violation. In January, 1993, the 7th Circuit Court of Appeals in Chicago ruled that distribution of Gideon Bibles to schoolchildren in an Indiana school is illegal.

1954 – M&Ms, "Melts in your mouth, not in your hands." Ted Bates & Co.

1954 – Winston cigarettes. "Winston tastes good - like a cigarette should," is the slogan that appears in newspaper, magazine, radio, and television advertisements for Winston cigarettes from the brand's introduction in 1954 until 1972. It is one of the best-known American tobacco advertising campaigns. In 1999, "Advertising Age" ranked the jingle eighth-best out of all the television jingles that aired in the United States in the 20th century.

1954 – Fifty–five percent of American homes have **television sets.**

1954 – The Senate Subcommittee on Juvenile Delinquency conducts hearings on comic books and warns the industry to effectively self-regulate or "other ways and means" would be found to protect children. The industry forms a new trade association and formulates a new Code to self-censor comic book content.

1954 – Lyndon Johnson, future President. Until 1954 it was considered normal for religious leaders to speak openly from the pulpit about any political candidate or issue. It was called **freedom of speech** and had been around since the beginning of our Nation's history. So what happened? How did we loose this right to free speech?

In 1948 Johnson overcame a 20,000-vote deficit to achieve his famous 87-vote victory in the Democratic runoff primary against former Governor, Coke Stevenson. Johnson was elected to the Senate by a margin of 87 votes: 202 ballots in Precinct 13 had been cast in alphabetical order and all just at the close of polling. Fraud? By Johnson? Most historians acknowledge Johnson stole a lot of votes but then go on to say "Everyone was doing it."

In 1954 Lyndon Johnson was trying to get reelected to the senate and was being aggressively opposed by two non-profit anti-Communist groups that were attacking Johnson's liberal agenda. What could Johnson do to win? He inserted language into

the IRS code that prohibited non-profits, including churches, from endorsing or opposing candidates for political office. In effect, he used the power of the IRS to silence his opposition.

Churches and Pastors were expected to speak out on issues of the day. The House of Representatives sponsored church services in its chambers for nearly 100 years, until transportation improved to the point where representatives could go home for the weekends. **Lyndon Johnson** forced a "gag order" on the American people for his own political gain. His "get elected at any cost" policies ended this right. He will be appointed President after John F. Kennedy is assassinated. Lyndon Johnson will then undo most of what President John Kennedy was trying to accomplish.

The oldest Boomer is only eight years old when this basic civil right is taken away.

Business / Technology:

January 1, 1954 – Regular color TV broadcasts begin in the U.S. The first nationwide view of NTSC color comes on January 1 with the coast-to-coast broadcast of the **Tournament of Roses Parade,** viewable on prototype color receivers at special presentations across the country.

January 20, 1954 – The National Negro Network is established. The National Negro Network, with 40 charter member radio stations, is the first black-oriented radio programming service in the United States founded on January 20, by W. Leonard Evans. It was the first black-owned radio network in the country.

1954 – Portable transistor radio, the Regency TR-1. The Regency TR-1 is the first commercially-sold transistor radio, and is the first widely sold transistorized product. It is designed and manufactured in the United States, has beautiful and daring styling and demonstrates the significance of engineering and technology in the 20th century. The TR–1 is introduced and rock n roll is breaking out at the same time. It was manufactured for only one year and approximately 100,000 TR–1 radios were sold for $49.95 each.

1954 – Kodak introduces Tri-X, high speed black-and-white film.

1954 – Texas Instruments produces transistors. The first commercial production of silicon transistors, each about the size of a kernel of corn, replace vacuum tubes.

1954 – The acoustic suspension loudspeaker. Acoustic Research introduces the small AR-1 bookshelf loudspeaker that uses the acoustic suspension principle developed by company co-founder Edgar Villchur.

1954 – IBM writes a computer operating system for the 704.

1954 – Disney ends the Hollywood freeze and leads studios in producing television programs.

1954 – California Eastern Aviation, Inc., (DynCorp) begins as an Air Force contractor. *Head Office:* 1510 H Street NW, Washington 5, DC, USA

    It has since gained a reputation as a CIA front company, for the Agency's dirty tricks. DynCorp uses high-level insider connections to provide services that make it a link between the private and public sectors. It can easily make funding difficult if not impossible to trace and the U.S. government has "plausible deniability" when things go wrong. The US Government is DynCorp's biggest client, accounting for more than 95% of its revenues. Its clients include the **Drug Enforcement Agency**, the **Department of Defense, Department of State, Department of Justice, Internal Revenue Service, Securities and Exchange Commission, FBI, CIA,** and **HUD.**

    DynCorp will go on to have ties to **almost everything, everywhere, all the time.**

Finance:

April 15, 1954 – The deadline for filing individual **income tax returns** is set by the Internal Revenue Code.

May 29-31, 1954 – The first meeting of the **Bilderbergers** at **Hotel de Bilderberg** in Oosterbeek, Netherlands is held. Reporters are not admitted, confidential minutes of meetings are taken but names are not noted, and anyone even attempting to interfere is dealt with harshly by the host government. Bilderberg founding member and, for 30 years, a steering committee member, Denis Healey has said: "To say we were striving for a one-world government is exaggerated, but not wholly unfair. Those of us in Bilderberg felt we couldn't go on forever fighting one another for nothing and killing people and rendering millions homeless. So we felt that a single community throughout the world would be a good thing."

Books:

1954 – **Saul Bellow.** "The Adventures of Augie March."

1954 – **The Los Angeles-based Church of Scientology** is founded by the science fiction writer **L. Ron Hubbard.**

1954 – **"Seduction of the Innocent"** by American psychiatrist Fredric Wertham warns that comic books are a bad form of popular literature and a serious cause of juvenile delinquency. The book alarms parents and motivates them to campaign for censorship while at the same time, a U.S. Senate investigation is launched into the comic book industry.

1954 – **Book 1: J.R.R. Tolkien's, "The Fellowship of the Ring,"** is published in Boston by Houghton, Mifflin. With the addition of **"The Two Towers," published in 1954,** and **"The Return of the King,"** published in 1955, the trilogy, **"The Lord of the Rings"** has been translated into 38 languages. It is one of the most popular stories in 20th-century literature and has been an important book for the fantasy genre.

1954 – **"The Two Towers," J.R.R. Tolkien**, Book 2. Boston. Houghton, Mifflin.

1954 – **"Animal Farm."** George Orwell. Published in England in 1945, in the U.S. in 1946, and animated in 1954, is required reading in English class for most Boomers.

1954 – William Golding. **"Lord of the Flies."**

1954 – **"Horton Hears a Who!"** Theodor Seuss Geisel, Dr. Seuss.

1954 – **"The Alice B. Toklas Cook Book,"** Alice B. Toklas.

TV:

1954 – **The Academy Awards** are first watched on television.

1954 – **The U.S. Senate** holds hearings on societal effects of televised violence.

1954 – **The U.S. is alarmed by Edward R. Murrow's** TV documentary on **Senator. Joseph McCarthy.** Murrow uses excerpts from McCarthy's speeches to point out episodes where he has contradicted himself. Murrow understands he is using the medium of television to attack a single man and expose him to nationwide scrutiny, and was often quoted as having doubts about the methods he used for the report.

Murrow and his producer Fred Friendly financed the promotion themselves because they were not allowed to use CBS' money for the publicity campaign or even use the CBS logo. Murrow and Friendly paid for their own newspaper advertisement for the program. After the broadcast contributed to a nationwide backlash against McCarthy it was considered **a turning point in the history of television.** The power of TV is shown as the program receives tens of thousands of letters, telegrams and phone calls at CBS headquarters, running 15 to 1 in favor.

Sports:

1954 – **Sporting events are broadcast live in color.**

May 6, 1954 – **Sir Roger Gilbert Bannister**, is an English athlete best known as the first man to run the **mile in less than 4 minutes.**

1954 – *"Sports Illustrated"* magazine begins publishing.

Music:

1954 – **Pre-recorded open-reel stereo tapes** go on sale for $12.95, from RCA Victor.

1954 – **"Earth Angel," by "The Penguins."** It is a common practice for radio stations to feature segregated playlists. This means the same song is often recorded by both black groups and white groups at the same time and "Earth Angel" is no exception when it is simultaneously recorded by the white group, **"The Crew-Cuts"**. In 1955 "The Crew-Cuts" cover peaked at #3 on the Hot 100 chart, five spots higher than the Penguins version (black group). The single's success launched the "Crew-Cuts'" own successful career of recording "crossover"-friendly covers of R&B hits.

Natural Disasters:

January 12, 1954 – An avalanche in Blons, Austria kills over 200 people.

March 29, 1954 – A 7.9 magnitude earthquake hits Spain.

March 1, 1954 – A 5.5 magnitude earthquake hits Adelaide, South Australia. It lasts only 20-30 seconds but causes 3 serious injuries and 3,000 buildings are damaged.

July 6, 1954 – A 6.6 magnitude earthquake hits Rainbow Mountain, Nevada.

August 24, 1954 – A 6.8 magnitude earthquake hits Stillwater, Nevada.

August 25-31, 1954 – Hurricane Carol strikes from North Carolina to New England killing 60 people on Long Island and the New England area.

October 5–18, 1954 – Hurricane Hazel is the worst hurricane of the 1954 Atlantic hurricane season and one of the worst hurricanes of the 20th century. Hazel kills as many as 1,000 people in Haiti before striking the United States just north of Myrtle Beach, South Carolina as a Category 4 hurricane. In the Carolinas alone, there were 19 deaths, 39,000 buildings were damaged and an additional 15,000 buildings were destroyed leaving property damage at 136 million dollars. When it hits Toronto, Canada, 81 people are killed. It is the strongest hurricane ever recorded to strike so far inland.

August 1954 – Farahzad, Iran. A Flash flood strikes a gorge where a Muslim shrine is located. The shrine is swept away by the torrential water, killing 2,000 pilgrims.

December 16, 1954 – A 7.1 magnitude earthquake hits Fairview Peak, Nevada.

December 16, 1954 – A 6.8 magnitude earthquake hits Dixie Valley, Nevada.

Man vs. Man / Wars:

1954 – CIA. President Harry S. Truman authorized the creation of the C.I.A. in 1947, and during his administration it carried out covert actions. **Truman refused, however, to authorize the overthrow of governments.** That changed when **Dwight D. Eisenhower** became President in 1953.

1954 – Guatemala. Guatemalan coup. The CIA helps to overthrow **Jacobo Arbenz Guzmán,** the democratically-elected President of Guatemala. **President Arbenz,** himself a former military officer, permitted free expression, legalized unions and diverse political parties, and initiated basic socio-economic reforms. The land reform programs upset the U.S. based multinational **United Fruit Company** because they owned vast tracts of land. The Guatemalan government purchased any unused land at the price that the land owner claimed it was worth when they paid taxes. The property was then sold to peasant cooperatives. To set an example, President Arbenz started with his own lands. Since most owners of vast tracts of land lied when it came time to declare their worth they were not happy with the price they were being paid. The United Fruit Company was one of the largest landowners in the country and they were outraged when the government took over various parcels of their land at such low prices. **United Fruit Company** leaders hurried to Washington and cried "Communism." With the help of the CIA Guatemalan dissidents were organized, armed and trained to carry out a coup and drive President Arbenz from the country. Thousands of people were killed, unions and political parties were broken, and peasant cooperatives were destroyed. CIA documents released after 1995 include a **CIA hit list** prepared before the coup, identifying political and intellectual leaders as military targets. A military dictatorship was installed and remained until the election of civilian President Venizio Cerezo in 1986.

The U.S. involvement in overthrowing the government of Guatemala **effectively ended** the experimental period of **representative democracy** in Guatemala known as the "Ten Years of Spring", which ended with Arbenz's official resignation. Within a few years Guatemala will be involved in a guerrilla war and state terror in which **hundreds of thousands of people will die** due to the violence, assassination and torture.

The Guatemalan intervention of 1954 set the precedent for later interventions in Cuba, British Guiana, Brazil and Chile. The tactics were the same, the mindset was the same, and in many cases the people who directed those covert interventions were the same. After the CIA coup, hundreds of Guatemalans were rounded up and killed.

November 1, 1954-1962 – The Algerian War of Independence. Algeria vs. France. A French colony since the 1830s, Algeria won independence from France after a very bloody war characterized by guerrilla warfare, terrorism against civilians, and the use of torture on both sides along with counter-terrorism operations by the French Army. Algeria's war of Independence is started by members of the National Liberation Front on November 1, 1954 during the "Toussaint Rouge conflict" and shook the French Fourth Republic's foundations, leading to its collapse. It has been estimated that between 350,000 and 1,000,000 people were killed. French military authorities listed their losses at nearly 18,000 dead. According to French figures, security forces killed 141,000 rebel combatants, and more than 12,000 Algerians died in internal FLN purges during the war. An additional 5,000 died in the "café wars" in France between the FLN and rival Algerian groups. French sources also estimated that 70,000 Muslim civilians were killed, or abducted and presumed killed, by the FLN. **The war uprooted more than 2 million Algerians, who were forced to relocate in French camps or to flee to Morocco, Tunisia, and into the Algerian backcountry, where many thousands died of starvation, disease, and exposure.** In addition large numbers of pro-French Muslims were murdered when the FLN settled accounts after independence. One of the bloodiest episodes was the six month long "battle of Algiers" in 1957.

1954 – Cambodia. Batdambang Massacre. Prince Norodom Sihanouk, now Prime Minister Sihanouk, presided over a regime that was oppressively reactionary and, in some instances, as violent in its suppression of political opposition as the **Khmer Rouge.** The Royal Armed Forces under Lon Nol slaughtered women and children in pro-Khmer Issarak regions of Batdambang in 1954 using methods that were later to become routine under Pol Pot.

The Thais forced ethnic Khmer residents of Battambang to dress in Thai clothing, and forbid the use of public display of the Khmer language. They even forbid the speaking of Khmer in pagodas, but the monks resisted, and thereby prevented the success of the program. During WWII Battambang residents suffered economically and even the rice harvest, fell to almost zero. Beatings, torture and rape were common. A concentration camp was set up at Boueng Chhouk Market, near the present day taxi stand to Sisophan. Three thousand people were interned there, and the women and girls were systematically raped by their captors. At the end of the Second World War, the new French government forced the Thais to return Battambang and other occupied territory to what remained of Cambodia. After the Thais looted the areas of everything of value, they left. The Khmer Rouge rebels continued fighting and plundering in the province after the civil war through the 1970's and 1980's until the end of 1998.

1946-1954 – The Huk Rebellion in the **Philippines** is a communist-led peasant uprising in central Luzon, Philippines. The name of the movement is a Tagalog acronym for Hukbo ng Bayan Laban sa Hapon, which means "People's Anti-Japanese Army." The Huks consider Filipinos who collaborated with the Japanese traitors and feel they should pay with their lives.

By the end of the war the Huks had seized most of the large estates in central Luzon. They established a regional government, collected taxes, and administered their own laws. The Huks had an estimated 500,000 rifles, and were reluctant to turn them in to a government they did not trust. The Manila government steadily decreased while the Huk strength increased and by 1950 the guerrillas were approaching Manila, and the communist-dominated Huks decided to seize the government.

The Huks almost obtained victory but were defeated by a combination of advanced U.S. weaponry supplied to the Philippine government and administrative reforms under the charismatic Philippine President Ramon Magsaysay. In 1954 Luis Taruc came out of the jungle and surrendered. This marked the end of the uprising in which 9,633 people were killed.

1945-1954 – First Indochina War. The Japanese ousted the French in March 1945 and then ruled through Bao Dia, who renamed the country Vietnam. The first Indochina War was fought between the French Union's, **French Far East Expeditionary Corps**, led by France and supported by Bao Dia's Vietnamese National Army against the Việt Minh, led by **Ho Chi Minh** and General Vo **Nguyen Giap**. The war will last eight years and marks the end of French colonial rule in Indochina. While most of the fighting takes place in North Vietnam it also extends to Laos and Cambodia. When the French lose the war, the Geneva Conference on July 21, 1954, divides Vietnam at the 17th parallel, with control of the north given to the Viet Minh as the Democratic Republic of Vietnam under Ho Chi Minh, and the south becoming the State of Vietnam under Bao Dia. This was done to prevent Ho Chi Minh from gaining control of the entire country. A year later, Bao Dai was deposed by his Prime Minister, **Ngo Dinh Diem**, creating the Republic of Vietnam.

The Geneva Conference called for mandatory nationwide elections in 1956 but Diem refused to negotiate with North Vietnam. This will lead to war breaking out again in South Vietnam in 1959, the Second Indochina War (Vietnam War). It has been estimated that 3 to 4 million Vietnamese from both sides died during this war.

1954-Present – India. Naga Rebellion. After India became independent in 1947, the Naga territory initially remained a part of Assam. A strong nationalist movement began seeking a political union of the Naga tribes, and extremists demanded outright secession from the Indian Union. This movement led to a number of violent incidents, and in 1955 the Indian army was called in to restore order.

1954 – Paraguayan Coup. Alfredo Stroessner leads a coup on May 4 and removes **President Federico Chavez' from office**. Fierce resistance by police left almost fifty dead.

Alfredo Stroessner was dictator in Paraguay from 1954-1989, when he was ousted by a coup led by General Andrés Rodríguez, who had been his friend and comrade-in-arms for many years. **Stroessner** placed many of his supporters in positions of power within the government and then through bribery, fear, and torture, he made Paraguay a safe haven for evil. Smugglers, ex-dictators, Nazi war criminals, all were welcome for a price.

1954 – India. Chinese incursions into Indian Territory began along the U.P.-Tibet border, just after India signed the infamous Border Trade Agreement between **"The Tibet Region of China and India,"** on April 29, 1954, which conceded Chinese Sovereignty over Tibet. The Agreement included handing over Indian property, the withdrawal of Indian military escorts and the handing over of telephone, telegraph and communications equipment and facilities in Tibet, to China. When **Prime Minister Nehru** took up the wrong depiction of borders on Chinese maps with the smooth and suave **Chou en Lai** in October 1954, he was assured that the maps in question "were really reproductions of old 'pre-liberation' maps and that he (Chou) had not time to review them."

1954-1959 – Laos. Pathet Lao Insurgency. In 1951, Prince Souphanouvong organized the **Pathet Lao,** a Communist independence movement, in North Vietnam. Viet Minh and Pathet Lao forces invaded central Laos, and civil war resulted. By the **Geneva agreements of 1954** and an armistice of 1955, two Northern provinces are given to the Pathet Lao, and the rest go to the royal regime. Full sovereignty is given to the kingdom by the Paris agreements of December 29, 1954.

In May 1954 the French suffer a defeat at **Dien Bien Phu** in northern Vietnam which, while of no great consequence militarily, is a political disaster. **The French government resigns** and Pierre Mendès-France becomes Prime Minister on a policy of **getting out of Indochina.** An international conference on Indochina has already been convened in Geneva, and as it met it was confronted with the new situation following Dien Bien Phu. Laos was a secondary issue at Geneva, and the decisions made about Laos were dictated by the settlement in Vietnam.

April 1954 – Cambodia. Viet Minh Incursion. Although **Cambodia** had achieved independence by late 1953, its military situation remained unsettled. Noncommunist factions of the **Khmer Issarak** had joined the government, but communist **Viet Minh** activities increased at the very time **French Union forces** were stretched thin elsewhere. In April 1954, several Viet Minh battalions crossed the border into Cambodia. Royalist forces engaged them but could not force their complete withdrawal. In part, the communists were attempting to strengthen their bargaining position at the Geneva Conference that had been scheduled to begin in late April.

1954

May 7, 1954 – Vietnam. The Viet Minh overrun the French fortress at Dien Bien Phu. After a 55-day siege, the Vietnamese Nationalist, and Communist-led, Vietminh army defeat French forces at Dien Bien Phu and the French are compelled to accede to the creation of a Communist Vietnam north of the 17th parallel while leaving a non-Communist entity south of that line.

As 900,000 Vietnamese people flee from the North to the South, the **United States** refuses to accept the arrangement. **President Dwight D. Eisenhower** undertakes instead to build a nation from the spurious political entity that was South Vietnam by fabricating a government there, taking over control from the French, dispatching military advisers to train a South Vietnamese army, and unleashing the Central Intelligence Agency to conduct psychological warfare against the North. The United States entered the war to prevent a communist takeover of South Vietnam as part of their wider strategy of containment. Military advisors had been in country since 1950.

1955

The Oldest Boomer is 9 years old.

Median Family Income: $4,400	**Minimum Wage:** 75cents/ hr
New House: $11,000	**Gallon Gasoline:** 29 cents

Government	Private Sector
Lawyer: $7,900	**Lawyer:** $8,700
Payroll Clerk: $3,700	**Payroll Clerk:** $3,200
Typist: $3,200	**Typist:** $2,800
Engineer: $9,400	**Engineer:** $19,600
Division Head: $12,000	**Plant Manager:** $25,000

New Car: Buick Special: $2,263	**Chevrolet Corvette:** $2,774
Unemployment Rate: 4.9%-4.0%-4.2%	**First-class Stamp:** 3 cents

12 cents buying power in 1955 = **$1.00 in 2008.**
In 1955 what cost our parents 12 cents to purchase
now costs us $1.00 in 2008.

Movies: "Rebel Without a Cause," "Marty," "Love is a Many-Splendored Thing," "Guys and Dolls," "Picnic," "The Rose Tattoo," "Lady and the Tramp," "Cinerama Holiday,"-filmed for curved screen Cinerama. "Mister Roberts," "The Seven Year Itch," "East of Eden," "Ma and Pa Kettle at Waikiki." "Abbott and Costello Meet the Mummy," "The Man with the Golden Arm," "Oklahoma!" "To Catch a Thief,"
"You're Never Too Young," starring Dean Martin and Jerry Lewis.

Broadway: "Plain and Fancy," "Silk Stockings," "Kismet,"London. "Damn Yankees," "Cat on a Hot Tin Roof."

TV: "Gunsmoke," "Captain Kangaroo," "The Adventures of Spin and Marty," "The $64,000 Question," "Ed Sullivan Show," "Highway Patrol," "Adventures of Robin Hood," "The Lawrence Welk Show," "The Mickey

Mouse Club," "Fury," "Life and Legend of Wyatt Earp," "My Friend Flicka," "Cheyenne," "Alfred Hitchcock Presents," "The Adventures of Kit Carson," "Sergeant Preston of the Yukon," "Tales of the Texas Rangers," "Steve Donovan, Western Marshal," "Sheriff of Cochise," "Phil Silvers Show," "Frankie Laine Show," "Patti Page Show". "The Great Gildersleeve". "TV's TOP Tunes."

Music: Alex North, "Unchained Melody." Rodgers and Hammerstein, "Oklahoma!" Elmer Bernstein, "The Man With the Golden Arm." First rock 'n' roll song to top the chart: Bill Haley's, "Rock Around the Clock." "East of Eden," "Mister Roberts," "The Rose Tattoo." Fats Domino, "Ain't That A Shame." Chuck Berry, "Maybellene." Ray Charles, "I've Got A Woman." Webb Pierce, "In The Jailhouse Now." Tennessee Ernie Ford, "Sixteen Tons."

Deaths: Shemp Howard, Carmen Miranda, Theda Bara, **David Millar, Jr.**

President: Dwight D. Eisenhower (R) Presbyterian; vetoes 181/ 2 overrides

Vice President: Richard M. Nixon (R) Quaker

House: D-232 ; R-203

Senate: 84th Congress (1955-1957) Majority Party: Democrat (48 seats) Minority Party: Republican (47 seats) Other Parties: 1 Independent Total Seats: 96

Federal Debt: $274.37 billion or 66 % of the GDP

Consumer Price Index CPI-U (1982 Base of 100): 26.80

GDP: $414.8 billion	**Inflation Rate:** -0.28%

Dow Jones: 469.63 (09-01)/ 409.70 (02-01)

Prime Rate: 3.50% (10-15)	**Average Home Mortgage Rate:** 5.18%
1 oz Gold: $35.15	**1oz of Silver:** $0.89

Average Monthly S.S. Benefits Paid: $69 / month

Federal Debt: $274,374,222,802.62

Federal Deficit: $3.0 billion dollars	
Defense Spending: $47.17 billion	**Interest Spending:** $4.85 billion
Health Care Spending: $910 million	**Pensions Spending:** $4.76 billion
Welfare Spending: $1.98 billion	**Education Spending:** $1.32 billion
Transportation Spending: $1.46 billion	**Misc. Other Spending:** $8.27 billion
Protection Spending: $130 million	**Total Government Spending:** $73.44 billion
% of GDP that goes towards just the interest payment: 1.17%	
$1.00 = 2.460 Yuan, China NPC	
U.S. Population: 165,275,000	**World Population:** 2,779,669,781
U.S. Birth Rate: 4,104,000	**U.S. Abortions:** 328
U.S. Homicide Rate: 4.5/ 100,000 population	
Annual Average Domestic Crude Oil Prices: $2.93 / barrel, $23.47 (2007 adjusted)	

Oil:

1955 – Soviet gains in the Middle East are particularly threatening. Moscow has leveraged the 1955 Czech Arms deal with **President Nasser's Egypt** into rapidly expanding influence across the region at a time when Middle East petroleum resources are increasingly **critical to the West.**

1955 – George H.W. Bush becomes president of Zapata. Various writers have alleged links between the company and the United States Central Intelligence Agency. Zapata Off-Shore concentrated its business in the Caribbean, the Gulf of Mexico, and the Central American coast.

1955

Zapata's filing records with the U.S. Securities and Exchange Commission are complete for the years 1955-1959, and from 1967 onwards. However in October of 1983, or possibly in 1981 shortly after **George Bush** became Vice President, the records for the years 1960-1966 were accidently destroyed.

1955 – Italy's ENI and Egypt sign an oil concession treaty which grants Egypt 75 % of the oil profits.

Major News:

February 8, 1955 – U.S.S.R., Nikolai A. Bulganin becomes the Soviet Premier, replacing Malenkov.

February 12, 1955 – The U.S. agrees to help train the **South Vietnamese** army.

April 5, 1955 – Sir Winston Churchill has **resigned** as Prime Minister of Britain due to his failing health. The news was announced in a statement from Buckingham Palace this afternoon. It said: "The Right Honorable Sir Winston Churchill had an audience with the Queen this evening and tendered his resignation as Prime Minister and First Lord of the Treasury, which Her Majesty was graciously pleased to accept." Churchill, a superb wartime leader, was received less favorably in peacetime and in the general election of July 1945 he was heavily defeated. **Churchill** became Prime Minister again in 1951.

May 5, 1955 – West Germany becomes a sovereign state. **The Federal Republic of Germany** becomes a sovereign state and joins **NATO,** (the North Atlantic Treaty Organization). In response the government of the German Democratic Republic signs the Warsaw Treaty of Friendship Cooperation and Mutual Assistance with **Albania, Bulgaria, Czechoslovakia, Hungary, Poland, Romania** and the **Soviet Union.**

May 11, 1955 – The Western European Union (WEU) comes into being. On May 11, the Foreign Ministers of **Belgium, France,** the **Federal Republic of Germany, Italy Luxembourg,** the **Netherlands** and the **United Kingdom** sign the Agreement on the

Status of the Western European Union (WEU), its National Representatives and International Staff, in Paris.

May 14, 1955 – The Warsaw Pact east European mutual defense agreement is signed. The Warsaw Pact is the Soviet-sponsored military-treaty organization and the European Communist Bloc's counterpart to **NATO.**

May 31, 1955 – The Supreme Court orders **"all deliberate speed"** in the integration of public schools.

July 18-23, 1955 – A summit meeting of the **U.S., Britain, France,** and the **USSR** takes place in Geneva, Switzerland. It is considered the first big meeting between leaders from the United States (**Dwight D. Eisenhower**) and Soviet Union (**Nikita Khrushchev**) in the 10 years since the **Potsdam Conference** following **World War II.** The countries discuss Germany and various disarmament methods, but are not able to agree. The Geneva Summit showed to the world that tensions are easing between the two superpowers, and is often referred to as **"The Spirit of Geneva."**

September 20, 1955 – An Argentine military coup removes President Juan Perón and he goes into exile for 18 years.

On June 15, Peron is excommunicated by Pope Pius XII and on the following day he calls for a rally of support on the Plaza de Mayo, gathering thousands. As Perón addresses the crowd Navy fighter jets fly overhead and drop bombs onto the square killing 364 people. The army did not back Perón and on September 20, he fled the country, eventually settling in Spain.

Juan Peron is perhaps the most famous Argentinean, other than Diego Maradona and many people know of him through the musical and film, **"Evita."** The reality, though, is that he was populist, nationalist and pro-capitalist, what Marxists call a 'Bonapartist'. He destroyed independent working-class politics in Argentina for half a century. He will return to power in 1973 and serve for nine months, until his death, when he is succeeded by his third wife, Isabel Martinez.

September 24, 1955 – President Eisenhower has a heart attack in Denver.

1955

December 5, 1955 – AFL-CIO. America's two largest labor organizations merge creating the AFL-CIO. The American Federation of Labor merges with the Congress of Industrial Organizations to become the AFL-CIO. Labor unions are capable of bringing down governments in the 1950's and there seems to be a **U.S government, Mafia, AFL-CIO connection** beginning here and flexing its muscle around the world.

Civil Rights Movement:

August 28, 1955 – Emmett Till, at the age of 14, is beaten and shot to death for allegedly whistling at a white woman in Money, Mississippi, a small town in the state's Delta region. His brutal murder combined with the acquittal on September 23 of the two white men charged with the crime attracts widespread public attention. The main suspects boast about committing the murder, after their acquittal by an all white jury, and the public outrage generated by the case helps spur the civil rights movement.

The State of Mississippi wanted things to just go away and even tried to control Emmett Till's funeral service in Chicago. Till's mother insisted on a public funeral service, with an open casket to show the world the brutality of the killing in which Till had been beaten and his eye had been gouged out, before he was shot through the head and thrown into the Tallahatchie River with a 70-pound cotton gin fan tied to his body with barbed wire. His body was in the river for three days before it was discovered and retrieved by two fishermen.

The State of Mississippi insisted it would not allow the funeral home in Chicago to open the casket, so Emmett Till's mother, Mrs. Mamie Till Bradley, threatened to open it herself, insisting she had a right to see her son. After viewing the body, she also insisted on leaving the casket open for the funeral and allowing people to take photographs because she wanted people to see how badly Till's body had been disfigured, she has famously been quoted as saying, **"I wanted the world to see what they did to my baby."** "We cannot afford the luxury of self-pity. Our top priority now is to get on with the building process." **"Death of Innocence," by Mamie Till Mobley**

December 1, 1955 – Rosa Parks refuses to give her seat to a white man on a bus in Montgomery, Alabama, and is arrested. In response to her arrest the Montgomery black community launches a successful year-long bus boycott.

The Montgomery Bus Boycott is a political and social protest campaign intended to oppose the city's policy of racial segregation on its public transit system. This causes deficits in public transit profits because a large percentage of people who use the public transportation were now boycotting it. The ensuing struggle will last from December 1, 1955, to December 20, 1956, and lead to a United States Supreme Court decision that declares the Alabama and Montgomery laws requiring segregated buses unconstitutional.

Women's Movement:

1955 – California. The Daughters of Bilitis is the first lesbian rights organization in the United States. It is formed in San Francisco, California in 1955. The group was conceived as a social alternative to lesbian bars, which were considered illegal and thus subject to raids and police harassment.

Popular Culture:

1955 – Rosa Parks refuses to sit at the back of the bus.

1955 – Tennessee Williams' "Cat on a Hot Tin Roof" wins the Pulitzer Prize for Drama.

1955 – Movie studios open their vaults for television rentals, sales.

1955 – The felt-tip-pen is marketed by **Esterbrook** in England.

1955 – The Comic book code censors horror stories. This hurts sales hitting the whole industry hard.

1955 – As Ronald Reagan hosts a live ABC special, **Disneyland** opens in Anaheim, California. The first major destination theme park spurs growth in travel and tourism nationwide. Today Disney's parks alone are a $5 billion annual business, and **Walt Disney World** in Orlando, Florida, which has more than 5,000 employees, is the largest single-site employer in the U.S.

1955

1955 – "The Marlboro Man," Marlboro. Leo Burnett Co.

When the brand is changed from the former feminine brand ("Fresh as the month of May") into a masculine product it soon began to sell millions.

Wayne McLaren, rodeo rider, actor, Hollywood stuntman and one of the Marlboro cigarette cowboys, became an anti-smoking advocate after he developed cancer. A former pack-and-a-half day smoker, he died in 1992 at the age of 51. The original Marlboro Man, **David Millar, Jr.** died of emphysema in 1987. The widow of Marlboro Man **David McLean,** who died of lung cancer in 1995, sued the company for damages.

Other tobacco spokesman such as David Goerlitz, the Winston Man from 1981 to 1987, was disabled by a stroke in his mid-30s. **Will Thornbury,** a Camel model, died of lung cancer at age of 56 in 1992. **Janet Sackman,** a former Lucky Strike girl in the 1950s lost her voice box and part of a lung to cancer.

1955 – United Artists withdraws from the Motion Picture Association when it refuses to issue a Production Code seal to the company's film "The Man With the Golden Arm," which deals with **drug addiction.**

1955 – The American Law Institute's model penal code omitted **sodomy laws** for the first time, without fanfare.

1955 – Walt Disney produces "Lady & The Tramp," offering a starkly desolate depiction of dogs on death row at the pound.

1955 – The **Riviera Hotel in Los Vegas** becomes the first high rise casino on the strip with a height of nine stories.

1955 – Robert Schuller receives his Bachelor of Divinity from Western Theological Seminary in Holland, Michigan and is ordained by the Dutch Reformed Church of America. In 1955, with his wife Arvella he establishes a congregation in Garden Grove, California. From the snack bar roof of the Orange drive-in theater, he begins conducting Sunday Services. The Crystal Cathedral comes later.

Business / Technology:

1955 – Archaeologists set the **carbon dating** base year.

1955 – TRADIC, the first fully transistorized computer contains nearly **800 transistors** instead of vacuum tubes. Instead of being the size of a small room the computer occupies only 3 cubic feet. It can perform a million logical operations every second, still not quite as fast as the vacuum tube computers of the mid 1950's, but pretty close. It is small and light enough to be installed in a B-52 Stratofortress, operates on less than 100 watts of power and is much more reliable than its vacuum tube counterparts.

November 22, 1955 – The first **Soviet** test of a **"true" hydrogen bomb** in the megaton range is dubbed **RDS-37** by the Soviets. It was of the multi-staged, radiation implosion thermonuclear design called Sakharov's "Third Idea" in the USSR and the Teller-Ulam design in the USA.

1955 – For the first time since they were introduced in 1949, **45 rpm discs** begin to outsell the old standard 78s.

July 17, 1955 – Disneyland, opens in Anaheim, California, with the backing of the new television network, ABC. Disneyland is the brainchild of **Walt Disney,** whose father had worked at the world's fair and inspired his son.

1955 – Marcel Dassault unveils its swept wing fighter, the **"Mirage."** The "Mirage" can fly at speeds **in excess of Mach 2** and can climb to 57,000 feet. The "Mirage" is possibly best known for its success as an air superiority fighter during the **Arab-Israeli War of 1967**.

1955 – The U-2 is tested. Lockheed presents the C.I.A. with a proposal for a high altitude spy craft. The C.I.A. accepts the proposal and, in eight months, Lockheed produces the "U-2." In its first flight, the lightly-loaded U-2 refuses to land and test pilot Tony LeVier makes five attempts before succeeding in landing the craft.

1955

Finance:

1955 – Textile workers strike. In both New Bedford and Fall River, Massachusetts workers strike over a nickel raise.

1955 – The August Consumer Price Index will not be this low again until March 2009. Prices actually fell by 0.4% for a twelve month period ending in August.

1955 – H&R Block is founded in Kansas City when the IRS stops preparing tax returns for free. Founders, Harvard business graduate Henry and his brother Richard "Bloch", changed the firm's name to "Block" to prevent mispronunciation.

Books:

1955 – Rudolf Flesch, **"Why Johnny Can't Read."**

1955 – "Guinness Book of Records" is published.

1955 – "Lolita," Vladimir Nabokov's scandalous novel of middle-age lust for nymphet, Lolita.

1955 – William Golding, **"Lord of the Flies."**

1955 – "The Return of the King," J.R.R Tolkien, Book 3.

1955 – South Africa's apartheid regime banned a number of classic books, for instance, the **New York Times** reported that Mary Shelley's **"Frankenstein"** was banned there as "indecent, objectionable, or obscene". At one time, the regime also reportedly banned Anna Sewell's **"Black Beauty,"** a story about a horse.

TV:

1955 – Captain Kangaroo. One of the longest-running **children's TV** shows of all time, Bob Keeshan, as Captain Kangaroo, taught lessons in morality with the help of his friends: **Mr. Green Jeans**, **Mr. Moose**, and **Mr. Rabbit**, among others. Captain Kangaroo taught us good manners, respect and fair play. Mr. Green Jeans taught us to be nice to animals.

1955 – **Research shows TV viewing** correlates inversely with education and income.

1955 – Radio's $64 Question becomes **TV's $64,000 Question.**

1955 – On TV, the Broadway hit **"Peter Pan"** pulls a big audience.

1955 – The Dumont television network gives up.

1955 – The **"Adventures of Spin and Marty"** premiers on **"The Mickey Mouse Club."**

1955 – **Granville Oral Roberts** makes the transition from tent crusader as the **"King of Faith Healers"** into radio and television broadcasting. His radio audience is larger than any other faith healer. Roberts is the national leader of paid religious television.

Sports:

1955 – **The Canadian Broadcasting Corporation** invents the first form of **instant replay** when director George Retzlaff uses a "hot processor" to develop kinescope footage of goals within 30 seconds to replay on **"Hockey Night in Canada."**

Music:

August 19, 1955 – WINS radio station in New York City adopts a policy of not playing white cover versions of black R&B songs.

1955 – **Elvis Presley's** third Sun Records single, **"Milk Cow Blue Boogie"** / "You're a Heartbreaker" is released.

September 3, 1955 – **Little Richard** records **"Tutti Frutti"** with significantly cleaned up lyrics. The original lyrics included "Tutti Frutti, good booty" among other things.

1955

Natural Disasters:

May 25, 1955 – A tornado in Udall, Kansas kills 80 people.

August 7–21, 1955 – North Carolina to New England. Hurricane Diane kills 184 people. Damages are calculated at $755 million with the majority occurring in New England.

September 10–24, 1955 – Hurricane Ione is the third hurricane to pass through eastern North Carolina within a six-week period. Total damage is estimated at $88 million and seven people are killed.

September 19, 1955 – Mexico. "Hurricane Hilda" kills 200 people.

September 22-28, 1955 – "Hurricane Janet" kills 200 people in Honduras and 300 people in Mexico.

October 14-21, 1955 – Hurricane Katie causes major damage in Hispaniola near the border between Haiti and the Dominican Republic. It crosses into Hispaniola on the evening of October 16, with damage estimated at $200,000. Seven people are killed.

August 31,-September 7, 1955 – Los Angeles, California. An eight day period of 100°F-plus heat leaves 946 people dead.

October 24, 1955 – A 5.4magnitude earthquake strikes Concord, California. One person is killed.

Man vs. Man / Wars:

Assassinated – Jose Antonio Remon, was **President of Panama** from October 1, 1952 until his murder by **machine-gun fire** at a Panama City racetrack on January 2, 1955. General José Remón was the man behind the scenes of several coups that ousted Dr. Arnulfo Arias from power, and arguably the true founder of the social reforming militarism. The crime has never been solved.

September 19, 1955 – Argentina. Juan Peron is overthrown by a military coup and goes into exile in Spain for 18 years.

1955 – Argentina. Military Revolt in Buenos Aires. President and dictator of Argentina, Juan Domingo Perón, began to lose power after the death of his wife Eva (Evita), who had a strong political following among women, labor, and the poor. Many Argentines were also upset by the deteriorating economy and increasing violence. Perón failed because he either went too far or not far enough. He just could not figure things out. He raised rural wages and forced landowners to sell cheap to the AIPE, but when they refused to sell he failed to nationalize the land. This reduced the amount of land under cultivation from nearly 22 million hectares in 1934-1938 to just over 17 million in 1955. When Peron turned against the Roman Catholic Church and arrested Priests, he went too far. Priests were arrested for supposedly meddling in labor unions, politics, and student organizations. Clerical teachers were fired from state-controlled schools and universities, the government stopped all financial support of church educational institutions, and outdoor religious celebrations were prohibited. As opposition increased many government officials resigned in protest. Then Peron introduced bills to end religious instruction in the schools and to tax church property. Catholic religious processions turned into anti government demonstrations, which the police ruthlessly suppressed by clubbing the protesters.

After a Corpus Christi celebration in June 1955, two high-ranking bishops were deported and in June the Vatican retaliated by excommunicating Peron. The next day the navy and air force staged an unsuccessful revolt in Buenos Aires. On September 20, 1955, Peron was overthrown by a military coup, fled the country and did not return for eighteen years. In the period following the overthrow of Perón, wages went up 400 percent while the price of food went up 750 percent.

February 28, 1955 – Israeli Raid on Gaza. Israeli forces conduct a raid, in response to repeated guerrilla attacks and the seizure of an Israeli ship by Egypt, killing 38 people and exposing Egypt's military weakness. Chinese Premier Chou En-Lai suggested to Nasser that the Soviets might be responsive to a request for arms. The Egyptian Czech arms deal, which ended Egypt's dependence on the West for weapons, was announced on September 27, 1955, and by the end of 1955 Egypt had successfully negotiated the British evacuation. This makes the Egyptian army, equipped with soviet weapons, the ultimate repository of power for the first time since the 1882 British occupation.

January 1955 – Nicaragua vs. Costa Rica. When an attempt to kill **Somoza,** the **President of Nicaragua,** was found to be backed by the Costa Rican President, Somoza used this as an excuse to invade Costa Rica. A small airborne force of Costa Rican "rebels" landed in the northern border town of Villa Quesada in Costa Rica and seized control of the area. Despite denials, President Jose Figueres of Costa Rica, charges Nicaraguan aggression and asks for OAS military aid and the town is recaptured by Costa Rican forces on January 12. **President Somoza is so upset he challenges President Figueres to a duel** on the border.

Both countries ask the OAS to establish a peace commission to settle further disputes and U.S. Vice-President Richard Nixon is involved in the peace process.

April 23, 1955 – Singapore "Black Thursday." Members of the Singapore Bus Workers' Union from the Hock Lee Amalgamated Bus Company get a lot of encouragement from the communists and go on strike. They are protesting against poor working conditions, long work hours and low pay.

A lot of the civil unrest began at the recent Legislative Assembly Election in April when the Labor Front led by David Marshall formed a minority government after winning a narrow victory. Two pro-communist leaders decided to encourage social unrest to discredit the British authorities and Marshall's local government and they started a campaign of strikes and student protests in an attempt to destabilize the government. There campaign is fairly successful with over 275 strikes in 1955 even though many labor union officials are arrested and sent to prison. Riots broke out on May 12 when police attempted to break up an illegal picket line formed by striking bus workers and Chinese school students. Thirty-one people are injured and four people are killed in what became known as **"Black Thursday."**

1955-1972 Sudan – First Sudanese Civil War is a civil war between the largely Muslim Arab north and the mostly Christian Black south from 1955 to 1972. **Half a million people are killed** over the 17 years of war.

February 12, 1955 – **Vietnam**. President Eisenhower's administration sends the **first U.S. advisers** to South Vietnam to train the South Vietnamese Army while French forces are leaving Vietnam.

1955 – Buddhist Rebellion in South Vietnam. The Geneva Accord promised free elections to determine the government for a unified Vietnam. France and the Viet Minh had signed the document but the United States and **Ngo Dinh Diem's** government refused to honor the agreement because they knew **Ho Chi Minh** would win. Instead of allowing Free Elections, Edward Lansdale's team from the CIA was instructed to help Diem continue to rule.

Lansdale was able to show an economic miracle for the South by manipulating the figures using $250 million dollars in aid per year to South Vietnam. The U.S. Navy program **Operation Passage to Freedom** helped almost **one million North Vietnamese** move to the south. Most of these refugees were Catholic. A referendum was scheduled for October 23, 1955 to determine the future direction of the south and the ballots were red and green. Lansdale felt that since local superstition held that red signified good luck while green indicated bad fortune this would help Diem. Emperor **Bao Dai** wanted the restoration of "his" monarchy, while Diem ran on a republican platform. In October 1955, Ngo Dinh Diem deposed Bao Dai and proclaimed himself President of the newly established Republic of Vietnam. **In Saigon Diem received over 600,000 votes even though there were only 450,000 registered voters.** He won the elections with 98.2 percent of the vote. Lansdale warned him that these figures would not be believed and suggested that he publish a figure of around 70 per cent. Diem refused and the outright arrogance of his voter theft undermined his authority.

The oldest Boomer is nine years old, and has no idea what is in store for him/her.

1956

The Oldest Boomer is 10 years old.

Median Family Income: $4,800	**Minimum Wage:** $1.00/ hr **Average Hourly Wage:** $1.95
New Car: Ford: $1,611 **Studebaker:** $1,844	**Hershey Bar:** 5 cents/ 1oz **Gallon Gasoline:** 30 cents
Unemployment Rate: 4.0%-4.4%-4.2%	**First-class Stamp:** 3 cents

13 cents buying power in 1956 = **$1.00 in 2008.**
In 1956 what cost our parents 13 cents to purchase
now costs us $1.00 in 2008.

Movies: "Forbidden Planet," "Friendly Persuasion," "Giant," "The Searchers," "Around the World in Eighty Days," "The King and I," "The Ten Commandments," "Anastasia," "Bus Stop". "The Kettles in the Ozarks."

Broadway: "My Fair Lady," "Irma La Douce," Paris. "Li'l Abner," "Bells Are Ringing," "Candide." Eugene O'Neill's, "Long Day's Journey Into Night."

TV: Ralph Kramden's "$99,000 Answer." "Queen For A Day," "The Price is Right," "The Hardy Boys," "Heckle and Jeckle," "To Tell The Truth," "Steve Allen Show," "Twenty One," "Judge Roy Bean," "Adventures of Jim Bowie," "As the World Turns," "Nat King Cole Show," "The Edge of Night," "Rock 'n Roll Dance Party," "Adventures of Sir Lancelot," "Dinah Shore Chevy Show," "Tic Tac Dough". Elvis, rocked the "Ed Sullivan Show." Elvis' first appearance on "The Milton Berle Show."

Music: "Carousel" & "The King and I," Rodgers and Hammerstein. Fats Domino, "I'm In Love Again" & "Blueberry Hill". Frank Sinatra, "All the Way". Pat Boone, "I Almost Lost My Mind" & "Don't Forbid Me." The Platters, "The Great Pretender" & "My Prayer." Little Richard, "Long Tall

1956

Sally" & "Tutti Frutti." Elvis Presley, "Heartbreak Hotel," "Don't Be Cruel," "Anyway You Want Me" & "Love Me Tender." Little Willie John, "Fever." Dean Martin, "Memories Are Made Of This." Johnny Cash, "I Walk The Line." Carl Perkins, "Blue Suede Shoes." Ray Price, "Crazy Arms." Frankie Lymon and the Teenagers', "Why Do Fools Fall in Love." Gene Vincent and His Blue Caps, "Be-Bop-A-Lula." Chuck Berry, "Roll Over Beethoven." Bill Haley and His Comets, "See You Later Alligator." The Four Lads, "Standing on the Corner." Doris Day, "Whatever Will Be, Will Be. Que Sera, Sera." Five Satins, "In the Still of the Night." Roy Orbison, "Ooby Dooby."

President: Dwight D. Eisenhower (R) Presbyterian; vetoes 181/ 2 overrides

Vice President: Richard M. Nixon (R) Quaker

House: D-232 ; R-203

Senate: 84th Congress (1955-1957) Majority Party: Democrat (48 seats) Minority Party: Republican (47 seats) Other Parties: 1 Independent Total Seats: 96

Federal Debt: $272.75 billion or 62 % of the GDP

Consumer Price Index CPI-U (1982 Base of 100): 27.20

GDP: $437.5 billion	**Inflation Rate:** 1.52%

Dow Jones: 518.69 (08-01)/ 468.70 (10-01)

Prime Rate: 4.00% (08-21)	**Average Home Mortgage Rate:** 5.19%
1 oz Gold: $35.20	**1oz of Silver:** $0.91

Federal Debt: $272,750,813,649.32

Federal Deficit: ($3.9 billion dollar surplus)

Defense Spending: $47.11 billion	**Interest Spending:** $5.31 billion
Health Care Spending: $970 million	**Pensions Spending:** $5.87 billion

Welfare Spending: $1.96 billion	**Education Spending:** $1.42 billion
Transportation Spending: $1.67 billion	**Misc. Other Spending:** $8.62 billion
Protection Spending: $160 million	**Total Government Spending:** $75.99 billion
% of GDP that goes towards just the interest payment: 1.21%	
$1.00 = 359.84 Yen, Japan	
U.S. Population: 168,221,000	**World Population:** 2,832,623,670
U.S. Birth Rate: 4,218,000	**U.S. Abortions:** 337
U.S. Homicide Rate: 4.6/ 100,000 population	
Annual Average Domestic Crude Oil Prices: $2.94 / barrel, $23.25 (2007 adjusted)	

Oil:

May 1956 – Oil is discovered in Nigeria. Shell Oil Company discovers oil in Oloibiri in the Niger Delta. Nigerians become over-elated and extremely optimistic as the countries leaders become lazy after realizing that little or no effort is required to pump and sell oil. Since 1956 oil production has grown to place Nigeria as the 10th largest producer in the world on par with Kuwait, however the demands of a huge population and recurring government corruption has meant the populace has seen little benefit. Nigeria's oil production in 2005 is 2,600,000 barrels per day and over **60% of Nigerians still live below the poverty line in 2000.**

1956 – Algeria. Oil is discovered in Algeria. Extensive deposits of sulfur-free light crude oil are discovered in the Algerian Sahara Desert. Production will begin in 1958 from three major fields: Hassi Messaoud, in the northeastern part of the Sahara; Zarzaïtine-Edjeleh, along the Libyan border; and El-Borma, on the Tunisian border. Algeria's proven reserves are primarily located in the eastern half of the country where the Hassi Messaoud basin contains 70 percent of the country's total proven reserves. Even in 2005 industry analysts will consider the country under explored. Algeria's oil production in 2005 is 2,080,000 barrels per day.

June 29, 1956 – The Interstate Highway Act popularly known as the **National Interstate and Defense Highways Act,** becomes law when President Eisenhower signs the bill. It is the largest public works project in American history up to 1956, appropriating **$25 billion** for the construction of 41,000 miles of interstate highways over the next thirteen years. The money is handled in a highway trust fund that pays for 90 percent of highway construction costs with the states required to pay the remaining 10 percent. The money for the project will come from new taxes on fuel, automobiles, trucks and tires. As the interstate highway system is constructed more and more Americans travel by automobile and the U.S. dependence on oil grows.

October 31-November 7, 1956 – The Suez Crisis. Israel, Britain and France vs. Egypt. The Suez Crisis begins on July 26th as Egypt stops the supply of oil from moving through the Suez Canal. **Israel, Britain, and France attack Egypt** after Egyptian President Nassar nationalizes the Suez Canal and oil prices temporarily soar.
    On October 30, Britain and France send an ultimatum to Egypt and on October 31, they initiate a bombing campaign. On November 3, F4U-7 Corsairs take off from the French carriers Arromanches and La Fayette and attack the Cairo airport. **Nasser responds** by **sinking all 40 ships** present in the canal which effectively closes it to all shipping until early 1957. A Cease-fire is forced by the U.S. and stops the British, French, and Israeli advance on November 6. Nasser loses militarily but emerges as the most influential political figure in the Arab world. Some argue that the crisis also marked the final transfer of power to the new superpowers, the **United States** and the **Soviet Union.**

1956 – Libya. The first oil well is drilled in western Fezzan. It is a dry well. The first oil is struck in 1957. Esso/ Exxon make the first **commercial strike** in 1959, just as several firms are planning to give up exploration.

1956 – The U.S. is producing twice as much oil as the Middle East and African oil states combined.

1956 – Griffin, Indiana. In 1938 oil was struck north of Griffin, Indiana, at Fitzpatrick and Hayes #1 Cooper well. The field will be expanded to include 25 square miles and produce over 83 million barrels by 2003.

Annual oil production in Indiana peaks in 1956 at over 12 million barrels.

Major News:

October 1956 – Communist Hungary Rebellion. The Soviet invasion of Hungary comes at a time in the rebellion when the Hungarian people considered their government out of control. The economy is not healthy, the country is suffering from food shortages, high prices, and there is a complete disinterest in communism. The Soviets took the Hungarian resources and did nothing to enhance the standard of living and the people find the idea of working for the State only to pay inflated prices and face shortages, repugnant.

The rebellion moves through the country and threatens not only the Soviet hierarchy, but also their ability to retain a stranglehold over all of Eastern Europe. The rebellion infuriates the Communist party leaders in Moscow as they apply first the carrot and then the stick. First they seem to bend giving them false optimism that they may yet possess freedoms and then the club and stranglehold of Communism. This optimism will lead to deadly and catastrophic consequences.

March 2, 1956 – Morocco gains independence from France on March 2, and from Spain, April 7. French activity in Morocco began during the 1800's and in 1904 France and Spain secretly partitioned the territory of the Sultanate, with Spain later creating Spanish Morocco from its portion.

March 20, 1956 – Tunisia gains independence from France. Nationalist Habib Bourguiba, 52, imprisoned by the French from 1938 to March 1943, convinced militants to support the Allies and appealed Tunisia's case for independence to the United Nations.

1956

March 23, 1956 – Pakistan proclaims herself an Islamic republic, but remains within the British Commonwealth. President Iskander Mirza rules with army support.

April 21, 1956 – Indonesia's parliament revokes the 1949 Hague Agreement with the Netherlands as animosity continues between Dutch and Indonesian nationalists.

May 1956 – Secretary-General Dag Hammarskjold feels his month-long peacemaking mission to the Middle East is a success. Israel and the four neighboring states all promised to observe a ceasefire and further agreed not to retaliate even if provoked. At the same time Egyptian forces are "working day and night seven days a week" learning to use new Stalin tanks, MIG fighters and IL-28 jet bombers, and for the first time, submarines. However, Western military observers think it will take the Egyptians months before they can effectively use the new weapons.

September 18, 1956 – Great Britain grants Gold Coast independence after 54 years in which the former Asante state has been a colony. Gold Coast is a British colony on the Gulf of Guinea in West Africa that became the independent nation of Ghana in 1957.

1956-1957 – The United States Army requests 151,000 nuclear warheads. (History of the Custody and Deployment of Nuclear Weapons, July 1945 Through September 1977, Prepared by the Office of the Assistant Secretary of Defense (Atomic Energy), February 1978, p. 50 (formerly Top Secret)

Civil Rights Movement:

February 3, 1956 – Alabama graduate student Autherine Juanita Lucy, 26, enters the University of Alabama at Tuscaloosa February 3, as the first black student ever admitted to a white public school or university in the state. She is allowed to attend classes but is barred from all dormitories and dining halls. As its first African-American student, she attends classes for only a few days before riots break out and then the board of trustees suspends her for "her own safety." During her first four days of classes she is pelted with rotten eggs by a racist mob screaming, **"Let's kill her,"** and chanting, "Hey, hey, ho, where did Autherine go?"

NAACP lawyer **Thurgood Marshall** made the comment, "That girl sure has guts," as he worked in her defense. The U.S. district court rules on February 29 that she must be readmitted. Instead she is charged with slandering the University and expelled on March 1. The University of Alabama **finally overturned her expulsion 24 years latter** in **1980**, and in 1992, she earned her Masters degree in Elementary Education.

March 11, 1956 – Southern congressmen issue a manifesto pledging to use "all lawful means" to upset the Supreme Court's 1954 desegregation ruling.

April 19, 1956 – A South Carolina law enacted April 19 forbids city employees from affiliating with any civil-rights organization. Schoolteacher Septima Poinsette Clark, 58, loses both her job and her retirement benefits when she refuses to resign from the **NAACP** and stop protesting the new law. Clark will travel throughout the South over the next 5 years, teaching prospective voters how to write their names, write letters, balance their checkbooks, and vote in elections. Her retirement pay will be restored in 1976 **after 20 years of fighting the system.**

September 2, 1956 – Governor Frank Clement orders the National Guard to restore order in Clinton, Tennessee, after **white mobs** attempt to block the desegregation of the high school.

1956 – South Africa's Nationalist government reveals plans January 13 to remove 60,000 mixed-blood "coloreds" from the Cape Province voting roll. On August 8, civil rights worker **Helen Joseph** leads a march of 20,000 women to the Union Buildings at Pretoria to protest the extension of laws requiring blacks to carry passes. She is arrested, charged with treason, and is placed under a ban order in 1957. **Helen Joseph** is pivotal figure in the formation of the Federation of South African Women and August 8, will later be commemorated as **South African Women's Day.**

1956 – A special session of the Virginia legislature in August adopts a program of **"massive resistance"** to school desegregation that calls for the closing of schools under desegregation orders.

1956

November 13, 1956 – The Supreme Court affirms the ruling of a lower federal court in "Browder vs. Gayle" declaring segregation on Alabama intrastate buses to be unconstitutional.

December 21, 1956 – After more than a year of boycotting the buses and a legal fight, Desegregated bus service begins in Montgomery, Alabama.

Women's Movement:

1956 – Egypt, Tunisia, Comoros, and **Mauritius** grant women the right to vote on the same basis as men.

August 1956 – About 20,000 women march to the Union Buildings in Pretoria to protest against legislation aimed at tightening the apartheid government's control over the movement of black women in urban areas.

Popular Culture:

1956 – The first transatlantic telephone calls are made using cable laid by submarine.

1956 – Elvis Presley spreads rock to a world audience with his first film, **"Love Me Tender."**

1956 – *Christianity Today* is published. An Evangelical Christian magazine, it is the flagship publication of its parent company Christianity Today International. The founder, **Billy Graham,** stated that he wanted to "plant the evangelical flag in the middle-of-the-road, taking the conservative theological position but a definite liberal approach to social problems."

January 1956 – The Narcotics Control Act. The Subcommittee concluded **the United States had more addicts than any other Western nation,** with an alarmingly large percentage under the age of twenty-one. They also found the drug problem is multiplying at an alarming rate with an incalculable cost in human lives. Drug addiction is responsible for over one half of all crime in urban areas and one quarter of the crimes reported in the entire U.S. Drug use was found to be contagious and unstoppable with only 20% of the known addict population in custody. The subcommittee recommends that all known addicts could be rounded up and placed in treatment and those that can not be "cured" should be "placed in a quarantine type of confinement or isolation." They are aware that international drug smuggling is growing and feel sub-version through drug addiction is a major goal of Communist China, which is officially pushing the exportation of Chinese-manufactured heroin to enslave Americans.

The Subcommittee accused the Supreme Court of allowing major drug dealers to escape trial by its too-liberal interpretation of constitutional safeguards. They recommended that the Narcotics Bureau should be freed to tap telephones and Bureau agents should have statutory authority to carry weapons. Existing penalties were said to be too lenient and bail was far to low. The committee still felt drug addiction could be contained with stronger laws and harsher penalties and claimed where penalties were increased, addiction and drug smuggling decreased. Little did they know the billions upon billions of illegal drug dollars that would be generated need to find there way back into the economy. Investment banks, Mortgage brokers, hedge funds, politicians pockets, Presidents? Countries have been bought. Leaders have been compromised. Institutions such as the **Federal Reserve** have been knowingly laundering drug money such as "cash from Columbia" with no pedigree.

1956 – A first-offense for marijuana possession carries a minimum sentence of 2-10 years with a fine of up to $20,000.

1956 – "Uncle Milton's Ant Farm," sends the ants through the mail to the purchaser, upon receipt of the coupon enclosed with the Ant Farm. "Uncle Milton" has sold over 20 million Ant Farms since 1956.

September 1956 – President Eisenhower tells a news conference that the French are "involved in a hopelessly losing war in Indochina."

1956 – *Playboy* magazine circulation hit the 800,000 mark by the end of 1956, thus surpassing that of the formerly most widely read men's magazine, *Esquire.*

1956

1956 – The film industry permits references to **abortion, drugs, kidnapping,** and **prostitution** under certain circumstances.

1956 – Pepsodent Toothpaste, **"You'll wonder where the yellow went,"** Foote, Cone & Belding.

1956 – Chet Huntley and **David Brinkley** bring the star system to U.S. TV News casting.

1956 – CBS evening news is videotaped on the West Coast for a 3-hour delay rebroadcast.

Business / Technology:

January 1956 – The peak number of operating domestic **uranium mines** is 925. "Nineteenth Semiannual Report of the Atomic Energy Commission."

1956 – Zenith sells a **cordless remote** for television sets.

1956 – M.I.T. builds a transistorized computer, TX-O, the first general-purpose, programmable computer built with transistors.

1956 – Congress passes the **Federal Water Pollution Control Act.** The act creates the Federal Water Pollution Control Administration, which approves and regulates **new water quality standards.**

1956 – England's first **nuclear power** station at Calder Hall comes online.

1956 – Bendectin, a prescription drug used to alleviate morning sickness and nausea in pregnant women, is first sold. Merrell Dow formed after a merger with Richardson-Merrell in 1980 will continue selling Bendectin until 1983 when there are more than 1,800 lawsuits from women claiming the drug caused birth defects. At this point it is estimated 33 million women have taken the drug. **Facing mounting lawsuits by thousands of women** claiming their children had been born with **birth**

defects, pharmaceutical manufacturer **Merrell Dow Pharmaceuticals Inc** stops the production of Bendectin.

April 1956 – The largest Canadian trade union umbrella organization, the Canadian Labor Congress (CLC), is formed.

1956 – The first Pager is made available and Hospitals are quick to buy them.

1956 – Transistors go into car radios.

April 5, 1956 – Columnist Victor Riesel, a crusader against labor racketeers, is blinded in New York City **when a hired assailant throws sulfuric acid in his face.**

1956 – Bell Labs Picturephone sends one image every two seconds.

1956 – IBM ships a hard drive, the 5 MB, 305 RAMAC is as big as two refrigerators.

1956 – Liquid Paper is created on the kitchen table of a Dallas secretary, **Bette Nesmith Graham.** Trained as an artist she remembered that artists painted over their mistakes on canvas, so why couldn't typists paint over their mistakes? She mixed up some tempera water based paint colored to match the stationery she used, put it in a bottle and used it in the office. Her boss never noticed the touchups. Gram and her son **Michael Nesmith** (known best for his **Monkees fame**) started mixing the product at home and worked nights and weekends to fill orders. Graham died in 1980, six months after selling her corporation for $47.5 million.

Finance:

May 9, 1956 – The Bank Holding Company Act is passed.

July 30, 1956 – President Dwight D. Eisenhower signs a Joint Resolution declaring that the motto **"In God We Trust"** will be the national motto.

1956 – The Ford Foundation sells 20 percent of its Ford Motor stock to Wall Street investors, permitting the public to buy into Ford for the first time and bringing in

1956

some $643 million to the Foundation, which announces that **it will give away more than $500 million in the next 18 months,** $150 million more than in the 20 years since 1936.

1956 – Telephone Company **AT&T** is accused of antitrust violations by the Federal Communications Commission. The FCC's intends to remove AT&T subsidiaries Western Electric and Bell Laboratories from the company's system. AT&T agrees to a consent decree, allowing the company to keep control of the two subsidiaries but forbidding it to expand into other areas of communication.

1956 – **Congress amends the Social Security Act** of 1935 to provide benefits to workers aged 50 to 64 who have become permanently and totally disabled, and to provide benefits to disabled adult children whose disability began before the age of 18. Dependents' benefits were added in 1958, and the age 50 requirement was eliminated in 1960. In 1967, disability benefits were added for disabled widows or widowers.

1956 – **DJIA.** The Israelis, British and French invaded Egypt after it seized the Suez Canal. **The Dow lost 10 percent** during the four-month period.

1956 – Omaha investor **Warren Buffett**, 25, starts the Buffet Partnership with $5,000 of his own money and **$100,000 from family and friends.** Buffett **began** working at **his father's brokerage** at the age of 11, and then joined a friend in high school in managing a pinball-machine business that earned him $50 per week. He used $1,200 of profits to buy 40 acres of farmland which he then rented to tenant farmers. Buffet attended Wharton School at the University of Pennsylvania, and then transferred to the University of Nebraska. He obtained a Master's degree in economics in 1951 at Columbia Business School, studying under **Benjamin Graham,** alongside other future value investors including **Walter Schloss** and **Irving Kahn** where he learned to look for undervalued stocks. Buffett wanted to work for Graham–Newman but was turned down so he worked for his father's brokerage firm as a salesman for three years until Graham offered him a position. Warren Buffett will become one of the richest men in America by buying undervalued stocks and holding them for appreciation.

June 29, 1956 – The Federal Aid Highway Act is signed by President Eisenhower. It authorizes twenty-five billion dollars to be spent over the next thirteen years on the highways. President Eisenhower considered it one of the most important achievements of his two terms in office.

Books:

1956 – Allen Ginsberg, **"Howl and Other Poems."** The poem is considered to be one of the principal works of the Beat Generation along with Jack Kerouac's **"On the Road"** (1957) and William S. Burroughs's **"Naked Lunch"** (1959). "Howl" was originally written as a performance piece, but it was later published by poet **Lawrence Ferlinghetti** of **"City Lights Books."** Although the poem was originally considered to be obscene and Ferlinghetti was arrested and charged with its publication, "Howl" went on to become one of the most popular poems of the **Beat Generation.**

1956 – Michael John Moorcock is the new editor of *Tarzan Adventures* and he is just sixteen years old.

1956 – Isaac Asimov, *"The Naked Sun"* is first published as a serial in *Astounding Science Fiction* between October and December.

1956 – "Peyton Place," by Grace Metalious. "Peyton Place" has become an expression to describe a place whose inhabitants have sordid secrets.

TV:

January 28, 1956 – Elvis Presley makes his national television debut on **"The Dorsey Brothers Stage Show."**

1956 – Elvis' first appearance on **"The Ed Sullivan Show"** is seen by **60 million people** which is about 80% of all TV owners in America. Ed Sullivan was having an intense Sunday-night rivalry with **Steve Allen.** Allen had Elvis on his July 1 show and trounced Sullivan in the ratings. When asked to comment, Sullivan said that he wouldn't consider presenting Elvis Presley before a family audience, but less than two

1956

weeks later he changed his mind. **Elvis appeared** and contrary to myth, Presley's whole body was shown in the first and second shows. By the time Elvis appears on the show for the third time in January 1957, he's only shown from the waist up, but most of his songs were ballads.

Sports:

October 8, 1956 – Game 5, Yankee right-hander Don Larsen pitches the only **World Series perfect game** when the New York Yankees beat the Brooklyn Dodgers in the 5th game of the 1956 World Series.

Music:

1956 – **Harry Belafonte's "Calypso"** is the first album in history to sell more than one million copies.

April 10, 1956 – Followers of Asa Earl Carter, a group of racial segregationists, rush the stage at a **Nat King Cole concert** in Birmingham, Alabama, but are quickly captured.

July 9, 1956 – **Dick Clark hosts "American Bandstand for the first time."**

November 5, 1956 – **Nat King Cole** becomes the first major black performer to host a variety show on national television. **"The Nat King Cole Show."**

1956 – The First **Eurovision Song Contest** begins as an annual competition between active member countries of the European Broadcasting Union. Each country selects a singer and a song to represent their country in competition. Each member country then casts votes for the other countries' songs to determine the most popular song.

1956 – **Aretha Franklin gives birth** to her first child, at the age of fourteen, **interrupting her career as a gospel singer.** Her biographies give various ages from 13 to 15 years of age. Her parents separated before she was six years old and her mother died when she was ten years old. She overcame this, along with her early pregnancies.

In 2003, Franklin released her final studio album on Arista, *So Damn Happy*, and left the label to found Aretha Records. Two years later, she was awarded the Presidential Medal of Freedom and became the second woman ever to be inducted into the UK Music Hall of Fame. In 2008, she received her 18th Grammy Award for "Never Gonna Break My Faith," a collaboration with Mary J. Blige, and was tapped to sing at the 2009 inauguration of President Barack Obama. Most recently, Franklin released her first album on her own label, *A Woman Falling Out of Love*.

1956 – Chrysler Corporation offers an **in-car turntable** 16⅔ rpm record player with 7-inch ultramicrogroove records in its luxury model, the "Imperial."

Man vs. Man / Wars:

Assassination – Nicaragua. Anastasio Somoza. After **Anastasio Somoza** is assassinated in León, he is succeeded by his elder son, **Luis Somoza Debayle,** director of the National Guard. His innovative projects were supported by the U.S. Kennedy administration, which in return was graciously granted full use of Puerto Cabezas for launching its disastrous 1961 invasion of Cuba. Luis Somoza Debayle called for "free elections" and then installed family friends as President from 1963-1967. His younger brother, **Anastasio Somoza Debayle,** wins the Presidency in 1967. Although **Luis Somoza Debayle,** gave up the Presidency he never lost control of Nicaraguan government and his family increased their land holdings to include 50% of the entire country.

Executed – Mau Mau leader Dedan Kimathi is captured and executed in Kenya.

March 5, 1956 – Representative Thomas J. Lane (D-Massachusetts) is **indicted** for **Federal income tax evasion**. Thomas Lane pleads guilty and on April 30, he is sentenced to 4 months in prison and fined $10,000. He is released on September 4, 1956.

November 18, 1956 – Nikita Khrushchev tells Western ambassadors, **"History is on our side. We will bury you!"** at a reception at the Polish embassy in Moscow.

1956

1956-1959 – Cameroon Rebellion. In 1955, the outlawed Union of the Peoples of Cameroon, based largely among the Bamileke and Bassa ethnic groups, began an armed struggle for independence in French Cameroon. This rebellion continued, with diminishing intensity, even after independence. Estimates of death from this conflict vary from thousands to hundreds of thousands of people being killed.

1956 – Ceylon Tamil-Sinhalese Unrest. Sri Lanka was colonized by Portugal and the Netherlands beginning in the 1500's. Almost 400 years later it gained its independence in 1948 as the Commonwealth of Ceylon. In the 1950's Tamil demonstrators demanded recognition of their language and culture.

1956 – Chinese who resist communization continue to be **liquidated** as they have been since 1949 (and especially since 1952). By 1960 when **Mao Zedongs' Great Leap Forward** ends some **26,300,000 Chinese will be killed** according to some estimates, the largest massacre in world history. Overall the Great Leap Forward is responsible for between 30 million and 72 million Chinese deaths.

1956 – Burma. Sino-Burma Border War. The key issue is the 1956-1957 construction of a Chinese military highway in the disputed territory of Aksai China just west of Tibet. India protested the Chinese incursion, and diplomatic exchanges continued for three years without progress or compromise, while each side firmly asserted its claim to the Aksai Chin area. Large sections of the North East Frontier Agency, east of Tibet, are also in dispute.

October 29, 1956 – Kafr Kassem. Israeli border police massacre 47 Arab men, women, and children at the village of Kafr Kassem. Acting on shoot-to-kill orders designed to discourage curfew breakers, the police have fired on people returning from their fields. Eight of the men responsible will be tried and convicted, despite their pleas that they were merely following orders, but none will serve more than 3½ years in prison. Arabs will commemorate the atrocity each year, and Israelis will acknowledge in 1999 that the massacre was a "disgrace."

October 22, 1956 – Hungarian revolution. Premier Nagy goes on the radio to promise Hungarians free elections and a prompt end to the one-party dictatorship. Premier Nagy also announces Hungary's unilateral withdrawal from the Warsaw Pact on November 1, and **16 Soviet divisions** move in 3 days later with **2,000 tanks** to crush the Hungarian defiance. Nagy is imprisoned and eventually executed while János Kádár is made the head of government by the Soviets.

Hungarians stage a general strike in December to protest the János Kádár regime. Nearly 200,000 people emigrate, including some of the country's best minds and talents. An estimated 40,000 people are killed by domestic violence along with 2,587 political executions.

1956-1960 – Guerilla / Occupational warfare. The Kenyan insurgency is a barely known insurgency from the last days of the British Empire. The British were caught off guard and had failed to recognize the scale of the threat the Mau Mau posed. In Kenya the armed enemy numbered 1,500 with personal weapons, and no source of external support. Still **it took 56,000 security forces four years to substantially defeat the 1,500 Mau Mau.**

1952-1956 – Kenya. Mau-Mau Rebellion. The Mau Mau are a militant African nationalist movement active in **Kenya** whose main aim is to remove British rule and European settlers from the country. In October 1955 official reports suggest that over 70,000 Kikuyu tribesmen suspected of Mau Mau membership have been imprisoned, while over 13,000 people have been killed by British troops and Mau Mau activists. On **January 7, 1956** the official death toll for Mau Mau activists killed by British forces in Kenya since 1952 is put at 10,173. Despite British victory in 1956, thousands of lives are lost and negotiations finally forced preparations for Kenyan independence.

June 24, 1956 – After being released from prison in Cuba on May 15, 1955, **Fidel Castro** and his younger brother Raul went to **Mexico City** to organize the war against Cuba's Dictator **Fulgencio Batista.** On June, 28 Cuban revolutionaries and supporters are arrested in Mexico City and **Castro** is not released until July 24, while **Che Guevara** is released a week later. On November 25, 1956, they are aboard the leisure yacht *Granma* heading for Cuba. The craft is overcrowded with weapons, ammunition, and 82 soldiers. To make matters worse, the ship's tanks hold only 1,200 gallons of fuel, not nearly enough to reach Cuba, so an additional 2,000 gallons of fuel are stored in cans on deck.

1956 – Morocco acquires limited home rule from France in February after more than four decades of French rule. The abolition of the Spanish protectorate and the recognition of Moroccan independence by Spain are finalized in April.

June 28, 1956 – Polish workers riot at Poznan June 28 to protest social and economic conditions under the communist regime. **More than 100 demonstrators are killed** as the militia move in to suppress the riots.

1956 – Suez Canal Crisis. A cease-fire forced by the U.S. stops the British, French, and Israeli advance. Approximately 2,800 people are killed.

March 1951-1959 – Tibetan resistance. The U.S. Ambassador to India advised the young Dalai Lama to leave his country and seek asylum abroad. By 1956, armed resistance against the Chinese occupation was underway and covert support began modestly, with the training of six Tibetans to engage in intelligence collection. A rebellion against the Chinese occupation was led by noblemen and monasteries and broke out in Amdo and eastern Kham in June 1956. The insurrection, supported by the American CIA, eventually spreads to Lhasa and is crushed by 1959. During this campaign, tens of thousands of Tibetans were killed and the 14th Dalai Lama and other government principals fled to exile in India.

1956 – Tunisia gains its independence from France. 2,500 people are killed.

1957

The Oldest Boomer is 11 years old.

Median Family Income: $5,000 **Secretary, executive:** $75/ week	**Minimum Wage:** $1.00/ hr **Clerk-typist:** $50/ week
Grape Jelly: 19 cents **Magazines:** *Woman's Day* or *Family Circle*: 7 cents/ issue	**Gallon Gasoline:** 31 cents **Daily Newspaper:** 5 cents **RCA Victor TV, personal** & **portable:** $78
New Car: 57 Chevrolet **Bel Air Convertible:** $2,611 **Ford T-Bird:** $3,151	**Hamburger:** 89 cents/ 3 pounds **Perch:** 49 cents/ lb **Record, 45 RPM:** 79 cents
Unemployment Rate: 4.2%-3.7%-5.2%	**First-class Stamp:** 3 cents

13 cents buying power in 1957 **= $1.00 in 2008.**
In 1957 what cost our parents 13 cents to purchase
now costs us $1.00 in 2008.

Movies: "The Bridge on the River Kwai," "Paths of Glory," "Peyton Place," "Sayonara," "12 Angry Men," "Witness for the Prosecution," "The Man Who Knew Too Much," "Bernadine," "April Love," "The Kettles on Old MacDonald's Farm."

Broadway: "Shinbone Alley," "The Music Man," "Jamaica," "West Side Story," "Free As Air," London.

TV: Ed Sullivan Censors Elvis. "Leave It To Beaver," "Tom Terrific," "American Bandstand," "Gray Ghost," "Bachelor Father," "Perry Mason," "Have Gun—Will Travel." "Maverick," "Sugarfoot," "Tales of Wells Fargo," "Wagon Train," "Zorro," "Cimarron Strip," "Blondie," "Colt 45," "Tombstone Territory," "The Frank Sinatra Show," "The Real McCoys," "Casey Jones," "Restless Gun," "Hawkeye and the Last of the Mohicans,"

"The Lucy-Desi Comedy Hour," "Divorce Court," "The Spike Jones Show," "Man Without a Gun," "Woody Woodpecker," "How To Marry A Millionaire," "Overland Trail."

Music: Elvis Presley, "Jailhouse Rock," "Treat Me Nice," "All Shook Up" & "Let Me Be Your Teddy Bear." The Coasters, "Searchin'" & "Young Blood." Everly Brothers, "Wake Up Little Susie" & "Bye Bye Love." Sam Cooke, "You Send Me." Nat King Cole, "After Midnight" & "An Affair To Remember." Count Basie, "April in Paris." Miles Davis, "Birth of the Cool." Pat Boone, "A Closer Walk with Thee," "April Love" & "Love Letters In The Sand." Tab Hunter, "Young Love." Debbie Reynolds, "Tammy." McGuire Sisters, "Sugartime." Frank Sinatra, "Witchcraft." Jerry Lee Lewis, "Whole Lotta Shakin' Goin' On." Buddy Holly & The Crickets, "That'll Be the Day." Johnny Mathis, "The Twelfth Of Never." Little Richard, "Lucille." Buddy Holly, "Not Fade Away" & "Oh Boy." Johnny Cash, "There You Go," "Next In Line," "Train of Love" & "Home of The Blues."

President: Dwight D. Eisenhower (R) Presbyterian; vetoes 181/ 2 overrides

Vice President: Richard M. Nixon (R) Quaker

House: D-234 ; R-201

Senate: 85th Congress (1957-1959) Majority Party: Democrat (49 seats) Minority Party: Republican (47 seats) Other Parties: 0 Total Seats: 96

Federal Debt: $270.53 billion or 59 % of the GDP

Consumer Price Index CPI-U (1982 Base of 100): 28.10

GDP: $461.1 billion	**Inflation Rate:** 3.34%
Dow Jones: 506.21 (08-01)/ 434.71 (11-01)	**S&P Price Index:** The S&P 500 index in its present form began on March 4, 1957.
Prime Rate: 4.50% (08-06)	**Average Home Mortgage Rate:** 5.42%
1 oz Gold: $35.25	**1oz of Silver:** $0.91

Federal Debt: $270,527,171,896.43

Federal Deficit: ($3.4 billion dollar surplus)	
Defense Spending: $51.30 billion	**Interest Spending:** $5.50 billion
Health Care Spending: $1.03 billion	**Pensions Spending:** $7.11 billion
Welfare Spending: $2.10 billion	**Education Spending:** $1.57 billion
Transportation Spending: $2.01 billion	**Misc. Other Spending:** $8.24 billion
Protection Spending: $160 million	**Total Government Spending:** $81.78 billion
% of GDP that goes towards just the interest payment: 1.19%	
$1.00 = 359.84 Yen, Japan	**$1.00** =75.750 Iranian Rial
U.S. Population: 171,274,000	**World Population:** 2,888,444,047
U.S. Birth Rate: 4,308,000	**U.S. Abortions:** 336
U.S. Homicide Rate: 4.5/ 100,000 population	
Annual Average Domestic Crude Oil Prices: $3.14 / barrel, $24.00 (2007 adjusted)	

Oil:

1957 – Libya. The first well was drilled in western Fezzan in 1956. It was a dry well. The first oil is struck in 1957. By 2003 Libya is OPEC's eighth largest producer.

1957 – Congo. Shortly before gaining independence oil and gas is discovered in large quantities. This changes the country and its impact on the outside world, especially France. In 1957 in what came to be known as Pointe Indienne field, the French found oil and gas reserves offshore in exploitable quantities. French geologists first discovered oil and gas in 1926, but it was not until 1957 that France started exploiting these reserves. The French are losing the Algerian war of independence, and Algeria until 1956 is the main source of oil and gas supplying the French market. To remain independent of the American and British oil companies France needs to find another source of supply.

The Republic of Congo will become one of the top oil producers in Africa, ranking fourth after Nigeria, Angola, and Gabon. Production will peak in 2000 and start declining. For some the discovery of oil off the Congolese coast is a blessing, but for the majority of the local population it will prove to be a curse as the IMF in its yearly report on the Congo sadly observed in 2006-2007.

1957 – The first oil is discovered in the gulf off Texas.

1957 – Alaska. The large Swanson River oil field on the Kenai Peninsula in Alaska is discovered by Richfield Oil. They struck oil with their first well reported on July 15, 1957. The well tested at 900 barrels a day, the first major, commercial discovery in Alaska.

Major News:

January 5, 1957 – The Eisenhower Doctrine calls for aid to Mideast countries which resist armed aggression from Communist-controlled nations.

March 25, 1957 – European Union. The Treaties establishing the European Economic Community and the European Atomic Energy Community are signed by the Six, **Belgium, France, Germany, Italy, Luxembourg,** and the **Netherlands,** in Rome. They will be referred to as the **"Treaties of Rome."**

April 20, 1957 – The Mayflower Replica Set Sail with her crew of 33. They sailed 5,500 nautical miles in 54 days to reach New England. Bad weather forced her to sail further but they did it in 12 days less time than the original. A fascinating story.

October 25, 1957 – Organized crime figure Albert Anastasia is killed. Albert Anastasia, also known as the **"Mad Hatter"** and "Lord High Executioner," was a New York City **Cosa Nostra** boss remembered for his brutality and his role in running the contract killing gang known as **Murder, Inc.**

November 14, 1957 – **Appalachian Conference. Over sixty organized crime** figures including **Vito Genovese, Carlo Gambino, Paul Castellano, Joseph Bonanno, Joseph Profaci, Joseph Magliocco** and **John Montana** are arrested at the home of **Joseph Barbara, Sr.** during the Appalachian Conference. Following this incident, federal authorities are forced to admit the possibility of the existence of organized crime.

1957 – Genovese, Costello organized crime war. Vito Genovese tries to take control of the Mafia but ends up being taken out by the Feds. Don Vito (Genovese) was **one of the most feared of the Mafia dons**. He ordered the deaths of Willie Moretti in 1951, Steve Franse in 1953, and Albert Anastasia in 1957, and was the obvious choice for the failed hit on Frank Costello. Don Vito can also be credited with keeping the mob in the narcotics business, something not all Mafioso agreed on.

Civil Rights Movement:

January 11, 1957 – **The Southern Negro Leadership Conference** on Transportation and Nonviolent Integration, later known as the **Southern Christian Leadership Conference**, is organized in Atlanta on January 11 with Martin Luther King, Jr. as its chairman.

April 14, 1957 – **Malcolm X,** born Malcolm Little, minister of Temple No. 7 of the **Nation of Islam** since 1954, leads a demonstration outside a police station in **Harlem**, to protest the beating of a **Black Muslim** and demands that he be transferred to a hospital.

August 29, 1957 – **The First federal civil rights bill since 1875** is passed on August 29, after it is significantly weakened in the Senate to avoid a filibuster. The act makes conspiring to deny citizens their right to vote in federal elections a federal crime and gives federal prosecutors the power to obtain injunctions against discriminatory practices used to deny citizens their voting rights.

September 4, 1957 – **The "Little Rock Nine"** integrate Little Rock, Arkansas **high school**. Several segregationist councils threatened to protest admitting black students to **Central High** and physically block the **9 black students** from entering the school and the President of the United States warned the governor not to interfere with the Supreme Court's ruling.

"STATE GUARD TROOPS HALT DESEGRAGATION AT ARKANSAS SCHOOL" is a local newspaper headline, as **Governor Orval Faubus** deployed the **Arkansas National Guard** to support the segregationists on September 4. The sight of a line of soldiers blocking nine black students from attending high school made national headlines and polarized the city. Regarding the accompanying crowd, one of the nine black students, Elizabeth Eckford, recalled "they moved closer and closer." "Somebody started yelling, 'Lynch her! Lynch her!' I tried to see a friendly face somewhere in the crowd, someone who maybe could help, I looked into the face of an old woman and it seemed a kind face, but when I looked at her again, she spat on me."

September 25, 1957 – 1,000 soldiers of the crack 327th Airborne Battle Group of the **101st Airborne Division** are deployed in **Little Rock, Arkansas** as ordered by **President Eisenhower.** They are sent to stop the white mob and protect school integration. Eisenhower also federalized the entire 10,000 member Arkansas National Guard to take it out of the hands of the Governor. The 101st patrolled outside the school and escorted the black students into the school. In addition, the black students were assigned a personal guard from the 101st that followed them around the school. Still, they were subjects of unspeakable hatred. White students yelled insults in the halls and during class. They beat up the black students, particularly the boys. They walked on the heels of the blacks until they bled. They destroyed the black students' lockers and threw flaming paper wads at them in the bathrooms. They threw lighted sticks of dynamite at Melba Pattillo, stabbed her, and sprayed acid in her eyes. The acid was so strong that had her 101st guard not splashed water on her face immediately, she would have been blind for the rest of her life.

1957 – Garfield High School becomes the **first Seattle high** school with a more than 50 percent nonwhite student body.

September–October 1957 – More than 200 reporters, according to U.S. Army estimates, converge on Little Rock to cover the integration of Central High School.

Women's Movement:

1957 – Dorothy Irene Height is appointed president of the **National Council of Negro Women,** a position she holds for 41 years. She later launches a crusade for justice for black women and works to strengthen the black family.

1957 – For her college reunion in 1957, **Betty Friedan** circulated a questionnaire among her classmates and learned that many were dissatisfied with their lives.

Popular Culture:

1957 – The Supreme Court finds in Roth vs. United States that banning the mailing of **obscene materials** is a proper exercise of postal power and defines obscene materials as something the "average person" applying contemporary community standards will find appealing to prurient interest.

May 13, 1957 – Magic mushrooms. "Life" magazine publishes an article by R. Gordon Wasson that documents and popularizes the use of **psilocybin mushrooms** in the religious ceremony of the indigenous Mazatec people of Mexico. Timothy Leary goes to Mexico to experience hallucinogenic mushrooms firsthand and when he returns to Harvard in 1960, he and Richard Alpert start the Harvard Psilocybin Project, promoting psychological and religious study of psilocybin and other hallucinogenic drugs. Leary and Alpert are dismissed by Harvard in 1963 and they turn their attention toward evangelizing the psychedelic experience to the hippie counterculture. **Tune-in, turn-on, drop-out. The "culture of drugs" and drug lifestyle is being promoted by the major news media as being the thing to do.**
    The oldest Boomer is eleven years old and does not stand a chance.

July 12, 1957 – The U.S. surgeon general says studies show a "direct link" between cigarette **smoking and lung cancer**.

November 3, 1957 – Sputnik II is the second spacecraft launched into Earth orbit, and the **first to carry a living animal**, a dog named Laika, in a 13 foot high cone-shaped capsule with a base diameter of 6.5 ft. Sputnik 2 does not contain a TV camera and TV images of dogs on Sputnik 5 are commonly misidentified as Laika.

The capsule contains scientific instruments, radio transmitters, a telemetry system, a programming unit, and an oxygen and temperature control system for the cabin. A separate sealed cabin contains Laika. Both scientific data and data on Laika's health are transmitted for a 15 minute period during each earth orbit. It is believed Laika survived for only a few hours instead of the planned ten days because of the missing heat shields and a cabin temperature of 104 degrees. The orbit of Sputnik 2 slowed and the capsule reentered Earth's atmosphere on April 14, 1958 after 162 days in orbit.

1957 – Frisbee. Wham-O co-founder Richard Knerr, decided to stimulate sales by giving the **Pluto Platter** discs the additional brand name **"Frisbee"** after hearing that East Coast college students were calling the Pluto Platter by that name.

1957 – Clairol, "Does she...or doesn't she?" Foote, Cone & Belding.

1957 – The Supreme Court modifies its 1951 holding regarding the Smith Act. In Yates vs. United States, the Court overturned the conviction of several Communist Party leaders under the Smith Act. The Smith Act made it a crime to advocate the violent overthrow of the government, to distribute any material that teaches or advocates such, or to belong to a group with such an aim. **The Supreme Court** modifies this, saying that merely urging a person to believe something, as opposed to urging a person to do something, can not be made illegal.

1957 – Greyhound, **"It's such a comfort to take the bus and leave the driving to us."** Grey Advertising.

1957 – Baseball cards. 1957 Topps Mickey Mantle, Yogi Berra GAI graded EX, Book-$600.00 / Sale-$225.00 - 02/2009.

Business / Technology:

1957 – The first Japanese car, a Toyota, is sold in the U.S.

1957 – Gordon Gould, an American physicist, invents the laser. Gould is working toward a Ph.D. in Physics at Columbia University, where Physics research is booming. Among others, Charles Townes, the inventor of the maser (1951), is teaching there.

Gould's former specialty was classical optics, and he is now doing research in microwave spectroscopy. One Saturday night, Gould was inspired, "in a flash," with a revolutionary idea: "Light Amplification by Stimulated Emission of Radiation," or the "laser." It will take him until 1977 to win a protracted legal battle over patent rights, and he will not start receiving royalties on his work until 1988. Gould was elected to the National Inventors Hall of Fame in 1991.

1957 – FORTRAN becomes the **first high-level computer programming language**. FORTRAN short for FORmula TRANslator, enabled a computer to perform a repetitive task from a single set of instructions by using loops.

October 4, 1957 – The Soviet satellite Sputnik I is launched into a successful orbit. This is the first Earth-orbiting satellite and the **Space Age** begins.

December 6, 1957 – The first attempt by the **United States** to launch a satellite into space fails when it **explodes on the launch pad.**

Finance:

January 16, 1957 – A peace time budget of seventy-two billion eight-hundred and seven million dollars is proposed.

June 30, 1957 – The Reconstruction Finance Corporation is abolished and some of its functions are transferred to the Treasury Department.

September 9, 1957 – "IN GOD WE TRUST" is first used on paper money in 1957. The first currency bearing the motto **"IN GOD WE TRUST"** is delivered by the Bureau of Engraving and Printing. The motto "In God We Trust" first appeared on United States paper currency when it was added to the one-dollar silver certificate. "IN GOD WE TRUST" first appeared on the 1864 **two-cent coin**. In 1865 the motto was placed on the **gold double-eagle coin**, the **gold eagle coin**, and the **gold half-eagle coin**. It was also placed on the **silver dollar coin**, the **half-dollar coin** and the **quarter-dollar coin**, and on the nickel **three-cent coin** beginning in 1866. A law passed by the 84th Congress (P.L. 84-140) and approved by the President on July 30, 1956, approving a Joint Resolution of the 84th **Congress, declared "IN GOD WE TRUST" the national motto of the United States.**

October 1, 1957 – The processing of **United States Savings Bonds** is first done by **computer.**

Books:

1957 – John Cheever's novel, **"The Wapshot Chronicle"** a satire on, among other subjects, the misuses of wealth and psychology, earned him the National Book Award.

1957 – Jack Kerouac's novel, **"On the Road."** Jack Kerouac alongside William S. Burroughs and Allen Ginsberg is considered a pioneer of the Beat Generation. Kerouac's work was very popular, but received little critical acclaim during his lifetime. Today, he is considered an important and influential writer who inspired others, including Hunter S. Thompson, Tom Robbins, Lester Bangs, Richard Brautigan, Ken Kesey, Haruki Murakami, and writers of the New Journalism.

1957 – "Atlas Shrugged," Ayn Rand. It was Rand's fourth, longest, and last novel, and she considered it her magnum opus in the realm of fiction writing. As indicated by its working title "The Strike," the book explores a dystopian United States where leading industrialists and businessmen refuse to allow the government to exploit their labor for the "general good." "Atlas Shrugged" received largely negative reviews after its publication.

TV:

January 6, 1957 – The Ed Sullivan Show. Elvis Presley performs a medley of "Hound Dog," "Love Me Tender," and "Heartbreak Hotel," followed by a full version of "Don't

Be Cruel." For a second set later in the show he did "Too Much" and "When My Blue Moon Turns to Gold Again." For his last set he sang "Peace in the Valley." much has been made of the fact that Elvis was shown only from the waist up, however, except for the short section of "Hound Dog," all of the songs on this show were ballads.

1957 – Tom Terrific, his sidekick Mighty Manfred the Wonder Dog and Crabby Appleton. Tom Terrific is a serialized animated series created by the Terrytoons studio specifically for the **Captain Kangaroo show.** At home kids would place a thin sheet of plastic on their TV screens and then draw on it with special crayons to help Tom. In one episode kids drew an elevator to help Tom escape to another floor in the building and thwart the villain, Crabby Appleton.

1957 – When **Nat King Cole's** television show is unable to get a sponsor, **Frankie Laine** becomes **the first artist to cross TV's color line.** Laine is the first white artist to appear as a guest, foregoing his usual salary of $10,000 as Cole's show only paid scale. Other top performers followed suit, including **Mel Tormé** and **Tony Bennett**, but despite an increase in ratings, the show still failed to pick up a national sponsor.

January 24, 1957 – Steve Allen hosts his last *"The Tonight Show,"* on NBC.

1957 – Before it airs, **CBS** yanks the pilot episode of **"Leave It To Beaver"** because of its plot: Wally and the Beav mail-order a baby alligator and are forced to hide it in the tank of the family's toilet. CBS finally decides the show will air, but only if all shots of the toilet seat are excised. The toilet tank is left unharmed, marking **the first time a toilet, or half of one, appears on TV.**

Sports:

July 6, 1957 – Althea Gibson becomes the first African American to win the Women's Singles Division of the British Tennis Championship at Wimbledon.

Music:

1957 – Iran begins the move to ban all rock 'n' roll music.

1957

1957 – Former Vice President of the United States (1924-1928) Charles Dawes co-wrote **"It's All in the Game,"** which is recorded by **Tommy Edwards** and goes to Number One. Dawes had died in 1951.

1957 – Paul Simon and Art Garfunkel name themselves *Tom and Jerry* and begin their recording career.

March 1957 – Chicago's Cardinal Stritch High School bans all rock and roll, and rhythm and blues music from Catholic-run schools, saying that "its rhythms encourage young people to behave in a hedonistic manner."

June 22, 1957 – The first public performance of **The Quarry Men.** They play in the Roseberry Street Empire Day celebration on the back of a lorry. They are paid nothing for their performance, **George Harrison is 14, Paul McCartney is 15, John Lennon is 16, Richard Starkey (Ringo Starr) is 17.**

1957 – The music business was never comfortable with **Black Rhythm & Blues** even after the name change to **Rock & Roll.** In a successful attempt to broaden their market they promoted safer, more innocent looking recording stars to capture the Teen Audience. Teen Idols Paul Anka and Ricky Nelson rocked to the top of the charts.

Natural Disasters:

1957 – The Worldwide, Influenza pandemic kills 69,800 people in the U.S. Estimates of worldwide death vary widely depending on the source, ranging from 1 million to 4 million people being killed.

1957 – AIDS. Polio vaccine. The oral polio vaccine. The AIDS hypothesis argues that the AIDS pandemic originated from live polio vaccines prepared in chimpanzee tissue cultures and then administered to up to one million Africans between 1957 and 1960 in experimental mass vaccination campaigns. The earliest known cases of AIDS occurred in central Africa, in the same regions where Koprowski's polio vaccine was given to over a million people in 1957-1960.

March 9, 1957 – Alaska. A 9.1 magnitude earthquake hits the Andreanof Islands, Alaska.

June 25–28, 1957 – Southwest Louisiana, and Northern Texas. Hurricane Audrey flattens Cameron, Louisiana, killing 390 people.

October 7, 1957 – Windscale Pile No. 1, North of Liverpool, England. A fire in a graphite-cooled reactor spews radiation over the countryside, contaminating a 200-square-mile area.

1957 – Soviet Union, South Ural Mountains. An explosion of radioactive wastes at a Soviet nuclear weapons factory 12 miles from the city of Kyshtym forces the evacuation of over 10,000 people from the contaminated area. No casualties are reported by Soviet officials, but that does not mean they did not occur.

December 4, 1957 – Turkey. A 6.8 magnitude earthquake hits Turkey along the North Anatolian Fault.

Man vs. Man / Wars:

Assassination - Guatemala. Carlos Castillo Armas, was President of Guatemala from July 8, 1954 until his assassination on July 26, 1957. The U.S. CIA had helped install Armas in 1954 by destabilizing the Guatemalan Government and recruiting Guatemalan exiles in Honduras.

March 6, 1957 – Ghana becomes independent. **Gold Coast** was a British colony on the Gulf of Guinea in West Africa that became the independent nation of Ghana in 1957. This marks the beginning period of decolonization in sub-Saharan Africa.

1957 – Brazil. The Indian population of Brazil declined from 1,000,000 to 200,000 between 1900 and 1957, a net loss of 800,000 ("Century of Genocide," Samuel Totten 1997). **Most were killed because they were Indian** and they were in the way of *"progress"*.

1957

1957-1958 – The Invasion of Ifni by Moroccan Irregulars. Spanish Morocco's territory of Ifni is invaded by Moroccan irregulars, who are driven out by Spanish troops. Ifni was later ceded to Morocco on April 1, 1958.

July 1957-1959 – The Muscat and Oman Intervention. An uprising in central Oman brings about a collapse in the **Sultan Said bin Taimur**'s authority in the area and threatens his control of the country as a whole. Ghalib bin Ali is forced by the British and the Sultan's Trucial Scouts to resign as Imam, while his brother Talib flees to Saudi Arabia and reorganizes tribal forces with Saudi support.

Said bin Taimur is backed by the British and on July 18, Britain decides to use air power to soften up and scatter the rebels. The following month ground troops are dispatched to join the fighting. As soon as the British gained a military solution and restored the Sultans power base they withdrew.

Sultan Said bin Taimur rules an oppressive regime with all resources and political power under his total control, but he is afraid for his life and stays in his palace with hundreds of slaves. His rule is erratic, changing with the wind, and he punished people for appearing in his dreams and discouraged wearing eyeglasses. There was no development to speak of and the main city did not even have electricity available to the public until 1971, one year after the Sultan was deposed. There were hardly any schools or health care, and diseases were rampant. Without the British governments support he would have been deposed or assassinated. Finally in 1970 with the support of China and some of the nationalist Arab states Sultan Said bin Taimur was overthrown in a coup and exiled to England.

September 1957 – The Federal district court orders nine African-American students admitted to Central High School in Little Rock, Arkansas, on September 3, but Governor Orval Faubus **uses the National Guard to prevent them** from entering the school. After the district court orders Faubus to end his interference on September 20, the governor withdraws the Guard, and on September 23 the students are attacked by a large mob. **President Eisenhower sends more than 1,000 paratroopers** of the 101st Airborne Division to Little Rock on September 24 and places the 10,000 members of the Arkansas National Guard under federal control. Students are escorted to class by armed soldiers on September 25.

1957 – Vietnam. The insurgency of those the Diem government dub the **"Viet Cong"** begins in South Vietnam and within two years the North is sending assistance to the guerrillas along what becomes known as the **Ho Chi Minh Trail.**

1957 – Warsaw Riot. Poland. Exploding tear-gas bombs push thousands of rioting Polish university students back as the police smacked them with rubber truncheons in the worst civil disturbance since the bloody Poznan rebellion of 1956. The students gathered to protest the banning of the country's boldest and best-known crusading student weekly, *Po Prostu* (Plain Speaking). The 1,000 steel-helmeted police ordered the students to disperse, then waded in with tear gas and rubber truncheons viciously clubbing those that refused to leave. The demonstrators throw bricks, paving stones and hurl teargas canisters back at the police. The riot lasts four days and nights.

1957 – Nicaragua vs. Honduras. 1,000 people are killed.

1958

The Oldest Boomer is 12 years old.

Median Family Income: $5,100   **Minimum Wage:** $1.00/ hr

De Soto Adventurer convertible: $4,369   **Nash Metropolitan:** $1,626
Lincoln Continental: $4,802   **Edsel Citation:** $3,500
The country is in a recession. DeSoto sales are down 54% from 1957.
Buick is down 33%, Mercury 48%, Oldsmobile 18%, Dodge 47%, and
Pontiac is down 28%.

Unemployment Rate:
5.8%-7.4%-6.2%

First-class Stamp: 4 cents

13 cents buying power in 1958 **= $1.00 in 2008.**
In 1958 what cost our parents 13 cents to purchase
now costs us $1.00 in 2008.

Movies: "Vertigo," "Gigi," "Auntie Mame," "Cat on a Hot Tin Roof,"
"The Defiant Ones," "Separate Tables," "The Old Man and the Sea,"
"South Pacific."

Broadway: "My Fair Lady," London. "Irma La Douce," London. "The
Flower Drum Song," "Say, Darling," "Plume de Ma Tante, La" Revue.

TV: "77 Sunset Strip," "Donna Reed Show," "Wanted: Dead or Alive,"
"Rifleman," "Yancy Derringer," "Casey Jones," "Cimarron City," "Jefferson
Drum," "Northwest Passage," "Frontier Doctor," "The Texan," "Mackenzie's
Raiders," "Nine Lives of Elfego Baca," "Texas John Slaughter," "Rough
Riders," "Sea Hunt," "The Huckleberry Hound Show, "The Yogi Bear
Show," "Mike Hammer," "Andy Williams Show," "Peter Gunn," "The
Invisible Man," "Bat Masterson," "Concentration," "The Lux Show with
Rosemary Clooney."

Music: Bernard Herrmann, "Vertigo." Chuck Willis, "What Am I Loving
For." Bobby Day, "Rock-In' Robin." Elvis Presley, "Don't," "I Beg Of You" &

"Hard-Headed Woman." Nat King Cole, "Looking Back" & "Do I Like It." Everly Brothers, "All I Have To Do Is Dream," "Claudette," & "Bird Dog." Johnny Cash, "Guess Things Happen That Way," & "Come In, Stranger." Don Gibson, "Oh, Lonesome Me," & "I Can't Stop Loving You." Marty Robbins, "Just Married" & "Stairway Of Love." Jerry Lee Lewis, "Great Balls of Fire." Ricky Nelson's, "Poor Little Fool." Brenda Lee, "Rockin' Around the Christmas Tree." Sheb Wooley, "The Purple People Eater." Chuck Berry, "Sweet Little Sixteen." Connie Francis, "Who's Sorry Now?" & "Stupid Cupid." Ritchie Valens, "Come On Let's Go." The Chipmunks, "The Chipmunk Song." The Silhouettes "Get a Job." Dion & the Belmonts, "I Wonder Why." The Kingston Trio, "Scarlet Ribbons," & "Tom Dooley." Frankie Laine, "Rawhide."

President: Dwight D. Eisenhower (R) Presbyterian; vetoes 181/ 2 overrides

Vice President: Richard M. Nixon (R) Quaker

House: D-234 ; R-201

Senate: 85th Congress (1957-1959) Majority Party: Democrat (49 seats) Minority Party: Republican (47 seats) Other Parties: 0 Total Seats: 96

Federal Debt: $276.34 billion or 59 % of the GDP

Consumer Price Index CPI-U (1982 Base of 100): 28.90

GDP: $467.2 billion	**Inflation Rate:** 2.73%

Dow Jones: 560.07 (12-01)/ 436.00 (January)

Prime Rate: 4.00% (09-11)	**Average Home Mortgage Rate:** 5.58%
1 oz Gold: $35.25	**1oz of Silver:** $0.88

Federal Debt: $276,343,217,745.81

Federal Deficit: $2.8 billion dollars

Defense Spending: $51.75 billion	**Interest Spending:** $6.12 billion
Health Care Spending: $1.10 billion	**Pensions Spending:** $8.74 billion

Welfare Spending: $2.56 billion	**Education Spending:** $1.77 billion
Transportation Spending: $2.55 billion	**Misc. Other Spending:** $8.49 billion
Protection Spending: $160 million	**Total Government Spending:** $86.05 billion
% of GDP that goes towards just the interest payment: 1.31%	
$1.00 = 359.84 Yen, Japan	
U.S. Population: 174,141,000	**World Population:** 2,944,942,787
U.S. Birth Rate: 4,255,000	**U.S. Abortions:** 345
U.S. Homicide Rate: 4.5/ 100,000 population	
Annual Average Domestic Crude Oil Prices: $3.00 / barrel, $22.33 (2007 adjusted)	

Oil:

July 14, 1958 – A coup in Iraqi sets off debate within the U.S. government over the benefits of military and covert intervention in the Arab Middle East.

1958 – Africa. Oil production in Africa for 1958 establishes a new all-time high of 31,930,880 bbls, which represents an increase of 72% over 1957. Gabon, Algeria, and Nigeria are largely responsible for the increase. Production in Egypt is up 33% and represents 69% of the African total.

1958 – The recession of 1958 coupled with Cold War issues like Sputnik, Hungary, and increased Soviet influence both globally and in the Middle East put the **Eisenhower** administration on the defensive. By the end of 1958, **Gamal Abdel Nasser,** the second President of Egypt, has concluded that the most immediate threat to his leadership of the pan-Arab movement and to his vision for the UAR lay in Baghdad, Iraq.

1958

1958 – In their authoritative book about the CIA entitled "The Invisible Government," Washington correspondents Thomas Ross and David Wise relate how the U.S. supplied a right-wing rebel force in Indonesia with arms and a small air force of B-26 bombers in an attempt to overthrow **Sukarno**. The attempt failed, but not before one of the American pilots, **Allen Pope,** was captured by loyalist forces.

In January officers meet in Padang, plot a coup and set up a rival PRRI government. After Sukarno returns from a tour to Japan and India, he has his Air Force bomb Padang, Bukittingi, and Manado. Army units from Diponegoro and Siliwangi divisions land in Sumatra and take Medan while Padang falls to central government forces along with Bukittingi and Gorontalo.

Armed Indonesians return to Sumatra by U.S. B-26 bombers from the Philippines and from U.S. submarines. On May 18, U.S. pilot Alan Pope is shot down over Ambon while secretly helping PRRI rebels. Manado falls to government forces and by July Sukarno is in control.

In 1957 Dutch petroleum assets were nationalized and in September 1958 Cabinet Minister Ibnu Sutowo began working with American and Japanese businessmen to build Permina as a state oil company.

Many in the CIA and the State Department saw a great many positive aspects to these covert operations. They thought destabilizing the Sukarno government would encourage Sumatra, Indonesia's big oil producer, to succeed keeping the Americans and Dutch in control of the oil.

In September 1961 after the **Eisenhower** Administration left office President Kennedy arranged for Allen Pope's exchange and Sukarno came to Washington uninvited. Kennedy was more candid in speaking about the U.S. attempt to unseat Sukarno. During the visit **Kennedy** commented to one of his aides: "No wonder Sukarno doesn't like us very much. He has to sit down with the people who tried to overthrow him."

Major News:

February 1, 1958 – Egypt and Syria merge into the **United Arab Republic.** This short-lived union will see its dissolution in 1961.

March 27, 1958 – Khrushchev becomes Premier of the Soviet Union as Bulganin resigns.

June 1, 1958 – General Charles de Gaulle becomes the French Premier. He will remain in power until 1969.

July-October 1958 – U.S. Marines are sent to Lebanon at the request of President Chamoun **to protect** the elected government from threatened overthrow.

July 29, 1958 – President Eisenhower signs the act creating **NASA.**

September 22, 1958 – White House Chief of Staff for President Dwight D. Eisenhower, **Sherman Adams resigns** over a scandal involving alleged improper gifts. A House subcommittee revealed Adams had accepted an expensive vicuña overcoat and oriental rug from **Bernard Goldfine,** a Boston textile manufacturer who was being investigated for Federal Trade Commission violations.

October 4, 1958 – A New French constitution is adopted. It is typically called the **Constitution of the Fifth Republic**, and replaced that of the Fourth Republic dating from 1946. Charles de Gaulle is the main driving force in introducing the new constitution and inaugurating the Fifth Republic, while the text was drafted by Michel Debré. Since then the constitution has been amended eighteen times, most recently in 2007. However, Parliament began the process for further amendment on July 21, 2008.

November 1958 – Nikita Khrushchev, Premier of the Union of Soviet Socialist Republics, demands withdrawal of U.S. troops from Berlin.

December 10, 1958 – The first domestic **jet airline passenger service** in U.S. is opened by **National Airlines** between New York and Miami.

1953-1959 – Guantanamo Bay Naval Base. GiTMO, Cuba. Thousands of Cubans commute daily from outside the base to jobs on base until the summer of 1958 when vehicular traffic is stopped and workers are required to walk through the base's several gates. Public Works Center buses are pressed into service almost overnight to carry the tides of workers to and from **Guantanamo Bay Naval Base.** The Cuban government allows those with employment on base to continue working but prohibits new recruitment and by 2006, only two elderly Cubans still enter through the base's North East Gate to work. With over 9,500 U.S. sailors and Marines, Guantanamo Bay is the only U.S. base in operation in a Communist led country.

Civil Rights Movement:

January 18, 1958 – The Battle of Hayes Pond refers to an armed confrontation between the Ku Klux Klan and Lumbee Native Americans near Maxton, North Carolina. The Ku Klux Klan waged a campaign of terror throughout the South in the 1950's. In 1957, Klan Wizard James W. "Catfish" Cole of South Carolina began a campaign of harassment against the Lumbee whom he felt had overstepped their place in the segregated Jim Crow South. Catfish Cole told newspapers: "There's about 30,000 half-breeds up in Robeson County and we are going to have some cross burnings and scare them up."

On January 13, 1958, a group of Klansmen burned a cross on the lawn of a Lumbee woman in the town of St. Pauls, North Carolina as "a warning" because she was "having an affair" with a White man. Cole felt the time was right for a large rally and predicted 5,000 Klansmen would attend and remind the Lumbee of "their place." The rally was set for the small town of Maxton, North Carolina but only 50 Klansmen showed up. As Cole gathered the Klansmen and started to organize the evening's event over 500 well armed Lumbee suddenly appeared, fanned out across the highway and encircled the Klansmen. The Lumbee began making whooping noises and then opened fire on the Klansmen. Four Klansmen were wounded in the first volley fired by the Lumbee, but none were seriously injured. The remaining Klansmen however panicked and **fled the scene, leaving their families**, public address system, unlit cross, and various Klan regalia behind. James W. "Catfish" Cole reportedly left his wife and escaped through a nearby swamp. Catfish Cole was later apprehended, charged, and convicted for inciting to riot for which he served a sentence 1959-1960.

May 8, 1958 – Adam Clayton Powell Jr. (D-New York) **is indicted** on Federal income tax evasion, Criminal contempt of court for avoiding payment of a $160,000 defamation of character judgment and failing to appear in court for a civil suit. A Federal judge throws out 2 of 3 counts on April 22, and Powell goes on trial on the 3rd count which ends in a hung jury. After the judge denies a motion for acquittal the case is dismissed. Almost ten years later in January 1967 the House Democratic Caucus stripped Powell of his committee chairmanship after allegations that he misappropriated Committee funds for his personal use. The full House refused to seat him until completion of an investigation by the Judiciary Committee and in March the House voted 307 to 116 to exclude him. Powell won the special election in April to fill the vacancy caused by his exclusion, but did not take his seat.

September 12, 1958 – The Supreme Court decides "Cooper vs. Aaron," **unanimously overturning** a district court decision allowing the Little Rock school board to postpone desegregation until 1960 because of the threat of continued violence. In an opinion signed by all nine justices, Warren writes that governors and state legislators are bound by the Constitution to uphold Supreme Court decisions.

Popular Culture:

1958 – Videotape can now deliver color.

1958 – Number of **drive-in theaters** in the U.S. peaks near 5,000.

1958 – Edsel. "Once you've seen it, you'll never forget it. Once you've owned it, you'll never want to change."

1958 – **"The Smurfs,"** created by Belgian cartoonist Peyo.

1958 – Crest toothpaste, **"Look, Ma! No cavities!"** Benton & Bowles.

1958 – Hula hoops. Plastic hula hoops were first manufactured and sold in Australia. In 1957, Coles department store sold bamboo hoops, but the supplier couldn't produce enough to meet demand so they invited Alex Tolmer, the founder of Toltoys, to produce plastic ones. Toltoys sold 400,000 plastic hoops in 1957. In 1958, Melin and Knerr of Wham-O started to market hula hoops in the U.S., selling **100 million over that summer.** The craze lasted from January to October, and then suddenly died. In only four months, an estimated 80 to 100 million Hula Hoops were sold in 1958 at $1.98 each.

1958 – Stereo LP records go on sale.

Business / Technology:

1958 – The International News Service is taken over by United Press. It's now **UPI.**

1958 – Broadcast TV signals are bounced off a **rocket** and this marks the beginning of pre-satellite space communication.

1958 – An early version of Pong uses an analog computer with an oscilloscope.

January 16, 1958 – The European Economic Community, Common Market, has its first meeting as part of the Hallstein Commission.

January 31, 1958 – The first U.S. **earth satellite** to go into orbit, **Explorer I,** is launched by the Army from Cape Canaveral, Florida. The mission discovers the Van Allen radiation belt.

1958 – The microchip is invented by **Jack Kilby.** His invention of the monolithic integrated circuit, the microchip, at Texas Instruments lays the conceptual and technical foundation for the entire field of modern microelectronics. It is this breakthrough that makes possible the sophisticated high-speed computers and large-capacity semiconductor memories of today's information age.

1958 – SAGE, Semi-Automatic Ground Environment, linked hundreds of radar stations in the United States and Canada in the first large-scale computer communications network. An operator directed actions by touching a light gun to the screen.

August 5, 1958 – The Nuclear sub "Nautilus" makes the first undersea crossing of the North Pole.

1958 – The Tokyo Tower opens. It is a dramatic structure that was built, in part, to relay broadcast signals.

1958 – Pizza Hut begins after a neighbor read a *Saturday Evening Post* article about pizza's newfound popularity in New York City. Dan and Frank Carney **borrowed $600 from their mother** and set up shop in a tavern in 1958 and by 1963, Pizza Hut had locations in states as far away as Arizona and its only threat was the California-based **Shakey's.** In 1975, when the chain boasted 1,800 franchises, PepsiCo made its first offer to buy Pizza Hut. Frank ended up selling the company two years later for $320 million.

While Pizza Hut grows, Shakey's will go from 500 stores throughout the United States, when Hunt International bought the company in 1974, to 63 stores as of 2008, 55 of them in California. The chain is now much bigger in the Philippines than in the United States.

1958 – The National Aeronautics and Space Administration, NASA, begins operations at Cape Canaveral.

February 1958 – The Defense Department creates the ARPA, precursor of the Internet. The single most influential agency in the history of computer development in the United States is the Advanced Research Projects Agency (ARPA). **ARPA is the central** research and development organization for the U.S. Department of Defense. Established in February 1958 by President Eisenhower, and later supported by the Kennedy Administration, ARPA's creation is in direct response to the launching of **"Sputnik"** by the former U.S.S.R.

Finance:

January 13, 1958 – The fiscal deficit is up to twelve billion, four hundred twenty-seven million dollars.

August 7, 1958 – President Eisenhower signs into law an appropriations bill for defense in the amount of thirty-nine billion, six hundred and two million, eight hundred and twenty-seven thousand dollars.

1958

Books:

1958 – Truman Capote. "Breakfast at Tiffany's."

1958 – "Exodus," Leon Uris novel about the ship *Exodus 1947,* carrying 4,500 Jewish men, women, and children, all displaced persons or survivors of the Holocaust trying to illegally immigrate into **Palestine** while being blocked by the British. *Exodus* became an international publishing phenomenon, the biggest bestseller in the United States since *Gone with the Wind.* Uris sold the film rights in advance.

Exodus 1947 had initially sold as scrap for slightly more than $8,000 and the ship was acquired by the Hagana, an underground Jewish military organization. Hagana personnel arranged to dock the ship in Europe in order to transport Jews who sought to illegally immigrate into Palestine. The plight of the ship's passengers captured the world's attention as the British refused to allow them to dock and they were returned to Hamburg in the British-occupied zone of Germany. The free world was outraged.

TV:

1958 – Louis E. Lomax becomes the first African American newscaster. He works for WNTA-TV in New York City.

1958 – Live television drama is replaced by videotaped programs. Up to this time almost every TV show was performed **"Live" on stage.**

1958 – Quiz show fraud rocks U.S. television. Top-rated prime-time game show "Twenty One" is abruptly dropped by NBC in October after former contestant Herb Stempel charged that the show was rigged and that he had been ordered to lose a match to the popular **Charles Van Doren.**

"The $64,000 Question." The sponsors of the TV programs expected and sometimes demanded that popular contestants be supplied with answers in advance. It was good business for the more popular contestant to defeat unpopular competitors. This proved to be the central factor in the quiz show scandal.

1958 – **Three Stooges** short-films first aired in 1949 but it was not until 1958 that Screen Gems packaged 78 short-films for national syndication. After the films initial success this was enlarged to include the entire library of 190 short-films. In 1959, KTTV in Los Angeles purchased the Three Stooges films for air, but by the early 1970s, rival station KTLA began airing the Stooges films, keeping them in the schedule until early 1994.

Sports:

1958 – **Golf. Arnold Palmer's** 284 wins the Masters. It is the first of 4 wins at the Masters for Palmer. Tommy Bolt wins the U.S. Open golf tournament.

1958 – **Heavyweight Floyd Patterson** KOs Roy Harris.

1958 – In the **NBA** Finals it's Boston Celtics over the **Minneapolis Lakers. Rookie of the Year:** Elgin Baylor, Minneapolis Lakers **Most Valuable Player:** Bob Pettit, St. Louis Hawks.

1958 – **The Brooklyn Dodgers move to Los Angeles. The New York Giants move to San Francisco.** Other baseball teams that may be thinking of making a move include, Milwaukee Braves, Cincinnati Redlegs, Kansas City Athletics, and the Washington Senators. Not the Phillies, the **Philadelphia Phillies** have been loyal since 1883.

Music:

February 14, 1958 – The Iranian government bans rock & roll because they claim that the form of music is against the concepts of Islam and also a health hazard. Iranian doctors warn people of the risk of injuries to the hips from the "extreme gyrations" of rock & roll dances.

March 12, 1958 – Billie Holiday is given a year's probation by a Philadelphia court following her arrest and guilty plea on narcotics possession charges in 1956.

1958

March 12, 1958 – "The controversial Miles Davis," saxophonists John Coltrane and Cannonball Adderley, pianists Bill Evans and Red Garland, bassist Paul Chambers and drummers Philly Joe Jones and Jimmy Cobb recorded live at clubs for radio and TV broadcasts between May 1958 and January 1959. The oldest Boomer is only 12.

March 24, 1958 – Elvis Presley enters the U.S. Army. Elvis received his draft notice at age 23 in Memphis, Tennessee and is inducted, and processed at Fort Chaffee, Arkansas on March 24.

Natural Disasters:

1956-1958 – The Asian flu sweeps around the world, **killing an estimated two million** people and making it the second biggest flu pandemic of the century. "Asian Flu" is a category 2 flu pandemic outbreak of **avian influenza** that originates in China in early 1956 and ends in 1958. It originated from a mutation in wild ducks that combines with a pre-existing human strain. The virus was first identified in Guizhou, spread to Singapore in February 1957, and reached Hong Kong by April and the U.S. by June. The Death toll in the U.S. was approximately 69,800 people.

July 8, 1958 – Tsunami. The Lituya Bay, Alaska earthquake registers 7.5 on the Richter scale. This shock produces a landslide causing a mega tsunami with a 1,706 foot high wave. Because the area is so remote only two people are killed. The waves dissipated when they reached open sea.

September 27, 1958 – Honshu, Japan. Super Typhoon Vera is the strongest typhoon to hit Japan up to this time, causing $260 million ($1.9 billion 2009). Winds of 160 mph slammed into the southern coast of Japan, causing widespread damage and flooding. Over 120 square miles of land is flooded. **Typhoon "Vera" kills nearly 5,000 people,** 39,000 people are injured and 1.5 million people are left homeless.

1958 – Ethiopia. Famine in Tigray kills 100,000 people. Famine is the most negative state of food consumption under which people, unable to replace even the energy they loose in basal metabolism, consume whatever is stored in their bodies. This means they literally **consume themselves to death.**

April 7, 1958 – A 7.3 magnitude Earthquake hits Huslia, Alaska.

Man vs. Man / Wars:

1958 – Charles Starkweather mass murder case. Charles Starkweather's first crime took place on December 1, 1957, when he robbed a service station in Lincoln, Nebraska, abducted an employee, and shot him in the head. Charlie is only 19.

Charles had proposed to Caril Ann Fugate numerous times and Caril, who is fourteen, is in love with Charlie. When he was forbidden see Caril after an argument with Caril's stepfather, Marion Bartlett, 57, and her mother, Velda Bartlett, 36. Starkweather shot them both in the head. Caril's two-and-a-half-year-old baby sister, Betty Jean, was clubbed, strangled, and stabbed to death in her bed.

After the murders, the two lived in the house for several days. Twice they told relatives stopping by that everyone was sick with the flu and could not come to the door. Caril Ann's grandmother became suspicious and after a few days she called the police and asked them to investigate. They found the bodies in the chicken house but the young couple had already left to begin their killing and stealing spree across Nebraska. Mass murder, especially by two people so young, was a relatively rare occurrence in 1958 and held onto the National conscience for a long time.

Assassinated – Cameroon. Ruben Um Nyobé, leader of the Union of the Peoples of Cameroon was an anti-imperialist Cameroonian leader, slain by the French army on September 13, 1958, near the village of Boumnyebel. He created on April 10, 1948 the Cameroon People's Union which used armed struggle to obtain independence. After his death, he was replaced by Félix-Roland Moumié, who was assassinated by the **SDECE** (French intelligence agency) in Geneva in 1960.

Assassinated – Iraq. Military Coup. Colonel Abd al-Karim Qassim took control of the government on **July 14, 1958** and ordered the royal family to leave ar'Rihab Palace in Baghdad. When **King Faisal, Crown Prince 'Abd al-Ilah, his wife Princess Hiyam,** his mother **Princess Abadiya** and assorted other royals and several servants arrived in the courtyard they were lined up against the wall where Captain Abdus Sattar As Sab', a member of the coup, shot them all. With the monarchy overthrown the military coup then declares Iraq a republic. General Abdul Karim Qassim becomes Iraq's leader, and begins reversing the monarchy's pro-western policies. On the same day a huge mass demonstration in Baghdad with at least 100,000 people came out onto the streets in support of the coup and swept away the last remnants of the old regime.

May 1958 – Ceylon. Ethnic Violence in Ceylon. A rumor that a Tamil has killed a Sinhalese sparks nationwide riots. Hundreds of people, mostly Tamils, are killed. This disturbance is the first major episode of ethnic violence on the island since independence and the riots leave a deep psychological scar between the two major ethnic groups. The government declares a state of emergency and forcibly relocates more than 25,000 Tamil refugees from Sinhalese areas to Tamil areas in the North.

1958 – China. Mao Zedong. The "Great Leap Forward" is supposed to accelerate the development of all sectors of the economy at once by simultaneously improving both industry and agriculture. The idea is to forcibly move surplus rural labor to either vast infrastructure projects or to small-scale, farm-based industries. The "Great Leap Forward" is also supposed to instill communist principles into the structure and functioning of social systems, by the development of people's communes in the countryside and selected urban areas. Between April and September 1958, **98% of the farm population** is organized into communes.

Everyone is required to work in the communes. This includes intellectuals, communist party members, even professionals such as Doctors and nurses. Literally everyone is required to work in factories, mines, or public works projects in order to gain firsthand experience about how those facing manual labor live day-to-day. **The "Great Leap Forward" is a failure from the onset.** Rather than boosting production, the Great Leap Forward brings shortages of food and raw materials and the demoralization and exhaustion of the workforce. Poor harvests caused by bad weather increase the inability to bring things under control.

Mao refused to hear of failures and insisted that the overall plan would work out. Mao knew of the vast suffering and he was dismissive of it, blaming bad weather or other officials for the famine. Although slaughter was not his purpose with the Leap, he was more than ready for a very large, indefinite number of deaths to result, and hinted to his top echelon that they should not be too shocked if they happened.

The "Great Leap Forward" was a disaster for China. Millions of peasants were forced to work on and die for public works projects such as dams, canals that were not built with the input of trained engineers or other professionals and were disasters waiting to happen. Mao had rejected the use of trained professionals on ideological grounds. Although the steel quotas were officially reached, almost all of the steel made in the countryside was useless lumps of iron, as it had been made from assorted scrap metal in home made furnaces with no reliable source of fuel such as coal.

"We took all the furniture, pots, and pans we had in our house, and all our neighbors did likewise. We put all everything in a big fire and melted down all the metal."

From 1958 to 1961, 30 million **more people died** than in similar years of poor harvests. Various other sources have put the figure between 30 and 72 million deaths. At the "Conference of the Seven Thousand," in Beijing in January 1962, Mao and Defense Minister Lin Biao, were overruled and State President Liu Shaoqi and Deng Xiaoping rescued the economy by disbanding the people's communes, introducing elements of private control of peasant landholdings and importing grain from Canada and Australia to mitigate the worst effects of famine.

May, 1958 – Algeria. French Officers' Revolt. The Algiers coup of May 13 is a political crisis in France during the turmoil of the Algerian War of Independence which led to Charles de Gaulle's return to political power after a ten year absence. Its aim is to prevent the constitution of Pierre Pflimlin's government and to impose a change of policies in favor of the right-wing partisans of French Algeria. It also sets in motion the events which will lead to a new constitution on October 5, and the establishment of the Fifth Republic in France.

1948-1958 – Colombia. Colombian Civil War. The National Front ended "La Violencia," and National Front administrations attempt to institute far-reaching social and economic reforms in cooperation with the Alliance for Progress. In the end, the contradictions between each successive Liberal and Conservative administration made the results decidedly mixed. Despite the progress in certain sectors, many social and political injustices continued. Colombia has a long history of violence and unrest, including La Violencia, the 1948-1958 civil wars that claimed more than 200,000 lives. Another "culture of violence" that will emigrate with them.

November 1, 1958 – Cuba. A Cubana Vickers Viscount airplane en route from Miami to Varadero to Havana is hijacked by Cuban militants. The hijackers are trying to land at Sierra Cristal in Eastern Cuba to deliver weapons to Raúl Castro's rebels. As night approaches the plane runs out of fuel and tries an emergency landing at the Preston sugar mill but misses the landing area and lands in the ocean instead. The plane breaks apart killing 13 of the 16 passengers and all four crew members on board.

1958 – France. Basque Separatist Campaign. The Basque region is divided between Spain and France. The Basque liberation front, ETA, has carried out a campaign of urban terrorism in an attempt to gain independence. As most Basque territory is in Spain, the bulk of the campaign has been directed at the Spanish, though French targets have also been hit. France and Spain largely cooperate in suppressing ETA.

1958 – Philippines. CIA and Filipino counterinsurgents had, by early 1958, set up special operations training bases, with **United States Army Special Forces** trainers, and made clandestine air bases on Palawan and Mindanao available to Indonesian rebels.

February 9, 1958 – Sumatra. Indonesia. A coup led by the CIA fails to affect the rule of President Sukarno of **Indonesia.** They had better luck in 1965.

Rebel Colonel Maluddin Simbolon issues an ultimatum in the name of a provincial government, the **Central Sumatran Revolutionary Council,** calling for the formation of a new central government. **Sukarno** refuses and calls upon his loyal army commander, General Abdul Haris Nasution, to destroy the rebel forces.

The CIA supports the Indonesian rebellion from the main Far East base in Naha, Okinawa. Another support facility is on Taiwan, where B-26 bombers are prepared to ferry men and supplies to the Philippine bases that will support the Indonesian rebels. The CIA, from U.S. Marine and Army stores provides 42,000 rifles.

In May 1958 a B-26 operated by CIA proprietary Civil Air Transport is shot down after bombing the Indonesian port of Amboina, and the resulting publicity ended the American attempt when the pilot, Allen Lawrence Pope, was captured. Pope was clearly not the only U.S. pilot involved in Indonesia's civil war.

TIME -From Zamboanga, in the southern Philippines, last week came word that during March and April some 20 transport planes had touched down at the dirt airport to refuel and continue on their way to or from rebel-held Menado. The planes reportedly had Nationalist Chinese markings covered over with hasty coats of paint, their pilots were Chinese and Americans from Chennault's swashbuckling CAT, the cargoes were rumored to be guns and munitions.

July 14, 1958 – Iraq. The 14th July Revolution and the Massacre of al-Zuhoor Palace is a military coup responsible for the overthrow of the Iraqi Hashemite monarchy under Faisal II and the regime of Prime Minister Nuri al-Said. **The Royal Family** was lined up against the wall of the Palace and shot by Captain Abdus Sattar As Sab. The coup ended the Iraqi Hashemite dynasty.

1958 – Jordan Intervention. Britain airlifts troops to Jordan in response to a request for aid from Jordan's **King Hussein.** Hussein feels threatened by the violent revolution in **Iraq, the assassination** of the Iraq King, who was a member of Hussein's family, and the recent union of Syria and Egypt. After the situation calms down, British troops leave Jordan.

1958 – Lebanon crisis. The Lebanon crisis, caused by political and religious reasons, **is calmed by a U.S. military intervention.** Lebanon is threatened by a civil war between Maronite Christians and Muslims. Lebanese Muslims pushed the government to join the newly created United Arab Republic, while the Christians wanted to keep Lebanon aligned with Western Powers. A Muslim rebellion armed by the U.A.R. through Syria causes President Chamoun to complain to the United Nations Security Council. The U.N. sends inspectors that find no evidence of significant intervention from the U.A.R.

The military coup in Iraq that is responsible for the assassination of the King, the Royal Family, and many household staff along with the internal instability in Lebanon, caused President Chamoun to call for U.S. assistance.

1958

October 7, 1958 – Pakistan, coup d'etat. Pakistan's first President, Iskandar Mirza, throws out the constitution and declares **martial law.** Various political factions in the East Pakistan legislative assembly confront each other in what becomes a brawl that results in the death of the Deputy Speaker. Martial law has now shifted the power into the hands of the military making it difficult for Mirza to remain in charge and on October 27, **General Ayub Khan** overthrows Iskander Mirza and assumes the Presidency in a **bloodless coup.**

1958 – Paraguayan Exile Insurgency. A national plebiscite elects Stroessner to a second term, but dissatisfaction with the regime turns into a **guerrilla insurgency as small groups of** exiled Liberals and Febreristas begin to slip across the border from Argentina. Well armed and supplied, the Colorado Party's peasant irregulars, have a well deserved reputation for ferocity, and often torture and then execute their prisoners. These guerrilla groups receive aid from both Venezuela and Cuba.

Stroessner's response is to employ the state's virtually unlimited power by giving a free hand to the military and to Minister of Interior Edgar Ynsfrán, who began to harass, **terrorize, and occasionally murder family members** of the regime's foes. People considered enemies of Stroessner's government are rounded up and placed in jungle concentration camps. Army troops and police break up striking labor unions by taking over their organizations and arresting their leaders and a cycle of terror and counter-terror began to make life in Paraguay precarious. The average person is afraid and the guerrillas receive little support from Paraguay's conservative peasantry.

1958 – South Africa. White, Dutch-descent, Afrikaners officially gain independence from Great Britain in South Africa.

1958 – Sudanese Military Coup. Abdullah Khalil, a former army general, put together an Umma Party/ Mahdist coalition on July 5, 1956 and became Prime Minister. On the night of November 16, 1958, the army under General Ibrahim Abboud occupies Khartoum and seizes power. The military coup d'etat was unopposed and bloodless, and the civilian government collapsed with little protest. Abdullah Khalil helped carry out the coup against his own government, putting the government under the control of the military junta that abolished all political parties and imprisoned many politicians.

1958 – Thai-Cambodian Border Clash. A border dispute over less than sixty square kilometers of land is responsible for the relatively steady occurrence of border clashes involving cross-border violations and the exchange of small-arms fire. In 1958 the two governments decide not to settle their border differences until one or the other has achieved victory in their dispute over territorial waters in the Gulf of Tonkin. This border dispute has been going on since 1887 because of agreements reached between China and France.

1958 – Tunisia. French-Tunisian Clashes. Relations with France remain on the whole good, in spite of a few periods of intense crisis. These include the bombing of a Tunisian village in 1958 by French planes, with the French claiming the right to pursue Algerian rebels across the border. On February 7, French planes cross into Tunisia, and are shot at by Tunisian artillery. In retaliation French military planes bomb the Tunisian village of Sekiet Sidi Youssef on February 8, where 68 persons are killed.

1958 – Venezuelan Military Revolt. Several air force units bomb the capital city of Caracas on January 1, destroying many buildings and causing many deaths. Perez Jimenez's forces quickly regain control but momentum builds for his overthrow when a week later part of the Navy mutinies. Perez Jimenez frantically reorganizes his cabinet several times in an effort to obtain strong leadership. Although initially unsuccessful, the rebellion led by the air force triggers widespread popular unrest that bring more of the armed forces into the anti-Pérez coalition. On January 21, a general strike shuts down Caracas and the armed forces join the protest. At this point Perez Jimenez realizes he can no longer rule and flees to Miami, Florida, with a multi-million dollar fortune. The Military wastes no time in setting up a junta to govern until elections can be held.

On May 13, When Vice President Richard Nixon visits Venezuela his motorcade faces a mob that ends his South American tour. Neither the President nor Mrs. Nixon is injured but their motorcade is attacked by the rock-throwing mob and their car is damaged.

1959

The Oldest Boomer is 13 years old.

Cost of the Average House: $12,400	
Median Family Income: $5,400	**Minimum Wage:** $1.00/ hr
Cigarettes: 25cents/ pack **Coca-Cola:** 6.5 oz 5 cents, **Gallon Gasoline:** 31cents	
New Car: Buick LeSabre: $1,495 **Cadillac Convertible:** $5,400 **Chevrolet Impala:** $3,451	
Unemployment Rate: 6.0%-5.8%-5.3%	**First-class Stamp:** 4 cents

13 cents buying power in 1959 = **$1.00 in 2008.**
In 1959 what cost our parents 13 cents to purchase
now costs us $1.00 in 2008.

Movies: "Some Like it Hot," "North by Northwest," "Ben-Hur," "Anatomy of a Murder," "The Diary of Anne Frank," "The Nun's Story," "Room at the Top," "Have Rocket, Will Travel."

Broadway: "Once Upon a Mattress," "Gypsy," "Saratoga," "The Sound of Music," "Destry Rides Again," "The Nervous Set."

TV: "The Twilight Zone." "Rawhide," with Clint Eastwood as Rowdy Yates. "Dennis the Menace," "Many Loves of Dobie Gillis," "Hawaiian Eye," "Adventures in Paradise," "Bourbon Street Beat," "Bonanza," "Riverboat," "Hotel de Paree," "Laramie," "Johnny Ringo," "The Deputy," "Law of the Plainsman," "Swamp Fox," "Man From Blackhawk," "The Untouchables," "Wichita Town," "Playboy's Penthouse," "Rocky and His Friends," (Rocky and Bullwinkle). "Mr. Lucky."

Music: "Ben-Hur." "Anatomy of a Murder." Wilbert Harrison, "Kansas City." Jackie Wilson, "Lonely Teardrops." Lloyd Price, "You've Got

Personality." Brook Benton, "It's Just A Matter Of Time." Johnny Horton, "Battle Of New Orleans." Stonewall Jackson, "Waterloo." Johnny Cash, "Don't Take Your Guns To Town." Connie Francis, "Lipstick On Your Collar." Bobby Darin, "Mack The Knife," "Beyond The Sea" & "Dream Lover." Frankie Avalon, "Venus." Paul Anka, "Lonely Boy" & "Put Your Head On My Shoulder." Bo Diddley, "Say Man." Buddy Holly, "Peggy Sue Got Married" & "Crying, Waiting, Hoping." The Drifters, "There Goes My Baby." Tommy Edwards, "It's All In The Game." Ritchie Valens, "La Bamba." Ricky Nelson, "Lonesome Town." Dion & the Belmonts, "A Teenager In Love." Brenda Lee, "Sweet Nothin's." The Clovers, "Love Potion Number Nine." The Fleetwoods, "Mr. Blue." Hank Ballard, "The Twist."

President: Dwight D. Eisenhower (R) Presbyterian; vetoes 181/ 2 overrides	
Vice President: Richard M. Nixon (R) Quaker	
House: D-283 ; R-153	
Senate: 86th Congress (1959-1961) Majority Party: Democrat (65 seats) Minority Party: Republican (35 seats) Other Parties: 0 Total Seats: 100	
Federal Debt: $284.71 billion or 56 % of the GDP	
Consumer Price Index CPI-U (1982 Base of 100): 29.10	
GDP: $506.6 billion	**Inflation Rate:** 1.01%
Dow Jones: 679.36 (12-31)/ 580.00 (January)	
Prime Rate: 5.00% (09-01)	**Average Home Mortgage Rate:** 5.71%
1 oz Gold: $35.25	**1oz of Silver:** $0.91
Federal Debt: $284,705,907,078.22	
Federal Deficit: $12.8 billion dollars	
Defense Spending: $53.98 billion	**Interest Spending:** $5.54 billion
Health Care Spending: $1.34 billion	**Pensions Spending:** $10.18 billion

Welfare Spending: $2.80 billion	**Education Spending:** $1.66 billion
Transportation Spending: $3.92 billion	**Misc. Other Spending:** $10.39 billion
Protection Spending: $170 million	**Total Government Spending:** $93.53 billion
% of GDP that goes towards just the interest payment: 1.09%	
$1.00 = 359.97 Yen, Japan	
U.S. Population: 177,130,000	**World Population:** 2,997,268,998
U.S. Birth Rate: 4,295,000	**U.S. Abortions:** 357
U.S. Homicide Rate: 4.6/ 100,000 population	
Annual Average Domestic Crude Oil Prices: $3.00 / barrel, $22.11 (2007 adjusted)	

Oil:

1959 – Libya. Oil is discovered. In 1959, Esso (ExxonMobil) makes the first commercial discovery of oil in Libya. Forty two foreign companies conduct exploratory drilling activities under concession contracts that cover an area of 231 square miles leading to many more. This discovery of significant oil reserves in 1959 and the subsequent income from petroleum sales enables what had been **one of the world's poorest countries** to become extremely wealthy, as measured by per capita GDP.

Resentment grows within the country as the oil and gas wealth is concentrated in the hands of the elite. The idea of Arab unity, Nasserism, begins to take hold as the average person seeks a way to better their life.

1959 – Abu Dhabi. The first big oil reserve is discovered just off the coast of Abu Dhabi. Oil is also found in Abu Dhabi's desert within eight months.

1959 – Lake Erie is the site of 100 purposed offshore oil wells. What happened?

The Energy Policy Act of 2005 permanently protects the American Great Lakes from future oil and gas development. According to an Ontario Ministry of Natural Resources report, **there are 1,161 oil wells and 744 gas wells operating** along the north Lake Erie shoreline in **Canada.** In addition, 478 gas wells operate offshore on Crown land under the lake itself. In total, these reserves provide just one to two percent of Ontario's oil and gas requirements. **Only a handful of wells operate** from the **U.S.** side of the lake and most were directionally drilled beneath the Great Lakes in Michigan. Geologists estimate that about half of the original deposits still remain in the ground. It is estimated 1.1 trillion cubic feet of gas minimum are recoverable from the U.S. side of Lake Erie.

1959 – Netherlands. The massive Groningen land gas field, the biggest in the world at this time, estimated to contain 3 trillion cubic meters of gas, is discovered in the Netherlands. **The Dutch petroleum company** was drilling for oil and is disappointed to find gas. The Groningen gas field will become very profitable for the partnership of the Dutch government, Royal Dutch Shell and ExxonMobil and will lead to the **North Sea** becoming the centre of one of the world's most productive energy industries. **Oil reserves** are small, estimated to be between 100 and 200 million barrels, gas is huge making Holland Europe's second-largest producer of natural gas and the ninth-largest in the world with estimated reserves of between 50 and 60 trillion cubic feet. Both onshore and offshore gas has been easily accessible and is found at low depths, encouraging 40 years of extensive activity.

1958-1959 – Iraq. The situation in Iraq **appears to warrant preemptive intervention** to prevent it from falling under Soviet Communist domination. The intelligence community, the State Department, and the Pentagon, in the **Eisenhower Administration** debate the necessity of preemptive intervention in Iraq's politics to maintain our supply of oil.

President Eisenhower served as Supreme Commander of the Allied forces in Europe, with responsibility for planning and supervising the successful invasion of France and Germany in 1944–1945. As a five-star General he understands the military, military occupations, diplomacy, and how to take a conservative approach to serving the interests of the United States. Eisenhower keeps the U.S. from preemptive intervention and allows the situation to continue on its way to a dictatorship which is the norm for Iraq. Lives are not squandered and the U.S. cost in dollars is minimal.

December 18, 1959 – USSR Pipeline. The 10th session of the Council for Mutual Economic Assistance is held in Prague. They adopt an agreement to construct a **trunk crude oil pipeline** from the **USSR** into **Poland, Czechoslovakia, GDR** and **Hungary.** Each country will supply all necessary construction materials, machinery and equipment.

Major News:

January 3, 1959 – Alaska becomes the 49th State.

August 21, 1959 – Hawaii becomes the 50th State.

January 7, 1959 – Cuba is taken over by rebel forces led by **Fidel Castro.** Cuban **President Batista resigns** and flees. Castro takes over and the United States recognizes the new Cuban government. Castro becomes the Premier of Cuba on February 16.

March 31, 1959 – Tibet's Dalai Lama escapes to India. The spiritual leader of Tibet, the Dalai Lama, crosses the border into India after an epic 15-day journey on foot from the Tibetan capital, Lhasa, over the Himalayan Mountains.

July 24, 1959 – Vice President Richard Nixon, on a tour of the USSR, holds the "kitchen debate," a series of impromptu exchanges with Soviet Premier **Nikita Khrushchev** at the U.S. exhibit in Moscow. The debates took place at a number of places, but were primarily in the kitchen of a cut–away suburban model home.

Vice President Richard M. Nixon became the highest ranking U.S. official to visit the Soviet Union since 1945, when Franklin Roosevelt attended the Yalta Conference. Nixon's ten-day visit was widely publicized and called "one of the greatest adventures in modern diplomacy."

September 1959 – Nikita Khrushchev visits the United States and is denied access to **Disneyland**. Nikita Khrushchev is the first Soviet Premier to set foot on American soil and his visit was heralded as "one of the most dramatic episodes in post-war history." In 1949 the world was on the verge of possible nuclear war with the increased tensions over the Berlin blockade, the Korean War, the victory of the Chinese People's Army and the establishment of the People's Republic of China. As both the United States and the Soviet Union began to realize the limits of their power there is hope for peaceful coexistence.

When Khrushchev came to the U.S. the visit went fairly well, and then in Los Angeles, California several famous Hollywood stars, including Ronald Reagan, refused to meet the Soviet leader. But what appeared to anger Khrushchev the most was that he was **denied access to Disneyland** due to security concerns. Hollywood stars that were still present when the Premier was denied access to the amusement park found the incident humorous, but were also aware the Soviet leader was disappointed. **Frank Sinatra told his friend,** "Screw the cops! Tell the old broad (Khrushchev's wife) you and I'll take 'em down to Disneyland this afternoon."

1959 – Khrushchev ridiculed Nixon for the Captive Nations Resolution that had been passed shortly before the Vice President left for Europe. **Khrushchev** said the resolution would not change anything in Europe and would only cause more problems between the United States and the Soviet Union, and then kept baiting Nixon with comments about the issue while Nixon continued trying to change the subject. **Finally Khrushchev told Nixon that the resolution "stinks like fresh horse shit,** and nothing smells worse than that." The Vice President, remembering from his preparation that the Premier had begun his life as a pig breeder, decided not to back down and crudely replied, **"I am afraid that the Chairman is mistaken.** There is something that smells worse than horse shit, and that is pig shit." Khrushchev, clearly angered, attempted to smile and finally agreed to change the subject. Two "world leaders," with their countries debating whether or not a preemptive nuclear strike is possible, make friends.

September 4, 1956 – At 10:38 a.m. Elementary school children participate in a nuclear drill by sitting on the floor under their desk. They are told, "In case we are attacked by Soviet Nuclear Weapons you will all take this position and stay there until the threat is lifted." This was the best response, of the best and the brightest, to a real nuclear threat and was practiced often, just as a "fire drill" was practiced. Although unable to fully articulate the situation many of the children, small enough to "fit under a desk while sitting upright" instinctively knew, "This is stupid!" The fog lifted all over America as these little ones look up at their teachers and adults in general, and know without a doubt, authority figures do some pretty stupid things and then lie about the reasons why. The oldest Boomer is 13 years old. **Little hippies in process.**

Civil Rights Movement:

January 19, 1959 – The Virginia Supreme Court rules the school closing law passed in 1956 violates the state constitution.

April 25, 1959 – Mack Charles Parker, an African-American man accused of raping a white woman, is taken from jail in Poplarville, Mississippi, and **lynched by a mob.** Gunmen wearing masks and gloves raided the jail in Poplarville, Mississippi, and seized Mack Charles Parker, 23, who was accused of raping a white woman. "The raiders dragged Parker from the building by his heels, his head bumping from steel tread to steel tread of the stairs. Blood flicked about marked progress of the party, a bloody handprint on the doorstep giving the last trace of Parker, who screamed and struggled, "Please, let me up. I'll walk." Inmates watched the scene below, "You could hear him hollering. Cars were lining up, almost as far as you could see." And then the cars sped away.

Mack Charles Parker was beaten, shot twice and thrown over a bridge railing into the Pearl River. The FBI files are online. http://foia.fbi.gov/foiaindex/parker.htm

June 26, 1959 – After the **Virginia legislature** repeals its compulsory school attendance law, Prince Edward County closes its schools to avoid **desegregation.**

Women's Movement:

1959 – Less than two years **after FDA approval of Enovid** for therapeutic purposes, an unusually large number of American women mysteriously develop severe menstrual disorders and ask their doctors for the drug. By late 1959, over half a million American women are taking Enovid, presumably for the "off-label" **contraceptive purposes.**

1959 – **Women still only earn,** on average, 60% of what their male counterparts earn.

1959 – **Margaret Sanger,** a radical activist in her eighties serves her last year as President of the International Planned Parenthood Federation, the largest private international "family planning" organization in 1959. She is on her way to make "the pill" available on demand. **This will change the world** as profoundly as any invention of the 20th century.

Popular Culture:

March 1959 – Barbie dolls. Barbie is a fashion doll manufactured by Mattel, Inc. The value of the 1959 Barbie doll in mint condition has sold for up to $8,000 apiece, while the **original value was $3 dollars.**

1959 – **Baseball cards, Topps, Billy Martin** EXMT. Book-$30.00   Sale- $13.50 (02/2009).

1959 – **Lenny Bruce** and Mort Sahl, remake stand-up comedy by loosening the language and skewering politics and religion.

1959 – **Atomic Bunny Comic Book #16** original cost 10 ten cents 02/2009 VG $10.50

1959 – **President Dwight Eisenhower** states in a press conference that **birth control** "is not a proper political or government activity or function or responsibility" and adds emphatically that it is "not our business."

March 11, 1959 – Lorraine Hansberry's "A Raisin in the Sun" opens with Sidney Poitier in the starring role. It is the first play by an African American woman to be produced on Broadway.

February 5, 1959 – "Beatnik" Allen Ginsberg gave a poetry reading at Columbia University before a crowd of 1,400. It was a big night for Ginsberg, his triumphant return to the campus that had suspended him over a decade earlier for scrawling obscenities on a windowpane. And you can hear the generation gap *crack* a little wider.

1959 – Princess telephones in 5 colors go on sale.

September 26, 1959 – President Dwight D. Eisenhower hosts Soviet premier Nikita Khrushchev at his farm in Gettysburg, Pennsylvania during the first visit of any Soviet Union leader to the United States.

1959 – Volkswagen, "Think Small." Doyle Dane Bernbach.

1959 – Maxwell House, "Good to the last drop." Ogilvy, Benson & Mather.

Business / Technology:

January 1, 1959 – Mafia casinos are seized by Fidel Castro's government after Cuban dictator Fulgencio Batista flees the country following the Cuban Revolution. Suffering a major financial setback, Meyer Lansky returns to Miami, Florida and begins looking into the possible relocation of syndicate casinos in the Bahamas and Caribbean.

January 2, 1959 – Lunar Probe. Russian satellite Lunik 1 passes the Moon. It is the first spacecraft to reach the Moon and the first of the Luna program of Soviet automatic interplanetary stations successfully launched in the direction of the Moon. While passing through the outer Van Allen radiation belt, the spacecraft's scintillator makes measurements indicating that there are very few high energy particles in the outer belt.

1959 – The U.S. Post Office first tries and then abandons a plan to move mail by submarine-fired missiles.

1959 – Xerox manufactures a plain paper copier.

1959

1959 – Twenty-one million radios are sold this year.

April 25, 1959 – The St. Lawrence Seaway is opened along the Canada and United States borders allowing oceangoing vessels to reach the American Midwest.

September 12, 1959 – Lunar Probe. Russian satellite Lunik 2 crashes on the Moon.

September 14, 1959 – The Landrum-Griffin Act passes, **restricting union activity.**

1959 – Magnetic ink character recognition is developed to process checks.

1959 – The U.S. Senate begins committee hearings into allegations that the largest electrical equipment makers in the United States are conspiring to **fix prices.** Among the manufacturers are major providers: **General Electric, Westinghouse, Allis Chalmers, and Federal Pacific Electric.**

1959 – There are now more than 50 million **television sets** in the United States.

1959 – The first computer chip is patented. Jack Kilby, an engineer with a background in ceramic-based silk screen circuit boards and transistor-based hearing aids, started working for Texas Instruments in 1958. A year earlier, research engineer **Robert Noyce** had co-founded the Fairchild Semiconductor Corporation. From 1958 to 1959, both electrical engineers are working on an answer to the same dilemma: how to make more of less. They both applied for and received patents separately in the same year, 1959. This small step triggers the digital age.

1959 – Grace Hopper writes the COBOL programming language for business.

1959 – The Austin Mini 7 goes on sale from the British Motor Corporation for close to $1,000.

October 4, 1959 – Lunar Probe. Russian satellite Lunik 3 photographs the far side of the Moon. **The third spacecraft makes a successful voyage to the Moon.** Although the photos that it sends back to earth are of poor quality, the historic, **never-before-**

seen views of the Moon's far side cause excitement and interest when they are published around the world.

November 7, 1959 – On October 12, **President Eisenhower** issues an injunction which is upheld and made effective by the Supreme Court invoking the **Taft-Hartley Act** November 7, ending a record 116-day **steel strike.**

Finance:

April 8, 1959 – The Charter of the InterAmerican Development Bank is signed.

1956-1959 – The Church of Scientology is denied tax exempt status in 1969 because payments during 1956-1959 were disguised and a portion of Scientology's income was secretly going to Scientology's founder, L Ron Hubbard and his family.

Books:

1959 – Boris Pasternak, "**Dr. Zhivago.**"

1959 – "**Naked Lunch.**" William Burroughs' novel about drug addiction.

1959 – Philip Roth's first novel, **"Goodbye, Columbus."**

1959 – **Grove Press** publishes an unexpurgated version of "Lady Chatterley's Lover," by D. H. Lawrence and the **U.S. Post Office confiscates copies sent through the mail.**
      The **U.S. rules D.H. Laurence novel, "Lady Chatterley's Lover,"** first printed in Florence, Italy, in 1928, **is not obscene.** The publication of the book caused a scandal due to its explicit sex scenes, including previously banned four-letter words and perhaps because the lovers were a working-class male and an aristocratic female. **"Lady Chatterley's Lover"** along with **"Tropic of Cancer,"** and **"Fanny Hill,"** had previously been banned. Barney Rosset, the owner of Grove Press, and attorney Charles Rembar sued the government's censors toppling obscenity laws forever.

1959

The Grove Press edition of "Lady Chatterley's Lover," went on to sell more than 2,000,000 copies.

1959 – "A Separate Peace," John Knowles.

1959 – James Michener, **"Hawaii."**

1959 – "Things Fall Apart," Chinua Achebe.

TV:

1959 – NBC offers a western in color. **"Bonanza"** will continue to run for 14 years.

1959 – The public is shocked to learn that most big-money **TV quiz shows are fixed**. In a **quiz show scandal**, Columbia University Professor **Charles Van Doren** admitted to a U.S. House subcommittee in November that he had been coached before appearances on NBC-TV's *21* in 1956. He had won $129,000.

1959 – Moscow, USSR. The Nixon Khrushchev Kitchen Debate in a model home modestly furnished by Macy's makes it to TV in COLOR via videotape. It has been described by Max Frankel as, "sparring at the kitchen of the Macy's house, mixing boasts and accusations like adolescents comparing sexual exploits."

1959 – The Hate That Hate Produced" a television documentary about the Nation of Islam produced by Mike Wallace and Louis Lomax catapulted Malcolm X to national attention from being relatively unknown.

Radio:

1959 – Disk jockey payola scandals smear radio broadcasting. The acceptance of cash or gifts for radio airplay of songs flourished among rock 'n' roll disc jockeys. Independent labels recording rock had broken the stranglehold Columbia, RCA and Decca, had on the industry.

1959 – The Japanese have exported 6 million transistor radios to the United States at a cost of $63 million. The American Zenith Royal 500 line is released at $75 dollars but reduced to $59.95 to be more competitive. The majority of both Japanese and American radios had excellent sensitivity and sound quality.

Sports:

February 22, 1959 – The Daytona 500 stock car race is run for the first time with Lee Petty taking the first checkered flag.

1959 – The Boston Red Sox are the last major league team to integrate its roster.

Music:

January 12, 1959 – Berry Gordy, Jr. founds **Motown Records** in Detroit. Berry Gordy, moves black urban music into mainstream pop culture.

February 2, 1959 – "The Day the Music Died." A plane crash kills **Buddy Holly, Richie Valens,** and **The Big Bopper.** This date becomes known as **"The Day the Music Died."** Future country star Waylon Jennings was scheduled to be on the plane, but instead gave his seat up to Richie Valens.

November 29, 1959 – First Grammys. The first **Grammy Award telecast** took place. Ceremonies are held in both **New York** and **Los Angeles** and the winners have their choice where they will accept the award.

1959 – The Supremes are founded as a quartet, "The Primettes."

1959 – Roy Orbison signs with Monument Records.

Natural Disasters:

1959 – Bubonic plague. The Third Pandemic is the designation of a major plague pandemic that began in the Yunan province in China in 1855. This episode of bubonic plague spread to all inhabited continents, and ultimately **killed more than 12**

million people in India and China alone. According to the World Health Organization, the pandemic is **considered active until 1959**, when worldwide casualties dropped to 200 per year.

1930-1959 – "Mortality from tobacco in developed countries: indirect estimation from national vital statistics," "Lancet," 23 May 1992. 1930-1959: **11,000,000 deaths.**

1959 – AIDS. Scientists isolate what is believed to be the earliest known case of AIDS. The discovery suggests that the multitude of global AIDS viruses all shared a common African ancestor within the past 40 to 50 years. This will be disputed later.

August 18, 1959 – Montana. A 7.3 magnitude earthquake hits Hebgen Lake, Montana killing 28 people.

August 20, 1959 – Fukien province, China. Typhoon "Iris" kills 2,334 people.

December 2, 1959 – Fréjus, France. A flood caused by the collapse of the Malpasset Dam kills 412 people.

1959 – India. Mautam Famine. The Mizo Hills are devastated by a great famine attributed to the flowering of bamboo which results in an explosion of the rat population. After eating bamboo seeds, the rats turn to crops, infest the huts and houses and become a plague to the villages. The havoc created by the rats is devastating and very little of the grain is left for harvest. For sustenance, many Mizos collect roots and leaves from the jungles. Still others move to far away places, and a considerable number die of starvation. Several welfare organizations become involved in the effort to help starving villagers.

Man vs. Man / Wars:

Assassinated – Ceylon (Sri Lanka 1972). The Prime Minister of Ceylon, Solomon Bandaranaike is assassinated by Talduwe Somarama a Sri Lankan Sinhalese Buddhist monk as part of a conspiracy. He later openly converts to Christianity, just weeks prior to being hanged in the Welikada gallows. Solomon Bandaranaike's widow, Sirimavo Bandaranaike, became the Prime Minister in 1960.

October 10, 1959 – Fatah. A group of about 20 Palestinians meet in Kuwait and secretly form Fatah, The Movement for the National Liberation of Palestine. **Cairo-born Palestinian** Mohammed **Yasser Arafat**, who had been working as a construction engineer in Kuwait, soon emerges as the leader of Fatah. Yasser Arafat studied civil engineering at the University of Cairo, where he headed the Palestinian Students League. Egypt, Syria, Jordan, and other Arab nations have organized the **Palestine Liberation Organization** (PLO) and will ignore Arafat until 1967. With Fatah, Arafat recruits terrorists and leads fedayeen raids into Israeli territory. Among the offshoots of Fatah are the infamous **"Black September"** who murder the Israeli athletes at the 1972 Munich Olympics.

1959 – Cuba. Fidel Castro's regime executes 550 people in the first six months of 1959. Overall it has been estimated that between 1,500 and 2,000 people were killed as a direct consequence of the political crisis between 1952 and 1959.

April 15, 1959 – Cuba. A plane is hijacked from Cuba to Miami. The hijackers are four members of Batista's Army, three were from the SIM, the Military Intelligence, and one was an aviation mechanic. The airplane is returned by the U.S.

1955-1959 – Cyprus. Archbishop Makarios, Greece and Turkey accept reality and agree on independence as a solution to the sectarian violence that killed 109 people. British Prime Minister Harold Macmillan proposes a seven-year partnership of separate communal legislative bodies and separate municipalities. This is not acceptable but leads to further discussions of the Cyprus problem between representatives of Greece and Turkey.

When Makarios endorses a Greek-Turkish plan to make Cyprus an independent state, under international guarantee within the Commonwealth they find a possible solution. One-hundred forty-two British soldiers were killed, eighty-four Turkish Cypriots were killed and two-hundred and seventy-eight Greek Cypriots were killed.

1959 – Cambodia. Sieu Heng's defection. Prince Norodom Sihanouk of Cambodia is a valuable asset in Hanoi's struggle to liberate South Vietnam. In 1959 Sieu Heng defected to the government and provided the security forces with information that enabled them to destroy as much as 90 percent of the opposition party's rural apparatus. Although communist networks in Phnom Penh and in other towns under Tou Samouth's jurisdiction fared better, only a few hundred communists remained active in the country by 1960.

1959 – Kirkuk. Kurds and the People's Resistance Force kill ethnic Turkomen in Kirkuk. During the celebration of the first anniversary of the Republic twenty-five Turcoman citizens were brutally killed and many Turkmens' houses and shops were looted and destroyed. The Kurdish mayor buried the Turkmens, who were killed by communist Kurds, in a mass grave in the city. General Kasım accused the Communist Party and Kurdish political groups of the massacre. There are oil fields in the area and the fighting for control will still be going strong in 2010.

1959-1962 – Maldives. Prime Minister, Ibrahim Nasir, is challenged in 1959 by a local secessionist movement in the southern atolls that benefit economically from the British presence on Gan. This group breaks from the Maldives government and forms an independent state with Abdulla Afif Didi as President. In 1962 Nasir will send gunboats from Male with government police on board to eliminate elements opposed to his rule and Abdulla Afif Didi flees to the British colony of Seychelles, where he is granted political asylum.

1959-1960 – Paraguayan State of Siege. General Alfredo Stroessner tries to calm the unrest by allowing opposition exiles to return, freeing political prisoners, and ending press censorship. Two months later the political opposition was so great Stroessner dissolved the government and an upsurge in guerrilla violence followed. Stroessner's paranoid witch hunts of "communists" gave Paraguay the highest number of unsentenced prisoners in the western world. Most of them were tortured and disappeared. He will rule Paraguay for 35 years, until he is deposed by a military coup in February 1989.

1959 – Spain. The ETA is founded with the aim of creating an independent homeland in Spain's Basque region. **In 1937,** General Franco occupied Basque country and the Basques had enjoyed a degree of autonomy which they now were denied. The Franco regime ruthlessly repressed their aspirations for independence. Both sides will still be fighting and people will be dying in 2009.

March 1, 1959 – Tibet. Tibetan Uprising. An unusual invitation to attend a theatrical performance on March 9 at the Chinese military headquarters outside Lhasa is extended to the **Dalai Lama** which he postpones until March 10. When Chinese army officers visit the head of the Dalai Lama's body guard on March 10 and insist the Dalai Lama will attend unaccompanied by his traditional armed escort, and that no public ceremony for the Dalai Lama's procession from the palace to the camp should take place, his officers fear an abduction of the Dalai Lama by the Chinese. They spread word to the inhabitants of Lhasa and on March 10 close to 300,000 **Tibetans surrounded the palace** to prevent the Dalai Lama from leaving or being removed.

An estimated 86,000 Tibetans died in the uprising and the **Dalai Lama** fled on foot from the Tibetan capital, Lhasa, over the Himalayan Mountains. An estimated 40,000 Chinese soldiers died in Tibet from 1956-1959.

July 8, 1959 – Vietnam. Two Americans are killed and one wounded during a Viet Minh attack 20 miles north of Saigon.

1960

The Oldest Boomer is 14 years old.

Cost of the Average House: $12,500	
Median Family Income: $5,600	**Minimum Wage:** $1.00/ hr
Major Magazines: 35 cents	**Gallon Gasoline:** 31cents

New Car: Jaguar E Type: $5,990 **Ford Falcon:** $1,975
Ferrari 250 GT California Spyder: $13,600
1961 Ferrari 250 GT SWB California Spyder: formerly owned by
actor, James Coburn, sold for $10,894,400 (2008)

Unemployment Rate: 5.2%-6.1%-6.6%	**First-class Stamp:** 4 cents

14 cents buying power in 1960 = **$1.00 in 2008.**
In 1960 what cost our parents 14 cents to purchase
now costs us $1.00 in 2008.

Movies: "Psycho," "The Apartment," "The Alamo," "Elmer Gantry," "Sons and Lovers," "The Sundowners," "Exodus," "Spartacus," "Flaming Star," starring Elvis Presley.

Broadway: "Flower Drum Song," London. "The Fantasticks," off Broadway. "Camelot," "Unsinkable Molly Brown," "Bye, Bye, Birdie."

TV: The Kennedy-Nixon Debate. "The Andy Griffith Show," "Flintstones," "Checkmate," "Route 66," "Mr. Mago," "Surfside 6," "The Tall Man," "Tate," "National Velvet," "Shari Lewis Show," "Stagecoach West," "The Bugs Bunny Show," "My Three Sons."

Music: Bernard Herrmann, "Psycho." Elmer Bernstein, "The Magnificent Seven." Alex North, "Spartacus." Chubby Checkers', "The Twist," becomes a dance craze. John Coltrane leads jazz new wave. Ike & Tina Turner, "Fool In Love." Brook Benton & Dinah Washington, "Baby." Sam Cooke, "Chain

Gang." Hank Locklin, "Please Help Me, I'm Falling." Ray Price, "One More Time." Buck Owens, "Above And Beyond." Percy Faith, "Theme From A Summer Place." Jim Reeves, "He'll Have To Go." Everly Brothers, "Cathy's Clown." Johnny Preston, "Running Bear." Mark Dinning, "Teen Angel." Elvis Presley, "Are You Lonesome Tonight?" & "It's Now or Never." The Miracles, "Shop Around." Freddy Cannon, "Way Down Yonder In New Orleans." The Drifters, "Save the Last Dance for Me." Johnny Horton, "Sink the Bismarck." Joe Jones, "You Talk Too Much." Johnny Burnette, "You're Sixteen." Ray Peterson, "Tell Laura I Love Her." Larry Verne, "Please, Mr. Custer." Anita Bryant, "Paper Roses." Brian Hyland, "Itsy Bitsy Teenie Weenie Yellow Polka Dot Bikini." Roy Orbison, "Only The Lonely." Bobby Vee, "Rubber Ball."

President: Dwight D. Eisenhower (R) Presbyterian; vetoes 181/ 2 overrides

Vice President: Richard M. Nixon (R) Quaker

House: D-283 ; R-153

Senate: 86th Congress (1959-1961) Majority Party: Democrat (65 seats) Minority Party: Republican (35 seats) Other Parties: 0 Total Seats: 100

Federal Debt: $286.33 billion or 54 % of the GDP

Consumer Price Index CPI-U (1982 Base of 100): 29.60

GDP: $526.4 billion	**Inflation Rate:** 1.46%

Dow Jones: 675.50 (January)/ 585.24 (11-01)

Prime Rate: 4.50% (08-23)	**Average Home Mortgage Rate:** 6.30%
1 oz Gold: $36.50	**1oz of Silver:** $0.91

Average Monthly S.S. Benefits Paid: $81 / month

Federal Debt: $286,330,760,848.37

Federal Deficit: ($0.3 billion dollar surplus)

Defense Spending: $53.29 billion	**Interest Spending:** $7.66 billion

Health Care Spending: $1.45 billion	**Pensions Spending:** $11.69 billion
Welfare Spending: $3.01 billion	**Education Spending:** $1.64 billion
Transportation Spending: $4.45 billion	**Misc. Other Spending:** $9.63 billion
Protection Spending: $170 million	**Total Government Spending:** $97.28 billion

% of GDP that goes towards just the interest payment: 1.46%

$1.00 = 359.97 Yen, Japan

The **Saudi Arabian Riyal** is devaluated 16.7% in terms of gold, changing the Official Rate from SRls3.75 to SRls4.50 **per U.S. Dollar.** Paper Riyals replace "pilgrim" receipts and gold coins are no longer legal tender.

U.S. Population: 180,760,000	**World Population:** 3,039,332,401
U.S. Birth Rate: 4,257,850	**U.S. Abortions:** 292
U.S. Homicide Rate: 4.7/ 100,000 population	**U.S. Violent Crime:** 160.9/ 100,000 population

Annual Average Domestic Crude Oil Prices:
$2.91 / barrel $21.16 (2007 adjusted)

Oil:

1960 – OPEC. The Power Begins to Shift to the Middle East. OPEC, a federation of oil-producing nations, is formed. In August 1960 it was the last straw for the Middle Eastern countries, as the major Western oil companies lowered oil prices yet again. OPEC was formed with five founding members **Iran, Iraq, Kuwait, Saudi Arabia** and **Venezuela.** Two of the representatives at the initial meetings had studied the **Texas Railroad Commission's** methods of influencing price by lowering the amount of oil produced. By the end of 1971 six other nations had joined the group: **Qatar, Indonesia, Libya, United Arab Emirates, Algeria** and **Nigeria.**

1960

1960 – Oil depletion allowance. During the 1960 Presidential election **John F. Kennedy** gave his support for the oil depletion allowance which allowed oil companies to avoid taxes on their wealth. In October, 1960, he said that he appreciated "the value and importance of the oil-depletion allowance. I realize its purpose and value . . . The oil-depletion allowance has served us well."

The depletion allowance is intended as an incentive to stimulate investment in this high-risk industry, though critics argue that mineral deposits are valuable enough to justify high levels of investment without tax incentives. The federal government allows owners of oil wells to take a tax savings for selling their oil. Specifically, a firm could reduce its corporate income tax by an oil depletion allowance equal to roughly 27.5 percent of the value of the crude oil sold. Oil companies are actually paid by the taxpayer for selling their own reserves.

Major News:

May 1, 1960 – The U-2 incident. The Soviet Union produces the wreckage of a U.S. covert surveillance aircraft and the United States government denies the plane's purpose and mission. The U.S. denied involvement because the **U–2 spy plane** flies at such high altitudes they thought it was near impossible to be shot down. They were wrong. When the Soviet government produced the pilot, **Francis Gary Powers**, the U.S. was forced to admit the plane and pilot were theirs. The incident was a great embarrassment to the United States causing the Big Four summit in Paris to fail even before it started. President Eisenhower, Soviet leader Nikita Khrushchev, General de Gaulle and Harold Macmillan, never got beyond preliminary procedural meetings.

May 11, 1960 – Israeli Capture of Adolf Eichmann. Karl Adolf Eichmann was the head of the **German Gestapo Department of Jewish Affairs** from 1941 to 1945 and during World War II Eichmann oversaw the deportation of European Jews to ghettos. In 1942, he organized the Wannsee Conference, a meeting of **Nazi officials** to devise the **"Final Solution,"** the Nazi euphemism for the **extermination** of European Jews. Eichmann is often referred to as "the architect of the Holocaust." He supervised the creation and operation of **death camps**, and set Nazi policy on the seizure of Jewish property. In 1944 he was sent to Hungry and began deporting Jews, sending 430,000

Hungarians to their deaths in the gas chambers.

After WWII Eichmann was captured and held by the American Army who did not know his true identity. He escaped in 1946 and lived in Germany, Italy and then fled to Argentina in July 1950. It was later reveled the CIA received at least one report from the German BND agency which stated that Eichmann was reported to have lived in Argentina since 1952 using the alias "Clemens", but the CIA took no action on this information. The U.S. government did not have a policy of seeking out Nazi war criminals and bringing them to trial.

After Eichmann arrived in Argentina he sent for his family and his son Klaus began dating an Argentinean girl. Klaus had no idea the girl was Jewish and made many anti-Semitic remarks and boasted of his father's deeds during the war. This coupled with the fact he used his real last name from time to time made the girl's father suspicious enough to contact his friend, Fritz Bauer, in Germany. Bauer had been imprisoned by the Nazis twice during the war and now spent his time hunting and capturing Nazi war criminals. Bauer checked the information, notified Israeli authorities and worked with them for several years as they made a positive ID and formulated a plan to capture Eichmann and smuggle him out of the country to stand trial.

Eichmann was captured by a team of **Mossad and Shabak agents** in a suburb of **Buenos Aires** on May 11, 1960. He was drugged, disguised, placed in a wheelchair, and smuggled out of the country on a commercial airline. Eichmann landed safely in Israel on May 22, 1960 and stood trial for war crimes and crimes against humanity in Israel from April 2 to August 14, 1961. He was convicted and sentenced to death. Eichmann was executed on May 31, 1962.

October 24, 1960 – The Nedelin disaster. During the development of the Soviet R-16 ICBM, a prototype of the missile was being prepared for a test flight. A switch was turned on unintentionally igniting the rocket's second stage motors and it exploded on the launch pad, killing over 100 Soviet missile technicians and officials. In his memoirs, Sergei Khrushchev quotes a witness in the command bunker who reportedly overheard someone ask: "So should I move PTR to zero?" and someone else reply: "Go ahead." While moving towards the "zero" position, the PTR switch activated an electrically-driven pneumatic valve controlling the ignition of the engine on the second stage of the rocket.

1960

Thirty minutes prior to the scheduled launch, an estimated 250 people were still around the rocket when the second stage engine ignited. In seconds the roaring flame cut through the fuel tank of the first stage causing a huge explosion. A four hundred foot diameter fireball spread out from the launch pad instantly incinerating most people while more deaths took place over the next few seconds as people were burned alive. Eyewitnesses described the scene of **burning people running from the rocket** as horrifying.

November 8, 1960 – The Presidential race to succeed President Dwight D. Eisenhower is won by Senator **John F. Kennedy**, the Democratic candidate from Massachusetts, over incumbent Vice President **Richard M. Nixon**. With almost 63 % of the voters casting ballots, Kennedy was a narrow victor in the popular vote, by slightly more than 120,000 votes, but won a more substantial victory in the Electoral College, 303 to 219. The 1960 campaign for President had the first televised debate on September 26 in one of the closest elections in history. Those that saw the debate on TV thought Kennedy had won the debate, while those that heard the debate on radio were certain Nixon had won.

December 15, 1960 – Laos. Today in the *New York Times*, a summary of U.S. policy towards Laos: "...the State Department made it clear this week that the United States would not hesitate to give Laos every possible assistance in case of aggression from outside. It plans to go ahead with its long-standing program of economic and military aid to the Government of Laos. The stakes in Laos are high indeed. Its location at the heart of Southeast Asia makes **the small and backward land** of utmost strategic importance. Its loss to the Communists would open up long borders of friendly powers such as Thailand and South Vietnam to infiltration by the Communists. It is also felt here in Washington that the loss of Laos to the Communists would prove an irreparable blow to United States and Western prestige (pride) throughout Asia." The Souvanna Phouma government is recognized by the communist bloc; Prince Boun Oum's Vientiane government is recognized by the West; heavy fighting breaks out and North Vietnamese troops are involved.

December 16, 1960 – **The midair collisio**n between a United Airlines DC-8 and a TWA Super-Constellation **over New York City kills all 128** on both planes and 6 persons on the ground.

Civil Rights Movement:

February 1, 1960 – Sit-ins begin when four students from **North Carolina Agricultural and Technical College** in Greensboro, North Carolina, refused to move from a **Woolworth lunch counter** when denied service. By September 1961 over **70,000 white and black** students had participated in sit-ins across the nation.

February 2, 1960 – The home of one of the first black students to enter Little Rock High School is bombed. A crude bomb rips a hole in the side of the home of Carlotta Walls.

1960 – Durham, North Carolina. Blacks demonstrate against standup service only at lunch counters.

1960 – North Carolina. Whites join Negro students in sit-ins at Winston Salem Woolworth store.

1960 – Chattanooga, Tennessee. Rioting hits lunch counter sit-ins and seven whites are arrested.

1960 – Nashville, Tennessee. Police arrest 100 Negro and white students after fights break out in two stores where the Negroes are conducting lunch-counter sit-ins.

1960 – Fifty are arrested by Nashville police after refusing to leave lunch counters of the **Greyhound** and **Trailways** bus stations in the face of bomb threats.

March 1, 1960 – Black students at **Tuskogee Institute** begin a full scale boycott of local white merchants to protest a 1957 Alabama State law that redrew Tuskagee city boundaries to exclude nearly all Negroes as residents and voters.

1960

April 19, 1960 – Z. Alexander Looby is a Nashville Tennessee black city councilmen and **NAACP lawyer. He has a** Bachelor of Law degree from Columbia University, and a Doctor of Juristic Science from New York University. His home is destroyed by a bomb after he represented 153 students arrested for lunch counter sit-ins. Twenty-five hundred students and community members in Nashville, Tennessee, stage a march on city hall, the first major demonstration of the civil rights movement, following the bombing.

April 15, 1960 – **One hundred and fifty black and white students** gather at Shaw University in Raleigh, North Carolina to form the Student Nonviolent Coordinating Committee.

April 21, 1960 – Congress approves a strong **voting rights act.** The Civil Rights Act of 1960 is signed into law by **President Dwight D. Eisenhower** on May 6. The Act establishes federal inspection of local voter registration rolls and introduces penalties for anyone who obstructs a citizen's attempt to register to vote or to cast a ballot.

1960 – **Biloxi, Mississippi,** experiences the worst race riots to date. Between 40 and 50 blacks **attempted to swim in the Gulf of Mexico.** The entire 26 mile beach was for **whites only.** A group of whites attacked the blacks with sticks, chains and blackjacks wounding 4, before being dispersed by the police. Later that night 2 white men and 8 black men suffered gunshot wounds. Biloxi blacks began boycotting stores that were anti-black and on May 17, the Justice Department filed suit in Unites States District Court to force Biloxi, Mississippi and Harrison County to open a beach on the Gulf of Mexico that blacks could use.

May 7, 1960 – **Houston, Texas. Felton Turner** is found hanging upside down from a tree, with **"KKK"** carved in his chest.

After a sit-in demonstration against segregation at Weingarten's store by students from **Texas Southern University,** Turner was abducted at gunpoint as he was walking home. Turner, was not involved in the student's actions, but just happened to be "available." Abducted at gunpoint and transported to a deserted area five blocks away his captors carved KKK into his chest with a knife. Following the departure of his kidnappers Turner was able to free himself and quickly called police. On March 15, 18-year-old Ronald Gene Erickson was arrested for the crime following a routine traffic stop.

The attack helped gain support for the students' actions and expanded the sit-ins to the downtown's Walgreen's stores. Over the next three years, virtually all businesses in downtown Houston will be desegregated.

June 1960 – Trailways and several southern department store chains desegregate their lunch counters.

1960 – United States District Judge Davidson orders Dallas, Texas schools to integrate.

July 2, 1960 – Miami Beach. The First U.S. Negro competes in the Miss Universe contest, representing Ohio.

August 8, 1960 – A Negro family swims at an all-white beach in Miami, Florida.

August 18, 1960 – Negroes attempting "kneel-ins" in **white churches** in **New Orleans** are turned away at two, and preached against in one.

September 11, 1960 – Negroes attend an all-white church in New Orleans. Negroes accompanied by whites attend services at 6 or 7 white churches.

September 14, 1960 – U.S. Federal marshals escorted four Negro girls into two desegregated white schools in New Orleans.

September 16, 1960 – New Orleans. Two thousand people riot in the streets **against integration.** (*Integration* not segregation)

November 14, 1960 – The nation watched as **six-year-old Ruby Nell Bridges** walked into William Frantz Elementary School and into history. **First grader Ruby Bridges, six years old,** is the first African American to attend William Frantz Elementary School in New Orleans. **She becomes a class of one** as parents remove all Caucasian students from the school and all but one teacher refused to teach a black child.

1960

Ruby Bridges Hall, born Ruby Nell Bridges September 8, 1954, in Tylertown, Mississippi, moved with her parents to New Orleans, Louisiana at the age of 4. In 1960, when she was 6 years old, her parents responded to a call from the (NAACP) and volunteered her to participate in the integration of the New Orleans School system. She is known as the first African-American child to attend William Frantz Elementary School and the first African-American child to attend an all-white school in the South.

Ruby Bridges Hall: That first morning I remember mom saying as I got dressed in my new outfit, "Now, I want you to behave yourself today, Ruby, and don't be afraid. There might be a lot of people outside this new school, but I'll be with you." That conversation was the full extent of preparing me for what was to come. I didn't give much thought to the events of my childhood until my youngest brother died in 1993. For a time, I looked after his daughters. They happened to be students at William Frantz, and when I took them there every morning, I was literally walking into my past, into the same school that I'd help integrate years earlier.

1960 – Civil rights groups launch voter registration drives in the South.

1960 – Alabama. Gomillion vs. Lightfoot. **The Court outlaws "gerrymandering,"** which is dividing a geographic area into voting districts so as to give unfair advantage to one party in elections. The city of Tuskegee, using a 28 sided figure, excluded all but a handful of potential African-American votes.

1960 – The Civil Rights Movement attracted both black and white students to the South in the 1960s from all over the country to work on voter registration and other issues. The intervention of people from outside the communities and threat of social change aroused fear and resentment among many whites.

August 27, 1960 – Jacksonville, Florida. On "Ax Handle Saturday." A group of white men that includes some members of the Ku Klux Klan are armed with ax handles and baseball bats when they attack civil rights protesters staging sit-ins at downtown restaurants. As the violence spread the whites begin attacking any black within sight. The youth council at Laura Street Presbyterian Church began leaving in groups of twos and threes that morning to join in the protests at W.T. Grant on Main Street and the Woolworth's on Hogan Street. When they sat down at the W.T. Grant lunch counter "Closed" signs were placed on the counter, the overhead lights went off and the salt and pepper were taken away. They sat for about ten minutes to intentionally disrupt the day's lunch business and then left the store. As the students exited a group of white men swooped down on them and they ran.

At Woolworth's a few blocks away the lunch counter was also closed. As the students were leaving the attackers came into the store swinging ax handles. The Boomerangs, a local black gang, joined in and tried to help the students get free from the mob of about 200 people.

"We were out there trying to save a community," said Perry Raines, a Boomerang member. "Everybody had to run; if you didn't, you wouldn't live." Students sought the white Memorial Church at Monroe and Laura streets, less than a block away, as a safe haven, but it seemed like a mile. They couldn't go the shortest distance through Hemming Park (now Hemming Plaza) because that's where people were being beaten.

Most simply did not believe that adults would attack teens with baseball bats and ax handles. Some of the protesters were as young as 13.

The police made no attempt to stop the violence until the blacks, with the help of the Boomerangs, started holding their own. Then they jumped into the violence. Within weeks after the clash, white and black committees started meeting to discuss how to integrate the city's private and public establishments.

1960 – A filibuster record of 82 hours, 3 minutes is set as sessions regarding the **Civil Rights Act** end.

December 5, 1960 – The U.S. Supreme Court rules 7 to 2 that racial discrimination in bus terminal restaurants serving passengers who cross state lines is a violation of the Interstate Commerce Act.

Women's Movement:

1960 – The Birth control pill is OK'd by the FDA. In the early 1960s, the Pill became available, at first **for married women only**, but demand and changes in attitudes later led to it becoming available to unmarried women as well.

1960

1960 – Oveta Culp Hobby becomes the first woman to serve as Secretary of Health, Education, and Welfare. She is also the first director of the Women's Army Auxiliary Corps (WAAC), and the first woman to receive the U.S. Army Distinguished Service Medal.

1960 – Jacqueline Cochran breaks the sound barrier by flying an F-86 over Roger's Dry Lake, California, at the speed of 652.337 miles per hour. Eleven years later, she flies at a speed of 1,429.2 miles per hour, more than twice the speed of sound.

1960 – *Playboy* **Magazine.** The 1960s were Playboy's golden age. **Playboy Enterprises'** "private key" clubs, staffed by **"bunny"** waitresses in skintight costumes complete with ears and tails, opened in major American cities and abroad. The company built hotel resorts and soon added not only modeling agencies but film, book, and record companies to the empire.

Popular Culture:

1960 – Nikita Khrushchev pounds his shoe at a UN General Assembly session.

1960 – Mattel's Chatty Cathy doll speaks 11 phrases in random order.
So does Nikita.

1960 – San Diego. The El Cajon Boulevard Riot is the official name of what the San Diego Union called the Drag Strip Riot. Socialists consider the El Cajon Boulevard Riot one of the first major youth riots of the 1960s.

1960 – Sex. During the 1960s and 1970s, shifts in regards to how society views sexuality begin to take place, moving some away from old moral codes, and developing new codes of sexual behavior which are now integrated into the mainstream. The 1960s and 1970s proclaim a new culture of **"free love"** with millions of young people embracing the **hippie** ethos and preaching the power of love and the beauty of sex as a natural part of ordinary life. Hippies believe that sex is a natural biological phenomenon which should not be denied or repressed. Beginning in San

Francisco in the mid 1960s, a new culture of **"free love"** emerges, with thousands of young people becoming hippies who preach the power of love and the beauty of sex as part of ordinary student life. This behavior is closer to the norm by 1980.

1960 – TV. 90% of American homes now have television sets.

1960 – Sexual liberalization changed values. Sexual experimentation is encouraged with the pill and contraception. Open sex within and outside of marriage is claimed as a basic right that should be celebrated. Public nudity, gay Liberation, liberalization of abortion, interracial marriage, a return to birth control and natural childbirth, women's rights and feminism all move into the mainstream. Some affect the culture in a more positive way and some are found later to definitely have a negative impact.

   The perception that all hippies are excessively promiscuous and the sexual revolution is an uncontrolled orgy of group sex is a myth without basis. Many of the era's countercultural people are celibate due to personal preferences. All of this change came at the expense of morality rooted in the Christian tradition. The oldest Boomer is fourteen, and quick to agree that a self indulgent lifestyle sounds pretty groovy.

1960 – Taking a food order by telephone, **Domino's delivers a pizza.**

February 29, 1960 – A Playboy Bunny is a waitress at the Playboy Club. The first club opening at 116 E. Walton in downtown Chicago, Illinois, is a bar with entertainment, featuring Playboy Bunnies serving drinks to keyholders, and performances by some big names in entertainment.

1960 – Fascination with all things French makes the poodle America's favorite dog.

1960 – Sea-Monkeys, Brine shrimp. By the mid-1960s, in addition to the standard packet of Sea Monkey "eggs" and plastic tank, optional extras included Sea Monkey Ocean Zoos of every size, a cardboard Sea Monkey Circus, complete with audience and ticket booth, and the Deluxe Sea Monkey Speedway.

1960 – SDS is formed. Students for a Democratic Society (SDS) is formed, as the youth group of the social-democratic League for Industrial Democracy. It grows out of the rejection of the hypocrisy and ineffectual conservatism of the Cold War period, **the constant threat of nuclear war** and the growing movement against blatantly immoral segregation in the South. SDS is a one of the main student activist movements in the United States that represents the New Left. They denounce anti-communism as being a social problem and an obstruction to democracy. They criticize the United States for its exaggerated paranoia and exclusive condemnation of the **Soviet Union.** By the end of the 1963 academic year, there were over 200 delegates at the annual convention at Pine Hill, New York, from 32 different colleges and universities. At this same time student unrest is responsible for overthrowing some foreign governments.

1960 – Etch A sketch. The Ohio Art Company launched "Etch A Sketch." in the United States, for the 1960 holiday season, with a televised advertising campaign. Etch A Sketch was manufactured in Bryan, Ohio until the company moved the manufacturing plant to Shenzhen, China in 2001.

1960 – Animated cartoon, "The Flinstones," comes to prime time and stays there until 1987.

September 26, 1960 – Vice President Richard Nixon and **Senator John F. Kennedy** face each other in the first of a series of televised **debates.** Kennedy defeated Nixon to win the presidency on November 8. Those that heard the debates on radio thought Nixon had won while those that had seen the debates on TV thought that Kennedy had won. Politics changed forever as the power of TV is exploited.

1960 – Smell-O-Vision comes to the movies but the public stays upwind.

1960 – Off-Broadway, "The Fantasticks" begins a 42-year-run.

1960 – The census includes a United States population of 179,323,175, an 18.5% increase since 1950. For the first time, two states, **New York** and **California** have over fifteen million people within their borders. The geographic population center of the United States is located six and one half miles northwest of Centralia, Illinois.

Business / Technology:

April 1, 1960 – "TIROS I," the first weather satellite, is launched from Cape Canaveral, now Cape Kennedy, Florida on a three-stage Thor-Able rocket system. It opens a new era for weather science and humanity's appreciation for the beauty of the global Earth.

May 13, 1960 – Echo I, a U.S. balloon in orbit, reflects radio signals back to Earth. The **Echo satellites** are NASA's first passive communications satellite experiment. Each spacecraft was designed as a metalized balloon satellite acting as a passive reflector of microwave signals. Communication signals were bounced off of it from one point on Earth to another.

May 16, 1960 – Theodore Harold Maiman using a synthetic **ruby crystal** grown by Dr. Ralph L. Hutcheson, builds the first true laser at Hughes Research Laboratories in Malibu, California. He will be nominated twice for a Nobel Prize due to his work on the laser as this discovery paves the way for multiple innovations, including high-quality printing, new forms of surgery, fiber-optic communications, bar-code scanners, CDs, DVD's, and Blu-ray.

1960 – AT&T installs the first electronic switching system**.**

1960 – FAX. The Post Office experiments with facsimile mail.

1960 – A hologram is constructed.

1960 – Digital Equipment Corporation's first computer, the PDP-1, with 18 bit integers, sold for only **$120,000** at a time when other computers sold for over $1,000,000. Only 50 units were manufactured. The company employed more than 120,000 people worldwide at its peak in 1990 and earned more than $14 billion in revenue. By 1997 Digital had subsidiary companies in more than two dozen countries. DEC was bought by Compaq Computer Corporation in 1998.

1960 – Techs at MIT, write the first **computerized video game, "SpaceWar"**, for the PDP-1 computer.

1960

Finance:

1960 – Bernard L. Madoff, founder of Bernard L. Madoff Investment Securities, starts his firm with $5,000 of savings. He will take advantage of securities-law changes in the 1970s, designed to spur competition in U.S. stock markets, to build a 50 billion dollar Ponzi scheme that steals from both the rich and the poor.

1960 – The International Brotherhood of Teamsters Pension Fund managers, loan money from the fund to organized crime, usually through an intermediary, for casinos, hotels, and resorts in **Las Vegas**, Nevada. The recipients of the fund "proceeds" included such noteworthy establishments as **Rancho La Costa, Circus Circus, Caesar's Palace,** the **Dunes,** and the **Sands.**

1960 – For the first eighteen years after WW II, President Truman (1945-1953), **President Eisenhower** (1953-1961) **and President Kennedy** (1961-1963) all worked vigorously to **keep spending under control.** Of the seven years Truman was in office, the national debt came down in four. In 1946 & 1947, with a Republican Congress for his first two years in office he brought down spending. The following year, with a Democratic Congress he reduced what was commonly called the "War Debt" again. Two of the eight years Eisenhower served as President saw debt reduction during the years when Democrats were in charge of Congress, 1956 & 1957.

Books:

1960 – John Updike. **"Rabbit, Run."**

1960 – **Henry Miller** completes his trilogy, **"Sexus, Plexus, and Nexus."**

1960 – **To Kill a Mockingbird,"** Harper Lee.

1960 – George Selden, **"The Cricket in Times Square."**

1960 – **"The Rise and Fall of the Third Reich**," William L. Shirer.

TV:

1960 – The Gillette Razor Company announces that NBC decides to drop **Friday night boxing** due to sensitivity over criminal allegations in the sport.

1960 – The largest television audience ever, 75 million Americans, watch the first of four debates between presidential candidates **John F. Kennedy** and **Richard M. Nixon.**

February 1960 – Jack Paar walked off the original "**Tonight Show**" when his monologue was cut due to a news update. It was still live TV and he said, "There's got to be a better way to make a living," announced that he was quitting and walked off the stage. He returned a month later with, "As I was saying before I was interrupted..."

November 24, 1960 – "Harvest of Shame," arguably U.S. television news' finest documentary. **Harvest of Shame** is a television documentary focusing on the plight of **American migrant workers by Edward R. Murrow** and shown on CBS. Fred W. Friendly, who co-produced another of Morrows' TV shows, is the executive producer.

Fred Friendly got the idea for the show after a colleague's assistant visited Senator Harry Byrd's Northern Virginia farm and was outraged by the conditions of the migrant laborers. It seemed perfect for Murrow, who had an image of being a champion of the oppressed. The show opened and closed with voice-over footage of migrant workers.

This scene is not taking place in the Congo. It has nothing to do with Johannesburg or Cape Town. It is not Nyasaland or Nigeria. This is Florida. These are citizens of the United States, 1960. This is a shape-up for migrant workers. The hawkers are chanting the going piece rate at the various fields. This is the way the humans who harvest the food for the best-fed people in the world get hired. One farmer looked at this and said, **"We used to own our slaves; now we just rent them."**

Murrow's closing words: The migrants have no lobby. Only an enlightened, aroused and perhaps angered public opinion can do anything about the migrants. The people you have seen have the strength to harvest your fruit and vegetables. They do not have the strength to influence legislation. Maybe we do. Good night and good luck.

1960

Sports:

1960 – Track star **Wilma Rudolph** of Tennessee State University is the first woman to win **three gold medals** at the Olympic Games which are held at the Summer Olympics in Rome.

1960 – **Wilt Chamberlain,** after being drafted by the **Philadelphia Warriors** in 1959, dominates the league right away winning the Rookie of the Year, and NBA MVP, while leading the league in scoring (37.6) and rebounds (27.0).

1960 – **Summer Olympics. Cassius Clay / Muhammad Ali** wins a gold medal in the light heavyweight division at the Summer Olympics in Rome.

Music:

1960 – **Big Band Music** is popular up until the sixties then **rock n roll** fueled by the **Boomers** and their money starts the shift.

January 20, 1960 – **Elvis Presley,** age 25, is promoted to Sergeant E-5 at Tank Range 42, in Grafenwoehr, Germany. His total time on active Army duty is 2 years, from 3/24/1958-3/5/1960. **Elvis Presley** accomplished a singing career that lasted from 1954 to 1977, during which he charted more hits, spent more weeks at the top of the chart, and scored more consecutive #1 hits than any other artist in the history of popular music.

February 8, 1960 – A New York Grand Jury begins looking into **disc jockey "payola,"** in the recording industry with disc jockeys from Boston and Cleveland testifying. **Dick Clark** is accused of taking money for showing bands on **"American Bandstand"** and denies the charges of Payola. On May 19, 1960 eight men are charged with receiving $116,580 in illegal gratuities. This probe leads to Alan Freed, the deejay who coined the term **"rock-n-roll,"** being charged with income tax evasion by the IRS. Freed is the only deejay subpoenaed by the House Oversight Committee and refuses to testify despite being given immunity. His trial begins in December of 1962 and ends with Freed pleading guilty to 29 counts of commercial bribery. Though he only receives a $300 fine and 6 months suspended sentence his career is over.

1960 – "Billboard" reports the findings of a **"Seventeen" magazine** survey: the average teen girl listens to the radio two hours and 13 minutes a day and plays records two hours and 12 minutes a day.

August 5, 1960 – Chubby Checker debuts **"The Twist"** on **'The Dick Clark Saturday Night Beechnut Show."** On September 19, "The Twist," tops the charts at #1.

1960 – Aretha Franklin joins the Blues Circuit singing gospel.

January 1960 – The Quarry Men, now reduced to **John Lennon, Paul McCartney,** and **George Harrison,** after failing fortunes in 1959, are joined by **Stuart Sutcliff** on bass. They have no work and few prospects. In May, Allen Williams becomes their agent and part-time manager, they recruit drummer Tommy Moore and change their name to the **"Silver Beetles."** The following month Tommy Moore quits the group and drummer **Norman Chapman** joins and then leaves the band. In August, **Pete Best** takes over on drums and they change their name to the **"Beetles"** while playing at the **Indra Club in Hamburg, West Germany.**

Before the year ends they are banned from the Indra club for playing too loud, George Harrison is deported from West Germany for being underage (17) and McCartney and Best are jailed for arson and are also deported. They pinned a condom to the wall and lit it on fire. In December McCartney takes over on base.

Natural Disasters:

February 29, 1960 – Agadir, Morocco. 10,000 to 12,000 people are killed as the earthquake sets off a tidal wave and fire, destroying most of city.

April 22-26, 1960 – Philippines. "Typhoon Karen", a Category 1 typhoon with an intensity of 85 mph strikes. Moving westward from the Philippine Sea a tropical depression forms and moves northwestward through the Philippines, strengthening quickly to a typhoon on the 24th due to its small size. When Karen turns to the northeast it rapidly weakens and ends on the 26th. Typhoon Karen left 56 people dead, 7,000 people homeless, and caused $2 million dollars crop and property damage.

May 22, 1960 – Chile. The strongest earthquake ever recorded at a 9.5 magnitude strikes near the coast, causing a **tsunami** that travels as far as **Hawaii, Japan,** and **New Zealand,** killing 4,000–5,000 people.

May 25-June 1, 1960 – Philippines. "Tropical Storm Lucille." On May 25, a tropical depression forms to the east of the Philippines, developing simultaneously with another low pressure system to the west. The depression moves to the northwest over the Philippines, and turns merging the two storms. The new system strengthened into **Tropical Storm Lucille** with winds of 50 mph and quickly moves northeast. Lucille causes flash flooding in Manila that kills nearly 300 people.

June 9, 1960 – Fukien province, China "Typhoon Mary." "Bloody Mary." The typhoon is the worst to hit Hong Kong in 23 years with 14 inches of rain, mudslides and strong winds causing damage across Hong Kong and southern China. Over 100 people are killed and 18,000 people are left homeless. The only positive aspect of the storm was its rainfall, which helped end a severe drought, but brought flooding to Taiwan, especially in the capital city of Taipei. Landslides trigged by the remnants of the storm kill 1,600 people.

July 29, 1960 – Typhoon Shirley, a Category 4 super typhoon with 155 mph winds strikes on July 29. A tropical depression forms to the east of northern Luzon and moves to the northwest where it rapidly builds to a 155 mph super typhoon with an eyewall only 7 miles wide. Shirley strikes northeastern Taiwan on July 31. The mountainous terrain rips apart the typhoon's circulation, and after crossing the Formosa Strait it makes landfall in southeastern China as a tropical storm.

Shirley's high winds and torrential rains devastated Taiwan, overflowing many rivers and trapping thousands. Nearly a foot of rain was reported on the island, causing extensive road and property damage. Little crop damage occurred due to

Typhoon Mary having destroyed most of the crops in June. Typhoon Shirley killed 104 people, destroyed or damaged 9,890 houses, and left 50,194 people homeless.

August 29-September 13, 1960 – From Florida to New England. **"Hurricane Donna"** kills 50 in the U.S. and kills 115 in the Antilles. Hurricane Donna holds the record for retaining major hurricane status Category 3 or greater. For nine days, September 2-11, Donna consistently had maximum sustained winds of at least 115 mph.

October 10, 1960 – East Pakistan. A cyclone and tidal wave kill about 6,000 people in East Bengal State (Bangladesh). The disaster has a large effect on the economy because from 1948-1960 East Pakistan produced 70% of all of Pakistan's exports while it received 25% of import earnings.

December 24,-January 2, 1960 – Philippines. "Typhoon Harriet," a Category 4 super typhoon with an intensity of 150 mph. Typhoon Harriet hits the eastern Philippines and weakens as it crosses the islands, dissipating over the South China Sea on January 2. Harriet brought strong winds and rainfall to Luzon, causing considerable property and crop damage. Typhoon Harriet killed 5 people and leaves more than 12,000 people homeless.

Man vs. Man / Wars:

May 11, 1960 – Adolf Eichmann is captured in Argentina by Mossad, Israeli secret service, and tried in an Israeli court on 15 criminal charges, including crimes against humanity and war crimes. He is found guilty and hanged at Ramleh on May 31, 1962.

Assassinated – Japan. Inejiro Asanuma, Japanese politician, and head of the Japanese Socialist Party. He is chiefly famous for the manner of his death. He is assassinated by 17-year old Otoya Yamaguchi, a sword-wielding right-wing extremist, while making a speech, at a televised rally. Although the stabbing was not shown live by NHK network, the videotape of the killing caused a sensation when it was broadcast.

1960

Attempted Assassination – Venezuelan Dictator Rafael Leonidas Trujillo frequently interfered in the affairs of neighboring countries while he ruled the Dominican Republic. When men who had **attempted to assassinate Venezuelan President Rómulo Betancourt** early in 1960 admitted that they had been sent by Trujillo, a special conference of the Organization of American States proclaimed a partial economic boycott of the Dominican Republic.

Attempted Assassination – U.S. Richard Paul Pavlick, a 73-year-old postal worker from New Hampshire, stalked and then attempted to assassinate U.S. **President John F. Kennedy** on Sunday December 11in Palm Beach, Florida. Pavlick's plan was to serve as a suicide bomber by crashing his dynamite-laden 1950 Buick into Kennedy's vehicle, but the plan was disrupted when Pavlick saw Kennedy's wife and daughter bidding him goodbye. That attack of conscience foiled the opportunity. Pavlick's arrest by the Secret Service came three days later after he was stopped for a driving violation, with the dynamite still in his car. Pavlick spent the next six years in both federal prison and mental institutions before being released in December 1966.

June 1960 – Albania. Soviet Plot. Nikita Khrushchev attempts to secure condemnation of Beijing at the **Romanian Workers' Party** congress. **Albania's delegation** is the only European delegation to support the Chinese and the Soviet Union immediately retaliates by organizing a campaign to oust the Albanian government by force. Moscow cut promised grain deliveries to Albania during a drought, but because the Albanian government leaders had such tight control of the party machinery, army, and secret police, the Albanian leaders easily parried the threat. Five pro-Soviet Albanian leaders were eventually tried and executed.

1960 – Algeria. French Army Revolt. Convinced Charles de Gaulle had betrayed them, some units of **European volunteers in Algiers led by student leaders** stage an insurrection in the Algerian capital. As the army, police and supporters standby, civilians threw up barricades in the streets and seize government buildings. General Maurice Challe, declared Algiers under siege, but prevented the troops from firing on the students. Twenty rioters were killed and eight arrest warrants were issued in Paris against the initiators of the insurrection.

1960-1963 – Cameroon Rebellion. Cameroon gained independence on January 1, 1960 as the Republic of Cameroon and there is a rebellion against the newly independent government by the Cameroon People's Union, a pro-Communist group. French forces aid the government in defeating the rebels.

1960 – Central African Republic gained its independence on August 13.

1960 – Chad gained its independence on August 11.

August 15, 1960 – Congo. Army Coup. The Belgian Congo achieves independence. Congolese Prime Minister Patrice **Lumumba,** establishes a Soviet-backed secessionist government by military coup.

1960 – Dahomey gained its independence on August 1.

1960-1964 – Ethiopia-Somalia. Border Clashes. Somali people in the **Horn of Africa** are divided among different territories that were arbitrarily partitioned by the **former colonial powers.** Besides Somalia proper, other historically and almost exclusively Somali-inhabited areas of the Horn of Africa now find themselves governed by neighboring countries, such as the Somali Region in Ethiopia and the North Eastern Province in Kenya. The Somali people seem to want all ethnic Somalis under one Nation and one flag. Most "average" Somalis more than likely just want to be left alone to eat, sleep, raise their families, and develop opportunities. However cross border raids by Somali insurgents and violent crackdowns by Ethiopian troops from 1960 to 1964, erupt into war between Ethiopia and Somalia. When it is over Ethiopia and Kenya sign a mutual defense pact to protect their newly acquired territories from the Somali separatists.

1960 – Gabon gained its independence on August 17.

November 13, 1960 – Guatemalan Army Revolt. Guatemalan President General Miguel Ydigoras Fuentes is supported by the **United States** because he allows **Guatemala** to be used as a base for the attempted invasion of **Cuba.** When a revolt breaks out in some army units on November 13, the United States provides B-26 bombers, with exiled Cuban pilots, to bomb the rebel bases. The revolt is crushed, but two young lieutenants, Marco Aurelio Yon Sosa and Luis Turcios Lima, are so disgusted by the episode that they start a guerrilla movement of their own. It is the beginning of a long war.

1960 – Ivory Coast gained its independence on August 7.

August 9, 1960 – Laotian Kong Le Military Coup. The Laos government is really controlled by about 20 powerful Lao families and the King is nothing more than a figurehead doing as he is told.

The Second Paratroop Battalion of the Royal Lao Army, led by Captain Kong Le, takes over the government in a bloodless coup d'état, which by chance took place when the entire cabinet was meeting with the King. Captain Kong Le says he will stop the widespread corruption and end the Loa civil war. He hopes to stop the American aid to Laos because the influx of money allows opportunities for corruption.

General Phoumi Nosavan is unwilling to accept the new government and decides to stage his own coup. On September 10, General Phoumi sets up a revolutionary Committee which is a second government in southern Laos. The U.S. suspends all aid and takes a wait–and–see attitude until the Kong Le government establishes diplomatic relations with the Soviet Union and the Pathet Lao. Then the **CIA orders Air America** to deliver supplies to General Phoumi's forces in the south.

China views the collapse of the Kong Le government as unacceptable to Chinese communist influence in the area and offers support. The Soviet Union also supplies Kong Le who then supplies the Pathet Lao and for the first time, the Pathet Lao are equipped with heavy weapons allowing them to play a major role in their military alliance with Kong Le's troops. Kong Le will also request four battalions of North Vietnamese troops on January 7, 1961.

1960 – Malagasy Republic gained its independence on June 26.

1960-1986 – Mali-Burkina Faso, formerly Upper Volta, Border Disputes. There are several instances of armed clashes from 1960-1986, the most serious being a four-day battle in December 1985. The World Court will end up mediating and dividing the 100 mile-long, 12-mile wide Agacher Strip.

1960 – Mali Federation gained its independence on June 20, 1960 and dissolved on August 20, 1960 into Senegal and the Sudanese Republic.

October 26, 1960 – Salvadoran Military Coup. José María Lemus President of **El Salvador** becomes increasingly harsh and dictatorial after an attempt is made to assassinate him. He is finally deposed in October 1960 by a leftist group and deported. A second coup, in January 1961, brings Lieut. Col. Julio Adalberto Rivera to power.

1960 – Mauritania gained its independence on November 28.

1960-1964 – Somalia. Greater Somalia Movement. British Somaliland gained its independence on June 26, 1960 as the State of Somaliland and was joined by the Trust Territory of Somalia (Italian Somalia) on July 1, 1960 becoming the Somali Republic.

1960 – Niger gained its independence on August 3.

1960 – Nigeria gained its independence on October 1.

1960 – Senegal became independent by withdrawing from the Mali Federation on August 20.

March 21, 1960 – South African Civil War. A large group of blacks in Sharpeville refused to carry their passes and the government declared a state of emergency. South African police opened fire on unarmed demonstrators killing 67 people, with more than 200 people wounded. The emergency lasted for 156 days. Wielding the Public Safety Act and the Criminal Law Amendment Act, the white regime had no intention of changing the laws of apartheid.

This is a major event in the development of the long South African guerrilla war. It moves the African National Congress away from nonviolence and into armed action, and South Africa isolates itself even more from the world community. The African National Congress, the principal anti apartheid organization, is banned and in 1964 its leader, Nelson Mandela, is sentenced to life imprisonment.

1960

1960 – **Togo** gained its independence on April 27.

1960 – **Upper Volta** gained its independence on August 5.

November 1960 – VietNam. John F. Kennedy is elected President. After taking office, **Vice President Lyndon Johnson travels to Vietnam** and affirms his support for Diem's increasingly autocratic government. Kennedy increases the number of American military advisors in Vietnam and forms the **Green Berets,** a Special Forces group trained to conduct counterinsurgency.

November 11, 1960 – South Vietnamese Military Revolt. A failed coup attempt against President Ngo Dinh Diem of South Vietnam is led by officers in the Army of the Republic of Vietnam (ARVN).

Diem, trapped inside the Independence Palace, stalls the coup by holding negotiations and promising reforms. He is really buying time until his forces enter Saigon and free him. When the Fifth and Seventh Divisions of the ARVN do enter Saigon they quickly defeat the rebels. More than 400 people are killed in the battle. Colonels Dong and Thi flee into Cambodia and Diem begins removing protesters from his government. Seven officers and two civilians are sentenced to death in absentia, while 14 officers and 34 civilians are jailed.

1961

The Oldest Boomer is 15 years old.

Median Family Income: $5,700	**Minimum Wage:** $1.15/ hr **Average Hourly Wage:** $2.32
Dozen Eggs: 30 cents	**Gallon Gasoline:** 31cents
New Car: Austin Mini Cooper: $1,950 **Triumph TR3 Roadster:** $2,699	
Unemployment Rate: 6.6%-7.1%-6.0%	**First-class Stamp:** 4 cents

14 cents buying power in 1961 **= $1.00 in 2008.**
In 1961 what cost our parents 14 cents to purchase
now costs us $1.00 in 2008.

Movies: "West Side Story," "Fanny," "The Guns of Navarone," "The Hustler," "Judgment at Nuremberg," "Breakfast at Tiffany's," "Splendor in the Grass," "101 Dalmatians," "Snow White and the Three Stooges." " El Cid."

Broadway: "The Gay Life." "How To Succeed in Business Without Really Trying." "Stop the World - I Want to Get Off," London. "Carnival!" "Milk and Honey." "Evening with Yves Montand." "Night of the Iguana."

TV: "The Dick Van Dyke Show," "Ben Casey," "Car 54, Where Are You?" "Defenders," "Dr. Kildare," "Mr. Ed," "Klondike," "The Bob Cummings Show," "Gunslinger," "Whispering Smith," "Whiplash," "The Asphalt Jungle," "Frontier Circus," "Top Cat," "Snagglepuss," "The Avengers," "The Wonderful World of Disney," "Bozo the Clown," "Password," "Wide World of Sports," "The Rocky and Bullwinkle Show," renamed "The Bullwinkle Show," when it moved to NBC in 1961.

Music: "West Side Story," Leonard Bernstein. Miracles, "Shop Around." Bobby Lewis, "Tossin' And Turnin'." Connie Francis, "Where the Boys

Are." Ike & Tina Turner, "It's Gonna Work Out Fine." Freddy King, "Hideaway." Bobby Bland, "Don't Cry No More." Patsy Cline, "Crazy" & "I Fall To Pieces." George Jones, "Tender Years." Buck Owens, "Foolin' Around." Highwaymen, "Michael." Ernie K-Doe, "Mother-In-Law." Roy Orbison, "Crying." Del Shannon, "Runaway." Gary and the U.S. Bonds, "Quarter To Three." Blue Moon, "The Marcels." Neil Sedaka, "Calendar Girl." Ricky Nelson, "Hello Mary Lou" & "Travelin' Man." Pat Boone, "Moody River." The Marvelettes, "Please Mr. Postman." Dion, "Runaround Sue" & "The Wanderer." The Tokens, "The Lion Sleeps Tonight." Dee Clark, "Raindrops." The Shirelles, "Will You Still Love Me Tomorrow." Gene Pitney, "Town Without Pity."

Deaths: Dashiell Hammett, author of "Maltese Falcon, Thin Man."

President: John F. Kennedy (D) Roman Catholic; vetoes 60/ 0 overrides

Vice President: Lyndon B. Johnson (D) Disciples of Christ

House: D-263 ; R-174

Senate: 87th Congress (1961-1963) Majority Party: Democrat (64 seats) Minority Party: Republican (36 seats) Other Parties: 0 Total Seats: 100

Federal Debt: $288.97 billion or 53 % of the GDP

Consumer Price Index CPI-U (1982 Base of 100): 29.90

GDP: $544.7 billion	**Inflation Rate:** 1.07%

Dow Jones: 728.8 (12-01)/ 598. (January)

Average Home Mortgage Rate: 6.97%

1 oz Gold: $35.50	**1oz of Silver:** $0.91

Federal Debt: $288,970,938,610.05

Federal Deficit: $3.3 billion dollars

Defense Spending: $56.99 billion	**Interest Spending:** $7.49 billion
Health Care Spending: $1.60 billion	**Pensions Spending:** $12.85 billion

Welfare Spending: $3.24 billion	**Education Spending:** $1.72 billion
Transportation Spending: $4.36 billion	**Misc. Other Spending:** $12.45 billion
Protection Spending: $190 million	**Total Government Spending:** $104.86 billion
% of GDP that goes towards just the interest payment: 1.37%	
$1.00 = 361.14 Yen, Japan	
U.S. Population: 183,742,000	**World Population:** 3,080,114,361
U.S. Birth Rate: 4,268,326	**U.S. Abortions:** 292
U.S. Homicide Rate: 4.7/ 100,000 population	**U.S. Violent Crime:** 158.1/ 100,000 population
Annual Average Domestic Crude Oil Prices: $2.85 / barrel, $20.48 (2007 adjusted)	

Oil:

June 19, 1961 – Kuwait gains its independence on June 19. Kuwait spent the early 1920s fighting off the army commanded by Abdulaziz bin Abdul Rahman Al Saud, the founder of modern **Saudi Arabia**. In 1923 the fighting ended with a British-brokered treaty and as a result, an oil concession was granted in 1934 to a U.S.-British joint venture known as the **Kuwait Oil Company.** The first wells were sunk in 1936, and by 1938 it was obvious that Kuwait was virtually floating on oil. WWII forced the KOC to suspend operations, but when oil exports took off after the war so did Kuwait's economy. As the country became wealthy, health care, education and the general standard of living improved dramatically.

June 25, 1961 – Iraq. Kuwait gains its independence on June 19, and **President Abdul Karim Kassem of Iraq** asserts a long-standing Iraqi claim to Kuwait's oil fields on June 25. Fearing an Iraqi invasion the Sheikh asked for and received British military aid. In the UNSC, where the majority approach was vetoed, and then in the Arab League, the problem was seen as one of seeking British withdrawal rather than of Iraqi threats. The Sheikh demanded and received an Arab protective force, despite an Iraqi threat to withdraw from the Arab League, in return for a percent of oil royalties for Arab development.

The Anglo-Kuwait Treaty of 1899 governed relations between London and Kuwait until 1961. This treaty did not allow Kuwaiti territorial concessions without British approval, and implied military protection in return for Kuwait's allowing the U.K. to conduct Kuwaiti foreign relations. The UK's defense of Kuwait is chronicled in an extensive collection of declassified CIA documents. After **President Abdul Karim Kassem of Iraq** is killed during a coup in 1963 the threat of an Iraqi invasion is diminished. He was overthrown and executed by military and civilian members of the Ba'ath party in February 1963 with some help from the CIA.

September 1961 – Libya. Oil production starts and by 1965, Libya is the world's sixth-largest exporter of oil.

Major News:

January 3, 1961 – The U.S. severs diplomatic and consular relations with **Cuba** after disputes over the nationalization of U.S. firms in Cuba.

January 1961 – Two of the high-wire "Flying Wallendas" are killed when their famous seven-person pyramid collapses during a performance in Detroit, Michigan.

January 16, 1961 – Cambridge Five. A Russian espionage ring is detected in Great Britain. The American policy of sharing its nuclear secrets with the British has always made life easier for Russian spies. Anthony Blunt, Donald Duart Maclean, Kim Philby and Guy Burgess, are four agents within this spy ring. The group is well placed in Royal SIS circles and even has posts in the United States. Fellow KGB operative and defector Anatoliy Golitsyn gave them all up in 1961.

In the late 50's Anatoliy Golitsyn turned on the Soviet Union and became a mole for the United States. The U.S. did not recruit him, he volunteered. The CIA could not believe that such a high ranking officer in the KGB would willingly give information to the United States. They tested him for years. They tried every way possible to prove this man a fraud but they couldn't.

March 29, 1961 – The 23rd Amendment, giving **District of Columbia** citizens the right to vote in presidential elections is ratified.

April 17, 1961 – The Bay of Pigs Invasion on the south coast of Cuba is less than stellar. In a U.S. backed attempt to overthrow the regime of Fidel Castro 1,400 Cuban exiles launch an invasion at the Bay of Pigs. Preparations began in March of 1960, when **President Eisenhower approved a CIA plan** to train Cuban exiles at camps in Guatemala and by late November the operation had trained a small army in guerilla tactics and conventional assault landing procedures. President Kennedy authorized the Cuban invasion plans with the understanding the U.S. would not surface as an obvious participant. With the idea of keeping the operation covert the landing site was moved to the Bay of Pigs, a remote area on the southern coast of Cuba and more than 80 miles from possible refuge in Cuba's Escambray Mountains.

On April 15, 1961, eight obsolete World War II B-26 bombers painted to look like they were a part of the Cuban air force, left Nicaragua to bomb Cuban airfields. They failed to destroy very many planes and left most of Castro's air force intact. As news of the attack begins to surface photos of the repainted planes help to make American involvement transparent and President Kennedy cancels the second airstrike.

On April 17, the **Cuban exiles land at the beaches** along the Bay of Pigs and come under heavy fire. The Cuban air force strafes the invaders, sinks two escort ships and destroys at least half of the exiles air support while the Cuban exile forces are running low on ammunition. By April 18, Castro has 20,000 Cuban regular army troops advancing on the beach while the Cuban air force continues to control the sky.

As the situation worsened, President Kennedy authorized an "air-umbrella" at dawn on April 19. He authorized six unmarked American fighter planes to help defend the Brigade's B-26 aircraft flying in from Nicaragua. The B-26s arrived an hour late (most likely due to time zone confusion) and were shot down by the Cubans and the invasion was crushed later that day.

Bay of Pigs: President Richard M. Nixon came up with the idea, President Dwight D. Eisenhower planned it, President John F. Kennedy approved it, and the

CIA carried it out. Out of 1,400 invaders, 1,197 are captured, 200 of them had been soldiers in Batista's army, and 14 of those were wanted for murder in Cuba. A CIA soldier fired the first shot. A volunteer teacher is the first Cuban casualty. Four American pilots and over 100 Cuban invaders are killed in battle.

President Kennedy was never given a full and truthful pre-Bay-of-Pigs intelligence briefing because the CIA wanted to embarrass him and drag him into a full-scale invasion of Cuba. Kennedy was so angered by the duplicity he was determined to dismantle and reorganize the CIA.

May 27, 1961 – President Kennedy signs a bill creating the **Alliance for Progress**, for Latin America.

July 1961 – President Kennedy requests a 25% spending increase for the military.

August 13, 1961 – Berlin Wall. Between 1949 and 1961 "approximately 2.7 million East Germans fled to the West," giving Berlin the nickname the "Brain Drain," as many of the brightest people in East Germany sought to leave the communist bloc for a clearly better life in West Berlin or Western Europe.

On August 13, **the Berlin border is closed.** Early in the morning of Sunday, August 13, the German Democratic Republic began under the leadership of Erich Honecker to block off **East Berlin** and the **German Democratic Republic** from West Berlin by means of barbed wire and antitank obstacles. Streets are torn up, and barricades of paving stones are erected. **Tanks and armed troops gathered** at crucial places and the subway and local railway service between East and West Berlin is stopped. Inhabitants of East Berlin and the GDR are no longer allowed to enter West Berlin. Sixty-thousand commuters, who had jobs in West Berlin the day before, are no longer allowed across the border. In the following days, construction crews began replacing the provisional barriers with a solid wall. Because the three essentials of American policy regarding Berlin are not affected, 1) presence of allied troops, 2) free access to Berlin, and 3) the right of self-determination of the West Berliners, this further complicated the situation and removed any easy solution.

The wall will remain for 28 years, until November 9, 1989, separating East Germany from West Germany. The East German government issued orders to shoot all people trying to escape from East Berlin. The Berlin Wall was a border designed to keep people inside of the country unlike most borders in the world which are designed to keep people out. Although the Berlin wall was meant to keep people from leaving they escaped by digging tunnels under the wall and people escaped by flying over the wall. They broke through the wall and many were shot as they tried to climb over the wall. Over 200 **people were killed trying to** flee to the West.

October 5, 1961 – The Soviet Union's first big open spy trial since the U-2 case opened today linking an unidentified American to two self-confessed Dutch agents.

Civil Rights Movement:

1961 – The Federal District Court orders the **University of Georgia** to admit Hamilton Holmes and Charlayne Hunter, January 6. They were suspended after a riot on campus by white students, January 11, but are reinstated by court order on January 13. They became the first two African American students admitted to the University of Georgia.

   Charlayne Hunter (later Hunter-Gault) makes good use of the situation to observe and interact with reporters. This motivates her towards a career in journalism. ….. (2009) **Charlayne Hunter-Gault has staked her claim as one of the leading journalists in the United States,** having won many of the top honors in her field for excellence in investigative reporting. She wrote for the "New Yorker," 1964-1967; "New York Times," 1968-1977, became Harlem bureau chief; **"MacNeil/Lehrer NewsHour,"** New York City, general correspondent, 1978-1983, national correspondent and substitute anchor, 1983-1997; National Public Radio, chief correspondent for Africa, 1997-1999; CNN, Johannesburg Bureau Chief, 1999-

1961 – President John F. Kennedy issues Executive Order 10925, which mandates that projects financed with federal funds **"take affirmative action"** to ensure that hiring and employment practices are free of racial bias. This establishes the **President's Committee on Equal Employment Opportunity** to investigate racial discrimination by government contractors.

1961

February 1, 1961 – Ten people are convicted of "Trespass" for a sit-in at McCrory's lunch counter in Rock Hill, S.C. They are sentenced to fines of $100 each or 30 days hard labor on the county chain-gang. They begin serving their sentence on February 2nd. The protesters (the Friendship Nine) are from **Friendship Junior College.**

1961 – "Freedom Rides" from Washington, DC, across the Deep South are launched on May 20 to desegregate public transportation in the South. In the spring and summer, student volunteers begin taking bus trips through the South to test new laws that prohibit segregation in interstate travel facilities, which includes bus and railway stations. The program, sponsored by The Congress of Racial Equality **(CORE)** and the Student Nonviolent Coordinating Committee **(SNCC), involves more than 1,000 volunteers, black and white.**

Several of the groups of **"freedom riders,"** are **attacked by angry mobs** along the way. "Freedom Riders" are **beaten by mobs in Birmingham,** May 14, and Montgomery, May 20, and arrested in Jackson, Mississippi, May 24.

On May 24, twenty-seven Freedom Riders boarded two Greyhound buses from Montgomery, Alabama to Jackson, Mississippi, and then on to New Orleans. National Guard patrols were stationed in all three cities to protect the riders and when the **Alabama National Guard** escorted the Freedom Riders out of Montgomery on May 24, it was a national news event. The two buses were escorted by 16 highway patrol cars each containing three National Guardsmen and two highway patrolmen. When the **Freedom Riders** arrived in **Jackson, Mississippi,** they entered the whites-only waiting room and were immediately escorted by local police into a paddy wagon and taken to jail where they were charged with violating the state law against trespassing. As defense attorney Jack Young spoke in defense of the riders, the judge would turn his back and look at the wall. When Young finished, the judge immediately sentenced the activists to **60 days in the state penitentiary.** The riders announce **"Jail No Bail"** they will not pay fines for unconstitutional arrests and illegal convictions. Each prisoner remains in jail for 39 days, the maximum time they can serve without loosing their right to appeal the unconstitutionality of their arrests, trials, and convictions. After 39 days, they file an appeal and post bond. This keeps the issue before the public for almost two months. **These convictions were eventually overturned** with the help of the NAACP.

May 21, 1961 – Governor Patterson declares martial law in Montgomery and calls out the National Guard following more violent clashes between blacks and whites. The trouble at the **Negro First Baptist Church** erupted when a crowd of white men, women and children began throwing stones through the windows as black civil rights leader **Dr Martin Luther King** was speaking. **Attorney General Robert Kennedy orders three hundred federal marshals armed with tear gas** to disperse the angry mob and within minutes local police baton-charged the crowd, which finally broke up.

The attack is the latest in a string of violent incidents that have followed the **Freedom Riders, a multi-racial group** on a bus tour of the southern U.S. states challenging racial segregation. In his address to the congregation, Dr. King called for a massive campaign to end segregation in Alabama.

August 1961 – George Collins and several other Afro-American newspapermen pretend to be African diplomats from an imaginary country and have lunch at a Maryland restaurant known to refuse service to African-Americans. Collins writes about this experience in **"Everybody Eats But Americans."**

September 22, 1961 – The Interstate Commerce Commission issues new rules effective November 1, forbidding interstate carriers to use **segregated terminals.**

November 17, 1961 – A Coalition of civil rights groups and local African-American organizations in Albany, Georgia, form **Albany Movement,** to conduct protest campaigns against segregation. In a series of demonstrations, December 10–16, more than 700 people are arrested. Demonstrations are suspended December 18 to allow for negotiations with the city government.

Women's Movement:

1961 – President John Kennedy establishes the President's Commission on the Status of Women and appoints **Eleanor Roosevelt** as chairwoman. The report issued by the Commission in 1963 documents substantial discrimination against women in the workplace and makes specific recommendations for improvement, including fair hiring practices, paid maternity leave, and affordable child care.

1961

1961 – President Kennedy makes **women's rights** a key issue of the New Frontier, and names women, such as Esther Peterson, to many high-ranking posts in his administration.

1961 – There is a secret program to test women pilots for space flight. *The Mercury 13: The Untold Story of 13 American Women and the Dream of Space Flight.* The testing program was halted and eventually scrapped, in large part, Ackmann writes, because of a pervasive "boy's club" attitude at NASA, even though women proved they can hold their own against the men.

1961 – Tainted milk. More than 50,000 women in 60 cities, mobilized by **Women Strike for Peace,** protest above ground testing of nuclear bombs and tainted milk. By 1963 a record high national daily level of 32 picocuries of radioactive stronium-90 per liter of milk will be reported by the Public Health Service. This is nearly double the level of 17 picocuries recorded in June 1962 and four times that recorded in 1961.

Popular Culture:

1961 – Time-Life Books begins publication.

1961 – The Single Convention on Narcotic Drugs is an international treaty to prohibit production and supply of specific **drugs** and of drugs with similar effects unless they have been licensed. The Paris Convention of July, 1931 set down similar standards but since most of the synthetic opioids were **invented in the last 30 years they had not been added.** Earlier treaties had only controlled **opium, coca,** and derivatives such as **morphine, heroin** and **cocaine.**

March 1, 1961 – U.S. President John Kennedy establishes the **Peace Corps** where volunteers work to improve living standards in Africa, Asia, and Latin America.

May 1961 – President Kennedy sends **400 American Green Beret 'Special Advisors'** to **South Vietnam** to train South Vietnamese soldiers in methods of 'counter-insurgency' in the fight against **Viet Cong guerrillas.**

October 8, 1961 – Albert Agueci, the French Connection heroin smuggler for the Buffalo crime family, is severely tortured and murdered. He confronted crime boss Stefano Magaddino because Magaddino did not provide bail money and assistance to his family. He also made accusations that Joe Valachi had become an informer.

Agueci's remains were found in a field near Rochester, N.Y. on November 23. He was naked, his hands were bound behind his back, his front teeth were knocked out and 30 lbs. of flesh had been cut from his body while he was still alive. The coroner's report said he was tortured. This will encourage Joe Valachi to become the government's star witness when he thinks the mob gave him the kiss of death.

1961 – Texas enacts a state sales tax.

1961 – The Illinois legislature revised their criminal code without prohibiting **sodomy.** The law went into effect the following year.

1961 – Bob Dylan, originally named Robert Zimmerman, is discovered singing in Greenwich Village by Columbia Records and produces his first album. His songs become symbolic of the civil rights movement and the hippie culture.

1961 – Mattel introduced Ken in March of 1961: *"Here he is...the Boyfriend for Barbie the Teen-Age Fashion Model. All Barbie fans will want Ken and his smartly-tailored wardrobe of finest quality materials for perfect fit and finish...with miniature accessories...plus a special arm tag identity for the only genuine Ken Doll."* In the 1960s, Ken was the boy next door, and his persona and outfits reflected that. He came with flocked hair and red swim trunks. The flocked hair easily rubbed off or came off totally in water. Then Ken had a deep tan (Malibu Ken), and in 1975 hair below his shoulders. The original first Ken, Flock Hair Ken, sells for $250-$300 in 2010.

December 21, 1961 – The National Park Service extends its lands into the U.S. Virgin Islands when President John F. Kennedy proclaims the **Buck Island Reef** as a National Monument. The reef includes an underwater nature trail and one of the best marine gardens in the **Caribbean Sea.**

1961 – Hertz, "Let Hertz put you in the driver's seat." Norman, Craig & Kummel.

1961

Business / Technology:

April 12, 1961 – Russian, Yuri Alexeyevich Gagarin a Soviet cosmonaut and hero of the Soviet Union, is the first human in space and the first to orbit the Earth.

May 5, 1961 – In the first U.S.-crewed suborbital space flight Commander **Alan B. Shepard Jr**. is rocketed from Cape Canaveral, Florida in a Mercury capsule. Shepard is the second person and the first American in space. Twenty days later, **President Kennedy announces his intention to place a man on the moon by the end of the decade.**

July 21, 1961 –Gus Grissom, piloting the Mercury-Redstone 4 capsule "Liberty Bell 7," is the second American to go into space (sub-orbital). Upon splashdown, the hatch prematurely opens, and the capsule sinks. It will be recovered in 1999.

1961 – The Fairchild Semiconductor makes the first commercially available integrated circuits. All computers are then made using chips instead of the individual transistors and their accompanying parts. Texas Instruments first used the chips in Air Force computers and the **Minuteman Missile** in 1962. "What we didn't realize then was that the integrated circuit would reduce the cost of electronic functions by a factor of a million to one, nothing had ever done that for anything before," Jack Kilby.

October 30, 1961 – Tsar-bomb. The most powerful thermonuclear device ever tested is the 50-megaton Soviet Tsar Bomba (King of Bombs). **"Tsar-bomb,"** is the nickname for the hydrogen bomb codenamed **"Ivan"** by its developers. It is the largest, **most powerful nuclear weapon** ever detonated. Developed by the Soviet Union, **the bomb** was originally designed to have a yield of about 100 megatons of TNT, but was reduced by half in order to limit the amount of nuclear fallout that would result. One bomb was built and tested on October 30, in the Arctic Sea above Novaya Zemlya Island. The weapon never entered service and this type of delivery system, low altitude aircraft, is considered obsolete. New nuclear weapons are needed that can strike anywhere, under any conditions, at any time. The intercontinental ballistic missile **(ICBM) is now King.**

1961 – **Bell Labs** tests communication by light waves.

1961 – **Frances Kelsey** blocks the U.S. approval of **thalidomide.** Worried about its potential for side effects, **Food and Drug Administration** medical officer **Dr. Frances Kelsey** delays the application for approval of **thalidomide, a sleeping pill** that later turns out to cause serious birth defects. Her action leads to the overhaul of the FDA and the creation of drug approval standards. The overhaul brings regulation to the enormous and powerful pharmaceutical industry and forces them to conduct scientifically rigorous clinical trials.

   Unfortunately by 2009 the FDA operates under the direction of the powerful pharmaceutical companies once again. Starting with the Prescription Drug User Fee Act (PDUFA)], passed in 1992, the influence of powerful pharmaceutical companies is exerted by their directly funding, paying cash right up front, for an FDA review. So in many ways, the FDA started looking upon the industry as their client, instead of the public and the public health, which should be the client. It goes downhill from there. In the last twelve years there have been essentially one or two days of congressional oversight hearings, as opposed to dozens and dozens of oversights during the previous twelve years. This means **powerful pharmaceutical companies** are also getting away with no congressional oversight.

1961 – **UNIMATE, the first industrial robot**, begins work at **General Motors**. Obeying step-by-step commands stored on a magnetic drum, the 4,000-pound arm sequences and stacks hot pieces of die-cast metal.

1961 – *LIFE* publishes a photo of a woman wearing an **anti-aging** magnetic collar.

1961 – **Advertel of Canada** designs the world's first electronic **videotape editing machine**.

1961 – **A compact stand-alone transistorized videotape recorder** is first introduced. **RCA TR-22, Sony SV-201.**

1961 – **FM stereo** is introduced in what is the last great leap ahead in commercial radio.

1961

1961 – Dwight D. Eisenhower's Military-Industrial Complex Speech. Until the latest of our world conflicts, the United States had no armaments industry. American makers of plowshares could, with time and as required, make swords as well. But now we can no longer risk emergency improvisation of national defense; we have been compelled to create a permanent armaments industry of vast proportions. Added to this, three and a half million men and women are directly engaged in the defense establishment. We annually spend on military security more than the net income of all United States corporations.

1961 – Kodak announces a new method for direct electron-beam recording on silver halide film.

April 14, 1661 – The first live television broadcast from the Soviet Union.

1961 – Speaking in general conference in 1961, Ezra Taft Benson stated, *"In connection with attack on the United States, the Lord told the Prophet Joseph Smith there would be an attempt to overthrow the country by destroying the Constitution. Joseph Smith predicted that the time would come when the Constitution would hang, as it were, by a thread, and at that time "this people will step forth and save it from the threatened destruction"* (*Conference Report*, October 1961, p.70).

1961 – Ham is the first primate in space, 158 miles, aboard **Mercury/Redstone 2.**

1961 – Sputnik 9 carries Chernushka, a dog into orbit.

1961 – Siemens and Halke of Munich develop a **magnetic video disc** for recording single frames.

1961 – Ray Kroc buys McDonald's.

Finance:

1961 – Multinational conglomerates General Electric, Westinghouse, and other manufacturers of heavy electrical equipment are **convicted of price-fixing** and other charges for electrical equipment valued at $1.74 billion per year. It is the largest price-fixing case in the history of the Sherman Antitrust Act up to this time, and it is the first time individual white-collar criminals are jailed for their offenses. This seems to be a move in the right direction but GE's fine is equivalent to a person earning $175,000 per year having to pay a $3 parking ticket.

1961 – The London gold pool is established in which U.S. central banks and seven other nations agree to buy and sell gold to support the $35 per troy ounce price that had been established on January 31, 1934. By the beginning of the 1960s, the $35/ oz U.S. gold ratio is becoming more and more difficult to sustain. Gold demand is rising and U.S. gold reserves are falling because of the ever increasing trade deficits. Shortly after President Kennedy is Inaugurated in January 1961, newly-appointed Undersecretary of the Treasury Robert Roosa suggests that the U.S. and Europe pool their Gold resources to prevent the private market price of Gold from exceeding the mandated rate of $35 /oz. this gives the green light to the Central **Banks of the U.S., Britain, West Germany, France, Switzerland, Italy, Belgium,** the **Netherlands,** and **Luxembourg** as they set up the **"London Gold Pool"** in early 1961.

Books:

1961 – "Franny and Zooey," a collection of J.D.Salinger's short stories.

1961 – Robert Heinlein's sci-fi novel, **"Stranger in a Strange Land."**

1961 – John Updike, "Rabbit, Run."

1961 – "Catch 22," Joseph Heller.

1961 – Henry Miller's "Tropic of Cancer" is published in the U.S. after 27 years of being banned. "Tropic of Cancer," has explicit **sexual passages** and could not be published in the United States until now.

An edition was printed by the Obelisk Press in Paris and copies were smuggled into the United States. In 2003 used book dealers asked $7,500 and up for copies of this edition.

1961

In 1961 when Grove Press releases a copy of the work dozens of lawsuits are brought against booksellers in a number of states for selling it. The issue is ultimately settled by the U.S. Supreme Court's 1973 decision in Miller vs. California. In this decision, the court defines obscenity by what is now called the Miller test. **The Miller Test consists of three parts. 1)** Whether the average person, applying contemporary community standards, would find that the work, taken as a whole, appeals to the prurient interest. **2)** Whether the work depicts/describes, in a patently offensive way, sexual conduct or excretory functions specifically defined by applicable state law. **3)** Whether the work, taken as a whole, lacks serious literary, artistic, political or scientific value. The work is considered obscene only if all three conditions are satisfied. This limits what may be classified as obscene.

TV:

1961 – As TV censors allowed couples to have one bed in their bedroom, the rule was both spouses could not both be in the bed at the same time. One of the two had to have at least one foot on the floor. In 1962 we make the jump to TV's "Peyton Place."

1961-1966 – The Dick Van Dyke Show. When the first scripts called for **Mary Tyler Moore** to vacuum the living room in a dress and high heels she refused. In real life Mary is a young mother and wore comfortable cloths around the house. **Laura Petrie's** trademark Capri pants gave network censors fits and set suburban housewives free of their **pantyhose.** Mary Tyler Moore was pushing the boundaries with her figure-revealing Capri pants and her tight-fitting pencil skirts that cupped her cheeks. The skirts hugged her rear end, outlining the curves. In 1961 women wore clothes. In 2010 clothes will wear the woman. In 2010 you can take women's pants, stuff them to capacity with anything remotely moldable, hang them from a clothes line and jiggle the rope. The pants all look great! You can stuff them with anything or anyone and the pants look great. The female has been reduced to nothing, she is not even necessary. Progress?

1961 – Newton Minow, chairman of the FCC calls TV a vast wasteland.

1961 – "Sing Along With Mitch," Mitch Miller, premieres on NBC TV. Mitch is the "inventor" of what would become modern day karaoke. Just **"follow the bouncing ball"** and sing along with us.

Sports:

February 15, 1961 – The entire United States figure skating team is killed in a plane crash near Brussels, Belgium on their journey to the World Championships. Seventy-three people are killed.

1961 – Roger Maris breaks **Babe Ruth's** single-season home run record. Roger Maris hit 61 home runs to break baseball's single-season record of 60, set by Babe Ruth in 1927.

Natural Disasters:

September 3-15, 1961 – Texas coast. Hurricane "Carla" devastated Texas gulf cities, killing 46 people when it hit the coast as a Category 4 hurricane and increased to Category 5 levels. Evacuation efforts reduced the number of deaths.

October 31, 1961 – British Honduras. Hurricane "Hattie" destroys the capital of Belize, killing at least 400 people.

1959-1961 – The "Great Leap Famine" killed an estimated **30 to 40 million people** in China as the policies of Mao Zedong resulted in massive social and economic upheaval. China was also hit by large famines in 1907, 1928-1930, 1936 and 1941-1942.

Man vs. Man / Wars:

Assassinated – Burundi. Louis Rwagasore, Burundian Prince and Prime Minister is assassinated on October 13, 1961. Louis Rwagasore demanded complete independence for Burundi, called on the local population to boycott Belgian stores and refused to pay taxes. Because of his calls for civil disobedience, he was placed under house arrest.Rwagasore was assassinated 2 weeks later while having dinner at the Hotel Tanganyika. He was killed by a Greek national named Georges Kageorgis, allegedly in the pay of the pro-Belgian Christian Democratic Party.

Assassinated – Congo. Patrice Lumumba, Prime Minister of the Congo. After Lumumba helped to win independence for the Republic of the Congo from Belgium in June 1960 he was the first legally elected Prime Minister. Ten weeks later, Lumumba's government is deposed in a coup during the Congo Crisis.

Lumumba fled house arrest on November 27 in an attempt to reach his supporters in Stanleyville. Mobutu was told by Belgian advisors that Lumumba was a liability, still able to bring down the government with a coup, and needed to be eliminated. He was soon captured by soldiers loyal to Mobutu.

On January 17, 1961 Mobutu sent Lumumba to Élisabethville and in full view of the press Lumumba was beaten and forced to eat copies of his own speeches. He was taken away by guards and had not been seen or heard from for three weeks when Katangan radio announced that he had escaped and been killed by some villagers. This later proved to be untrue. Lumumba had been tortured and killed along with two others shortly after his arrival.

A Belgian inquiry in 2001, established that Lumumba had been shot by Katangan gendarmes in the presence of Belgian officers. Lumumba was beaten, placed in front of a firing squad with 2 other allies, shot, cut up, buried, dug up and what remained was dissolved in acid.

Assassinated – Rafael Leonidas Trujillo, Dominican Republic dictator. During the Revolution in Santiago in 1930 Trujillo and his followers overthrew the government and in October 1937, Trujillo made agreements with the Haitian President, Stenio Vincent, stating that he would permit Haitians to cross the border. He then changed his mind and took control of the border. It was decided that if a person could not pronounce the letter r in "perejil," the Spanish word for parsley (the R is difficult for Haitians to pronounce), they would be killed. Haitians are clearly not welcome in the Dominican Republic. The numbers of **Haitians** killed was never confirmed but it is said to be **from 12,000 to 25,000, men, women and children.** To make it look like it was not his fault Trujillo used as scapegoats some of the people that committed this atrocity under his orders. They were jailed and Trujillo paid $525,000 to the Haitian government.

Trujillo, 71 years old, is murdered by his own armed forces on May 30, 1961, after leaving the home of Doña Trujillo. He went to **El Pony Bar,** where he was shot.

Trujillo completely dominated the economy of the country. Various family members including his current wife and his two brothers controlled everything from prostitution to agriculture. While he was in office he forced all but one of the sugar plantations to sell out to him. He forced Dominican landowners of large estates to turn their holdings over to him and was considered a "partner" of every industry in the country. His fortune was estimated in the late 1950s at about **$500 million.** Within 6 months of his assassination his whole family was in exile. This ended the **"Era of Trujillo, the goat"** and his 31 year reign.

The **"Haitian immigrant" situation** in the Dominican Republic will still be dealt with by the army in the same way in 2006.

April 2, 1961 – John F. Kennedy. President and Mrs. Kennedy attend Easter service in Palm Beach, Florida. A week-old report had said the church would be the scene of an attempt by pro-Castro Cubans to assassinate the President and his family or to kidnap his three-year-old daughter Caroline. Security is doubled.

April 11, August 14, 1961 – Adolf Eichmann is on trial in **Jerusalem** for crimes against the Jewish people, crimes against humanity and war crimes. Eichmann is found guilty and hanged at Ramleh on May 31, 1962. A fellow Nazi reported Eichmann once said "he would leap laughing into the grave because the feeling that he had five million people on his conscience would be for him a source of extraordinary satisfaction."

1961 – Angola. The **Popular Movement for the Liberation of Angola** led by Agostinho Neto and the **Angolan War of National Liberation** begins. A rebellion by workers, undergoing forced labor in coffee and cotton plantations in the north, plunges the country into chaos. Starting with a strike by workers in the cotton fields owned by **Portuguese, German,** and **British** investors, the peasants burn their identification cards and attack the Portuguese traders. Within four weeks the Portuguese military bomb area villages and kill up to 7,000 men, women, and children. The MPLA militants in Luanda storm a police station and São Paulo prison and kill seven policemen. Around forty of the attackers are killed and no prisoners are set free. In retaliation the Portuguese backed police help vigilantes organize nightly slaughters in the Luanda slums where they drag Africans from their huts, shoot them, and leave their bodies in the streets. A Methodist missionary testified that he personally knew of the deaths of almost three hundred people.

As the government pushes the MPLA out of Luanda, Holden Roberto, the **Union of Peoples of Angola** leader, enters northern Angola, leading 4,000 to 5,000 militants. His forces take farms, government outposts, and trading centers, killing everyone they encounter, including women, children and black Angolan workers. They proceeded to massacre the civilian population killing 1,000 whites and 6,000 blacks. Angola will gain independence in 1975 but war within the country will continue through 2002. In the first year of the war 2,000 Portuguese and 50,000 Africans died while between 400,000 and 500,000 refugees went to Zaire. **Angola is known for its diamonds,** iron ore, gold, copper, and oil. The money made from diamonds alone from 1992-1998 is **three to four Billion dollars**, based on UN estimates. Diamond reserves are estimated at 180 million carats. Add oil, gold, copper, iron ore and we are talking about a lot of money.

1961 – Burma. The Shan States of Burma. Although **the CIA** has no real interest in an independent Shan land, it supports individual rebel armies in order to accomplish its intelligence gathering missions inside China, and without the CIA's tolerance of its **opium-arms traffic,** the Shan National Army could never have occupied so much of Kentung State. The local warlords are selling opium and then making the trek to Gnar Kham's forward caravan camp at Huei Krai, Thailand where they buy U.S. automatic weapons from the Laotian army. As the warlords become wealthier and more powerful their first priority is to protect their areas, expand operations and sell more opium.

May 1, 1961 – U.S. Cuba. A National Airlines Corvair is **hijacked** at gunpoint after leaving Miami International Airport and forced to fly to Havana, Cuba by Antulio Ramirez Ortiz. He is given asylum but is jailed for twenty years when he returns to the U.S. in 1975.

1961 – Ecuador. President J. M. Velasco Ibarra of Ecuador is overthrown by a **CIA-backed coup** for being too friendly with **Cuba.** According to a book by ex-CIA agent Philip Agee, the CIA staged a Communist takeover of Ecuador before backing a military coup, ousting elected President J. M. Velasco Ibarra, and again in 1963 the government of Carlos Julio Arosemena. Philip Agee now lives in Cuba and is accused of being a **"KGB shill."**

1961 – El Salvador. A coup by young officers overthrows the junta, in January 1961, and brings Lieutenant Colonel Julio Adalberto Rivera to power from 1962-1967. Under the banner of the **Alliance for Progress,** Rivera advanced programs aimed at economic growth and diversification, which enabled El Salvador to take advantage of the increased trade opportunities offered by the recently formed **Central American Common Market.**

1961 – Eritrea. Ethiopia. Eritrean Secession. The war will go on for 30 years, from September 1, 1961-May 29, 1991, when the Eritrean People's Liberation Front, having defeated the Ethiopian forces in Eritrea, take control of the country. In April 1993, in a referendum supported by Ethiopia, the Eritrean people vote almost unanimously in favor of independence. Formal international recognition of an independent and sovereign Eritrea follows later the same year. The **Eritrean War of Independence** is fought as a guerilla campaign by the two main liberation fronts and major civilian massacres occur, with around 150,000 people being killed.

1961 – Guatemala. The Guatemalan Civil War, the longest civil war in Latin American history will be fought from 1960 to 1996. By the end of the war 200,000 Guatemalans were killed by military and paramilitary forces, according to the United Nation's Commission for Historical Clarification. The report of the **Archbishop's Office for Human Rights** attributed almost 90% of the atrocities and over 400 massacres to the Guatemalan army and paramilitary, and less than 5% of the atrocities to the guerrillas including 16 massacres.

1961-1963 – Iraq vs. Kurds. Kurdish Revolt. The Kurds located in northern Iraq demand autonomy. September 10, 1961, when an Iraqi army column is ambushed by a group of Kurds, the Kurdish revolt truly begins. In response to the attack the Iraqi

1961

Air Force indiscriminately bombs Kurdish villages and these bombings rally the entire Kurdish population. Fighting between the Kurds and the government continues into 2009 with no end in sight. According to CIA "World Factbook," Kurds formed approximately 20% of the population in Turkey (approximately 14 million) in 2008 and Kurds makeup about 17% of Iraq's population. They are the majority in at least three provinces in northern Iraq which are together known as Iraqi Kurdistan.

Mustafa Barzani, the legendary Kurdish leader, is a KGB agent code-named "RAIS," and the Kurdish armed revolution he starts September 11, 1961, is in reality a **KGB covert action** to destabilize Western interests in the Middle East and put additional pressure on Abdel Karim Kassim's government of Iraq. On May 23, 1999, the *Denver Rocky Mountain News* estimated the number of people killed between 1961 and 1999 to be 280,000 which includes 180,000 between 1976 and 1988, and 10,000 in 1991.

1961 – Iraq-Kuwait. After Kuwait's independence in 1961, Iraq claimed Kuwait, under the pretense that Kuwait had been part of the Ottoman Empire subject to Iraqi suzerainty, and that the 1932 recognition had never been ratified by the Iraqi Parliament. General Abdel Karim Kassim holds a press conference on June 19, 1961 at which he states **"Iraq regards Kuwait as an integral part of its territory."** Following that press conference, Britain quickly masses troops in Kuwait with naval support in the Persian Gulf. Kassim will be assassinated in a CIA backed coup by the Arab Socialist **Ba'ath Party** of Iraq in 1963.

1961-1962 – Laos. Laotian Civil War. A second Geneva conference provides for the independence and neutrality of Laos, but the agreement is subverted by both the **United States and North Vietnam.** The war soon resumes and the government and army of Laos are generally neutral during the conflict. The United States and North Vietnam, however, undermine the agreement by forming private proxy armies. Growing American and North Vietnamese military presence in the country increasingly draws Laos into the Second Indochina War (1954-1975). Eastern Laos was subjected to the heaviest bombing in the history of warfare, as the U.S. sought to destroy the **Ho Chi Minh Trail** that passed **through Laos** and the country was also repeatedly invaded by both North and South Vietnam. This continued until April

1975 when the Pathet Lao with the support of North Vietnam take control of Laos. Non-communist elements of the national government decided that allowing the Pathet Lao to take power would be better than having them take it by force. There is little resistance and the King is forced to abdicate his throne.

December 26, 1961 – Nepal. King Mahendra appoints a council of five ministers to help run the administration and then declares political parties to be illegal. At first the Nepali Congress leadership tried a nonviolent struggle against the new order and formed alliances with several political parties. King Mahendra then substitutes a **"National Guidance"** system under his absolute control. By late 1961, violent actions organized by the Nepali Congress in exile begin along the Indian border, and increase in size and number during early 1962.

1961 – Nicaragua. The Sandinista National Liberation Front, founded in 1961 by a small group of university students, is trying to overthrow the **Somoza government**.

From 1945 to 1960, the U.S.-owned Nicaraguan Long Leaf Pine Company (NIPCO) directly paid the Somoza family millions of dollars in exchange for favorable benefits to the company, such as not having to re-forest clear cut areas. NIPCO had cut all of the commercially viable coastal pines in northeast Nicaragua by 1961 and continued to expand; forcing peasant families from the areas they had farmed for decades. **The National Guard forces some families to relocate** to colonization projects in the rainforest and some move east where they began to clear-cut forests so they can plant crops. Soil erosion will force them deeper into the rainforest where they again clear-cut. Cattle ranchers move in right after they abandon the land and by 1970 Nicaragua is the number one beef supplier to the United States. President Anastasio Somoza Debayle owned the largest slaughterhouse in Nicaragua, as well as six meat-packing plants in Miami, Florida.

1961 – Sierra Leone gains independence from Britain and establishes the Dominion of Sierra Leone.

January 1961 – Soviet Premier Nikita Khrushchev pledges support for **"wars of national liberation."** greatly encouraging Communists in North Vietnam to escalate their armed struggle to unify Vietnam under **Ho Chi Minh.**

1961

John Fitzgerald Kennedy is inaugurated as the 35th U.S. President on January 20, and outgoing **President Eisenhower** tells him, I think you're going to have to send troops to Southeast Asia. Kennedy, with lots of advice from the academic community wages a limited war to force a political settlement, while Ho Chi Minh is sworn to total victory of a unified Vietnam.

July 18, 1961 – **In Spain the Basque separatist group ETA** tries to derail a train carrying supporters of dictator General Francisco Franco.

May 16, 1961 – **Park Chung Hee, a South Korean** military officer stages the **"May 16th Coup"** and sets up a military government that will last until he is assassinated in 1979. The **Korean Central Intelligence Agency** (KCIA) is created on June 19, 1961 to prevent a countercoup and to suppress all potential enemies, domestic and international. It has investigative power, and the power to arrest and detain anyone suspected of wrongdoing. **The KCIA soon extends its power** to economic and foreign affairs and becomes a much-feared agent of political repression.

Park Chung Hee adheres to a policy of guided democracy, with restrictions on personal freedoms, suppression of the press, suppression of opposition parties, control over the judicial system, and the universities. Park claims this is all necessary to fight communism. While keeping close ties with the U.S., Park Chung Hee is largely responsible for South Korea's "economic miracle" as his major programs give South Korea one of the fastest-growing economies in the world.

May 31, 1961 – **South Africa** ended its dominion status and established the **Republic of South Africa.** By withdrawing from the British Commonwealth, South Africa became isolated in the international community. In June of the same year, the African National Congress rose against the racist rule of the South African Government.

1961 – **Syria and Egypt.** In February 1958, Syria and Egypt merged as the **United Arab Republic.** They were joined by Yemen in March, creating the **United Arab States.** The union was soon torn by personal and political differences, and a Syrian revolt in 1961 leads to its virtual dissolution.

1961 – Tunisia tells the French military to leave their base in Bizerte and go home. Fighting breaks out and France will not leave Bizerte until 1963. 2,000 people die.

December 11, 1961 – Vietnam. The U.S. aircraft carrier "Core" arrives in Saigon with 33 helicopters and 400 air and ground crewmen assigned to operate them for South Vietnam. The United States also sends the first of **11,000 military advisors** to South Vietnam. When advice failed to stem the Communist tide, the United States in 1965 launched an air war against North Vietnam and committed ground troops to combat guerrilla insurgencies in the south. American strength peaked at 540,000 in 1969, and then rapidly declined.

1961 – Yemen. There is a failed assassination attempt on King Saif al-Islam Achmad of Yemen.

1961 – Western New Guinea is the western half of the island of New Guinea. It is the easternmost part of Indonesia, consisting of two provinces: Papua and West Papua. The Dutch government began to prepare **Netherlands New Guinea** for full independence in the 1950's and allowed elections in 1959. The **New Guinea Council** took office on April 5, 1961 after elections.

Indonesia wanting control of Papua and West Papua, receives military help from the Soviet Union, mobilizes its army and threatens to invade. The Dutch are prepared to resist an Indonesian attack but are pressured into a peace agreement by the Kennedy administration and on October 1, 1962, the Dutch will hand over the territory to a temporary UN administration. On May 1, 1963, Indonesia illegally takes control and renames the territory **West Irian** and then **Irian Jaya**. In 1969 Indonesia will annex the areas under the **"Act of Free Choice."** Many people are killed and most people do not think they had a choice.

A recently declassified cable reveals that **Freeport Sulphur** had by April **1965** reached a preliminary "arrangement" with Indonesian officials for what would become a $500 million investment in West Papua copper. *West Papua,* which was not even a part of Indonesia.

Freeport-McMoRan Copper & Gold Inc. is the world's lowest-cost **copper** producer, one of the world's largest producers of **gold**, and the largest publicly traded copper and **molybdenum** producer in the world. Best known for its Grasberg mine in

1961

Papua province, Indonesia, the company is the largest taxpayer to the Indonesian government. It mines and mills ores containing copper, gold, molybdenum **and silver. McMoRan Exploration Company,** is an **oil and gas** exploration company.

1962

The Oldest Boomer is 16 years old.

Cost of the Average House: $15,700	
Median Family Income: $6,000	**Minimum Wage:** $1.15/ hr
Gallon of Milk: 49 cents **Loaf of Bread:** 20 cents	**Gallon Gasoline:** 31cents **Daily Newspaper:** 10 cents
New Car: **Chevrolet Corvette:** $4,038 **Ford Galaxie 500** **XL Skyliner:** $3,350 **Austin Mini Cooper S:** $1,295	**45 rpm record:** $1.00 **Music Album 33 1/3 rpm:** $3.00 **Movie Ticket:** 50 cents, **popcorn** +20cents
Unemployment Rate: 5.8%-5.4%-5.5%	**First-class Stamp:** 4 cents

14 cents buying power in 1962 = **$1.00 in 2008.**
In 1962 what cost us 14 cents to purchase now costs us $1.00 in 2008.

Movies: "Lawrence of Arabia," "To Kill a Mockingbird," "The Manchurian Candidate," "La Dolce Vita," "The Longest Day," "The Music Man," "Mutiny on the Bounty," "The Miracle Worker," "The Three Stooges in Orbit." "Dr. No-James Bond." "The Three Stooges Meet Hercules."

Broadway: "I Can Get It for You Wholesale." "No Strings." "This Was Burlesque," off-Broadway-revue. "A Funny Thing Happened on the Way to the Forum."

TV: "The Alfred Hitchcock Hour," "The Lucy Show," "McHale's Navy," "Beverly Hillbillies," "I'm Dickens—He's Fenster," "Benny Hill," "Combat," "The Roy Rogers-Dale Evans Show," "The Saint," "The Jetsons," "The Virginian," "The Tonight Show Starring Johnny Carson," "Stump the Stars," "Stoney Burke," "Beany and Cecil," "Merv Griffin Show". John Glenn's earth orbit is televised for 135 million viewers.

Music: Maurice Jarre, "Lawrence of Arabia." Meredith Willson, "The Music

Man." Elmer Bernstein, "To Kill a Mockingbird." Soundtrack of "West Side Story" tops the music charts for 54 weeks. Isley Brothers, "Twist And Shout." James Brown & The Famous Flames, "Lost Someone." King Curtis, "Soul Twist." Ray Charles, "I Can't Stop Loving You." Sam Cooke, "Bring It On Home To Me." Claude King, "Wolverton Mountain." Porter Wagoner, "Misery Loves Company." Dee Dee Sharp, "Mashed Potato Time." Bobby Vinton, "Roses Are Red." David Rose, "The Stripper." Elvis Presley, "Good Luck Charm," "Return To Sender," "Follow That Dream" & "Can't Help Falling in Love." Marcie Blane, "Bobby's Girl." Neil Sedaka, "Breaking up Is Hard to Do" & "King of Clowns." Roy Orbison, "Dream Baby." Gene Chandler, "Duke of Earl." James Darren, "Goodbye Cruel World." Shelley Fabares, "Johnny Angel." Little Eva, "The Loco-Motion." The Beatles Love, "Me Do." Walter Brennan, "Old Rivers." Joey Dee and the Starliters, "Peppermint Twist." Shirelles, "Soldier Boy." Bobby "Boris" Pickett, "The Monster Mash." Mark Wynter, "Venus in Blue Jeans."

President: John F. Kennedy (D) Roman Catholic; vetoes 60/ 0 overrides	
Vice President: Lyndon B. Johnson (D) Disciples of Christ	
House: D-263 ; R-174	
Senate: 87th Congress (1961-1963) Majority Party: Democrat (64 seats) Minority Party: Republican (36 seats) Other Parties: 0 Total Seats: 100	
Federal Debt: $298.20 billion or 51 % of the GDP	
Consumer Price Index CPI-U (1982 Base of 100): 30.20	
GDP: $585.6 billion	**Inflation Rate:** 1.20%
Dow Jones: 650 (December)/ 535.76 (06-26)	
Average Home Mortgage Rate: 5.93%	
1 oz Gold: $35.35	**1oz of Silver:** $1.12
Federal Debt: $298,200,822,720.87	
Federal Deficit: $7.1 billion dollars	
Defense Spending: $63.60 billion	**Interest Spending:** $6.89 billion

Health Care Spending: $1.20 billion	**Pensions Spending:** $11.72 billion
Welfare Spending: $6.59 billion	**Education Spending:** $1.74 billion
Transportation Spending: $4.29 billion	**Misc. Other Spending:** $9.02 billion
Protection Spending: $430 million	**Total Government Spending:** $106.82 billion

% of GDP that goes towards just the interest payment: 1.21%

$1.00 = 360.86 Yen, Japan

U.S. Population: 186,590,000	**World Population:** 3,136,197,751
U.S. Birth Rate: 4,167,362	**U.S. Abortions:** 292
U.S. Homicide Rate: 4.8/ 100,000 population	**U.S. Violent Crime:** 162.3/ 100,000 population

Annual Average Domestic Crude Oil Prices:
$2.85 / barrel, $20.24 (2007 adjusted)

Oil:

1962 – During the year of the **Cuban Missile Crisis,** oil prices didn't rise.

October 16, 1962 – President Kennedy decides to take on the oil industry. On October 16, Kennedy is able to persuade Congress to pass an act that removes the distinction between repatriated profits and profits reinvested abroad. While this law applies to industry as a whole, it especially affects the oil companies. As a result of this legislation, wealthy oilmen saw their earnings on foreign investment cut in half.

1962 – Algeria is granted independence and most Europeans leave the country. Terror, counter-terror, and violence are what observers bitterly record when they describe the circle of hate that is so tenacious and evident as Algeria has consistently tried to regain its Arab and Islamic heritage even though the influence of the French language and culture remain strong. At the same time, the development of oil, natural gas and other mineral deposits in the Algerian interior bring new wealth and a modest rise in the standard of living. In 2001 its economy is among the largest in Africa.

1962 – Abu Dhabi begins to export petroleum. Massive amounts of money start to flow into Abu Dhabi, now part of UAE, when it begins to export petroleum. Foreign workers are hired by the hundreds of thousands because the small local population cannot meet the need for planned construction of hospitals, roads, and schools.

1962 – Libyan oil. From 1954 to 1962 in search of water and minerals large areas of Libya were photographed by the petroleum industry supplementing the information gleaned from the large portions that had been mapped by the Italians, British, American military personnel, and by the United States Geological Survey. Active exploration in Libya had started in 1953 after oil was discovered in neighboring Algeria.

1962 – Onam. Oil is discovered at Yibal. By the end of 1984 average daily production had risen to 400,000 barrels per day and reserves stood at 3.8 billion barrels.

Major News:

February 14, 1962 – President John F. Kennedy says that U.S. military advisers in **Vietnam** would fire if fired upon; one of the first signs of the Vietnam conflict.

April 21, 1962 – The Seattle Century 21 Exposition, the first **World's Fair** held in the United States since World War II, opens in central Seattle under the theme of space exploration. Over 9.6 million visitors will attend the exposition over the next 184 days. Knowing that the Fair needed some eye-catching icons for the world press the two most futuristic and lasting legacies of Seattle Century 21, **the Monorail** and **the Space Needle,** were built and are still in operation in 2010.

October 22, 1962 – A Soviet offensive missile buildup in Cuba is revealed by President Kennedy. U.S. forces around the world are placed on alert and more than

100,000 troops are deployed to Florida for a possible invasion of Cuba. Additional naval vessels are ordered to the Caribbean and **B-52s loaded with nuclear weapons** are in the air at all times.

The United States catches the Soviet Union building offensive nuclear missile bases in Cuba, just 90 miles from U.S. soil, and the two superpowers are joined in **the first direct nuclear confrontation in history.** Reconnaissance flights over Cuba begin in June/July, and surveillance photographs taken on October 14 show the construction of a Soviet medium-range ballistic missile base near San Cristobal. The President immediately meets with his most trusted advisers to serve as an Executive Committee of the National Security Council and they discuss several courses of action from doing nothing to a full invasion of Cuba. After thirty-eight days of debate, in what many think was the closest the Cold War came to breaking into armed conflict, a naval blockade of the island emerges as the leading choice and lowers the risk of all out war.

October 22, 1962 – President Kennedy gives a key warning in his first public speech on the **Cuban Missile Crises**. "It shall be the policy of this nation to regard any nuclear missile launched from Cuba against any nation in the Western Hemisphere as an attack on the United States, requiring a full retaliatory response upon the Soviet Union."

Civil Rights Movement:

1962 – Students for a Democratic Society proclaim the Port Huron Statement, an early step in the era of student protest.

1962 – Mass demonstrations resume in Albany, Georgia, in late July but are suspended in August when the local leadership decides to concentrate on voter registration.

August 27, 1962 – Congress submits the Twenty-fourth Amendment to the Constitution, abolishing poll taxes in federal elections, to the states for ratification.

October 1, 1962 – The Fifth Circuit Court of Appeals orders **James Meredith** admitted to the **University of Mississippi** and he becomes the first black student at the University after **3,000 troops** put down riots. His enrollment is bitterly opposed by segregationist Governor Ross Barnett, sparking riots on the Oxford campus, which require **federal troops** and **U.S. Marshals,** to be sent by **President John F. Kennedy.** The riots lead to a violent clash leaving two people dead, including French journalist Paul Guihard, who was on assignment for the London *Daily Sketch.* Guihard, was found behind a dormitory block with a gunshot wound to the back. Forty-eight soldiers are injured and twenty-eight U.S. Marshals are wounded by gunfire. **Mississippi Governor Ross Barnett is fined $10,000 and sentenced to jail** for contempt, but the charges are later dismissed by the 5th Circuit Court of Appeals.

1962 – In South Carolina the all-white legislature votes to fly the **Confederate Naval Jack** over the capitol dome to mark the hundredth anniversary of the Confederate secession.

November 20, 1962 – President John Kennedy issues Executive Order 11063 on November 20, prohibiting racial discrimination in federally owned housing, in public housing built with federal funds, and in new housing built with loans from federal agencies.

Popular Culture:

1962 – Touch-tone phones are a hit at the Seattle World's Fair.

March 26, 1962 – In "Baker vs. Carr," the Supreme Court backed **"one-man one-vote"** apportionment of seats in state legislatures.

1962 – Timothy Francis Leary "Turn on, tune in, drop out." Leary and Richard Alpert begin a research program known as the **Harvard Psilocybin Project.** The goal is to analyze the effects of psilocybin on human subjects, in this case, prisoners and later students of the **Andover Newton Theological Seminary,** using a synthesized version of one of two active compounds found in a wide variety of hallucinogenic mushrooms including Psilocybe Mexicana. The drugs are legal in 1962 and are produced according to a recipe developed by research chemist Albert Hofmann of

Sandoz Pharmaceuticals. Research participants reported profound mystical and spiritual experiences, which they claim permanently, altered their lives in a very positive manner.

Leary and Alpert establish the **International Foundation for Internal Freedom** in 1962 in Cambridge, Massachusetts. This was run by Lisa Bieberman, a disciple of Leary and one of his many lovers. The hallucinogenic drug research attracted a great deal of public attention and many people wanted to participate in the experiments but were turned away. **This lead to a black-market in psychedelic drugs** being developed near the Harvard University Campus by various chemistry majors. Leary's Harvard colleagues are not pleased with the various rumors and complaints associated with the drug research.

1962 – **The Supreme Court**, in Engel vs. Vitale disallows a government-composed, nondenominational "Regents" prayer which is recited by students. **Any kind of prayer,** composed by public school districts, even nondenominational prayer, is unconstitutional government sponsorship of religion, so says the Supreme Court.

1962 – **Baseball cards.** Topps Mickey Mantle, Willie Mays PSA 7, Book-$200.00, Sale-$175.00. (02/2009)

November 4, 1962 – The U.S. carries out its last nuclear test in the Pacific; Tightrope.

1962 – **Andy Warhol** paints 32 images of **Campbell's Soup cans.** "Campbell's Soup Can, 19¢" by Andy Warhol. Warhol became the most-renowned American pop art artist, and also the highest-paid living American artist.

1962 – **MIT students** Slug Russell, Shag Graetz, and Alan Kotok wrote **"Spacewar"** considered the first interactive computer game. It can be played by competitors on a variety of computers.

1962 – Ideals' **Odd Og, Half Turtle-Half Frog.** He walks backwards and you roll the balls, hit him, and he rolls forward making a low-croaking sound. Miss him and he retreats, sticks out his tongue and makes a "razzing" frog noise. $5.97

1962

Business / Technology:

1962 – An estimated 44% of the world population is **illiterate.**

February 20, 1962 – **Lt. Colonel John H. Glenn Jr.,** 40, becomes the first American in orbit when he circles the earth 3 times in the Mercury capsule "**Friendship 7.**" He lands safely in the Atlantic Ocean after travelling about 81,000 miles as he circled the globe three times at more than 17,000 mph.

1962 – **The Communications Satellite Corporation COMSAT** begins operations with its headquarters in Washington, DC, It is created to launch and operate global satellite system.

1962 – The concept of **Packet-Switching Networks** is first explored by Paul Baran.

1962 – **The first Taco Bell** is built and in 1964 it was not uncommon for a franchise to clear $10,000 in one month.

1962 – **Silicone Breast Implants** are deemed successful and much safer than inserting foam and other materials directly into the breast. There will be lawsuits. There were 32,000 in 1992 and 347,000 in 2007, over ten times the number of implants done in 1992. In 2007 breast augmentation is the number one cosmetic procedure performed annually. In 1992 it was number six.

   "**We are hammering our children with the notion that how they look** is more important than who they are and what they can do. And that is just wrong," said Joseph Kelly, President of **Dads and Daughters.**

1962 – The U.S. Congress passes the **Kefauver Harris Drug Amendments,** requiring that drug companies show evidence their products are safe to a relative degree.

1962 – **President John F. Kennedy** issues Executive Order 10988 establishing limited **collective bargaining rights** for federal employees and widely regarded as the impetus for the expansion of public sector bargaining rights at state and local levels in the years to come.

August 27, 1962 – Mariner II sends radio signals from Venus. The primary mission is to receive communications from the **spacecraft in the vicinity of Venus** and to perform radiometric temperature measurements of the planet. A second objective is to measure the Interplanetary Magnetic Field and charged particle environment.

Finance:

1962 – DJIA. In August, when the markets endured the **Cuban missile crisis**, the Dow was at 615. It fell to 550 in October and rose to 650 in December.

1962 – The first Wal-Mart opens. Discount retailing is highly controversial as it threatens the manufactures control of the market. **Ben Franklin** variety store owner **Sam Walton** feels the heat from discount merchandisers, so he creates one of his own. Walton opens **Wal-Mart Discount City** in Rogers, Arkansas. That same year, **S.S. Kresge Co.** launches **Kmart**, **F.W. Woolworth** starts **Woolco** and **Dayton Hudson begins** its **Target** chain and discounting is here to stay. Sam Walton borrows ideas freely from other discounters and places his stores on the outskirts of small towns where the cost is low. Although Sam promotes "Made in America," he imports as much as he can from China at lower costs and the consumers love the everyday low prices. This may be the first footfalls of the rush to a super–consumer economy. By 1989 Sam is **the richest man in America** with 39% ownership of Wal-Mart's stock.

September 28, 1962 – Authority over the trust powers of national banks was assigned to the Comptroller of the Currency.

Books:

1962 – Rachel Carson's "Silent Spring" launches the environmentalist movement.

1962 – Helen Gurley Brown. "Sex and the Single Girl." In 1959 Helen Gurley married David Brown, a motion picture producer. She left advertising in 1962 when her first book, *Sex and the Single Girl*, became an immediate best-seller. Her advice to young single women on such topics as career, fashion, love, and entertainment emphasized the **positive benefits of unmarried life.**

1962

1962 – **Alexander Solzhenitsyn,** "One Day in the Life of Ivan Denisovitch."

1962 – **"One Flew Over the Cuckoo's Nest,"** Ken Kesey.

1962 – Muriel Spark, **"The Prime of Miss Jean Brodie."**

1962 – **"A Clockwork Orange,"** Anthony Burgess.

TV:

1962 – **"The Mickey Mouse Club"** show returns to TV, as a half-hour syndicated re-run.

Sports:

March 2, 1962 – Wilt Chamberlain set the NBA single-game scoring record by tallying 100 points for the **Philadelphia Warriors** in a 169-147 victory over the **New York Knicks.** Chamberlain also holds the second-place spot on the points-in-a-single-game list, 78, and 15 of the top 20.

1962 – Ernie Davis, a running back at Syracuse University, becomes the first African American athlete to receive football's Heisman Trophy.

Music:

January 1, 1962 – "The Beatles" and **"Brian Poole and the Tremeloes"** both audition at **Decca Records,** a company which has the option of signing one group only. After recording 15 songs the Beatles are rejected. The Tremeloes are one of the longest surviving English rock and roll bands and are still playing regularly more than 50 years after the group's founding in 1958. They had fourteen UK and two U.S. **Top 20 hit singles.** They were the first south of England group to top the chart in the beat boom era. Brian Poole, Chip Hawkes and The Tremeloes toured the UK as part of their 40th anniversary reunion in September 2006.

August 16, 1962 – The Beatles replace Pete Best on drums with **Ringo Starr.**

1962 – Mick Jagger and **Keith Richards** meet **Brian Jones** at *The Ealing Club,* a blues club in London.

1962 – Otis Redding's musical career begins.

April 10, 1962 – Stuart Fergusson Victor Sutcliffe dies of a brain hemorrhage on the way to the hospital. He was a painter and the original bassist of **The Beatles** for eighteen months. Sutcliffe and John Lennon are credited with coming up with the name for the Beatles, as they both liked Buddy Holly's band, the Crickets.

1962 – Booker T. & the MG's' musical career begins.

1962 – The Rolling Stones form in London.

1962 – Isaac Hayes' recording career begins.

1962 – Paul & Paula make their first appearance together while attending Howard Payne College in Brownwood, Texas.

November 14, 1962 – Little Richard and the Beatles perform at the *Star Club* in Hamburg, West Germany. **"Love Me Do"** is released in October in the UK and **"Please, Please Me,"** is released in November.

Natural Disasters:

January 10, 1962 – Peru. An avalanche down the extinct **Huascaran Volcano** kills more than 3,000 people.

October 12, 1962 – The Columbus Day Storm strikes the U.S. Pacific Northwest with record wind velocities leaving 46 people dead. The storm is a contender for the title of most powerful extratropical cyclone recorded in the U.S. in the 20th century. The storm leaves nearly $200 million dollars in damage to Oregon, and another $40-

$80 million in damage to California and Washington. Adjusted to early 2000 dollars the amount of damage is 3 to 5 Billion dollars.

November 5, 1962 – A moderately strong earthquake with a 4.75 magnitude causes minor damage in the Vancouver, Washington—Portland, Oregon, area.

Man vs. Man / Wars:

Attempted Assassination – February 27, 1962. President of the Republic of Vietnam, Ngo Dinh Diem survives an attempted assassination by two dissident Republic of Vietnam Air Force pilots. The pilots targeted the Independence Palace, the official residence of the President of South Vietnam, with the aim of assassinating President Diem and his immediate family, who act as his political advisors. The pilots stated later that their assassination attempt was in response to Diem's autocratic rule, in which he focused more on remaining in power than on confronting the Vietcong.

Attempted Assassination – August 22, 1962. French President Charles de Gaulle survives an assassination attempt by Jean Bastien-Thiry and the OAS (Organization of the Secret Army). They were trying to prevent Algerian independence.

October 16, 1962 – **Representative** Thomas F. Johnson (D-Maryland) is **indicted** on eight counts of conspiracy and conflict of interest. The indictment alleges that Johnson received more than $20,000 for giving a speech in the House favorable to savings and loan institutions. He is also accused of interceding with the U.S. Attorney General to obtain a dismissal of an indictment against a Maryland savings and loan association. He is convicted, on June 13, 1963, of conflict of interest and sentenced to **six months in prison.** The sentence is reversed on September 13, 1964.

October 16, 1962 – **Representative** Frank W. Boykin (D-Alabama) is **indicted** for conflict of interest and conspiracy to defraud the government. Boykin tried to get the Department of Justice to dismiss indictments against a Maryland savings and loan association. In October 1963, he was placed on six months' probation and fined $40,000. He will be **pardoned by President Lyndon Johnson.**

1954-1962 – Algeria gains its independence from France on July 5, 1962. The **Algerian War of Independence** is a conflict between France and Algerian independence movements from 1954 to 1962. The summer of 1962 saw 1.4 million refugees, including almost the entire Jewish community and some pro-French Muslims, join the exodus to France. **Nearly 700,000 people died** during the eight year war. Thousands of Muslim civilians lost their lives in French army ratissages, bombing raids, and vigilante reprisals. The war forced more than 2 million Algerians, to relocate in French camps or to flee to Morocco, Tunisia, and into the Algerian interior, where many thousands of people died of starvation, disease, and exposure. In addition large numbers of pro-French Muslims were murdered when the FLN settled accounts after independence.

1961-1962 – Angola Atrocities. The uprisings are responsible for up to 40,000 deaths, with many people dying from disease or because of famine. About 400 Europeans are killed, as well as many black Angolans and Africans deemed sympathetic to colonial authorities. By summer the Portuguese had reduced the area controlled by the rebels to one-half its original extent, but major pockets of resistance remain. Portuguese forces, relying heavily on air power, attacked many villages. The result was the mass exodus of Africans toward First Republic of the Congo (Belgian Congo, Zaire, or Democratic Republic of the Congo: they are all the same country at different times.)

1962-1963 – Argentina's "Black Year." Argentina's local and congressional elections in 1962, allow Peronist candidates on the ballot for the first time since the ouster of their leader Juan Domingo Peron as President in 1955. The Peronistas win 45 out of 86 seats in the Chamber of Deputies and 9 of 14 governorships. The anti-Peronist military leaders, ultraconservatives known as the "Gorillas," are so outraged they refuse to permit the elected Peronistas to take their seats in the government. The majority of the people go on strike, the country goes into chaos and when Argentina's President Arturo Frondizi refuses to resign the Gorillas forcibly remove him from office and seize control of the government. There is much infighting until free elections are held in 1963.

1962

1962-1966 – Brunei Rebellion. Brunei is emerging as a major oil producer and the **Indonesia-Malaysia confrontation** is an undeclared war over the future of the island of Borneo, between British-backed Malaysia and Indonesia. In Brunei, the Indonesian-backed North Kalimantan National Army revolts on December 8, 1962. They try to capture the Sultan of Brunei, seize the oil fields and take European hostages but the Sultan escapes and receives help from British and Gurkha troops from Singapore. On December 16, the British Far Eastern Command claimed that all major rebel centers had been occupied, and on April 17, 1963, the rebel commander was captured and the rebellion ended.

1962 – Burma Army Coup. General Ne Win leads a **military coup** that removes Prime Minister U Nu and his civilian government. The Burmese path to Socialism drives the formerly prosperous country into deep poverty as Burma remains under the tight control of the military-led State Peace and Development Council.

July 1, 1962 – Burundi becomes an independent republic and joins the United Nations in August. A constitutional monarchy is established and the **Hutu** and **Tutsi** hold equal representation in Parliament.

Hutu forces are not happy with the arrangement and take control of the country forcing thousands of **Tutsi** out of the country into Rwanda. In 1962-1963 12,000 Tutsi are killed and 200,000 to 250,000 people flee the country.

1962-1971 – The Cameroon Rebellion. In February 1961 the inhabitants of British Cameroon have a choice of joining independent **Cameroon** or neighboring **Nigeria.** In the largely Muslim northern areas the vote favors Nigeria, but in the mostly Christian south, they vote for reunification with Cameroon. The Bamilekes, supported by many communist states and newly independent **Ghana** and **Guinea,** demand a separate autonomous state and the Bamilekes rebels increasingly reject the authority of their traditional rulers. Civil war breaks out forcing many to move to large cities. The Cameroon government, with French military assistance, will defeat the continuing Bamileke revolt in 1963. The five year rebellion will be responsible for over 70,000 people's deaths.

1962-1963 – China vs. India. Sino-Indian War. Fighting begins in June 1962 between the People's Liberation Army and the Military of India. Official military casualty figures for China, as confirmed by the Chinese government, stand at 722 people killed, 1,047 people wounded, and 2 people captured. Official military casualty figures for India, as confirmed by the Indian government, stand at 3,128 people killed, 3,123 people captured, and 1,697 people wounded.

1962 – Cuban Missile Crisis. In the fall of 1962, the United States and the Soviet Union come very close to **global nuclear war.** American **U-2 aircraft** photographed missile sites in western Cuba and further intelligence indicated that the missiles, SS-4 and SS-5, both with 1 megaton warheads, had the ability to reach almost the entire continental USA, including every Strategic Air Command base. In what becomes known as the Cuban Missile Crisis, **President John F. Kennedy** considers an invasion of Cuba and possible **all out nuclear war with the Soviets.** After six tense days of deliberation between the Soviet Union and President Kennedy's cabinet, President Kennedy secretly agreed to remove all missiles set in Turkey on the border of the Soviet Union in exchange for Nikita Khrushchev removing all missiles and offensive weapons in Cuba.

December 1962 – Cuba. Castro releases 1,113 captured rebels from the Bay of Pigs in exchange for $53 million in food and medicine raised by private donations in the United States.

1962 – Eritrean-Ethiopian War. In 1952 the United Nations tried to satisfy the demand for self-determination by creating an Eritrean Ethiopian Federation. **Haile Selassie** unilaterally abolishes the federation and imposes imperial rule throughout Eritrea. Formally a province of Ethiopia, Eritrea gains its independence in 1993 after a long guerrilla war. Between 1998 and 2000, they will be at war again, spending hundreds of millions of dollars and killing up to 100,000 people.

1962 – Guatemalan Student Riots. In March 1962, there are student riots in Guatemala City, costing 20 lives. Between 1962 and 1970 in order to defeat a couple of hundred rebels, the counterinsurgency in Guatemala killed about 10,000 people.

1962

1962-1974 – Guinea-Bissau Independence. In late 1962, small guerrilla bands begin attacking Portuguese army posts and police stations, and many areas are soon cleared of foreigners. Each band establishes a base in the forest from which it stages its operations. The Portuguese retaliate by bringing in warplanes and more troops from Lisbon to better attack guerrilla bases.

1962-1975 – Cambodia-Pathet Lao Insurgency. In the 1960s, more attempts at neutrality agreements and coalition government are attempted but as North Vietnam has no intention of withdrawing from Laos, these agreements fail. By the mid 1960s, the country has fallen into proxy warfare between pro-U.S. and pro-Vietnamese irregular military groups. This will continue until 1975 when the Pathet Lao convince the King to abdicate and establish the People's Democratic Republic.

April 1962 – Dutch New Guinea Guerrillas. Indonesia's President Sukarno is at last going to do more than talk about grabbing the disputed territory that he calls **West Irian.** Indonesia broadcast reports of widely spaced troop landings on New Guinea's coast and Waigeo Island, forcing the Dutch to spread out their meager defenses consisting of 5,800 combat troops. The Dutch Parliament is about to debate the situation in New Guinea and they are forced to send more troops which proves to be unpopular in **The Netherlands.**

Sukarno is training **25,000 Indonesians** to lead the invasion. Even young boys and girls drill in Djakarta parks while Sukarno shops for landing craft to ferry the invaders across 1,600 miles of open sea to New Guinea.

1962-2009 – Indonesia gained its independence from the Netherlands in 1949. October 1, 1962, the Dutch handed over the territory of **West Papua** to a United Nations Temporary Executive Authority. On May 01, 1963, with heavy pressure on the UN by the U.S. Administration, Indonesia takes control of the territory from the UN. Many argue that the takeover of West Papua was an invasion by the Indonesian military. The territory was renamed West Irian and then Irian Jaya.

Since **1961, West Papuan people** in the 'Indonesian Province' of Papua raising the Morning Star flag in public have been shot by Indonesian soldiers. West Papuan resistance to Indonesia began in 1962 when temporary authority was first given to Jakarta, and continues into 2010.

1962 – Nepal. Declaring parliamentary democracy a failure, King Mahendra carries out a royal coup.

1962-1975 – Portugal vs. Mozambique - Eduardo Mondlane forms the political and military Mozambique Liberation Front in neighboring Tanzania. He holds the organization together by obtaining support from both communist and western European countries while building a rebel army of several thousand guerrillas who are active in northern Mozambique. The war officially starts on September 25, 1964.

1962-1963 – The Rwandan Civil War. The Tutsi are ruled by a King from the 15th century until 1961 when the monarchy is abolished by the Belgians, in response to the desires of both **Tutsi and Hutu,** following a national referendum leading up to independence. Two new countries emerge: **Rwanda, dominated by the Hutus,** and **Burundi by the Tutsis,** and the ethnic fighting flared on and off in the following decades.

In 1962 Civil war begins in Rwanda as Tutsi military forces try to gain control of the new country after the majority Hutus had won control in free elections. Between 1961 and 1962, Tutsi guerrillas stage attacks into Rwanda from neighboring countries. Rwandan Hutu-based troops respond and thousands more are killed in the clashes.

January 12, 1962 – Vietnam. American forces participate in the first combat actions against the Viet Cong. Later in the year, defoliant **Agent Orange,** manufactured by several American companies including **Dow Chemical,** is used for the first time in Vietnam.

May 15, 1962 – Vietnam. President Kennedy orders an immediate build-up of U.S. troops in Thailand to a total of 5,000 due to Communist attacks in Laos and movement toward the Thailand border.

1962-1970 – The North Yemen Civil War. Shortly after assuming power in 1962, Crown Prince Muhammad al-Badr is deposed by revolutionary forces, which take control of Sana'a and create the **Yemen Arab Republic. Egypt, with backing from the Soviet Union,** sends troops to support the Yemeni Republican government against Royalist rebels supported by **Saudi Arabia.**

The Imam escapes to the Saudi Arabian border and rallies popular support. The royalist side receives support from Saudi Arabia. **Egyptian President Gamal Abdel Nasser** supports the republicans with 70,000 troops. Despite several military moves and peace conferences, the war sinks into a stalemate until 1967 when Egyptian troops are withdrawn.

1963

The Oldest Boomer is 17 years old.

Cost of the Average House: $19,300	
Median Family Income: $6,200	Minimum Wage: $1.25/ hr Average Hourly Wage: $2.46
Gallon of Milk: 49 cents Zenith Portable 19" TV: $149.99	Gallon Gasoline: 30cents Dozen Eggs: 54 cents
New Car: Buick Riviera: $4,300 Pontiac Tempest: $2,418 Studebaker Avanti: $4,450	Loaf of Bread: 23 cents RCA Whirlpool Washer & Dryer: $298
Unemployment Rate: 5.7%-5.9%-5.5%	First-class Stamp: 5 cents

14 cents buying power in 1963 = **$1.00 in 2008.**
In 1963 what cost us 14 cents to purchase now costs us $1.00 in 2008.

Movies: "8 ½," "Tom Jones," "America, America," "Cleopatra," "How the West Was Won," "Lilies of the Field". "Hud," "It's a Mad, Mad, Mad, Mad World." "The Three Stooges Go Around the World in a Daze."

Broadway: "Oliver!" "Danny Kaye," revue. "She Loves Me," "110 in the Shade," "The Girl Who Came to Supper."

TV: The "I Have a Dream," speech. Jack Ruby Shoots Lee Harvey Oswald on live TV "Petticoat Junction," "The Fugitive," "Quick Draw McGraw," "Temple Houston," "Dakotas," "Doctor Who," "Richard Boone," "Beetle Bailey," "General Hospital," "The Art Linkletter Show," "My Favorite Martian," "The French Chef" with Julia Child. "Let's Make a Deal." John-John's Salute on November 25.

Music: Little Stevie Wonder, "Fingertips." Martha & The Vandellas, "Heat Wave." Little Johnny Taylor, "Part Time Love." Jackie Wilson, "Baby Workout." Buck Owens, "Act Naturally." Johnny Cash, "Ring Of Fire."

Jimmy Gilmer & The Fireballs, "Sugar Shack." Beach Boys, "Surfin' U.S.A." Cascades, "Rhythm Of The Rain." Chiffons, "He's So Fine." Skeeter Davis, "The End Of The World." Buddy Holly, "Brown Eyed Handsome Man" & "Bo Diddley." Paul & Paula, "Hey Paula." Roy Orbison, "In Dreams," "Blue Bayou" & "Mean Woman Blues." The Beatles, "Please Please Me," "She Loves You," "Love Me Do," "From Me to You," "I want to Hold Your Hand." Jan & Dean, "Surf City." Lesley Gore, "It's My Party." The Surfaris, "Wipe Out." Trini Lopez, "If I Had A Hammer." The Drifters, "Up On The Roof." Dusty Springfield, "I Only Want to Be With You." Bobby Vee, "The Night Has a Thousand Eyes." Kingsmen, "Louie-Louie."

Deaths: Patsy Cline, Addie Mae Collins, Carole Robertson, Cynthia Wesley, Denise McNair. **Thích Quảng Đức**, a Vietnamese Buddhist monk, burns himself to death in front of reporters at a busy intersection in Saigon. He was protesting against the persecution of Buddhists by South Vietnam's Ngo Dinh Diem administration.

President: John F. Kennedy (D) Roman Catholic; vetoes 60/ 0 overrides
President: Lyndon B. Johnson (D) Disciples of Christ; vetoes 30/ 0 overrides

Vice President: Lyndon B. Johnson (D) Disciples of Christ
(no Vice President, 1963–65)

House: D-259 ; R-176

Senate: 88th Congress (1963-1965) Majority Party: Democrat (66 seats) Minority Party: Republican (34 seats) Other Parties: 0 Total Seats: 100

Federal Debt: $305.86 billion or 50 % of the GDP

Consumer Price Index CPI-U (1982 Base of 100): 30.60

GDP: $617.7 billion	**Inflation Rate:** 1.24%

Dow Jones: 775. (December)/ 659.72 (03-01)

Average Home Mortgage Rate: 5.81%

1 oz Gold: $35.25	**1oz of Silver:** $1.29

Federal Debt: $305,859,632,996.41

Federal Deficit: $4.8 billion dollars

Defense Spending: $64.22 billion	**Interest Spending:** $7.74 billion
Health Care Spending: $1.45 billion	**Pensions Spending:** $13.23 billion
Welfare Spending: $6.44 billion	**Education Spending:** $1.99 billion
Transportation Spending: $4.60 billion	**Misc. Other Spending:** $9.70 billion
Protection Spending: $470 million	**Total Government Spending:** $111.32 billion
% of GDP that goes towards just the interest payment: 1.29%	
$1.00 = 361.49 Yen, Japan	
U.S. Population: 189,300,000	**World Population:** 3,205,706,699
U.S. Birth Rate: 4,098,020	**U.S. Abortions:** 390
U.S. Homicide Rate: 4.9/ 100,000 population	**U.S. Violent Crime:** 168.2/ 100,000 population
Annual Average Domestic Crude Oil Prices: $2.91 / barrel, $20.43 (2007 adjusted)	

Oil:

1963 – OPEC acts unilaterally to raise prices for the first time.

January 17, 1963 – President Kennedy presents his proposals for tax reform. This includes relieving the tax burdens of low-income and elderly citizens. Kennedy also claims he wants to remove special privileges and loopholes. He even says he wants to do away with **the oil depletion allowance.** It has been estimated the removal of the oil depletion allowance will cost Texas oilmen around $300 million a year.

After the assassination of President John Kennedy, **President Lyndon Johnson** stops the government plans to remove the oil depletion allowance. **Richard Nixon** does the same and it is not until the arrival of **Jimmy Carter** that the oil depletion allowance is removed.

May 29, 1963 – The United States starts a last-minute effort to persuade **President Sukarno of Indonesia** from imposing severe restrictions on three foreign oil companies, two of them American.

November 11, 1963 – Argentina has threatened to cancel oil contracts with American companies. W. Averell Harriman, in high-level weekend meetings, warned Argentine leaders if they cancel the contracts worth $300 million in investments, the U.S. may no longer subsidize these loans with taxpayer funded economic aid. When he left for the Alliance for Progress' annual meeting in San Palo, Brazil, he still had no word on the oil contracts.

November 16, 1963 – The Argentine Government issued decrees last night voiding all foreign oil contracts. Most heavily affected were United States companies. The decrees signed by President Arturo Illia made no mention of compensation and announced the appointment of a federal attorney to "initiate action" to recover alleged losses from the contracts.

1963 – Cook Inlet, Alaska. Shell strikes oil.

November 17, 1963 – Peru has indicated that her decision on changing the status of an oil subsidiary of **Standard Oil of New Jersey** is still open to negotiation. This assurance is given to W. Averell Harriman, Under Secretary of State for Political Affairs.

Major News:

November 22, 1963 – President Kennedy is assassinated in Dallas, Texas.

1963 – The Great Train Robbery, England, 2.6 million pounds sterling is stolen from the Glasgow to London mail train in used £1, £5 and £10 notes, the equivalent of £38 million (U.S. $56 million) adjusted for 2008 inflation. An anonymous tip leads the police to a Farm in Leatherslade near Oakley, Buckinghamshire five days later where they find fingerprints of the robbers on a Monopoly board game using real money. They had used two Land Rovers with identical plates to confuse any potential witnesses but it did not help as 13 of the robbers are caught, tried, sentenced by April 16, 1964, and sent to prison.

The robbery was investigated by Detective Chief Superintendent **Jack Slipper** of the Metropolitan Police, known in the press as **"Slipper of the Yard,"** who became so involved with its aftermath that he continued to hunt many of the escaped robbers in retirement.

Ronnie Biggs escaped from prison 15 months into his sentence, and fled to Brazil with a lot of the money. He lived openly in **Rio de Janeiro** for 27 years while the British authorities could not extradite him. An extradition treaty between Brazil and Britain was later signed and Biggs now broke and in poor health willingly returned to England and was imprisoned. Slipper believed Biggs should not be released from prison after returning to the UK in 2001 and he often appeared in the media to comment on any news item connected to the robbery before his death on August 24, 2005 at the age of 81. Ronnie Biggs was released from custody on August 6, 2009, the day before his 80th birthday, on 'compassionate grounds'.

March 18, 1963 – In Gideon vs. Wainwright the Supreme Court rules that all **criminal defendants** must have counsel.

June 17, 1963 – **The Supreme Court rules** that laws requiring **recitation of the Lord's Prayer** or Bible verses in public schools are unconstitutional.

June 23, 1963 – **President Kennedy**, on his European trip, addresses a huge crowd in **West Berlin**. In Kennedy's speech, considered one of his best, he makes the statement: **"Ich bin ein Berliner"** ("I am a Berliner"). It was a huge boost to moral for West Berliners who feared East German occupation.

July 25, 1963 – **The Nuclear Test Ban Treaty is ratified.** The United States, Soviet Union, and Great Britain agree to a limited nuclear test-ban treaty, barring all nuclear testing above ground.

1963

September 1963 – **Joseph Valachi** becomes the highest level **Mafia informer** to date. Despite the notoriety, Joe Valachi's testimony before a Senate committee never leads to the jailing of any criminal. Valachi is a barely literate, low-ranking member of the Mafia whose first hand experience is limited to fairly unimportant events and most of his information is second hand, hearsay or rumor.

November 22, 1963 – **President John F. Kennedy is shot and fatally wounded** as he rides in a motorcade through downtown Dallas, Texas. Vice President Lyndon B. Johnson, riding in the third car behind the President, is unhurt and is sworn in as President. **Lee Harvey Oswald is arrested within hours of the assassination** and charged with President Kennedy's murder. On November 24, while Oswald's transfer from jail is being broadcast on live TV, **Jack Ruby steps out from the crowd and shots Oswald point blank, killing him.** Jack Ruby, a strip–club owner, is convicted of Oswald's murder and dies of lung cancer in **1967,** while awaiting retrial following a reversal of his conviction.

   President Kennedy was most likely shot by a person unknown who was in the storm sewer in front of the grassy knoll at street curb level. The shot that killed President Kennedy came from below the President and from his right front. The shooter then walked underground out of the storm sewer and exited towards the trains on the other side of the grassy knoll. The walk takes just a few minutes.

November 22, 1963 – **Prince Norodom Sihanouk of Cambodia** has asked the French Government for economic and military aid to replace the United States program, which he canceled Tuesday. As French officials studied the request, it was announced that **Paris has renewed a commercial agreement with the Communist regime of North Vietnam.** The indications were that **diplomatic relations between Paris and Hanoi would follow.**

1963 – **India.** To meet the threat from Communist China, **India wants $1 billion** in military aid from the **United States** and the **British Commonwealth**. India's entire national budget for fiscal 1963 is less than $3 billion. The request for help, to be spread over three years, is reported to have been made to top U.S. officials by Indian officials in Washington. By May 25, the Kennedy Administration will pledge long-term military aid to India.

1963 – **An Associated Press survey** shows that **Senator Barry Goldwater** is far ahead of former **Vice President Nixon** and **Governor Rockefeller** for the Republican Presidential nomination.

1963 – **The Profumo Affair. John Profumo, Britain's Secretary of State for War,** is sharing **Christine Keeler,** a good-looking **prostitute,** with the **Russian Naval Attach,** Yevgeny Ivanov. Profumo then lied to the House of Commons about this affair even though he should have known **MIS was involved** because of the Russian connection. Profumo was forced to resign, and soon afterwards Prime Minister Harold Macmillan, also has to resign. In the following general election the Conservative party was swept from power, and a Labour government was elected, with Harold Wilson as Prime Minister.

Civil Rights Movement:

April 23, 1963 – William Lewis Moore, a postal worker and Congress of Racial Equality (CORE) member who staged lone protests against racial segregation, is **murdered** on his final protest. He was thirty–five years old.

William Moore's three protests consisted of walking to the Capital and hand-delivering letters he had written denouncing racial segregation. On April 23, 1963, Moore was interviewed by Charlie Hicks, a reporter from radio station WGAD in Gadsden, Alabama while he walked along a rural stretch of highway. In the interview Moore stated "I intend to walk right up to the governor's mansion in Mississippi and ring his door bell. Then I'll hand him my letter." Less than an hour after the reporter left, Moore's body was found by a passing motorist about one mile further down the road. William Moore had been shot twice in the head at close range with a .22 caliber rifle. The gun's ownership was traced to Floyd Simpson, whom Moore had argued with earlier that day, but no charges were ever filled.

Moore's letter was found and opened. In it Moore wrote "the white man cannot be truly free himself until all men have their rights," and he asked Governor Barnett to "Be gracious and give more than is immediately demanded of you . . ."

1963

After Moore's death ten Freedom Walkers set out from Chattanooga, Tennessee, to complete Moore's walk but they were arrested at the Alabama border by the highway patrol.

Forty-five years later on April 23, 2008, Ellen Johnson and Ken Loukinen walked the 320 miles from Reese City, Alabama to Jackson, Mississippi and delivered Bill Moore's original letter to Dr. Bob Zellner (one of the original Freedom walkers in 1963). Zellner attempted to present the letter to the current Governor of Mississippi, Haley Barbour on May 6, 2008, but **the Governor of Mississippi would not meet with them to accept the letter.**

April 12, 1963 – The Reverend Martin Luther King Jr. is arrested on April 12, and writes his **"Letter from Birmingham Jail,"** responding to the city's white ministers who called for an end to the protests. The clergymen agreed that social injustices existed but argued that the battle against racial segregation should be fought solely in the courts, not in the streets. **King responded that without nonviolent forceful direct actions** such as his, true civil rights could never be achieved. As he put it, "This 'Wait' has almost always meant 'Never.'" He asserted that not only was civil disobedience justified in the face of unjust laws, but that **"one has a moral responsibility to disobey unjust laws."** The letter was first published as "Letter from Birmingham Jail" in the June 12, 1963, edition of "The Christian Century," and in the June 24, 1963, issue of "The New Leader." King was released on bail April 20.

May 2, 1963 – Police arrest close to 1,000 demonstrators as the march for civil rights begins in **Birmingham, Alabama.** This leads to a desegregation agreement, which in turn sparks rioting and violence. The police make more than 2,400 arrests between May 2 and May 7.

May 10, 1963 – Malcolm X, the leader of the **Black Muslims,** warned that Birmingham would look like a picnic compared to racial strife elsewhere unless whites gave into the Negro's demands for equality. Malcolm X criticized **Reverend Martin Luther King** for using children in the demonstrations. After Klansmen set off two bombs in Birmingham on the night of May 11, rioting breaks out despite pleas of movement leaders for continued nonviolence.

May 12, 1963 – Birmingham, Alabama. A riot breaks out in the streets near Birmingham's business district as 2,500 people pour into the streets in protest of the bombing of a Negro motel and the home of the younger brother of the Reverend Dr. Martin Luther King Jr. Several people are injured in the riot when they confront firemen and the police. Dr. Martin Luther King Jr., head of the **Southern Christian Leadership Conference** led an integration drive in Birmingham recently. The first bombing demolished the front half of the home of the Reverend A.D. King. The second bombing rocked the A.G. Gaston Motel, which has served as headquarters for the Negroes' integration campaign.

The rioters burned many automobiles and six small stores. The city police broke up the riot with the help of Negro ministers and civilian defense workers. About 50 persons were injured.

May 13, 1963 – President Kennedy dispatches Federal troops to areas near Birmingham in case more racial violence flares. **President Kennedy** was concerned over a riot of about 2,500 Negroes following bombings of a motel and an integration leader's home. The President also ordered preliminary steps taken toward **federalizing the Alabama National Guard,** which then could be ready in minutes. As he spoke at the White House, armed forces units trained in riot control were already on their way. President Kennedy warned citizens of the Alabama city against repetition of yesterday's demonstrations and urged them to restore the atmosphere of last week's agreement. **Alabama's Governor George Wallace** wired the President that there were enough state and local forces to handle the situation and questioned the President's right to send troops. On May 14, some 3,000 infantrymen, paratroopers and other troops move into Alabama, while F.B.I. agents investigate charges of police brutality lodged by demonstrators.

March 23, 1963 – Birmingham, Alabama. Reinstatement of the 1,100 Negro pupils who were suspended after the demonstrations was ordered by Chief Judge Elbert P. Tattle in Atlanta. His ruling comes only six hours after **a Federal judge in Birmingham refused to issue the order.**

May 25, 1963 – Three days after a Federal judge ordered the **University of Alabama** to admit two Negroes on June 10, the Justice Department asked a Federal court to enjoin Governor George C. Wallace from interfering. The Governor has pledged to **"stand in the schoolhouse door"** to prevent their admission. A hearing was set for June 3.

June, 1963 – Jackson, Mississippi. Students in Jackson poured out of their schools to protest the beatings and arrest of demonstrators at downtown sit-ins. In response, Jackson officials put police and firemen on 24 hour alert with orders to contain the crowds. Hundreds are arrested and Mayor Allen Thompson announces that Jackson could handle 10,000 if necessary. The attitude of Jackson city officials was another reminder that blacks in Mississippi would have no real power until they had the power to elect those who governed them.

1963 – Attorney General Robert Kennedy, after signing the Alabama complaint, **met secretly** in New York with a group of prominent Negroes to get their views on ways to fight segregation and discrimination in the North. The group, which included writers and other professional persons, was understood to have told Mr. Kennedy that race relations in the North had become "explosive."

1963 – The Justice Department is studying a broad proposal for legislative action that would **prohibit racial discrimination** in stores and restaurants selling products that have crossed state lines. Virtually all commercial enterprises would be affected by the invocation of the commerce power of the Constitution.

May 30, 1963 – In Alabama, a resolution **endorsing Governor George C. Wallace's** promised defiance of a court order to integrate the University of Alabama is **approved in the State Senate.** A compromise agreement that includes an appeal against mob violence ends the lengthy filibuster. A Federal judge rules that the Justice Department did not have the right to sue for desegregation of two Alabama school systems.

1963 – As desegregation demands continue in the South, the police in **Tallahassee, Florida,** use tear gas to disperse a group of 150 Negro students.

1963 – Memphis, Tennessee. Acting under a court order, **city officials in Memphis** agree to desegregate all recreational facilities, but they announce that public swimming pool and wading pools will be **closed "for the time being."**

June 11, 1963 – President Kennedy gives a televised address on June 11 in which he calls racial discrimination **"a moral crisis"** and proposes passage of a new civil rights bill.

June 11, 1963 – The University of Alabama is desegregated after **Governor George Wallace** steps aside when confronted by federally deployed **National Guard troops** on June 11.

June 12, 1963 – Civil rights leader Medgar Evers, NAACP leader**, is assassinated** as he enters his home in Jackson, Mississippi. On February 6, 1994 Byron De La Beckwith is convicted of the 1963 murder of civil rights leader Medgar Evers and dies in prison while serving a life term for the murder.

August 28, 1963 – The March on Washington, DC, gathers over 200,000 people in support of **black demands** for equal rights. The highlight is the **"I have a dream" speech by Reverend Martin Luther King Jr.**

September 15, 1963 – The 16th St. Baptist Church in Birmingham, Alabama is bombed. On Sunday, September 15, 1963, a white man was seen getting out of a white and turquoise Chevrolet. He walked to the church and placed a box under the steps. Soon afterwards, at 10.22 a.m., the bomb exploded killing **Denise McNair** (11), **Addie Mae Collins** (14), **Carole Robertson** (14) and **Cynthia Wesley** (14). The four girls had been attending Sunday school classes at the church. Twenty-three other people were also hurt by the blast. **Civil rights activists blamed George Wallace**, the Governor of Alabama, for the killings. Only a week before the bombing he had told the *New York Times* that to stop integration Alabama needed a "few first-class funerals."

October 18, 1963 – University of Wisconsin at Madison has its first substantial antiwar protest on the campus.

1963

November 2, 1963 – A three-judge Federal court in Americus, Georgia, decided to prohibit prosecution of four civil rights workers on charges of insurrection against the state. By a 2-to-1 vote, the panel also directed local authorities to set bail for the defendants and two others, five of whom were held since an anti-segregation demonstration on August 8.

1963 – Harvey Gantt becomes the first African-American to enroll in Clemson University, with little vocal opposition. Years later Gantt becomes Mayor of Charlotte, and runs for the U.S. Senate in North Carolina.

Women's Movement:

1963 – The Presidential Commission on the Status of Women, that President Kennedy established in 1961 reports. The report finds discrimination against women in every aspect of American life and outlines plans to achieve equality. Specific recommendations for women in the workplace include fair hiring practices, paid maternity leave, and affordable child care.

June 10, 1963 – Twenty years after it is first proposed, the **Equal Pay Act** makes it illegal for employers to pay a woman less than what a man would receive for the same job. However, it does not cover domestics, agricultural workers, executives, administrators or professionals.

  "Help Wanted, Male." Until John F. Kennedy signs the Equal Pay Act classified ads are full of that perfectly legal heading. The job market for women is smaller than the job market for men and they earn just 59 cents for every dollar earned by men. The new legislation reverses the practice of paying women less than men for the same job, simply because they are women. By the first quarter of 1998, women would be earning more than 76 cents for every male dollar, and it only took 35 more years for the 30% increase. At this rate women should finally be paid the same as men in another 32 years (2030). Maybe.

1963 – Betty Friedan publishes her highly influential book *The Feminine Mystique*, which describes the dissatisfaction felt by middle-class American housewives with the narrow role imposed on them by society. The book becomes a best-seller and galvanizes the modern women's rights movement.

June 16, 1963 – Russian Cosmonaut, Valentina Vladimirovna Tereshkova, is the first woman in space.

Popular Culture:

March 21, 1963 – Alcatraz. The last twenty-seven prisoners of Alcatraz, the island prison in San Francisco Bay, are ordered removed by **Attorney General Robert F. Kennedy**, and the federal penitentiary is closed.

1963 – Hippies. The hippie subculture is originally a youth movement that began in the United States during the early 1960s and spread around the world. The word **hippie** derives from hipster, and was initially used to describe beatniks who had moved into San Francisco's Haight-Ashbury district. These people inherited the countercultural values of the Beat Generation, created their own communities, listened to psychedelic rock, embraced the sexual revolution, and used drugs such as cannabis and LSD to explore alternative states of consciousness.

1963 – Easy Bake Oven, America's first working toy oven, is turquoise and has a carrying handle and fake stove top. It is manufactured by Kenner Products and sells for $15.95. In its first year, over 500,000 kids talked their parents into buying one.

1963 – Thích Quảng Đức, a Vietnamese Buddhist monk, sits down in the middle of a busy intersection in Saigon, covers himself in gasoline, and lights himself on fire, burning himself to death. Đức was protesting President Ngô Đình Diệm's administration for oppressing the Buddhist religion.

April 30, 1963 – Governor John King signs the Sweepstakes bill and New Hampshire is the first state to sponsor a lottery, New York follows three years later.

May 26, 1963 – A march by 2,000 demonstrators in Scotland protests the **Polaris missile,** a submarine-launched, two-stage solid-fuel nuclear-armed ballistic missile built by Lockheed for the United States Navy.

1963

1963 – **Valium is introduced.** Valium is powerful, inexpensive, and socially acceptable. It quickly becomes **mother's little helper** for millions of housewives during the '60s and beyond. More prescriptions are written for it than for any other drug between 1969 and 1982, as Diazepam (Valium) is used to treat a wide range of conditions and is one of the most frequently-prescribed medications in the world. Valium is the first billion-dollar medicine and profits pour in as it launches the era of superstar prescription drugs.

1963 – **TV is now the principal source of news in the U.S.**, according to a Roper Poll.

June 17, 1963 – The Supreme Court of the United States ruled in the case of "Abington School District vs. Schempp" that laws requiring the recitation of the **Lord's Prayer or Bible verses in public schools** are unconstitutional. The vote is 8 to 1. In a number of major decisions (Murray vs. Curlett; Abington Township School district vs. Schempp) mandatory Bible verse recitation was ruled unconstitutional.

1963 – **Instamatic cameras** with drop-in film cartridges are released. You no longer have to thread the film yourself in a dark place. More than 50 million will be sold.

August 30, 1963 – **Hot Line.** A telephone "hot line" is set up between the White House and the Kremlin to prevent a possible **Nuclear War.** Instead of relying on telegrammed letters that had to travel overseas, the new technology was a momentous step toward the very near future when American and Soviet leaders could simply pick up the phone and be instantly connected 24 hours a day, seven days a week.

1963 – **There are now 81 million telephones** in the United States and 159 million telephones worldwide.

1963 – **Avis, "We try harder."** Doyle Dane Bernbach.

Business / Technology:

May 2, 1963 – **The Government of France** will build a nuclear test center in the **Tahiti** Islands in the Pacific. The center will be used for the development of a French thermonuclear bomb. The new move follows Algerian and African protests on nuclear tests in the Sahara.

1963 – Jimmy Hoffa, President of the **Teamster's Union,** explains plans for overseas picketing.

1963 – A Federal aviation official in Washington claims the **Russians** are designing a **supersonic airliner** in an effort to beat the West to it. The official said the Soviet Union had a good start.

1963 – A 27-year-old Teamsters Union shop steward who opposed the chief of his local, Anthony (Tony Pro) Provenzano, was fatally shot as he left his home in Hoboken to go to work. The victim was Walter Glockner, a former marine.

1963 – The Navy's atomic submarine Thresher, with 129 men aboard, appears to be lost in the Atlantic. Accompanied by the submarine rescue ship USS Skylark the craft took a test dive in water 8,400 feet deep 220 miles east of Boston, and then was silent. At such a depth, according to the **Chief of Naval Operations,** "rescue would be absolutely out of the question." The Navy releases photographs of the lost submarine within weeks clearly showing six major sections of the Thresher's hull. An investigation finds that while the Thresher is operating at test depth, a leak developed in a silver-brazed joint in an engine room seawater system. Water from the leak would have most likely short-circuited electrical equipment, causing a reactor shutdown and leaving the submarine without primary and secondary propulsion systems. The submarine would be unable to blow its main ballast tanks, and due to the boat's weight and depth, the power available from the **emergency propulsion motor** is insufficient to bring the submarine to the surface.

All hands were lost, 129 people.

May 7, 1963 – The Air Force said that another attempt would be made to put copper "needles" in a 2,000-mile-high belt around the earth. On May 13, the successful release in space of **400,000,000 copper needles** is confirmed by radar. Thinner than human hair, the needles are ejected from a satellite to study world radio communication.

1963

1963 – Five-hundred Europeans, most of them West Germans, are working in the **United Arab Republic** as aircraft designers and technicians. About 10 of the scientists are developing ground-to-ground rocket designs.

May 8, 1963 – The second Telstar satellite is placed in orbit.

May 21, 1963 – The Soviet Union has offered to sell machine tools to Britain, the same ones the United States has supplied in the past. Leaders of a British trade mission to Moscow favored the deal.

June 11, 1963 – A patent for the first manned space capsule, the Mercury, is issued to Maxime A. Faget, Andre J. Meyer, Jr., Robert G. Chilton, William S. Blanchard, Jr., Alan B. Kehlet, Jerome B. Hammack, and Caldwell C. Johnson, Jr.

August 29, 1963 – A peaceful settlement to the land dispute between Mexico and the United States is enacted with the signing of the Chamizal Treaty, establishing the boundary in the El Paso Juarez Valley. The dispute, which had been ongoing for ninety-nine years, is now commemorated by the Chamizal National Memorial in El Paso, Texas.

1963 – The U.S. is still moving from an **agricultural** economy to a highly industrial one.

1963 – Sony offers an open-reel videotape recorder for the home, $995.

1963 – The Labor Department announces that an all time high of 70.9 million Americans had jobs in July and unemployment dropped. More civilians than ever are working for the **nation's biggest employer,** government.

1963 – AT&T. The American Telephone and Telegraph Company announced that in June it would split its stock two for one. The world's largest corporation also announced a 10-cent increase in its quarterly dividend and said that it would offer one additional share next February for each 20 shares held. One effect of all the news was a $7.62 a share increase in price on the N.Y. Stock Exchange.

1963 – **Polaroid** instant photography adds color.

April 1, 1963 – The 1962 **New York City newspaper strike**, the longest newspaper strike in U.S. history ends. The 9 major newspapers in New York City had ceased publication for over 114 days.

1963 – **U.S. Car Maker Studebaker** goes out of business and ends production.

November 16, 1963 – In New York City, President Kennedy tells an overflow crowd of unionists at the Americana Hotel that **providing jobs** is the country's most important issue, even ahead of civil rights. Delegates to the A.F.L.-C.I.O. convention, who represent major Democratic resources, gave the President a warm response.

July 1, 1963 – **Postal ZIP codes** begin as business mail makes up 80 percent of the total volume. The computer, brought centralization of accounts and a growing mass of utility bills and payments, bank deposits and receipts, advertisements, magazines, insurance premiums, credit card transactions, department store and mortgage billings, and payments, dividends, and Social Security checks traveling through the mail. A five-digit code had been assigned to every address throughout the country. The first digit designated a broad geographical area of the United States, ranging from zero for the Northeast to nine for the far West. This was followed by two digits that more closely pinpointed population concentrations and those sectional centers accessible to common transportation networks. The final two digits designated small post offices or postal zones in larger zoned cities.

1963 – The **audio cassette** is released by Phillips of Holland.

1963 – Douglas Engelbart gets a patent for the **computer mouse.**

1963 – **Syncom II, a communications satellite,** goes into geo-synchronous orbit.

1963 – **While preparing for the 1964 elections**, the **A.F.L.-C.I.O.** indicated that one of its prime political aims was to fight what it called "the growing threat of the right wing." One major effort in its early start on the election will be a $750,000 register-and-vote campaign directed at union members.

1963

Finance:

1963 – Executive Order 11110 is issued by **President John F. Kennedy** on June 4, 1963. This executive order delegates to the Secretary of the Treasury the President's authority to issue silver certificates under the Thomas Amendment of the Agricultural Adjustment Act. **Six days prior to President John F. Kennedy's assassination,** he ordered the Treasury to print United States Notes to be used as legal tender. These notes were to be backed by silver owned by the U.S. government and would have had real value unlike Federal Reserve Notes which are not backed by anything. A limited number of the notes were printed before his assassination.

   "The high office of President has been used to foment a plot to destroy the American's freedom, and before I leave office I must inform the citizen of his plight," John F. Kennedy at Columbia University, 10 days before his assassination. Virtually all of the nearly $9 trillion in federal debt has been created since 1963 and the government could have avoided most, if not all of it.

   Executive Order 11110 allowed the government to repay its debt without going to the Federal Reserve and **this would have removed the Federal Reserves financial and political control over the United States.** The Federal Reserve actually creates out of nothing the money we use and then loans it to us and charges us a fee (interest) for its use. We are then taxed by the government to repay this debt. The government has the right to print its own money debt free. No interest and no instant debt owed to bankers worldwide.

   One of the first acts of **President Lyndon Johnson** is to reverse this Executive Order and allow the Federal Reserve to continue to be a money–machine printing money pretty much as it chooses.

   "Each Federal Reserve Bank is a separate corporation owned by commercial banks in its region. The stock-holding commercial banks elect two thirds of each Bank's nine member board of directors." Lewis vs. United States: Federal Reserve Banks are not U.S. government institutions, are private credit monopolies which prey upon the people of the United States for the benefit of themselves and their foreign customers. Many, many good books have been written on this subject and most Americans don't have a clue. **"If a nation expects to be ignorant and free it expects something it cannot be."** Thomas Jefferson.

1963 – Production of $1 Federal Reserve notes with the motto **"In God We Trust"** begins.

May 24, 1963 – **The Securities and Exchange Commission and Wall Street leaders** have agreed on several proposals for enlarging the commission's authority to police securities trading. The accord involves setting up minimum qualifications for securities dealers and changes in penalties for violating regulations.

1963 – **The leaders of 30 independent African nations agree** to unite in an Organization of African Unity.

June 4, 1963 – An Act of Congress allowing the exchange of **silver certificates for silver dollars** is signed into law. Five months *after* Kennedy was assassinated Series 1958 "Silver Certificates" are no longer issued and silver certificates are removed from circulation. **"I believe that banking institutions are more dangerous to our liberties than standing armies,"** Thomas Jefferson.

July 1, 1963 – **The official Flag of the Treasury Department** is displayed for the first time.

July 8, 1963 – **The Cuban Assets Control Regulations** are issued. **The Johnson Administration** places obstacles to maritime transport of goods to and from **Cuba** by exerting pressure on a number of European countries. Secretary of State Dean Rusk indicated to President Kennedy that the U.S. efforts to reduce the navigation of allies of Cuba had been successful. The governments of **Liberia, Turkey, Honduras** and **Panama** had officially prohibited their ships to trade with Cuba. **West Germany** had issued a decree to prohibit ships under its registry to participate in the trade between Socialist countries and Cuba The U.S. Postal Service Regulations were amended (28 FR 11763) thus suspending the sending of postal parcels to Cuba, except those containing medicines only.

November 14, 1963 – It was disclosed yesterday that the **United States and nine other industrial nations are considering creation of a new unit of international currency**. Made up of such currencies as the dollar, the German mark, the French franc and the British pound, the new unit would be the center of a plan to improve the international monetary system and lessen the burden on the dollar. The plan, now under study, is aimed at allowing currencies of prosperous Western European nations to play a greater role in the money system.

November 18, 1963 – In the deserts and mountains of **Nevada,** a large group of investigators are looking into the gambling industry with an annual turnover of **hundreds of millions of dollars.** The reinvestment of this cash has created a new force in American life that extends **from the underworld to the Government** and the careers of public figures. What happens here will eventually set a precedent for the billions of dollars from drug trafficking working its way back into the U.S. economy.

November 22, 1963 – **President John F. Kennedy is assassinated** and the market falls 20 points in 20 minutes before being shut down. DJIA: rose to 767 by December 1963 for the high point of 1963. The low was 647 on January 2.

Books:

1963 – **Maurice Sendak**'s children's book, **"Where the Wild Things Are."**

1963 – Betty Friedan's **"The Feminine Mystique,"** is published, becomes a best-seller, and lays the groundwork for the feminist movement.

1963 – **"The Spy Who Came in From the Cold,"** John Le Carre.

1963 – Sylvia Plath, **"The Bell Jar."**

1963 – **Rod Serling, "Triple W: Witches, Warlocks and Werewolves,"** is an anthology of fantasy and horror stories edited by Rod Serling and ghost edited by Gordon R. Dickson. Most of the stories originally appeared in popular science fiction magazines.

1963 – Kurt Vonnegut, Jr. **"Cat's Cradle."** A satire of the arms race, built from science technology, and religion.

1963 – **James Baldwin,** "The Fire Next Time."

1963 – **"Hop on Pop,"** Dr. Seuss.

TV:

1963 – **Astronaut, Major L. Gordon Cooper Jr.,** circles the earth at 17,546 miles an hour every 88 minutes 45 seconds. Major Cooper and his **"Faith 7"** capsule are in fine shape, following a path so close to plan that he speeds over each point in the global tracking net within seconds of the timetable worked out weeks ago. The flight enables the first transmission of **TV pictures** from an orbiting American space capsule.

1963 – **TV news "comes of age"** in reporting JFK's assassination. It was a time of sadness rather than anger, a time of confusion rather than vengeance. Everyone instinctively knew that nothing would ever be the same again.

1963 – **Jack Ruby shoots Lee Harvey Oswald on Live TV.** The first televised murder.

1963 – **The Dick Van Dyke Show.** "That's My Boy?" almost didn't make it to the TV. Rob Petrie is convinced the hospital sent him and Laura home with the wrong baby. Another couple with the last name Peters had a baby the same day, with a similar room number, and the Petries had even received some of their gifts in a mix-up. The controversial and very funny twist comes when the Mr. and Mrs. Peters arrive at Rob and Laura's home and it is revealed they are a black couple played by Greg Morris and Mimi Dillard. The positive response from the studio audience gave producer Sheldon Leonard the confidence to sign **Bill Cosby** for a co-starring role in a new series he was producing; **"I Spy,"** which is **the first television show to feature a Black actor.**

1963 – **Most TV evening News broadcasts** expand their time from fifteen minutes to one half hour. They also begin to rely less on outside news sources.

December 7, 1963 – **Instant replay.** The first instant replay occurs during the **Army-Navy Game** played in Philadelphia and telecast by CBS-TV. The first form of instant replay occurred in 1955 on **"Hockey Night in Canada."**

1963

Sports:

1963 – **Mount Everest.** Two members of an **American expedition** conquer Mount Everest in **the first attempt by Americans** to scale the 29,028-foot peak, the worlds highest. Two teams of the United States, Mount Everest Expedition reached the summit of the world's highest mountain, one by the hitherto unclimbed West Ridge.

1963 – **Sonny Liston** wins the Heavyweight Championship of the world by knocking out **Floyd Patterson** in the 1st round of their bout in Las Vegas, Nevada.

Music:

January 11, 1963 – The Beatles, "Please Please Me" is released in the United Kingdom by The Beatles, with "Ask Me Why" as the B-side. It is the first Beatles' single to reach #1 in the UK.

January 11, 1963 – The first disco in the U.S. opens, *Whisky a Go Go* night club in Los Angeles.

April 29, 1963 – Andrew Loog Oldham, 19, becomes the manager of **The Rolling Stones.** Oldham had seen the band in concert the previous day at the *Crawdaddy Club* in London.

1963 – **Dalida is rejected by Decca** in the UK, again.

1963 – **The Righteous Brothers** begin performing together.

1963 – **The Kinks** form.

1963 – **The Rolling Stones** first single **"Come on"** is released in the UK and reaches #21 on the charts.

1963 – **The Animals** and **Herman's Hermits** both get noticed this year.

Natural Disasters:

September 30-October 12, 1963 – Hurricane Flora, a massive storm kills 7,200 people in Haiti, Cuba, Trinidad, Tobago, and Grenada. It is among the deadliest Atlantic hurricanes in recorded history.

July 26, 1963 – An Earthquake Strikes Skopje, Yugoslavia destroying 80% of the city. The city is leveled, paralyzed, almost wiped from the face of the earth in only a few seconds. More than 3,300 inhabitants of Skopje were injured and 1,066 were killed. Three minutes after the first earthquake another earthquake strikes of the same intensity (8.5 degrees of the Mercali scale), followed by hundreds of tremors of smaller intensity.

1963 – An earthquake in Libya destroys the village of Barce killing 500 people.

April 30, 1963 – Typhoon Olive with 110 MPH Winds destroys most of the homes on the **Island of Saipan** when its center passes only 5 mi northwest of Saipan Harbor, producing estimated peak gusts of 200 mph. It destroys 95% of the crops and buildings on the island.

1963 – Paraná Forest fires. Brazil's most catastrophic forest fire burns out of control in the state of Paraná, in the southern Brazil. It burns close to **2,000,000 hectares,** destroys more than 5,000 homes and kills 110 people.

May 28–29, 1963 – East Pakistan. A cyclone lashes the **Chittagong coast** in modern-day Bangladesh, killing at least 11,500 people and damaging about 1 million homes.

October 9, 1963 – Italy. One of the highest dams in the world at 860 feet, the Vaiont Dam disaster is caused when engineers disregard warning signs during the early stages of filling the reservoir. While the area behind the dam is being filled with water numerous landslides and earthquakes occur in the area. By the time the reservoir authority begins to draw down the water level **the mountain moves more than 3 feet** and a landslide of about 341 million cubic yards of forest, earth, and rock moving at 68 mph pours into the reservoir displacing 50 million cubic meters of water to over-top the dam in an 820 foot high wave killing 2,000 people.

1963 – One of America's favorite toys is the Easy Bake Oven and during this time in China **"The Great Leap Forward"** is responsible for **31,000,000 to 33,000,000 deaths** due to starvation and famine which remain mostly unknown to the western world until 1980. However, I remember being told as a child to "Eat all your dinner, there are people starving in China". So was the world aware or not? All told Mao was responsible for the deaths of 70 Million people, mostly Chinese.

Man vs. Man / Wars:

Assassinated – South Vietnam President Ngo Dinh Diem on November 2, 1963. President Diem, refuses an American offer of safety contingent upon his resignation, and is **killed by the** CIA's Secret Death Squad; Military Assistance Command Strategic Operational Group Special Detachment, Department of Defense, Vietnam. This is a Black ops group. With the military in control, the capital is the scene of jubilation as youths ransack homes and offices of Government officials.

On November 1, the Army of the Republic of Vietnam laid siege to the Gia Long Palace in Saigon. The next morning Diem and his brother Ngo were cornered at a loyalist camp in Cholon. After they were promised safe exile they were arrested, and then executed in the back of an armored personnel carrier by ARVN officers on the journey back to military headquarters at Tan Son Nhut Air Base. **The arrest and assassination of Ngo Dinh Diem**, marks the culmination of a successful CIA-backed coup d'état led by General Duong Van Minh.

The United States extends diplomatic recognition to South Vietnam's provisional government less than a week after the overthrow. In an announcement timed to coincide with a note delivered in Saigon, the State Department expressed to South Vietnam's military leaders **the hope that cordial relations would continue.** The note was a formal reply to a request for recognition, the extension of which opens the door for renewal of a **$95-million-a-year** commercial-imports **aid program.**

Assassinated – Algeria. Algeria's 33-year-old Foreign Minister, Mohammed Khemisti, lay near death from an assassin's bullet on April 12. He will die three weeks later.

Assassinated – Togo. Sylvanus Olympio, the President of Togo is assassinated.

1963 – Greece. A bloodless military coup removes **President George Papadopoulos.** He will be back as the leader of another coup in 1967.

1963 – Cyprus. On Christmas Eve 1963 the Greek Cypriot militia attacked Turkish Cypriot communities across the island. Large numbers of men, women, and children are killed and 270 mosques, shrines and other places of worship are desecrated. The *Daily Express* reported from Cyprus: "We went tonight into the sealed-off Turkish Cypriot quarter of Nicosia in which 200 to 300 people had been slaughtered in the last five days. We were the first Western reporters there, and we have seen sights too frightful to be described in print. Horror was so extreme that the people seemed stunned beyond tears." There is in place an ethnic cleansing or attempted genocide of Turkish Cypriots by Greek Cypriots.

October 1963 – Honduras. Conservative military officers preempt constitutional elections and depose **Dr. Ramón Villeda Morales** in a bloody coup. Villeda had been elected in 1955 to oversee the transition to democracy and he immediately worked to help the poor and working class. These officers exiled Liberal Party members and took control of the national police. The armed forces, led by General Lopez Arellano, governed until 1970.

January 13, 1963 – Togolese Military Coup. President Olympio is assassinated in an uprising of army noncommissioned officers dissatisfied with conditions following their discharge from the French army. In 1963, the Togolese adopted a new constitution which reinstated a multiparty system and elected Grunitzky as President. President Grunitzky formed a government in which all political parties were represented.

1963

November 2, 1963 – President John F. Kennedy survived an attempted assassination in Chicago by unknown assailants, believed to be from the mob. Kennedy was set to arrive in the morning on November 2 to attend the Army-Air Force football game at Soldier Field and ride in a parade. Secret Service officials in Chicago had information that the Presidents life was in danger. Thomas Vallee an expert marksman was arrested with an M1 rifle, a handgun and 2,500 rounds of ammunition. A motel manager called with information concerning what she had seen in a room rented by two Cuban nationals. She had seen several automatic rifles with telescopic sights lying on the bed and a map of the route President Kennedy was supposed to take in Chicago, according to a former Secret Service agent.

November 22, 1963 – Assassinated. United States President, John F. Kennedy, is assassinated in Dallas, Texas. By 1990 it is common knowledge to anyone who looks into the facts that the Warren Commission was a cover-up, Lee Harvey Oswald was a patsy, and there were actually three gunmen and four shots fired. Three shots were fired by two gunmen from the rear and the shot that killed President Kennedy was fired from the storm sewer at curb level in front of the grassy knoll. Of the shots fired from the rear, one missed the car altogether and struck the curb well ahead of the motorcade cutting an eye witness with at least one small concrete chip. It was a conspiracy and the U.S. government was involved in the cover up. That part is well known. Who is responsible? Unfortunately that part is still open to conjecture.

1963 – Colombian bandit, also known as **"Chispas," confessed to 592 murders**, but is supposed to have killed up to 3,500 people. The Minister of War, General Ruiz Novoa, announced to the Congress that the bandit problem is no longer merely a political inspiration having domestic interest alone. He goes on to state, that although it began as a result of political party rivalry, today bandit activity is influenced and directed from outside the country, with directorial centers situated in urban areas being used as the principal means of directing and controlling subversive activities within the country. This is subversion in its most refined form.

Colombian bandit, Desquite, is killed in a shootout with police. "Brutal mass killings of people by bandits have plagued Colombia for over fifteen years. Since the late 40's, more than 300,000 people have been killed. The situation has been marked not only by the intensity of the killings but also by the practice of mutilation of the victim's bodies. In the past year, combined police and military action has achieved striking results." Bryon Engle, director Office of Public Safety, Colombia.

October, 1963 – Algerian-Moroccan Border War. The Sand War or Sands War along the Algerian-Moroccan border is a Moroccan attempt to claim the mostly uninhabited Tindouf and the Bechar areas that France had annexed to French Algeria in 1952 after the discovery of large deposits of oil, iron, and manganese.

1963 – British Honduras Crisis (Belize). In 1963, troops are massed along the British Honduras/Guatemala border, and Britain has to send a small army of its own to deter an invasion. British Honduras, now Belize, became fully independent from the United Kingdom in 1981. Belize was the last continental possession of the United Kingdom in the Americas.

1963-1970 – Canada. FLQ Terrorism begins. FLQ is a nationalist and Marxist revolutionary group in Quebec, Canada with at least two terrorist cells that is responsible for more than **200 bombings**, including the bombing of the Montreal Stock Exchange in 1969 and the deaths of at least five people. During the "October Crisis" in October 1970 British Trade Commissioner James Cross is kidnapped and Quebec Labor Minister Pierre Laporte is murdered. FLQ supported the Quebec sovereignty movement.

August 15, 1963 – Congolese Military Coup. In the Congo (Zaire, or Democratic Republic of the Congo), **President Fulbert Youlou** is removed by a coup and formally resigns on August 15. Anti-government rioting is so rampant it almost turns the country towards civil war. President Youlou is succeeded by Alphonse Massamba-Debat who becomes Provisional President and is formally elected to the Presidency on December 19. Immediately after he is elected a new constitution is approved by national referendum.

October 28, 1963 – Dahomey. Military Coup. Colonel Christophe Soglo, chief of staff, assumes power as head of a 3-man provisional government, and takes control of the country to prevent a civil war. He overthrew Hubert Maga, whose Presidency faced extreme economic stagnation and a host of other problems.

September 3, 1963 – Dominican Republic. Juan Bosch is overthrown by a right-wing military coup supported by the U.S. in September, and flees into exile in Puerto Rico. A civilian government is created, while power remains with the military.

July 11, 1963 – Ecuadoran Coup. On July 11, 1963, the Presidential Palace in Quito is surrounded by tanks and troops. **President** Carlos Julio Arosemana, who became President after a coup in 1961, is **removed by a Junta** whose first act is to outlaw communism. The Junta begins seizing and arresting communists and other extreme leftists. It has been reported they used the CIA's Subversive Control Watch List which named the person, their family and friends. People on the list were "questioned" and then their friends or family members with supposed communist ties were arrested.

1963-1974 – The Guinea-Bissau War of Independence is an armed conflict and national liberation struggle in Guinea-Bissau. January 1963 PAIGC guerrilla fighters attack the Portuguese garrison in Tite, south of the capital Bissau and the conflict quickly spread across the country. Portugal responds by deploying troops in what is mostly a defensive position.

May 4, 1963 – Haiti. Without giving a reason, the regime of **President-Dictator Francois "Papa Doc" Duvalier** declared Haiti under martial law yesterday. Underground forces have promised to overthrow the Government by May 15, but no unusual military activity is apparent. United States support of anti government forces is futile and efforts to involve the Dominican military only weaken that nation's elected government. Francois "Papa Doc" Duvalier was responsible for 30,000 deaths and the exile of thousands.

1963 – Honduran Military Coup. Colonel Lopez Arellano overthrows the Liberal Party government of Ramon Villeda Morales in a coup. The Agrarian Reform Law is ended and the country's two peasant unions are harassed. A new organization of rural workers, the National Union of Peasants, with Christian Democratic ties, will take over and draw even more members.

In 1962 and 1963 coups in El Salvador, Guatemala, Peru, Argentina, the Dominican Republic, and Ecuador were followed by the U.S. in every case suspending relations, publicly exclaiming support of democracy, and then quickly renewing relations with the generals. This coup is no different and the Johnson Administration recognizes the military government in early 1964 and renews military aid.

1963-1966 – Indonesia Confronts Malaysia. Sukarno was jailed and exiled by the Dutch at various times in the 1930s. During World War II, Sukarno cooperated with the Japanese when Indonesia was occupied by them, while still continuing his agitation for Indonesian independence. After the war he and Mohammad Hatta played a crucial part in the establishment of the Republic of Indonesia in August of 1945.

In 1963, **Sukarno proclaims himself President for life,** and increases his country's ties to Communist China. Sukarno orders sporadic raids on Dutch New Guinea, intensifying a conflict that result in UN intervention. His actions will bring Dutch New Guinea under Indonesian administration in May 1963.

February 8, 1963 – Iraq. Abdul-Karim Qassem is overthrown, with the help of the CIA's electronic command center in Kuwait and brings the Ba'ath Party to power. Qassim was one of the first to die in the coup. The common people of Iraq never stopped loving Qassim, yet they were never able to prevent the coup. The separation of the political process in Iraq with the average Iraqi is now nearly complete.

In November civil war begins between two factions of the Baath party. It stops for one day while both sides lay down their weapons to attend a U.S. Embassy memorial service for John F. Kennedy and then resumes the following day.

Iraqi-Kuwaiti relations improved following Qasim's death, but the UK remained on alert to the threat of an Iraqi invasion of Kuwait.

1963 – Iraq. A national security official in Washington, DC, with Iraq oversight duties reports that he was called back to the office the evening of February 8, 1963, to find that **the CIA station chief in Baghdad** was reporting that members of the Ba'ath party had overthrown and killed `Abd al-Karim Qasim and that "to convince the public of the demise of Qasim, Iraqi TV showed a film of a Ba'ath officer holding up Qasim's severed head." This U.S. government old-timer writes, "I assure you that the

1963

Ba'ath coup came as a Total surprise to the U.S. intelligence and diplomatic community . . . No one in the Washington community had ANY prior knowledge that this coup would take place, let alone having been involved in fomenting it . . ."

1963 – Kenya. Multi-ethnic Kenya declares independence from the British.

1963 – Kuwait gains admission to the United Nations in 1963.

1963-2010 – Papua New Guinea. Indonesia invades West Papua and Papuans **will endure horrific violence** through 2010 in a modern example of genocide. Amnesty International estimates that at least 100,000 Papuans, one sixth of the total population, have been killed as a result of government-sponsored violence against West Papuans. Many more have been "disappeared" or starved to death from forced relocation to inhospitable areas. It's almost impossible to document the exact number of victims, since academics, human-rights defenders and journalists are targets themselves of intimidation, torture and murder. Popular civic and cultural leaders are also strategically assassinated in order to wipe out the Papuan culture as well as the people. Throughout most of the occupation, simply raising the Papuan flag has been punishable by death.

1963 – USA. Air America, owned by the CIA is a corporation that hires plots and owns an aircraft maintenance facility on Taiwan. It has been reported that its planes often carry drugs for the Kuomintang (KMT) Chinese while they are in the process of taking over the drug trade within the Golden Triangle. In 2010 it has been reported for years that the U.S. government was determined to keep the drug business under the control of the KMT and did so with logistical and air support while **Chiang Kai-shek's** Kuomintang were expanding their control over the **opium** trade. Civil Air Transport/ renamed Air America, allowed the KMT to remain in control so they would supposedly supply the troops to hold back the rise of communism. Instead Southeast Asia is destabilized and millions of people will die.

The amount of money involved is significant. As early as 1930 the Chinese based in Shanghai under the leadership of Boss Tu were taking in over $1 million dollars a week. **They produced 90% of the world's opium.** They had a cut of everything;

gambling, drugs, and over 100,000 prostitutes. **Boss Tu kidnapped Chiang Kai-shek's bride** just to show him who was really in control. Corruption is widespread and reaches out wherever drugs are used. This is REAL POWER.

    President John Kennedy had been gradually disengaging from the goals of the KMT and the powerful China lobby. The drug trade is growing and with the money it fuels an **endless series of corruption, greed and lies.** President Kennedy has been trying to disengage the U.S. from trafficking in illegal drugs among other things and this does not make him very popular with the CIA, or the Mafia, or the KMT or the drug lords. And the list goes on and on.

1963 – Vietnam. The world is shocked when a **Vietnamese Buddhist monk** named **Quang Duc burns himself to death** in front of reporters at a busy intersection in Saigon. He did so to protest religious persecution of Buddhists by the pro-Catholic, U.S.-backed Diem regime.

March 8, 1963 – Syrian Nasserite Coup. The Baath Arab Socialist Party comes to power in a coup known in Syria as the **March Revolution.** The Baathists dissolve the Parliament and introduce a one-party regime that is later destabilized by conflicts within the Baath itself. In February 1966, the right wing of Baath will take over party leadership and place radical Salah Jadid as the strongman of the country.

1963-1973 – Uruguay. Tupamaros Terrorism. The Tupamaros are a group of urban guerrillas who operate in Montevideo, Uruguay, from the early 1960's to the 1980's. The Tupamaros will grow to over 5,000 strong and initially see bloodshed as a last resort. As the military becomes more violent the Tupamaros become increasingly violent until the mid 1980's when democracy returned to Uruguay and the Tupamaro movement laid down their weapons in favor of joining the political process.

1963 – Rwanda. The Tutsi Invasion of Rwanda. Tutsi Massacre. Following the failed Tutsi revolt in Rwanda, the Hutu-dominated government massacred 10,000 to 15,000 Tutsis. An estimated 200,000–250,000 Tutsis fled into exile.

December 1963 – Zanzibar. The islands gain independence from Britain in December as a constitutional monarchy. A series of parliamentary elections results in the Arab minority retaining their hold on power. A month later, the bloody Zanzibar Revolution, in which several thousand Arabs and Indians are killed and thousands more expelled leads to the overthrow of the Sultan of Zanzibar and his mainly Arab government by African revolutionaries.

1964

The baby boom ends: 1946-1964

The Oldest Boomer is 18 years old.

Cost of the Average House: $20,500	
Median Family Income: $6,600	**Minimum Wage:** $1.25/ hr **Average Hourly Wage:** $2.53
1964 Silver Kennedy Half Dollar: 90% silver, 10% copper, 12.5 grams, The melt value is $5.05 in 2009	
New Car: Pontiac Catalina: $3,149 **Chevrolet Corvair Monza:** $2,335	**Gallon Gasoline:** 30 cents **Loaf of Bread:** 24 cents
Unemployment Rate: 5.6%-4.9%-5.0%	**First-class Stamp:** 5 cents

14 cents buying power in 1964 **= $1.00 in 2008.**
In 1964 what cost us 14 cents to purchase now costs us $1.00 in 2008.

Movies: "Dr. Strangelove," "My Fair Lady," "Mary Poppins," "Becket," "Zorba the Greek."

Broadway: "Hello, Dolly!" "What Makes Sammy Run?" "Funny Girl," "I Had a Ball."

TV: The Beatles First Appearance on The Ed Sullivan Show is February 9. "The Addams Family," "Bewitched," "Flipper," "Gilligan's Island," "Gomer Pyle U.S.M.C.," "The Munsters," "Man From U.N.C.L.E.," "Peyton Place," "Jonny Quest," "Jeopardy!" "The Famous Adventures of Mr. Magoo," "Daniel Boone," "The Porky Pig Show," "Twelve O'Clock High," "Underdog," "Voyage to the Bottom of the Sea," "Bewitched."

Music: John Barry, "My Fair Lady." "Mary Poppins," "Goldfinger." Henry Mancini, "The Pink Panther." Jim Reeves, "Welcome To My World" & "I Guess I'm Crazy." Buck Owens, "My Heart Skips A Beat." Beatles, "I Want To Hold Your Hand," "A Hard Day's Night," "She Loves You."

Roy Orbison, "Oh, Pretty Woman." Beach Boys, "I Get Around." Louis Armstrong, "Hello, Dolly!" The Animals, "The House of the Rising Sun." Lorne Greene, "Ringo." Beach Boys, "I Get Around." The Kinks, "You Really Got Me." Manfred Mann, "Do Wah Diddy Diddy." The Rolling Stones, "It's All Over Now." Jan and Dean, "Little Old Lady from Pasadena." Little Anthony and The Imperials, "Goin' Out of My Head."

Deaths: Andrew Goodman, Michael Schwerner, James Chaney, Kitty Genovese, Bill Hunter, Hugh Ward, Mary Pinchot, C. D. Jackson.

President: Lyndon B. Johnson (D) Disciples of Christ; vetoes 30/ 0 overrides

Vice President: (no Vice President, 1963–65)

House: D-259 ; R-176

Senate: 88th Congress (1963-1965) Majority Party: Democrat (66 seats) Minority Party: Republican (34 seats) Other Parties: 0 Total Seats: 100

Federal Debt: $311.71 billion or 47 % of the GDP

Consumer Price Index CPI-U (1982 Base of 100): 31.00

GDP: $663.6 billion	**Inflation Rate:** 1.28%

Dow Jones: 875. (December)/ 776. (January)

Average Home Mortgage Rate: 5.95%

1 oz Gold: $35.35	**1oz of Silver:** $1.30

Federal Debt: $311,712,899,257.30

Federal Deficit: $5.9 billion dollars

Defense Spending: $65.38 billion	**Interest Spending:** $8.20 billion
Health Care Spending: $1.79 billion	**Pensions Spending:** $14.16 billion
Welfare Spending: $6.42 billion	**Education Spending:** $2.32 billion
Transportation Spending: $5.24 billion	**Misc. Other Spending:** $12.79 billion

Protection Spending: $490 million	Total Government Spending: $118.53 billion
% of GDP that goes towards just the interest payment: 1.28%	
$1.00 = 361.99 Yen, Japan	
U.S. Population: 191,927,000	World Population: 3,276,816,764
U.S. Birth Rate: 4,027,490	U.S. Abortions: 823
U.S. Homicide Rate: 5.1/ 100,000 population	U.S. Violent Crime: 190.6/ 100,000 population
Annual Average Domestic Crude Oil Prices: $3.00 / barrel, $20.78 (2007 adjusted)	

Oil:

1964 – The Druzhba Pipeline is the world's longest pipeline starting in southeast **Russia** and ending in **Germany** with points in between. Construction of the Druzhba-Pipeline began in December of 1959. In 1962, the first oil reached **Czechoslovakia**, in September 1963 **Hungary**, in November 1963 **Poland**, and in December 1963 the **German Democratic Republic**. The completed pipeline is put into operation in October 1964. The first oil pumped through the Druzhba pipeline originates in the oil fields in Tatarstan and Samara Oblast. The Druzhba pipeline has a capacity of 1.2 to 1.4 million barrels per day in 2001.

Major News:

May 17, 1964 – The U.S. reports it is sending military planes to **Laos.**

1964 – Judge John L. Coffey's "John Doe" inquiry into corruption in the Milwaukee Police Department and the Milwaukee County Sheriff's Department includes **gambling, prostitution and bribery.** The inquiry results in more than 30 police officers losing their jobs. The head of the city vice squad and deputy sheriffs are fired but the investigation fails to indict local Mafia boss Frank Balistrieri.

1964

August 7, 1964 – Congress passes the Tonkin Gulf Resolution, authorizing broad powers to the President to take action in Vietnam, after North Vietnamese boats **reportedly attacked** two U.S. destroyers. On August 2, 1964, the destroyer USS Maddox engages three North Vietnamese P-4 torpedo boats, resulting in damage to the three boats. Two days later the Maddox, having been joined by the destroyer USS Turner Joy, reported a second engagement with North Vietnamese vessels. This second report was later claimed to be in error.

September 27, 1964 – The Warren Commission releases a report concluding that Lee Harvey Oswald was solely responsible for the **assassination of President John F. Kennedy.** It outlines the famous **"zig-zag" bullet,** refuses to interview eyewitness testimony, helps to cover up the autopsy, and produces a long boring work of fiction. Many, many eyewitnesses die under suspicious circumstances over the next ten years.

The House Select Committee on Assassinations (HSCA) found both the original FBI investigation and the Warren Commission Report to be seriously flawed.

November 3, 1964 – Lyndon B. Johnson is elected to a full term, defeating Republican Senator **Barry Goldwater** (Arizona) in a landslide. Lyndon Johnson, a Democrat, succeeded to the Presidency following the assassination of President John F. Kennedy and completed Kennedy's term before being elected President in his own right. He escalates the **American involvement in the Vietnam War** from 16,000 American soldiers in 1963 to 500,000 in early 1968.

December 18, 1964 – Panama suspended relations with the U.S. January 9, after the Panama Canal incident, when Panamanian mobs engage United States troops, leading to the death of twenty-one Panama citizens and four U.S. troops. The U.S. offers on December 18, to negotiate a new canal treaty.

1962-1964 – Boston Strangler. The city of Boston is terrorized by a serial killer for eighteen months. In 1964, Albert DeSalvo gave a detailed confession of his activities as the Boston Strangler after he was charged with rape. Both authorities and the city at large breathed a collective sigh of relief, believing the killer was finally behind bars.

Now, 46 years later, some investigators, are not sure that DeSalvo was the lone killer. The murders were so varied and the M.O. was inconsistent. More than likely three killers were responsible although it is doubtful they knew each other. There is a persuasive case to be made that DeSalvo wasn't the only killer after all.

Civil Rights Movement:

February 17, 1964 – The Supreme Court orders that congressional districts have equal populations.

March 8, 1964 – Malcolm X, born **Malcolm Little**, the son of an African American **Baptist preacher,** Earl Little, was born in Omaha, Nebraska, on May 19, 1925. Malcolm's mother, Louise Little, was born in the West Indies. Her mother was black but her father was a white man. On March 8, Malcolm X announces his resignation from the Nation of Islam and forms the **Muslim Mosque, Inc.,** an Islamic movement devoted to working in the political sphere and cooperating with civil rights leaders. Later in the year he made his first pilgrimage to Mecca and visited several African and Arab Countries. When Malcolm X returned to the United States he renamed himself El-Hajj Malik El-Shabazz, adopted from Sunni Islam, and announced that he had found the "true brotherhood" of man.

June 10, 1964 – The U.S. Senate votes to limit further debate on the civil rights bill, ending the **longest filibuster in Senate history**, and passes a revised civil rights bill on June 19.

June 1964 – Three civil rights workers have been missing for six weeks. Michael Schwerner a 24-year-old white Jewish CORE organizer and former social worker from New York, **Andrew Goodman,** a 20-year-old white Jewish anthropology student also from New York, and **James Chaney,** a 21-year-old black man from Meridian, Mississippi are missing and feared dead because they had not checked in with other workers. It was not until J. Edgar Hover, the head of the FBI, was threatened by President Johnson, that the FBI made the case top priority, codenamed Miburn (Mississippi burning), and sent agents down to Mississippi to investigate. The FBI found the bodies of Michael Schwerner, Andrew Goodman, and James Chaney, buried in a partially constructed dam near Philadelphia, Mississippi about six miles from the town where they were last seen on the night of June 21.

The three young men were members of CORE, the Congress of Racial Equality, and had been sent down to Mississippi to investigate the burning of a Church with a black Church in Longdale, that was used as the site for a "freedom school." They were found buried on August 4 and twenty-one white men were arrested. On **October 20, 1967**, an all-white federal jury will prosecute 18 men and convict 7 of conspiracy in the slayings. **Two are released** because of a deadlocked jury and **the others are acquitted.**

In 2005, 80-year-old **Edgar Ray Killen**, one of the men who earlier went free, was convicted in a new trial of manslaughter for the killings and sentenced to 60 years in prison. During the investigation, searchers including Navy divers and the FBI discovered the bodies of at least seven other Mississippi blacks, whose disappearances over the past several years had not attracted attention outside their local communities. The local sheriff and his deputy were implicated in the murders. In Mississippi, in 1964, it was business as usual.

June 1964 – The First of approximately 550 "Freedom Summer" volunteers begin arriving in Mississippi in mid-June to register voters, work in community centers, and teach in **"Freedom Schools."** In the small town of the South where I was born and lived until I was 9 years old, white people called us "red niggers." In truth, our family was a mix of Scottish, African-American and Seminole. Most of us were light-skinned enough to "pass white" when we rode up to Americus or Valdosta. This deception got us into places we couldn't otherwise have gone, like front row center at the movie theater instead of the "coloreds-only" balcony. Back home, however, where we were known, it was another story. Nobody in my family voted. Nobody on our side of town did. They couldn't pass the trumped-up "literacy test," nor pay the poll tax. Most wouldn't even set foot in the county clerk's office. Even attempting to register to vote was met with humiliation, intimidation and the barely veiled threat of retaliation. So, year after year, white men were elected to every office from sheriff to senator, each of them dedicated to ensuring that Mr. Jim Crow continued to rule the land. With philosophical help from the Supreme Court and more direct applications by the Klan, they had succeeded since the notorious "compromise" of 1876. All that was about to change.

I signed up for Freedom Summer on March 20, 1964, the same day I got my official university acceptance. I lied about my age. The Freedom Summer organizers at the Student Non-Violent Coordinating Committee and Congress of Racial Equality wanted volunteers who were at least 18. I was barely 17. In June, we all went to Ohio for training in voter registration and non-violent resistance. **Most of the 550 or so activists who showed up were white,** and most had never been in the South. Although everyone knew about the **assassination of Medgar Evers**, most were unaware that other blacks who had themselves registered or tried to register others in the past three years had been murdered in Mississippi. Meteor Blades, 1964 Freedom Summer. **Boomers we can all be proud of.**

July 2, 1964 – The Civil Rights Act of 1964 is signed by **President Johnson** July 2: the most sweeping civil rights legislation since Reconstruction. The act strengthens federal power to protect voting rights; prohibits discrimination in public accommodations; authorizes the attorney general to file suits for the desegregation of schools and public facilities; bars discrimination in federally assisted programs; prohibits discrimination by employers and unions; and establishes an Equal Employment Opportunity Commission with investigative powers. On July 2, 1964 the **24th Amendment** bans the poll tax as a requirement for voting in federal elections which originally had been established in the South after Reconstruction to make it difficult for poor blacks to vote.

August 25, 1964 – The Mississippi Freedom Democratic Party delegation, led by Fannie Lou Hamer, **is denied seating at the Democratic National Convention** in Atlantic City. The credentials committee votes on August 25 to seat regular Democrats while offering Freedom Democrats two at-large seats, but the Freedom Democrats reject this offer.

October 14, 1964 – Martin Luther King, 35, becomes the youngest recipient of the **Nobel Peace Prize,** which is awarded to him for leading non-violent resistance to end racial prejudice in the United States.

1964 – St. Augustine, Florida. The event that brought the civil rights movement in St. Augustine to international attention was the arrest of **Mary Parkman Peabody**

1964

(1891-1981), the **72-year old mother** of the **Governor of Massachusetts,** for trying to be served in a racially integrated group at the Ponce de Leon Motor Lodge on March 31, 1964. The socially prominent Mrs. Peabody's husband is an Episcopal bishop, and she is related to Eleanor Roosevelt.

1964 – The Seattle City Council agrees to put together an open-housing ordinance but insists on putting it on the ballot. Voters defeat it by a 2-to-1 ratio. It will be four more years before an open-housing ordinance becomes law.

1964 – Sidney Poitier wins the Academy Award for Best Actor for his performance in the film **"Lilies of the Field."**

Women's Movement:

1964 – Title VII of the Civil Rights Act of 1964 bars employment discrimination on account of sex, race, etc. by private employers, employment agencies, and unions. The Equal Employment Opportunity Commission is established; in its first five years, 50,000 complaints of gender discrimination are received.

1964 – Margaret Chase Smith, of Maine, becomes the first woman nominated for President of the United States by a major political party, at the Republican National Convention in San Francisco. **She is a Republican Senator** from Maine, and one of the most successful politicians in Maine history. She is the first woman to be elected to both the U.S. House and the Senate, and the first woman from Maine to serve in either.

Popular Culture:

February 2, 1964 – GI Joe is released. In 1963, noting the commercial success of the Barbie doll for girls, Stan Weston, a toy creator and licensing agent, came up with the idea of a line of Barbie-sized dolls with a military theme that would be marketed to boys. He pitched the idea to Don Levine, the creative director of **Hasbro,** who saw the potential of the idea and approved development. The prototypes are originally named

"Rocky," a marine, "Skip," a sailor, and "Ace," the pilot, before Don Levine, inspired by the popular 1945 film "The Story of G.I. Joe," decided on the generic name "G.I. Joe."

March 6, 1964 – Elvis Presley's 14th motion picture, **"Kissin' Cousins"** is released to theaters. Synopsis: An Army officer returns to the Smoky Mountains and tries to convince his kinfolk to allow the Army to build a missile site on their land. Once he gets there, he discovers he has a lookalike cousin.

May 2, 1964 – Anti War Demonstrations. In the first major student demonstrations against the war hundreds of students march through Times Square in New York City, while another 700 march in San Francisco. Smaller numbers also protest in Boston; Seattle; and Madison, Wisconsin.

1964 – Birth Control. Less than a decade after President Eisenhower declared that the government should not get involved with birth control, President Lyndon B. Johnson pushes through legislation for **federal support of birth control** for the poor. Despite the competition, Searle earns $24 million in net profits from the sale of birth control Pill sales.

1964 – Kitty Genovese, Catherine Susan Genovese. Kitty Genovese, a young 28 year old woman, is stabbed to death outside her apartment building in Queens, New York. She is attacked repeatedly over the course of an hour.

As she cries for help: Oh my God! He stabbed me! Please help me! Please help me! Lights go on in some apartments overlooking the crime.

Irene Frost, according to her affidavit, at 82-68 Austin Street heard Catherine's screams plainly. Q. Now, sometime on the early morning, did you hear something? A. I heard a shriek. I got out of bed, went to the window and I saw a man and a woman standing across the street. They were standing across the street. A. The second time she screamed, "Please help me, God. Please help me. I have been stabbed," and he ran up the street. I was looking out one window. I have two windows in my bedroom and he ran up the street. I went to the other one, so I could look up Austin Street. Then I went back to the other window, the front window, and she was on her knees. She got up. Then it looked like she was reaching for her purse. She bent down again and picked something up. I don't know what it was; walked down to the drug store, walked along into the back of that building.

According to Robert Mozer's trial testimony he heard a girl. A. "Yes. I heard a girl saying, "Help me, help me." It wasn't a scream. It wasn't a cry. It was more just like a talk like, "Help me, help me." "I hollered, "Hey, get out of there" or "What are you doing?" And he jumped up and run. Then it was quiet again." Catherine, by now bleeding from several stab wounds tried to make her way around the side of the building by the parking lot to get to her apartment. Within five minutes, the assailant returned and stabbed her again.

Trial testimony states some of the witnesses heard her cry, "I'm dying! I'm dying!" and as several people looked to see what was going on the assailant got into his car and drove away.

Miss Genovese staggered to her feet. Marjorie and Samuel Koshkin witnessed the attack from their window. Mr. Koshkin said he "looked out the window and I saw a man hurrying to his car, a little car parked under my window." Mr. Koshkin wanted to call the police, but did not, thinking that several people must have already called. Miss Andre Picq, a French girl, who lived on the second floor, said at the trial, "I heard the scream, "Help, help," three times." "I saw a girl laying down on the pavement. That moment she was completely laying down and a man was bending over her and beating her."

Despite her screams, only one person called the police some time after the attack began. Some were afraid. Some didn't want to get involved. Some thought someone else would do it. The incident became a symbol of the increased callousness, self-centeredness, and fearfulness of a society where bad guys act with confidence that onlookers won't interfere. Catherine was the murders third victim. She was picked at random. Trial testimony is available online. *People v. Moseley* (June 8, 1964)

1964 – Pepsi-Cola, "The Pepsi generation." Batton, Barton, Durstine & Osborn.

1964 – Charmin, "Please don't squeeze the Charmin." Benton & Bowles.

August 11, 1964 – Congress approves the **War on Poverty** bill providing for a domestic Peace Corps (**VISTA**), a **Job Corps,** and antipoverty funding.

1964 – The "Pentagon Papers" (published in 1971) **show that President Lyndon Johnson had planned** to bomb North Vietnam **well before the 1964 Election.** Johnson had been outspoken against doing so during the election and claimed that his opponent Barry Goldwater was the one that wanted to bomb North Vietnam.

After the release of the "Pentagon Papers" Goldwater said: "During the campaign, President Johnson kept reiterating that he would never send American boys to fight in Vietnam. As I say, he knew at the time that American boys were going to be sent. In fact, I knew about ten days before the Republican Convention. You see I was being called a trigger-happy, warmonger, bomb happy, and all the time Johnson was saying, he would never send American boys, I knew damn well he would." The "Pentagon Papers" first surfaced on the front page on the *New York Times* in 1971. The *Washington Post* soon followed.

Business / Technology:

January 11, 1964 – The surgeon general reports that smoking causes lung cancer. Surgeon General **Luther Terry**, who picked tobacco in Alabama as a boy, startles Americans with the news that deliberately inhaling smoke deep into your lungs dozens of times every day may not be good for your health. Cigarette sales drop 20% during the next three months. A pack of Lucky Strike Cigarettes cost 25 cents.

1964 – The Picturephone is tested between Disneyland and the N.Y. World's Fair. AT&T installs their earliest commercial videophone unit, the **Picturephone Mod I**, in Picturephone booths in three cities: New York's Grand Central Station, Washington, D.C. and Chicago. The use of reservation time slots and their initial cost of $16 per three minute call at public booths leave the public unimpressed and they are discontinued in 1968.

1964 – CDC′s 6600 supercomputer, designed by Seymour Cray, performs up to 3 million instructions per second (**3 MIPS**), a processing speed three times faster than that of its closest competitor, the **IBM Stretch**. Today in 2009 the AMD Phenom II X4 940 Black Edition 42,820 MIPS at 3.0 GHz.

1964

1964 – The estimated construction costs for more than 1,000 **ICBM launch pads**, silos, and support facilities, from 1957-1964 is **nearly $14,000,000,000.**

1964 – IBM's OS/360 is the first mass-produced computer operating system. When the development looks like it will take a lot longer than projected and the OS/360 will not fit into the limited memory available on the smaller System/360 models IBM introduced a series of stop-gaps to prevent System/360 hardware sales from collapsing.

April 22, 1964 – The New York World's Fair opens in Queens, New York on the site of the 1939 event. One of the largest world fairs in United States history, it is not a sanctioned Bureau of International Exhibitions event, due to a conflict over the dates of the Seattle fair of 1962. This world's fair will last for two seasons, and include exhibits from eighty nations. **Over 50 million visitors will attend.**

November 21, 1964 – The Verrazano-Narrows Bridge opens in New York City.

1964 – A local area network (LAN) is created for atomic weapons research. The first LAN is put into service at the Livermore Laboratory to support atomic weapons research. LANs spread to the public sector in the late 1970s and are used to create high-speed links between several large central computers at one site. Of many competing systems created at this time, **Ethernet** and **ARCNET** are the most popular.

1964 – Transpacific submarine telephone cable service begins. AT&T opens TPC-1, the first submarine telephone cable across the Pacific. It stretches from **Japan to Hawaii,** where it connects to two cables linking Hawaii with the mainland. This brings the same improvements to trans-Pacific service that TAT-1 had brought to trans-Atlantic service in 1956.

1964 – Japan's NHK begins HDTV development NHK (Japan Broadcasting Corporation) performed much of the initial "high risk" research and development on HDTV, then split up specific product areas to interested companies for further development, such as **Toshiba, NEC** and **Matsushita.**

1964 – The Capitol Beltway highway completed around Washington, D.C., originally intended as a bypass, becomes a crowded commuter route.

1964 – BASIC programming is developed at **Dartmouth** to provide computer access to non-science students. At the time, nearly all computer use requires writing custom software. BASIC remains popular to this day in a handful of highly modified dialects and new languages influenced by BASIC such as Microsoft Visual Basic. As of 2006, 59% of developers for the .NET platform used Visual Basic as their only language.

1964 – President Lyndon B. Johnson. Brown & Root reaps obscene profits with the help of LBJ and the "cost plus" contracts it receives from our government. "Cost plus" means that Brown & Root can recoup all expenses plus a guaranteed profit based on a pre-negotiated percentage. Basically, it's a blank check from the government. When your profit is a percentage of the cost, the more you spend, the more you make. This same scam was run on the American people by Halliburton in Iraq under the Cheney administration. **LBJ raised the troop levels from 16,000 to 500,000** and the money poured in while the U.S. taxpayer was being mugged.

Finance:

April 1964 – DJIA. After the assassination of President Kennedy when the markets reopened under Lyndon B. Johnson, the Dow went from 712 in November to 825 by April 1964.

April 24, 1964 – The Secretary of the Treasury removes the restrictions on acquiring or holding **gold certificates**. The gold certificate had been used from 1882 to 1933 in the United States as a form of paper currency. In 1933 the practice of redeeming these notes for gold coins was ended by the U.S. government and until 1964 it was actually illegal to possess these notes. In 1964 these restrictions were lifted, primarily to allow collectors to own examples legally.

September 18, 1964 – The United States Customs Service establishes four new offices.

1964

Books:

1964 – **Saul Bellow,** "Herzog."

1964 – "Sometimes a Great Notion," **Ken Kesey.**

1964 – **"Harriet the Spy,"** Louise Fitzhugh.

1964 – **"Chitty Chitty Bang Bang: The Magical Car,"** Ian Fleming.

TV:

February 9, 1964 – The Beatles arrive in the U.S. for the first time and appear on CBS-TV's "Ed Sullivan Show."

1964 – **Olympic Games** in Tokyo are telecast live globally by satellite.

1964 – **Mariner IV** sends television images back **from Mars.**

1964 – The first televised negative political ad skewers Barry Goldwater. Although even Eisenhower's original spot campaign in 1952 contained a large number of critical or negative messages, Lyndon Johnson's 1964 campaign spots attacking Barry Goldwater are considered classics, particularly the **"Daisy Girl"** spot, in which a mushroom cloud suggests GOP candidate Barry Goldwater would not hesitate to use nuclear warfare.

October 22, 1964 – The first television couple to share a bed when the actors were not married in real life was Samantha and Darrin Stephens of **"Bewitched."**
      Herman and Lily Munster are often mistakenly named as the first couple to share the same bed on American television, in the episode "Autumn Croakus" on November 26, 1964. The honor actually goes to "Mary Kay and Johnny," in an episode that aired on November 18, 1947 on the DuMont network. "Mary Kay and Johnny" stared, Mary Kay and Johnny Stearns.

October 1964 – We still have some **"Live TV."** Jackie Mason appears on *The Ed Sullivan Show* and is subsequently banned after some think he gives Ed "the finger" on the air. Ed tried to mess with quite a few stars which may have been part of the shows charm. Ed once turned off Buddy Holly's microphone but was forced to invite him back because the audience loved his act. Holly said No thanks.

1964-1969 – "Peyton Place." Love affairs, illegitimate births, and narratives of unrepressed desire, are showcased as the "new" single girl sexuality with its primary goal of self-fulfillment in TV's Peyton Place.

Sports:

February 25, 1964 – 1960 Olympic champion Cassius Clay, (Muhammad Ali,) wins the World Heavyweight Championship in Boxing from current champ **Sonny Liston**. **Cassius Clay,** 22, has been crowned heavyweight champion of the world after beating Sonny Liston in one of the biggest upsets in boxing history. Clay, from Kentucky, was announced the winner after the hot favorite retired at the end of the sixth round in Miami. When the bell rang for the start of the seventh round, Liston stayed on his stool in the corner of the ring, saying he did not want to continue. **Cassius Clay, (Muhammad Ali)** will win the world heavyweight boxing championship three times.

Music:

January 13, 1964 – Beatlemania hits the shores of the United States with the release of **"I Want to Hold Your Hand,"** which becomes the Liverpool group's first North American hit. One week later, their first U.S. album, **"Meet the Beatles"** is released.

January 18, 1964 – The Beatles appear on the Billboard magazine charts for the first time.

February 1, 1964 – Indiana Governor Matthew E. Welsh declares the song **"Louie, Louie" by the Kingsmen pornographic.** He requests that the Indiana Broadcasters Association ban the record. Governor Welsh claimed that hearing the song made his "ears tingle." Publisher Max Firetag offers $1,000 to anyone that can find anything "suggestive" in the song's lyrics.

April 4, 1964 – The Beatles occupied all five top positions on Billboard's Hot 100 with their singles "Can't Buy Me Love," "Twist and Shout," "She Loves You," "I Want to Hold Your Hand," and "Please Please Me."

1964 – Marianne Faithfull's musical career begins.

April 16, 1964 – The Rolling Stones release their eponymous début album and on June 5 The Rolling Stones start their first US tour.

1964 – 11 year old Keith Green becomes the youngest person ever to sign a contract with the American Society of Composers, Authors and Publishers (ASCAP) after publishing, recording and releasing the song **"The Way I Used to Be."** At age eleven in February 1965, with forty original songs already under his belt, Green signs a five-year contract with Decca Records.

1964 – MC5 forms.

1964 – Sonny and Cher begin performing together. They appear at Geauga Lake Park outside rock and roll capitol, Cleveland, Ohio, and play to a "respectful" crowd of less than 100 people.

Natural Disasters:

March 28, 1964 – Alaska. The strongest earthquake ever to strike North America at 9.2 magnitude, hits 80 mi east of Anchorage. It is a powerful megathrust earthquake that generates a 50 ft high tsunami that traveled 8,445 mi at 450 mph. One hundred and thirty-one people are killed.

April 11, 1964 – East Pakistan. The Bangladesh Observer reports as many as 500 people may have died as a tornado destroyed villages in the Narail and Magura regions of Jessore. The presence of bodies in trees and cooking utensils imbedded in trees left little doubt that this was a true tornado. Another tornado killed 4 people in Narail just nine days earlier, on April 2nd.

June 16, 1964 – Chūbu region, Japan. Twenty-six people are killed when a 7.2 magnitude earthquake hits.

August 24, 1964 – Hurricane Cleo blasted Key Biscayne and then moved north along the Florida coastline. The hurricane caused massive flooding, structural damage and destroyed much of the citrus crop. It also prevented the "Fort Lauderdale News" from publishing, for the only time in its history. Hurricane Cleo caused property damage of $115.3 million dollars.

November-December 1964 – Mekong Delta, South Vietnam. Flooding kills 5,000 people.

Man vs. Man / Wars:

Assassinated – Bhutan. Jigme Palden Dorji, **Prime Minister of Bhutan is assassinated.** King Jigme Dorji Wangchuck, eventually assumes the duties of the Prime Minister. Namgyal Bahadur **is later executed for his part in the assassination.**

November 1964 – Bolivia. The Vice Presidential coup. The elected government of President Victor Paz Estensoro is deposed by a military coup mounted by Vice President Rene Barrientos Ortuno, who then becomes co-president of a military government with General Alfredo Ovando Candia. After the 1964 coup, Bolivia experienced a number of weak, short-lived governments, along with successive coups and counter-coups on behalf of the military.

1964-1967 – British. Aden Conflict. During the early 1960s President Nasser of Egypt began meddling, not very successfully, in the affairs of neighboring Yemen. Nationalist elements in Yemen liked his proposal to absorb Aden and its Protectorate territory to the north of Aden and in November terrorists, made a number of grenade attacks during the visit of the Colonial Secretary. In these attacks, a number of servicemen were killed or injured when **explosive devices were hurled into**

restaurants and bars. As a result of this, all bars and places of entertainment were placed out of bounds to all service personnel. December saw more bombings in Aden and further casualties among service personnel and civilians alike. The importance of Aden as a naval refueling station disappeared when the United Kingdom withdrew from its far eastern colonies.

March 31, 1964-1985 – Brazilian Military Revolt. President Johnson told his aids that he felt the U.S. should do everything they could to support the **coup in Brazil** on March 31, 1964.

On the 40th anniversary of the 1964 coup in Brazil the National Security Archive at The George Washington University, posted recently declassified documents on U.S. policy leading up to the overthrow of **President João Goulart** by the Brazilian military on the night of March 31, 1964. The documents show President Lyndon Johnson was prepared to back the coup by sending a naval task force to anchor off the coast of **Brazil and airlift ammunition** and CS gas for mob control.

On April 2, CIA agents in Brazil send a cable stating that João Goulart has been overthrown and fled Porto Alegre about 1pm local time for Montevideo. After the coup, **Brazil underwent a period of tremendous economic growth** under the military governments that instituted a policy emphasizing foreign investment, industrialization, economic growth, and internal repression.

1964-Present – The Colombian Civil War. The current low-intensity armed conflict in Colombia has existed since approximately 1964, when the Revolutionary Armed Forces of Colombia (FARC) and later the National Liberation Army (ELN) were founded and subsequently started their guerrilla insurgency campaigns against the Colombian government. The civil war developed out of the previous conflict known as La Violencia, which began after the 1948 assassination of Jorge Eliécer Gaitán, a populist political leader.

The fighting continues through 2010 between the wealthy, the poor, the drug lords, and the government. Colombia, the centre of the world cocaine trade, remains beset by violence and poverty while some three million people have been internally displaced by the fighting. Every group in Columbia has been tied to drug trafficking.

In 2009 Columbia allows the U.S. to fight drug-trafficking in Venezuela from bases inside Columbia and FARC members continue laying down their weapons.

1960-1964 – Congo Crisis. After a violent showdown between UN troops and Tshombe's forces, the Katanga secession ended in January 1963. The last of the pro-Lumumba Stanleyville government is defeated in 1964 after 11 more months of fighting. Then six months later, a year and a half after his defeat by the UN forces, Tshombe is back as the providential leader of the besieged central government.

Much of the Congo Crisis began around 1910, when the agents of King Leopold II of Belgium massacred 10 million Africans in the Congo. Forced labor was used for the very profitable rubber plantations in the French territories west and north of the Congo River, in Portuguese-ruled Angola, and in nearby Cameroon under the Germans. King Leopold II controlled vast rubber producing areas that were divided among various companies. Forced labor, hostages, slave chains, starving porters, burned villages, paramilitary company 'sentries', and the chicotte were business as usual. Mens wives were held captive until enough rubber was produced and members of the *Force Publique* were not paid unless they brought back the hands of those they killed. More hands, more pay. The chicotte was a vicious whip made out of raw, sun-dried hippopotamus hide, cut into a long sharp-edged cork-screw strip. It was applied to bare buttocks, and left permanent scars. Twenty strokes of it sent victims into unconsciousness. One-hundred or more strokes were often fatal. The chicotte was freely used by both Leopold's men and the French. There is still no peace in 2010.

1964 – The Cook Islands gain self-government from **New Zealand.**

February 18, 1964 – France. The Gabon Intervention, Coup. Gabon is thought to be one of the most politically stable countries in Africa. Gabonese President Léon M'ba removes the legislature on January 21, and Gabonese military officers rise up and arrest him and some of the remaining government officials. The military take over the government and go on the radio asking the people to remain calm. They assure the people that the country's pro-France foreign policy would remain unchanged. The people take a wait and see attitude with no major uprising and the new government takes this as a sign of popular approval.

French President Charles de Gaulle decides to restore the M'ba government and sends French paratroopers. The new government is toppled overnight and on February 19, the French reinstate M'ba as President.

President M'ba gets right to work and his troops round up and imprison more than 150 opponents, pledging "no pardon or pity" but rather "total punishment." President M'ba , now afraid for his life, will spend the next three years in the palace guarded by French troops until he dies of cancer on November 28, 1967.

September 25, 1964-1975 – The Mozambican War of Independence begins its fight against over 400 years of Portuguese rule. The Front for the Liberation of Mozambique (FRELIMO), initiates a guerrilla campaign against Portuguese rule in September 1964. Portuguese emigration to the colonies (**Angola, Portuguese Guinea, and Mozambique)** soared after WWII and the Portuguese control most of, if not all of, the wealth. Less than one-tenth of one percent of Mozambicans had been granted the right to vote by the Portuguese colonial government by 1950.

In surprise attacks, rebels kill Portuguese farmers and their families, including women, children and their black employees, on remote Angolan plantations. The U.S. supports independence for most colonized nations, and the UN also puts pressure on Portugal to grant independence. Portugal instead threatens to withdraw from NATO and the Nationalist groups in Mozambique are forced to seek help from the Soviet Union.

The war for independence is a guerrilla war that will officially end in 1975 but the Mozambican Civil War begins again in 1977 and continues through 1992. By 1975 almost all the Portuguese population had fled the African territory. The conflict creates more than 5 million refugees.

1964-1975 – Oman. Dhofar Rebellion. Oman is strategically located 35 miles directly opposite Iran on the Strait of Hormuz, the entrance to the Persian Gulf. A separatist revolt begins in Dhofar Province. The rebels form the **Dhofar Liberation Front,** which later merges with the Marxist-dominated **Popular Front for the Liberation of Oman and the Arab Gulf** (PFLOAG) and their main goal is to overthrow all traditional Arab Gulf regimes. Their cause is backed by communist and leftist governments such as the former South Yemen. By 1974, PFLOAG changed its name to the Popular Front for the Liberation of Oman (PFLO) and begins a political strategy to gain power in the other Gulf States, while continuing the guerrilla war in Dhofar.

January 9-12, 1964 – Panama. Anti-American Rioting. Pulling the Tigers tail.
Panamanians are angry with the Americans and looking for any excuse to express it. They are upset that the American flag is raised at many locations in the Canal Zone while their flag is only raised at one location and an agreement is soon reached allowing both flags to be flown side by side.

U.S. citizens residing in the Canal Zone feel they are above this agreement and the students of an American high school are encouraged by adults to hoist the American Flag by itself in front of their school. The local Panamanian students are shocked and close to 200 march into the Canal Zone with their flag. The Panamanian flag is torn when a fight erupts and thousands of Panamanians now storm the border fence. The rioting lasts 3 days, 20 people are killed, several hundred people are severely injured, and there is more than $2 million of property damage.

1964 – Singapore. The Race Riots are a series of riots that take place in Singapore during two separate periods in July and September between Chinese and Malay groups. The first incident occurs on July 21, during a Malay procession that marks Muhammad's birthday. In total, the violence kills 36 people and injures another 556. About 3,000 people are arrested.

1964-1987 – The Thailand War is greatly fueled by the **Vietnam War**. **Laos** and **Cambodia** allow the North Vietnamese to supply their troops in the south along the **Ho Chi Minh Trail,** which passes through southern Laos and northeastern Cambodia. They did not have a whole lot of choice. The Thais, with the backing of the U.S., quietly begin to conduct military operations in Laos, to which **North Vietnam** and **China** respond by supporting an anti-government insurgency in Thailand. The more the Thais feel threatened by the spread of communism, the more they look to the Americans for help. The U.S. will have around **45,000 military personnel on Thai soil** by 1968 as Thailand is used as a base for U.S. bombing raids against North Vietnam and Laos. Thailand is also used for covert operations into Laos. The Thai economy is flooded with American dollars and hundreds of thousands of Thais became reliant on the Americans for a living. There is also a direct increase in corruption and prostitution.

1964 – Rwanda. Tutsi Invasion of Rwanda. Following the failed Tutsi revolt in Rwanda, the Hutu-dominated government massacre 10,000 to 15,000 Tutsis and an estimated 200,000 Tutsis flee into exile.

1964-1967 – Somali Border Wars with Ethiopia and Kenya. Pan-Somali sentiment is aimed at uniting all territories settled by Somalis, including French Somaliland (Djibouti), the Ogaden (Ethiopian) and stretches of Kenya. The Somali government supports ethnic Somalis in Kenya and Ethiopia agitating for or committing acts of violence in order to achieve self-government and eventual unification with Somalia One of the first Somali-Ethiopian wars over Ogaden is fought.

Ogaden rebels will still be using guerrilla tactics to resist Ethiopian rule in 2009.

May 1964 and February 1966 – Syrian Urban Unrest. There were frequent changes of government reflecting the contest for power between the centrist and leftist wings of the **Baath Party** between 1964 and 1966. By April 1964 urban unrest had again become serious. In Hamah, for example, the military measures taken to suppress the uprisings resulted in what President Amin Hafiz described as **"frightful carnage."**

January 12, 1964 – Tanganyika, Tanganyika Army Mutiny. The British tri-service operation in January 1964 puts an end to the five-day mutiny by the army of newly-independent Tanganyika. Simultaneous but less serious military unrest in neighboring **Kenya** and **Uganda** is also dealt with relatively easily, and makes the military action against the Army Mutiny in Tanganyika business as usual. Neither the British nor the Tanganyika governments wanted to make too much of it.

January 1964 – Ugandan Army Mutiny. The army of Uganda, which had recently become independent of Britain, mutinies against the government of President Milton Obote. Unable to control the situation, Obote calls for help from British forces who put down the revolt rather quickly.

July 1964 – Vietnam. An announcement by the Johnson administration states that the U.S. military contingent in Vietnam would increase by **5,000, to 21,000 soldiers.**

August 2-4, 1964 – Vietnam. Gulf of Tonkin resolution. U.S. Navy destroyers **"Maddox"** and **"C. Turner Joy"** are reported attacked by **North Vietnamese** torpedo boats in the Gulf of Tonkin. On August 4, a U.S. retaliatory strike destroys 25 North Vietnamese boats at their bases. Congress overwhelmingly passes the **Gulf of Tonkin resolution** authorizing President Johnson to take "all necessary measures" in the region. Johnson describes the Tonkin resolution as **"like grandmother's nightshirt. It covers everything."**

Fall of 1964 – Vietnam. The U.S. turns down an offer of secret peace talks with North Vietnam.

November 1964 – Vietnam. Democrat Lyndon Johnson wins a landslide election over **Republican Barry Goldwater** just days after the **Viet Cong** shell an American air base. Operating with both legislative and electoral mandates, Johnson will soon significantly increase America's military presence in Vietnam. The war exacted a huge human cost in terms of fatalities, including 3 to 4 million Vietnamese from both sides, 1.5 to 2 million Laotians and Cambodians, and 58,260 names are listed at the Vietnam Veterans Memorial.

July 1964 – Zambia. A State of emergency is declared in July by the Governor of **Northern Rhodesia,** in connection with the rising of Alice Lenshina's separatist independent Christian Church, commonly called **'Lumpa'.** The most typical attitude towards the Lumpa episode among the Zambian elite has been one of embarrassment and silence.

In the rural areas of north-eastern Zambia the fighting between state troops and the church's members had ceased in October leaving an estimated death toll of about 1,500. The increased powers given to the government because of the state of emergency are allowed to continue. This was renewed every six months and survived both the attainment of territorial independence (October 1964) and the creation (December 1972) of the Second Republic under the exclusive leadership of Kaunda's United National Independence Party (UNIP). The Lumpa aftermath, including the continued presence of thousands of Lumpa refugees in Zaire just across the Zambian border was repeatedly cited as a reason for this continuation.

January 12, 1964 – Zanzibar. An uprising against the Sultan. The 2nd Scots Guards, who had made a previous visit to the island in August 1963 to supervise the elections, stood by to fly to the Sultan's aid. The British Government was against intervention and the **Scots Guards** flew instead to Aden.

The revolutionaries are overthrowing the government and the Sultan is looking for a way out of town. When the British community seemed to be in jeopardy, the Staffordshire Regiment standing by in place of the Scots Guards flew a company to Mombasa, where they embarked in the frigate H.M.S. Rhyl just to wait and see what happened. As it turned out **the Sultan made his escape by air,** to Tanganyika, and then fled to the UK.

1965

The oldest Boomer is 19 years old.

Cost of the Average House: $21,500	
Median Family Income: $6,900 (= $46,500 in 2006)	**Minimum Wage:** $1.25/ hr (= $8.10 in 2006) **Average Hourly Wage:** $2.61
21-inch color TV: $269	**Gallon Gasoline:** 31cents
New Car: Cadillac De Ville: $5,427 **Studebaker Daytona:** $2,405 **Ford Mustang:** $2,427 **Shelby Cobra:** $5,595	**A year at Harvard in 1965 cost $2,700** ($50,000+ in 2008) **Round Trip airfare, New York to Los Angeles:** $290
Unemployment Rate: 4.9%-4.3%-4.0%	**First-class Stamp:** 5 cents

15 cents buying power in 1965 = **$1.00 in 2008.**
In 1965 what cost us 15 cents to purchase now costs us $1.00 in 2008**.**

Movies: "Darling," "Doctor Zhivago," "Ship of Fools," "A Thousand Clowns," "The Sound of Music," "Cat Ballou." "The Pawnbroker," becomes the first major Hollywood film to feature frontal nudity.

Broadway: "On a Clear Day You Can See Forever," "Half a Sixpence," "Charley Girl," London. "Man of La Mancha."

TV: "A Charlie Brown Christmas," "Green Acres," "Hogan's Heroes," "I Dream of Jeannie," "My Mother the Car," "F.B.I.," "The Soupy Sales Show," "Get Smart," "Gidget, with 18 year old Sally Field. "I Spy," with Bill Cosby as Alexander Scott. "Big Valley," "A Man Called Shenandoah," "Convoy," "F Troop," "Lost in Space," "The Dating Game," "Supermarket Sweep," "The New Three Stooges," "The Smothers Brothers Show," "Roger Ramjet," "The Beatles, Animated," "The Wackiest Ship in the Army," "The Wild Wild West," "Laredo," "Loner," "Hullabaloo," "Shindig". The Vietnam War becomes the first war to be televised, and every night for years the

American public gets to watch the war. Most broadcasts are now in color.

Music: The Beatles, "Yesterday," "I Feel Fine," "Ticket to Ride" & "Help!" Sing-Out 65, in 1968 they changed the name to, "Up With People." Rodgers and Hammerstein, "The Sound of Music." Maurice Jarre, "Doctor Zhivago." Four Tops, "I Can't Help Myself." Billy Stewart, "I Do Love You." Wilson Pickett, "In The Midnight Hour." Jr. Walker & The All Stars, "Shotgun." Barbara Mason, "Yes, I'm Ready." Buck Owens, "I've Got A Tiger By The Tail." Eddy Arnold, "What's He Doing In My World." Warner Mack, "Bridge Washed Out." Sam The Sham & The Pharaohs, "Wooly Bully." Rolling Stones, "I Can't Get No, Satisfaction" & "The Last Time." Righteous Brothers, "You've Lost That Lovin' Feelin'" & "Unchained Melody." We Five, "You Were On My Mind." Herman's Hermits, "A Must to Avoid." The Beach Boys, "Help Me Rhonda." Sonny & Cher, "I Got You Babe." The Supremes, "I Hear a Symphony." The Dave Clark Five, "I Like It Like That." Herman's Hermits, "I'm Henry VIII, I Am." Bob Dylan, "Like a Rolling Stone." Roger Miller, "King of the Road." Tom Jones, "It's Not Unusual" & "What's New, Pussycat?" The Byrds, "Mr. Tambourine Man." James Brown, "Papa's Got a Brand New Bag." Johnny Rivers, "Seventh Son." Jackie DeShannon, "What the World Needs Now Is Love."

Deaths:

Alice Herz, the first activist in the United States known to have immolated herself in protest of the escalating Vietnam War.

Roger LaPorte, doused himself with gasoline outside of the United Nations and lit a match, to protest the war.

Norman Morrison, a Baltimore Quaker, handed his 1-year old daughter to horrified onlookers and lit himself on fire outside the Pentagon office of Secretary of Defense Robert McNamara, to protest the war. In a society where it is normal for human beings to drop bombs on human targets, where it is normal to spend 50 percent of the individual's tax dollar on war, where it is normal...to have twelve times overkill capacity, Norman Morrison was not normal. He said, "Let it stop".

Viola Liuzzo, Jimmie Lee Jackson, Ellen Church, William M. Branham.

President: Lyndon B. Johnson (D) Disciples of Christ; vetoes 30/ 0 overrides

Vice President: (no Vice President, 1963–1965)

House: D-295 ; R-140

Senate: 89th Congress (1965-1967) Majority Party: Democrat (68 seats) Minority Party: Republican (32 seats) Other Parties: 0 Total Seats: 100

Federal Debt: $317.27 billion or 44 % of the GDP

Consumer Price Index CPI-U: According to the official consumer price index, it costs $645 in 2006 to buy what $100 bought in 1965.

GDP: $719.1 billion	**Inflation Rate:** 1.59%

Dow Jones: 958.96 (11-01)/ 871.59 (07-01)

Prime Rate: 5.00% (12-06)

1 oz Gold: $35.50	**1oz of Silver:** $1.30

Average Monthly S.S. Benefits Paid: $82 / month

Federal Debt: $317,273,898,983.64

Federal Deficit: $1.4 billion dollars

Defense Spending: $61.61 billion	**Interest Spending:** $8.59 billion
Health Care Spending: $1.79 billion	**Pensions Spending:** $15.14 billion
Welfare Spending: $5.94 billion	**Education Spending:** $2.93 billion
Transportation Spending: $5.76 billion	**Misc. Other Spending:** $14.17 billion
Protection Spending: $540 million	**Total Government Spending:** $118.23 billion

% of GDP that goes towards just the interest payment: 1.25%

$1.00 = 361.51 Yen, Japan

U.S. Population: 194,347,000	**World Population:** 3,345,837,853

1965

U.S. Birth Rate: 3,760,358	**U.S. Abortions:** 794
U.S. Homicide Rate: 5.5/ 100,000 population	**U.S. Violent Crime:** 200.2/ 100,000 population
Annual Average Domestic Crude Oil Prices: $3.01 / barrel, $20.51 (2007 adjusted)	

Oil:

1965 – Oil prices fall from 1965 to 1972 as we become more involved in **Vietnam**.

1965 – British Petroleum makes the first British discovery of gas in the West Sole field, off the coast of East Anglia, by the British Petroleum jack-up drilling rig Sea Gem. This leads to more discoveries in the North Sea. Only days later, on Boxing Day, **the Sea Gem capsizes and thirteen people die.**

1957-1965 – Oman. Five years after the British finished propping up the Sultan's authority in the area and had withdrawn their forces, little had changed when a rebellion broke out in the province of **Dhofar.** (This is not Darfur, where over 400,000 people will die between 2003-2009.) After the rebels proclaimed the liberation of Dhofar in 1965 they received support from Egypt, Iraq and South Yemen. The British respond with another military intervention that will last until 1974. Oil is the main issue and Oman will begin production in 1967.

Major News:

January 4, 1968 – In his State of the Union address **President Johnson** outlines plans for his **"Great Society."**

February 7, 1965 – President Lyndon B. Johnson orders the continuous bombing of North Vietnam below the 20th parallel.

April 28, 1965 – The Johnson administration sends 14,000 troops to the **Dominican Republic** during their civil war. All troops are withdrawn by 1966.

July 1965 – The Johnson administration announces it will dispatch 150,000 U.S. troops to Vietnam. There were 16,000 last year. There will be 543,000 soldiers in Vietnam in 1968, the last year of the Johnson administration.

Civil Rights Movement:

March 7, 1965 – "Bloody Sunday." The Selma-to-Montgomery March for voting rights. On "Bloody Sunday," March 7, 1965, some 600 civil rights marchers headed east out of Selma on U.S. Route 80. They got only as far as the Edmund Pettus Bridge six blocks away, **where state and local lawmen attacked them with billy clubs** and tear gas and drove them back into Selma. Fifty marchers were hospitalized. Two days later on March 9, **Martin Luther King, Jr.,** led a "symbolic" march to the bridge. Then civil rights leaders sought court protection for a third, full-scale march from Selma to the state capitol in Montgomery. Federal District Court Judge Frank M. Johnson, Jr., weighed the right of mobility against the right to march and ruled in favor of the demonstrators. "The law is clear that the right to petition one's government for the redress of grievances may be exercised in large groups . . .," said Judge Johnson, "and these rights may be exercised by marching, even along public highways." On Sunday, March 21, about 3,200 marchers set out for Montgomery, walking 12 miles a day and sleeping in fields. By the time they reached the capitol on Thursday, March 25, **they were 25,000-strong.** Less than five months after the last of the three marches, President Lyndon Johnson signed the Voting Rights Act of 1965, the best possible redress of grievances.

March 25, 1965 – Martin Luther King speaks at a civil rights rally on the courthouse steps of the Alabama State Capitol, ending the Selma to Montgomery, Alabama march for voting rights.

1965 – Viola Liuzzo. Viola Fauver was a civil rights activist from the U.S. state of Michigan and mother of five, who was **murdered by Ku Klux Klan** members after the 1965 **Selma to Montgomery marches** in Alabama. Viola Liuzzo's name is one of those inscribed on a civil rights memorial in the state capital. She died at the age of 39.

Viola Liuzzo was deeply troubled by Bloody Sunday when the police broke up the march at the Edmund Pettus Bridge in Alabama. She took part in a protest at Wayne State University where had she attended classes and then afterwards she called her husband and told him she was going to Selma because there were "too many people who just stand around talking," the struggle "was everybody's fight."

On March 25, **Martin Luther King** led 25,000 people to the Alabama State Capitol and handed a petition to **Governor George Wallace,** demanding voting rights for African Americans. Viola was there and helped drive local marchers home with the assistance of 19 year old Leroy Morton. After they dropped off their second carload of people a car full of Klan members spotted Violas car at a stoplight. When they saw a white woman and black man in the car they started taunting them and then chased them for miles. The KKK members drove alongside and fired two shots that hit Viola in the head, killing her instantly. Leroy was uninjured and was able to get the car under control before it crashed.

The four Klan members in the car, Collie Wilkins (21), FBI informant Gary Rowe (34), William Eaton (41) and Eugene Thomas (42) were quickly arrested and within 24 hours **President Lyndon Johnson** appeared personally on national television to announce their arrest.

An all-white jury is selected for Wilkins' trial on May 3, and Gary Rowe is the key witness. The defendant's attorney made blatant racist comments during his final arguments, including calling Liuzzo a "white nigger," in order to sway the jury. The comments had their intended effect and caused a mistrial with 10-2 in favor of conviction. The three accused killers were part of a Klan parade on May 10 which closed with a standing ovation for them.

President Lyndon Johnson, instructed officials to arrange for the men to be charged under an 1870 federal law of conspiring to deprive Viola Liuzzo of her civil rights. Wilkins, Eaton and Thomas were found guilty and sentenced to 10 years in prison.

March 11, 1965 – James Reeb had been in Alabama less than a day when white assailants attacked him and two other white **Unitarian Universalist Ministers** on a **Selma** sidewalk, fatally injuring him with a blow to the head.

James Reeb's death on March 11, inspired a wave of **nationwide protests, memorial services, and calls for federal action,** transforming Reeb into a martyr and creating the political groundswell **President Lyndon Johnson** needed to introduce new voting rights legislation. Four days after Reeb's death, Johnson invoked his memory, "that good man," as he introduced the **Voting Rights Act** to a joint session of Congress.

1965 – Jimmie Lee Jackson. Close to 500 demonstrators leave the **Zion United Methodist Church** in Marion for a peaceful march to the Perry County Jail about a half a block away where young Civil Rights worker James Orange was being held. They were not allowed to march during the day because it would disrupt the local businesses. The plan is to **sing hymns and return to the church** in spite of the many **Marion City police officers, sheriff's deputies, and Alabama State Troopers.** As the marchers began to pass between them the police and State Troopers attacked the demonstrators. The street lights were either turned off or shot out by the police and the **police began to beat the protestors.** Two United Press International photographers had their cameras smashed, and **NBC News correspondent Richard Valeriani,** was beaten so badly he was hospitalized. The marchers turned and ran, some back towards the church, and some just trying to escape.

Jimmie Lee Jackson's 82 year old grandfather, Cager Lee, was badly beaten and bleeding. While being chased by Alabama State Troopers Jimmy Lee and his mother, Viola Jackson, rushed him over to Mack's Café behind the church. The State Troopers clubbed everyone inside the Café. They beat Cager Lee to the floor in the kitchen and then continued to beat him. When his daughter Viola attempted to pull the police off, she was also beaten. When Jimmy Lee saw the Trooper club his mother he tried to push the trooper away and was hit in the face by another State Trooper, pushed against a cigarette machine and shot twice in the stomach. Jimmy Lee managed to get out of the Café as the troopers chased him up the street and beat him until he dropped and collapsed in front of the bus station. He was first arrested and charged with assault and battery before being taken to the hospital two hours later. Jimmie Lee Jackson died at Good Samaritan Hospital in Selma, on February 26, 1965, from an infection caused by the shooting. He was 26 years old.

1965

1965 – National Voting Rights Act of 1965. President Lyndon B. Johnson, in a dramatic joint-session address, calls upon Congress to enact a strong voting rights bill. Johnson's administration drafted a bill intended to enforce the 14th and 15th Amendments, aiming to eliminate various previously legal strategies to prevent blacks and other minorities from voting. On August 6, The Voting Rights Act of 1965 is signed into law by **President Lyndon B. Johnson.** Two significant portions of the act; the outlawing of the requirement of potential voters to take a literacy test in order to qualify and the provision of federal registration of voters in areas with less than 50% of all voters registered.

February 21, 1965 – Malcolm X is assassinated by three black men. "It is a time for martyrs now, and if I am to be one, it will be for the cause of brotherhood. That's the only thing that can save this country." These prophetic words were spoken by **Malcolm X,** one of Americas most famous and controversial African-Americans just two days before his assassination by three black men.

By the time Malcolm X, born **Malcolm Little,** was 13, his father had died and his mother had been committed to a mental hospital. His childhood, including his father's lessons concerning black pride and self-reliance and his own experiences concerning race, played a significant role in his adult life. Although his father was an outspoken **Baptist** lay speaker, Malcolm became a **Sunni Muslim** and made a pilgrimage to Mecca.

August 11-15, 1965 – Los Angeles. A riot by blacks living in the **Watts** neighborhood of Los Angeles, California is a large-scale civil disorder which lasts six days. During the riots, 34 people are officially reported killed, 1,100 people are injured, 4,000 people are arrested, 600 buildings are damaged or destroyed, and there is an estimated $200 million in property damage.

1965 – Student Non-Violent Coordinating Committee. SNCC fielded the largest staff of any civil rights organization in the South. Their sit-ins combine non-violence and confrontation. SNCC organized nonviolent direct action against segregated facilities, as well as voter-registration projects, in **Alabama, Arkansas, Maryland, Missouri, Louisiana, Virginia, Kentucky, Tennessee, Illinois, North and South**

Carolina, Georgia, and Mississippi. SNCC helped candidates for agricultural stabilization and conservation service boards in five states, aided school board candidates in Arkansas in 1965, and worked toward solving the economic problems of southern blacks by organizing the Mississippi Freedom Labor Union and a poor people's corporation, and mounting economic boycotts against discriminatory merchants.

SNCC helped to build two independent political parties. One, the Lyons County Freedom Organization, will prove to be factor in black politics in Alabama for years to come. Other black civil rights organizations wanted to integrate blacks into the mainstream where SNCC wanted to change American society itself.

Women's Movement:

1965 – The case "Weeks vs. Southern Belle" marks a major triumph in the fight against restrictive labor laws and company regulations on the hours and conditions of women's work, opening many previously male-only jobs to women.

1965 – EEOC commissioners are appointed to enforce the Civil Rights Act. Among them is Aileen Hernandez, a future president of NOW.

1965 – Patsy Takemoto Mink, of Hawaii, is the first Asian-American woman elected to Congress. She will serve in the U.S. House of Representatives for 24 years.

Popular Culture:

October 15, 1965 – The first public burning of a draft card occurs in protest to the Vietnam War. It is coordinated by the anti-war group of students, National Coordinating Committee to End the War in Vietnam.

1965 – The Supreme Court case Griswold vs. Connecticut strikes down the only remaining state law banning the use of **contraceptives** by married couples.

1965 – Boomers. With the threat of disease and pregnancy now reduced, some of the post-WWII Boomer generation experiment with sex without considering marriage.

1965

1965 – "Super Ball" is invented by Norman Stingley, and manufactured by **Wham-O.** Dropped from shoulder level, a high energy Super Ball bounces nearly all the way back. Thrown down, it can soar over a three-story building. Thrown into a wall with spin, it flies back with remarkable reverse English. The supercharged sphere, about the size and color of a plum, is America's most popular plaything this summer and fall. By Christmas, just six months after it is introduced by Wham-O, seven million balls are sold at ninety-eight cents apiece.

1965 – Project Head Start, a preschool education program for children from low-income families, begins as an eight-week summer program. Part of the **"War on Poverty,"** the program continues to this day as the longest-running anti-poverty program in the U.S.

April 1, 1965 – Sociology department head William Sewell organizes a well-attended **antiwar teach-in** on the **University of Wisconsin at Madison** campus, reflecting his belief that the U.S. doesn't have "any business over there" in Vietnam. First attempted at the **University of Michigan** just a week earlier, the teach-in becomes a popular form of protest. Later in the month, **15,000 students demonstrate** against the war. In Washington; 35,000 **antiwar protesters** converge on the city in November. **War supporters** also draw large crowds, including 25,000 at a Washington, D.C. rally in October.

August 23, 1965 – "LIFE" magazine features a two page spread of photographs depicting the small but growing opposition to the war in Viet Nam. On the left is a black and white photo of an "all-American boy," crew cut hair and neatly dressed, his eyes fixed **on a draft card burning in his hand.** Unidentified by "LIFE," the young man is **Christopher Kearns,** associate editor of **"The Catholic Worker"** and a direct descendent of Benjamin Rush, a signer of the Declaration of Independence. On the opposite page is a color photo of a demonstration two weeks earlier when 1,500 people had marched from the Washington Monument to the Capitol. "As we marched peacefully, we were interrupted by an enraged right-winger. He threw a bucket of paint at our leaders, but we pressed on." This dramatic moment was immortalized by *LIFE* magazine.

These photographs caught the attention of some conservative Senators and Congress responded by amending the Universal Military Training and Service Act to make it a Felony when any person "knowingly destroys [or] knowingly mutilates" his registration certificate. They quickly framed a bill to make draft card burning a felony punishable by **five years in prison and $10,000 fine.** David O'Brien and the American Civil Liberties Union fought O'Brien's conviction for burning his registration certificate in front of some FBI agents and a large Boston crowd. The United States Court of Appeals held that the 1965 law unconstitutionally abridged Freedom of Speech because it interfered with O'Brien's "symbolic" protest against the war. The September issue of **"The Catholic Worker"** suggested it was time for us to burn our draft cards.

1965 – The United States Congress passes the **Federal Cigarette Labeling** and Advertising Act, requiring the surgeon general's health warnings on all cigarette packs and cartons. **Caution: Cigarette Smoking May be Hazardous to Your Health.**

1965 – As the United States goes to war, antiwar protest groups form on many of the nation's campuses. In June, the leftist organization **Students for a Democratic Society** decide to make the war its principal target, but major dissent does not begin until 1966 or later. Forming the core of the 1960s **New Left,** Students for a Democratic Society (**SDS**) is a radical organization. Its political manifesto, known as the Port Huron Statement, was adopted at the organization's first convention in 1962, based on an earlier draft by staff member **Tom Hayden**. It criticizes, among other things, racial discrimination, economic inequality, big businesses, trade unions and political parties.

Most Americans still support the administration's claim that it is fighting to stop communism in Southeast Asia and many if not most people simply go about their daily lives, unaware that this gradually escalating war will tear American society apart.

October 3, 1965 – The national immigration quota system is abolished.

October 1965 – In mid-October, the anti-war movement had significantly expanded to become a national and even global phenomenon, as anti-war protests drawing

100,000 are held simultaneously in as many as 80 major cities around the **U.S., London, Paris and Rome.**

November 9-10, 1965 – An electric power failure blacks out most of the northeastern U.S. and parts of two Canadian provinces. For 12 hours electricity is unavailable for 25 million in an area covering 80,000 square miles. The power outage falls on Tuesday-Wednesday, (no TV/-no sports/-no radio) and their will be an upsurge in births in nine months.

November 27, 1965 –40,000 protesters led by several student activist groups **surround the White House,** calling for an end to the war. They then march to the Washington Monument, while President Johnson announces a significant escalation of U.S. involvement in Indochina, from 120,000 to 400,000 troops.

December 6, 1965 – Pakistan's Islamic Ideology Advisory Committee recommends that **Islamic Studies be made a compulsory** subject for Muslim students from primary to graduate level.

1965 – Foster Grant, **"Who's that behind those Foster Grants?"** Geer, Dubois.

1965 – The Roman Catholic Church has supported the U.S. government's Vietnam policy since the 1950s on the now disproved theory that it will hold communism at bay.

Business / Technology:

1965 – Ford offers 8-track tape players on next year's model cars.

1965 – The PDP-8, or Straight-8 **minicomputer**, is manufactured by the Digital Equipment Corporation (DEC). It is the first minicomputer and the first DEC computer to be made with an automatic wire-wrapped backplane, which makes the machine **cheaper to produce and more reliable.** Over 5,000 are sold worldwide. The PDP-8 is used for industrial control, controlling experiments, running businesses, word processing, and many other uses. The PDP-8 sells for only **$18,000**, one-fifth the price of a small **IBM 360 mainframe.**

1965 – "Subway" restaurant sandwiches and salads. **Fred De Luca, 17,** is trying to raise money to pay for college when he **borrows $1,000** from a family friend to start his first sandwich shop. He chose a mediocre location for his shop, but by noon on the first day of the opening, customers were pouring in. On the radio advertisement they had promoted the name as "Pete's Submarines," which sounded like Pizza Marines, so they changed the name to "Pete's Subway." Eventually it is shortened to "Subway." As of December 30, 2008, the company has 19,310 franchised locations in 87 countries and produces $9.05 billion sales every year. In 2007, Forbes magazine named De Luca number 242 of the 400 richest Americans with a net worth of $1.5 billion.

1965 – Mobile radio telephone service is widely available in the U.S.

1965 – Computer-based telephone digital switching replaces electromagnetic systems.

1965 – Kevlar. Stephanie Kwolek, a DuPont research scientist, develops Kevlar by spinning fiber from liquid crystalline solutions. **She will patent the compound,** used extensively in bullet proof vests, in 1966.

1965 – Kodak offers Super 8 film for home movies.

1965 – Westinghouse Phonovid stores TV sound and pictures on phonograph records.

July 30, 1965 – Medicare. President Johnson signs Medicare into law in Independence, Missouri at the Truman Library. Former **President Truman** is seated beside him. LBJ held the ceremony there to honor President Truman's leadership on health insurance, which he first proposed in 1945. When Medicare went into effect in 1966, over 19 million people enrolled.

1965

June 28, 1965 – Early Bird, Intelsat I. The first commercial communications satellite, nicknamed Early Bird, introduces live commercial television across oceans.

1965 – Groups of Russian, American and British scientists bounce radio waves off Venus (in 1961), Mercury (in 1962) and Mars (in 1965) and detect the echoes. Simply measuring the time taken for these waves to make the journey from transmitter to planet to receiver, and dividing by the speed of light, gave them the round-trip distance to those planets. This method produces better results than parallax ever could achieve.

January 1965 – The first version of **Moore's Law:** microprocessor speed will double each year. Lewis Young, the editor of the widely circulated trade journal "Electronics," writes to Gordon Moore, inviting him to contribute to the magazine's 30th anniversary issue. In the cover letter accompanying his manuscript, Moore suggests a change to Young's assignment: "Enclosed is the manuscript for the article entitled 'The Future of Integrated Electronics' . . . I am taking the liberty of changing the title slightly from the one you suggested, since I think that 'integrated electronics' better describes the source for the advantages in this new technology than does the term 'microelectronics.'" Just over one month later, the edited version of Moore's paper appeared in the April 19, 1965 issue of **"Electronics,"** constituting the first public articulation of what came to be known as "Moore's law."

Finance:

1965 – This year marks the end of the last inflation-free economic expansion for a long time.

1965 – Medicare. Congress amends the Social Security Act of 1935 to create Medicare, which covers hospital and other health-care costs of the elderly.

Books:

1965 – Ralph Nader, "Unsafe at Any Speed."

1965 – Alex Haley publishes **"The Autobiography of Malcolm X."** It was written between 1964 and 1965, as told to him through conversations with Malcolm conducted shortly before Malcolm X's assassination. The book was named by *"Time"* magazine as one of the ten most important nonfiction books of the 20th century.

1965 – "Dune," Frank Herbert.

1965 – Bans on three books with **explicit erotic content** are challenged and overturned. Putnam publishes John Cleland's 1750 novel **"Fanny Hill."** This was the turning point, because Charles Rembar appealed a restraining order against it all the way to the U.S. Supreme Court and won. In Memoirs vs. Massachusetts, 383 U.S. 413, the court ruled that sex was "a great and mysterious motive force in human life," and that its expression in literature was protected by the First Amendment.

TV:

1965 – The TV show "I Spy" will be remembered as the first television show to feature a Black actor, **Bill Cosby,** in a lead role.

Music:

August 15 – The Beatles play at Shea Stadium, the first rock concert to be held in a setting of that size. The concert also sets new world records for revenue and a record for attendance at 55,600+.

November 26 – Arlo Guthrie is arrested in Great Barrington, Massachusetts for the crime of littering, perpetrated the day before Thanksgiving, in the nearby town of Stockbridge. The resultant events and adventure would be immortalized in the song **"Alice's Restaurant."**

Natural Disasters:

February 4, 1965 – A magnitude 8.7 earthquake hits the **Rat Islands** off Alaska's coast.

1965

May 11–12 & June 1–2, 1965 – **East Pakistan,** cyclones kill 35,000 to 40,000 people.

August 27, 1965 – "Billion-Dollar Betsy." Hurricane "Betsy" kills 75 people and cost more than $1.4 billion in the Bahamas, Florida, and Louisiana.

December 15, 1965 – Cyclone. Karachi, Pakistan, about 10,000 people are killed.

April 11–12, 1965 – Midwest–Great Lakes region, tornadoes in Iowa, Illinois, Indiana, Ohio, Michigan, and Wisconsin cause the deaths of 272 people.

April 29, 1965 – A magnitude 6.5 earthquake near Olympia, Washington causes about $12.5 million dollars in damage.

1965-1967 – Drought in India causes more than 1.5 million peoples deaths.

Man vs. Man / Wars:

Assassinated – Burundi. Pierre Ngendandume, **Burundi Prime Minister** from January 7, 1965–January 15, 1965. He was a member of the Union for National Progress and was an ethnic **Hutu.** Eight days after beginning his second term, he is assassinated by a Rwandan **Tutsi** refugee.

Assassinated – Burundi. Joseph Bamina, **Burundi Prime Minister.** Bamina was Prime Minister from January 26, to September 30. He was a **Hutu** and is replaced by Léopold Biha, October 13, 1965–November 28, 1966, **a Tutsi**

Assassinated – Iran. Hassan Ali Mansur, **Prime Minister of Iran.** He served during the **White Revolution** of **Shah Mohammad Reza Pahlavi** and was assassinated by a member of the Fadayan-e Islam.

1965 – There are 10 major wars under way. The United Nations defines "major wars" as military conflicts inflicting 1,000 battlefield deaths per year.

1965 – Boston Strangler. Albert DeSalvo confesses to the murders. Between June 14, 1962 and January 4, 1964, thirteen women in the Boston area were victims of a **serial killer** or possibly several killers. The middle-aged and elderly women were posed obscenely in the early cases and the later cases involve young women.

After Albert DeSalvo is charged with rape he gives a detailed confession of his activities as the Boston Strangler while he is interrogated under hypnosis.

Investigators have since suggested the murders, sometimes known as the **Silk Stocking Murders,** were not committed by one person. There was never any physical evidence to tie Albert DeSalvo with any of the crimes, so the only thing that ever connected him was his confession. In 2001 DNA tests on one of the victims cleared Albert DeSalvo.

October 1, 1965 – Indonesia. Military coup. Indonesia is an archipelagic country of 17,508 islands (6,000 inhabited) stretching along the equator in South East Asia.

General Sukarno is stripped of power by **General Suharto** on October 1, 1965. The coup leads to a violent army-led anti-communist purge in which **over half a million people are killed.** Suharto's New Order administration favors the West whose investment in Indonesia is a major factor during the next three decades of substantial economic growth. The ***Christian Science Monitor*** described General Suharto as Indonesia's new "moderate" leader after he had washed some of the blood off his hands. The respected ***London Economist*** assures us that General Suharto is "at heart benign," while he is behind the murder of hundreds of thousands of people in East Timor and elsewhere.

The reality is by 1965 Sukarno is precariously balancing between the military commanders, the Muslim organizations and the PKI, which has close to three million members and supporters, making it the third largest Communist Party in the world, after China and the Soviet Union.

So much of the world outside of Europe and the U.S. has a lifestyle of murder. To maintain order and control you simply kill everyone who disagrees with you. This attitude is also immigrating to an unprepared western world. It is estimated that General Suharto is responsible for the murder of between 500,000 and a million PKI members and supporters, as well as people of ethnic Chinese origin. Tens of thousands of people were detained in prisons and concentration camps and more than 7,000 soldiers were killed. Documents released in 2008/ 2009 show that throughout late 1965 and early 1966 U.S. and Australian officials reported to their respective governments that **army units and Muslim groups** were working hand-in-hand to **shoot, hack or club to death at least 1,500 suspected PKI sympathizers per day,** sometimes parading their heads on sticks. People were commonly denied basic rights and between 1969 and 1980, approximately 10,000 persons, primarily known to be communists or suspected of being communists, were detained without trial on Buru Island in the Moluccas. In terms of the numbers killed the massacres in Indonesia rank as one of the worst mass murders of the 20th century.

1965-1985 – Syria. Muslim Brotherhood. In 1964 and 1965, strikes and mass demonstrations spread throughout Syria's major cities, and were crushed by the military.

May 1965 – Bolivia. Tin miners occupy the mines and go on strike. The government sends in troops and begins to draft insurgent workers into the army. After the strike is stopped the army forces President Barrientos to accept General Alfredo Ovando Candia as his co-president.

January 1965 – Republic of Burundi. Tutsi vs. Hutu. Burundi borders Rwanda to the north, Tanzania to the south and east, and the Democratic Republic of the Congo to the west. Discord and violence have marked Burundi since independence in 1962 and ethnic conflict has resulted in **hundreds of thousands of deaths and hundreds of thousands of people being displaced** from their homes. In January 1965 Pierre Ngendandumwe, **a Hutu,** took office as prime minister for the second time, at the request of the King of Burundi, Mwambutsa. After only eight days and before he has a chance to establish a government, **Ngendandumwe is assassinated by a Tutsi gunman on January 15.** Joseph Bamina, **another Hutu,** then serves as Prime Minister from January 26, to September 30 **when he is assassinated.** Elections gave the Hutu a clear majority of seats in the National Assembly but King Mwambutsa ignored the results **and appointed** his private secretary, **a Tutsi,** Prime Minister.

King Mwambutsa insisted that power would continue to rest with the crown. After a failed coup in October, some 34 Hutu officers were executed and King Mwambutsa felt it may be a good time to leave the country. He decreed that his son, Prince Charles

Ndizeyeto, was to rule in his absence. Control of Burundi will be completely in the hands of the Tutsi before the end of the next year.

November 1, 1965 – Chad. In January 1962 President Tombalbaye had banned all political parties except his own Chadian Progressive Party (PPT), and started immediately concentrating all power in his own hands. He filled the prisons with thousands of political prisoners and was particularly hard on the regions of central and northern Chad, where the southern Chadian administrators came to be perceived as arrogant and incompetent.

In 1965 the Chadian civil war begins with a spontaneous peasant uprising in Guéra Prefecture because of new taxes imposed by President Tombalbaye. The rebellion gave the Muslim northern and central regions an opportunity to get back at the predominantly non-Muslim people of the south who had dominated the government and civil service since independence. This Muslim resentment at last exploded with the tax revolt on November 1, causing 500 deaths. The National Liberation Front of Chad, created to militarily oust Tombalbaye and the Southern dominance begins in Sudan in 1966. It is the start of a bloody civil war that will still be going on in 2009.

1965 – Republic of the Congo, Brazzaville. Not to be confused with its neighbor **Republic of the Congo, Leopoldville. The 1965 mission marks the beginning of the MPLA's twenty-six year alliance with Cuba.** Brazzaville is used as a rear-base for **Che'Guevara's guerrillas** in eastern Congo. The Cuban insurgents will build strong relationships with the **Popular Movement for the Liberation of Angola** (MPLA) which serve as a foundation for a large-scale intervention in 1975. **In late May 1965**, the first nine Cuban instructors under Rafael Moracen Limonta arrived in Brazzaville incognito. They obtained false ID's from the Congolese government and then traveled to the main MPLA camp thirty miles north in Loubomo.

1965 – Republic of the Congo, Leopoldville. Unrest and rebellion plague the government and from 1960 to 1964 the peacekeeping effort is the largest, most complex, and most costly operation ever carried out by the **United Nations.** In the chaos a number of temporary governments take over in quick succession. In 1965, Lieutenant General Joseph-Désiré **Mobutu,** commander-in-chief of the national army, stages a second coup d'etat and President Kasavubu retires for good. **Prime Minister Moise Tshombe flees** the country and Mobutu claims the Presidency. President Mobutu will keep his hold on the country until 1997 by establishing several military forces whose sole purpose is to protect him. According to Transparency International, Mobutu embezzled over $5 billion from his country, ranking him as the third-most corrupt leader in the past two decades and the most corrupt African leader during the same period.

1965 – Cuba. Ernesto 'Che' Guevara. Following the successful overthrow of Batista in 1959, Che was asked to assume numerous leadership responsibilities, including directing the National Bank, the land reform, and the ministry of industry, as well as representing Cuba at the UN and other international gatherings. **In 1965 he left these positions to lead combat operations** against imperialist intervention in the **Congo.** Then he tried to overthrow the **Bolivian** dictatorship and turn the Andes into the Sierra Maestra of the Americas. The Sierra Maestra was the base of Cuba's guerillas.

1965 – Dhofar. Not to be confused with Darfur. A counter-insurgency campaign, the **Dhofar Rebellion**, is fought by the **Sultan of Oman's Armed Forces** and the **British** in 1965-1975 against guerrilla fighters of the **Popular Front for the Liberation of Oman and the Persian Gulf** supported by **South Yemen** after that territory's independence. It aimed to depose the Sultan because of poverty, repression and general incompetence within the government. The Sultan's forces, assisted by the **United Kingdom, Iran, Jordan** and **India,** prevailed, and once the campaign ended in December 1975, the remainder of the active forces surrendered.

April 28, 1965 – Dominican Republic. A coup by reformist officers and civilian combatants loyal to former President Bosch seize the national palace. Conservative military forces strike back with tank assaults and aerial bombings. The anti-Bosch sections of the army request U.S. military assistance, officially to protect U.S. citizens and to evacuate U.S. and other foreign nationals in what was known as **Operation Power Pack.** On April 28, U.S. Marines land and ultimately, **23,000 troops are deployed to the Dominican Republic.**

August 5, 1965 to September 22, 1965 – Pakistan attacks India and achieves some early successes but ultimately the Indian armies not only stop Pakistan but are also able to occupy a good bit of Pakistani territory. With the help of the Soviet Union a cease fire is arranged.

Pakistan was not prepared when the U.S. declared its neutrality and also cut off military supplies. The U.S. felt the situation was largely Pakistan's fault and refused to come to Pakistan's aid under the terms of the Agreement of Cooperation. The **Pakistanis were angry** with the U.S. refusal to come to their aid and looked for support wherever they could find it. The clash did not resolve this dispute, but it did engage the **United States** and the **Soviet Union** in ways that would have important implications for subsequent superpower involvement in the region.

November 9, 1965 – Philippines. Marcos is elected President and pledges to reform the "old order" by removing bureaucratic inefficiency and corruption.

It was reported that, when Dictator Ferdinand Marcos fled the Philippines in 1986, U.S. Customs agents discovered **24 suitcases of gold bricks** and **diamond jewelry** hidden in diaper bags. In addition, certificates for gold bullion valued in the billions of dollars were allegedly among the personal property he, his family, his cronies and business partners surreptitiously took with them when the **Reagan administration** provided them safe passage to Hawaii. Testimony in a Los Angeles court reveled gold transfers by the Marcos family from 1986 through 1997. 1986: the first transfer involved 1.1 million troy ounces of gold (30+ tons) which were deposited in five separate banks. 1993: these were sold and the proceeds of this sale were deposited in the Swiss Bank Corporation. According to former Solicitor General Francisco Chavez, the Marcos family still keeps some US$13.4 billion in deposits at the Union Bank of Switzerland under the account of Irene Marcos-Araneta, and also a hoard of 1.241 tons of gold at an underground bunker at Kloten Airport in Zurich. In February 2001, the Philippine Daily Inquirer disclosed the alleged attempt of Irene Marcos Araneta to launder billions of dollars in deposits under the 885,931 accounts from Union Bank of Switzerland to Deutsche Banks in Dusseldorf, Germany. The Marco's gold is listed in the Guinness Book of World Records. **Former First lady Imelda Marcos** once bragged on American TV that the family owned everything worth owning in the Philippines.

1965

July 28, 1965 – The first physical battle between the OPM or **Free Papua Movement** and the **Indonesian military** occurs at Arfai.

February 7, 1965 – Vietnam. In the early hours of February 7th, the Viet Cong up the ante when they launch a guerilla assault against the military barracks at **Pleiku** where **U.S. military advisors** are housed. The attack leaves eight Americans dead, and President Johnson reacts as though the VC had delivered a personal insult. Johnson orders a retaliatory air-strike against North Vietnam the next day. Operation **"Rolling Thunder" begins** in mid-February and will last 3 years.

   "Rolling Thunder" is the most intense air/ground battle waged during the Cold War and North Vietnam fielded a potent mixture of sophisticated air-to-air and ground-to-air weapons that created one of the most effective air defense environments ever faced by American military aviators. **Rolling Thunder** was terminated as a strategic failure in late 1968 after achieving none of its objectives.

March 8, 1965 – Vietnam. Two U.S. Marine battalions arrive on the beach at **DaNang** in full battle gear. They are met not by enemy fire, but by curious onlookers. One soldier said, "The war was nowhere in sight."

March 16, 1965 – Vietnam. Alice Herz, an 82-year-old survivor of Nazi terror, **sets herself on fire in Detroit** as a protest against the war shortly after President Johnson announced major troop increases and the bombing of North Vietnam.

May 20, 1965 – Vietnam. Hanoi restates its peace proposal which "Washington" has already rejected.

November 2, 1965 – Vietnam. After handing his one year old daughter to onlookers, **Quaker Norman Morrison sets himself on fire** as a protest against the war and dies outside Secretary of Defense Robert McNamara's Pentagon office, a scene McNamara witnessed.

November 9, 1965 – Vietnam. Catholic Worker Roger LaPorte sets himself on fire as a protest against the war opposite the United Nations building, just days after the group draft card burning. At the time, he was a 22 year old, former seminarian, Catholic Worker Movement member.

1965 – Vietnam. The U.S. Congress provides $2.4 Billion for the Vietnam War effort, with little dissent in the U.S. House or Senate. President Johnson authorizes the use of napalm in Vietnam bombing runs, by years end roughly 200,000 U.S. troops will be **"in-country," and the United States of America is changed forever.**

1966

The Oldest Boomer is 20 years old.

Cost of the Average House: $23,300	
Median Family Income: $7,400	**Minimum Wage:** $1.25/ hr
Sugar: 38 cents/ 5 pounds **Lettuce, iceberg:** 25 cents/ head	**Gallon Gasoline:** 32 cents **Gerber's Baby Food:** 25 cents/ 3
New Car: Buick Skylark GS: $2,596	**Triumph TR6:** $3,275
Unemployment Rate: 4.0%-3.6%-3.8%	**First-class Stamp:** 5 cents

15 cents buying power in 1966 = **$1.00 in 2008.**
In 1966 what cost us 15 cents to purchase now costs us $1.00 in 2008.

Movies: "A Man For All Seasons," "Who's Afraid of Virginia Woolf?" "Blow-Up," "The Sand Pebbles," "The Battle of Algiers," "Alfie," "Hawaii," "The Russians Are Coming, The Russians Are Coming."
"Georgie Girl" becomes the first film to carry the label "recommended for mature audiences."

Broadway: "It's a Bird . . . It's a Plane . . . It's Superman," "Sweet Charity," "Cabaret," "I Do! I Do!" "Mame."

TV: "Star Trek," "The Avengers," "Batman," "Dark Shadows," "Green Hornet," "Girl From U.N.C.L.E." "Mission: Impossible," "The Monkees," "Iron Horse," "Batman," "Abbott & Costello, Animated," "Cool McCool," "The All-New Truth or Consequences," "Daktari," "The Adventures of Superboy," "Captain America," "Family Affair," "Sammy Davis Jr. Show," "That Girl," "Tarzan," "Dr. Seuss' How The Grinch Stole Christmas," "The Road Runner Show," "Hulk, Animated," "Hollywood Squares," "The Lone Ranger, animated." "The Monroes," "The Rat Patrol," "The Time Tunnel," "The Road West."

Music: Simon and Garfunkel, "The Sound of Silence" & "Parsley, Sage, Rosemary and Thyme." The Beatles, "We Can Work It Out," "Yellow

Submarine" & "Paperback Writer." James Brown, "I Got You, I Feel Good." Cher, "Bang Bang, My Baby Shot Me Down." The Byrds, "Turn! Turn! Turn!" The Dave Clark Five, "Over and Over." The Four Seasons, "Let's Hang On!" The McCoys, "Fever." The Beachboys, "Good Vibrations." The Righteous Brothers, "Ebb Tide." Roger Miller, "England Swings." Nancy Sinatra, "These Boots Are Made For Walking." Eddy Arnold, "Make the World Go Away." Dusty Springfield, "You Don't Have to Say You Love Me." The Beach Boys, "Barbara Ann." The Marvelettes, "Don't Mess with Bill." Sam the Sham and the Pharaohs, "Lil' Red Riding Hood." The Mamas and the Papas, "California Dreamin'" & ""Monday, Monday." The Capitols, "Cool Jerk." The Lovin' Spoonful, "Summer in the City." The Monkees, "Last Train to Clarksville." The Supremes, "You Keep Me Hangin' On." Aaron Neville, "Tell It Like It Is." Dionne Warwick, "Message to Michael." Sgt. Barry Sadler, "Ballad of the Green Berets."

Deaths: Gloria Davy, Patricia Matusek, Nina Schmale, Pamela Wilkening, Suzanne Farris, Mary Ann Jordan, Merlita Gargullo, and Valentina Pasion.

President: Lyndon B. Johnson (D) Disciples of Christ; vetoes 30/ 0 overrides

Vice President: Hubert H. Humphrey (D)
Lutheran; Methodist; Congregationalist

House: D-295 ; R-140

Senate: 89th Congress (1965-1967) Majority Party: Democrat (68 seats) Minority Party: Republican (32 seats) Other Parties: 0 Total Seats: 100

Federal Debt: $319.91 billion or 41 % of the GDP

Consumer Price Index CPI-U (1982 Base of 100): 32.40

GDP: $787.8 billion	Inflation Rate: 3.01%

Dow Jones: 995.15 (02-09)/ 789.75 (12-01)

Prime Rate: 6.00% (08-16)	Average Home Mortgage Rate: 6.5%
1 oz Gold: $35.40	1oz of Silver: $1.40

Federal Debt: $319,907,087,795.43

Federal Deficit: $3.7 billion dollars	
Defense Spending: $69.61 billion	**Interest Spending:** $9.39 billion
Health Care Spending: $2.61 billion	**Pensions Spending:** $18.46 billion
Welfare Spending: $5.62 billion	**Education Spending:** $5.22 billion
Transportation Spending: $5.73 billion	**Misc. Other Spending:** $15.50 billion
Protection Spending: $560 million	**Total Government Spending:** $134.53 billion
% of GDP that goes towards just the interest payment: 1.25%	
$1.00 = 362.35 Yen, Japan	
U.S. Population: 196,599,000	**World Population:** 3,416,065,246
U.S. Birth Rate: 3,606,274	**U.S. Abortions:** 1,028
U.S. Homicide Rate: 5.9/ 100,000 population	**U.S. Violent Crime:** 220.0/ 100,000 population
Annual Average Domestic Crude Oil Prices: $3.10 / barrel, $20.52 (2007 adjusted)	

Oil:

1966 – Beirut, Lebanon. When Lebanon's largest bank, Intra, crashes their long period of economic growth comes to a temporary halt. **Beirut, the "Switzerland of the Middle East,"** had been the repository of choice for oil money from Saudi Arabia and the Gulf states. Beirut was also a favored destination for wealthy Europeans and Americans. After the banking crisis settled, the Lebanese economy is strong again until the civil war in 1975.

1966

1966 – Gulf Oil opens an oil field in Cabinda, Angola. On November 22, 1957, the Cabinda Gulf Oil Company was awarded its original concession covering 2,806 square miles of onshore and offshore acreage. On the concession's anniversary in 1966, additional offshore acreage was added. The oil companies provide their own security, completely closing themselves off from the rest of the country. Oil produced in Cabinda provides Angola with about half of its foreign exchange earnings. From 1961-1966 thousands have died and almost one million people have fled Angola for Zaire.

Major News:

January 17, 1966 – The cost of a nuclear weapons accident over Palomares, Spain, including two lost planes, an extended search and recovery effort, waste disposal in the U.S. and settlement claims, is **$182,000,000.**

May 1, 1966 – U.S. forces began firing into **Cambodia.**

June 29, 1966 – The bombing of Hanoi and **Haiphong** in North Vietnam by U.S. planes begins. By December 31, 385,300 U.S. troops are stationed in South Vietnam, plus 60,000 offshore and 33,000 in Thailand.

July 14, 1966 – Richard Speck, **mass murderer,** systematically kills eight student nurses from South Chicago Community Hospital in Chicago, Illinois. In 1973 **his sentence was reduced** to a new statutory maximum of 300 years in prison, making Speck eligible for parole in 1977. (That is not a misprint.) He was denied parole in seven minutes at his first parole hearing on September 15, 1976, and at six subsequent hearings in 1977, 1978, 1981, 1984, 1987, and 1990. Speck confessed to the murders for the first time publicly in 1979. Speck died of a heart attack at 6:05 a.m. December 5, 1991, one day before his 50th birthday, at Silver Cross Hospital in Joliet.

August 1, 1966 – Clock Tower Shootings. Charles Whitman, 25, **kills 14 students and wounds 32 others** from a clock tower at the **University of Texas campus** in Austin, before being shot dead by police.

September 9, 1966 – President Lyndon Johnson signs legislation creating the **San Juan Island National Historical Park.** The site, in Washington State, includes the location of British and United States army camps in the 1860s, with both nations claiming ownership of the island.

October 15, 1966 – The Department of Transportation (DOT) is established by an act of Congress, and signed into law by President Lyndon B. Johnson.

October 15, 1966 – The National Historic Preservation Act is made law. It expands the National Register of Historic Places to include historic sites of regional, state, and local significance.

Civil Rights Movement:

1966 – James T. Whitehead, Jr., becomes the first African American to pilot a **U-2 spy plane**.

1966 – Robert C. Weaver is named secretary of the newly created Department of Housing and Urban Development **(HUD)**, becoming the **1st black cabinet member**.

1966 – Harper vs. Virginia Board of Elections, 383 U.S. 663 is a case in which the U.S. Supreme Court finds Virginia's poll tax unconstitutional under the equal protection clause of the 14th Amendment. The Twenty-fourth Amendment to the United States Constitution prohibited poll taxes in federal elections and the Supreme Court extended this prohibition to state elections. A **poll tax** is still in use in **Alabama, Mississippi, Texas,** and **Virginia** in 1966.

May 14, 1966 – Black Power, SNCC. Stokely Carmichael, the new chairman of the SNCC, begins moving the group away from passivism and more toward militancy and **"Black Power."** Although Martin Luther King opposed the usage of the term, Black Power, the slogan caught on quickly. **Carmichael announces that SNCC will no longer send white organizers into black communities** and after the Freedom Rides, the focus of SNCC's work is primarily in voter registration, along with local protests about segregated public facilities.

1966

It has always been extremely difficult and dangerous to register to vote in the south. **Blacks who attempted to register often lost their jobs and their homes were often firebombed.** SNCC workers lived with local families and violence **was so widespread** the Kennedy Administration provided federal protection from time to time to curb mob violence. There were very few black FBI agents (James W. Barrow, 1962 is just one) and local FBI offices were usually staffed by Southern whites who refused to intervene to protect civil rights workers or local blacks who were attempting to register to vote. By no longer allowing whites to go into black communities it was safer for everyone involved. Organizers had more freedom of movement but their lives were still in danger.

SNCC believed that since the group's activities were often so dangerous that at best those involved may end up in prison and at worst they may be killed, everyone should be in agreement. Decisions were made from the bottom up and everyone had the right to speak freely during the meetings for as long as they wanted until every participant was in agreement with the decision.

June 6, 1966 – James Meredith, the first African-American student at the University of Mississippi, leads the *March Against Fear* from Memphis, Tennessee to Jackson, Mississippi. While en route **Meredith is wounded by sniper** Aubrey James Norvell on June 6 and Civil Rights leaders including **Martin Luther King, Floyd McKissick,** and **Stokely Carmichael** vow to continue the march which eventually reaches Jackson. On June 26 Carmichael gives his first **"Black Power"** speech in Greenwood.

James Meredith has characterized himself as an individual American citizen who demanded the rights extended to any American, not just as a participant in the U.S. civil rights movement. There is considerable animosity between James Meredith and the organized Civil Rights Movement. James Meredith said in an interview for CNN, "Nothing could be more insulting to me than the concept of civil rights. It means perpetual second-class citizenship for me and my kind."

July 10, 1966 – SCLC and Chicago civil rights groups begin a campaign against housing discrimination in Chicago with a mass rally and a series of marches through white neighborhoods that are often met with violence from mobs

October 15, 1966 – Oakland, California. **The Black Panthers** are founded by **Huey Newton** and **Bobby Seale.** In September 1968, FBI Director J. Edgar Hoover described the Black Panthers as, "The greatest threat to the internal security of the country."

November 8, 1966 – Former Attorney General of Massachusetts, **Edward Brooke** is elected November 8. He is a Republican and the first black U.S. senator in 85 years.

1966 – The U.S. Supreme Court upholds the Voting Rights Act in South Carolina vs. Katzenbach.

Women's Movement:

January 25, 1966 – Constance Baker Motley is appointed by President Lyndon Johnson to the Federal Bench in New York City. She becomes the first African American woman elevated to a **Federal judgeship.**

1966 – Betty Friedan along with a small group of women found the National Organization for Women (**NOW**). Its purpose is to act as a civil rights organization for women and Betty becomes its first President. The group is the largest women's group in the U.S. and pursues its goals through extensive legislative lobbying, litigation, and public demonstrations. The National Organization for Women is the largest organization of feminist activists in the United States. NOW has more than 500,000 contributing members and more than 500 local and campus affiliates in all 50 states and the District of Columbia. NOW's goal has been "to take action" to bring about equality for all women. Both the actions NOW takes and its position on the issues are principled, uncompromising and often ahead of their time. NOW is a leader, not a follower, of public opinion.

Popular Culture:

1966 – Louisville, Kentucky. Vice President Hubert H. Humphrey has paid a Louisville man **$10** for damages to a 30-foot hedge behind his house caused by a crowd that engulfed Humphrey at an impromptu political rally for local candidates.

1966

1966 – The peak number of **nuclear warheads and bombs** in the stockpile is **32,193.**

1966 – **"Food" becomes a highly processed industrial commodity**. During McDonald's early years french fries were made from scratch every day. Russet Burbank potatoes were peeled, cut, and fried in McDonald's kitchens. As the chain expands nationwide in the mid-1960s, it cuts labor costs and reduces the number of suppliers to ensure its fries taste the same at every restaurant.

To further cut costs and ensure uniform quality, McDonald's began switching to frozen french fries in 1966. This change will have a profound effect on the nation's agriculture and diet. An ordinary, common food has been transformed into a highly processed industrial commodity. McDonald's fries now come from huge manufacturing plants that can peel, slice, cook, and freeze two million pounds of potatoes a day.

1966 – **The Narcotic Addict Rehabilitation Act** (NARA) is passed allowing treatment as an alternative to jail. This legislation was designed to allow the use of the federal courts and criminal-justice system to compel drug addicts to participate in treatment. They were following the lead of New York and California's massive programs to implement compulsory treatment and civil commitment. The program assumes people want to behave according to basic Christian values and has limited success as evidenced by the increase in drug use worldwide over the next fifty years. More and more people are without hope, self-centered, self-serving and demand their right to impose their feelings on others as the mood strikes them.

1966 – **Public Law 358, the Veterans Readjustment Benefits Act** of 1966, provides not only educational benefits, but also home and farm loans as well as employment counseling and placement services for Vietnam veterans. More than 385,000 troops, serve in Vietnam during 1966. From 1965-1975, more than **nine million American military personnel are on active military duty**, about 3.4 million of whom serve in **Southeast Asia.**

February 1966 – A group of about **100 veterans** attempt to return their decorations to the **White House** in protest of the Vietnam War, but are turned back.

March 4, 1966 – John Lennon, says "We (the Beatles) are more popular than Jesus." A swift apology makes daily papers immediately as most Americans are incensed at this remark.

March 26, 1966 – Anti-war demonstrations are again held around the country and the world with 20,000 taking part in New York City.

1966 – A Gallup poll shows that **59 % believe** that sending troops to Vietnam **was not a mistake.** Among the age group of **21-29, 71 % believe** it was **not a mistake** compared to only **48 % of those over 50.**

Spring 1966 – Barry Bondhus. His Quaker father has been particularly vocal about not allowing any of his 10 sons to be drafted and sent to Vietnam and apparently he was ready to die for his beliefs. Barry took action; it seems, to keep his father from doing something even more dramatic. In preparation, his sons begin collecting their own excrement into two five-gallon buckets for a couple of weeks. Nineteen-year-old Bondhus, alone, then broke into the Big Lake, Minnesota, draft board and emptied the two buckets of excrement onto hundreds of draft files and then patiently waited to be arrested. He received 18 months in federal prison.

During the trial a Statement to the court by Barry and his parents read in part: **The boys don't deserve to die for the bungling of the politicians.**

I believed the propaganda thrust on us during the war with Hitler; when they said there would be no war with Germany if the people had refused to follow that mad man. We now have a mad power crazy feeling in the United States. Now I am going to follow that advice and try to stop the aggression of these **power crazy lunatics.**

The simplest way to tell an aggressor is to observe whose land they are fighting on. We are fighting on their land. We have bases all around Russia and they have none here so we are the aggressor.

I would like to think of myself as more of a man than to let my boy fight my battle for me. **YOU are a coward to send children to fight a war you believe in.**

May 15, 1966 – Another large demonstration, with 10,000 people calling for an end to the war, takes place outside the White House and the Washington Monument.

1966

June 13, 1966 – The U.S. Supreme Court rules in "**Miranda** vs. Arizona," that suspects must be read their rights before police questioning.

July 1, 1966 – Medicare begins.

July 3, 1966 – A crowd of 4,000 demonstrate in London against the U.S. war and scuffle with police outside the U.S. Embassy where 33 protesters are arrested.

November 8, 1966 – Julian Bond wins a seat in the Georgia State Senate. However he is **denied the seat** by the Georgia Legislature because of his opposition to the Vietnam War. Bond is eventually seated after a bitter court battle.

1966 – "Pot is not only the new party drug but also part of the emerging protest culture. **Beer, military conscription, and anticommunism are out of style.** A lot of the social life on Colleges centered around fraternities in the early 1960s because beer was going to be served at a party in the fraternity house all weekend, and this was how you **got dates.** Now pot is readily accessible and the in thing to do. Social culture is moving towards smaller groups and ultimately to a group of one.

April 12, 1966 – Daylight Saving Time. Congress decides to step in and end the confusion Daylight Saving Time brings to over 100 million Americans. Up to this point Daylight Saving Time has been based on local custom and local laws. You could cross an invisible line and change time by an hour or more and then back again.

The Uniform Time Act of 1966 is signed into Public Law, by President Lyndon Johnson. Daylight Saving Time begins on the last Sunday of April and ends on the last Sunday of October. Any State that wanted to be exempt from Daylight Saving Time could do so by passing a state law.

1966-1973 – GI Resistance During the Vietnam War. The Pentagon faced widespread opposition to military service and enlistment and retention rates hit all-time lows. College ROTC participation, the main source of junior officers, dropped to unacceptable levels. Two-hundred and six thousand young men never even reported for the draft and as U.S. involvement increased, there are five times the number of desertions. Most soldiers deserted due to disgust and not out of fear. AWOL rates stayed high. In 1971, the Army reported almost 18 unauthorized absences for every 100 enlisted personnel.

Business / Technology:

1966 – Charles Kao's waveguide light theory will lead to communication channels.

1966 – The U.S. Congress passes the **National Traffic and Motor Vehicle Safety Act** in mandating the incorporation of safety devices that were designed to prevent as many fatalities as possible in automobile accidents. During the next six years, automobile accidents decline at an average rate of 3.5 percent annually. The act also established the National Highway Traffic Safety Administration under the Department of Transportation to oversee safety and consumer programs, including motor vehicle crash testing and automotive recalls.

1966 – Xerox sells the Telecopier, a fax machine.

Finance:

October 15, 1966 – The United States Coast Guard, originally established within the **Treasury Department** in 1790, is transferred to the Department of Transportation.

Books:

1966 – China, the Cultural Revolution. "Quotations from Mao Tse-Tung." Millions read the **"Little Red Book."**

1966 – "Fanny Hill." The United States Supreme Court rules John Cleland's "Memoirs of a Woman of Pleasure" (aka Fanny Hill), does not meet the test for obscenity under the Roth law. By permitting the publication of **"Fanny Hill,"** the Supreme Court set the bar for any ban so high that Charles Rembar, who fought and won some of the most important censorship cases called the 1966 decision **"the end of obscenity."**

1966

1966 – Grove Press successfully publishes **"My Secret Life."** "My Secret Life," by "Walter," is a lengthy sexual memoir of a Victorian gentleman first printed in a private edition of eleven volumes, over seven years beginning around 1888. It is believed that only around 20 original copies were ever printed. The author of the book remains a mystery. **Henry Spencer Ashbee**, a book collector, writer, and bibliographer notable for his particular focus on sexuality is suspected by some to be "Walter."

1966 – "Valley of the Dolls," Jacqueline Susann. Valley of the Dolls is widely considered to be one of the most commercially successful novels of all time. *Dolls* is a slang term for downers, a mood altering drug.

1966 – John Barth's comic novel, **"Giles Goat-Boy."** It is a satire and allegory of the American campus culture of the time.

1966 – "In Cold Blood," Truman Capote.

TV:

1966 – Recent movies are played on prime time.

1966 – TV viewers are treated to **close-ups of the moon**, courtesy of Surveyor 1.

1966 – The Miss Universe Pageant and the **Academy Awards** are first broadcast in color.

1966 – Mary Ann from "Gilligan's Island," Jeannie from "I Dream of Jeannie" and "Gidget" are all barred from baring their navels. Actress Mariette Hartley receives the same treatment in a 1966 episode of "Star Trek," but the show's director, Gene Roddenberry, recasts Ms. Hartley in the pilot for his new show, "Genesis II," in 1973 and gives her two belly buttons.

1966 – The FCC blocks cable television wiring in large cities.

Sports:

March 19, 1966 – The Miners, with five black starters, win the NCAA men's basketball championship, defeating Kentucky 72-65. No. 1 Kentucky. All-white Kentucky. "We were just kids playing basketball having fun. ... It was not that big a deal to us," center David Lattin said. "We were just out there trying to win."

1966 – Ampex develops the **"instant replay"** videodisc recorder at the request of ABC in for the "Wide World of Sports" program.

January 2, 1966 – The Green Bay Packers beat Cleveland Browns 23-12 in **NFL** championship game.

May 25, 1966 – Peru & Argentina soccer fans fight in Lima and 248 people die.

1966 – Heavyweight boxing champion Muhammad Ali, formerly known as Cassius Clay, declares himself a **conscientious objector** and refuses to go to war. According to a writer for "Sports Illustrated," the governor of Illinois called Ali "disgusting" and the governor of Maine said that Ali "should be held in utter contempt by every patriotic American." In 1967 **Ali was sentenced to 5 years in prison** for draft evasion, but his conviction was later overturned on appeal. In addition, he was stripped of his title and banned from professional boxing for more than three years.

February 1966 – Sandy Koufax and Don Drysdale begin a joint holdout against the **Brooklyn Dodgers** seeking an unprecedented 3-year, $1.05 million contract to be divided evenly.

Music:

February 19, 1966 – Jefferson Airplane and **Big Brother and the Holding Company** with **Janis Joplin** perform at the **Fillmore.**

March 4, 1966 – The Beatles' John Lennon is quoted in the London newspaper, The Evening Standard as saying that the band was now more popular than **Jesus.** In

1966

August, following publication of this remark in *Datebook,* there are Beatles protests and record burnings in the Southern U.S. "Bible Belt."

April 1966 – Herb Alpert & the Tijuana Brass have a world record 4 albums in Billboard's Top 10.

1966 – The Jimi Hendrix Experience begins.

1966 – Cream begins performing.

Natural Disasters:

January 11-13 – Brazil, Rio de Janeiro. A landslide kills 550 people.

January 27-31, 1966 – The Blizzard of 1966. Winds above 100 mph push a snowfall that covers some homes. A total of 102" of snow was recorded at Oswego, New York. Fifty inches of snow fell on the last day of the storm.

1966 – AIDS. Proceedings of the National Academy of Sciences on November 1, 2007 dismisses the patient zero hypothesis and claim that **AIDS transited from Africa to Haiti in 1966** and from Haiti to the United States in 1969.

June 28, 1966 – A 6.1 magnitude earthquake hits Parkfield, California.

September 12, 1966 – A 5.9 magnitude earthquake hits Truckee, California.

September 24, 1966 – Hurricane Inez slams into the islands of the Caribbean, killing 293 people. The storm left death and destruction in its wake from Guadeloupe to Mexico over the course of its nearly three-week run. Inez is the most destructive hurricane of the 1966 storm season.

August 19, 1966 – Turkey. Varto Earthquake. A 6.6 magnitude earthquake hits the North Anatolian Fault killing 2,400 people.

October 21, 1966 – Aberfan, Wales. An avalanche of coal, waste, mud, and rocks kills 144 people, including 116 children in school.

Man vs. Man / Wars:

Assassinated – Central African Republic. Jean Izamo, head of the gendarmerie in David Dacko's government, **is killed following the Saint-Sylvestre coup d'état.** On January 1, 1966, **Jean-Bédel Bokassa** overthrows the Dacko government in a swift coup d'état. Bokassa considered both Izamo and the director of the Presidential security particularly dangerous individuals and "did not rest until they were eliminated." Izamo, was taken out of his cellar prison, moved to Camp de Roux, and then to Ngaragba Prison. At the end of January, Izamo died from mistreatment and neglect.

By January 1979, French support for Bokassa had all but eroded after riots in Bangui led to a massacre of civilians. On April 17-19 a number of schoolchildren were arrested after they had protested against wearing the expensive, government required school uniforms. Around 100 were killed. It was claimed that Bokassa had participated in the killings and even that he had eaten some of the bodies. With French support, using French troops, Bokassa is overthrown in a coup and David Daco is once again President until he is again overthrown in 1981.

Assassinated – Nigeria. Abubakar Tafawa Balewa, the Prime Minister of **Nigeria**, was a founder and Deputy President General of the country's largest political party. Sir Abubakar Tafawa Balewa was killed on January 15, 1966, in Lagos during a military coup d'état which ended The First Republic, Nigeria's first civilian government.

Assassinated – South Africa. Hendrik Verwoerd, the Prime Minister of South Africa, is stabbed in parliament by Dimitri Tsafendas. **Prime Minister Verwoerd** is considered to be the primary architect of the official policy of apartheid, and was Prime Minister during the Sharpeville Massacre, the banning of the African National Congress and Pan Africanist Congress, and the Rivonia Trial.

1966

March 27, 1966 – Hijacking. In an attempt to reach the U.S. Angel María Betancourt Cueto, armed with a pistol, tries to hijack a plane, with 97 persons onboard, flying from Santiago de Cuba to Havana. The pilot, Fernando Álvarez Pérez, opposed the hijacking and landed in Havana. The hijacker then killed Álvarez and air-steward Edor Reyes, seriously wounding the copilot Evans Rosales.

Havana. (AP) An airline flight engineer who killed two men when he tried to hijack a plane was executed immediately after his conviction Wednesday, and a Roman Catholic priest who gave him refuge was sentenced to 15 years in prison. Angel María Betancourt Cueto was executed by firing squad at dawn after a trial in La Cabana Fortress that began Tuesday afternoon.

February 1966 – Ghana. Kwame Nkrumah is removed from power in Ghana by coup d'état. In February, while Nkrumah is on a state visit to Vietnam, his government is overthrown in a military coup. Nkrumah never returned to Ghana, but he continued to push for his vision of African unity. Today, Nkrumah is one of the most respected leaders in African history. In 2000, he was voted Africa's man of the millennium by listeners to the BBC World Service.

1966 – Cambodian Civil War. Colombia's internal security has been disrupted by the actions of two guerrilla forces, the Revolutionary Armed Forces of Colombia, FARC and the National Liberation Army, ELN. It was not long before both FARC and ELN troops are hired by the drug cartels to protect labs, cultivation sites, runways, and warehouses. In the late 1990's the FARC and ELN gradually enter the drug business, cultivating, processing, and selling marijuana, cocaine and heroin. Most sales are to Colombian middlemen, although there are reports of FARC sales to traffickers in Panama, Venezuela, Peru and Ecuador.

1966–1993 – Chad and Sudan. A guerrilla war is conducted against the repressive government of **François Tombalbaye** in Chad from the Sudan-based group FROLINAT. On November 1, 1965, riots in Guéra Prefecture lead to 500 deaths which cause a series of small conflicts throughout the northern half of the country. **Libya** to the north and **Sudan** to the east also become involved in the conflicts before the situation produces massive numbers of refugees. Tombalbaye insists that France should come to his aid and the French agree if Tombalbaye initiates a series of reforms to the army, government, and civil service. France also wanted the arbitrary tax laws to restore the traditional Sultan's role as tax collector, for which he received 10%. Tombalbaye agreed in 1969 and Chad began a gradual liberalization process. Elections were held in 1969 but Tombalbaye was the only candidate on the ballot.

1966 – First Republic of the Congo, now the Democratic Republic of the Congo. President Mobutu consolidates power by **publicly executing** political rivals, and threats to his rule. To set an example, many were hanged before large audiences, including former **Prime Minister Evariste Kimba,** who, with three cabinet members, was tried in May 1966, and sent to the gallows on May 30, before an audience of 50,000 spectators.

1960–1966 – The Congo Crisis is a period of turmoil in the First Republic of the Congo that began with national independence from Belgium and ended with the seizing of power by Joseph Mobutu. In an attempt to regain their economical and political control in the region, the United States and Belgium sponsored guerrilla activities and secret assassinations, which led to the death of anti-colonist leader Patrice Lumumba, further complicating the situation. At various points, the United Nations peacekeeping force and the Soviet Union also participated in the conflict. The Crisis caused the death of some 100,000 people.

February 28, 1966 – India. Mizo Rebellion. The Mizo National Front (MNF) seeks independence from India for the Mizoram region. The Mizo rebellion is officially ended by negotiated settlement 19 years later, in 1985.

1965-1966 – The Indonesian killings are a violent anti-Communist purge following an abortive coup in the Indonesian capital of **Jakarta.** The most widely accepted estimates are that **over half a million people are killed.** The purge is a pivotal event in the transition to the "New Order." The Indonesian Communist Party is eliminated as a political force, and the upheavals lead to the downfall of **President Sukarno,** and to the commencement of **Suharto's thirty-year presidency.**

1966

1966 – Namibia. During the 1960s, as the European powers grant independence to their colonies and trust territories in Africa, pressure mounts on South Africa to do the same in Namibia, still named South-West Africa. Ethiopia and Liberia brought a complaint against South Africa's continued presence in the territory which was dismissed by the International Court of Justice. The South-West Africa People's Organization (SWAPO) began guerrilla attacks on South Africa, infiltrating the territory from bases in Zambia. After Angola becomes independent in 1975, SWAPO established bases in the southern part of the country and hostilities intensify through the 1990's.

January 15, 1966 – Nigerian Coup and Counter Coup. A military rebellion in Nigeria against the first republic is led by a group of Majors **who are predominantly of eastern origin.**

Oil was discovered in the Niger River Delta at the southernmost tip of the country. The area is mostly low-lying swamp and marsh lands, but holds the key to the southeastern part of the country becoming self–sufficient if they can control the oil, so they attempted to annex the land. Those from the eastern part of Nigeria are afraid the oil wealth will be taken by the north and west. After the coup by the easterners, the Prime Minister, a federal minister, two regional premiers, top Army officers and a number of civilians were brutally assassinated. General Johnson Aguiyi-Ironsi, an Igbo and head of the Nigerian Army, takes power as President and becomes the first military head of state in Nigeria. This coup benefits many Igbo.

On July 29, **the Northerners execute a counter-coup** led by Lt. Col. Murtala Mohammed and it places Lt. Col. Yakubu Gowon into power. This leads to large-scale massacres of Christian Igbo living in the Muslim north.

Up to this time Nigeria's wealth derived from agricultural products from the south, and minerals from the north and the North wanted to secede from Nigeria and retain its wealth for northerners. Now they also want the oil revenues from the south.

1966–1998 – Northern Ireland. The Ulster Volunteer Force is recreated by militant Protestant British loyalists in Northern Ireland to wage war against the Irish Republican Army and the Roman Catholic community at large.

1966 – Uganda's Buganda ethnic group. In January 1964, several army units rebel demanding higher pay and more rapid promotion. The situation becomes so extreme that Prime Minister Milton Obote is forced to request the assistance of the British military in putting down the revolt. Prime Minister Obote allowed the army to expand rapidly and gain more political control. He also chose a young army officer, **Idi Amin Dada,** as his personal protégé and set about consolidating power by stripping the monarchs of the five kingdoms of their titles and forcing them into exile. Obote ruled Uganda, sold weapons to groups in the neighboring Congo in return for gold and ivory, and eliminated opponents, but the average person lived a quiet life until 1971 when Idi Amin replaced Obote in a coup.

1966 – Vietnam, Philippines. President Ferdinand Marcos of the Philippines sends Filipino troops to Vietnam in support of the U.S. position. In all, over 10,450 Filipino soldiers are sent to South Vietnam under the designation of PHLCAAG or Philippines Civil Affairs Assistance Group.

January 29, 1966 – Vietnam. The U.S. begins bombing around **Haiphong and Hanoi**, North Vietnam. This is considered a major escalation of the air war.

1966 – Vietnam. As antiwar protests grow, President Johnson and American military leaders increase reliance on "search-and-destroy" missions in an effort to draw the Viet Cong into battles and inflict heavy casualties. But the Viet Cong prove difficult to pin down. By year's end, 6,000 American soldiers have died. Evening TV broadcasts the number dead on both sides every day and the U.S. military is encouraged to **improve the numbers.**

October 1966 – Vietnam. Horrified by the civilian casualties napalm is causing in Vietnam, student protesters begin targeting the military's only supplier, Dow Chemical. The first demonstrations occur this month in Detroit and Berkeley, and 43 more take place by March 1967.

May 16, 1966 – Vietnam. In a protest against changes to the draft policy that threaten some of their deferments, students stage the first **"sit-in"** at the **University of**

1966

Wisconsin, occupying an administration building peacefully for several days before a compromise is reached.

1966 – Vietnam. Operation Rolling Thunder. By early 1965 it became clear to the Americans that their cautious policy in Vietnam was not working. South Vietnam was at the point of "impending collapse" and a continuation of existing policies would necessarily lead to defeat for the U.S. and South Vietnam. The U.S. response is to greatly increase its troop levels in the South (184,000 by the end of 1965; 385,000 by the end of 1966) and to initiate Operation Rolling thunder, the sustained aerial **bombing of North Vietnam**.

January 1966-October 1968 – Vietnam. U.S. bombs dropped on North Vietnam total over 600,000 tons.

March 1 1966 – Vietnam. An attempt to repeal the **Gulf of Tonkin resolution** is defeated in the U.S. Senate. The Tonkin Gulf Resolution is of historical significance because it gave U.S. President Lyndon B. Johnson authorization, without a formal declaration of war by Congress, for the use of military force in Southeast Asia. Specifically, the resolution authorized the President to do whatever is necessary in order to assist "any member or protocol state of the Southeast Asia Collective Defense Treaty."

During the summer of 1966 U.S. troop increases are matched by the infiltration of North Vietnamese forces. **The Pentagon Papers** state " . . . the total number of individual flights against North Vietnam in Operation Rolling Thunder rose from 55,000 in 1965 to 148,000 in 1966, total bomb tonnage from 33,000 to 128,000, the number of aircraft lost rose from 171 to 318, and direct operational costs rose from $460-million to 1.2- billion." The 1966 bombing " . . . accomplished little more than in 1965." American military leaders felt the U.S. should step up the air war sharply and mobilize the reserves to provide additional manpower. They urged President Johnson to consider **invading Laos, Cambodia, and even North Vietnam** to force Hanoi to cease its support for the war in the South.

1967

The Oldest Boomer is 21 years old.

Cost of the Average House: $24,600	
Median Family Income: $7,200	**Minimum Wage:** $1.40/ hr **Average Hourly Wage:** $2.83

Twist 'N Turn Barbie: buyers would trade in an old doll, add $1.50 and they would get one of the new Twist 'N Turn dolls. In May when the promotion began, 1,250,000 dolls were traded in and donated to charity.

New Car: **Austin Healey Sprite:** $2,050 **Volkswagen beetle:** $1,769	**Gallon Gasoline:** 33 cents **Cigarettes:** 25 cents/ pack **McDonald's Big Mac:** 45 cents
Unemployment Rate: 3.9%-4.0%-3.8%	**Rolling Stone Magazine:** 25 cents **First-class Stamp:** 5 cents

15 cents buying power in 1967 = **$1.00 in 2008.**
In 1967 what cost us 15 cents to purchase now costs us $1.00 in 2008.

Movies: "The Graduate," "Bonnie and Clyde," "Guess Who's Coming to Dinner," "In The Heat of The Night," "Doctor Dolittle," "Cool Hand Luke." "I Am Curious, Yellow."

Broadway: "You're a Good Man, Charlie Brown," off Broadway. "How Now, Dow Jones," "Hair," off Broadway. "Thoroughly Modern Millie."

TV: "The Smothers Brothers Comedy Hour." The Final Episode of "The Fugitive." "The Carol Burnett Show," "Dragnet-revival," "Captain Nice," "George of the Jungle, Animated," "The Jonathan Winters Show," "The Atom Ant/ Secret Squirrel Show," "The Flying Nun," "Invaders," "Ironside," "Guns of Will Sonnett," "Cowboy in Africa," "Hondo," "Dundee and the Culhane," "Legend of Custer," "Gentle Ben," "Ironside," "Good Morning, World," "Mannix," "Spider-Man," Animated. "Super Bowl," "NYPD," "Washington Week in Review."

Music: "The Graduate," Simon & Garfunkel. The Monkees, "I'm a Believer" & "Pleasant Valley Sunday." Nancy Sinatra, "Sugar Town." Sonny and Cher, "The Beat Goes On." Johnny Rivers, "Baby I Need Your Loving." The Turtles, "Happy Together." The Mamas & the Papas, "Dedicated to the One I Love." Aretha Franklin, "I Never Loved a Man the Way I Love You" & "Respect." Scott McKenzie, "San Francisco, Be Sure To Wear Flowers in Your Hair." Engelbert Humperdinck, "Release Me." Donovan, "Mellow Yellow." Martha and the Vandellas, "Jimmy Mack." The Royal Guardsmen, "Snoopy vs. the Red Baron." The Buckinghams, "Kind of a Drag." The Supremes, "Love Is Here and Now You're Gone" & "The Happening." Neil Diamond Girl, "You'll Be a Woman Soon." The Temptations, "All I Need Is You." The Seekers, "Georgy Girl." Tommy James & the Shondells, "I Think We're Alone Now." Frank Sinatra, "That's Life." The Young Rascals, "Groovin'." Aaron Neville, "Tell It Like It Is." Peaches & Herb, "Close Your Eyes." The Fifth Dimension, "Up, Up and Away." The Beatles, "Penny Lane" & "Strawberry Fields Forever." Stevie Wonder, "I Was Made to Love Her." Bobbie Gentry, "Ode to Billie Joe." Bill Cosby, "Little Ole Man." John Fred & His Playboy Band, "Judy in Disguise, with Glasses." Diana Ross & the Supremes, "Reflections." The Doors, "Light My Fire." Gladys Knight & the Pips, "I Heard It Through the Grapevine." The Mamas and the Papas, "Words of Love."

Deaths: Jack Ruby.

President: Lyndon B. Johnson (D) Disciples of Christ; vetoes 30/0 overrides

Vice President: Hubert H. Humphrey (D)
Lutheran; Methodist; Congregationalist

House: D-247 ; R-187

Senate: 90th Congress (1967-1969) Majority Party: Democrat (64 seats) Minority Party: Republican (36 seats) Other Parties: 0 Total Seats: 100

Federal Debt: $326.22 billion or 39 % of the GDP

Consumer Price Index CPI-U (1982 Base of 100): 33.40

GDP: $832.6 billion	**Inflation Rate:** 2.78%

Dow Jones: 912.97 (08-01)/ 792. (January)	**S&P Price Index:** 96.47/20.09%
Prime Rate: 6.00% (11-20)	**Average Home Mortgage Rate:** 6.42%
1 oz Gold: $35.50	**1oz of Silver:** $1.50

Monthly S.S. benefits paid: $84 / month

Federal Debt: $326,220,937,794.54

Federal Deficit: $8.6 billion dollars

Defense Spending: $83.72 billion	**Interest Spending:** $10.27 billion
Health Care Spending: $6.10 billion	**Pensions Spending:** $19.60 billion
Welfare Spending: $5.73 billion	**Education Spending:** $7.35 billion
Transportation Spending: $5.94 billion	**Misc. Other Spending:** $16.11 billion
Protection Spending: $620 million	**Total Government Spending:** $157.46 billion

% of GDP that goes towards just the interest payment: 1.26%

$1.00 = 362.15 Yen

U.S. Population: 198,752,000	**World Population:** 3,485,807,350
U.S. Birth Rate: 3,520,959	**U.S. Abortions:** 2,016
U.S. Homicide Rate: 6.8/ 100,000 population	**U.S. Violent Crime:** 253.2/ 100,000 population

Annual Average Domestic Crude Oil Prices:
$3.12 / barrel, $20.10 (2007 adjusted)

1967

Oil:

1967 – Oil prices fall from 1965 to 1972.

1967 – Nigeria. The Biafra Secession War is partially fought over Nigeria's oil fields.

June 5, 1967 – Egypt closes the Suez Canal in conjunction with the Six-Day War.
The Egyptians close the Suez Canal during the Six-Day War and it becomes part of the boundary separating Egypt and the Israeli-occupied Sinai Peninsula after the war. The Suez Canal remains closed for the next eight years while Egypt loses considerable revenue and many ships built after the closing, especially tankers, are too large to navigate the canal.

August 1967 – Oman. Commercial oil production in Oman begins. Oil production is modest, averaging less than 30,000 barrels per day but this will reach 332,000 barrels per day in 1970. The country subsists on farming and fishing.

1967 – The People's Democratic Republic of Yemen. Southern Yemen is in economic shambles with the closing of the Suez Canal following the Six-Day War and the loss of British trade. Southern Yemen accepts Soviet economic aid and becomes the first and only Marxist Arab state.

1967 – Alaska. The Middle Ground Shoal oil field was discovered off Port Nikiski, at the same latitude as the onshore Swanson River field in 1962. Commercial production begins this year.

Major News:

January 27, 1967 – Gus Grissom, Ed White, and Roger B. Chaffee, NASA astronauts, die on the launch pad when a flash fire began in their pure oxygen environment during a training exercise for the first Apollo/ Saturn mission.

February 10, 1967 – The 25th Amendment, providing for **Presidential succession,** and passed by Congress on July 6, 1965, is ratified February 10. It states: "In case of the removal of the President from office or of his death or resignation, the Vice President shall become President." It also provides for the transfer of temporary power in situations such as a President undergoing surgery. The 25th Amendment provides two remedies when a President is disabled. 1) The President of his own volition may turn over the power of his office to the Vice President. 2) The Vice President, with the assent of a majority of the leading members of the cabinet, may make himself acting President on a temporary basis.

February 27, 1967 – The Outer Space Treaty is signed by the United States, Great Britain, and the Soviet Union. It will take effect on October 10, 1967.

April 24, 1967 – Soviet cosmonaut Vladimir Komarov is killed when the parachute of his **Soyuz 1** craft fails to deploy upon landing. He is the first person to die on a space mission.

June 23-25, 1967 – President Johnson and Soviet Premier Aleksei Kosygin met at Glassboro State College in New Jersey. They agree not to let any crisis push them into war.

July 12-17, 1967 – Newark and Detroit political violence. When two white Newark policemen, John DeSimone and Vito Pontrelli, arrest a black cabdriver, John W. Smith, for improperly passing them on 15th avenue a rumor is started that he has been killed while in police custody. Although Smith had been moved to a local hospital this still sets off six days of riots, looting, violence, and destruction. During the riots in **Newark, New Jersey,** July 12-17, 1967, **1,000 people are arrested,** 26 people are killed and 1,500 are injured. Property damage exceeds $10 million.

July 23-30, 1967 – Detroit, Michigan. Vice squad officers execute a raid at the **Blind Pig,** or speakeasy, on the corner of 12th street and Claremount on the cities near Westside. The confrontation with the patrons evolves into one of the deadliest and most destructive riots in modern U.S. history, lasting five days and far surpassing the 1943 riot the city endured. Before the end, the state and federal governments, under orders from President Lyndon B. Johnson, send in over **12,500 National Guard** and **United States Army troops.** Forty-three people were killed, 470 were injured, over 7,200 arrests were made and more than 2,000 buildings burned down. Five-thousand people are left homeless by the rioting, looting, and burning in city's black neighborhoods.

October 2, 1967 – Thurgood Marshall is sworn into office as the first black Supreme Court Justice.

October 21-22, 1967 – Over 100,000 people participate in an **antiwar march** on Washington, D.C.

Civil Rights Movement:

1967 – In Loving vs. Virginia, the Supreme Court strikes down all state miscegenation laws. There have been laws against interracial marriage and interracial sex since the original Thirteen Colonies from the 1600's onwards and subsequently in several states and U.S. territories until 1967. Sixteen states still have anti-miscegenation laws in 1967 when they are ruled to be unconstitutional. First, legal segregation in the army, in education and in basic public services were removed, and then restrictions on the voting rights of African-Americans were lifted. These victories were ensured by the Civil Rights Act of 1964. But the bans on interracial marriage were the last to go, in 1967.

1967 – Black U.S. Representative Adam Clayton Powell (D, New York) is denied his seat March 1, because of charges he misused government funds. He is reelected in **1968,** and seated, but fined $25,000 and stripped of his seniority.

April 4, 1967 – Speaking before the Overseas Press Club in New York City, **Revered Dr. Martin Luther King, Jr.,** announces his opposition to the Vietnam War. This is King's first sermon devoted entirely to the issue of **Vietnam.**

May 12, 1967 – H. Rap Brown becomes chairman of SNCC.

November 7, 1967 – Carl B. Stokes (D-Cleveland) and **Richard G. Hatcher** (D-Gary, Indiana) are elected the first black mayors of major U.S. cities.

1967 – Sam Smith is elected Seattle's first black city councilman.

December 1967 – The Pittsburgh branch of the NAACP charges that Planned Parenthood clinics provide birth control in low income and minority neighborhoods as an instrument of racial genocide. The term "black genocide" catches on.

Women's Movement:

1967 – Executive Order 11375 expands President Lyndon Johnson's **affirmative action** policy of 1965 to cover discrimination based on gender. Federal agencies and contractors must now take active measures to ensure that women as well as minorities enjoy the same educational and employment opportunities as white males.

1967 – NOW begins petitioning the EEOC to end sex-segregated want ads and adopts a Bill of Rights for Women.

1967 – Senator Eugene McCarthy introduces the Equal Rights Amendment (ERA) in the U.S. Senate.

1967 – New York Radical Women is formed by Shulie Firestone and Pam Allen. **Anne Koedt organizes** "consciousness raising" groups.

1967 – Women's Liberation groups begin springing up all over the nation.

1967 – The National Welfare Rights Organization is formed.

1967 – Muriel "Mickey" Siebert becomes the first woman to own a seat on the New York Stock Exchange and the first woman to head one of its member firms.

December 28, 1967 – The Pill. Katharine McCormick dies at the age of 92 in Boston, Massachusetts. No major newspaper gives her an obituary, and with her passing, her contribution to the birth of **the Pill** is forgotten.

1967

Popular Culture:

1967 – The U.S. population reached 200 million in November. World population reached 3.5 billion.

December 3, 1967 – Dr. Christiaan Bernard performs the first successful heart transplant.

1967 – One of the top secret A-12 spy planes operating out of **Area 51** crashes shortly before landing when it runs out of fuel. It reportedly flew on the edge of space at five times the speed of sound.

January 14, 1967 – 20,000-30,000 people stage a "Human Be-In" anti-war event in Golden Gate Park in San Francisco, near the **Haight-Ashbury** neighborhood that has become the center of **hippie activity.**

January 1967 – *Ramparts* **magazine** publishes photographs of **Vietnamese children** burned by napalm, spurring the involvement of Martin Luther King Jr., who will publicly denounce the war at a speech in New York in April.

February 1967 – Recruiters from Dow Chemical visit the Madison campus, where they are confronted by protesters bearing *Ramparts* photographs. The next day students stage a sit-in at the university chancellor's offices, but the confrontation is defused when the chancellor uses his own money to bail out arrested protesters. Within weeks a proposal is defeated that would have barred Dow from recruiting on campus.

February 8, 1967 – Christian groups opposed to the war stage a nationwide protest, **"Fast for Peace."**

1967 – Wacky Packages. A series of collectible stickers featuring parodies of consumer products and well-known brands and packaging are produced by **Topps Chewing Gum,** Inc. Wacky Packages had higher sales than **Tops Baseball cards** for the first two years.

March 12, 1967 – A three page anti-war ad appears in *The New York Times* bearing the signatures of 6,766 teachers and professors. The advertisement spanned two and a quarter pages in Section 4, **The Week in Review.** The advertisement itself cost around $16,500 and was sponsored by the Inter-University Committee for Debate on Foreign Policy.

April 15, 1967 – 400,000 people march from Central Park to the UN building in New York City to protest the war, where they are addressed by critics of the war such as Benjamin Spock, Martin Luther King, and Jan Barry Crumb, a veteran of the conflict. On the same date **100,000 marched in San Francisco. Martin Luther King, Jr.,** addresses the crowd strongly condemning American involvement in Vietnam.

April 28, 1967 – On a chilly, rainy day in Houston, **Muhammad Ali refuses** to be inducted into the U.S. Army and is immediately stripped of his heavyweight title. Ali ignored the calling of his name by an induction officer at the U.S. Armed Forces Examining and Entrance Station and it was all over. One newsman asked, "What do you think about the Vietcong?" to which Ali replied, **"I ain't got no quarrel with those Vietcong."** On June 20, 1967, Ali was convicted of draft evasion, sentenced to five years in prison, fined $10,000 and banned from boxing for three years. He appealed his case and returned to the ring on October 26, 1970, knocking out **Jerry Quarry** in Atlanta in the third round. On March 8, 1971, Ali fought **Joe Frazier** in the "Fight of the Century" and lost after 15 rounds, the first loss of his professional boxing career. On June 28 of that same year, the U.S. Supreme Court overturned his conviction for evading the draft.

May 1967 – 70,000 supporters of the war march in New York City.

May 30, 1967 – Vietnam Veterans Against the War is founded by six Vietnam war veterans, including Jan "Barry" Crumb, Mark Donnelly, and David Braum, in New York City in June, 1967 after they marched together in the April 15, 1967, **Spring Mobilization to End the War** with **over 400,000 other protesters.** While talking to members of the **"Veterans for Peace"** group at that march, Barry discovered there was no organization representing Vietnam veterans and on June 1 "**Vietnam Veterans Against the War"** was born.

1967

May 30, 1967 – Evel Knievel jumps his motorcycle over 16 cars lined up in a row.

1967 – The "Summer of Love" is a high point of the San Francisco counterculture.

1967 – Over 12.5 million women worldwide are on **the Pill**. The pharmaceutical industry awakens to the huge market for effective contraception, and 13 major drug companies, nine of them American, work to develop new birth control methods and their own versions of the Pill.

1967 – LSD is made illegal in the U.S. Swiss chemist Albert Hofmann synthesized LSD and accidentally discovered its hallucinogenic effects in 1933. He took what he believed was a tiny dose and discovered LSD's astonishing potency.

October 1967 – Protests become more militant at many college campuses. Members of radical groups including, Students for a Democratic Society, are elected to the student governments at more than a few colleges and universities. **Demonstrations against Dow Chemical Company** and other campus recruiters are widespread as draft issues grow in importance. Harassment by the authorities is also on the rise as the FBI and other law enforcement agencies are exposed as having spies and informers in the colleges.

A demonstration at the University of Wisconsin, Madison, on October 17, is peaceful at first, and then turns into a sit-in that is violently dispersed by the Madison police and riot squad, accompanied by many injuries and arrests. The situation escalates into a mass rally and student strike that closes the university for several days.

After conventional civil rights tactics of peaceful pickets seem to have failed, the Oakland, California **"Stop the Draft Week"** ends in mass hit and run skirmishes with the police. The huge October 21 **"March on the Pentagon" gathered over 100,000** protesters and hundreds were arrested and injured. Night-time raids on draft offices begin to spread.

1967 – Opium War. The Shan States of Burma. The 1967 Opium War opens the country to many, many warlords trafficking in opium, and heroin, as a precursor for illegal recreational drugs or tightly regulated legal prescription drugs.

1967 – In Loving vs. Virginia, the United States Supreme Court rules in favor of a mixed race couple whose marriage had been judged illegal by Virginia law. The decision put an end to state prohibitions against interracial marriage.

October 17, 1967 – The Baltimore Four. Philip Francis Berrigan began taking more radical steps to bring attention to the anti-war movement and on October 17, the "Baltimore Four," Francis Berrigan, Tom Lewis, David Eberhardt, and United Church of Christ missionary and pastor The Reverend James L. Mengel, **poured blood**, on Selective Service records in the Baltimore Customs House. Reverend James Mengel agreed to the action and donated blood, but decided not to actually pour blood on the records. He distributed editions of the New Testament, **"Good News for Modern Man,"** to draft board workers, newsmen, and police. As the group calmly waited to be arrested they explained to draft board employees the reasons for their actions. Berrigan stated in the written statement, "This sacrificial and constructive act is meant to protest the pitiful waste of American and Vietnamese blood in Indochina." Philip Francis Berrigan was sentenced to six years in prison.

October 21, 1967 – An enormous antiwar protest draws more than 100,000 people to Washington, including a contingent from the University of Wisconsin. In Madison, two thousand students march to the Wisconsin State capital in what they term a "funeral procession" to protest police brutality. By early next year, **the American death toll in Vietnam will reach 25,000.**

October 1967 – Stop the Draft Week. More than a thousand registrants return their draft cards to induction centers across the country during "Stop the Draft Week". Many more draft cards are turned in at events across the country and then delivered to the Justice Department on October 20.

The next day, October 21, 1967, a large demonstration takes place at the Lincoln Memorial in Washington and over **100,000 demonstrators** are there. At least 30,000 later march to the Pentagon for another rally and an all night vigil. Some, including Abbie Hoffman and Jerry Rubin, attempt to "exorcise" and "levitate" the building, while others engage in civil disobedience on the steps of the Pentagon, interrupted by clashes with soldiers and police. In all, 647 arrests are made. When a plot to **airdrop**

1967

10,000 flowers on the Pentagon is foiled by undercover agents, these flowers end up being placed in the barrels of MP's rifles, as seen in some famous photographs.

1967 – Vietnam War. U.S. Secretary of State Dean Rusk states during a news conference that proposals by the U.S. Congress for peace initiatives were futile because of North Vietnam's opposition.

1967 – The Pentagon Papers, officially titled "**United States–Vietnam Relations, 1945–1967: A Study Prepared by the Department of Defense,**" are a top-secret United States Department of Defense history of the United States' political-military involvement in Vietnam from 1945 to 1967. Commissioned by United States Secretary of Defense Robert S. McNamara in 1967, the study was completed in 1968. **The "Pentagon Papers" first surfaced** on the front page on *The New York Times* in 1971. The study was classified as **top secret** and was not intended for publication, however, contributor Daniel Ellsberg gave most of the "Pentagon Papers" to *New York Times* reporter Neil Sheehan, with Ellsberg's friend Anthony Russo assisting in their copying. The Times began publishing excerpts in a series of articles on June 13, 1971. Street protests, political controversy and lawsuits followed.

Business / Technology:

1967 – Pre-recorded movies on videotape are sold for home TV sets.

June 27, 1967 – Automatic Teller Machine. The first mechanical cash dispenser was developed and built by Luther George Simjian and installed in 1939 in New York City by the City Bank of New York, but removed after 6 months due to the lack of customer acceptance. The history of ATMs paused for over 25 years, until De La Rue Instruments developed the first electronic ATM, which was installed first in Enfield Town in North London, United Kingdom on June 27, 1967 by Barclays Bank.

January 1967 – President Johnson asked Congress to approve "a sensible course of fiscal and budgetary policy," including a 6 percent surcharge on personal and corporate income taxes. The special levy, designed to help pay for the war, would last a maximum of two years, less if swift victory allowed U.S. forces to withdraw sooner.

1967 – Jimmy Hoffa begins an 8 year prison term for defrauding the union and jury tampering.

Finance:

June 30, 1967 – The Treasury Department begins compiling data on the United States Government's foreign loans.

1967 – Congressman Wright Patman, the **Chairman Of The House Banking And Currency Committee, states** in Congress, **"In the United States today, we have in effect two governments...**We have the duly constituted government...Then we have an independent, uncontrolled and uncoordinated government in the **Federal Reserve System,** operating the money powers which are reserved to Congress by the Constitution."

1967 – The deficit is announced to be twenty five billion dollars and President Johnson submits a record budget of one hundred and eighty six billion dollars. This is approximately one sixth of the 2007 budget.

1967 – Social Security. The Supplementary Medical Insurance Program began in April 1965 and there is now a balance of $394 million dollars in the Trust Fund at the end of October 1967.

Books:

1967 – Novelist Joyce Carol Oates, "A Garden of Earthly Delights."

1967 – "An Expensive Place to Die," Len Deighton.

1967 – "Rosemary's Baby," Ira Levin. Supposedly inspired by the publicity surrounding the Church of Satan of Anton LaVey.

1967

1967 – **"The Confessions of Nat Turner,"** William Styron.

1967 – **"Coffee, Tea or Me?"** Donald Bain. The anecdotal lives of two lusty young stewardesses.

TV:

1967 – **Censorship.** It's a difficult year for network censors struggling to keep up with the **hippie** culture's profusion of **drug slang**. Ed Sullivan requests that The Doors change the lyric "Girl, we couldn't get much higher," since it sounds suspiciously like a drug reference. Meanwhile, "The Smothers Brothers Comedy Hour" has a recurring skit about Goldie, a housewife with her own talk show called "Share a little tea with Goldie." The skit constantly plays on the tea/marijuana connection, which goes straight over the censors' heads. Goldie's opening lines include "Hi[gh]! …And glad of it!"

1967 – Dr. George Gerbner reports to the nation on **TV violence**.

1967 – **ABC joins CBS and NBC** in presenting 30-minute television newscasts.

January 15, 1967 – Super Bowl Sunday. The Green Bay Packers defeat the Kansas City Chiefs in the first Super Bowl. This begins a new cultural tradition in the United States as Super Bowl Sunday quickly becomes an unofficial holiday. Worldwide viewership of the 2002 Super Bowl was estimated to be 800,000,000 people. Audiences for other sports such as soccer can be even higher. Estimates for World Cup matches are **over one billion people!**

Sports:

1967 – **Althea Gibson** is the first African-American tennis player to win a singles title at Wimbledon.

January 15, 1967 – The Green Bay Packers beat the Kansas City Chiefs, 35-10, in the **first Super Bowl,** in Los Angeles.

1967 – ABC uses the Ampex HS-100 disk recorder for slow-motion playback of downhill skiing on the program **"World Series of Skiing"** in Vail, Colorado. This is the first use of slow-motion instant replay in sporting events.

Music:

January 4, 1967 – The Doors release their début album of the same name.

January 15, 1967 – The Rolling Stones appear on The Ed Sullivan Show. At Ed Sullivan's request, the band changed their lyrics from "Let's spend the night together" to "Let's spend some time together."

February 6, 1967 – Micky Dolenz of the Monkees flies into London. On this trip he sees "Til Death Us Do Part" on British TV and uses the term "Randy Scouse Git" from the program for the title of The Monkees next single release "Randy Scouse Git," which is based on the program. The British censors force the title to be changed to "Alternate Title" in the UK. "Randy Scouse Git" is composed of 3 British slang words, roughly translated as follows, "Randy": Horny, in search of sex., "Scouse": A person from the north of England., "Git": Sort of a jerk, or an idiot.

February 12, 1967 – Following a tip British police raid 'Redlands', the Sussex home of **Keith Richards.** No arrests are made at the time but it was reported that Richards, **Mick Jagger** and art dealer Robert Fraser were subsequently charged with possession of drugs.

March 31, 1967 – Kicking off a tour with The Walker Brothers, Cat Stevens and **Engelbert Humperdinck** at The Astoria London, **Jimi Hendrix** sets fire to his guitar on stage for the first time. He is taken to the hospital suffering burns to his hands. This guitar-burning act soon becomes a trademark of Hendrix's performances.

1967 – The Who destroy their instruments during a performance on **"The Smothers Brothers Comedy Hour."**

May 1967 – Paul McCartney announces all four of the Beatles have dropped acid.

1967

1967 – Toots & the Maytals release "54-46 That's My Number," one of the first **reggae** songs.

1967 – New Bands: Blue Öyster Cult, The Stooges, Creedence Clearwater Revival, The First Edition (fronted by Kenny Rogers), Chicago, Genesis.

Natural Disasters:

1965-1967 – India. Three years of drought in India results in an estimated 1,500,000 peoples deaths from starvation and disease. Severe Indian droughts also killed millions in 1900 and 1942.

April 21, 1967 – In Northern Illinois, Missouri, Iowa, and Lower Michigan a series of 52 tornadoes causes 58 deaths.

July 22, 1967 – Turkey. A 7.1 magnitude earthquake strikes the North Anatolian Fault line.

December 10, 1967 – Koynanagar, India. A 6.3 magnitude earthquake strikes in and around the town of Koynanagar in Maharashtra near the site of Koyna dam. The earthquake kills at least 180 people and injures over 1,500. The earthquake also damaged more than 80% of the houses in Koyana Nagar Township.

1967 – Ebola Virus. Germany and Yugoslavia. Marburg hemorrhagic fever is a severe and highly fatal disease caused by a virus from the same family as the one that causes Ebola hemorrhagic fever. Marburg hemorrhagic fever is initially detected following simultaneous outbreaks in Marburg and Frankfurt, Germany, and Belgrade, Yugoslavia. The initial cases occurred in laboratory workers handling **African green monkeys** imported from **Uganda**. The outbreaks involved 25 primary infections, with 7 deaths, and 6 secondary cases, with no deaths. The primary infections were in laboratory staff exposed to Marburg virus while working with monkeys or their tissues. The secondary cases involved two doctors, a nurse, a post-mortem attendant, and the wife of a veterinarian. All secondary cases had direct contact, usually involving blood, with a primary case. Both doctors became infected through accidental skin pricks when drawing blood from patients.

Man vs. Man / Wars:

1967 – Algerian-Moroccan Border Clash. The Algerian-Moroccan border had been determined by the former colonial power, **France**, to the satisfaction of neither state. The **Moroccan King, Hassan II,** wished to create a Greater Morocco and this led to a series of border clashes and regional wars. Morocco really wants to establish its control over the western Algerian region around Tindouf, **an area rich in iron ore, oil, and natural gas.** Relations between Algeria and Morocco remain strained after the cease-fire of 1963. Border clashes resume in 1967.

1967 – An aircraft carrying Katangan rebel leader Moise Tshombe is hijacked en route to Ibiza, Spain, and forced to land in Algeria in a bid to extradite him to his native **Congo.** The Algerians kept him under house arrest until he died two years later.

1967 – A British European Airways Comet aircraft is destroyed over Rhodes, Greece by a bomb detonated in the passenger cabin. All 66 people on board are killed.

1967 – Angola. Forced resettlement becomes the focus of Portuguese counter insurgency efforts. Over 1,000,000 **Africans** will be driven from their homes, often at gun point, and beaten if they resist. Their huts are burned and they are trucked to villages organized by the military. The "Sanzala de Paz." or **"Village of Peace"** policy will be imposed throughout much of the Angolan Countryside.

May 30, 1967-January 15, 1970 – The Biafra Secession. The Republic of Biafra is a secessionist state in south-eastern Nigeria. The Igbo people are the majority in the area and due to economic, ethnic, cultural and religious tensions they break away from Nigeria and form a separate state. The main source of income, **Nigeria's oil**, is located in the southeast with the Igbo.

    In 1960, Nigeria became independent of the United Kingdom. Its borders were not drawn according to earlier territories and this left the northern desert region of the country with semi-autonomous feudal Muslim states, while the southern population was predominantly Christian and animist. The creation of the new country, named after the Bight of Biafra (the Atlantic bay to its south), is among the complex causes for the **Nigerian Civil War,** also known as the **Nigerian-Biafra War.**

June 24, 1967 – Bolivia, Catavi-Siglo Massacre. Catavi is a tin mine in Bolivia. The mine was nationalized after the "Bolivian National Revolution" of 1952. The Catavi-Siglo complex employs some 5,000 workers. President Barrientos discovers a guerrilla force operating in the rural Bolivian mining camps under the leadership of Cuban **"Che" Guevara.** Barrientos is very concerned with Guevara's rising insurgency there, and clamps down in the area with some very heavy handed measures including the **"Massacre of San Juan,"** when soldiers opened fire on the miners and killed around 30 men and women on Saint John's Day.

July - October 1967 – Bolivia ELN Insurgency. Bolivia's army **consists mostly of untrained Indian conscripts** and has fewer than 2,000 troops ready for combat so while the army keeps Che Guevara's guerrilla force contained in a southwestern area of the country, an 800-man Ranger force begins training an elite military group in counterinsurgency and three well-trained, well-equipped Bolivian Ranger battalions are ready by late July 1967.

The Bolivian Rangers and the Eighth Division attack Guevara's demoralized, ill-equipped, and poorly supplied band. **Guevara's capture and summary execution** on October 7 ends the Cuban-sponsored insurgency. Some people say, the body has been returned to Cuba, others say, it's still in Bolivia.

1967 – Burma. The Shan Rebellion, Opium Wars. For Chan Shee-fu the 1967 Opium War marked the beginning of the end and his defeat is the last real attempt by any warlord to gain significant control of the Shan States. When the rebellion began in 1958, there were only three or four rebel groups active in the entire Shan States. In mid 1971 there were more than a hundred different armed bands prowling the highlands and the people become progressively alienated from the independence movement as opium is now the main focus of the rebels. Even though opium means wealth and power many of the lesser Shan warlords tax the people at gunpoint as they move around the country reducing the peasants to a continuing state of poverty.

1967-1970 – Cambodian Tax Revolt. In January an insurrection breaks out in the area around Samlot in Batdambang, an area of large landowners with a majority peasant class. When the government continues to tax the peasants and expropriate land to build a sugar refinery the peasants attack a tax collection brigade. Encouraged by the North Vietnamese the insurrection quickly spreads through the whole region. In March 1967, **Norodom Sihanouk** personally controlled Cambodia and supervised counterinsurgency measures. He later mentioned, in an offhand way, that the effectiveness of the royal armed forces had restored the peace but that approximately **10,000 people had died.**

November 20, 1967 – Cuba. Louis Gabor Babler, born in Hungary, successfully hijacks a Crescent Airline Piper Apache from Hollywood, Florida, to Cuba.

1967 – Cypriot Crisis. The island's Turkish Cypriot and Greek Cypriot communities have been in a constant power struggle following independence in 1960. On February 17, 1964 the *Washington Post* reported that "Greek Cypriot fanatics appear bent on a policy of genocide." As Greece and Turkey became increasingly involved in the situation, Greece sends 20,000 troops to the island, and Turkey responds to attacks on Turkish Cypriot areas with air strikes. In 1964 the United Nations sent peacekeeping troops to support British soldiers manning the so-called "Green Line."

In 1967 a military junta seizes power in Greece **which again brings** George Papadopoulos to power. **Greek President Papadopoulos** is determined to end the deadlock with force, and relations between **Archbishop Makarios,** the Greek Cypriot President and the Greek dictator Papadopoulos are strained at best. This will continue until 1974 when the regime in Athens Greece supports a coup by Greek Cypriot army officers. Archbishop Makarios is overthrown and flees to Britain where he dies unexpectedly in 1977 from a heart attack. During the autopsy his heart was removed and is now preserved in his former bedroom in the Archbishopric.

1967

1967 – Congo Katanga Revolt. A failed revolt in Katanga is joined by some mercenaries and is defeated by Congolese (Democratic Republic of the Congo) government forces, which also used mercenaries.

August 25, 1967 – Egypt Officials' Plot. **Abd al-Hakim 'Amir** and fifty other high-ranking military and civilian officials are arrested and accused of plotting to overthrow **Nasser.**

In June 1967 the Six-Day War erupted between Egypt and Israel. Egypt suffered a disastrous defeat, and Āmir was relieved of his post as field marshal on June 9, 1967. On September 5, he was arrested and accused of heading a coup to overthrow the government. Approximately two weeks later, the government announces that Amir, who was once considered Nasser's closest associate among the Free Officers, had **committed suicide** by taking poison while under house arrest.

April 21, 1967 – Greece Colonels Coup. The coup leaders gained control of the city by placing tanks in strategic positions around Athens and by the early morning Greece was in the hands of the colonels. All leading politicians, including acting Prime Minister Panagiotis Kanellopoulos, had been arrested. Martial music was continuously broadcast over the radio. Announcements with the junta issuing orders interrupted the music often and always started with the introduction **"We decide and we order."** Political freedoms and civil liberties, that had been taken for granted and enjoyed by the Greek people for decades were gone. **President George Papadopoulos** is the head of the military coup d'état and leader of the military government that rules the country from 1967 to 1974.

May 25, 1967 – Present. India. Naxalite Guerrilla War. Beginning with a peasant uprising in the town of Naxalbari, this Marxist/Maoist rebellion sputters on in the Indian countryside through 2010.

June 5-10, 1967 – Six Day War. Israel vs. Egypt, Jordan & Syria & Iraq. Egyptian President Gamal Abdel **Nasser** expels the United Nations Emergency Force (UNEF) from the Sinai Peninsula in May 1967. The Six Day War between the Israel army and the armies of Egypt, Jordan, Syria, and Iraq begins on June 5.

The peacekeeping force had been stationed there since 1957, following a British-French-Israeli invasion which was launched during the Suez Crisis. Egypt placed 1,000 tanks and nearly 100,000 soldiers on the Israeli border and closed the Straits of Tiran to all Israeli ships or carrying strategic materials. Israel responded with a similar mobilization that included the call up of 70,000 reservists to augment the regular IDF forces. On June 5, 1967, Israel launched a pre-emptive air strike against the Egyptian air force. Jordan, then attacked western Jerusalem and Netanya. At the war's end on June 10, Israel had gained control of the **Sinai Peninsula,** the **Gaza Strip,** the **West Bank, East Jerusalem,** and the **Golan Heights.**

1967-1970 – The Nigerian Civil War or "Biafra War." The Nigerian Civil War, also known as the Nigerian-Biafra War, July 6, 1967 to January 15, 1970, is a political conflict caused by the attempted secession of the southeastern provinces of Nigeria as the self-proclaimed Republic of Biafra.

1967-1979 – The Rhodesian Civil War can also be considered the **Zimbabwe War of Independence**. Rebels of the black majority fight a guerilla war against the white minority government of **Ian Smith.** Smith had declared unilateral independence from Britain rather than end white rule. The war concluded with a peace agreement in 1979 in which each adult received the right to vote regardless of race.

1967 – Sierra Leone. In 1961 Sierra Leone became an independent state within the British Commonwealth. The nation has considerable wealth from diamonds which are easy to misappropriate. Democracy ends in Sierra Leone in 1967 with the election of an opposition party led by Siaka Stevens and the country declines into a long era of repressive rule, military coups and, by the end of the century, terrifying and violent anarchy. Siaka Stevens remains in control for eighteen years by dismantling the country's checks on the abuses of power, executing his political opponents, and controlling its wealth. The Sierra Leone government recorded exports of only 8,500 carats in 1998, the Diamond High Council (HRD) in Belgium recorded imports of 770,000 carats from Sierra Leone.

In 2009 the Sierra Leone Civil War, 1991–2002 is barely over. Fifty thousand people were killed. Two million people were displaced, and it is reported September

17, 2009: "A U.S. oil company has found what could be commercially viable reserves of oil off the coast of Sierra Leone."

March 1967 – Vietnam. **"Operation Pop Eye."** It is later revealed in the **"Pentagon Papers"** that "Operation Pop Eye," a rain-making project, was designed to reduce traffic along the **Ho Chi Minh trail in Laos.**

September 3, 1967 – Vietnam. Nguyen Van Thieu is elected President of South Vietnam.

October 1967 – Vietnam. Congressman Thomas P. ("Tip") O'Neill breaks publicly with President Johnson and **opposes continuation of the Vietnam War.** O'Neill supports **Senator Eugene McCarthy** (D-Minnesota) for President in 1968.

1968

The Oldest Boomer is 22 years old.

Cost of the Average House: $26,600	
Median Family Income: $7,700	**Minimum Wage:** $1.60/ hr **Average Hourly Wage:** $3.01
Monthly Rent: $130 average	**Gallon Gasoline:** 34 cents
New Car: **Alfa Romeo Spider:** $3,950 **Cadillac Elderado:** $6,605	**Pepsi:** 59 cents/ 6 pack 10oz bottles **Loaf of Bread:** 22 cents **Gallon of Milk:** $1.22
Unemployment Rate: 3.7%-3.5%-3.4%	**First-class Stamp:** 6 cents

16 cents buying power in 1968 = **$1.00 in 2008.**
In 1968 what cost us 16 cents to purchase now costs us $1.00 in 2008.

Movies: "2001: A Space Odyssey," "Oliver!" "The Producers," "Barbarella," " Funny Girl," "The Lion in Winter," "Rachel, Rachel," "Romeo and Juliet," "Rosemary's Baby," "Planet of the Apes," "The Odd Couple."

Broadway: "The Happy Time," "People Is the Thing That the World Is Fullest Of," off Broadway. "Hair."

TV: LBJ's announcement that he would not run for President for a second term. Nixon Asks, "Sock it to me?" on "Rowan and Martin's Laugh-In." Elvis's '68 Comeback Special. "Adam 12," "Hawaii Five-O," "Mod Squad," "Lancer," 'Here Come the Brides," "60 Minutes," "Mister Rogers' Neighborhood," "Adam 12," "Julia," "Mayberry R.F.D.," "The Ghost and Mrs. Muir," "Aquaman," "Dick Cavett Show," "Playboy After Dark," "The Archie Show," "Here's Lucy," "Dean Martin Presents The Golddiggers," "Land of the Giants," "Julia."

Music: "Up With People," "2001: A Space Odyssey," "Oliver!" "Planet of the Apes". Tom Jones, "Delilah." The Temptations, "I Wish It Would Rain."

Cream, "Sunshine of Your Love." Steppenwolf, "Born to Be Wild." Tommy James & the Shondells, "Mony Mony." Bobby Womack, "California Dreamin.'" Bobby Goldsboro, "Honey." O. C. Smith, "Little Green Apples." Simon and Garfunkel, "Mrs. Robinson." Rolling Stones, "Jumpin' Jack Flash." Sammy Davis, Jr., "I've Gotta Be Me." The Who, "Magic Bus." Sly & The Family Stone, "Dance to the Music." Kenny Rogers and The First Edition, "Just Dropped In To See What Condition My Condition Was In." Big Brother and the Holding Company, "Piece of my Heart." Diana Ross & The Supremes, "Love Child." Otis Redding, "Sittin' On The Dock of the Bay." Diana Ross & the Supremes and The Temptations, "I'm Gonna Make You Love Me." The Beatles, "Hello, Goodbye," "Hey Jude," "Revolution" & "Lady Madonna." Deep Purple, "Hush." Herb Alpert, "This Guy's in Love With You." Aretha Franklin, "Chain of Fools." Tiny Tim, "Tiptoe Through The Tulips With Me."

Deaths: Little Willie John, Roy Orbison & Anthony Orbison, Helen Keller.

President: Lyndon B. Johnson (D) Disciples of Christ; vetoes 30/ 0 overrides

Vice President: Hubert H. Humphrey (D)
Lutheran; Methodist; Congregationalist

House: D-247 ; R-187

Senate: 90th Congress (1967-1969) Majority Party: Democrat (64 seats) Minority Party: Republican (36 seats) Other Parties: 0 Total Seats: 100

Federal Debt: $347.58 billion or 38 % of the GDP

Consumer Price Index CPI-U (1982 Base of 100): 34.80

GDP: $910.0 billion	**Inflation Rate:** 4.27%
Dow Jones: 948.41 (11-01)/ 840.44 (03-01)	**S&P Price Index:** 103.86/7.66% 100.38 June 4,1968
Prime Rate: 6.75% (12-18)	**Average Home Mortgage Rate:** 6.8%
1 oz Gold: $40.06	**1oz of Silver:** $2.57

Federal Debt: $347,578,406,425.88

Federal Deficit: $25.2 billion dollars	
Defense Spending: $94.26 billion	Interest Spending: $11.09 billion
Health Care Spending: $9.04 billion	Pensions Spending: $22.00 billion
Welfare Spending: $6.59 billion	Education Spending: $8.57 billion
Transportation Spending: $6.32 billion	Misc. Other Spending: $17.62 billion
Protection Spending: $660 million	Total Government Spending: $178.13 billion
% of GDP that goes towards just the interest payment: 1.28%	
$1.00 = 360.56 Yen, Japan	
U.S. Population: 200,745,000	World Population: 3,557,675,690
U.S. Birth Rate: 3,501,564	U.S. Abortions: 6,211
U.S. Homicide Rate: 7.3/ 100,000 population	U.S. Violent Crime: 298.4/ 100,000 population
Annual Average Domestic Crude Oil Prices: $3.18 / barrel, $19.61 (2007 adjusted)	

Oil:

1968 – Billions of barrels of crude oil are discovered in **Prudhoe Bay** on the Alaskan North Slope, significantly affecting U.S. oil and oil-shipping industries. The oil reserves are close to the center of Alaska's coastline and a web of pipelines, roads, and power lines begin to spread out from the site. Oil companies will leave a steady accumulation of harmful environmental and social effects over the next thirty-five years because environmental damage does not heal easily in the area's harsh climate and it is uneconomical to remove structures or restore damaged areas once drilling is over. Even though oil companies make record profits in 2008 and 2009, a particular problem is the lack of specific state or federal rules requiring cleanups of degraded areas.

1968 –The U.S. Gulf of Mexico has had over 9,000 wells drilled.

Major News:

January 1968 – A massive surprise attack by North Vietnamese troops makes a U.S. victory seem more remote. Opposition to not only the war but to the administration and its policies erupts on campuses, and at both national conventions. From the Olympics to the Miss America Beauty Pageant in Atlantic City, people are dissatisfied and protest. Martin Luther King, Jr. and Robert Kennedy are assassinated and President Johnson announces that he will not seek reelection. Federal troops put down race riots across the country.

January 23, 1968 – North Korea. The USS Pueblo and its 83 man crew are captured by the North Koreans. It is the first U.S. Navy ship to be hi-jacked on the high seas by a foreign military force in over 150 years. Through 2009 the capture has resulted in no reprisals against the North Koreans. No military action was taken at the time, or at any later date. This lack of military response guarantees the Pueblo's place in history as a watershed event in our national conscience. Eighty-two men are released on December 22. U.S. sailor, Fireman Apprentice Duane Hodges, was killed.

　　North Korea announces the **USS Pueblo** strayed into their territorial waters and the **United States** maintains that the vessel was in international waters at the time of the incident. More recently, facts have come to light that indicate that the USS Pueblo was captured by North Korea at the instigation of the **Soviet Union**, which was seeking a cryptographic machine onboard to match with a "key" provided to the Soviets by the **spy John Walker.** The Pueblo, is still held by North Korea today, officially remains a commissioned vessel of the United States Navy, and is currently located in Pyongyang, where it is used as a museum ship.

January 31, 1968 – Vietnam. "Tet offensive." The Tet Offensive is a series of surprise attacks by the Vietcong and North Vietnamese forces. Throughout South Vietnam communist troops attack Saigon and over 30 cities, towns, and hamlets in South Vietnam on January 31, the first day of the Lunar New Year, Vietnam's most important holiday. In Saigon, they attacked the Presidential Palace, the airport, the ARVN headquarters, and fight their way onto the U.S. Embassy grounds. The U.S. and ARVN forces are caught off guard, but quickly respond, and within a week have regained most of the lost territory. Hue is a different story as the Vietcong hold their ground. The historic city has been all but leveled by the time it is retaken on February 24. During the **"Massacre at Hue,"** thousands of civilians are executed and 100,000 residents loose their homes. It will be weeks before U.S. and South Vietnamese troops retake all of the captured cities, including the former Imperial Capital of Hue. The Tet Offensive is considered to be a turning point in the Vietnam War.

March 27, 1968 – Robert Kennedy declares his candidacy for the Democratic Presidential nomination on an **anti-war platform**. Kennedy's platform included racial and economic justice, non-aggression in foreign policy, decentralization of power and social improvement. Robert Kennedy worked on bringing the young voter into his campaign because he feels they are the future of a reinvigorated American society based on partnership and social equality.

   Kennedy's policy objectives do not sit well with the business world, which opposes the tax increases necessary to fund his proposed social programs. When asked after a speech, "And who's going to pay for all this, senator?" Kennedy replied with typical candor, "You are." Robert Kennedy continued with this open and honest dialogue. Not all Boomers agreed with him, but they admired his candor and most agree it is time for change.

March 31, 1968 – President Lyndon B. Johnson halts the bombing of **North Vietnam** and announces that he will not seek reelection as President. Peace talks began in Paris on May 10, and all bombing of North Vietnam is halted on October 31, 1968.

April 4, 1968 – Martin Luther King Jr., 39, is **assassinated** in Memphis, Tennessee. **James Earl Ray**, a fugitive from Missouri State prison who was serving 20 years for armed robbery is arrested at London's Heathrow Airport on June 8. Ray is extradited to the U.S., pleads guilty to murdering King and is sentenced to 99 years in prison.

1968

During the civil rights movement, Martin Luther King Jr. captured the attention of the nation with his philosophy and commitment to the method of **nonviolent resistance** and **in his memory** the assassination leads to a nationwide wave of riots in more than 60 cities. President Lyndon B. Johnson declares a national day of mourning and a crowd of 300,000 attend **Martin Luther King Jr.**'s funeral. Vice President Hubert Humphrey attended on behalf of Lyndon B. Johnson, because President Johnson felt he would attract war protestors to the funeral making his presence disruptive.

Findings of the Select Committee on Assassinations in the Assassination of Dr. Martin Luther King, Jr.: Based on its investigation, the committee determined that James Earl Ray fired the shot that killed Dr. Martin Luther King, Jr.

April 9-10, 1968 – Riots erupt in Trenton, New Jersey, and throughout the country following the assassination of Martin Luther King. The upscale shopping district of Trenton is left in shambles. Riots occur in large cities across the U.S.

April 23-24, 1968 – Students at Columbia University take control of campus buildings in protest demonstrations. The Columbia protests erupt after students discover links between the university and the institutional apparatus supporting the United States' involvement in the Vietnam War, as well as their concern over an **allegedly segregated gymnasium** to be constructed in the nearby Morningside Park. The protesters had to be forcibly removed from the university buildings by the New York City Police Department.

May 1968 – Bloody Monday. France is on the verge of a total revolt with 11 million workers on strike, 122 factories occupied, and students fighting against the old archaic system in which they find themselves. On March 22, eight students break into the Dean's office at the **University** of Paris, **Nanterre, to protest** the recent arrest of six members of the National Vietnam Committee. They have occupied the building for one month when a meeting that calls for solidarity with the working class is attended by 1,500 students.

When the college decides to discipline eight of the students there is a protest march through Paris. The students are savagely attacked by the police. The students tear up paving stones and overturn cars to form barricades while police toss tear gas into the crowds and call for reinforcements. This day was to go into the annals of 1968 as **"Bloody Monday,"** with 422 arrests and 345 policemen injured.

The average citizen is appalled by the brutality of the police. It is no longer "business as usual" as people stand up to authority run amuck. By Friday, May 10, 30,000 students, including high school students gather and march in protest. By May 14, thousands of workers join in with the beginning of nationwide strikes. To prevent a run on the banks, withdrawals are limited. Fuel and food supplies run low as people stock up. Air traffic controllers, auto workers, the textile industry, department stores and French television are all on strike. **Within two weeks eleven million workers are out on strike.**

May 1968 – The USS Scorpion, a 3,500-ton Skipjack class nuclear-powered attack submarine begins another Mediterranean cruise in February. In May, while homeward bound from that tour, she is lost with her entire crew some 400 miles southwest of the Azores. In late October 1968, her remains are found on the sea floor over 10,000 feet below the surface by a towed deep-submergence vehicle. Photographs taken show that her hull suffered fatal damage while she was running submerged and show even more severe damage occurred as she sank. The cause of the initial damage continues to generate controversy more than four decades later.

November 6, 1968 – San Francisco State University. November 6, 1968, is the first day in the **longest student strike in American history.** At San Francisco State University in California, members of the Third World Liberation Front, as well as other political, social, and ethnic groups, marched for an education that would be more relevant and accessible to their communities. By the end of this historic five-month battle, SFSU founded the first school of Ethnic Studies in the nation. San Francisco State's strike for Ethnic Studies prompted a similar strike on UC-Berkeley's campus. The resulting Ethnic Studies departments at both SFSU and Berkeley were the first of their kind in the nation.

When George Murray, a part-time English professor and Minister of Education for the Black Panther Party, was suspended for calling for an "armed student revolution on campus," the Black Student Union objected. This was the beginning of the student strike.

1968

September 22, 2008 – "This fall San Francisco State commemorates the 40th anniversary of the 1968 student-led strike, the longest campus strike in United States history. The five-month event defined the University's core values of equity and social justice, laid the groundwork for establishment of the College of Ethnic Studies, and inspired the establishment of ethnic studies classes and programs at other universities throughout the country."

June 5, 1968 – Senator Robert F. Kennedy (D-New York), 42, **is assassinated** in Los Angeles, after celebrating his Presidential Primary victories. He dies on June 6. The assassin, a twenty-four year old Palestinian immigrant named Sirhan Sirhan, is convicted of murder in 1969. His death sentence is commuted to life in prison in 1972. The shooting is recorded on audio tape by a freelance newspaper reporter, while the aftermath is captured on film.

August 26-29, 1968 – Democratic National Convention in Chicago. "The whole world is watching." Opposition to the Vietnam War is the catalyst and one of the end results is to forever change how the Democratic Party selects presidential candidates, opening up the political process to millions.

Anti war leaders coordinate efforts with over 100 anti–war groups with the goal of bringing 100,000 young adults to Chicago. They planned a counter convention, a **YIPPIE convention,** and applied for the necessary permits but were denied. Permits for marches were also denied and a permit is granted for only one rally.

President Johnson, a Democrat, is given a favorable rating of around 32 % by most polls and his war policies are favored by only 23 %. All of this tempts many Democrats to move their national convention from Chicago to Miami, but politically powerful Mayor Richard J. Daley did not want the convention to leave Chicago. He vowed to enforce the peace and not allow outrageous demonstrations. John Kennedy won Illinois and the Presidency in 1960 by less than 10,000 votes and most of those were probably stolen gratis Mayor Daley.

Only a few thousand demonstrators showed up. Some came to protest and some just came to support their favorite Democratic candidates. The Chicago police did show up and **law enforcement outnumbered** the **demonstrators** by five to one. There are 11,900 Chicago police, 7,500 Army troops, 7,500 Illinois National

Guardsmen and 1,000 Secret Service agents that riot against the demonstrators for five days. Five hundred and eighty–nine people are arrested and many more are injured.

Demonstrators tried to get permits to sleep in Lincoln Park and those permits were denied. When they decided to sleep in Lincoln Park anyway the Chicago police moved in with tear gas bombs and billy–clubs swinging. Many innocent bystanders, reporters and doctors offering medical help were severely beaten by the police. Seventeen reporters will be attacked by the police as nightly battles occur in Lincoln Park on live TV. A legal rally in Grant Park ended when the police clubbed a teenager who was lowering an American flag. They also clubbed others who tried to protect the teen.

During the final day of the convention, protestors tried to march to the convention center while the police and National Guard tried to remove everyone from the area. Party volunteers, candidate supporters and tourists along Michigan Avenue in front of the convention headquarters were attacked by police. Heads are cracked, tear gas is thrown, many are beaten with billy–clubs and a few people were pushed through plate glass windows. TV cameras kept running and when these images are played inside the convention almost everyone stops what they are doing to watch in amazement. **"The whole world is watching"** was reality and not just a slogan.

The **"police riot"** was widely covered and led to a government funded study which placed most of the blame on the Chicago Police; Mayor Daley disagreed and gave the police a pay raise.

1968 – Democratic National Convention. The barbed wire-laced jeeps in Grant Park evoke images of Russian tanks in the streets of Prague. After the Tet offensive in January many Americans begin to change their opinion of the war in Vietnam. After Chicago 1968 they begin to doubt the ability of American institutions to tolerate active dissension. The acknowledged right to dissent within certain limits, and the equally valid right of a city to protect its citizens go head to head in Chicago.

Chicago changed politics. Chicago changed minds. Chicago '68, **"The whole world is watching!"** shaped our current political and cultural life. Although Chicago '68 was termed a Police Riot, many felt Chicago's police had struck a notable blow for law and order as U.S. culture and values are further divided.

1968

August 21, 1968 – Czechoslovakia. The Soviet army invades Czechoslovakia along with troops from four other Warsaw Pact countries. The occupation is the beginning of the end for the Czechoslovak reform movement known as the **Prague Spring** when between 5,000 and 7,000 tanks roll in, accompanied by 400,000 Warsaw Pact troops. The tanks occupy the streets while the troops seek out the 'antisocialist' elements. Soviet troops crush the Czechoslovakian revolt and Czechoslovakia remained occupied until 1990.

August 1968 – Republican National Convention, Miami, Florida. Richard M. Nixon wins the Republican Presidential nomination.

Authorities refuse to comment about how many Secret Servicemen, FBI agents, private security, and state and local law enforcement are on duty. The Southern Christian Leadership Conference and a contingent of Cuban exiles are the only groups that plan on demonstrating during the convention.

August 22, 1968 – Czechoslovakia. Czech students are hurling Molotov cocktails at Russian tanks on the streets of Prague as they vainly seek to repel a Soviet invasion of their country.

October 14, 1968 – The Presidio Mutiny in San Francisco. Twenty-seven soldiers serving brig time attempt to stage a sit-in protesting prison conditions and all are tried as mutineers. The Presidio mutiny is the first of a number of protests and riots that focus attention on anti-war dissent within the military. The news media investigates the conditions at the stockade and the situations of the protesters. The protesters had learned that you cannot trust army recruiters, as none of those convicted had been given the non-combatant assignment promised them.

October 22, 1968 – The Gun Control Act is signed into law. The Bureau of Alcohol, Tobacco and Firearms is charged with its enforcement.

October 20, 1968 – Former First Lady, Jacky Kennedy came to fear for her life and the lives of her children after the assassination of her brother-in-law **Robert F.**

Kennedy in June 1968. Afraid she will be killed next, **Jacqueline Kennedy marries Aristotle Onassis.**

November 5, 1968 – Richard Milhous Nixon, the 55-year-old former Vice President who lost the Presidency for the Republicans in 1960, reclaims it by defeating **Hubert Humphrey** in one of the closest elections in U.S. history. Nixon captures 301 Electoral College Votes to 191 for Humphrey and 46 for Wallace.

1968 – West Berlin. The International Vietnam Congress is held in West Berlin and 10,000 demonstrate against the American War in Vietnam. **Rudi Dutschke, 28,** leads the way as the authorities failed to get the courts to ban the demonstration. Student leader Rudi Dutschke is shot three times in an **attempted assassination** outside the SDS-office in West Berlin. Josef Bachmann, shoots him twice in the head and once in the chest. This sparks extensive riots in West Berlin where 300,000 participate in a protest demonstration.

Civil Rights Movement:

1968 – Aaron Dixon becomes the first leader of the **Black Panther Party** branch in Seattle. In the spring of 1968, at the funeral of Bobby Hutton in Oakland, California, Dixon meets Bobby Seale and later is appointed Captain of Seattle's Black Panther Party, the first chapter outside of Oakland. He is 19 years old.

In 2006, Aaron Dixon runs for the United States Senate in Washington State on the Green Party ticket. While a member of the Black Panthers, Dixon started the Free Breakfast for Children program that fed thousands of hungry African American children; and he helped to open a free community medical and legal clinic. At the same time, according to the "**Seattle Weekly**," the Panthers were involved in the "firebombing of businesses and institutions that they considered racist." The clinic continues to this day as the Carolyn Downs Clinic, now part of Country Doctor Community Health Center.

April 4, 1968 – Martin Luther King Jr. preached and taught nonviolent resistance and in response to his death Seattle residents hurled firebombs, broke windows, and pelted motorists with rocks. Ten thousand people also marched to Seattle Center for a rally **in his memory.**

April 6, 1968 – The Oakland Police and Black Panther shootout results in the death of 18 year-old Bobby Hutton, an early party member. **Eldridge Cleaver** later said that he had led the Panther group on a deliberate ambush of the police officers, thus provoking the shoot-out. In September 1968, FBI Director J. Edgar Hoover described the Black Panthers as, "The greatest threat to the internal security of the country."

April 11, 1968 – President Johnson signs the Civil Rights Act of 1968, prohibiting discrimination in the sale, rental, and financing of housing.

May 12, 1968 – The Rev. Ralph Abernathy succeeds Martin Luther King as President of the SCLC and leads the **Poor People's March** to Washington, where protestors build **"Resurrection City,"** a plywood shantytown near the **Washington Monument.**

June 24, 1968 – Poor People's Campaign. The six-week-old Poor People's Campaign ends with the government's 'closing' of its camp site, **Resurrection City, USA,** on Monday June 24. On May 12, 1968 the first wave of demonstrators arrived in Washington, D.C. and Resurrection City was built on the Washington Mall, a settlement of tents and shacks to house the protesters. Demonstrators were sent out to various federal agencies to protest and spread the message of the campaign but **Ralph Abernathy's leadership lacked** the momentum that Martin Luther King might have provided. Bad press, Robert Kennedy's assassination, and an underwhelming number of protesters (7,000 at its peak) further limited the campaign's effectiveness. The protesters demanded a $30 billion anti-poverty package that would include a commitment to full employment, a guaranteed annual income, and increased construction of low-income housing. Failing to force a response from legislators, the Poor People's Campaign closed camp on June 24, 1968.

July 1968 – The Black Panthers sponsor the **"Free Huey" Rally** in front of the Alameda County Courthouse for release of Party Defense Minister, Huey P. Newton who was convicted of manslaughter and sentenced to 2–15 years in federal prison.

Women's Movement:

September 1968 – Women's liberation groups protest the Miss America Beauty Pageant in Atlantic City. Among them was **Robin Morgan** who led members of the *New York Radical Women* to protest the sexist and racist Miss America Pageant.

1968 – The first national women's liberation conference is held in Lake Villa, Chicago, Illinois.

1968 – The National Abortion Rights Action League (NARAL) is founded by **Betty Friedan** and others.

1968 – Coretta Scott King assumes leadership of the African-American Civil Rights Movement following the death of her husband, and expands the movement's platform to include women's rights.

1968 – The EEOC rules sex-segregated help wanted ads in newspapers illegal, a ruling which is upheld in 1973 by the Supreme Court. Women now are able to apply for higher-paying jobs previously opened only to men.

1968 – New York feminists bury a dummy of "**Traditional Womanhood**" at the all-women's Jeanette Rankin Brigade demonstration against the war in Vietnam in Washington, D.C.

1968 – For the first time, feminists use the slogan "**Sisterhood is Powerful.**"

1968 – The first public speakout against abortion laws is held in New York City.

1968 – NOW celebrates Mother's Day with the slogan **"Rights, Not Roses."**

November 1968 – Shirley Chisholm of New York is the first black woman elected to the U.S. Congress.

1968 – Feminists disrupt the Students for a Democratic Society (SDS), national convention to protest sexism within the organization.

1968

Popular Culture:

1968 – Overview. The Boomers are between 4 and 22 years old. At its root, 1968 is the key year of the war in Vietnam as it pushes the rapid growth of a mass antiwar movement. My Lai massacre of women and children by the U.S. army and the subsequent attempted cover-up brings the most dishonorable side of the war home to Americans. The strains and pressures this puts on the world economy leads to the end of the "long boom" and a decade of sharp economic crises. It is the year that the U.S. Civil Rights Movement turns into "Black Power", triggered by the assassination of Martin Luther King. The voice of all those who are denied equal rights, jobs and wages, inspires women to demand their rights as well. Gays and lesbians find their voice. It is the year of hundreds of student occupations, of barricade fighting in Paris, which turns into a general strike by eleven million workers. The cry for revolution is heard as the decisive split in the U.S. is forming between change and business as usual. **The stakes are high and every aspect of American life is changing.**

1968 – The film industry announces a rating system: **"G"** for general audiences; **"M"** for mature audiences; **"R,"** no one under 16 admitted without an adult guardian; and **"X,"** no one under 16 admitted.

1968 – 24,500 U.S. military reservists are called to action for a two-year commitment.

1968 – The Student Mobilization Committee holds the largest student strike against the war and thousands of protesters march in San Francisco and New York.

February 13, 1968 – Ford's Theatre, the site of the **assassination** of **President Abraham Lincoln** in 1865, is reopened to the public. It had been restored to its original appearance and use as a theatre, now comprising the Ford's Theatre National Historic Site.

February 8, 1968 – Orangeburg, South Carolina. The Orangeburg Massacre. Students from an almost all-black college attempt to bowl at the city's only bowling alley and the owner refuses to allow them. Two nights later the students start a bonfire and gather in protest. As an officer attempts to put out the fire he is injured by a piece of banister thrown at him. The police later said they thought they were under attack by small weapons fire. Protesters said they did not fire on the police but only threw things at them. Tension is high and the police fire into a crowd of young people protesting the segregation of the bowling alley. The police kill three and injure twenty–seven, shooting most of them in the back. Evidence that police were being fired on was inconclusive.

1968 – The Pill. David Niven and Deborah Kerr star in the Hollywood film **"Prudence and the Pill."** Birth control once considered obscene and vulgar, is now a pop culture icon.

1968 – The Park Theater in Los Angeles is the first theater to commercially show films with **male nudity** and gay themes.

1968 – The "**Ride-a-Roo**" ball is launched in England with the help of the "Ride a Roo" song by Theresa Brewer. It never really caught on in the U.S. although the multi-color cube game called **Instant Insanity** did very well.

1968 – The "Monkey Trial" revisited! In the case of Epperson et al. vs. Arkansas, the U.S. Supreme Court finds the state of Arkansas' law prohibiting the teaching of evolution in a public school or university unconstitutional. A state cannot alter any element in a course of study in order to promote a religious point of view. A state's attempt to hide behind a nonreligious motivation will not be given credence unless that state can show a secular reason as the foundation for its actions.

March 16, 1968 – Mai Lai. A group of **U.S. soldiers attack the South Vietnamese village of My Lai,** believed to be a Communist stronghold, and kill between 347 and 504 civilians as well as committing rape and other crimes. U.S. helicopter pilot, Hugh Thompson and two crewmen, who were flying a reconnaissance mission over My Lai, see the dead bodies and stop to investigate. In the process, they managed to rescue a group of Vietnamese civilians from American troops. Although Thompson reports the incident to his superiors, the American public did not learn about it until over a year later, after a former soldier named Ronald L. Ridenhour wrote letters about what happened at My Lai to President Richard Nixon and other government officials. Ridenhour had found out about the events a month after they occurred from soldiers who were there and gathered eye witness and participant accounts.

The Army eventually launched an investigation that led to the conviction of platoon leader **Lt. William L. Calley, Jr.,** for the **murder of 22 unarmed men, women and children**. In 1971, Calley was sentenced to life in prison, which was later reduced to 10 years. Ultimately, he served three years under house arrest. **The My Lai massacre** left many Americans even further disillusioned about the Vietnam War. The average person is horrified that U.S. soldiers would commit such atrocities against women and children. As they then looked at the military cover-up they lost faith in our government for allowing it to happen and in our military for thinking it was not that important. They asked, "Why was Lt. Calley the only person convicted for the murders?"

In the spring of 1972, the camp (at My Lai 2) where the **survivors of the My Lai Massacre had been relocated was largely destroyed by Army of the Republic of Vietnam artillery and aerial bombardment**. The destruction was officially attributed to "Viet Cong terrorists." However, the truth was revealed by Quaker service workers in the area, through testimony, in May 1972, by Martin Teitel at hearings before the Congressional Subcommittee to Investigate Problems Connected with Refugees and Escapees. They were attacked by the South Vietnamese army, ARVN, which existed from October 26, 1955 until the fall of Saigon on April 30, 1975. In the U.S. we cover-up the evidence, in most of the rest of the world they just kill the evidence.

May 1968 – Catonsville Nine. Philip Francis Berrigan, after being released on bail, decided to repeat a 1967 protest when he and others poured blood on draft records. A local high-school physics teacher helped Berrigan mix homemade napalm and nine activists, who later became known as the Catonsville Nine, walked into the **draft board** of Catonsville, Maryland, removed draft records and **burned 378 draft files** in a lot outside of the building. The Catonsville Nine, who were all Catholic, issued a statement: "We confront the Roman Catholic Church, other Christian bodies, and the synagogues of America with their silence and cowardice in the face of our country's crimes. We are convinced that the religious bureaucracy in this country is racist, is an accomplice in this war, and is hostile to the poor." Berrigan is again arrested and sentenced to three and a half years in prison. **The Catonsville Nine,** priests, nuns, and lay Catholics, consisted of: **Father Daniel Berrigan**, a Jesuit priest, **Philip Berrigan**, a former Josephite priest, **Brother David Darst**, **John Hogan**, **Tom Lewis**, **Marjorie Bradford Melville**, **Thomas Melville**, a former Maryknoll priest, **George Mische**, and **Mary Moylan**, a former nun.

August 1968 – An August Gallup poll shows 53% said it was a mistake to send troops to Vietnam.

September 1968 – Mattel's Hot Wheels toy cars are introduced.

1968 – Drug Abuse Control Amendments. DACA Amendments Provide that the sentence may be suspended and the record expunged if no further violations occur within 1 year. The **Bureau of Narcotics and Dangerous Drugs** (BNDD), a predecessor agency of the Drug Enforcement Administration (DEA) is formed as a subsidiary of the United States Department of Justice.

1960-1968 – Lava Brand Motion Lamps are advertised as "head trips that offered a motion for every emotion."

April 23, 1968 – The United Methodist Church is created by the union of the former Methodist and Evangelical United Brethren churches.

1968 – American Tourister invents, "The Gorilla" commercials. Doyle, Dane Bernbach.

1968 – The price of a **Hershey bar** doubles in price from 5 to 10 cents.

1968 – Wisk detergent, **"Ring around the collar."**

1968 – U.S. Student Strike. In the spring of 1968, **National SDS** activists led an effort on the campuses called **"Ten Days of Resistance"** and local chapters cooperated with the **Student Mobilization Committee** in rallies, marches, sit-ins and teach-ins, which

1968

culminate in a one-day strike on April 26. **About a million students** stayed away from classes that day, the **largest student strike** in the history of the United States.

1968 – *LIFE* magazine confronts Americas Drug Problem: Diet pills to acid trips.

December 1968 – The son of former President **Dwight D. Eisenhower, David Eisenhower,** marries **Julie Nixon**, the daughter of U.S. President-elect **Richard Nixon**. And the beat goes on . . .

Business / Technology:

July-August 1968 – Farm Workers Union. Cesar Estrada Chavez founded and led the first successful farm workers' union in U.S. history. He conducted a 25 day fast in 1968 to reaffirm the UFW's commitment to non-violence. The late Senator **Robert F. Kennedy** called Cesar "one of the heroic figures of our time," and flew to Delano to be with him when he ended the fast.

1968 – Sony develops the Trinitron color television tube.

1968 – Data General Corp., started by a group of engineers that left Digital Equipment Corp., introduces the Nova minicomputer, with 32 kilobytes of memory, for $8,000.

May 1968 – France. What began as a student protest developed into a nationwide general strike with 11million workers on strike, 122 factories occupied, and students fighting against **"the system."**

1968 – Sales of the Pill hit the $150 million mark and American women can now select from 7 different brands.

1968 – An Intel 1 KB RAM microchip reaches the market.

1968 – Douglas Engelbart links the keyboard, keypad, and mouse. He invented the computer mouse.

December 21, 1968 – Apollo 8 is the first manned space voyage to achieve enough velocity to escape from the gravitational field of planet Earth; the first to escape from the gravitational field of another celestial body; and the first manned voyage to return to planet Earth from another celestial body, Earth's Moon. The three-man crew consisted of Mission Commander **Frank Borman,** Command Module Pilot **James Lovell,** and Lunar Module Pilot **William Anders.** The three become the first humans to see the far side of the Moon with their own eyes, as well as the first humans to see planet Earth from orbit about another celestial body. The mission was the second manned mission of the Apollo Program and the first manned launch of a Saturn V rocket.

1968 – Hospital Corp. of America is founded.

Finance:

1968 – Marks the first time in United States history that a paper currency designated as legal tender, is not directly or indirectly redeemable in **silver or gold coin or bullion.** On March 25, 1964, C. Douglas Dillon, the 57th Secretary of the Treasury announced that silver certificates would no longer be redeemable in silver dollars. This decision was pursuant to the Act of June 4, 1963 (31 U.S.C. 405a-1). The Act allowed the exchange of silver certificates for silver bullion until June 24, 1968. This was the deadline set by the Congress. Since that date, there has been no obligation to issue silver in any form in exchange for these certificates. Congress took this action because there were approximately three million silver dollars remaining in the Treasury Department's vaults. These coins had high numismatic values, and there was no way to make an equitable distribution of them among the many people holding silver certificates. Silver certificates are still legal tender and do still circulate at their face value. Depending upon the age and condition of the certificates, they may have a numismatic value to collectors and dealers.

1963-1969 – The National Debt increased every year Johnson was in office, and he was also the last President, until **President Clinton,** to submit a **balanced budget.** Johnson increased the debt on average 3% and he had a Democratic Congress to work with all his years in office. Johnson used the veto power 30 times and is the last President to have no overrides.

1968 – The U.S. Congress passes the **Truth in Lending Act**, designed to promote economic stability by protecting the credit rights of consumers by requiring clear disclosure of key terms of the lending arrangement and all costs. The act states consumers will no longer be subject to fine print and misleading credit applications.

   Monday, July 07, 2008. The Courts **may Begin Enforcing** Truth-in-Lending Act. "A lawsuit filed by a Wisconsin couple against their mortgage lender could have major implications for banks should a U.S. appeals court agree that borrowers can cancel their loans en masse when their lenders violate a federal lending disclosure law."

1968 – **King of the fugitive financiers. Robert Vesco** grew up in Detroit, Michigan. He dropped out of engineering school in his early twenties to go to work for an investment firm and after a brief period of time, he borrowed $800 to start his own business matching buyers and sellers in the aluminum market. While gaining market knowledge he acquired a portion of the profits of a floundering aluminum plant and by 1965, he was in a position to borrow enough money to acquire **International Controls Corporation.** Through aggressively hostile expansions and debt-financed takeovers of other businesses he grew ICC quickly and by 1968 the company owned an airline and several manufacturing plants. Robert Vesco held shares totaling $50 million. In 1970 he went on to buy **Investors Overseas Service** from Bernie Cornfeld, loot the company of $220 million dollars and survive as **"the undisputed king of the fugitive financiers."**

1968 – **The London gold pool sustains enormous losses** and is discontinued. The two-tier gold price is established, one tier is for official monetary transactions, the other is for open-market transactions.

Books:

1968 – Tom Wolfe, **"The Electric Kool-Aid Acid Test."**

1968 – "Notes from the First Year," a women's liberation theoretical journal is published by the New York Radical Women.

1968 – "Welcome to the Monkey House," Kurt Vonnegut.

1968 – Arthur C. Clarke, **"2001: A Space Odyssey."**

1968 – "The Whole Earth Catalog" is an American counterculture catalog that granted "Access to Tools" published by Stewart Brand between 1968 and 1972, and occasionally thereafter, until 1998. Apple Inc. founder and entrepreneur Steve Jobs has described the catalog as the conceptual forerunner of the World Wide Web.

TV:

January 21-April 8, 1968 – The siege of Khe Sanh. Khe Sanh Combat Base is a United States Marine Corps outpost in South Vietnam that is under siege for 77 days from North Vietnamese/ Vietcong mortar attacks. A force estimated at between 20,000–40,000 North Vietnamese troops attacks the U.S. Marine garrison and Military Assistance Command Vietnam is convinced that the communists plan to overrun the base and then make an all-out effort to seize the two northernmost provinces of South Vietnam. To prevent this enemy advance General William Westmoreland deployed 250,000 men, including half of MACV's U.S. maneuver battalions, to the I Corps Tactical Zone.

On July 5, 1968, the U.S. Army citing the vulnerability of Khe Sanh to enemy artillery abandons the base. The closure allows the 3rd Marine Division to construct mobile firebase operations along the northern border area.

January 31, 1968 – The Tet Offensive begins. The North Vietnamese and Vietcong simultaneously attack all major South Vietnamese cities and briefly occupy the American embassy in Saigon. South Vietnamese and U.S. military intelligence estimated that communist forces in South Vietnam during January 1968 totaled 323,000 men, including 130,000 North Vietnamese regulars, 160,000 Viet Cong and members of the infrastructure, and 33,000 service and support troops.

January 31, 1968 – The Battle of Hue, one of the bloodiest and longest battles of the Vietnam War, begins. House by house fighting destroys thousands of homes, inflicting heavy civilian casualties. The Communist forces suffered heavy losses, losing 8,200 men in and around Hue. Eighty percent of the city was destroyed by American firepower.

The Vietnam War is brought to the evening news day-after-day-after-day. Each news cast gives the number of VC dead and the number of American causalities. The "score" is important and often the numbers are made up out of thin air. And America watched it on TV every night as families ate dinner together. The oldest Boomer is 22 years old; the youngest Boomer is 4 years old.

April 4, 1968 – James Brown appears on national television, in an attempt to calm feelings of anger in the United States following the **assassination** of **Reverend Martin Luther King Jr.**

December 1968 – Apollo 8. The largest audience to ever hear a human voice. After launching on December 21, 1968, the crew takes three days to travel to the **Moon.** They orbit ten times over the course of 20 hours, during which the crew make a **Christmas Eve television broadcast**, in which **they read the first 10 verses from the Book of Genesis.** The crew timed this reading to coincide with a full view of planet Earth hanging in the empty blackness of space clearly showing the rich diversity of the living planet. On the Earth, seas, landforms, and weather patterns, are visible in color as the dull gray horizon of the lifeless Moon is shown simultaneously in the foreground. At the time, the broadcast was the most watched TV program ever. Apollo 8's successful mission paved the way for Apollo 11 to fulfill U.S. President John F. Kennedy's goal of landing a man on the Moon before the end of the decade.

Sports:

1968 – Student riots in Mexico City threaten the Mexico Olympic Games. Thousand of students are gathered together by the National Strike Council to protest against the military occupation of the National Polytechnic Institute. Many of the protesters are women and children planning to march through a working–class suburb but are surrounded by Mexican military personnel in armored vehicles. The Mexican government will later say "agitator groups" among the students began shooting into the crowds. Protesters say the Mexican military began shooting into the crowd. Whoever started the shooting it led to a 90-minute gun fight that killed more than 25 people and injured hundreds more, just days before the Olympic Games are to begin.

1968 – Peggy Fleming an American figure skater wins an Olympic gold medal.

1968 – Jean-Claude Killy, alpine skier, wins three gold medals at the Winter Olympics.

1968 – Summer Olympic Games in Mexico City Bob Beamon's incredible record-setting long jump is 29 feet, 2 1/2 inches, (8.9m)

1968 – Arthur Ashe becomes the first African American to win the Men's Singles competition in the U.S. Open. He will go on to win two more and win both the U.S. Amateur and the U.S Open championships in 1968. This is the only time such a double win has been accomplished.

October 16, 1968 – The Summer Olympic games in Mexico City. Black sprinters raise their fists for civil rights. San Jose State athletes Tommie Smith and John Carlos raise their fists in the black power salute during their medal ceremony to protest the treatment of African Americans. Smith and Carlos wear wraps around their necks to protest lynching and they are not wearing shoes to protest poverty. Australian silver medalist Peter Norman wears a solidarity patch on his Olympic jacket so the world will know which side he is on. It is still being talked about when their statue is commemorated some 40 years later.

November 17, 1968 – Heidi Football. "Heidi" is a character in Johanna Spyri's 1880s children's tale, and when it was adapted for the movies she still did not play football. On November 17, at 7 p.m. EST she became forever linked to Joe Namath in the minds of pro football fans.

With **65 seconds** remaining in the game, the **New York Jets take a 32-29 lead** over Oakland when Jim Turner kicks a 26–yard field goal. The Raiders returned the kickoff to their 23-yard line. NBC is televising the game and cuts to a commercial break **and**

1968

never comes back to the game! The TV schedule called for the movie "Heidi" to begin at 7 p.m. and it starts right on time.

What the nation didn't see was this: Oakland quarterback Daryle Lamonica's 20-yard pass to Charlie Smith and a face-mask penalty put the ball at the Jets 43-yard line. On the next play, Lamonica and Smith come together on a touchdown pass. Oakland leads 36-32 with 42 seconds to play. The Jets fumble the kickoff, Oakland's Preston Ridlehuber recovers at the 2 yard line and scores! **Oakland wins 43-32, with two TDs in nine seconds.**

Music:

January 13, 1968 – Johnny Cash performs his famous concert at **Folsom Prison** in California.

January 1968 – The Beatles launch Apple Corps, Ltd., a disastrously mismanaged entertainment company that included a recording studio, a record label, and clothing store.

February 16, 1968 – The Beatles, Mike Love, Mia Farrow, Donovan and others travel to India to visit the **Maharishi Mahesh Yogi** at Rishikesh.

February 18, 1968 – Pink Floyd, founder Syd Barrett, checks himself into a psychiatric hospital.

May 14, 1968 – The Beatles announce the creation of **Apple Records**, a division of Apple Corps, in a New York press conference.

May 17, 1968 – The Catonsville Nine enter the Selective Service offices in Catonsville, Maryland, take dozens of selective service draft records and burn them with napalm as a protest against the Vietnam War.

1968 – New Jersey Police confiscate 30,000 copies of **John Lennon and Yoko Ono**'s *Two Virgins* album at Newark Airport, saying that the cover, which features a nude photo of the two artists, is **"pornographic."** In Chicago, Illinois, police officers shut down a record shop for displaying the album cover.

Natural Disasters:

1968 – The Hong Kong flu becomes the third flu pandemic of the 20th century and kills about 1,000,000 people worldwide. The Hong Kong Flu is also the last pandemic until the Swine Flu pandemic of 2009. Ordinary flu kills about 250,000 to 500,000 people each year.

August 31-September 1, 1968 – Iran. The Dasht-e Bayaz and Ferdows earthquakes are two successive earthquakes that kill between 7,000 and 12,000 people. More than 175 villages are destroyed or damaged in these earthquakes.

Man vs. Man / Wars:

Assassinated – Canada. Sergio Perez Castillo, a Cuban diplomat is killed by anti-Castro forces in Montreal.

August 13, 1968 – Greece. Georgios Papadopoulos, the leader of the military government, is in route from his summer residence in Lagonisi to Athens when his motorcade is attacked. Alexandros Panagoulis detonates a bomb near, but not directly under the limousine, which fails to harm Papadopoulos. A few hours later Panagoulis is captured in a cave by the sea while he is waiting for the boat sent to pick him up. The boat had arrived but the currents were too strong for him to swim out to it. Panagoulis is arrested beaten, tortured and sentenced to death. He will be released from prison in five years after the restoration of Democracy.

Assassinated – The U.S. Ambassador to Guatemala. August 28, 1968. The U.S. Ambassador to Guatemala, **John Gordon Mein,** is assassinated by a rebel faction when gunmen force his official car off the road in Guatemala City and rake the vehicle with gunfire.

1968

1968 – The Zodiac Killer. A serial killer who operates in Northern California, murders at least 5 people but claims responsibility for as many as 17 murders in the San Francisco area. The killer sends a total of 21 letters to the media with details only the killer would know. He sends in diagrams of plans to bomb a school bus, but the attack never takes place. "School children make nice targets, I think I shall wipe out a school bus some morning," the Zodiac wrote. Over 2,500 people are considered suspects. The killings stopped, but the letters kept coming until 1974. No one knows if the Zodiac is still alive. His identity remains unknown.

1973 – The Popular Front for the Liberation of Palestine attack an El Al aircraft with machine guns at Athens airport in Greece. An Israeli is killed and two terrorists are captured but later released by the Greek government after a Greek aircraft is hijacked to Beirut. Three days after the Athens attack, Israeli commandos raid Beirut airport in Lebanon and blow up 13 Arab airliners worth $43 million dollars.

1930-1968 – Political assassination. There were 57 incidents of political assassination **in the U.S.** from 1930 to 1968.

February 9, 1968 – A military charter flight out of South Vietnam is involved in an unsuccessful hijacking attempt by a U.S. Marine.

February 17, 1968 – Thomas J. Boynton hijacks a private charter Piper Apache from Marathon, Florida to Cuba. November 1, 1969 he returned to the United States by way of Canada on and was sentenced to 20 years for kidnapping.

February 21, 1968 – Lawrence Rhodes hijacks a DC-8 from Tampa, Florida to Cuba. He surrenders in Spain on February 10, 1970. A January 4, 1971 hijacking charge against him is dismissed. He is committed to a mental institution and is returned to prison on July 8, 1971. He is sentenced to 25 years for robbery on July 17, 1972.

March 12, 1968 – Three Cuban fugitives hijack a DC-8 from Tampa, Florida to Cuba.

July 1, 1968 – Velasquez Fonseca, born in Cuba, hijacks a Boeing 727 from Chicago to Cuba.

July 12, 1968 – Leonard Bendicks hijacks a Cessna 210 from Key West, Florida, to Cuba. He is deported to the U.S. in September 1968. On March 4, 1971, he is sentenced to 10 years for kidnapping.

July 17, 1968 – Hernandez Leyva, a Cuban, hijacks a DC-8 from Los Angeles to Cuba.

July 23, 1968 – An El Al 707 carrying 10 crew and 38 passengers is the target of the first Arab hijacking of an El Al plane. Three members of the Popular Front for the Liberation of Palestine (PFLP) hijacked the plane which was enroute from Rome, Italy to Lydda, Israel and diverted it to Algiers. Negotiations last 40 days until both the hijackers and the 21 Israeli hostages went free. This was the first and only successful hijacking of an El Al flight.

August 4, 1968 – A Cessna 182 from Naples, Florida is hijacked by Jessie Willis and forced to fly to Cuba. He will voluntarily return to the U.S. on January 10, 1969 and will be sentenced to 10 years for kidnapping. He will be paroled on July 28, 1971.

August 22, 1968 – A Cessna 336 is hijacked by Bill McBride from Nassau and forced to fly to Cuba.

October 23, 1968 – A Cessna 177 from Key West is hijacked by Alben Truitt, the grandson of former U.S. Vice President Alben Barkley, and forced to fly to Cuba. He returns to the U.S. in February 1969 and is sentenced to 20 years for aircraft piracy and 20 years for kidnapping.

November 4, 1968 – A Boeing 727 from New Orleans is hijacked by Raymond Johnson and forced to fly to Cuba.

November 23, 1968 – Five Cubans hijack a Boeing 727 from Chicago to Cuba.

November 24, 1968 – Three Cubans hijack a Boeing 707 from New York to Cuba.

November 30, 1968 – Montesino Sanchez, a Cuban, hijacks a Boeing 720 from Miami to Cuba.

1968

December 5, 1968 – A Boeing 727 from Tampa is hijacked by Eduardo Castera and forced to fly to Cuba.

December 11, 1968 – Two men hijack a DC-8 from St. Louis to Cuba.

1968 – Cambodia. Prince Sihanouk of Cambodia tells U.S. representatives that he will not stop American forces from pursuing the Vietcong across the Cambodian border.

1968 – Congo. Military Coup. President Massamba-Debat's term ends abruptly in August, when Captain Marien Ngouabi and other army officers topple the government in a coup. After a period of consolidation under the newly formed National Revolutionary Council, Major Ngouabi assumes the Presidency on December 31, 1968.

August 20, 1968 – Czechoslovakia. Prague Spring. Around midnight citizens of Czechoslovakia are awakened to the sound of tanks rolling through their cities. At first no one knew what was happening. Then as the troops followed the tanks, residents became aware this is a full scale invasion of **Czechoslovakia** by the **Soviet Union.** Warsaw Pact forces, including troops from Bulgaria, the German Democratic Republic (East Germany), Hungary, Poland, and the Soviet Union, will reach approximately 500,000 troops and the country will remain occupied until 1990.

1968 – Colombia. FARC Insurgency. The FARC was founded in 1966 by Manuel Marulanda Vélez, and other members of the Central Committee of the Communist Party of Colombia. As many as 500 armed militants and several thousand peasants were recruited. FARC operations included raids on military posts and facilities, which enabled the organization to accumulate weapons, ammunition, military uniforms, and communications equipment. The government's counterinsurgency campaign and the opening of diplomatic relations between Colombia and the Soviet Union weaken the organization and by the early 1970s, FARC is no longer a threat.

1968 – Congo Coup. President Massamba-Debat is removed from office in August when Captain Marien Ngouabi and other army officers topple the government in a coup. After a period of consolidation under the newly formed National Revolutionary Council, Major Ngouabi assumes the Presidency on December 31.

1968-1974 – Dhofar Revolt. (not to be confused with the genocide in Darfur). In early 1968 the Dhofar rebels changed the name of their organization to the Peoples Front for the Liberation of Oman and the Arabian Gulf. Their emblem, showing an arm holding an **AK-47 rifle in red, has a background** with a map delineating the territory they hope to liberate, including what are now the independent states of Bahrain, Qatar, the United Arab Emirates, and Oman. With a secure supply base in the new Peoples Democratic Republic of South Yemen, the PFLOAG rebels present a considerable threat not only to Dhofar but the rest of the sultanate. When the British withdrew in 1971 Sultan Qaboos moved quickly to suppress the Dhofar revolt. He brought in troops from Iran and also sought to win the allegiance of the disaffected tribes in Dhofar. Unlike the rebels he stressed his allegiance to Muslim values and promised to work for the independence and development of the country. Combining these policies removed support for the rebels and Sultan Qaboos had effectively defeated them militarily by 1975.

1968-1970 – Egypt. The War of Attrition is a limited war fought between forces of **Egypt and the Palestine Liberation Organization** against **Israel.** It is initiated by Egypt as a way to force Israel to negotiate on favorable terms the return of the Sinai Peninsula, which was captured by Israel in the 1967 Six-Day War. When the hostilities end with a ceasefire in 1970 the borders are the same as when the war began and there is no real commitment to serious peace negotiations.

1968 – Equatorial Guinea, officially the **Republic of Equatorial Guinea** becomes independent from Spain. Pre-independence Equatorial Guinea counted on cocoa production for hard currency earnings and it had the highest per capita income of Africa in 1959.

   Francisco Macías Nguema is the first President of Equatorial Guinea, from 1968 until his overthrow in 1979. The country had become well known for it's for political executions and virulent anti-Spanish radio speeches. The country's pre-independence Prime Minister, Bonifacio Ondó Edu, was starved and executed in prison. A former Vice President, "committed suicide" while in detention. Macías Nguema's was one of the worst African dictators of all time. His violations of human rights caused more than two-thirds of Equatorial Guinea's population to flee to other countries. In May of 1971, he repealed parts of the 1968 Constitution and granted himself "all direct powers of Government and Institutions," and in July he declared himself President for Life.

Nguema had 150 alleged coup plotters executed to the sound of a band playing Mary Hopkin's tune "Those Were the Days" in a national stadium on Christmas day 1975. He is responsible for up to 80,000 people's deaths in a country that had an estimated population of only 500,000 people.

1968 – Honduran-Salvadoran Tension. The nation's economic problems become worse and the Honduran government and many others blame the 300,000 undocumented Salvadoran immigrants for the high unemployment. Salvadoran immigrants have moved onto land they do not own and simply take possession and set up residence illegally.

July 17, 1968 – Iraq. Baath Party Coup. Ahmad Hasan al-Bakr **overthrows** Abdel-Rahman **Aref.** The Ba'ath coup includes street fighting as Communist activists and supporters resist the coup attempt and the fighting in Baghdad continues for three days, concentrated in the party's strongholds in the poorer, mainly **Shia, districts.** Following the takeover thousands of people are executed, assassinated, and intimidated as the Baath party removes any opposition to **Saddam Hussein,** a relative of Bakr, as he consolidates his power.

The CIA and Saddam Hussein seemed to have some things in common. Saddam Hussein was not an Islamic fundamentalist along the lines of the Iranian ayatollahs and he did not appear to be a communist.

1968 – Ireland. Violence erupts in Ireland between Catholics and Protestants.

December 28-29, 1968 – Israeli Raid on Beirut. The commandos are from the Army's elite Sayeret Matkal. They blow up 13 Arab airliners worth $43 million belonging to Middle East Airlines in response to an attack on an Israeli airliner in

Athens by the Popular Front for the Liberation of Palestine. There were no casualties reported.

November 1968 – Republic of Mali. Military Coup. In November 1968, following progressive economic decline, the Keïta regime is overthrown in a military coup led by Moussa Traoré. The subsequent military-led regime, with Traoré as President, attempts to reform the economy, but his efforts are frustrated by political turmoil and a devastating drought from 1968 to 1974. As the government continues to reform the economy the people continue to call for democratic free elections and the regime allows some limited political liberalization, without giving up control.

1968 – Peru. Military Coup. By the mid-1960s, many intellectuals and government officials see land reform as an urgent economic problem as well as a matter of social justice. Even the army believes that land reform must change the people's lifestyle before any real industrial development can take place.

Tanks surround the Presidential Palace on October 3, and General Velasco and the army seize power. Peru is now ruled by a military junta consisting of the President and the commanders of the three armed forces.

The new government goes about giving the land back to the peasants in 1969 and the great plantations are turned into cooperatives overnight. The peasant class is given control of their futures while the **guerrilla leaders are brought to trial.** Political activity is banned in the universities, indigenous banks are controlled, foreign banks are nationalized and diplomatic relations are established with East European countries. The return to civilian rule begins in July 1979.

1968 – The Corregidor Massacre of 1968. Historically, the Bangsamoro people settled the geographical areas of Mindanao and Sabah. Following the eviction of the Japanese and the departure of the formal American influence, the **Philippine government** reestablished control over the Bangsamoro settled areas of Mindanao, Basilan, Sulu, Tawi-Tawi and the Palawan islands on July 4, 1946. During the early 1960's President Macapagal wanted control over Sabah's wealth but Malaysia had already colonized Sabah and paid a tax to the family of the Sultanate of Sula. In 1967 **President Marcos of the Philippines** established a force of commandos to destabilize Saba so he could send in troops to "protect" the Filipinos living there. On December

1968

30, 1967, 150–180 recruits were sent to the island of Corregidor in Luzon for special training but the recruits found out their true mission may involve fighting their brother Muslims and maybe killing their own Tausug and Suma relatives. They demanded to be sent home. Under the pretext of going home groups of twelve were led out of their barracks and taken to a nearby airstrip where they were executed by gunfire. Jibin Arula, the loan survivor, said that he heard a series of shots and saw his colleagues fall. He ran towards a hill and rolled off the edge into the sea where he held onto a piece of driftwood until morning when he was rescued by fishermen.

1968 – Oman. The 1960s bring a threat to the imams' power base in the formation of a Marxist guerrilla movement, the Popular Front for the Liberation of Oman. The PFLO involve themselves in an existing minor rebellion in the hill regions of the southern province of **Dhofar**, and from 1968 they succeed in escalating this into a serious threat to the regime.

October 11, 1968 – Panama. Military Coup. Panama had consented to the U.S. military presence only for purposes of defending the Panama Canal and not as a major base of operations. The **Johnson Administration** wants increased U.S. military presence in Panama to be granted after the May 1968 elections. Charismatic and unpredictable **Arnulfo Arias** is elected Panama's President for the third time and the U.S. pushes for swift approval of the "three-in-one" treaties. Almost immediately after his inauguration, President Arias takes steps to reduce the power of the National Guard, which was supported financially by the U.S., and the Guard retaliated by staging a military coup on October 11, 1968, to keep their benefits and privileges.

1968 – Spain. Basque Terrorism. The economic pain inflicted on the Basque Country of Spain can be tied to the terrorist struggle that began in 1968 and continues through 2010. After **terrorism** became a way of life within the region, fears of violence, extortion and kidnapping by ETA separatists are responsible, on average, for a 10 percent drop in the area's per capita GDP. Furthermore, during a 1998-1999 cease-fire, stocks in the region responded by outperforming stocks from outside the region. Then, when the cease-fire was over, those same Basque-centered stocks, seemingly taking a cue from the return to trouble, drop below those of other regions.

January 1968 – VietNam. Tet Offensive. The war is coming to a stalemate and the guerrillas in the south are being slowly pushed back. General Vo Nguyen Giap, known for his audacity, is aiming for a quick and decisive victory to influence the result of the 1968 U.S. Presidential campaign. The attack on the small military base at Khe Sanh will draw necessary U.S. troops north leaving the southern areas more vulnerable to attack. And in fact it works brilliantly; the Americans were caught off guard by the rapidity and scope of the offensive.

The Tet Offensive is a series of surprise attacks by close to 85,000 combined Vietcong and North Vietnamese forces, on a multitude of cities, towns, and hamlets throughout South Vietnam. North Vietnam realizes it cannot continue to sustain the heavy causalities inflicted by the Americans and must have a military victory. The timing had to be now because Ho Chi Minh is close to death. The Tet Offensive is considered a turning point in the Vietnam War.

February 1968 – Vietnam. An additional 206,000 U.S. troops are requested by General Westmoreland and his request is **denied**. The Republic of Vietnam announces the call-up of 65,000 additional men for its armed forces.

1968 – Vietnam. A U.S. Gallup poll shows 50% of Americans disapprove of the President's management of the war.

1968 – Vietnam. Troops of the Republic of Vietnam retake the Citadel of the **Imperial Palace** at Hue. The remains of **2,000 Hue residents executed by the Communists** are discovered by South Vietnamese authorities.

March 16, 1968 – Vietnam. My Lai Massacre. In the hamlet of My Lai, north of Da Nang, unarmed civilians, consisting mostly of women, children and the elderly, are massacred by members of Charlie Company, Americal Division. Between 347 and 504 people are killed. Many of the victims were sexually abused, beaten, tortured, and some of the bodies were found mutilated. The massacre took place in the hamlets of Mỹ Lai and My Khe of Sơn Mỹ village. The memorial at the site of the massacre lists 504 names, with ages ranging from one year old to 82 years old.

General William C. Westmoreland, MACV commander, congratulated the unit on the "outstanding job," and the Army's *Stars and Stripes* magazine reported U.S.

infantrymen killed 128 Communists in a bloody day-long battle.

The 11th Light Infantry Brigade's commanding officer, Colonel Henderson, began initial investigations of the My Lai operation. The orders to investigate came from the Americal Division's executive officer, Brigadier General George H. Young.

Six months later Tom Glen, a 21-year-old soldier of the 11th Light Infantry Brigade, wrote a letter to General Creighton Abrams, the new overall commander of U.S. forces in Vietnam, accusing the Americal Division (and other entire units of the U.S. military) of routine and pervasive brutality against Vietnamese civilians. The letter was detailed and its contents echoed complaints received from other soldiers.

General Colin Powell, then a 31-year-old Army Major, is charged with investigating the letter, which does not specifically reference My Lai (Glen had limited knowledge of the events there). In his report Powell wrote: "In direct refutation of this portrayal is the fact that relations between American soldiers and the Vietnamese people are excellent." Powell's handling of the assignment is later characterized by some observers as "whitewashing" the atrocities of My Lai.

Eventually, LT Calley is charged with several counts of premeditated murder in September 1969, and 25 other officers and enlisted men are later charged with related crimes. On March 29, 1971, LT Calley is sentenced to life imprisonment at hard labor. On April 1, 1971, only a day after Calley was sentenced, **U.S. President Richard Nixon** ordered him transferred from prison to house arrest at Fort Benning, pending appeal. This leniency was protested by Melvin Laird, the Secretary of Defense. The prosecutor, Aubrey Daniel wrote, "The greatest tragedy of all will be if political expedience dictates the compromise of such a fundamental moral principle as the inherent unlawfulness of the murder of innocent persons." His sentence is later reduced to 20 years "hard labor". Ultimately, Calley would serve only three and a half years of house arrest in his quarters at Fort Benning. When the incident became public knowledge in 1969, it prompted widespread outrage around the world. The massacre also reduced U.S. support at home for the Vietnam War.

Three U.S. servicemen who made an effort to halt the massacre and protect the wounded were **denounced by U.S. Congressmen**, received hate mail, death threats and mutilated animals on their doorsteps. Only 30 years after the event were their efforts honored.

March 16, 1968 – My Lai. Hugh Thompson, Jr., a U.S. military helicopter pilot and his crew came upon U.S. troops killing civilians at the village of My Lai on March 16, 1968. He put his helicopter down between the soldiers and villagers, ordering his men to shoot their fellow Americans if they attacked the civilians. "There was no way I could turn my back on them," he later said of the victims. Mr. Thompson, a warrant officer at the time, called in support from other U.S. helicopters, and together they airlifted at least nine Vietnamese civilians, including a wounded 4 year old boy, to safety. He returned to headquarters, angrily telling his commanders what he had seen. They ordered soldiers in the area to stop shooting and the My Lai massacre was covered up, for awhile. Hugh Thompson was shunned for years by fellow soldiers, received death threats, and was once told by a congressman that he was the only American who should be punished over My Lai. **Chief Warrant Officer Hugh Thompson, Jr., the man who helped stop the My Lai massacre, has died at 62 on January 7, 2006. Thank you Hugh for having a moral compass and doing what needed to be done. America is grateful and in your debt.**

March 31, 1971 – President Richard Nixon; "Calley's crime was inexcusable. But I felt that many of the commentators and congressmen who professed outrage about My Lai were not really as interested in the moral questions raised by the Calley case as they were interested in using it to make political attacks against the Vietnam War. For one thing, they had been noticeably uncritical of North Vietnamese atrocities. In fact, the calculated and continual role that terror, murder, and massacre played in the Vietcong strategy was one of the most underreported aspects of the entire Vietnam War. . . .On March 31, 1971, the court-martial sentenced Calley to life in prison at hard labor. Public reaction to this announcement was emotional and sharply divided. More than 5,000 telegrams arrived at the White House, running 100 to 1 in favor of clemency. **John Connally** and **Jerry Ford** recommended in strong terms that I use my powers as Commander in Chief to reduce Calley's prison time. . . ."

As governor of Georgia, **Jimmy Carter** responded to the 1971 sentencing of Lt. William Calley by calling upon his fellow Georgians to **"honor the flag" as Calley had done,** and to leave their headlights on to show their support.

President Richard Nixon; "I called Admiral Moorer on April 1 and ordered that, pending Calley's appeal, he should be released from the stockade and confined instead to his quarters on the base. When this was announced to the House of

Representatives, there was a spontaneous round of applause on the floor." **"My Lai: a brief history with documents,"** By **James Stuart Olson, Randy Roberts**. A very good account of My Lai, an American Tragedy.

Indiana's governor, Edgar. Whitcomb, ordered all flags on state property to be flown at half-staff *in support of* LT. Calley. The **Arkansas, Kansas, Texas, New Jersey, and South Carolina legislatures** *requested clemency* **for Calley. Alabama's governor George Wallace** visited Calley in the stockade and requested that Nixon pardon him.

March 31, 1968 – Vietnam. President Johnson commits the U.S. to a non-military solution of the war when he announces he will not seek re-election, and orders a bombing halt, north of the 20th Parallel. This encompasses over 75% of North Vietnam.

May 1968 – Vietnam. The U.S. and North Vietnam agree to preliminary peace talks in Paris. The Vietcong launch a Mini-Tet with rocket and mortar attacks against Saigon and other towns across South Vietnam. The U.S. responds with air strikes on North Vietnam.

July 1968 – Vietnam. GIs serving time in the stockade at Fort Bragg, North Carolina take control of the prison from military police, while three American POWs are released by Hanoi.

October 1968 – An Anti-war protest organized and led by **Vietnam veterans** is held in San Francisco.

October 31, 1968 – Vietnam. President Johnson announces a halt to all bombing of North Vietnam on November 1, and increases bombing of Laos. U.S. bombing "sorties" are shifted to Laos. From November 1, 1968 through 1972, over 25,000 sorties are flown, with the most occurring in 1971.

1968 – Vietnam. "Draftees" account for 38% of all American troops in Vietnam. Over 12% of the draftees are college graduates.

1968 – Vietnam. Robert F. Kennedy concluded that victory in Vietnam was "probably beyond our grasp," and called for a peaceful settlement.

1968 – Historian Robert Dallek writes, "Lyndon Johnson's escalation of the war in Vietnam divided Americans into warring camps... cost 30,000 American lives by the time he left office, (and) destroyed Johnson's presidency..." His refusal to send more U.S. troops to Vietnam was seen as Johnson's admission that the war was lost. It can be seen that the refusal was a tacit admission that the war could not be won by escalation, at least not at a cost acceptable to the American people. As Secretary of Defense Robert McNamara noted, "the dangerous illusion of victory by the United States was therefore dead."

1968 – Vietnam. U.S. troops in Vietnam number **536,000** at the end of the year.

1968 – Vietnam. South Vietnamese forces number approximately **800,000.**

July 26, 1968 – Vietnam. South Vietnamese opposition leader Truong Dinh Dzu is sentenced to 5 years hard labor, for advocating the formation of a coalition government as a way to move toward an end to the war.

1968 – Vietnam. There are more than 16,000 total U.S. deaths in Vietnam for the year.

1968 – Vietnam. There are approximately 28,000 deaths of South Vietnamese troops for the year.

1969

The Oldest Boomer is 23 years old.

Cost of the Average House: $27,900	
Median Family Income: $8,389	**Minimum Wage:** $1.60/ hr **Average Hourly Wage:** $3.19
Gallon of Milk: $1.08	**Gallon Gasoline:** 35 cents
New Car: **Pontiac Firebird Trans Am:** $4,366 **BMW 2002:** $4,200	
Unemployment Rate: 3.4%-3.7%-3.5%	**First-class Stamp:** 6 cents

17 cents buying power in 1969 = **$1.00 in 2008.**
In 1969 what cost us 17 cents to purchase now costs us $1.00 in 2008.

Movies: "Midnight Cowboy" is the first major film that is x-rated. "Butch Cassidy and the Sundance Kid," "The Wild Bunch," "Easy Rider," "They Shoot Horses, Don't They?" "Anne of a Thousand Days," "Z," "Hello, Dolly!" "True Grit," "The Italian Job" with Michael Caine. "Cactus Flower".

Broadway: "Oh Calcutta!" off-Broadway-revue. "Promises, Promises," London.

TV: "The Eagle Has Landed; Two Men Walk on the Moon," Buzz Aldrin and Neil Armstrong, July 20. "The Brady Bunch," "Turn-On," "Monty Python's Flying Circus," "Marcus Welby, M.D." "The Dudley Do-Right Show," "The New Beat the Clock," "Sesame Street," "Love, American Style," "The Galloping Gourmet." "The Bill Cosby Show," "Scooby-Doo, Where Are You!" "Hot Wheels," "The Courtship of Eddie's Father."

Music: "Once Upon a Time in the West," "Easy Rider." Woodstock: 500,000 in attendance. Diana Ross Presents, "The Jackson 5." Diana Ross & The Supremes, "Someday We'll Be Together." The Archies, 'Sugar Sugar." Creedence Clearwater Revival, "Proud Mary." Zager and Evans, "In the

Year 2525." Kenny Rogers and The First Edition, "But You Know I Love You" & "Ruby, Don't Take Your Love to Town." Stevie Wonder, "My Cherie Amour." Blood, Sweat & Tears, "Spinning Wheel." Crazy Elephant, "Gimme, Gimme Good Lovin'." Bob Dylan, "Lay Lady Lay." Crosby, Stills & Nash, "Judy Blue Eyes." Dionne Warwick, "You've Lost That Lovin' Feeling." Led Zeppelin, "Whole Lotta Love." The Rolling Stones, "Honky Tonk Woman." Tommy James & the Shondells, "Crimson and Clover." The Who, "Pinball Wizard." Sly & the Family Stone, "Everyday People." The Beatles, "Get Back." Stevie Wonder, "Yester-Me, Yester-You, Yesterday." Fifth Dimension, "Aquarius, Let the Sunshine In." Jethro Tull, "Living In The Past." B. J. Thomas, "Raindrops Keep Fallin' on My Head." The Beach Boys, "I Can Hear Music." Elvis Presley, "Suspicious Minds" & "In the Ghetto."

Deaths: Meredith Hunter.

President: Richard M. Nixon (R) Quaker; vetoes 43/7overrides

Vice President: Spiro T. Agnew (R) Episcopalian

House: D-243 ; R-192

Senate: 91st Congress (1969-1971) Majority Party: Democrat (57 seats) Minority Party: Republican (43 seats) Other Parties: 0 Total Seats: 100

Federal Debt: $353.72 billion or 36 % of the GDP

Consumer Price Index CPI-U (1982 Base of 100): 36.70

GDP: $984.6 billion	**Inflation Rate:** 5.46%
Dow Jones: 949.22 (05-01)/ 806.89 (10-01)	**S&P Price Index:** 92.06/-11.36%
Prime Rate: 7.00% (01-07)/ 8.50% (06-09)	**Average Home Mortgage Rate:** 7.82%
1 oz Gold: $41.51	**1oz of Silver:** $1.88
Federal Debt: $353,720,253,840.45	**Federal Deficit:** ($3.2 billion dollar surplus)
Defense Spending: $94.73 billion	**Interest Spending:** $12.70 billion

Health Care Spending: $10.86 billion	**Pensions Spending:** $25.56 billion
Welfare Spending: $7.26 billion	**Education Spending:** $8.49 billion
Transportation Spending: $6.53 billion	**Misc. Other Spending:** $14.64 billion
Protection Spending: $770 million	**Total Government Spending:** $183.64 billion
% of GDP that goes towards just the interest payment: 1.34%	
The highest rate of world population growth (2.04 per cent) occurred in the late 1960s. The rate (1995-2000) is 1.31 per cent.	
$1.00 = 358.38 Yen, Japan	**$1.00** = 76.25/ 76.50 Iranian Rial
U.S. Population: 202,736,000	**World Population:** 3,632,341,351
U.S. Birth Rate: 3,600,206	**U.S. Abortions:** 27,512
U.S. Homicide Rate: 7.7/ 100,000 population	**U.S. Violent Crime:** 328.7/ 100,000 population
Annual Average Domestic Crude Oil Prices: $3.32 / barrel, $19.45 (2007 adjusted)	

Oil:

January 29, 1969 – Santa Barbara, California. A blowout occurs at a Union Oil Co. platform five miles off the coast of Summerland. Oil workers had drilled a well down 3,500 feet below the ocean floor and riggers began to retrieve the pipe in order to replace a drill bit. The pressure difference created by the extraction of the pipe was not sufficiently compensated for by the amount of drilling mud being pumped back down the well. This resulted in a natural gas blowout. The initial attempt to cap the hole is successful but leads to a tremendous buildup of pressure and the expanding mass creates five breaks in an east-west fault on the ocean floor. Oil and gas is released from deep within the earth beginning an environmental nightmare.

1969

Chemical mud finally sealed the cracks in the ocean floor after 11 days and 3,000,000 gallons of oil had leaked. The winds, ocean currents, and tides spread the oil to a long stretch of shoreline.

1969 – Libya. By the end of 1969, Libya's oil production reached 15.4% of OPEC's total and 7.5% of the world's total oil production. In 1969 a major oil field is discovered at Sarir, which is well to the southeast of the Sirt Basin fields.

December 1969 – Phillips Petroleum discovers oil in Norwegian waters in the central North Sea making **Ekofisk** one of the most important oil fields in the Norwegian sector. Production begins in 1971 after the construction of a series of off-shore platforms by Phillips Petroleum and oil production is planned to continue until at least 2050.

1969 – Saudi Arabia. The Barqan oil field is discovered.

May 1969 – The Arbroath Field is discovered by the Amoco operated group comprising Amoco (UK) Exploration Company, Gas Council (Exploration), Amerada Hess Ltd and Texas Eastern (UK) Ltd, and is the first commercial oil field to be discovered in any sector of the northern North Sea. The Arbroath Field is under development and the first oil is produced in April 1990.

Major News:

January 18, 1969 – Vietnam peace talks begin. President Nixon set the Vietnamization policy November 3, to encourage the South Vietnamese to take more responsibility for fighting the war. It is hoped that this policy will eventually enable the United States to gradually withdraw all U.S. soldiers from Vietnam.

June 23, 1969 – Earl Warren retires upon swearing in **Warren Burger**, as Supreme Court chief justice.

July 8, 1969 – Vietnam. U.S. forces peak at 543,400. Withdrawal starts on July 8.

July 18, 1969 – Chappaquiddick. The FBI file known as Chappaquiddick, is also known as the **Mary Jo Kopechne** investigation. This investigation is opened when an overturned car is found in the water in Martha's Vineyard, Massachusetts. Ms. Kopechne's body is in the car. Ms. Kopechne was a former secretary to late Senator, Robert F. Kennedy and it was determined the driver of the automobile was **Senator Edward M. Kennedy.** It was alleged he was on the wrong road and drove off Dike's Bridge, with the automobile overturning in the water. Senator Kennedy managed to get out of the car, but Ms. Kopechne did not make it out of the car and drowned.

Sometime around midnight, on July 18, 1969 Senator Edward Kennedy drove his Oldsmobile 88 off of a small bridge on Chappaquiddick Island, into eight feet of chilly water. The vehicle landed upside-down. While Kennedy managed to free himself from the wreck and swim to safety, his passenger, **28-year-old Mary Jo Kopechne** was left in the car and died. Once he reached shore, Kennedy claims to have made seven or eight attempts to rescue Kopechne, but could not free her. Kennedy then walked back to the cottage where he and four other men, were partying with several young women known as the **"Boiler Room Girls"** who had worked on Robert Kennedy's campaign. Though Kennedy passed by a fire station and a private home to return to the cottage, he never stopped to ask for help for the trapped Kopechne.

He returned to the party and according to Kennedy himself, informed his cousin and a friend of the situation. The two men, Joseph Gargan and Paul Markham claim to have returned to the scene of the accident and made several unsuccessful attempts to free Kopechne. Then Kennedy's story takes an even stranger turn. After the failed rescue attempts, **Kennedy claims to have jumped back into the water** and made the 500-foot swim across the channel back to Edgartown. He then walked back to his hotel and spent the night. He even took the time to change clothes and pay a visit to the front-desk, to complain about a noisy party, no doubt Kennedy's sloppy attempt at securing an alibi.

Ted Kennedy pled guilty to the charge of leaving the scene of an accident, was sentenced to two months in jail and the sentence was suspended.

July 20, 1969 – Apollo 11 lands on the moon. Apollo 11 carries the first men to the moon. Launched on July 16, 1969, it carried Mission Commander **Neil Alden Armstrong,** Command Module Pilot **Michael Collins** and Lunar Module Pilot **Edwin Eugene 'Buzz' Aldrin, Jr.** On July 20, Armstrong and Aldrin become the first humans to land on the Moon, while Collins orbited above. As Armstrong steps off Eagle's footpad and into history as the first human to set foot on another world, he says, "one small step for **a** man, one giant leap for mankind." This comment about "a man" upsets the many thousands of people responsible for putting a man on the moon and **some** (not all) newspapers remove the "a" in the next mornings headlines. Within a week the newly accepted quote, "one small step for man, one giant leap for mankind," is considered factual.

July 25, 1969 – President Richard M. Nixon announces his new Vietnam policy, declaring the **Nixon Doctrine** that expects Asian allies to provide for their own military defense. This policy, and all Vietnam War policies, are heavily protested throughout the remainder of the year.

1969 – The Weather Underground Organization, also known as **The Weathermen,** is an American radical left organization founded in 1969 by leaders and members who split from the Students for a Democratic Society **(SDS).** The group is notable for a campaign from 1969 through the middle 1970s of **bombings, riots,** and a **jailbreak.** The **"Days of Rage,"** the group's first public demonstration on October 8, 1969, **is a riot** in Chicago coordinated with the trial of the **Chicago Seven**. In 1970 the group issues a "Declaration of a State of War" against the United States government, under the name "Weather Underground Organization." The bombing attacks are mostly against government buildings and some banks. Most are preceded by communiqués that provided evacuation warnings, along with statements regarding the particular matter which motivated the attack.

October 15, 1969 – Vietnam Moratorium Day. Anti-Vietnam-War demonstrations are held in cities across the U.S. on November 15. Over 250,000 demonstrators march in Washington, D.C. to protest the war. Millions participated throughout the world. About 100,000 attended a speech by anti-war **Senator George McGovern** in Boston. **Bill Clinton** helps to organize the demonstration in England while he is a Rhodes Scholar at Oxford. This will become an issue in his Presidential campaign.

November 16, 1969 – My Lai Massacre. The massacre of between 347 and 504 unarmed citizens, all of whom are civilians and the majority of whom are women, children, and elderly people by members of Charlie Company, Americal Division, **March 16, 1968**, is reported on November 16.

November 20, 1969 – Alcatraz Island, the former prison in San Francisco Bay, is occupied by fourteen **American Indians** in a long standoff over the issues of Indian causes. This symbolic occupation turns into a full scale occupation which lasts nineteen months until June 11, 1971. When it starts the occupation force consists of 100 young urban Indian college students from U.C.L.A.

December 1969 – The Chicago Police Department, in conjunction with the **FBI,** conducts a raid on the home of **Black Panther Fred Hampton**, in which he and Mark Clark are killed. Seven other people in the apartment are wounded and charged with assault and attempted murder. The police claimed they shot in self-defense but the Panthers submitted evidence that they were asleep and not resisting arrest. The government later dropped the charges and the families of those killed won a $1.8 million settlement. It was discovered in 1971 that Hampton had been targeted by the FBI's **Counter Intelligence Program** which was a series of covert, and often illegal, projects conducted by the FBI under **J. Edgar Hoover.**

1969 – Charles Manson. Manson Family, a type of cult "family," led by Charles Manson into numerous murders.

Manson tells Family members at Spahn Ranch, on August, 8 "Now is the time for **Helter Skelter."** The Manson family members stabbed to death, Wojciech Frykowski, **Sharon Tate** (eight and a half months pregnant), Jay Sebring, a noted hairstylist; and Abigail Folger, heiress to the Folger coffee fortune.

During the trial, "Manson Family" members loitered near the entrances and corridors of the courthouse. They were not allowed to enter the courtroom because the prosecution subpoenaed them as prospective witnesses and they were not allowed to be present during the testimony of others. While the Manson group wandered around outside, each of the "hard-core" members carried a sheathed hunting knife, legally in plain view and wore an X on his or her forehead.

Charles Manson is convicted of conspiracy to commit the Tate/LaBianca murders, carried out by members of the group at his instruction. He is also found guilty of the murders themselves through the joint-responsibility rule, which makes each member of a conspiracy guilty of crimes his fellow conspirators commit in furtherance of the conspiracy's object. After a 1972 decision by the Supreme Court of California temporarily eliminated the state's death penalty Manson's death sentence was automatically reduced to life imprisonment. When California's reestablished the death penalty it did not affect Manson, who is still an inmate in 2010.

Civil Rights Movement:

January 26, 1969 – On the snowy night of January 26, **Edwin T. Pratt is killed by a shotgun blast** in the doorway of his home in Shoreline, Seattle, by an unknown assailant. The city is shocked by his murder. Pratt was a voice of calm during the racial turmoil of the 1960s. He had worked for the Urban League in Cleveland, Ohio and Kansas City, Missouri before arriving in Seattle in 1956 to be the Seattle league's Community Relations Secretary. In 1961, he became the Executive Director of the Seattle Urban League. Among his achievements was the Triad Plan for the desegregation of the Seattle Public Schools. He also led an initiative for equal housing opportunities. The murder has never been solved.

May 5, 1969 – **Moneta Sleet, Jr. of *Ebony* magazine**, becomes the first African American to win a Pulitzer Prize in Photography.

May 21, 1969 – **Police and National Guardsmen fire on demonstrators** at North Carolina A&T College. One student is killed and five policemen are injured.

June 27, 1969 – **Gay Rights.** Patrons of a the Stonewall Inn, a gay bar in New York's Greenwich Village, fight back during a police raid on June 27, **sparking three days of riots credited with launching the gay-rights movement.** The Stonewall riots transform the gay rights movement from one limited to a small number of activists into a widespread protest for equal rights and acceptance.

June 27, 1969 – **The Department of Labor announces** the "Philadelphia Plan," requiring federal building contractors in Philadelphia to meet specific "goals" for hiring minority workers.

August 8, 1969 – **President Richard Nixon** issues Executive Order 11478, requiring all federal agencies to adopt "affirmative programs for equal employment opportunity."

September 22, 1969 – **The African American Studies Program** begins offering courses at **Harvard University.**

October 29, 1969 – **The Supreme Court declares** the **"all deliberate speed"** standard is no longer constitutionally permissible and orders the immediate desegregation of 33 Mississippi school districts.

November 1969 – Robert Chrisman and Nathan Hare publish the first issue of **"The Black Scholar."**

November 21, 1969 – **The nomination of Clement Haynsworth to the Supreme Court** is rejected by the Senate after it is opposed by civil rights groups.

1969 – **Alfred Day Hershey, Ph.D. geneticist**, becomes the first African American to share a Nobel Prize in Medicine when he is recognized for his work on the replication and genetic structure of viruses.

1969 – **Howard N. Lee** becomes the first African American **Mayor of Chapel Hill, North Carolina**. At the time he is the first African American Mayor of a predominately white Southern city.

1969 – **The Ford Foundation gives one million dollars** to Morgan State University, Howard University, and Yale University to help prepare faculty members to teach courses in African American studies.

December 4, 1969 – **Chicago police kill Black Panther leaders** Fred Hampton and Mark Clarke during a raid.

1969

Women's Movement:

1969 – Three-hundred female workers at the Medical University of South Carolina hospital go on strike with the support of labor and civil rights groups protesting poor working conditions and low wages. After confrontations with police and the arrival of **National Guard troops,** the mostly African-American workers win a settlement while violence is narrowly averted.

1969 – The radical organization, Redstockings, organizes. Members of Redstockings disrupt a hearing on abortion laws of the New York State legislature when the panel of witnesses turns out to be fourteen men and a nun. Repeal, not reform, of abortion laws is demanded. Redstockings popularizes slogans such as **"Sisterhood is Powerful,"** and **"The Personal is Political"** which become buzzwords of the feminist movement. There were 27,512 reported U.S. abortions this year. In 2004 there will be 1,293,000 abortions in the U.S. and there will be **over 40 million abortions** total in the U.S. during the years 1973-2004.

1969 – Golda Meir, born in Kiev (Ukraine) and raised in Milwaukee, Wisconsin, becomes the first female to hold the position **of Prime Minister of Israel.**

1969 – Shirley Chisholm, of New York, becomes the first African-American woman in Congress. Her motto is, **"Unbought and unbossed."** She will serve in the U.S. House of Representatives for 14 years.

Popular Culture:

1969 – Astronauts send live color photos from the moon to a worldwide audience.

1969 – Internet. A U.C.L.A. computer sends data to a Stanford computer, foreshadowing the Internet.

1969 – The first draft lottery in 27 years is held. This was one most young men did not want to win.

1969 – Since 1960 the U.S. population rose 13% while crime went up 148%.

1969 – Anton LaVey, called "the black pope" by many of his followers, publishes the "**Satanic Bible.**" Over the years the book has been translated into every major language, and has been an inspiration for many well-known criminals.

April 30, 1969 – The number of U.S. military personnel in Vietnam stands at 543,482, the most at any time during the war. College enrollments swell as many young men seek **student deferments** from the draft. Anti-war protests become commonplace on college campuses, and **grade inflation** begins as professors realize that low grades may change male students' draft status.

August 15-18, 1969 – Woodstock. The **Woodstock Festival,** held at Max Yasgur's 600 acre dairy farm in the rural town of Bethel, New York is a three-day concert, extended a fourth day that involves lots of **sex, drugs, and rock 'n roll.** An icon of the 1960s **hippie** counterculture, Woodstock is held despite the constant rain and acres of mud. Thirty-two of the best-known musicians of the day appear during the sometimes rainy three day event in front of nearly **half a million concertgoers.**

October 15, 1969 – The Moratorium to End the War in Vietnam demonstrations take place. Millions of Americans take the day off from work and school to participate in local demonstrations against the war. These are the first major demonstrations against the Nixon administration's handling of the war.

November 15, 1969 – Crowds estimated at up to **half a million people** participate in an anti-war demonstration in Washington, D.C. and a similar demonstration is held in San Francisco. These protests are organized by the New Mobilization Committee to End the War in Vietnam, and the Student Mobilization Committee to End the War in Vietnam.

1969 – High school students take the school district to court and win. Petitioner John F. Tinker, 15 years old, and petitioner Christopher Eckhardt, 16 years old, attended high schools in Des Moines, Iowa. Petitioner Mary Beth Tinker, John's sister, was a 13-year-old student in junior high school.

1969

The Constitution protects students who wear armbands in school to protest the Vietnam War. Petitioners, three public school pupils in Des Moines, Iowa, were suspended from school for wearing black armbands to protest the Government's policy in Vietnam. They sought nominal damages and an injunction against a regulation banning the wearing of armbands. The District Court dismissed the complaint stating that it is within the Board's power to ban armbands. The Supreme Court, in Tinker vs. Des Moines School District, ruled 7 to 2 that the First Amendment applied to public schools, and that administrators would have to demonstrate constitutionally valid reasons for any specific regulation of speech in the classroom. The United States Supreme Court defined the constitutional rights of students in U.S. public schools. The **"Tinker test"** is still used by courts today to determine whether a school's disciplinary actions violate students' First Amendment rights.

1969 – California adopts a "no fault" divorce law which allows couples to divorce by mutual consent. Legislation is also passed regarding equal division of common property. California is the first state to adopt **No Fault Divorce** and leads a landslide that by 1985 will have every state adopt a similar law.

1969 – Herbert R. Kohl's book, "The Open Classroom," helps to promote open education, an approach emphasizing student-centered classrooms and active, holistic learning. The conservative back-to-the-basics movement of the 1970s begins at least partially as a backlash against open education.

Business / Technology:

1969 – PASCAL. The Computer powerful programming language PASCAL is completed. It will be launched in 1970 as a small and efficient language intended to encourage good programming practices using structured programming and data structuring.

Pascal is the primary high-level language used for development in the **Apple Lisa,** and in the early years of the **Mac.** Parts of the original Macintosh operating system are hand-translated into Motorola 68000 assembly language from the Pascal sources.

1969 – Kenneth Thompson with help from Dennis Ritchie creates the UNIX Operating System for computers.

November 21, 1969 – The Internet, called Arpanet during its initial development, is invented by the Advanced Research Projects Agency at the U.S. Department of Defense. The first operational packet switching network in the world is deployed connecting the IMP at UCLA and the Stanford Research Institute. By December 5, it includes the entire four node system, with the UCSB and the University of Utah.

1969 – 3/4" U-Matic. Sony brings out the first videotape cassette editing system.

Finance:

1969 – Lyndon Johnson's effort to conduct a war in Vietnam and a War on Poverty at the same time causes inflation to triple from 1.9% in 1965 to 6.2% four years later. There is a mild recession in the U.S. 1969-1970 and the price hikes give Americans their first taste of the double-digit inflation.

1969 – Arkansas Gets Ready. Hot Springs Arkansas. In the 1930s, Hot Springs represented the western border of organized crime in the U.S with the local syndicate headed by **Owney Madden,** a New York **killer** who had taken over the mob's resort in Arkansas. Owney Madden was an English born gang member who had been arrested more than 40 times in New York by the time he was 21. **Myer Lansky** placed Madden in charge and the plan for Arkansas was modeled on an earlier one in which Louisiana Governor Huey Long opened a Swiss bank account into which the mob would put $3 to $4 million annually for the right to run casinos in the state. Lansky then moved to Hot Springs where he hired Madden, former operator of **Harlem's Cotton Club.** According to one account, "The Hot Springs set up was so luxurious and safe that it became known as a place for gangsters on the lam to hole up until the heat blew over." Hot Springs was where **Lucky Luciano** was arrested, brought back for trial and prosecuted by Thomas E. Dewey.

A federal investigation in the 1960's concludes that **Hot Springs has the largest illegal gambling operations in the United States** and the income from illegal gambling exceeds that of Las Vegas well into the 1960's.

1969

Bill Clinton's uncle, Raymond G. Clinton, a prosperous local Buick dealer, and Gabe Crawford a family friend and wealthy businessman were thought to be well known members of the **Dixie Mafia.** They are both instrumental in keeping Bill from being drafted and make it possible for him to be elected Governor of Arkansas. Gabe Crawford was indeed a successful "business man", it is said he presided over a backroom bookie operation that was one of Hot Springs' most lucrative criminal enterprises. Many think Uncle Raymond is involved in illegal gambling, and drug money laundering, bribery, and politics.

Twenty-three year old Bill is in England for a second year as a Rhodes Scholar at Oxford University. This also keeps him from being drafted which is a common pursuit of many 23 year old men.

April 11, 1969 – The export ban on U.S. silver coins, which began on May 18, 1967, is lifted.

April 26, 1969 – Ownership of pre-1934 gold coins no longer requires a license from the Treasury Department.

July 14, 1969 – The Department of the Treasury and the Federal Reserve System announce that currency notes in **denominations of $500, $1,000, $5,000, and $10,000** are to be discontinued immediately due to lack of use. Although they are issued until 1969, they were last printed in 1945.

1969 – Congress approves laws authorizing the Federal Reserve to accept the International Monetary Fund's (IMF), Special Drawing Right (SDR), as reserves in the United States and to issue Federal Reserve Notes in exchange for SDR's. The **SDR** is an international reserve asset, created by the IMF in 1969 to supplement the existing official reserves of member countries. So-called "paper gold" is just an accounting transaction within a ledger of accounts, which eliminates the logistical and security problems of shipping gold back and forth across borders to settle national accounts. It also may allow those who wish to diversify away from the dollar, to do so without weakening the value of the dollar at the same time.

1969 – Auto makers settle a lawsuit by the Justice Department for conspiracy to delay the development of **pollution-control** devices.

1969 – CompuServe goes into business and is the first major commercial online service in the United States. It will dominate the field during the 1980s and remain a major player through the mid-1990s, when it is sidelined by the rise of information services such as **AOL** that charge monthly subscription fees rather than hourly rates. Today the CompuServe Information Service operates as an online service provider and an Internet service provider, owned by AOL.

1969 – Xerox Corporation buys **Scientific Data Systems** for nearly **$1 billion dollars.** Ninety times Scientific Data System's earnings.

1969 – ATM. The first modern automated teller machine begins operating in Rockville Centre, N.Y.

Books:

1969 – Novelist Kurt Vonnegut, **"Slaughterhouse Five."** or "The Children's Crusade: A Duty-Dance With Death," is a post-modern anti-war science fiction novel dealing with a soldier's (Billy Pilgrim) experiences during World War II and his journeys with time travel.

1969 – "The Andromeda Strain." Michael Crichton's first best-seller.

1969 – Mario Puzo, **"The Godfather."**

1969 – "Portnoy's Complaint," Philip Roth.

1969 – Joan Garrity, identifying herself only as "J.", publishes **"The Way to Become the Sensuous Woman."**

1969 – Dr. David Reuben's book **"Everything You Always Wanted to Know About Sex (But Were Afraid to Ask),"** is not only a bestseller, it also becomes required reading in some high schools across the U.S.

1969

1969 – "The Left Hand of Darkness," Ursula K. LeGuin.

1969 – "The Four-Gated City," Doris Lessing.

TV:

1969 – Body Counts. Night-after-night, on the evening news, "body counts" are given as the American press keeps score in Vietnam. This goes on for years.

1969 – "The Saturday Evening Post" stops publishing after 148 years and TV is blamed.

1969 – "Sesame Street" is launched on public TV which many have linked to shorter and shorter attention spans in children, resulting in falling mathematics scores across the U.S. and information only being palatable in thirty-second bites.

1969 – "Monty Python's Flying Circus" premieres on BBC1.

1969 – Non-event. Tiny Tim marries **Miss Vicky** on the *Tonight Show with Johnny Carson.*

1969 – Red Lion Broadcasting Co. vs. FCC. The Supreme Court rules that the 1st Amendment does not prohibit FCC regulation of broadcasting, stating that there is "no unabridged right to broadcast comparable to the right of every individual to speak, write, or publish." The tighter regulation of broadcasting is based on broadcasters' use of public airwaves.

Sports:

January 12, 1969 – The New York Jets win Super Bowl III over the Baltimore Colts after a bold prediction by quarterback **Joe Namath.** This is the first victory in the National Football League for a former American Football League team.

1969 – ABA Finals. Oakland Oaks defeat Indiana Pacers 4 games to 1.

Music:

1969 – At a Rolling Stones concert in Altamont, California, a fan is stabbed to death by a **Hells Angel's member.** The Hells Angels biker gang had been hired to provide security for the event. In retrospect, some commentators have concluded that the violence signaled **the end of the "hippie" movement**, which espoused an ethos of free love and peace.

January 30, 1969 – The Beatles perform for the last time in public, on the roof of the Apple building at 3 Savile Row, London. The performance, filmed for the "Let It Be" movie, is stopped early by police after neighbors complain about the noise.

February 15, 1969 – Vickie Jones is arrested for impersonating Aretha Franklin in a concert performance. Jones' impersonation was so convincing that nobody in the audience asked for a refund.

February 17, 1969 – Johnny Cash and Bob Dylan record together in Nashville, Tennessee. Only one song, **"Girl from the North Country,"** would be released from these sessions.

March 1, 1969 – During a performance at Miami's "Dinner Key Auditorium," **Jim Morrison of the Doors is arrested** for allegedly exposing himself during the show. Morrison is officially charged with lewd and lascivious behavior, indecent behavior, open profanity and public drunkenness.

April 20, 1969 – The L.A. Free Festival in Venice, California ends early following a riot. The police arrest 117 members of the audience.

1969 – Jimi Hendrix is arrested by Canadian Mounties at Toronto's International Airport for possession of narcotics. Hendrix is released on $10,000 bail.

May 10, 1969 – The Turtles perform at the White House. Singer Mark Volman falls off the stage five times.

1969

July 3, 1969 – Brian Jones is found dead in his swimming pool at his home in Sussex, England almost a month after leaving **The Rolling Stones.**

1969 – Black Sabbath forms in Birmingham, England.

1969 – Mott the Hoople begin recording.

1969 – King Crimson forms.

1969 – The **Doobie Brothers** forms.

1969 – The original line-up of UK pop group **Brotherhood of Man** forms.

1969 – Mashina Vremeni forms.

1969 – Judas Priest forms.

Natural Disasters:

January 18, 1969 – Southern California. Floods and mudslides from heavy rains cause widespread property damage and leave at least 100 people dead. Another downpour on February 23-26 causes further floods and mudslides resulting in at least 18 people being killed.

August 14, 1969 – "Camille." Mississippi, Louisiana, Alabama, Virginia, West Virginia. Two-hundred and fifty-six people are killed as a result of hurricane Camille. Damages are estimated at $1.4 billion.

October 2, 1969 – Santa Rosa, California. A 5.7 magnitude earthquake kills one person.

October 25 and 26, 1969 – Two earthquakes strike Banja Luka, Bosnia and Herzegovina. One is magnitude 6.2 and kills one person. The second is magnitude 7.0 and kills 20 people.

1969 – East Pakistan. A Tornado in Bangladesh kills 923 people.

1969 – The Hong Kong Flu pandemic of 1968 and 1969 kills up to 750,000 people. Fifty million people are infected in the United States, resulting in an estimated 34,000 deaths.

1969 – AIDS. Proceedings of the National Academy of Sciences on November 1, 2007 dismiss the patient zero hypothesis and claim that **AIDS is transmitted from** Africa to Haiti in 1966 and from **Haiti to the United States in 1969.**

1969 – Smoking deaths. "Mortality from tobacco in developed countries: indirect estimation from national vital statistics," Lancet, May23, 1992: 1930-1959: 11,000,000 people die from smoking; 1960s: 9,000,000 people die from smoking.

Man vs. Man / Wars:

Assassinated – Somalia. Ali Shermarke, the President of Somalia is shot dead by one of his own bodyguards on October 15, while paying a visit to the northern town of Las Anod. His assassination is quickly followed by a military coup on October 21, the day after his funeral, in which the army seizes power without encountering opposition. The coup is spearheaded by **Major General Muhammad Siad Barre,** the commander of the army. Barre nationalizes the economy with the help of Soviet advisers and Cuban troops. His Supreme Ruling Council formulates political and legal institutions based on the **Qur'an, Marx, Mao, Lenin,** and **Mussolini.** Siad Barre explained: "The official ideology consists of three elements: my own conception of community, a form of socialism based on Marxist principles, and Islam." **This coup caused anarchy and widespread starvation.**

Assassinated – Eduardo Mondlane is killed on February 3, by explosives. He served as **President of the Mozambican Liberation Front** from 1962 until his assassination.
   Many sources state that, in an attempt to rectify the situation in Mozambique, the **Portuguese secret police** assassinated Mondlane by sending a parcel to his office that exploded when it was opened. Other sources state he was killed when an explosive was detonated underneath his chair at the FRELIMO headquarters by unknown

assassins. The original investigations leveled accusations at **Silverio Nungo** and **Lazaro Kavandame,** FRELIMO leaders in Cabo Delgado. The Tanzanian police also accused Lazaro Kavandame of working with Portugal's secret police, to assassinate Mondlane.

Mondlane's successor is the moderate **Reverend Uria Simango,** the former Vice President of FRELIMO. Within two months the power struggle that followed Simango's appointment forced him to share control of the government and seven months later he is removed. **Reverend Uria Simango** is seen as a continuing threat and is expelled from FRELIMO. He is eventually arrested and executed in 1975.

Assassinated – Equatorial Guinea. Atanasio Ndongo Miyone, Saturnino Ibongo, Bonifacio Ondó Edu, Armando Balboa, Pastor Torao and many other Equatorial Guinean politicians, **are assassinated** in a murderous crackdown after a coup attempt against President Francisco Macías Nguema.

December 1, 1969 – Senator Daniel Brewster (D-Maryland) **is indicted** on charges of soliciting and accepting bribes. The case is dismissed October 9, 1970. Dismissal is reversed in 1972. He is convicted on November 17, 1972, however this conviction is also reversed and he pleads no contest.

December 18, 1969 – Representative Hugh J. Addonizio (D-New Jersey), **is indicted** on charges of extortion, conspiracy, and income tax evasion. He is convicted on July 22, 1970, sentenced to 10 years in prison and serves five.

1969-1970 – Beirut. Christian-Shia Violence. The Lebanese government's efforts to curtail guerrilla activities continue through late 1969 and 1970. The migration of large numbers of Shia increases from southern Lebanon and in Beirut the migrants, estimated to exceed 30,000, often can not find adequate shelter and meet with indifference on the part of predominantly Christian military leaders. These problems result in occasional clashes between the migrants and government forces.

1969 – Some of the many Terrorist Attacks and Hijackings. This list could go on-and-on-and-on so this is just one year. Although the number of Airline Hijackings seems to peak in 1969, terrorist attacks killing innocent people go on every year.

January 2, 1969 –A DC-8 from New York is hijacked by two Americans and is forced to fly to Cuba.

January 9, 1969 – Ronald Bohle, a 21-year-old Purdue University student, hijacks a Boeing 727 from Miami to Cuba. He returns by way of Canada on November 1, 1969, and is sentenced to 20 years for air piracy on July 6, 1972.

January 11, 1969 – A 727 from Jacksonville, Florida is hijacked and forced to fly to Cuba. When the hijacker returns to the U.S. on May 5, 1969, he is arrested and acquitted of air piracy and kidnapping on grounds of temporary insanity.

January 13, 1969 – A man attempts to hijack a Convair 880 from Detroit to Cuba. He is sentenced on July 31, 1969, to 15 years for interference with a flight crew. He had a history of mental illness.

January 17, 1969 – A DC-8 from New York is hijacked by a man from the Dominican Republic and forced to fly to Cuba.

January 24, 1969 – A 19-year-old Navy deserter who "didn't want to go to Vietnam," hijacks a Boeing 727 from Key West to Cuba.

January 28, 1969 – Two prison escapees successfully hijack a DC-8 from Los Angeles to Cuba.

January 31, 1969 – Allan Sheffield hijacks a DC-8 from San Francisco to Cuba. He says he is "tired of TV dinners and tired of seeing people starve in the world."

February 3, 1969 – A 21-year old student and his girlfriend attempt to hijack a plane from New York City to Cuba. When the pilot refuels in Miami, the hijackers allow the passengers to deplane and the police capture the hijackers.

February 3, 1969– A 727 from Newark, New Jersey, is hijacked by two Cubans and forced to fly to Cuba.

1969

February 10, 1969 – A Cuban hijacks a DC-8 from Atlanta to Cuba.

February 18, 1969 – A pilot and 3 passengers are killed by terrorists that attack an El Al Boeing 707 on the airport runway in **Zurich, Switzerland.**

February 25, 1969 – A DC-8 from Atlanta is hijacked and forced to fly to Cuba. The hijacker later surrenders to U.S. authorities in Prague and is sentenced to life imprisonment on July 7, 1970.

March 1, 1969 – Islamic terrorists use a bomb to destroy an **Ethiopian Airlines** Boeing 707 at the Frankfurt Germany, Airport, injuring several airline employees. The Government of Ethiopia blames the attack on the **Syrian-Egyptian Movement for the Liberation of Eritrea,** while the **Islamic Eritrean Liberation Front** claims credit for the bombing.

March 6, 1969 – Black Panther Tony Bryant hijacks a **National Airlines** plane en route from New York to Miami and forces it to land in Cuba. He is arrested in Cuba and spends a year and a half in jail. His 1984 book **"Hijack"** describes his experience in Cuban prisons.

March 6, 1969 – Muslims belonging to the **Popular Front for the Liberation of Palestin**e thought it would be a good idea to detonate a bomb in the Hebrew University cafeteria, so they did, mutilating and burning 29 Jewish students.

March 17, 1969 – A man hijacks an airliner from Atlanta and forces it to fly to Cuba. He returns to the U.S. on November 1, 1969 and is committed to a mental institution on February 1, 1972.

March 19, 1969 – A man tries to hijack a CV-880 from Dallas to Cuba but ends up in New Orleans where he is taken into custody. Charges are dismissed due to insanity.

May 5, 1969 – Jean-Pierre Charrette and Alain Alard successfully hijack a Boeing 727 from New York and force it to fly to Cuba.

May 22, 1969 – The attempted assassination of the first **Israeli Prime Minister, Ben-Gurion,** fails but the would-be killers are freed by **Denmark.**

May 23, 1969 – Three Cuban men successfully hijack a 727 from Miami and force it to fly to Cuba.

May 30, 1969 – The Trans-Arabian Pipeline in Jordan is sabotaged by **Popular Front for the Liberation of Palestine** terrorists. An explosive device causes a fire that disrupts the flow of oil. A spokesman of the PFLP claimed that his group had intended to have the spill pollute water supplied to Israeli settlements and fisheries in the Hutch Valley and they were somewhat successful. Oil was reported seeping into the northern part of the **Sea of Galilee,** and oil slicks were seen on the **Jordan River.**

June 17, 1969 – Willie Lee Brent, a **Black Panther** charged by the FBI with participating in a shoot-out with police in San Francisco in 1968, hijacks a TWA jet from Oakland, California, to New York. The plane is diverted to Havana, Cuba and no one is injured. This is the longest U.S. hijacking to date. Brent remained in jail in Cuba for two years.

June 17, 1969 – Rome, Italy. A Muslim student dies when a bomb he is preparing in his room explodes. Leaflets surrounding his body announced an impending attack by the **Eritrean Liberation Front.**

June 18, 1969 – Pakistan. Three armed members of the **Islamic Eritrean Liberation Front** assault and set fire to an Ethiopian Boeing 707 at the Karachi airport. The terrorists, all of whom are captured, told authorities that they carried out the attack to dramatize their opposition to Ethiopian rule in Eritrea. **Since the Islamic Pakistani government was sympathetic to their cause** the three men were jailed for less than one year.

June 25, 1969 – A DC-8 from Los Angeles is hijacked by an unidentified male and forced to fly to Cuba.

June 18, 1969 – A TWA plane is hijacked from Los Angeles and forced to Damascus.

1969

June 28, 1969 – A 727 from Baltimore is hijacked and forced to fly to Cuba. The hijacker returns to the U.S. in November 1969. He is tried and sentenced to 15 years for interference with a flight crew.

July 17, 1969 – In India, a bomb is detonated inside of a **U.S. Investigations Services reading room** in the American Consulate in **Calcutta,** burning one employee.

July 18, 1969 – In London, England, **Popular Front for the Liberation of Palestine terrorists fire-bomb** a department store owned by Jewish citizens of the U.K. The PFLP claimed responsibility for the bombing and warned that there would be more bomb attacks on Jewish-owned establishments in London and in the United States.

July 19, 1969 – **Islamic jihadists** associated with the Sudan government firebomb a United States Information Services library in Khartoum.

July 26, 1969 – A DC-8 from El Paso, Texas, is hijacked and forced to fly to Cuba. When the hijacker returns to the U.S. on November 1, 1969 he is arrested and tried. He is sentenced to 50 years for aircraft piracy on September 14, 1970.

July 31, 1969 – A 727 from Pittsburgh is hijacked by an unidentified male and forced to fly to Cuba.

August 5, 1969 – A Man unsuccessfully hijacks a DC-9 from Philadelphia to Cuba. Charges are dismissed on January 12, 1970 and he is committed to a mental institution. He is discharged on September 15, 1971.

August 14, 1969 – A 727 from Boston is hijacked by two unknown male Cubans and forced to fly to Cuba.

August 29, 1969 – An unidentified male Cuban hijacks a 727 from Miami to Cuba.

August 29, 1969 – A TWA 707 is hijacked from Rome to Damascus. Leaders of the **Popular Front for the Liberation of Palestine** learned that Yitzak Rabin was scheduled to be aboard the flight. Leila Khaled, born April 9, 1944, in Haifa, is a member of the **Palestinian National Council** and one of the hijackers. She will hijack another plane in 1970. Salim Issawi is the second hijacker. Rabin was not aboard but they did succeed in hijacking the plane and forcing it to fly to Damascus, the capital of Syria. The plane carried a crew of 12 and 101 passengers. Immediately upon landing, the passengers managed to jump from the plane before a bomb went off, destroying the aircraft. Four passengers were injured.

September 7, 1969 – An unidentified male hijacks a DC-8 from New York to Cuba.

September 10, 1969 – A Puerto Rican unsuccessfully tries to hijack a DC-8 (scheduled for San Juan) to Cuba. He is committed to mental institution on January 30, 1970 and is released in December 1971.

September 24, 1969 – A DC-8 from Charleston, South Carolina is hijacked by an unknown Cuban and forced to fly to Cuba.

October 9, 1969 – A DC-8 from Los Angeles is hijacked by an unknown man and forced to fly to Cuba.

October 26, 1969 – Muslims in Beirut, Lebanon bomb the car of a U.S. Embassy official in front of his home.

October 21, 1969 – An unidentified male hijacks a Boeing 720 from Mexico City to Cuba. He committed suicide in Cuba on September 28, 1970.

November 4, 1969 – Two armed men seize a Nicaraguan airliner en route from Miami to Mexico and divert it to Cuba.

November 27, 1969 – In Athens, Greece, **Muslim militants** associated with **Yasser Arafat's Fatah** throw hand grenades into the **El Al Israeli Airlines office.** A child is killed and 13 innocent civilians are wounded.

December 12, 1969 – **Islamic terrorists bomb** the West Berlin office of Israeli El Al Airlines. No one is injured in the blast.

1969

December 12, 1969 – **Muslim militants** associated with the **Islamic Eritrean Liberation Front** armed with pistols and explosives are killed by plainclothes security guards as they attempt to hijack an Ethiopian Airlines jet shortly after takeoff from Madrid on a flight to Addis Ababa.

December 21, 1969 – **Three Lebanese Muslims** are stopped as they try to hijack a TWA plane in Athens. The flight was bound for Rome and then on to New York. The three Muslim militants, who used handguns and explosives, said that they were members of the **Popular Front for the Liberation of Palestine**, and that they had received orders to divert the airplane to Tunis where they were to evacuate the passengers and blow up the aircraft.

One of the hijackers confessed that he and his colleagues had planned to destroy the plane "to warn the Americans to stop providing air communications with Israel." The three Islamic terrorists were freed after other terrorists hijacked an Olympic Airways plane to Cairo on July 22, 1970.

December 26, 1969 – A 727 from New York is hijacked by an unknown man, using the name M. Martinez (alias), and forced to fly to Cuba.

December 29, 1969 – **Philippine terrorists** attempt to assassinate **U.S. Vice President Spiro Agnew** by bombing his car. No one claimed credit for the assault but these same tactics were deployed countless times by local **Islamic groups** such as the Abu Sayyaf, Jemaah Islamiyah, and the Moro Islamic Liberation Front.

1969 – **Great Britain. The Ulster Troubles** is another of a long series of conflicts fought in Ireland by Britain. Northern Ireland is a part of the United Kingdom and the Protestant majority is loyal to London. The Irish Catholic minority wants to separate and join Irish Republic in the south. The **IRA** has fought the British in an urban guerrilla campaign since 1969.

In August the British army sends troops into Ulster (Northern Ireland) to put down widespread rioting and will remain for over thirty years. Eventually an on-again/off-again peace is reached with the IRA but they refuse to totally disarm.

January 2, 1969 – Guyana Rebellion. On January 2 ranchers living in the Rupununi District are involved in a rebellion which is crushed by soldiers of the Guyana Defence Force who are flown into the area. The leading conspirators come from the Hart and Melville clans which are associated with cattle ranches in the Rupununi.

1969 – The Sino-Soviet Border War. A series of armed border clashes between the Soviet Union and People's Republic of China at the height of the Sino-Soviet split. The most serious of these border clashes occurs in March in the vicinity of Zhenbao Island, also known as Damanskii Island, on the Ussuri River. Following the collapse of the Soviet Union, the island is given to China. As many as 3,000 people are killed.

July 14, 1969 – Soccer War. El Salvador vs. Honduras. El Salvador is a small country, the population is growing rapidly and there is not enough land. Honduras happens to be just across the border and is a much larger country with a smaller population and a less-developed economy. This leads to over three-hundred thousand Salvadorans moving across the border and illegally homesteading.

In June during and after a soccer match between the Honduran and Salvadoran national soccer teams, resentments build to a point of confrontation between the two countries. On July 14, 1969 the Salvadoran army launches major offensives against the military government in Honduras because it cannot deal with all of the displaced Salvadoran illegal immigrants being evicted from Honduras. The Honduran government has evicted over 100,000 illegal Salvadorians and moved them back across the border. In what came to be known as the Soccer War the Salvadoran air force attacks targets inside Honduras and the Salvadoran army attacks targets along the main road connecting the two nations. El Salvador also attacked the Honduran islands in the Golfo de Fonseca. Up to 2,000 people, mostly Honduran civilians are killed, and thousands of other Hondurans in the border area are now homeless. The border is closed and the economies of both countries suffer. For example, airline service between the two nations is disrupted for over ten years.

September 1, 1969 – Libyan Military Coup. Muammar al-Qaddafi, a 27-year-old Libyan army captain, leads a successful military coup against King Idris I of Libya. They waited until King Idris was out of the country, being treated for a leg ailment at a Turkish spa, and then toppled his government in a bloodless coup. The monarchy is abolished, Idris is deposed and **Muammar al-Qaddafi** is named chairman of Libya's new governing body, the Revolutionary Command Council. King Idris I traveled from Turkey to Greece before finding asylum in Egypt. He died in Cairo in 1983.

May 13, 1969 – Malaysia. After the May 13 race riots the controversial New Economic Policy was launched by Prime Minister Abdul Razak. The new policy was supposed to increase proportionately the indigenous people's share of the wealth. Malaysia then somewhat successfully tries to maintain a delicate ethno-political balance, with a system of government that attempts to combine overall economic development with political and economic policies that promote equitable participation of all races.

1969-2009 – New Guinea. The Free Papau Movement. In 1969, General Sarwo Edhi Wibowo oversaw the Indonesian **"Act of Free Choice."** Prior to the vote, the Indonesian military rounded up and detained a large group of Papuan tribal leaders. The Papuans were daily threatened with death at gunpoint if the entire group did not vote to continue Indonesian rule.

The U.S. and other Western powers ignored protests over the lack of freedom to vote and allowed Indonesia to formally annex the territory in August. The annexation of western New Guinea into Indonesia remains controversial in 2010. More than 100,000 Papuans, one sixteenth of the population, have died as a result of government sponsored violence against West Papuans.

March 1969 – Panama. January Coup. In January power rested in the hands of Omar Torrijos and Boris Martínez, commander and chief of staff, of the Guard. In early March, a speech by Martinez promising agrarian reform and other measures is radical enough to alarm landowners and businessmen. Threatened by a loss of wealth they stage a coup and Torrijos assumes full control. Martinez and a few of his supporters in the military government are exiled. Torrijos assured Panamanian and U.S. investors that their interests were not threatened while never denouncing the land reforms.

December 1969 – Panama. Attempted Coup. Amado Sanjur and Ramiro Silvera lead an unsuccessful coup attempt against Torrijos in December. 1969. The colonels followed earlier competitors of Torrijos into exile in Miami, Florida.

1969 – Philippines. The Muslim Rebellion in the Southern Philippines. Muslim rebel groups seek independence from the mostly Christian Philippines. One rebel group, the Abu Sayaf Group, is believed linked to **Osama bin-Laden's Al-Qaida.**

1969 – Rwanda. In 1969 another purge of **Hutus** by the **Tutsi military** occurs. Then in neighboring **Burundi** a localized Hutu uprising in 1972 is fiercely answered by the Tutsi-dominated Burundi army in the largest **Burundi genocide of Hutus,** with a death toll nearing **200,000 people.**

1969 – Shatt al Arab Dispute. Iraq and Iran. The first recorded treaty that involved the Shatt-al-Arab was the peace treaty of 1639 between the Persian and Ottoman Empires. This treaty established a border lacking in detail and conforming in large part to tribal loyalties. By 1969 the situation in the region had changed. Iran is now vastly superior in military terms to Iraq. This is due in part to the fact that the Ba'th party has recently taken power and is tied up domestically ensuring its power base within Iraq. The Iranians support the Kurdish uprising in the northern sector of the Iraq which brings the countries to the verge of open warfare again.

1969 – Sharpeville. South Africa. Fifty-six Africans, including women and children, were killed and 162 injured when South African police open fire on a crowd demonstrating against the pass laws yesterday at Sharpeville, a township of Vereeniging.

The Pan-Africanist Congress had urged its 31,000 union members to come out without their identity cards (required by law) and surrender themselves for arrest at the nearest police station. At Sharpeville a crowd of over 20,000 surrounded the police station, shouting and throwing stones. The Africans retaliated and then the police opened fire.

"I don't know how many we shot," said Colonel J. Pienaar, the local area police commander at Sharpeville. "It all started when hordes of natives surrounded the police station. My car was struck with a stone. If they do these things they must learn their lesson the hard way." An official at Vereeniging hospital put the casualties at 7 p.m. to-night at 56 dead and 162 injured. Forty-four people seriously injured are in this hospital and the other 118 injured have been transferred to Baragwanath hospital, near Johannesburg.

May 25, 1969 – Sudan. Sudanese Military Coup. Several young officers, led by Colonel Jaafar an Nimeiri, seize power in Sudan. Coups are being formulated by various army factions supported by the Sudanese Communist Party, Arab nationalists and conservative religious groups. Nimeiri's coup just got there first. Former chief justice Awadallah is appointed Prime Minister and a ten-member Revolutionary Command Council has collective executive authority under Nimeiri's chairmanship. They then go about the business of consolidating their power by eliminating their enemies.

April 5-6, 1969 – Vietnam. The only major anti-war demonstration in the early months of the Nixon presidency occurs on April 5 and 6.

Spring 1969 – Vietnam-Cambodia. During the 1973 Senate hearings, it is revealed that **secret bombings started** a year before the April 30, 1970 incursion into Cambodia.

May 8, 1969 – Vietnam. The "10-point peace plan" is offered in Paris by the National Liberation Front and endorsed by Hanoi.

May 14, 1969 – Vietnam. President Nixon, during a policy address on Vietnam, proposes an **"8-point peace plan"** that includes mutual withdrawal of all non-Vietnamese forces to designated bases over a 12-month period, after which remaining troops will be totally withdrawn from South Vietnam.

Mid 1969 – Vietnam. President Nixon abandons the idea of a "purely military victory," and starts bringing U.S. troops home. The President now talks of a **"Vietnamization"** program to prepare the South Vietnamese to take over the U.S. combat role. Withdrawals announced: June 8, 25,000 troops and September 16, 35,000 troops.

September 3, 1969 – Vietnam. Ho Chi Minh dies of heart failure in Hanoi. The Japanese occupation ended in 1945 and the Viet Minh Independence Movement took over Hanoi. Ho wrote the Declaration of Independence of the Democratic Republic of Vietnam and wanted to use the exact words from the American Declaration of Independence but could not find a copy. He paraphrased from his recollections: "All men are created equal; they are endowed by their Creator with certain inalienable Rights; among these are Life, Liberty, and the pursuit of Happiness."

Ho was the "George Washington" of his nation and the people affectionately called him "Uncle Ho." He was so popular that it was generally conceded Vietnam would have been unified under his leadership if the elections that were promised at Geneva had taken place.

In 1946 Ho was appointed President and he led the anti-French resistance. The Viet Minh controlled the countryside while the French controlled the large cities. In 1954 The Viet Minh overwhelmed the French stronghold at Dien Bien Phu. The French Government signed an armistice, and after negotiations Vietnam was divided along the 17th parallel.

North Vietnam followed a communist system of socialism and carried out brutal land reform. It is estimated that 70,000 people died and 70,000 to 100,000 were imprisoned. In 1959 the Ho Chi Minh Trail into the south moved weapons and guerrillas. The trail worked its way south through the neighboring kingdoms of Laos and Cambodia and will eventually consist of over 12,000 miles of roads and paths.

The United States support Ngo Dinh Diem and the Saigon regime in the South after the French leave.

October 15, 1969 – Vietnam. "Vietnam Moratorium." An estimated 1-2 million Americans across the U.S. participate in anti-war demonstrations, protest rallies and peace vigils. **50 members of the U.S. Congress also participate.**

November 3, 1969 – Vietnam. President Nixon says he plans withdrawal of all U.S. troops on a secret timetable. After much pressure President Nixon **announces the reduction** of another 50,000 troops by mid-April 1970.

November 19, 1969 – Vietnam. Draft Lottery. Congress gives the president the authority to **institute the "draft lottery"** system aimed at inducting 19-year-olds before older men. Nixon signs the bill into law November 26, 1969. Under the new law the period of prime eligibility is reduced from 7 years to 1 year. Maximum eligibility would begin on a man's 19th birthday and end on his 20th birthday. Nice thought but it did not exactly work this way.

December 1, 1969 – Vietnam. The first draft lottery in 27 years is held at Selective Service Headquarters in Washington, DC.

December 2, 1969 – Vietnam. The U.S. House approves, 334 to 55, a resolution endorsing Nixon's efforts to achieve **"peace with justice,"** following a 2 day debate. This is the first major Vietnam policy declaration since the 1964 Gulf of Tonkin resolution.

December 18, 1969 – Vietnam, Laos and Thailand. Senator John Cooper (R-Kentucky), after several attempts, succeeds in limiting U.S. activities in Laos and Thailand when a bill including $23.2 Billion for Vietnam war activities prohibited introduction of U.S. combat troops into Laos and Thailand.

1969 – Vietnam. A year of ever widening divisions in the U.S. **The "silent majority"** and **"middle America"** are pitted against the **war protestors.** Vice President Agnew called protestors "impudent snobs." President Richard **Nixon begins a secret bombing** of Viet Cong strongholds in Cambodia and also initiates a "Vietnamization" of the war, a policy which leads to a gradual withdrawal of American military forces.

April 1969 – U.S. deaths in Vietnam surpasses the 33,000 lost in the Korean War.

1969 – Philippines. Communist and Islamic Insurgency in the Philippines. There are two significant insurgencies in the Philippines, **a Muslim** insurgency fighting for autonomy in the Mindanao region and **a Communist** insurgency in the east. The Communist insurgency has been ongoing since 1969, while the Muslim groups have been operating since the early 1970s. The fighting is responsible for the **deaths of 160,000 people** and uprooting the lives of more than two million more people.

1970

The Oldest Boomer is 24 years old.

Cost of the Average House: $26,600	
Median Family Income: $8,730	**Minimum Wage:** $1.60/ hr **Average Hourly Wage:** $3.36
Gallon of Milk: $1.15	**Gallon Gasoline:** 36 cents
New Car: American Motors Ambassador SST Sedan: $3,722 **Buick LeSabre:** $3,337 **Dodge Challenger R/T Coupe:** $3,266	**Average Undergraduate Tuition / year:** **Public University:** $1,475 **Other 4-year:** $1,205 **Two-year:** $995
Unemployment Rate: 3.9%-4.9%-6.1%	**First-class Stamp:** 6 cents

18 cents buying power in 1970 = **$1.00 in 2008.**
In 1970 what cost us 18 cents to purchase now costs us $1.00 in 2008.

Why?

A part of the answer is we were on the gold standard until President Nixon eliminated it due to government excess. Yup-After WWII, a system similar to the Gold Standard was established by the Bretton Woods Agreements and many countries fixed their exchange rates relative to the U.S. dollar. The U.S. promised to fix the price of gold at $35 per ounce and all currencies pegged to the dollar also had a fixed value in terms of gold.

France, under President Charles de Gaulle, wanted to act as a powerful buffer between the U.S. and the Soviet Union and it reduced its dollar reserves, trading them for gold from the U.S. government. This reduced U.S. economic influence abroad. U.S. spending on the Vietnam war, President Johnson's Great Society, and the number of dollars being traded for gold led President Nixon to eliminate the fixed gold price in 1971. After some politics as usual this allowed the Federal Reserve to "create" dollars out of thin air, charge the American people for the privilege of using them (interest), and then confiscate much of their wealth through the inflation they created. When the U.S. government has the authority to "create" dollars out of thin air without paying interest for the privilege, **WHY** does it prefer to pay a "private" enterprise (The Federal Reserve) for this privilege?

Wednesday April 2, 2008 China, Japan and other countries own $2.4 trillion in U.S. Treasury debt, but there is only $182 billion (at $743 per ounce) total in gold reserves at Fort Knox. **"IF"** there is any gold in Fort Knox. An independent audit of Fort Knox has not been done since the Eisenhower administration even though it is required by law to be done on a yearly basis. **Who is hiding what?**

Movies: "M*A*S*H*," "Patton," "Airport," "Five Easy Pieces," "Love Story," "The Out-of-Towners," "Catch-22," "Beyond the Valley of the Dolls," "Ryan's Daughter," "There's a Girl in My Soup."

Broadway: "Last Sweet Days of Isaac," "The Me Nobody Knows," "Purlie," "Applause," "Rothschilds."

TV: "The Mary Tyler Moore Show," "The Odd Couple," "Men From Shiloh," "All My Children," "Flip Wilson Show," "Partridge Family," "The Phil Donahue Show starts its 26-year run. "Monday Night Football." Ringo Starr appears on "Laugh In" but it doesn't help his career. "The Harlem Globetrotters, Animated," "Josie and the Pussycats," "Night Gallery," "Nanny and the Professor," "Tim Conway Comedy Hour," "The Phil Donahue Show."

Music: "Isle of Wight Festival and 600,000 people attend the largest rock festival of all time. It outperformed Woodstock. Miles Davis, "Bitches Brew." The Beatles, "The Long and Winding Road." Norman Greenbaum, "Spirit in the Sky." Wilson Pickett, "Sugar-Sugar." Mungo Jerry, "In the Summertime." Diana Ross, "Ain't No Mountain High Enough." Stevie Wonder, "Signed, Sealed, Delivered I'm Yours." Badfinger, "No Matter What." Simon & Garfunkel, "Bridge Over Troubled Water." Three Dog

Night, "Celebrate." The Carpenters, "They Long to Be, Close to You," "Ticket To Ride" & "We've Only Just Begun." Creedence Clearwater Revival, "Who'll Stop The Rain." George Harrison, "My Sweet Lord." Nitty Gritty Dirt Band, "Mr. Bojangles." The Tee Set, "Ma Belle Amie." Led Zeppelin, "Whole Lotta Love." Tony Orlando and Dawn, "Candida." The Jackson 5, "ABC." Deep Purple, "Black Night." Neil Diamond, "Solitary Man." Aretha Franklin, "Son of a Preacher Man." Shocking Blue, "Venus." Eric Clapton, "After Midnight." Barbra Streisand, "Stoney End." Smokey Robinson & the Miracles, "The Tears Of A Clown." B. B. King, "The Thrill Is Gone." R. B. Greaves, "Take a Letter Maria."

Deaths: George Winne, Jr, is remembered as a protester of the Vietnam War who set himself on fire in a deliberate act of self-immolation.

President: Richard M. Nixon (R) Quaker; vetoes 43/7

Vice President: Spiro T. Agnew (R) Episcopalian

House: D-243 ; R-192

Senate: 91st Congress (1969-1971) Majority Party: Democrat (57 seats) Minority Party: Republican (43 seats) Other Parties: 0 Total Seats: 100

Federal Debt: $370.92 billion or 36 % of the GDP

Consumer Price Index CPI-U (1982 Base of 100): 38.80

GDP: $1,038.5 billion	Inflation Rate: 5.84%
Dow Jones: 800. (January)/ 687.64 (07-01)	S&P Price Index: 92.15/0.10%
Prime Rate: 8.00% (03-25)/ 6.75% (12-22)	Average Home Mortgage Rate: 8.13%
1 oz Gold: $36.41	1oz of Silver: $1.88

Monthly S.S. Benefits Paid: maximum was $123.82/ month

Federal Debt: $370,918,706,949.93

Federal Deficit: $2.8 billion dollars

Defense Spending: $94.69 billion	Interest Spending: $14.38 billion

Health Care Spending: $12.12 billion	**Pensions Spending:** $28.40 billion
Welfare Spending: $9.08 billion	**Education Spending:** $9.58 billion
Transportation Spending: $7.01 billion	**Misc. Other Spending:** $16.93 billion
Protection Spending: $960 million	**Total Government Spending:** $195.65 billion
% of GDP that goes towards just the interest payment: 1.42%	
$1.00 = 358.15 Yen, Japan	
U.S. Population: 205,089,000	**World Population:** 3,707,610,112
U.S. Birth Rate: 3,731,386	**U.S. Abortions:** 193,491
U.S. Homicide Rate: 8.3/ 100,000 population	**U.S. Violent Crime:** 363.5/ 100,000 population
Annual Average Domestic Crude Oil Prices: $3.39 / barrel, $18.77 (2007 adjusted)	

Oil:

1970 – **Food prices** are going up due to regional droughts **and high energy costs**. The cost of energy for transportation increases with the Arab oil embargo.

October 1970 – Egypt. Nasser dies. Nasser's political system was called **Arab Socialism.** He nationalized banks and industries as well as the **Suez Canal.** Following peaceful negotiations, he ended the **72-year British presence** in Egypt. As President, he formed a new constitution, giving himself increased power and then extended this power again in 1967, when he added the office of Prime Minister to the Presidential office. Nasser fought the British presence in Egypt, the landowning elite and the weak and morally corrupt King.

After Egyptian President Gamal Abdel Nasser dies he is succeeded by **Anwar Sadat** his former Vice President. Sadat has a close working relationship with **Saudi intelligence,** the **CIA, Henry Kissinger,** and **Islamic fundamentalists.** As a former member of the **Muslim Brotherhood** he welcomes them back with open arms. Sadat pushes for radical change and **Sheikh Omar Abdul-Rahman** and **Ayman al-Zawahiri** gain great power in Egypt during this period.

Anwar Sadat is **assassinated** in 1981 by **Islamic Jihad,** an offshoot of the Muslim Brotherhood, because of his accommodation with Israel.

1970 – Production of petroleum, crude oil and natural gas plant liquids, in the **U.S. lower 48 States** reaches its highest level at 9.4 million barrels per day. By 2005 the U.S. will consume 20 million barrels of crude oil every day and no new refineries have been built in 29 years. On April 25, 2005, **Crown Prince Abdullah of Saudi Arabia,** visiting **President Bush** at his Texas ranch, chided him with the message that his country could send more oil, but the United States would not have the ability to refine it. Soon afterward, Mr. Bush offered to provide closed military bases for new refineries.

1970s – Libya nationalizes its manufacturing and private-sector industries. Although Libya enjoys immense oil revenues coupled with a small population, most of the money stays within the centralized government, and little flows to the general population.

October 1970 – North Sea Oil. British Petroleum drills what turns out to be a dry hole in May 1970, followed by the discovery of the giant **Forties oilfield** in October. By the time British Petroleum sells the field in 2003, their reservoir engineers estimated the reserves are 4.2 billion bbl. Apache Corporation buys the field, immediately initiates an intensive re-evaluation and finds another 800 Mbbl, extending the field's life by at least 20 years.

1970 – Oman is now producing 332,000 barrels of oil a day which is a great improvement from the 30,000 barrels per day when it started producing oil in 1967. Oman is an undeveloped country with a population of almost one million people that have survived by farming and fishing. There is only one hospital, three primary schools and a few miles of paved road in the whole country. Oil revenues allow an ambitious social and economic development program.

Major News:

1970 – University of Wisconsin. A car bombing devastates a University of Wisconsin campus building, killing one person in the blast. Four student radicals protesting **weapons research at Sterling Hall** are responsible for the most powerful act of **domestic terrorism** on U.S. soil until the 1995 Oklahoma City bombing. The bomb blasted a crater in Sterling Hall, killing 33 year old research scientist, Robert Fassnacht, injuring three others and damaging dozens of other campus buildings. They targeted the building because its upper floors housed the Army Mathematics Research Center, where they believed scientists were conducting secret weapons research for the war in Vietnam. They said later they thought the building would be empty at the time. The Sterling Hall attack will help bring increasingly violent protests in Madison and across the country to a halt, although the movement to stop the war continues until the last U.S. forces finally leave Vietnam in defeat in 1975.

February 21, 1970 – The Weathermen. Gasoline-filled Molotov cocktails are thrown at the home of New York State Supreme Court Justice John Murtagh, who is presiding over the trial of the **Black Panther** members. The **"Panther 21,"** have been charged with plotting to bomb New York landmarks and department stores. One bottle full of gasoline broke against the front steps, setting the overhanging wooden frame on fire. Windows were broken, and another Molotov cocktail caused paint damage to a car. Painted in red on the sidewalk in front of his house were "Free The Panther 21," "The Viet Cong Have Won," and "Kill The Pigs." Molotov cocktails are thrown at a police car in Manhattan and two military recruiting stations in Brooklyn later that night. The son of Justice Murtagh claimed that the Weatherman are responsible for the attempted arson.

February 18, 1970 – The Chicago 7 are found **innocent of conspiring** to incite riots during the 1968 Democratic National Convention, but five defendants are **convicted of crossing state lines with intent** to incite riots.

March 6, 1970 – The Weathermen. As bombs are being built at a Greenwich Village safe house in preparation for the bombing of an officers' dance at the **Fort Dix U.S. Army base** and for **Butler Library at Columbia University,** there is an explosion. A nail bomb being built explodes killing **Weathermen** members Diana Oughton, Ted Gold, and Terry Robbins. Cathy Wilkerson and Kathy Boudin escape unharmed. The FBI reported that the group had enough explosives to level both sides of the street.

The Weathermen now go deep underground and refer to themselves as the **Weather Underground Organization.** They want to convince the American public that the United States is responsible for the calamity in Vietnam and they begin by bombing empty offices at night so that no people will be harmed. They always give advanced warning to allow for a safe evacuation. According to David Gilbert, "their goal was to not hurt any people, and a lot of work went into that. But we wanted to pick targets that showed the public who was responsible for what was really going on." The **FBI** placed the Weather Underground organization on the ten most-wanted list by the end of 1970.

Unrepentant Weather Underground terrorist Bill Ayers has never been implicated in a death among the high-profile bombings of the Capitol, the Pentagon and several other targets of the Weather Underground when he served as a leader. **Bernardine Dohrn,** his wife cannot make the same claim, according to FBI files. Ayers and Dohrn will go on to help launch **Barack Obama's political career.**

April 22, 1970 – The first Earth Day celebration is held with millions of American participating in anti-pollution demonstrations. These demonstrations included school children walking to school instead of riding the bus.

April 30, 1970 – U.S. and South Vietnamese forces cross Cambodian borders to attack enemy bases as **President Nixon** extends the Vietnam War into **Cambodia.** Nixon's declaration sets off a chain reaction, and 1.5 million students protest around the country. The President fueled the confrontation by calling them **"bums" who were "blowing up the campuses."**

May 4, 1970 – Kent State. Four students from Kent State University in Ohio are killed and nine wounded by **National Guardsmen** during a protest against the Vietnam War. Tensions in Kent, Ohio, escalated in the days leading up to May 4, as

1970

Mayor Leroy Satrom declared the city under a state of emergency after a disturbance downtown got out of hand. On May 2, the Mayor requested that the Ohio National Guard deploy. The protest ended when four students at Kent State University, two of them women, were shot to death by **National Guard gunfire.** At least 8 other students were wounded.

About **1,000 young people** were on a grassy hill, a campus gathering spot when the National Guard began lobbing tear gas at the crowd. More than 100 troops advanced on the students, up a hill and then down toward a practice football field. When they reached the fence at the far end, some of the troops knelt and aimed their weapons. The students had retreated into a parking lot between the buildings and some threw the tear gas back at the National Guard. Others threw rocks. The troops slowly moved back up the hill and when they reached the crest twenty-eight guardsmen turned quickly and fired in the direction of the protesters. They fired sixty-one rounds of ammunition. Of the thirteen people killed or injured, only two were actively involved in the protest. One student was killed while walking to class and another was an ROTC student. Others were more than one hundred yards away

May 14, 1970 – Jackson State University in Mississippi. A small group of non-students rioted and were throwing rocks at passing cars when police, Mississippi State Troopers, and National Guard troops (with no ammunition) cordoned off a thirty block area around the campus. Those rioting set several fires and firefighters asked for police backup. After the fire was extinguished the police and state troopers marched the students back up the street to Alexander Hall as the students hurled rocks and bricks at the officers. When state police warned them and then opened fire into the dormitory at the all-black school, killing two students and wounding twelve others. The five-story dormitory is struck with over 460 rounds shattering every window facing the street on each floor. **FBI investigators** counted at least 160 bullet holes in the outer walls of the stairwell alone.

A **U.S. Senate probe** conducted by **Senators Walter Mondale** and **Birch Bayh** will later reveal the police officers first picked up their shell casings before calling for ambulances to assist the many students that lay bleeding on the ground in front of the dormitory. After the area was "cleaned up," most of the students still made it to University Hospital within 20 minutes of the shooting.

September 1970 – Weather Underground Organization. The group takes a $20,000 payment from a psychedelics distribution organization called The Brotherhood of Eternal Love to successfully break **LSD** advocate **Timothy Leary** out of **prison.** Leary and his wife are then flown to **Algeria** where Leary joined **Eldridge Cleaver.**

Leary's initial press release contains revolutionary rhetoric sympathetic to the Weather Underground's cause. It is later alleged Timothy Leary tries to make a deal with the FBI in exchange for his freedom when he is finally captured. Leary did not pick up the "Get out of Jail, Free" card and spends a few more years in prison.

July 23, 1970 – The Houston Plan. President Richard Nixon approves a plan for greatly expanding **domestic intelligence-gathering** by the **FBI, CIA** and other agencies. **John Mitchell,** the first United States Attorney General ever to be convicted of illegal activities, hears about the Huston plan for the first time and goes to Nixon urging him to rescind it. Nixon has second thoughts a few days later and cancels the plan.

October 1970 – The United States Customs Service is charged with enforcing air security provisions of the Federal Aviation Act.

1970 – The Postal Reform Bill makes the U.S. Postal Service self-supporting.

Civil Rights Movement:

1970 – Census. U.S. population: 204,765,770; Black population: 22,580,289 (11.1%).

January 2, 1970 – Dr. Clifton Wharton, Jr., is named President of Michigan State University. He is the first African American to lead a major, predominately white university.

February 18, 1970 – Bobby Seale and six other six defendants, popularly known as the **Chicago Seven,** are acquitted of the charge of conspiring to disrupt the 1968 **Democratic National Convention. Five were found guilty** of **crossing state lines with intent** to incite riots.

1970

1970 – **African-American voter registration** reaches fifty-seven percent of the voting age population, sixteen percentage points behind the white figure.

July 1, 1970 – Kenneth Gibson becomes the **first black Mayor** of an eastern city when he assumes the post in Newark, New Jersey.

August 7, 1970 – Angela Davis. The San Rafael, California courthouse shooting results in the death of Judge Harold Haley and three others. UCLA Philosophy Professor Angela Davis is implicated in the shooting and is placed on the **FBI's Ten Most Wanted List.** In the escape attempt, a white judge and four blacks were killed, among them, Jonathan Jackson, a close friend of Angela Davis and the younger brother of imprisoned Black Panther George Jackson. Angela Davis is accused of supplying Jackson with some of the weapons used in the shoot-out. When brought to trial on June 4, 1972, she is acquitted of all charges.

In a 1990 interview with the *Los Angeles Times,* Angela Davis said that the reason she pushed for ethnic studies classes was that she feared that her generation of radicals would be forgotten and that she dreaded the question she sometimes heard, "Angela Davis, is she still alive?"

1970 – **Literacy requirements** are banned for five years by the 1970 renewal of the Voting Rights Act. **Eighteen states still have** a literacy requirement in place. In Oregon vs. Mitchell, the Court upholds the ban on literacy tests, which will be made permanent in 1975. Judge Hugo Black, writing the court's opinion, cited the "long history of the discriminatory use of literacy tests to disenfranchise voters on account of their race" as the reason for their decision.

In Alabama you had to go down to the courthouse to register to vote and the **Registrars Office** was only open two or three days a month for a few hours. So you were required to take time off of work. In most cases a black worked for a white business owner and if your employer gave you the time off to register, or did not fire you for just taking unauthorized time off to register, he could be driven out of business. When you did show up at the courthouse, the county Sheriff and his deputies would in many instances discourage "undesirables" from trying to register. **Once grandma got through all** of those hurdles, she then had to run the gauntlet of harassment and intimidation from the clerks. Then you were required to fill out a four page form and take oaths under the threat of perjury that you told the whole truth, all the while knowing this form would be sent to the local **Ku Klux Klan.** Some counties even required a registered voter to vouch for you, under oath and penalty of perjury. There were not many blacks who were registered, and the few who would vouch for you could always be intimated later.

If you made it this far you were given the Literacy Test. **Part A:** Read a section of the U.S. Constitution. You could then be required to write this same section while the clerk read (mumbled) it. And you would be judged as to whether or not you were literate. Then there were the questions from **Part B** and **Part C.** Freedom Schools helped people learn how to fill out the forms and pass the tests.

1970 – Albert W. Watson a conservative Republican congressman running for Governor, tells residents of Darlington County, South Carolina, to "use every means at your disposal to defend" the community against a Federal court order desegregating the local schools. Nine days later, a white mob attacks three buses carrying black children to school in the Darlington County town of Lamar. The state restores order and enforces the rule of law. No one is injured, but many of Mr. Watson's critics blame him for the incident.

October 12, 1970 – Charles Gordone becomes the first African American to win a Pulitzer Prize in Drama for his play, **"No Place to Be Somebody."**

1970 – November. I.S. Leevy Johnson, James Felder, and Herbert Fielding are elected to the South Carolina House in the General Assembly, the first African-Americans since 1902. County-wide at-large elections make winning difficult for African-Americans. Republican Albert Watson, basing his campaign for governor on opposition to the civil rights movement and integration, loses to Democrat John West, but Watson wins nearly three-fifths of the white vote.

Women's Movement:

1970 – A *Ladies' Home Journal* sit-in exposes the **sexism** of the "women's magazines."

1970

1970 – The North American Indian Women's Association is founded.

1970 – Feminist leader **Bella Abzug** is elected to Congress, famously declaring **"A woman's place is in the House."**

1970 – President Nixon vetoes the Comprehensive Child Development Act, which would have established federally, funded childcare centers.

1970 – Chicana feminists begin the Comision Femenil Mexicana Nacional.

August 26, 1970 – It is the 50th anniversary of woman suffrage in the U.S. and tens of **thousands** of women across the nation **participate** in the "Women's Strike for Equality," organized by **Betty Friedan**, to demand equal rights.

Popular Culture:

1960-1970 – Free Love. During the 1960s and 1970s, society's views of sexuality begin to change. The pill and birth control supposedly remove any of the consequences of sex outside of a commitment within marriage. This begins a break from Biblical "Truth" and a tolerance of worldly viewpoints, leading to the development of new codes of sexual behavior. Many of these "new" codes of sexual behavior become "normal" and are integrated into the mainstream. The 1960s and 1970s embraced a culture of **"free love"** and millions of young people live the hippie philosophy of the **power of love** and the **beauty of sex** as a natural part of ordinary life because many of the consequences were thought to be far removed with the advent of birth control. **Hippies** believe sex is a natural biological phenomenon which should not be denied or repressed and the **"era of Self"** is born. Experimenting with open sex within marriage and outside of marriage, contraception and the pill, public nudity, gay Liberation, liberalization of abortion, interracial marriage, a return to natural birth control and childbirth, women's rights and feminism now move into the mainstream. It is a myth that all hippies are promiscuous wallowing in an orgy of free sex. In fact many remain celibate as a matter of personal choice.

The **Jesus movement** is a movement in **Christianity** beginning on the West Coast of the United States in the late 1960s and early 1970s and it spreads through North America and Europe for ten to fifteen years. It is the **major Christian element** within the **hippie counterculture,** or, conversely, the major hippie element within some strands of Christianity. Members of the movement are called *Jesus people,* or *Jesus freaks.*

1970 – National Student Strike. More than 450 university, college and high school campuses across the country are shutdown by student strikes and both violent and non-violent protests that involve more than 4 million students, **in the only nationwide student strike in U.S. history.**

1970 – 55% of American adults have completed high school. Slightly more females than males have graduated.

1970 – Toni Cade, **"The Black Woman."**

1970 – National Right to Life Committee is established to block the legalization of **abortion.**

May 4, 1970 – Kent State/Cambodia Incursion Protest, Washington, D.C. A week after the Kent State Shootings, on May 4, **100,000 anti-war demonstrators** converge on **Washington, D.C.** to protest the shooting of the students in Ohio and the Nixon administration's incursion into Cambodia. In an almost spontaneous response to the events of the previous week the demonstration is quickly put together, as thousands of protestors march in the nation's capital.

As police surround the **White House** with buses to block the demonstrators from getting too close to the executive mansion, President Nixon meets early in the morning with the protesters at the Lincoln Memorial. (The President of the United States of America met with protest leaders!)

May 15, 1970 – President Nixon names two women Generals, the first in U.S. history.

May 1970 – The first issue of **Essence magazine.**

1970

1970 – The Joint Center for Political Studies is established in Washington, D.C.

May 1970 – A Gallup poll in May shows that 56% of the public believes that sending troops to **Vietnam** was a mistake, 61% of those over 50 expressed that belief compared to 49% of those between the ages of 21–29.

June 13, 1970 – President Nixon establishes the **President's Commission on Campus Unrest.** The commission is directed to study the dissent, disorder, and violence breaking out on college and university campuses.

1970 – The Lutheran Church in America and the American Lutheran Church allow **women to be ordained.**

1970 – The case of Diana vs. California State Board results in new laws requiring that **children referred for possible special education placement** will now be tested in their primary language.

1970 – Teams of players compete in shooting games on the **Internet.**

August 24, 1970 – Sterling Hall bombing. Close to 3:40 a.m., a van filled with an ammonium nitrate and fuel oil mixture is detonated on the **University of Wisconsin-Madison** in the Sterling Hall bombing.

1970 – Vortex I. A Biodegradable Festival of Life. To avert potential violence arising from planned anti-war protests, **a government-sponsored rock festival** is held near Portland, Oregon from August 28 to September 3, attracting 100,000 participants. The festival, arranged by the People's Army Jamboree, an ad hoc group, and Oregon Governor Tom McCall, is set up when the FBI tells the Governor that President Nixon's planned appearance at an American Legion convention in Portland could lead to violence worse than that seen at 1968 Democratic National Convention in Chicago.

August 29, 1970 – The Chicano Moratorium. Twenty-five thousand Mexican-Americans participate in the largest anti-war demonstration in Los Angeles. Police attack the crowd with billyclubs and tear gas. Two people are killed. Immediately after the marchers are dispersed, sheriff's deputies raid a nearby bar, where **Ruben Salazar**, KMEX news director and **"Los Angeles Times" columnist**, is shot with a tear-gas projectile.

A sheriff's deputy warned three men to come out of the bar with their hands up. Ruben Salazar was sitting on a bar stool just behind the men when he was shot in the head with a tear gas cartridge. Although it is ruled a homicide no one is ever prosecuted.

October 26, 1970 – Gerry Trudeau introduces "**Doonesbury.**"

November 1970 – CBS News broadcasts a report from Fire Base Aires in Vietnam where members of the First Air Cavalry Division gather for a **marijuana "smoke-in."** The image of soldiers using the barrel of a shotgun to smoke pot is shocking enough, but it suggested a larger problem that was to plague the military for the remainder of the war.

1970 – National Public Radio (NPR) begins.

1970 – The Comprehensive Drug Abuse and Control Act Replaces and updates all previous laws concerning narcotics and other dangerous drugs. The emphasis is on law enforcement.

1970 – Coca-Cola, "It's the real thing." McCann-Erickson.

1970 – 7 UP, "The Uncola." J. Walter Thompson.

1970 – The President's Commission on Obscenity and Pornography submits its controversial report to **President Richard Nixon**. In 1970, the Presidential Commission on Obscenity and Pornography concluded that "**there was insufficient evidence** that exposure to explicit sexual materials played a significant role as the cause of delinquent or criminal behavior." In general, with regard to adults, the Commission recommended that legislation **"should not seek to interfere with the right of adults who wish to do so, to read, obtain, or view explicit sexual**

materials." Regarding the view that these materials should be restricted for adults in order to protect young people from exposure to them, the Commission found that it is "inappropriate to adjust the level of adult communication to that considered suitable for children." The Supreme Court supported this view.

1970 – For the first time, the **1970 census** counted over **200 million people** living in the United States.

Business / Technology:

1970 – **Optical Fiber**. Corning Glass Works spins out optical fiber clear enough for light pulses.

1970 – **IBM System 370 allows time-sharing**, online computing. This will eventually allow **Bill Gates** to use a state of the art computer at his private school to log many hours and begin writing programs while **in the eighth grade.**

January 5, 1970 – **Joseph Yablonski,** is **murdered,** along with his **wife and daughter,** in their Clarksville, Pennsylvania home by **assassins.** Yablonski was a reform candidate that had challenged W. A. Boyle for the Presidency of the United Mine Workers the month before. Twenty–thousand West Virginia miners go on strike the following day in protest convinced Boyle was responsible for the murders. Boyle was later convicted of the three murders and died in prison in 1985.

1970 – **Cloning. Dr. John B. Gurdon (U.K.) clones a frog** by transplanting the intestinal cell of a tadpole into an enucleated frog egg, which develops into an adult frog.

1970 – **AFL-CIO meets to discuss the status of women** in unions. It endorses the ERA and opposes state protective legislation.

1970 – **Congress outlaws** tobacco ads in broadcasting.

1970 – Schultz vs. Wheaton Glass Co. The U.S. Court of Appeals rules jobs held by men and women must be **"substantially equal" but not "identical"** to fall under the protection of the Equal Pay Act. It is illegal for employers to change the job titles of women workers in order to pay them less than men.

1970 – In Germany, a **videodisk** is demonstrated.

1970 – Ford Motor Corporation unveils its new automobile, the **Pinto**, despite tests revealing that rear-end collisions sometimes caused fuel-line ruptures, setting the vehicle aflame. Ford was acquitted of criminal charges in the many lawsuits filled but limped away with a damaged reputation.

Over two million Pinto's are built and it is estimated 27 people died in rear end collisions, which is far below the national standard. Its fatality rates are lower than comparably sized imported automobiles.

March 18, 1970 – The first mass work stoppage in the 195-year history of the **United States Post Office Department** begins with a **walkout** of letter carriers in Brooklyn and Manhattan. By March 23rd, the strikers numbered almost 250,000 of the nation's 750,000 postal employees. With mail service virtually paralyzed in New York, Detroit, and Philadelphia, President Nixon declared a state of national emergency and assigned military units to New York City post offices.

Because of the high cost of living in New York City, many carriers were forced to work two jobs or go on welfare, if not both. The stand-off culminated two weeks later although it has been said that a lot of what had been promised was never delivered.

July 29, 1970 – United Farm Workers force California grape growers to sign an agreement after a five-year strike.

August 1970 – The first issue of *Black Enterprise* magazine makes it to the newsstands.

1970 – The AP, Associated Press, sends **news by computer.**

December 31, 1970 – President Richard Nixon signs the Clean Air Act, in response to growing concerns for the environment. **The Clean Air Act** is a bill calling for development of a cleaner auto engine and national air quality standards for 10 major pollutants. It also requires states to regulate sources of **air pollution** to specific air quality standards, and to have regulatory programs in order to attain improved levels of air quality.

1970 – U.S. Post Office and Western Union offer Mailgrams.

1970 – Picturephone services are offered in downtown Pittsburgh.

1970 – In response to rising concerns about **worker and workplace safety**, the U.S. Congress passes the **Occupational Safety and Health Act.** Enacted under the federal government's Constitutional right to regulate interstate commerce, the legislation aimed to guarantee that workers across the country have a workplace that is free from unreasonable dangers.

1970 – Xerox begins its Palo Alto Research Center.

Finance:

June 30, 1970 – The United States Savings Stamp Program ends. The **war savings stamp** was a patriotic program used by the United States Treasury to help fund participation in World War I and World War II, and was principally aimed at school-age children. Stamps were available in 25 cent and ten cent versions, and provided interest. In some cases collections of stamps could be redeemed for war bonds. The postal system had a program that allowed customers to purchase the stamps and place them into savings books that could be redeemed for savings bonds at the post office.

1970 – Bernard "Bernie" Cornfeld is tried and acquitted for orchestrating one of the most lucrative confidence games of his era. From his ancient French castle Bernie jets around the world building his company, **Investors Overseas Services**, into a $2.5 billion financial empire that fascinated the news media, attracted small investors and plagued market regulators. His trademark recruiting challenge, **"Do you sincerely want to be rich?"** helps build an intensely loyal sales force. At its peak, Investors Overseas Services includes an intensely loyal sales force, an insurance unit, real estate interests and many offshore investment funds operating beyond the reach of any single country's securities laws. Bernie pumped 450 million dollars into the American mutual funds industry with the help of his *Fund of Funds*, an offshore fund that invested in other mutual funds.

Robert L. Vesco, an American financier, took over Investors Overseas Services in 1970. Vesco drained more then $220 million dollars from the company and fled the country after being accused of securities fraud. He tried to buy a Caribbean island from Antigua in order to create an autonomous country and while he was living in Costa Rica he had a national law made to protect him from extradition. A 2001 Slate.com article labeled **Vesco "the undisputed king of the fugitive financiers."**

Robert Vesco finally settled in Cuba in 1982. He was charged with drug smuggling in 1989 and in the 1990s he was indicted by the Cuban government for "fraud and illicit economic activity" and "acts prejudicial to the economic plans and contracts of the state." Vesco was sentenced to 13 years in jail by Cuban authorities. The *New York Times* reported he died of lung cancer at a hospital in Havana, Cuba in November 2007.

Books:

1970 – Kate Millet publishes her revolutionary book, "**Sexual Politics.**"

1970 – Joseph Heller, "Good As Gold."

1970 – Germaine Greer, "**The Female Eunuch.**"

1970 – The Boston Women's Health Collective published "**Women and their Bodies**" This will become far better known a year later under its subsequent title, "**Our Bodies, Ourselves.**" This book would have been banned just 5 years ago. It now sells for 35 cents, as a newsprint booklet.

1970 – "**Human Sexual Inadequacy,**" **Masters and Johnson** declares that 90 percent of all impotence is caused by some form of psychological or emotional conflict.

1970 – "**One Hundred Years of Solitude,**" Gabriel García Marquez.

1970

1970 – James Dickey, "**Deliverance.**"

1970 – "**Fifth Business,**" Robertson Davies.

1970 – Jerzy Kosinski, "**Being There.**"

1970 – "**Sisterhood Is Powerful,**" An Anthology of Writings from the Women's Liberation Movement edited by Robin Morgan.

TV:

1970 – **U.S. movie ticket sales drop** from 3 billion plus in 1950 to under 1 billion. TV is thought to be the main cause of the decline in sales.

1970 – **Robert Schuller 's Hour of Power** is derived from Norman Vincent Peale's "**Power of Positive Thinking**" and shares his positive theology of "possibility thinking," the management of ideas, lessening negative self-talk, and exploring ideas for the possibilities they present.

1970 – **Monday Night Football begins** with the Cleveland Browns vs. the New York Jets. The Browns win 31/21.

Sports:

1970 – **Diane Crump** becomes the first female jockey to ride in the **Kentucky Derby.**

1970 – **Muhammad Ali** is allowed to fight again while his selective service draft case is still on appeal. With the help of a Senator, he is granted a license to box in Georgia because it is the only state without a boxing commission. In October 1970, he stops Jerry Quarry on a cut after three rounds. After wining a separate lawsuit the New York State Supreme Court ruled that Ali had been unjustly denied a boxing license. Able to fight in New York, he fought Oscar Bonavena at Madison Square Garden in December 1970. After a tough 14 rounds, Ali stopped Bonavena in the 15th, paving the way for a title fight against Joe Frazier, who was himself undefeated.

Music:

1970 – Isle of Wight Festival is held on August 26-31, on Afton Down an area on the Western side of the Isle of Wight. It is the last of three consecutive music festivals to take place on the island between 1968 and 1970 and is widely acknowledged as the largest musical event of its time (until Summer Jam at Watkins Glen in 1973), greater than the attendance of "Live Aid", "Woodstock" and "Rock in Rio". The Guinness Book of Records has cited its attendance as 600,000.

1970 – The disco hustle starts in New York.

January 7, 1970 – Max Yasgur, owner of the New York farm where the 1969 **Woodstock Festival** was held, is sued for $35,000 in property damages by neighboring farmers.

January 16, 1970 – John Lennon's London Art gallery exhibit of lithographs, *Bag One,* is shut down by Scotland Yard for displaying **"erotic lithographs."**

February 11, 1970 – The film **"The Magic Christian,"** starring **Peter Sellers and Ringo Starr** premieres in New York.

March 4, 1970 – Janis Joplin is fined $200 for using obscene language during a concert performance in Tampa, Florida.

March 6, 1970 – Cult leader and suspected murderer **Charles Manson** releases an album titled **"Lies"** to help finance his defense.

March 26, 1970 – Peter Yarrow, of Peter Paul and Mary, pleads guilty to "taking immoral liberties" with a 14 year old girl in Washington D.C.

July 26, 1970 – Guitarist Jimi Hendrix plays at his hometown of Seattle at Sicks Stadium where, under the influence of **drugs**, he starts verbally abusing members of the audience.

1970

September 6, 1970 – During his final European tour, guitarist **Jimi Hendrix** is greeted by booing and jeering German fans at his late appearance on stage and incoherent stage performance. Bassist Billy Cox quits the tour and returns to the United States.

September 18 – Jimi Hendrix dies from a barbiturate overdose at his London hotel at the age of 27.

October 30, 1970 – **Jim Morrison of The Doors,** is found guilty of indecent exposure and profanity because of his behavior during a March 1, 1969 concert, and is sentenced to eight months of hard labor and a $500 fine.

1970 – Some new bands are **The Doobie Brothers, Electric Light Orchestra, Ocean, Queen, and Aerosmith.**

December 21, 1970 – **Elvis** shows up at the white House gate with a letter for **President Nixon** requesting a personal meeting about how he could help the government fight the **drug trade**. The meeting took place and Nixon gave Presley an actual narcotics agent badge.

Natural Disasters:

January 5, 1970 – **Yunnan province, China**. A magnitude 7.5 earthquake kills more than 10,000 people.

May 31, 1970 – **Peru**. **Ancash earthquake** or **Great Peruvian Earthquake**. A magnitude 7.9 earthquake leaves more than 66,000 people dead. The **Ancash earthquake** is an undersea earthquake affecting the Peruvian regions of Ancash and La Libertad. Combined with a subsequent landslide, it is the most catastrophic natural disaster ever recorded in the history of Peru.

July 31, 1970 – **Columbian earthquake.** Buildings rocked in the capital cities of San Juan, Bogota, Caracas, Sao Paulo, and Buenos Aires. Light damage was noted in Peru. A combination of great depth (651 km) and high magnitude caused the widely impacted area, but also limited more serious effects and led to unprecedented discoveries about the Earth's interior. The shock is felt from Buenos Aires, Argentina, to Mexico City, Mexico, and throughout the Caribbean. One person is killed and several people are injured.

November 12-13, 1970 – East Pakistan. The Bhola cyclone and tidal waves kill up to 500,000 people and another 100,000 people are reported missing. The Bhola cyclone is the deadliest tropical cyclone on record and is one of the deadliest natural disasters in recent history. The exact death toll will never be known, but it is estimated that between 350,000 and 500,000 people lost their lives primarily as a result of the storm surge that flooded much of the low-lying islands of the Ganges Delta. There are an estimated 235,000 homes destroyed, 140,000 homes damaged, 470,000 livestock killed, 9,000 fishing boats lost, and 400,000 metric tons of rice destroyed.

Man vs. Man / Wars:

March 31, 1970 – Representative John V. Dowdy (D-Texas) **is indicted** on charges of conflict of interest, conspiracy, perjury, and interstate travel to facilitate bribery. Dowdy is accused of taking $25,000 from a Maryland home improvement firm accused of defrauding its customers in return for intervening in an investigation of the firm by the Justice Department. He is convicted on December 12, 1970 and sentenced to **18 months**.

October 18, 1970 – Representative Martin B. McNeally (R-New York) **is indicted** for failure to file federal income tax returns for four years. McNeally pleads guilty to one year's lapse.

Assassinated – Canada. Pierre Laporte, The Quebec Minister of Labour. Pierre Laporte was a prominent cabinet minister in the Bourassa Liberal government when he was kidnapped and killed by the Chénier cell of the FLQ during the October Crisis of 1970. For many years Pierre Laporte was the parliamentary correspondent for the Montreal newspaper "Le Devoir" and he was well known in the province of Quebec. He entered politics in 1961.

1970

February 21, 1970 – A Swiss airliner is blown up over Switzerland, killing all 47 people on board.

February 23, 1970 – **Terrorists** belonging to the **Palestine Liberation Organization** open fire on a busload of Christian pilgrims killing 1 and wounding 2.

April 21, 1970 – **A bomb explodes** aboard a Philippines airliner. All 36 civilians aboard are killed in the name of **Islamic Jiahd.**

September 6, 1970 – **"Skyjack Sunday" in Jordan** involves three planes. "Skyjack Sunday" took place at Dawson Field, Jordan. **TWA, Swissair, BOAC aircraft,** along with more than **four hundred hostages, are hijacked** and ordered to the Jordanian airport by the **Popular Front for the Liberation of Palestine.** Another terrorist team tried to hijack an El Al Boeing over London but the security staff foiled the attempt. The German, Swiss and British Governments all agreed to the PFLP's demands and released a number of terrorists held in their jails.

September 14, 1970 – **The Popular Front for the Liberation of Palestine hijacked** TWA flight to Ammon, 4 Americans were injured.

1970 – **The Baader-Meinhof Gang.** The **Red Army Faction**, shortened to **RAF,** in its early stages commonly known as **Baader-Meinhof Group** or **Gang**, is one of postwar West Germany's most violent and prominent left-wing militant groups. The RAF described itself as a communist "urban guerrilla" group engaged in armed resistance. The RAF s formally founded in 1970 by Andreas Baader, Gudrun Ensslin, Horst Mahler, Ulrike Meinhof.

May 14, 1970 – **Berlin. Ulrike Meinhof** tells prison officials that she has been contracted to write a book with Baader, and the two will need to study at a library outside of the prison. The prison grants her request which requires a brief leave from the prison under armed guard. Once outside the prison and under guard at Berlin's Dahlem Institute for Social Research, Journalist Ulrike Meinhof helps Baader to escape through a window.

The **Baader-Meinhof Gang** is held responsible for 34 deaths, including many secondary targets, such as chauffeurs and bodyguards, and many injuries over the next 30 years of activity.

1967-1970 – Biafra. Southeastern Nigeria. Major oil strikes were made in the non-Igbo section of the Eastern Region of Nigeria in the 1960's. Nigeria's first oil refinery, at Alesa Eleme near Port Harcourt, began operations in late 1965 with a capacity of 38,000 barrels per day. This oil in the Niger Delta will shape and change the future of the country. The Igbos see the oil wealth as the answer to the poverty in their region, unfortunately the oil revenues will go back to the central government. The Igbos want to secede and form a separate state so they can keep all of the wealth and this is one of the reasons for the civil war.

The Republic of Biafra was a secessionist state in south-eastern Nigeria. Biafra was inhabited mostly by the Igbo people and existed from May 30, 1967 to January 15, 1970. It has been estimated that up to **2,000,000 people were killed.** Many of these men women and children starved to death.

March 18, 1970 – Cambodian Civil War. Prince Sihanouk is away on a trip to Moscow and Beijing when General **Lon Nol** launches a successful coup. The National Assembly is hastily convened on March 18, and votes unanimously to depose Sihanouk as head of state. Lon Nol, who had been serving as Prime Minister, is granted emergency powers in a transfer of power that is both legal and constitutional.

The Cambodian Civil War begins between the Khmer National Armed Forces loyal to Lon Nol and the Cambodian People's National Liberation Armed Forces, which will progressively come under the total control of the Khmer Rouge.

The U.S. is frustrated by Prince Sihanouk allowing the Ho Chi Minh trail to operate within Cambodia's borders so when Lon Nol asks for help from the U.S., President Nixon requests Congress to approve $155 million in supplemental aid. Unfortunately, Lon Nol is unable to defeat either the North Vietnamese forces or the Khmer Rouge. With the backing of China, and to a lesser extent Vietnam, The Khmer Rouge, advance their control of the countryside.

March 11, 1970 – A man hijacks a 727 from Cleveland to Cuba. He is imprisoned in Cuba for attempting to escape and is fatally shot escaping from a Cuban prison on March 26, 1973.

1970

April 22, 1970 – In 1966 Ira David Meeks was diagnosed with paranoid schizophrenia. On April 22, Meeks hired a pilot to take him and his girlfriend on a sightseeing tour over Gastonia, North Carolina. Once in the air Meeks pulled a gun on the pilot and demanded he fly them to Cuba.

When they landed in Havana, they were imprisoned by Cuban soldiers. Meeks told Cuban authorities "he felt persecuted as a black man in America and had heard that things would be better in Cuba." Cuban authorities suspected him of being a spy and he was jailed and then deported in 1976. When he arrived in the U.S. he was arrested for the hijacking by the FBI. Meeks was freed in 1981 after spending years in jail and a mental hospital.

August 2, 1970 – **A Pan American Airways 747** bound for San Juan from New York is hijacked by an unidentified male and forced to fly to Cuba. This is the first hijacking of the newly-introduced Boeing 747 to Cuba and Premiere **Fidel Castro** came out to **Havana's José Martí Airport** to see the new airliner for himself. Castro reportedly met with the pilot and expressed concerns over the ability of the big plane to take off safely from the small airport, but the Pan Am captain convinced him it would not be a problem.

1970-1975 – **Dhofar Rebellion in Oman.** (No to be confused with Darfur.) Said ibn Taimur's reprisals against the Dhofari people drive many of them into the rebel camp and in 1970, the Dhofari guerrilla attacks increase. In response his son, Qabus ibn Said, with the help of the British, remove him from government with a coup. Qabus ibn Said, a Sandhurst graduate and veteran of British army service, begins a program to modernize the country and to develop the armed forces. The new Sultan is assisted by troops sent by the **Shah of Iran,** annual financial aid from Abu Dhabi and Saudi Arabia, while Britain, Jordan, Saudi Arabia, Egypt, and Pakistan provide training in military schools for the armed forces. The Sultan improved transportation, education, rural health, and religious facilities. Almost all of the development was for Dhofar, a small section of the country with only one-fifth of the population.

October 10, 1970 – **Fiji gains its independence** from Britain as a dominion within the British Commonwealth. Ratu Sir Kamisese Mara becomes its first Prime Minister.

November 1970 – Guinea. Mercenary Invasion of Guinea. Mercenaries supported by Portugal attack the Guinea government. Nigeria and the United Arab Republic (Egypt) send troops to help Guinea.

January 1970 – Iraq. Iranian Plot. The Shah of Iran-backs a right-wing coup attempt in Iraq. The Ba'th regime hangs or shoots 29 Iraqi military officers and 12 Iraqi civilians for allegedly being involved in the coup plot.

1969-1970 – Arab-Israeli War of Attrition. A limited war is fought between **Israel, Egypt,** and the **Palestine Liberation Organization** from 1967 to 1970. The **War of Attrition** was initiated by Egypt as a way to force Israel to negotiate, on favorable terms, the return of the **Sinai Peninsula**, which had been captured by Israel in the 1967 Six-Day War. Given the wide disparity in the populations of Israel and Egypt, Israel could not long tolerate trading casualties with the Egyptians. The Israeli government, now led by **Golda Meir,** pursued a policy of "asymmetrical response," retaliation on a scale far exceeding any individual attack. The hostilities end with a ceasefire signed in 1970 with frontiers remaining in the same place as when the war began. Over 5,300 people are killed as a direct result of this war.

November 1970 – Ivory Coast. Cote D'ivoire. The Bete Rebellion. Gnagbé Niabé proclaims himself **Grand Chancellor of Côte d'Ivoire**. When Houphouët-Boigny refuses to accept Gnabé's candidacy for President or grant his request for a cabinet post, Gnabé gatheres a large group of supporters and marches on Gagnoa. Again, government troops capture the rebel leader, ending the small rebellion. The West African state of Ivory Coast is known more as an **oil refining country** rather than an oil producing one. While it does not have the prolific offshore oil fields of Nigeria, it does possess a modest oil industry. Its recoverable oil reserves have been estimated at 100 million barrels. Oil producing fields are Lion and Panthere. The national oil company, Petroci, will be established in 1975.

September 1970 – Jordan. The partnership with the Palestinians desired by **King Hussein** falls apart in September and the pervasive and chaotic presence of armed **Palestinian fedayeen groups** who expect immunity from Jordan's laws is leading to a state of virtual anarchy throughout the Kingdom. Moderate Palestinian leaders are unable to reign in extremist elements, which ambush the King's motorcade twice and perpetrate a series of spectacular hijackings. Forced to respond decisively in order to preserve his country from anarchy, **King Hussein** orders the army into action.

While most Arab world leaders privately express sympathy for King Hussein's plight, they also favor the fedayeen in public. In September **200 Syrian tanks,** camouflaged rather unconvincingly as Palestinian Liberation Army tanks, cross into Jordan. The Syrians have no air cover, and Jordanian aircraft force a Syrian retreat within three days. In a brief yet intense campaign ending in July 1971, the Jordanian army puts an end to the chaotic actions of these Palestinians guerrillas in Amman.

1970 – Syria. Black September. In September the Jordanian army launches attacks on PLO camps and on Palestinian refugee camps that are under the control of PLO units. Jordan's King Hussein orders the assaults in response to efforts by the PLO to implement its avowed policy of deposing Hussein and other Arab monarchs. The hostilities in Jordan, which became known by the PLO and its supporters as **Black September**, have a profound impact on the Arab world and particularly on the government in Syria.

During a civil war that lasted only 10 days, Syria sent some 200 tanks, somewhat disguised as **Palestine Liberation Army tanks,** to aid the PLO forces. **The United States dispatched the Sixth Fleet** to the eastern Mediterranean, and the Israeli air force openly assumed a posture of military preparedness. The **Syrian air force refused** to provide air cover to the Syrian tank brigade, which came under severe attacks first by the Jordanian air force and then by **the Jordanian army.** Then on September 23 and 24, the **Syrian expeditionary force** withdrew from the battle zone and returned to Syria. By the time Syrian President Nureddin al-Atassi realized the threat from Hafez al-Assad it was too late. Assad swiftly launched a bloodless intra-party coup. Syria's intelligence and security services begin consolidating power and sponsoring terrorism.

1970 – Trinidad and Tobago. Black Power Revolution. The National Joint Action Committee is formed out of the Guild of Undergraduates at the St. Augustine Campus of the **University of the West Indies.** The Black Power movement appears as a serious challenge to Prime Minister Eric Williams' authority and this is coupled with a growing militancy by the Trade Union movement.

    The Black Power Revolution begins with a 1970 Carnival band named **"Pinetoppers"** whose presentation entitled "The Truth about Africa" included portrayals of "revolutionary heroes" including Fidel Castro, Stokely Carmichael and Malcolm X. This is followed by a series of marches and protests. Prime Minister Williams counters with a broadcast entitled "I am for Black Power." He introduced a 5% levy to fund unemployment reduction and later establishes the first locally-owned commercial bank. However, this intervention has little impact on the protests.

1966-1970 – Nigeria. (Biafra). The Nigerian-Biafra War also called the **Nigerian Civil War** is a political conflict caused by the attempted secession of the southeastern provinces of Nigeria as the self-proclaimed Republic of Biafra. Nigeria was an artificial structure initiated by the British which had neglected to consider religious, linguistic, and ethnic differences. **The discovery of vast oil reserves** in the Niger River delta, a sprawling network of rivers and swamps at the southernmost tip of the country, tempted the southeast to annex the region in order to become economically self-sufficient. Igbos feared the northerners had plans to strip eastern oil to benefit the North. The war cost Nigeria a great deal in terms of lives, money and its image in the world. **It has been estimated that up to 3,000,000 people are killed as a result of the conflict**, most from hunger and disease.

December 14 1970 – Polish Revolt. Thousands of workers from the **Gdansk shipyards** put down their tools and began marching into the city towards the local regional office of the Polish United Workers' Party because they are angered by the government's announcement that it will increase the prices of key consumer goods, such as clothing, coal and food, to deal with Poland's worsening economic situation. The protestors are met by police units and fighting between the two sides lasts into the evening. The uprising of 1970 is the first time Polish workers demanded changes of the regime through collective action and won.

January 1970 – Vietnam. "Washington Monthly Magazine" describes an **intelligence network** of "nearly 1,000 plain clothes investigators working out of some 200 offices from coast to coast" who wrote reports on "political protests of all kinds." **The domestic intelligence operation** stores and disseminates information on both groups and individuals who "might cause trouble to the U.S. Army." Senator Ervin reports in December 1970 that he was informed the surveillance included 800 Illinois citizens including Senator Adlai Stevenson, III (D-ILL), Rep. Abner Mikua (D-ILL) and U.S. Circuit Judge Otto Kerner. Ervin said "apparently anyone who in the Army's definition was 'left of center' was a prospective candidate for political surveillance." During lengthy Senate hearings on the Army's activities, Defense Secretary Melvin Laird ordered the spying stopped.

February 21, 1970 – Vietnam. A Presidential Commission recommends the institution of **an all-volunteer Army** and the elimination of the draft.

March-April 1970 – Vietnam. News of increased U.S. involvement in Laos and Cambodia surfaces when 1969 Senate transcripts are made public.

April 20, 1970 – Vietnam. President Richard Nixon announces during a TV address, the **withdrawal of another 150,000 troops** over the next 12 months. This reduction would lower U.S. troop strength to 284,000.

April 23, 1970 – Vietnam. President Nixon calls for far-reaching draft reform. Nixon also issues an Executive Order that **ends all occupational deferments** and most paternity deferments, with "extreme hardship" as the only exception.

April 30, 1970 – Vietnam. President **Nixon sends U.S. forces into Cambodia,** causing widespread war protest in the streets, and plunging Congress into a session-long debate over Congressional war powers.

May 2, 1970 – Vietnam. Senators McGovern, Hughes, Cranston, Goodell, and Hatfield announce they plan to introduce an "end the war" amendment which would work by suspending funds for military operations in Vietnam, Laos and Cambodia.

May 4, 1970 – Vietnam. Four Kent State college students are shot to death by Ohio National Guardsmen during an anti-war protest on the campus. This leads to widening anti-war protests.

May 9, 1970 – Vietnam. A peaceful anti-war rally held at the Ellipse in Washington, DC is attended by about **80,000 people** including about **10 members of Congress.**

May 11, 1970 – George Winne, Jr., (1947 – May 11, 1970) is remembered as a protester of the Vietnam War who **set himself on fire** in a deliberate act of self-immolation in Revelle Plaza on the campus of the University of California, San Diego on May 10, 1970, **to protest the United States involvement in the war.** The 23 year old student, a former member of a ROTC unit, had no previous affiliation with any organized protests. Winne had recently completed his studies towards a degree in History in March, and would have graduated in June.

He died ten hours later, asking his mother to write a letter to President Nixon. His last words were "I believe in God and the hereafter and I will see you there." After being buried, he was given the ensign "Most Beloved"

The bricks upon which he lit himself on fire were removed from their original location in Revelle Plaza and currently rest next to a small memorial plaque, located in a grove of trees east of the campus library.

August 1970 – An antiwar protest at the University of Wisconsin turns violent when a **bomb destroys** Sterling Hall, home of the Pentagon-sponsored Army Math Research Center. A physicist with no connections to the Army center is killed.

August 31, 1970 – Vietnam. During debate over the **McGovern-Hatfield Amendment** in the U.S. Senate, **Senator Eagleton** (D-Missouri) and Javits (R-NewYork) said that the Nixon policy of gradual de-escalation is leading to a wider war in Indochina. Senator Church said the Congress needed to keep pressure on President Nixon to hasten the withdrawal. Senators Scott (R-Pennsylvania) and Thurmond (R-South Carolina) expressed concern over the fate of U.S. P.O.W.'s and bargaining pressure if U.S. troops were removed. The amendment is defeated by the Senate September.

1970 – Vietnam. War Powers. By the time Congress learned that the naval incident leading to the Gulf of Tonkin Resolution in 1964 had been **misrepresented** and moved to repeal the resolution in 1970, **President Nixon** had already shifted to another legal rationale. Nixon used his constitutional powers as "Commander in

1970

Chief" for his Vietnam policies. In its 1969 "national commitments" resolution, the Senate made a bid to reassert a congressional voice in decisions committing the U.S. to the defense of foreign countries. The House passed war-powers measures in 1970, 1971 and 1972.

September 17, 1970 – Vietnam. The VC presented an **8-point peace plan** which is the first substantial initiative since Nixon's May 1969 plan. The Paris Peace Talks remain stalemated throughout 1970.

October 7, 1970 – Vietnam. President Nixon announces a new **5-point peace plan.**

1970 – Yemeni Civil War. The civil war in North Yemen is fought between royalists of the Mutawakkilite **Kingdom of Yemen** and factions of the **Yemen Arab Republic** from 1962 to 1990. The war began with a coup carried out by the republican leader, Abdullah as-Sallal, which dethroned the newly crowned Imam Al-Badr and declared Yemen a republic under his Presidency. The Imam escaped to the Saudi Arabian border where he rallied popular support. The royalist side received support from **Saudi Arabia,** while the republicans were supported by **Egypt** and the **Soviet Union.** Both foreign irregular and conventional forces were also involved. The Egyptian President, Gamal Abdel Nasser, supported the republicans with as many as 70,000 troops. In 1970 the civil war comes to a pause. The republicans have created alliances with tribal leaders and also receive aid from Saudi Arabia. There is now a **North Yemen** and a **South Yemen. Upwards of 100,000 people have died** as a direct result of the conflict.

Unification of the two Yemens remain a constant possibility. The North remains a market economy while the South becomes progressively communist. The Soviet Union desperately needs land within the Arab countries and is willing to provide money and technical assistance to get it. South Yemen renames itself the People's Democratic Republic of Yemen, a communist country, and this leads to another brief war between the two Yemens.

1971

The Oldest Boomer is 25 years old.

Cost of the Average House: $28,300	
Median Family Income: $9,030	**Minimum Wage:** $1.60/ hr **Average Hourly Wage:** $3.57
Movie Ticket: $1.60	**Gallon Gasoline:** 36 cents
New Car: **Chevrolet Pickup:** $2,229 **Oldsmobile Delta 88:** $3,826 **Ford Ranchero:** $2,995	**Walt Disney World's Magic Kingdom:** The admission price for a single day pass is **$3.50** for an adult (age 18+) and **$1.00** for a child. No rides are included.
Unemployment Rate: 5.9%-6.1%-6.0%	**First-class Stamp:** 8 cents

19 cents buying power in 1971 **= $1.00 in 2008.**
In 1971 what cost us 19 cents to purchase now costs us $1.00 in 2008.

Movies: "A Streetcar Named Desire," "The French Connection," "A Clockwork Orange," "Fiddler on the Roof," "Nicholas and Alexandra," "Klute," "The Last Picture Show."

Broadway: "Meeow!!" "Godspell," "Jesus Christ Superstar," "Ain't Supposed To Die a Natural Death," "Two Gentlemen of Verona."

TV: "Brian's Song," "All in the Family," "The Sonny and Cher Comedy Hour," "Rollin' On A River," "Alias Smith and Jones," "The New Dick Van Dyke Show," "Deputy Dawg," "You Asked For It," "Jackson 5ive, Animated," "Soul Train."

Music: Bread, "Baby I'm-a Want You" & "If." Van Morrison, "Blue Money." Sonny and Cher, "All I Ever Needed Is You." Lynn Anderson, "I Beg Your Pardon, I Never Promised You a Rose Garden." Paul & Linda McCartney, "Another Day." Tom Jones, "She's a Lady." John Denver and Fat City, "Take

Me Home Country Roads." James Taylor, "Country Road." The Partridge Family, "Doesn't Somebody Want To Be Wanted." Michael Jackson, "Got to Be There." The Bee Gees, "How Can You Mend a Broken Heart." Rod Stewart, "I'm Losing You" & "Maggie May." Tony Orlando and Dawn, "Knock Three Times." The Rolling Stones, "Brown Sugar." Santana, "Black Magic Woman." Cher, "Gypsys, Tramps & Thieves." The Carpenters, "For All We Know" & "Rainy Days and Mondays." Elton John, ""Friends" & "Tiny Dancer." Marvin Gaye, "What's Going On." James Taylor, "You've Got a Friend." Creedence Clearwater Revival, "Have You Ever Seen The Rain?" Alice Cooper, "I'm Eighteen." Paul Revere and the Raiders, "Indian Reservation." Ringo Starr, "It Don't Come Easy." Carly Simon, "Legend In Your Own Time." The Bee Gees, "Lonely Days." James Brown, "Hot Pants." Olivia Newton John, "If Not For You." The Jackson 5, "Mama's Pearl." Joan Baez, "The Night They Drove Old Dixie Down." Ike & Tina Turner, "Proud Mary." Aretha Franklin, "Spanish Harlem." Walter Matthau, "Ernie." Helen Reddy, "Crazy Love" & "I Don't Know How to Love Him." Donny Osmond, "Go Away Little Girl." David Cassidy, "Cherish."

Deaths: Jerome Irving Rodale, Manfred Bonnington Lee, Bobby Jones.

President: Richard M. Nixon (R) Quaker; vetoes 43/ 7 overrides

Vice President: Spiro T. Agnew (R) Episcopalian

House: D-255 ; R-180

Senate: 92nd Congress (1971-1973) Majority Party: Democrat (54 seats) Minority Party: Republican (44 seats) Other Parties: 1 Conservative; 1 Independent Total Seats: 100

Federal Debt: $398.13 billion or 35 % of the GDP

Consumer Price Index CPI-U (1982 Base of 100): 40.50

GDP: $1,127.1 billion	**Inflation Rate:** 4.30%
Dow Jones: 913.65 (06-01)/ 825.86 (11-01)	**S&P Price Index:** 102.09/10.79%
Prime Rate: 6.5% (01-06)/ 5.38% (04-23)	**Average Home Mortgage Rate:** 7.31/7.69%

1 oz Gold: $41.25 /$70	**1oz of Silver:** $1.60
Federal Debt: $398,129,744,455	**Federal Deficit:** $23.0 billion dollars
Defense Spending: $92.80 billion	**Interest Spending:** $14.84 billion
Health Care Spending: $13.47 billion	**Pensions Spending:** $35.01 billion
Welfare Spending: $14.75 billion	**Education Spending:** $10.86 billion
Transportation Spending: $8.05 billion	**Misc. Other Spending:** $16.43 billion
Protection Spending: $1.31 billion	**Total Government Spending:** $210.17 billion
% of GDP that goes towards just the interest payment: 1.37%	
$1.00 = 2.267 Yuan, China NPC	**$1.00 =** 347.48 Yen, Japan
After the U.S. Dollar floats on August 15, Jeddah announced that the Official Rate of the Saudi Arabian Riyal would remain unchanged. **$1.00 =** 75.750 Iranian Rial	
U.S. Population: 207,692,000	**World Population:** 3,785,190,759
U.S. Birth Rate: 3,555,970	**U.S. Abortions:** 485,816
U.S. Homicide Rate: 9.1/ 100,000 population	**U.S. Violent Crime:** 396.0/ 100,000 population
Annual Average Domestic Crude Oil Prices: $3.60 / barrel, $19.10 (2007 adjusted)	

Oil:

January 1971 – Iran. Negotiations begin in Tehran between 6 Gulf producing countries and 22 oil companies. In February **OPEC** mandates a "total embargo" against any company that rejects the 55 percent tax rate. Oil companies accept the agreement and there is an immediate increase in oil prices.

February 1971 – Algeria nationalizes 51 percent of all French oil concessions. They have had a fractured economic base since independence when they kicked the French out in 1963. The wealthy landowners fled the country in fear for their lives and the businesses and jobs the French abandoned were taken in a free-for-all rush by individuals and citizens as their basic human rights were reestablished.

March 1971 – Since 1945 oil exporting countries found increasing demand for their crude oil but a 40% decline in the purchasing power of a barrel of oil. In March 1971, the balance of power shifts. That month the **Texas Railroad Commission** allowed all-out production to meet rising demand and America's oil surplus just vanished. The power to control crude oil prices now shifts from the United States, Texas, Oklahoma and Louisiana, to OPEC. There is no more spare capacity within the U.S. and therefore no tool to put an upper limit on prices. A little over two years later OPEC will, through the unintended consequence of war, get a glimpse at the extent of its power to influence prices. Was this ignorance or greed? Probably a mixture of both.

1971 – Cabinda, Angola. Takula Oil Field. The Greater Takula area comprises four offshore fields. The largest field is Takula, where oil is first discovered in 1971. In 2006 Cabinda produces 700,000 barrels of crude oil per day. Cabinda Oil is associated with **Sonangol, Agip Angola Lda** (41%), **Chevron** (39.2%), **Total** (10%) and **Eni** (9.8%).

May 1971 – Nigeria. Nigeria's active participation in the oil economy begins with the formation of federal government owned Nigerian National Oil Corporation (NNOC).

July 1971 – Venezuela. The Hydrocarbons Reversion Law mandates a gradual transfer to government ownership of all "unexploited concession areas" by 1974 and "all their residual assets" by 1983.

August 15, 1971 – The United States pulls out of the Bretton Woods Accord taking the U.S. off the Gold Exchange Standard. The U.S. dollar had been pegged to the price of gold and all other currencies were pegged to the U.S. dollar. This allowed the dollar to "float." Then Britain allows the pound sterling to float and other industrialized nations follow suit with their respective currencies. The industrialized nations also increase their reserves by printing money in amounts far greater than ever before with the end result being the depreciation of the value of the U.S. dollar, as well as the other currencies. **Because oil is priced in dollars**, this means that oil producers are receiving less real income for the same price. OPEC issues a statement that they are **now pricing a barrel of oil against gold** and this forces the price of oil up and then up some more.

September 22, 1971 – **OPEC** directs members to negotiate price increases to offset the devaluation of the U.S. dollar.

1971 – **United Kingdom.** For more than a century, the **British** have policed the **Gulf States.** Now the British withdraw from the Middle East, leaving the Arab states to police themselves. **Nixon** chose the **Shah of Iran** to do the policing as the U.S. steadily became more involved in Vietnam. Oil prices fell from 1965 to 1972, adjusted for inflation.

1971 – **Libya** nationalizes the **British Petroleum** concession and operations are transferred to the state-owned National Oil Corporation.

1971 – **North Sea Oil. The Montrose Field** is discovered. **Amoco discovers** the Montrose field about 135 miles east of Aberdeen towards the northern end of the Central Graben area. It is later estimated to contain 12.71million tons of oil, and 0.08 billion cubic meters of natural gas.

1971 – **North Sea Oil. Shell Expro** discovers the giant Brent oilfield in the northern North Sea east of Shetland.

1971 – **Norway** begins to produce **North Sea Oil.**

1971 – **President Richard Nixon always had a special relationship with big oil** and a deep commitment to the depletion allowance. **Big Oil** is afraid they might see the price of oil crash toward the true cost of production in the Arabian fields which is about 15 cents per barrel. Nixon's National Security Advisor, and later Secretary of

State (1973), **Henry Kissinger,** is so wrapped up in himself and the "grand global plan" for his legacy he does not even pay attention to the coming oil crises and its impact on the United States and the world. It has long been said the coming "energy crisis" is created by collusion to justify higher oil prices.

1971 – Vietnam. According to *Oil & Gas Journal (OGJ)*, Vietnam held 600 million barrels of proven oil reserves as of January 2007.

Major News:

January 25, 1971 – Charles Manson and three of his cult followers are found guilty of first-degree murder in the 1969 murder of **Sharon Tate** and six others.

March 29, 1971 – A court-martial jury convicts **Lt. William L. Calley Jr.** in the **murder of 22 South Vietnamese** at **My Lai** on **March 16, 1968.** He is sentenced to life imprisonment at hard labor. **August 20, 1971**, the convening authority, the Commanding General of Fort Benning, **reduces Calley's sentence** to 20 years. The Secretary of the Army reviewed the sentence and findings and approved both, but in a separate clemency action **commuted confinement to ten years.**

Calley served only three and a half years of house arrest in his quarters at Fort Benning. He petitioned the federal district court for habeas corpus on February 11, 1974, which was granted on September 25, 1974, along with his immediate release, by Federal Judge J. Robert Elliott. Judge Elliott found that Calley's trial had been prejudiced by pretrial publicity.

June 1971 – Pentagon Papers. The government tries to stop the *New York Times* from publishing the "Pentagon Papers" about U.S. involvement in the **Vietnam War.** The Supreme Court on June 30 upholds the paper's right to publish the "Pentagon Papers" in *New York Times* vs. United States.

June 13, 1971 – The *New York Times* begins publishing the Pentagon Papers, the Defense Department's secret history of the Vietnam War. **The *Washington Post*** begins publishing the papers later the same week. **John Mitchell** sends a telegram to the *New York Times*, trying to prevent their publication. White House Chief of Staff H.R. Haldeman tells President Nixon not to be concerned about it because the material only makes the Kennedy and Johnson administrations look bad. National Security Advisor **Henry Kissinger** and special counsel **Charles Colson** feel overkill is a much better response to the leak and set about publicly discrediting former State Department and Defense Department analyst **Daniel Ellsberg** who leaked the "Pentagon Papers".

August 16, 1971 – John Dean, White House Counsel to **President Richard Nixon**, writes the memorandum **"Dealing with our Political Enemies"** where he describes "how we can use the available federal machinery to screw our political enemies."

September 3, 1971 – The White House "plumbers," are named for their orders to plug leaks in the administration.

The **Nixon** administration begins a campaign against further leaks (Pentagon Papers) and against **Daniel Ellsberg** personally. In August 1971, Egil Krogh and David Young, of the Special Investigations Unit met with **G. Gordon Liddy** and **E. Howard Hunt** in a basement office in the Old Executive Office Building. Both Hunt and Liddy wanted to gather damaging information about Ellsberg's mental state to discredit him. Krogh and Young agree and send a memo to **John Ehrlichman**, counsel and Assistant to the President for Domestic Affairs, seeking his approval for a covert operation to be undertaken to examine all of the medical files still held by Ellsberg's psychiatrist. Ehrlichman approves the operation with the understanding that it will not be traceable and on September 3, the break in of the office of **Daniel Ellsberg**'s psychiatrist is led by **E. Howard Hunt** and **Gordon Liddy.**

September 9, 1971 – Attica State Penitentiary. Two inmates are taken to isolation cells after a fight is broken up and rumors circulate they will be tortured as confrontations escalate between the prisoners and the guards. The next day, violence boils over when a group of inmates manage to leave their cells and force their way into the prison's nerve center, where they beat several guards with pieces of pipe, lengths of chain, and baseball bats, fatally injuring one of them. More than one thousand inmates quickly take control of the prison and set fire to several of its buildings. The state police are called in and manage to recapture part of the facility that afternoon containing the inmates in one of the yards where they are holding 38 hostages in a ring of wooden benches. The inmates demand: federal management of the prison, better conditions, amnesty for the crimes committed during the revolt and the removal of the prison's superintendent. In their statement, they criticized the "unmitigated oppression wrought by the racist administrative network of this prison throughout the year," and the "ruthless brutalization and disregard for the lives of the prisoners here and throughout the United States." The State began negotiating with the prisoners.

Hundreds of guards and riot police storm the facility, wound more than eighty inmates and kill twenty-nine. In the chaos, they also inadvertently shot ten hostages to death.

December 14, 1971 – Jack Anderson publishes a column concerning **President Nixon's** foreign policy plans with India and Pakistan. His sources are top secret documents taken from the **White House**, specifically notes from meetings held by **Henry Kissinger** on December 3 and 4, 1971. In his column of December 14, 1971; entitled "U.S. Tilts to Pakistan," information is revealed that could only have come from inside the highest levels of the Pentagon or the White House. Some thirty years later it will be reveled that top levels of the military set up a spy network that stole thousands of White House Top secret documents and delivered them to the offices of the Joint Chiefs of Staff. When Nixon found out about the spy ring he said it was a **federal offense of the highest order but instead of prosecuting he covered it up.**

December 26, 1971 – U.S. bombers strike North Vietnam for 5 days in retaliation for alleged violations of agreements reached prior to the 1968 bombing halt.

September 13, 1971 – Baker Street robbery of 1971. The robbers rented Le Sac leather goods shop, two doors away from the bank, and then tunneled a distance of 50 feet, passing under the **Chicken Inn restaurant.** They only dug during weekends to avoid being heard. The thieves successfully tunneled into the vault of **Lloyds Bank on Baker Street** in London and broke open the safety deposit boxes, making off with a haul in excess of £3million. This makes it the largest bank robbery in England up to this time. Newspapers covered the story every day. They were called **"The Moles of**

Baker Street" and the **"Sewer Rats,"** and then, suddenly, the story disappeared. The last reports ran on Thursday, September 16. Then there was silence.

This story was killed after a "D" Notice, which forbids the press from reporting on certain events, was issued by the government. Ordinarily, such a measure would be employed only if the story threatened national security. So why was it slapped on this particular story? What else did the robbers find in those safety deposit boxes? How was it tied in with the **Royal family?** Were **nude photos** of one of the Royals found? There is a lot of conjecture, but no facts have emerged.

Civil Rights Movement:

February 2, 1971 – The Congressional Black Caucus. The Caucus, founded in 1969 as a Democratic Select Committee, is renamed the Congressional Black Caucus, as increasing numbers of African-Americans are elected to public office. The Congressional Black Caucus is an organization representing the African American members of the **United States Congress.** The Caucus describes its goals as "positively influencing the course of events pertinent to African-Americans and others of similar experience and situation," and "achieving greater equity for persons of African descent in the design and content of domestic and international programs and services."

April 20, 1971 – The Supreme Court rules 9–0 in Swann vs. **Charlotte-Mecklenburg Board of Education** to uphold a court-ordered busing plan designed to achieve racial balance in a de jure segregated school system.

May 21, 1971 – Chattanooga, Tennessee. **The National Guard is mobilized** to quell a riot by **black youths.** One person is killed and four hundred are arrested. While firemen fight fires caused by firebombs, the mayor calls in the National Guard after local police have been on duty for 72 hrs. Tennessee National Guard Brigadier General Van Nunnally says ammunition will be issued to the troops if the situation calls for it. Over 300 people are arrested for curfew violations.

July 1971 – Captain Samuel L. Gravely, Jr. is promoted to **Rear Admiral**. He becomes the first African American to achieve Flag Rank in the U.S. Navy.

1971

December 18, 1971 – **Jesse Jackson resigns** from the **SCLC** (Southern Christian Leadership Conference) and announces the formation of his own organization in Chicago, Operation **PUSH** (People United to Save Humanity).

Women's Movement:

1971 – *Ms. Magazine* is first published as a sample insert in *New York* magazine and 300,000 copies sell out in 8 days. The first regular issue is published in July 1972. The magazine becomes the major forum for feminist voices, and cofounder and Editor Gloria Steinem is launched as an icon of the modern feminist movement.

1971 – **Help Wanted.** Reed vs. Reed is the first time the Supreme Court finds **sex-based classification** to be unconstitutional. In its ruling the Court strikes down an Idaho law giving fathers preference over mothers in the administration of children's estates.

August 26, 1971 – **Women's Equality Day** legislation is first introduced in Congress by **Bella Abzug**. Every President has published a proclamation for "Women's Equality Day" since 1971.

WHEREAS, the **women of the United States** have been treated as **second-class citizens** and have not been entitled the full rights and privileges, public or private, legal or institutional, which are available to male citizens of the United States; and

WHEREAS, the women of the United States have united to assure that these rights and privileges are available to all citizens equally regardless of sex; and

WHEREAS, the women of the United States have designated August 26th, the anniversary date of the passage of the Nineteenth Amendment, as symbol of the continued fight for equal rights: and

WHEREAS, the women of United States are to be commended and supported in their organizations and activities,

NOW, THEREFORE, BE IT RESOLVED, the **Senate and House of Representatives** of the United States of America in Congress assembled, that August 26th of each year is designated as "Women's Equality Day," and the **President is authorized** and requested to issue a proclamation annually in commemoration of that day in 1920, on which the women of America were first given the right to vote, and that day in 1970, on which a nationwide demonstration for women's rights took place.

Popular Culture:

1971 – Drugs. The UN Convention on Psychotropic Substances urges banning of synthetic drugs such as **amphetamines** and **LSD.**

1971 – State Lottery. New Jersey launches the first financially successful modern lottery. The New Jersey lottery is successful because it stresses frequent action at low cost, and it returns a higher percentage of lottery revenues as prizes.

1971 – The Reverend Philip Berrigan and five others are indicted on charges of conspiring to **kidnap Henry Kissinger** and of plotting to blow up the heating tunnels of federal buildings in Washington, D.C. Berrigan attracted the notice of federal authorities when he and six other anti-war activists were caught trading letters alluding to kidnapping Henry Kissinger and bombing steam tunnels. Although the government spent $2 million on the Harrisburg Seven trial in 1972, they could not win a conviction. Berrigan was for a time on the **FBI Ten Most Wanted Fugitives list** for acts of **vandalism** including destruction of government property.

1971 – SDS-WSA. Worker Student Alliance faction of SDS strongly opposes bombing and terrorism. In 1971 SDS-WSA publishes a pamphlet titled **"Who Are The Bombers?"** It warns readers against police agents sent into the anti-Vietnam War movement to foment violence to justify police attacks. It also sharply criticizes the **"Weathermen,"** which had begun its campaign of bombings.

March 1, 1971 – The Weathermen take credit for the **bombing** of the United States Capitol. They issue a statement saying it was "in protest of the U.S. invasion of Laos."

May 3, 1971 – Following **President Nixon**'s decision concerning **Laos**, Anti-Vietnam activists attempt to shutdown Washington by blocking roads with stalled cars, human blockades, garbage cans, and other materials. The protests result in over **12,000**

arrests. John Dean headed up the White House intelligence gathering during this protest.

1971 – The Stone Age Tasaday Tribe is discovered and the world swallows the hoax of a primitive Philippine Tasaday tribe of **cave dwellers.** Manuel Elizalde, Presidential Assistant to the Marcos Government said he had information from a hunter who found the Tasaday. The tribe is described as an unknown Filipino people who inhabit a vast forested area in the rugged mountainous interior of South Cotabato Province in Mindanao.

Anthropologists and archaeologists fly in to Mindanao to see 24 people Mr. Elizalde said are living in caves in a remote area, completely isolated from all of mankind since the Stone Age. NBC produces a *National Geographic* television special in December 1971, ***The Last Tribes of Mindanao.*** The *National Geographic* carries a story in August 1972 entitled, ***Stone Aged Cavemen of Mindanao*** and there is extensive television coverage. Expressing fear that the Tasadays' habitat would be destroyed by the encroachments of civilization, the Marcos Government created a 46,000-acre preserve for them and put it off limits to loggers and farmers while gaining control of all logging and oil exploration.

It has been said NBC paid Elizalde $50,000 for exclusive rights to the story. Manuel Elizalde Jr. died in May 1997, at his home in Makati, a Manila suburb. Manuel Elizalde Jr. was Harvard educated and from one of the Philippines' wealthiest families. He was 60.

Fourteen years later, after the fall of the Marcos government the Tasaday story was found to be a gigantic hoax, but the indigenous people involved are real and their exploitation has become one of the reasons why **indigenous peoples in the Philippines** are now struggling to retain or regain their land, resources, and self-determination. Imelda Marcos, wife of the dictator, once bragged her family owned everything worth owning in the Philippines. A little oil here, a little gas there . . .

April 23, 1971 – Vietnam. Veterans throw away over 700 medals on the West Steps of the Capitol building. The next day, antiwar organizers claimed that 500,000 marched, making this the largest demonstration since the November, 1969 March.

The U.S. Army has serious problems. Disciplinary problems deplete the ranks.

Administrative discharges for unfitness, unsuitability, or misconduct, inability to adapt to military life, drug use, or antiwar activity, continue to grow until they peak in 1971. Discipline and the chain of command are no longer held sacrosanct.

July 1, 1971 – The Twenty-Sixth Amendment to the Constitution is ratified, lowering the **voting age** from 21 to 18. Draftees into the armed services are any male over the age of 18. They are expected to fight and even die for their country but are not allowed to vote until Congress passes the 26th Amendment, specifically setting a national **voting age, in both state and national elections, to 18.**

August 1971 – The Camden 28 conduct a raid on the Camden, New Jersey, draft board offices. **The 28 included four Catholic priests and a Lutheran minister,** as well as a number of local blue-collar workers. The group's goal is to make a bold statement in opposition to the war in Vietnam. They planned to break into the draft board offices at night and search for, collect, and either destroy or remove all 1A-status draft registrations as both a symbolic and real blow to the draft process.

The U.S. government planted a 29th person who was very good at solving practical problems that otherwise baffled the well-meaning but un-handy activists. He even supplied the group with the buildings security plans and helped them gain access at which point the FBI agents moved in on the protesters during the sabotage. The eight inside the federal building are arrested as other agents round up the 20 other co-conspirators.

By the time The Camden 28 are brought to trial in the spring of 1973, their case is viewed by many as a referendum on the Vietnam War. Each of the 28 faces seven felony charges stemming from the raid and more than **40 years in prison if convicted**. The 28 choose to be tried together.

They turn down the offer of a **plea-bargain** in which they would each plead guilty to **a single misdemeanor charge** and all other charges would be dropped. After much debate the 28 decided that they would not take the plea and that as political activists they wanted to go to trial. On May 20, 1973, the jury returned "not guilty" verdicts for all counts against all 28 defendants, acquitting them.

Supreme Court Justice William Brennan said, of the trial, "I think Camden was one of the great trials of the 20th Century."

1971

September 9, 1971 – Attica. Prisoners riot and seize control of the maximum-security Attica Correctional Facility near Buffalo, New York. One prison guard is fatally beaten. Later in the day state police retake most of the prison, but 1,281 convicts still occupy an exercise field called D Yard, where they hold 38 prison guards and employees hostage for four days. After negotiations stall, **New York Governor Nelson A. Rockefeller** orders the state police to regain control of the prison by force. The inmates then threatened to kill their hostages if attacked but they did not kill anyone, even when the state police retake the prison. There are 43 deaths, 32 inmates and 11 state employees. More than a thousand inmates will sue state officials over the abuse they had suffered and after years of litigation, the prisoners win an $8 million settlement.

1971 – American Christian College. Billy James Hargis, author and radio evangelist forms American Christian College in order to teach **fundamentalist Christian principles**. A **sex scandal** at the College, involves claims that Hargis had **sex with both male and female students.** Hargis was forced out of American Christian College's presidency as a result. Further scandals erupted when members of Hargis' youth choir, the **"All American Kids,"** accused Hargis of **sexual misconduct** as well. The college eventually closed down in the mid-1970s. Hargis denied the allegations publicly. He told a Tulsa reporter in 1985, "I was guilty of sin, but not the sin I was accused of."

1971 – McDonald's, "You deserve a break today." Needham, Harper & Steers.

1971 – Keep America Beautiful, "Crying Indian." Advertising Council/Marstellar Inc.

1971 – Perdue chicken, "It takes a tough man to make tender chicken." Scali, McCabe, Sloves.

1971 – Pennsylvania Association for Retarded Children (PARC) vs. Pennsylvania, the federal court rules that students with mental retardation are entitled to a **free public education.**

Business / Technology:

1971 – Starbucks. The original Starbucks is opened in **Pike Place Market in Seattle**, Washington, by three partners: English teacher Jerry Baldwin, history teacher Zev Siegel, and writer Gordon Bowker. The three are inspired by Alfred Peet, to open their first store in Pike Place Market to sell high-quality coffee beans and equipment.

Entrepreneur Howard Schultz joined the company in 1983, and, after a trip to Milan, Italy, advised the group that the company should sell coffee and espresso drinks as well as beans. The owners rejected this idea, believing that getting into the beverage business would distract the company from its primary focus. Schultz started the "Il Giornale" coffee bar chain in 1985 confident that coffee to go would be very profitable. The original owners of Starbucks sold the Starbucks chain to Schultz's "Il Giornale", which rebranded the "Il Giornale" outlets as Starbucks and quickly began to expand. In the 1990s, Starbucks was opening a new store every workday, a pace that continued into the 2000s. By late March 2008 Starbucks was the largest coffeehouse company in the world, with 16,226 stores in 44 countries.

1971 – Newspapers switch from hot metal letterpress to offset.

February 5, 1971 – Apollo 14 is the third mission to land on the **Moon**. During the two lunar EVA's over 100 pounds of **moon rock** are collected and several surface experiments, including seismic studies, are carried out. Commander Alan Shepard famously **hit two golf balls** on the lunar surface with a make-shift club he had brought from Earth. Command Module Pilot Stuart Roosa took several hundred seeds on the mission, many of which were germinated on return resulting in the so called **Moon trees.**

April 14, 1971 – President Richard Nixon relaxes a 20-year trade embargo with **China**.

June 18, 1971 – Southwest Airlines begins flying between Houston, Dallas and San Antonio. With its get there on time at the lowest possible fares and make darn sure they have a good time doing it attitude the new carrier is an immediate success. In 2009 they will carry over 100 million passengers a year.

1971

September 17, 1971 – The advent of the **microprocessor age at Texas Instruments** includes the introduction of the 4-bit TMS 1000 with a calculator on the chip.

October 1, 1971 – Walt Disney World opens. Disney in Orlando, Florida, is the most visited and largest recreational resort in the world, containing four theme parks; two water parks; twenty-three themed hotels; and numerous shopping, dining, entertainment and recreation venues. Owned and operated by the Walt Disney Parks and Resorts segment of The Walt Disney Company, it is located southwest of Orlando, Florida. It is referred to by locals as simply "Disney."

November 15, 1971 – Intel releases the 4-bit 4004 microprocessor developed by Federico Faggin, which is a computer on a chip.

1971 – The Wang 1200 is the first word processor.

December 23, 1971 – Jimmy Hoffa, the head of the Teamsters Union has been serving a 15-year prison sentence for jury tampering and fraud when **President Richard Nixon pardons him.** Nixon had one condition, however: Hoffa should "not engage in direct or indirect management of any labor organization" until at least March 1980. Hoffa agrees and supports Nixon's re-election bid in 1972. It is believed that Hoffa was trying to reassert his power over the Teamsters, defying Nixon's requirement, when he disappeared in 1975.

1971 – MCI, founded in 1968, receives **FCC** approvals in 1969 that allows the company to build its first microwave route and interconnect with local phone companies. The upstart scores its big breakthrough in 1971, when it becomes the first company authorized to compete with **AT&T.** It is instrumental in pushing legal and regulatory changes that lead to the breakup of the AT&T monopoly that has dominated American telephony.

1971 – IBM first introduces the 8-inch Floppy Disk Drive as a read only program load device.

1971 – AM-FM radios are installed in new cars.

1971 – **The U.S. Congress bans** all broadcast advertising related to cigarettes.

1971 – **The Kenbak-1, the first personal computer,** is advertised for $750 in *Scientific American.* In 1973, after selling only 40 machines, Kenbak Corp. closed its doors.

Finance:

1971 – **President Richard Nixon "closes the gold window."** When Nixon took office U.S. gold reserves had declined from $25 billion to $10.5 billion. The French under Charles de Gaulle traded dollars for underpriced gold. Wealthy Europeans traded dollars for underpriced gold and Americans were still not legally allowed to own gold, although some tried to buy gold and funnel it to their Swiss accounts. The U.S. is on the verge of running its first trade deficit in over 75 years. Gold is still priced at $35/ounce and foreign countries acquire more dollar reserves, then the entire amount of gold the United States was said to possess. When President Nixon closed the gold window this prevented foreign governments from redeeming U.S. currency for gold. Some feel that the bill signed by Nixon is an admission that the U.S. can no longer pay its foreign obligations and the world markets reflect this line of thinking as the U.S. Dollar declines in value. The dollar is then allowed to float freely like other currencies.

By the end of 1971 the remaining gold in Fort Knox may all belong to the Federal Reserve, a privately owned bank controlled by foreign interests, as collateral on the U.S. debt. When most if not all of the gold is siphoned from the U.S., Americans will again be allowed to own gold and this will force the price to $850/ ounce. A nice profit for some.

January 19, 1971 – The Overseas Private Investment Corporation (OPIC) begins operations. The Overseas Private Investment Corporation is established as an agency of the U.S. government. OPIC helps U.S. businesses invest overseas, fosters economic development in new and emerging markets, complements the private sector in managing risks associated with foreign direct investment, and supports U.S. foreign policy. Because OPIC charges market-based fees for its products, it operates on a self-sustaining basis at no net cost to taxpayers.

1971

January 21, 1971 – The last **United States notes** are placed into circulation by the Treasury Department. President Nixon suspends convertibility of dollars into gold and the dollar is devalued by 7.9%.

January 29, 1971 – **President Nixon** announces that the **deficit** is thirty-eight billion seven hundred and eighty-three million dollars.

July 1971 – **Henry Kissinger,** while on a trip to Pakistan, feigned illness and did not appear in public for a day. He was actually on **a top-secret mission to Beijing** to open relations with the government of the **People's Republic of China**. On July 15, 1971, President Richard Nixon revealed the mission to the world and that he had been invited to visit the PRC and that he had accepted.

August 15, 1971 – **The value of the dollar** is allowed to float and the first peacetime price and wage controls are instituted. **President Nixon imposes wage and price controls** in a move widely applauded by the public and some economists. The 90 day freeze is unprecedented in peacetime, but such drastic measures are thought necessary. Inflation had exceeded 6% briefly in 1970 and persisted above 4% in 1971. Such inflation rates, in peacetime, are thought to be completely intolerable. The 90 day freeze turns into nearly 1,000 days of measures known as **Phase One, Two, Three, and Four.** The initial attempt to dampen inflation by calming inflationary expectations is a **monumental failure.**

December 18, 1971 – **The Smithsonian Agreement.** The Smithsonian Agreement ends the **fixed exchange rates** established at the Bretton Woods Conference of 1944. Affected by the devaluation of the dollar, the official U.S. gold price is raised to $38 per ounce on May 8, 1972. The unofficial rate is about $70/ ounce.

1971 – **Michael Milken. Drexel's junk-bond trading operation.** Young companies with no credit begin issuing bonds that start out as "junk" in order to get off the ground. **Drexel Harriman Ripley** has made a lot of money investing in **"fallen angels,"** once-investment-grade bonds that have fallen in price because of investor worries that their issuers will default. They are on the prowl for another easy score and **Michael Milken** convinces them there is a lot of money to be made if the firm will underwrite high-yield 'junk" bonds. **Milken** used junk bonds to finance **hostile takeovers** of companies. He would use junk bonds to generate cash to bid on, or take over, an unwilling company. The company would then be gutted to repay the debt it generated to make the bid in the first place. Tax laws assisted these hostile takeovers because the interest payments on debt are tax deductible and companies could more easily fund their takeovers with junk bonds.

Milken earned between $200 million and $550 million a year at the height of his success. Following his release from prison, he worked as a strategic consultant. This was in violation of his probation, and he was subsequently fined $42 million for these actions. Lost American jobs, disrupted lives, ruined families and huge profits for a few insiders; you are correct, if it was not illegal it should have been.

Books:

1971 – "Man's World, Woman's Place," Elizabeth Janeway.

1971 – Herman Wouk, **"The Winds of War."**

1971 – Project Gutenberg starts to enter great documents and literature online. Project Gutenberg is the first and largest single collection of free electronic books, or **eBooks.** Michael Hart, founder of Project Gutenberg, invented eBooks in 1971

1971 – "Angle of Repose," Wallace Stegner.

TV:

1971 – Television and radio ads for cigarettes are banned.

1971 – "All in the Family." TV's first flushing toilet is heard. A major breakthrough takes place as the toilet is finally allowed to perform on TV. The first flush is heard, but not seen, on a first-season episode of **"All in the Family."**
TV's first toilet flusher is **Archie Bunker.**

1971

Sports:

March 8, 1971 – The Fight of the Century. Ali and Frazier meet in the ring on March 8, at Madison Square Garden. The fight, known as "The Fight of the Century," is one of the most eagerly anticipated bouts of all time and one of the most famous. **"Smokin"" Joe Frazier** beats **Muhammad Ali** for the **world heavyweight** boxing title in one of the best matches of all time. It features two undefeated fighters, both of whom have legitimate claims to the heavyweight crown. **Frank Sinatra,** unable to acquire a ringside seat, took photos of the match for **Life** magazine. Legendary boxing announcer **Don Dunphy** and actor and boxing aficionado **Burt Lancaster** called the action for the broadcast to millions of people. The fight lived up to expectations and Frazier floored Ali with a hard, leaping left hook in the 15th and final round. Frazier retained the title on a unanimous decision, giving Muhammad Ali his first professional loss.

While **Joe Frazier** held the world heavyweight boxing title he had the highest knockout percentage in history. **Smokin Joe** was knocked down a few times; he was never knocked out.

April 12, 1971 – The U.S. Table Tennis team is in Japan on April 6, for the 31st World Table Tennis Championship. From the early years of the People's Republic, sports had played an important role in diplomacy, often incorporating the slogan "Friendship First, Competition Second." The U.S. team is invited to China and on April12, the **U.S. Table Tennis team** and accompanying journalists become the first American sports delegation to set foot in the Chinese capital **since 1949.** The meeting was facilitated by the National Committee on U.S.-China Relations.

Music:

July 3, 1971 – Jim Morrison of The Doors, is found dead in a bath tub in Paris, France. He was 27. It is widely believed that he inhaled **heroin** thinking it was **cocaine.**

1971 – Woodstock. Max Yasgur sold the farm in 1971 and died in 1973 at age 53.

Natural Disasters:

February 19, 1971 – A 6.7 magnitude earthquake in Slymar, California kills 65 people.

February 21, 1971 – Mississippi, Louisiana, Arkansas, and Tennessee are struck by a series of **10 tornadoes** that kill 121 people.

March 18, 1971 – A landslide kills 200 people in Chungar, Peru.

May 22, 1971 – A 6.8 magnitude earthquake strikes the North Anatolian Fault in Turkey.

August 1971 – Hanoi Flood. An estimated 100,000 people die when heavy rains led to severe flooding of the Red River Delta around **Hanoi, in North Vietnam.**

September 29, 1971 – Orissa state, India. A **cyclone** and **tidal wave kill** as many as 10,000 people off the Bay of Bengal.

Man vs. Man / Wars:

Assassinated – Prime Minister of Jordan. Wasfi at-Tall began his third term as Prime Minister on September 26, 1970. The following day, **King Hussein** and PLO chairman **Yasir Arafat** sign an agreement in Cairo that calls for the withdrawal of **Palestinian guerrillas** from the cities but allows them to continue the battle against **Israel** from the countryside. **Wasfi at-Tall and the military** are set on driving the guerrillas out of Amman, Irbid, Jarash, and Ajlun and were mostly successful by June 18, 1971. In revenge, during a visit to Egypt in September 1971, Prime Minister Wasfi at-Tall is assassinated by the **Black September Group** at the Sheraton Hotel in Cairo.

London, England – The Jordanian ambassador to London, England, former Prime Minister Zaid Rifai, is shot but not killed in an attempted assassination by **Black September.**

September 1971 – Iraq. Failed assassination attempt on **Mulla Mustapha Barzani,** the **Kurdish leader.** Several other people are killed in the attempt and the **Iraqi government** is accused of being involved in the plot. The **Ba'ath regime** also accused Barzani of getting arms from Iran, helping the **Iranian Intelligence Service** to gather information on the Iraqi army, having a broadcast radio station on Iranian soil, and training Kurdish guerrilla fighters.

March 30, 1971 – Iraq. Hardan al-Tikriti, Minister of defense, Deputy Premier, and former member of the RCC, was dismissed from all his functions in October of 1970. On March 30, while he is in Kuwait he is **assassinated.**

September 28, 1971 – Iraq. Abd al-Karim al-Shaikhli, Foreign Minister and member of the RCC is dismissed, appointed to a position at the UN and later **assassinated.**

1971 – Canada. Air Canada Flight 932 is hijacked while the plane is in-flight from Thunder Bay, Ontario, to Toronto. The hijacker is armed with a handgun and a grenade. He is flown to Cuba.

1971 – D.B. Cooper stopped the stewardess and told her calmly, "Miss, you'd better have a look at that note. **I have a bomb."** The note informed the flight crew that a hijacking is underway. Cooper wants $200,000 in cash and four parachutes, two main chutes and two emergency chutes which are worn over the chest. He also wants the plane to be refueled in Seattle. He ordered the items delivered to the jet when it landed at Sea-Tac, and he said he would blow up the plane if the airline failed to comply. The pilot had radioed information about the hijacking to Sea-Tac air traffic control, who alerted Seattle police, who in turn alerted the FBI. The airline complied.

    After landing in Seattle **the aircraft returned to the sky** and Cooper ordered the pilot to keep to an altitude not to exceed 10,000 feet, with wing flaps set at 15 degrees and airspeed of no more than 150 knots. Cooper warned the pilot he was wearing a wrist altimeter to monitor the altitude.

    Two Air Force F-106 fighters, far enough behind the 727 as to not attract attention, did not see anyone leave from the rear stairway at 8:13 when D.B. Cooper jumped into the fog and darkness, never to be seen again. Three bundles of 20 dollar bills will be dug up by an eight year old boy on the banks of the Columbia River in 1980. The $5,800 is positively matched by serial numbers to D.B. Cooper's loot.

May 19, 1971 – Juan Corona, mass murderer. A rancher is touring his peach orchard near Yuba City, when he sees a freshly dug hole, approximately seven feet long and three and a half feet deep. Returning that night, he finds the hole has been filled in and thinks someone is burying trash on his property so he calls the police. The following morning the police respond to the call and begin uncovering the hole to see what has been buried. In just a few minutes they are shocked to find the fresh corpse of a white American male, aged 40 years, named Kenneth Whitacre. Four days later on a nearby fruit ranch another shallow grave is discovered. Then in rapid succession another body is discovered and then another.

On July 12, the grand jury returns a 25-count murder indictment against **Juan Corona** a Mexican-born, licensed labor contractor. He was in charge of hiring workers to staff the local fruit ranches and is charged with the murder of 25 itinerant laborers, all found buried in shallow graves in the orchards of fruit ranches in Sutter County, California. These gruesome crimes represented the worst and most notorious mass murder in U.S. history at this time. The local sheriff said even more men may have been buried in the area.

June 28, 1971 – Joseph Colombo Sr., 48, the head of one of New York's five Mafia families is shot at the Italian-American Civil Rights League's second annual Unity Day. The turnout was quite large and Colombo was shaking hands, joking, and posing for photographers when he was shot. The noise of the happy crowd made the shots almost inaudible when Colombo dropped to the ground bleeding heavily from the head and neck.

Almost immediately, three more shots are fired into Colombo's killer by a still unidentified league captain or possibly a Colombo bodyguard who then escaped into the crowd. Colombo survived the shooting but remained in a coma for seven years. He died at his New York estate on May 22, 1978.

1962-1971 – Agent Orange. Approximately **20 million gallons of herbicides** were used in Vietnam between 1962 and 1971 to remove unwanted plant life and leaves which otherwise provided cover for enemy forces during the **Vietnam Conflict.**

1971

Shortly following their military service in Vietnam, some veterans reported a variety of health problems and concerns which some of them attributed to exposure to **Agent Orange** or other herbicides.

1971 – Bolivia. The arrest of 30 leaders of a right-wing demonstration in Santa Cruz, Bolivia, triggers a brief general revolt pitting peasants, students, miners, the air force, and other supporters of leftist President Juan Jose Torres against most of the army and the conservative middle and upper classes.

1971 – Bolivia. Hugo Banzer, a rightist colonel and head of the education ministry, staged a successful 'revolution' in 1971 against the leftist coup which had taken power from him and his allies one year previously and he then held onto power for seven years, banning leftist parties and closing the universities.

1971 – Air Piracy. There are at least eight hijackings from the U.S. to Cuba during the year. Some of the hijackers later returned to the U.S. voluntarily.

February 25, 1971 – An unidentified male successfully hijacks a 727 from San Francisco. He ends up in Canada and is deported to the U.S. on March 8, 1971, where he is sentenced to 10 years in prison for interference with a flight crew.

July 11, 1971 – A Cubana de Aviación aircraft is hijacked at Cienfuegos, Cuba resulting in one fatality. The two hijackers were taken down and the hijacking lasted less than one day.

September 3, 1971 – There is an attempted hijacking of a plane taking off from Chicago. The man is subdued and arrested. He is sentenced to 20 years for interference with a flight crew on March 6, 1972.

October 18, 1971 – A Canadian attempts to hijack a Boeing 737 from Anchorage to Cuba. The attempt ends in Vancouver where he is arrested. He is deported to the United States on October 19, 1971, and sentenced to 20 years for air piracy on May 12, 1972.

October 29, 1971 – A man, his two sons, and a third youth hijack an Eastern Airlines jet from Houston to Havana. They kill a ticket agent in the process.

1971 – East Pakistan / Bangladesh. The **mass killings** in East Pakistan (Bangladesh) are one of the worst acts of genocide in the twentieth century. People are seeking independence for **East Pakistan** after the elections favored them and the **West Pakistani military regime** unleashes a systematic campaign of **mass murder** for the purpose of **killing millions of Bengalis** as it refuses to give up control of the government. **Close to 1,500,000 Bengali men, women, and children are killed** by the **Pakistani military,** and some 10 million Bengalis flee to the neighboring Indian state of West Bengal. Women and children are tortured, raped and killed during the war. Exact numbers are not known, however Bangladeshi sources cite a figure of 200,000 women raped, giving birth to thousands of war-babies. The Pakistan Army also kept Bengali women as sex-slaves inside the Dhaka Cantonment, where most of the girls had been captured from Dhaka University and private homes. How many women and young girls (children) were kept for their personal use? As many as they wanted. What did they do with them? What ever they felt like doing at the time.

In early December 1971 the Indian military intervened in support of Bengali forces in East Pakistan. India's intervention was brief and decisive. The Pakistani military surrendered in mid-December. On December 16 of that year **East Pakistan became the sovereign nation of Bangladesh.**

Even in the closing days of the war professors, journalists, doctors, artists, engineers, and writers were rounded up by the Pakistan Army and the Razakar militia in Dhaka. They were blindfolded, taken to torture cells in Mirpur, Mohammadpur, Nakhalpara, and Rajarbagh where the were slaughtered in the killing fields just two days before the Pakistan Army and the Razakar militia surrendered to the Indian military on December 14, 1971. While they still had time to kill a few more innocent people an estimated 991 teachers, 13 journalists, 49 physicians, 42 lawyers, and 16 writers, artists and engineers were systematically executed. The atrocities of 1971 were an act of genocide by West Pakistan.

These same Pakistanis possess nuclear weapons. Their neighbor, India, who sent in military to defeat the West Pakistan (Pakistan) army, also has nuclear weapons. This **"culture of violence"** is still **"business as usual"** in 2010 Pakistan.

1971 – Haiti. François Duvalier, known as **"Papa Doc,"** is the **President of Haiti** from 1957 to 1971. In 1964 he made himself President for Life and ruled until his death in 1971. His rule was a dictatorship relying on corruption and state-sponsored terrorism through his private militia known as **Tonton Macoutes.** It has been estimated that he is responsible for the deaths of 30,000 people and the exile of thousands more. When Papa Doc finally died in 1971, he had managed to bring an already poor nation into unimaginable poverty and misery, as Haiti became the poorest nation in the Americas as a direct result of his wild kleptomania. It is fitting that his grandiose mausoleum in Port-au-Prince was demolished by angry mobs who had finally learned to stop fearing the quiet little country doctor, only 20 years after his death. **Bébé Doc,** the 19 year old son of Papa Doc, takes over as President but prefers to have his mother run the government.

1971 – Jordan, The Black September Uprising. Beginning in September 1970 the **Black September** or "era of regrettable events," was a month when **Hashemite King Hussein of Jordan** moved to quash the autonomy of **Palestinian organizations** and restore his monarchy's rule over the country. The violence results in the deaths of thousands of people, mostly Palestinians. Thousands of Palestinian fighters (PLO) are forced out of Jordan into Lebanon in July 1971 which ends most of the armed conflict between Jordan and the PLO. This will result in the Lebanese Civil War and many, many more innocent people will be killed.

1971 – Lebanon. Black September. In the September fighting, the **PLO** lost its main base of operations as the fighters were driven to **Southern Lebanon.** The growing PLO presence in Lebanon and increasing military actions on the **Israeli-Lebanese border** will usher in the **Lebanon Civil War. The PLO will be fighting in the Lebanon Civil War** until well after the mid-1980s. Many innocent men, women and children will be killed due to this **culture of violence.**

April 1971 – Madagascar. MONIMA Revolt. After an armed opposition to the central government which is quickly and harshly suppressed, MONIMA becomes a truly left-wing opposition movement with support among students and urban radicals. Though MONIMA is banned, their ideas lead a series of demonstrations against the Tsiranana regime that result in its fall in May 1972. The ban on MONIMA is lifted in June.

1971 – Morocco. A coup against **King Hassan** at the Skhirat Palace fails. Nearly 100 guests are killed and the coup leaders are executed three days later. The army officers were angered by Hassan's abandonment of thousands of square miles in an Algerian border war.

1971 – Rhodesian Civil War. The rival African factions working for black-majority rule in white-controlled **Rhodesia (Zimbabwe)** form a coalition, the **Front for the Liberation of Zimbabwe,** which became a joint guerrilla effort to overthrow the government. The black guerrillas operate from bases in **Zambia** and from FRELIMO-controlled areas in **Mozambique** and make periodic raids into **Rhodesia.**

1971 – Sri Lanka / Ceylon. An **uprising** is led by **the Sinhalese Sri Lankan People's Liberation Front**, or Janatha Vimukthi Peramuna, and is an unsuccessful Marxist youth rebellion that **claims the lives of 15,000 young people.** The **JVP** drew worldwide attention when it launched an insurrection against the Bandaranaike government in April 1971. Although the insurgents are young, poorly armed, and inadequately trained, they succeeded in seizing and holding major areas in Southern and Central provinces of Sri Lanka before they are defeated by the security forces. Their attempt to seize power created a major crisis for the government and forces a fundamental reassessment of the nation's security needs.

November 1971 – Thailand. Thai Government Coup. Prime Minister Thanom **executes a coup against his own government**, thereby ending the three-year experiment with what had passed for parliamentary democracy. The 1968 constitution is suspended, political parties banned, and undisguised military rule is imposed on the country. Under the new regime, executive and legislative authority is held by a military junta, the National Executive Council. Heading the council is a triumvirate that includes Thanom, who retained the office of Prime Minister; Field Marshal Praphat Charusathian, his Deputy Prime Minister; and Thanom's son (also Praphat's son-in- law), Narong Kittikachorn, an army colonel.

1971

January 25, 1971 – Uganda. A military coup d'état is executed by the Ugandan military and led by General **Idi Amin**, against the government of **President Milton Obote**. The seizure of power takes place while Obote is abroad attending the Commonwealth Heads of State conference in Singapore. Amin is largely supported by the British before and after the coup because President, Milton Obote, **was attempting to nationalize UK businesses.**

Idi Amin's rule is characterized by human rights abuses, political repression, ethnic persecution, extrajudicial killings and the expulsion of Asians from Uganda. The number of people killed as a result of his regime is unknown; estimates from international observers and human rights groups range from **100,000 to 500,000 people.**

February 8, 1971 – Vietnam. A forty-four day raid into **Laos** by South Vietnamese soldiers is begun with the aid of United States air and artillery.

February 23, 1971 – Vietnam. Senate Democrats vote (38-13) to adopt a "resolution of purpose" for the 92nd Congress to end U.S. involvement in Indochina and "bring about the withdrawal of all U.S. forces and the release of prisoners in a time certain."

March 1, 1971 – Vietnam. A powerful bomb explodes at 1:32am in a restroom in the original part of the Capitol Building in Washington, DC, with responsibility claimed by the "Weather Underground." **Senator McGovern** attributed the bombing to **"our Vietnam madness."**

March 29, 1971 – Vietnam. LT Calley is convicted for the **My Lai Massacre.**

March 30, 1971 – Vietnam. It was later found out that on this date; "a **confidential Army directive orders** personnel to intercept and confiscate personal mail containing anti-war and other dissident material sent to soldiers in Vietnam."

April 1, 1971 – Vietnam. Draft Bill. A two year extension of the draft passes the House (239-99) in a roll-call vote. The Senate also passes the bill, June 24, following a long debate, lasting from May 6 through June 24.

Forty-eight percent of Army manpower is from draftees or "draft motivated." Many young men "signed up" thinking they could get a better deal, instead of waiting to be drafted.

April 7, 1971 – Vietnam. During a speech, President Nixon says that in relation to setting a firm date for troop withdrawal, that it would "serve the enemy's purpose, not our own."

April 18, 1971 – Vietnam. Two-thousand-three-hundred Vietnam Veterans come to Washington, DC to participate in Dewey Canyon III, "a military incursion into the country of Congress," Led by **Vietnam Veterans Against the War** (VVAW). The vets camp on the mall 1/4 mile from the Capitol, and throw away military medals and ribbons at the foot of the statue of Chief Justice John Marshall.

April 24, 1971 – Vietnam. Ten days of protests by a group calling themselves the **"Mayday Tribe"** included attempted work stoppages at several federal offices in Washington, DC.

May 3, 1971 – Vietnam. Over 5,100 policemen backed by 10,000 federal troops result in an unprecedented mass arrest of approximately 10,000 persons, with another 2,700 arrested the next day. Protests end May 5, with the arrest of another 1,200 demonstrators on the Capitol's east steps **during a rally attended by some members of Congress.**

June 9, 1971 – Vietnam. The Senate adopted an amendment authorizing **drug control and rehabilitation programs** in the military.

June 1971 – Vietnam. The Pentagon Papers, a top-secret United States Department of Defense history of the United States' political-military involvement in Vietnam from 1945 to 1967, are published.

June 17, 1971 – Vietnam. Congressman Charles Whalen, Jr. (R-Ohio) co-sponsors an **"end the war" bill** which is rejected by the House (158-255).

1971

June 24, 1971 – Vietnam. The Mansfield Amendment is passed along with the **draft extension bill.** It is a controversial amendment by **Senate Majority leader Mike Mansfield** (D-Montana) setting a national policy of withdrawing troops from Indochina 9 months after the bill's enactment, however the wording is later softened to the "earliest practical date." It is the **first time in modern U.S. history** that the Congress had urged an end to a war in which the country was actively involved.

July 1, 1971 – Vietnam. During the peace talks, the **Viet Cong** proposed the return of all **American and allied prisoners** held in North and South Vietnam by the end of 1971, if all U.S. troops are withdrawn within that same period. The U.S. is cautious.

September 28, 1971 – Vietnam. The 2-year **draft extension** is signed into law after lapsing from June 30 until September 28. **Draft deferments are abolished** for 1971 college freshmen, and retained for upperclassmen. Also in the bill is a non-binding provision putting Congress on record as backing an early end to the Vietnam War.

October 3, 1971 – Vietnam. South Vietnam election. President Nguyen Van Thieu runs unopposed and is re-elected with more than **90% of the popular vote.** Vice President Ky and General Duong Van Minh earlier dropped out of the race amid charges that Thieu had rigged the election. **Thieu was advised by the CIA to not be so obvious.**

November 2, 1971 – Vietnam. A Senate subcommittee releases a 300-page report documenting **"corruption, criminality, and moral compromise" in a PX scandal** in Vietnam and other overseas areas.

November 12, 1971 – Vietnam. President Nixon announces a troop withdrawal of 45,000 more troops by February 1, but said it is particularly important to continue air strikes on enemy infiltration routes.

December 30, 1971 – Vietnam. The U.S. carries out the **heaviest air strikes** on North Vietnam since 1968 in **Operation Proud Deep**, consisting of 1,025 sorties.

1972

The Oldest Boomer is 26 years old.

Cost of the Average House: $30,500
In 1972, the average square foot home is about 1,634 square feet and sells for $30,500. There were 1,700,000 housing starts this year.

Median Family Income: $9,700	**Minimum Wage:** $1.60/ hr
Pay Phone, local call: 10 cents	**Gallon Gasoline:** 36 cents
New Car: **Cadillac De Ville:** $6,168 **Ford Pinto:** $2,078 **Ford Thunderbird:** $5,293 **MG Midget Convertible:** $2,559 **Triumph TR6 convertible:** $3,795	**Loaf of Bread:** 25 cents **F.W. Woolworth Lunch Counter** **Triple Decker BLT :** 50 cents **Egg Salad Sandwich:** 30 cents **Banana Split**: 39 cents
Unemployment Rate: 5.8%-5.7%-5.2%	**First-class Stamp:** 8 cents

19 cents buying power in 1972 = **$1.00 in 2008.** In 1972 what cost us 19 cents to purchase now costs us $1.00 in 2008.

Movies: "The Godfather," "Cabaret," "The Emigrants," "Deliverance," "Sounder," "The Poseidon Adventure," "Lady Sings the Blues."

Broadway: "Grease," "Man of La Mancha," "The Sunshine Train."

TV: The Munich Olympic Tragedy. Sammy Davis Jr. Kisses Archie Bunker on "All In The Family." "M*A*S*H," "The Bob Newhart Show," "Sanford and Son," "The A-Team," "The Waltons," "Bridget Loves Bernie," "The Joker's Wild," "The Osmonds, Animated," "Fat Albert and the Cosby Kids, Animated," "Black Beauty," "The Price Is Right," "Maude."

Music: "Superfly," Curtis Mayfield. "The Godfather,"Nino Rota. "Cabaret," John Kander and Fred Ebb. David Bowie, "Starman" & "John, I'm Only Dancing." Gilbert O'Sullivan, "Alone Again, Naturally." Harry Nilsson,

"Without You." Dr. Hook and the Medicine Show, "The Cover of Rolling Stone." Wayne Newton, "Daddy Don't You Walk So Fast." Jackson Browne, "Doctor My Eyes." Johnny Nash, "I Can See Clearly Now." The Fifth Dimension, "Last Night, I Didn't Get to Sleep At All." Elton John, "Honky Cat." The Doobie Brothers, "Jesus Is Just Alright" & "Listen to The Music." Paul Simon, "Me and Julio Down by the Schoolyard." Carly Simon, "You're So Vain." The Temptations, "Papa Was a Rollin' Stone." Joni Mitchell, "You Turn Me On I'm a Radio." Rod Stewart, "You Wear It Well." America, "A Horse With No Name" & "Ventura Highway." Love Unlimited, "Walking in the Rain With the One I Love." The Eagles, "Witchy Woman." Jim Croce, "You Don't Mess Around With Jim." Michael Jackson, "Ben." Looking Glass, "Brandy, You're a Fine Girl." Roberta Flack, "The First Time Ever I Saw Your Face." Helen Reddy, "I Am Woman." The Moody Blues, "Isn't Life Strange." Robert John, "The Lion Sleeps Tonight." Derek & The Dominos, "Layla." Three Dog Night, "The Family of Man." The Carpenters, "Goodbye to Love." Crosby & Nash, "Immigration Man." Elvis Presley, "Burning Love." The New Seekers, "I'd Like To Teach The World To Sing." Neil Diamond, "Song Sung Blue." Elton John, "Rocket Man." Don McLean, "American Pie." Harry Chapin, "Taxi." Neil Young, "Heart of Gold." Godspell, "Day by Day." Sammy Davis Jr. "The Candy Man." Sonny and Cher, "A Cowboy's Work Is Never Done." Carly Simon, "Anticipation." Donny Osmond, "Puppy Love." The Staple Singers, "Respect Yourself."

Deaths: Mahalia Jackson, Bobby Ramirez, Jackie Robinson.

President: Richard M. Nixon (R) Quaker; vetoes 43/ 7 overrides

Vice President: Spiro T. Agnew (R) Episcopalian

House: D-255 ; R-180

Senate: 92nd Congress (1971-1973) Majority Party: Democrat (54 seats) Minority Party: Republican (44 seats) Other Parties: 1 Conservative; 1 Independent Total Seats: 100

Federal Debt: $427.26 billion or 35 % of the GDP

Consumer Price Index CPI-U (1982 Base of 100): 41.80

GDP: $1238.3 billion	**Inflation Rate:** 3.27%

Dow Jones: 1023.93 (12-01)/ 890. (January)	**S&P Price Index:** 118.05/15.63%
Prime Rate: 4.75% (01-31)/ 6.00% (12-27)	**Average Home Mortgage Rate:** 7.29/7.44%
1 oz Gold: $58.60 Official U.S. gold price is increased to $38 per ounce.	**1oz of Silver:** $2.53

Monthly S.S. Benefits Paid: maximum is $133 / month
Social Security was created in 1935 and does not have
an automatic cost-of-living adjustment until 1972.

Federal Debt: $427,260,460,940.50

Federal Deficit: $23.4 billion dollars

Defense Spending: $94.67 billion	**Interest Spending:** $15.48 billion
Health Care Spending: $16.15 billion	**Pensions Spending:** $40.35 billion
Welfare Spending: $18.16 billion	**Education Spending:** $13.51 billion
Transportation Spending: $8.39 billion	**Misc. Other Spending:** $19.06 billion
Protection Spending: $1.69 billion	**Total Government Spending:** $230.68 billion

% of GDP that goes towards just the interest payment: 1.31%

$1.00 = 303.08 Yen, Japan

U.S. Population: 209,924,000	**World Population:** 3,862,197,286
U.S. Birth Rate: 3,258,411	**U.S. Abortions:** 586,760

U.S. Homicide Rate: 9.4/ 100,000 population
U.S. Violent Crime: 401.1/ 100,000 population

The reported crime rate was fairly level during the 1930s, 1940s, and
1950s, before sharply increasing until the early 1970s. It moved higher in

1980 and went higher again in 1991. **Drug arrests peak** in 1989 and again 1995-1997. The Federal prison population tripled from 1960-1997, from 20,000 to 1.3 million. In 1953, 131 persons were on death row, while 62 were executed, a ratio of 2:1. In 1960, the ratio of death sentences to executions was 4:1, and by 1984, the ratio was 67:1. The number of executions has increased 300% during the 1990s, with a doubling between 1996 and 1999. Annual drug sales in the U.S. increase, according to government court cases, so much that **$400 Billion** to **$500 Billion** is being laundered **a year!** by the early 1990's. This leads to politicians being bought, Presidents (and wannabe's) being paid, and the corruption of major banks and the mortgage meltdown as money is being laundered.

Annual Average Domestic Crude Oil Prices:
$3.60 / barrel, $20.48 (2007 adjusted)

Oil:

1972 – U.S. Oil. As we became more involved in Vietnam, oil prices, adjusted for inflation, actually fall from 1965 to 1972.

1972 – Oil well productivity for the **U.S.** reaches a high of 18.6 barrels per day per well. This figure will decline through 2008 when it reaches 9.4 barrels per day per well. Total U.S. production goes from 9,441 thousand barrels per day in 1972 to 4,995 in thousand barrels per day 2008.

1972 – Ecuador. Collusion between the **military and Chevron** has been commonplace and dates back to the **Texaco** years when the military served as the company's private security force. Texaco's contract for oil production is signed by **General Guillermo Rodriguez Lara, Ecuador dictator-in-chief** brought to power by a **military coup** in 1972.

Texaco promised to bring state of the art, modern U.S. oil industry technology and the first barrel of oil was paraded through Quito's historic center. People lunge to touch the barrel for luck and the archdiocese of the Catholic Church blesses the barrel.

Ecuador joins OPEC, and is granted access to international lines of credit which it uses with abandon while very little of the oil money trickles down to the local people. The land is polluted with toxic wastewater and crude oil byproducts. At one of Texaco's infamous "remediated" pits, the company claims it spent $40 million on clean up while the residents claim to have footage of the pits being covered over with nothing but dirt.

June 1, 1972 – Iraq becomes the first Arab country to nationalize a Western oil corporation. Iraq **nationalizes Iraq Petroleum Company's** (IPC) concession owned by British Petroleum, Royal Dutch-Shell, Compagnie Francaise des Petroles, Mobil and Standard Oil of New Jersey (now Exxon). The concessions are valued at over one billion dollars.

Prior to 1972, U.S. and British companies held a three-quarter share in Iraq's oil production. Soviet petroleum experts help Iraq develop its oil industry to the extent that Baghdad ends its reliance on Western companies. The Soviets also help Iraq nationalize the Iraq Petroleum Company and Iraq rapidly increases its oil output, becoming the world's second largest exporter of oil by 1979.

1972 – Saudi Arabia negotiates for control of 25 percent of the **Arabian American Oil Company** (Aramco). Until the early 1970s, Aramco is owned by California Arabian Standard Oil Company (Casoc), Texaco, Standard Oil Company of New Jersey (later renamed Exxon), and Socony-Vacuum (now Mobil Oil Company). In 1968 the **Saudi Minister of Petroleum & Mineral Resources** had publicly broached the idea of Saudi participation in Aramco. After long negotiations, it is agreed that the Saudi government will buy 25 percent of the company. Over the next 16 years, Aramco will be converted to a totally Saudi-owned company called Saudi Arabian Oil Company (Saudi Aramco).

Major News:

May 15, 1972 – While campaigning for president at a Laurel, Maryland shopping center, Governor **George C. Wallace** (D-Alabama) is **shot** and seriously wounded by Arthur Bremer. Bremer also wounds three others. Arthur Bremer is **convicted** on August 4 and sentenced to 63 years in prison for the shootings.

1972

May 26, 1972 – SALT I is signed. Strategic Arms Limitation Talks. In the **first visit of a U.S. president to Moscow,** President Richard Nixon arrives May 22 for summit talks with Kremlin leaders that culminate in a landmark strategic arms pact. SALT I freezes the number of strategic ballistic missile launchers at existing levels, and provides for the addition of new submarine-launched ballistic missile launchers only after the same number of older intercontinental ballistic missile (ICBM) and SLBM launchers had been dismantled.

May 28, 1972 – The first break-in at the **Watergate** office complex. Democratic National Committee chairman, Larry O'Brien's office is broken into. Photographs are taken of material from his desk and bugs are placed in his office. **Howard Hunt** and two of the burglars will later say the real target of the first break-in was not Larry O'Brien's office, but telephones in the portion of the DNC that contains the offices of **R. Spencer Oliver** and his secretary **Maxie Wells.**

June 17, 1972 – Five men, one of whom says he used to work for the **CIA,** are **arrested** at 2:30 a.m. trying to bug the offices of the **Democratic National Committee** at the Watergate hotel and office complex in **Washington, DC.** All five are wearing business suits and surgical gloves. One has $814 in cash and another $800. The walkie-talkie they are using operates on a channel authorized for the exclusive use of the **Republican National Committee.** James W. McCord is security coordinator of the Committee for the Re-election of the President and a retired security consultant at the CIA. Two of the five carry address books that list the name of E. Howard Hunt, who is on the White House payroll as a consultant to Charles Colson, one of Nixon's closest assistants. The investigation of **Republican "dirty tricks"** will eventually lead to the **White House.**

It has been speculated that **Maxi Wells** was running a **prostitution** ring that involved **politicians** and **some of their wives** at the Columbia Plaza Apartments, very close to the DNC at the Watergate office complex. One of the burglars was carrying a key to Wells' desk at the time of the arrest. The story may have been hushed up because they were caught before they could gather the hard evidence they wanted.

June 18, 1972 – *Washington Post.* **"Five Held in Plot to Bug Democratic Offices Here,"** says the headline **at the bottom of page one** in the *Washington Post.* This is the beginning of "Watergate" and will be kept in the news for two years as the story leads to the Nixon White House and the first resignation of a U.S. President.

August 1, 1972 – **A $25,000 cashier's check**, apparently earmarked for the **Nixon** campaign, winds up in the bank account of a **Watergate burglar**, The *Washington Post* reports.

September 29, 1972 – The **Washington Post reports that John Mitchell**, while serving as attorney general, controlled a **secret Republican fund** used to finance widespread intelligence-gathering operations against the Democrats.

October 10, 1972 – **The Washington Post reports that** FBI agents establish the Watergate break-in stems from a massive campaign of political spying and sabotage conducted on behalf of the Nixon reelection effort.

November 7, 1972 – **Richard Nixon is reelected** in one of the **largest landslides** in American political history, carrying 49 states and taking more than 60 percent of the vote to crush the Democratic nominee, Senator George McGovern of South Dakota. In one of the most lopsided races in American Presidential election history, incumbent President Richard M. Nixon wins 520 Electoral College votes to McGovern's 17.

December 8, 1972 – **Dorothy Hunt**, the wife of E. Howard Hunt, **is killed** in a plane crash while on her way to meet with CBS journalist Michelle Clark. Dorothy Hunt worked for the **CIA** after WWII, and was stationed in Shanghai, China, where she met her future husband, **E. Howard Hunt.** She then worked for the CIA in Paris. Dorothy and Howard returned to the U.S. and moved into a home in Maryland. Howard Hunt spent much of his time involved in covert operations in Mexico, Nicaragua, Guatemala, and Cuba. He was very active in the 1954 coup against democratically elected **Guatemalan President Jacobo Arbenz.**

    After Watergate Howard was going to fall on his sword like a good soldier but was frustrated when others equally guilty were given leniency and he threatened to reveal details of who paid him to organize the Watergate break-in. Dorothy Hunt took part in the negotiations with Charles Colson, and according to investigator Sherman Skolnick, Hunt also had information on the assassination of John F. Kennedy. Howard argued that if Nixon did not pay to suppress the documents they had showing he was implicated . . .

Former Attorney General John Mitchell, the head of Nixon's re-election organization, reportedly arranged to have Nixon aide Frederick LaRue pay the Hunts $250,000 to keep their mouths shut.

After United Airlines Flight 533, crashes into a Chicago neighborhood, there are over fifty **FBI agents** and a few **CIA agents** "unofficially" on the scene. The day after the crash Egil Krogh, one of Charles Colson's aides directly involved in overseeing Hunt's "Plumbers," is Nominated by President Nixon to be Under Secretary of Transportation. He assumes the post on February 2, 1973, and has direct control over the two agencies responsible for investigating the crash. What really happened is covered up. Egil Krogh will be sentenced to two to six years in prison, for his part in Watergate but will only serve four-and-a-half months.

James W. McCord claimed that Dorothy revealed that Hunt had information that would "blow the White House out of the water." In 1974, **Charles Colson,** Howard Hunt's boss at the White House, told *Time Magazine*: "I think they killed Dorothy Hunt." (07/08/1974)

Civil Rights Movement:

1972 – Tuskegee Syphilis Study. Peter Buxtun, a whistle blower, claims many blacks have been experimented on since 1932 when the Tuskegee Study of untreated syphilis began. The project involved 399 men with syphilis and 201 without. The men were told they were being treated for "bad blood." Dr. Dibble and Nurse Rivers, two African American health professionals, were involved in recruiting and retaining the men in the study. Once the project was leaked to the press it came to an end.

1936 – Researchers request that local physicians withhold treatment from study subjects. In addition, the decision is made to follow the men until death.

1940 – Researchers keep the men from receiving treatment ordered by the military draft.

1945 – Although accepted as the drug of choice for syphilis, USPHS researchers decide not to treat the men with Penicillin.

1968 – Peter Buxtun, a venereal disease investigator with the USPHS, voices concern over the study.

1969 – The CDC and local chapters of the AMA and NMA reaffirm their support for the study.

1972 – Whistle blower Peter Buxtun, informs Associated Press writer Jean Heller about the study. The public learns about the study in local newspapers.

1972 – The study ends; participants are offered some monetary and medical reparations.

1973 – Congressional hearings begin. A class action law suit filed by the NAACP results in a $9 million dollar settlement.

1997 – On May 16th, President Bill Clinton offers a formal apology on behalf of the nation.

March 10-12, 1972 – Several thousand African Americans gather in Gary, Indiana, for the first **National Black Political Convention.**

March 24, 1972 – Congress passes the Equal Employment Opportunity Act, giving the Equal Employment Opportunity Commission the power to file class-action lawsuits and extending its jurisdiction to cover state and local governments and educational institutions.

November 1972 – Andrew Young is elected to the House of Representatives from Georgia, and **Barbara Jordan** is elected to the House from Texas. They are the first African-Americans elected to Congress from the South since 1898.

1972 – In the Philippines, President Marcos' martial law silences one of Asia's freest presses as Marcos begins to gather all the wealth of the Philippines for himself and his family.

Women's Movement:

1972 – Sally Jean Priesand is ordained as the first woman **rabbi** in the United States.

March 22, 1972 – The Senate, approves the Equal Rights Amendment banning discrimination on the basis of sex, and sends the measure to the states for ratification. The vote is 84 to 8.

In 1848 Elizabeth Cady Stanton and four other women in Seneca Falls, New York invited the public to the **First Women's Rights Convention** to discuss expanding the role of women in America. Seventy–two years later women will be given the right to vote.

The 19th Amendment: "The right of citizens of the United States to vote shall not be denied or abridged by the United States or by any state on account of sex."

The 19th Amendment affirming a woman's right to vote came out of congress in 1919 and got more than half the ratifications it needed in the first year. Then it was stopped by states'-rights advocates, the liquor lobby, business interests against higher wages for women, and a number of women themselves, who believed claims that the amendment would threaten the family. The amendment still needed ratification by three-quarters of the states and the battle was narrowed down to a struggle in Tennessee. **It passed by a single vote on August 18, 1920.**

Many laws and practices in the workplace and in society still perpetuated men's status as privileged and women's status as second-class citizens.

Seneca Falls, 1923. The 75th anniversary of the 1848 Women's rights Convention. Alice Paul introduced the "Lucretia Mott Amendment," which read, in part: "Men and women shall have equal rights throughout the United States and every place subject to its jurisdiction." **The amendment was introduced in every session of Congress until it passed in 1972.**

1972 – Equal Rights Amendment The amendment reads: "Equality of rights under the law shall not be denied or abridged by the United States or by any State on account of sex." **President Ford,** in support for the Equal Rights Amendment, issued Presidential Proclamation 4383. "In this Land of the Free, it is right, and by nature it ought to be, that all men and all women are equal before the law." **The amendment died in 1982 when it failed to achieve ratification by a minimum of 38 states.** In 2009 the ERA had been ratified by only 35 states. Still three states short of passing.

1972 – **Juanita Kreps** becomes the first woman director of the **New York Stock Exchange.** She later becomes the first woman appointed Secretary of Commerce.

1972 – **The National Women's Political Caucus** is founded by **Betty Friedan**, **Gloria Steinem, Myrlie Evers,** several congresswomen, including **Shirley Anita St. Hill Chisholm** and **Bella Abzug**, several heads of national organizations, and others who shared the vision of gender equality.

1972 – **Abortion.** With the majority of **feminists being pro-choice** advocates of the legalization of abortion, **pro-life women form** the organization **Feminists for Life** to counter them.

1972 – **Battered Women's Shelter.** The first battered women's shelter opens in the U.S., in Urbana, Illinois, founded by Cheryl Frank and Jacqueline Flenner.

1972 – Over the summer New York **Congresswoman Shirley Chisholm** makes an unsuccessful bid for the **Democratic Presidential nomination.** She is the first African American to campaign for the nomination. She is the first woman to win primaries in a Presidential election.

1972 – **Title IX of the Education Amendments of 1972**, passed by Congresswoman Patsy T. Mink of Hawaii, states "No person in the United States shall, on the basis of sex, be excluded from participation in, be denied the benefits of, or be subjected to discrimination under any education program or activity receiving Federal financial assistance." This revolutionary legislation ended **sex discrimination** in high schools and colleges.

1972 – *Ms. Magazine*. Headed and edited by journalist and activist **Gloria Steinem**, *Ms. Magazine* becomes an independent publication, and is considered the magazine of the feminist movement. It was originally published in the *New Yorker,* for which Steinem was a columnist.

1972 – **The Feminist Women's Health Center** is founded in Los Angeles by Carol Downer and Lorraine Rothman.

1972

1972 – New York Radical Feminists hold a series of **speakouts** and a conference on rape and women's treatment by the criminal justice system.

Popular Culture:

1972 – Reporters have long asserted a right to keep their **sources confidential**. In Brandzburg vs. Hayes, however, the Court rules that reporters must respond to questions put to them in valid grand jury inquiries or criminal trials, and that protection for reporters who don't disclose their sources must be granted by Congress or State legislatures. Some 36 states have passed shield laws to protect reporters.

1972 – Dunn vs. Blumstein. The Supreme Court ruled that **Tennessee**'s lengthy residence requirements for voting in state and local elections is unconstitutional and suggests that 30 days is an ample period.

1972 – The first Haitian "boat people" arrive in south Florida.

February 13, 1972 – Led Zeppelin's concert in Singapore is canceled when government officials won't let them off the airplane because of their long hair.

1972 – "Deep Throat" starts the **porn movie** industry explosion. Thirty years later in 2002 Hollywood will be releasing 11,000 adult movies per year, more than 20 times the mainstream movie production. The U.S. Customs Service estimates that there are more than 100,000 websites offering **child pornography** in 2002.

1972 – HBO starts pay-TV service for cable.

1972 – Atari's Pong, a hit in arcades and taverns, starts the video game industry. Pong, designed as a ping-pong game for his Odyssey gaming console, is released by Ralph Baer.

May 19, 1972 – The Weathermen take credit for the bombing of The Pentagon. They stated it was "in retaliation for the U.S. bombing raid in Hanoi."

1972 – SDS-WSA Worker Student Alliance faction of SDS demonstrated at the **Democratic National Convention in Miami** against Democratic Presidential candidate **George McGovern**'s retreating from his original stronger campaign positions against the Vietnam War. Several hundred SDS members staged a sit-in at the Doral Hotel as McGovern and his staff met upstairs with protesting members of "Grassroots", McGovern Volunteers and sympathizers angry over the same issues. SDS-WSA strongly opposed bombing and terrorism. A few early SDS leaders went on to careers as **Democratic Party politicians.**

1972 – Wozniak´s "blue box." Steve Wozniak builds his "blue box," a tone generator to make free phone calls.

June 29, 1972 – The Supreme Court in Furman vs. Georgia rules **capital punishment** as currently practiced is unconstitutional. On July 2, 1976 The Supreme Court reinstates the death penalty, subject to conditions.

1968-1972 – Skyjackings. Between 1968 and 1972 there were a total of 159 U.S.-registered aircraft involved in skyjack incidents and 335 hijacking incidents in the world. Up to the, end of 1969, the desire to reach Cuba was the almost exclusive factor which caused skyjackings of U.S. aircraft. During the years 1970 and 1971 this factor declined to account for roughly, one half of all incidents.

In 1972, a new breed, of skyjacking extortionists, called **'parajackers'** demanded parachutes for escaping from the hijacked airplane with the ransom money. They are the single most important group of "true" air pirates in the U.S.

1972 – The Supreme Court rules, in Eisenstadt vs. Baird, that the right to privacy includes the **right to use contraceptives** even if unmarried.

1972 – e-mail. Ray Tomlinson of the research firm Bolt, Beranek and Newman sends the first e-mail when he was supposed to be working on a different project. Tomlinson, who is credited with being the one to decide on the '@" sign for use in e-mail, sent his message over a military network called ARPANET. When asked to describe the contents of the first email, Tomlinson said it was "something like "QWERTYUIOP"

1972

1972 – Budweiser, "This Bud's for you." D'Arcy Masius Benton & Bowles.

1972 – Life cereal, "Hey, Mikey." Doyle Dane Bernbach.

Business / Technology:

1972 – Apollo 16 lands on the moon. John Young and Charles Duke spend three days exploring the Descartes highland region, while Ken Mattingly circles overhead in Casper. This is the only Apollo landing to target the lunar highlands. The astronauts discovered that what was thought to have been a region of volcanism was actually a region full of impact-formed rocks. Their collection of returned specimens included a 25 pound chunk that was the largest single rock returned by the Apollo astronauts. After Apollo 16 planetary geologists revised previous interpretations of the lunar highlands and concluded that meteorite impacts were dominant in shaping the moon's ancient surface.

The Apollo 16 astronauts conducted performance tests with the lunar rover. The Rover reached a maximum speed of eleven miles an hour which is still a moon record according to the Guinness Book of Records.

1972 – Sony sells a videotape system for the home, the **Betamax.**

1972 – The **Xerox Alto,** first computer with a **mouse** and a graphical interface.

February 15, 1972 – The United States gives federal **Copyright protection** to sound recordings. Prior to this, phonograph records were only protected at the state level, and not in all states.

July 1. 1972 – The Bureau of Alcohol, Tobacco and Firearms, becomes a division of the Treasury Department, separate from the Internal Revenue Service.

1972 – Landsat I, "eye-in-the-sky" satellite, is launched.

1972 – The Consumer Product Safety Act is enacted as a response to perceptions that product liability laws did not sufficiently protect consumers from unsafe products. To implement the act, the Consumer Product Safety Commission is created and given the responsibility for administering additional consumer protection laws, including the **Federal Hazardous Substances Act** and the **Flammable Fabrics Act.**

1972 – **Hewlett-Packard** announced the HP-35 as **"a fast, extremely accurate electronic slide rule"** with a solid-state memory similar to that of a computer.

1972 – **Canada**, a programmable word processor with a video screen, the AES 90 is developed in Canada.

Finance:

February 21, 1972 – President Richard Nixon arrives in Beijing, China for an 8-day visit, in a **"journey for peace."** A joint communiqué released February 27 calls for increased Sino-U.S. contracts.

1972 – **BCCI. Pakistan**'s Agha Hassan Abedi establishes **Bank of Credit and Commerce International** in Luxembourg to avoid possible nationalization by the **Pakistan banking industry**. BCCI will become one of the most corrupt banks in the world, with ties to the CIA, U.S. presidents, terrorists, and, of course, the major money launderers; drug traffickers. By the early 1990's between $400 Billion and $500 Billon dollars a year in drug money is being laundered in the United States. Only 1% of it is traceable by the U.S. government. BCCI is set up from the start deliberately to avoid centralized regulatory review, and operates extensively in bank secrecy jurisdictions. Its affairs are extraordinarily complex. Its officers are sophisticated international bankers whose objective is to keep their affairs secret, to commit fraud on a massive scale, and to avoid detection. BCCI operates a "full service" money laundering operation that does business with anyone and everyone. BCCI was created with capital from Sheikh Zayed bin Sultan Al Nahyan, the ruler of Abu Dhabi in the United Arab Emirates and Bank of America (25%).

   "On the other side of the isle, the bank had alliances with the Bush family. George W. Bush, later forty-third President of the United States, ran a huge company supplying heavy drilling and pumping equipment to companies in Saudi Arabia owned by BCCI's major shareholders. The bank also enjoyed a good friendship with his brother Jeb Bush, introduced to the bank's senior management by George Barbar, a Lebanese multimillionaire businessman in Boca Raton who had millions in the London, Paris, Holland, and Florida branches of BCCI." "The Infiltrator," Robert Mazur. LittleBrown.

BCCI was involved in some of the most sensitive intelligence operations of the Reagan-Bush years, including the secret sales of arms to Iran. Investigators believe a portion of money stolen from BCCI's depositors financed covert operations sponsored by the U.S. government.

NEW YORK, Apr 4 (IPS) - Now that the U.S. Congress is investigating the truth of President George W. Bush's statements about the Iraq war, they might look into one of his most startling assertions: that there was a link between Saddam Hussein and Osama bin Laden.

Critics dismissed that as an invention. They were wrong. There was a link, but not the one Bush was selling. The link between Hussein and Bin Laden was their banker, BCCI. But the link went beyond the dictator and the jihadist; it passed through Saudi Arabia and stretched all the way to George W. Bush and his father.

BCCI was the Bank of Credit and Commerce International, a dirty offshore bank that then-president Ronald Reagan's Central Intelligence Agency used to run guns to Hussein, finance Osama bin Laden, move money in the illegal Iran-Contra operation and carry out other "agency" black ops. The Bushes also benefited privately; one of the bank's largest Saudi investors helped bail out George W. Bush's troubled oil investments. "FINANCE: Questions Linger About Bushes and BCCI," Analysis by Lucy Komisar(Investigative journalist Lucy Komisar's chapter, "The BCCI Game: Banking on America, Banking on Jihad," appears in the book "A Game as Old as Empire," published by Berrett-Koehler (San Francisco). **And the beat goes on . . .**

February 1972 – Successive waves of speculation drive many currencies up to their official ceilings. Throughout the spring of 1972 pressure is building on the British pound. In June it is floating and in trying to beat back successive waves of speculation and to defend the pound, Common Market currencies are all driven off their Smithsonian parities as well, and yet simultaneously there is a total absence of any commitment by the United States to help defend the new structure of parities. The United States stands by idly while the entire burden for protecting the Smithsonian parities falls on its allies and their central banks. The Treasury finally does agree to a limited resumption of the Federal Reserve swap network on July 18, in defense of the dollar. The very next day Treasury officials call for a stop to any more trading.

May 5, 1972 – The United States notifies the International Monetary Fund of its intent to change the par value of the dollar and on April 27, the Treasury Department announces a drawing of sterling from the International Monetary Fund.

October 20, 1972 – The State and Local Fiscal Assistance Act authorizes the Office of Revenue Sharing as a bureau of the Treasury Department.

1972 – The Commonwealth Bank of Detroit is the first bank with **more than $1 billion in assets to be bailed out.** The bank is considered essential to Detroit's inner city, so the Federal Deposit Insurance Corp provided $35.5 million in loans. It will never be paid back.

November 14, 1972 – The Dow Jones Industrial Average rises 6.09 to close at 1,003.16. This is the first time it closes above 1,000.

Books:

1972 – "Watership Down," Richard Adams. A rabbits' odyssey.

1972 – Down Alex Comfort's "The Joy of Sex: A Gourmet Guide to Love Making." This would have been banned just 7 years ago.

TV:

January 21 – Star Trek fans hold their first convention. New York's Statler-Hilton hotel had the honor of hosting.

1972 – Bob Keeshan airs as **Captain Kangaroo** for the 5,000th show.

1972 – A satellite is used for live television transmission.

1972

Sports:

September 1972 – Mark Spitz wins 7 gold medals in world record times, at the Munich Olympics.

September 5, 1972, 4:30 a.m. – The Munich massacre. War, politics and religion invade the Munich Olympics when members of the **Israeli Olympic team** are taken hostage and eventually murdered by **Black September,** a militant group with ties to **Yasser Arafat's Fatah** organization.

    The **Palestinian guerrilla** group broke into the **Olympic Village** dressed as athletes and carried their weapons in gym bags. By the end of the ordeal, the terrorist group had **killed eleven Israeli athletes and coaches and one West German police officer.** Five of the eight members of Black September were killed by police officers during an abortive rescue attempt. The **three surviving terrorists** were captured, and **later released by West Germany** following the hijacking by Black September of a Lufthansa airliner. This release led to speculation that West Germany helped stage the Lufthansa hijacking. Israel responded to the massacre with **a series of airstrikes and assassinations** of those suspected of planning the killings.

1972 – Munich Olympics. Basketball. In one of the most chaotic, confusing and controversial endings in the history of basketball, the Soviets were given three chances to score with three seconds remaining. Despite several apparent violations, they did it on their third try, beating the United States 51-50 for the gold medal at the 1972 Munich Olympics to end the Americans' 63-game winning streak.

Music:

February 8, 1972 – Frank Zappa's concert at London's Royal Albert Hall is canceled because of Zappa's obscene lyrics.

February 19, 1972 – Paul McCartney's single "Give Ireland Back to the Irish," which was inspired by the **"Bloody Sunday" massacre** in Ireland on January 30, 1972, is banned by the BBC. The controversy caused by the banning only increases the song's popularity and it ends up in the Top 20 in England.

Natural Disasters:

February 1972 – The Iran Blizzard kills 4,000 people. The blizzard also ends a four-year drought.

February 26, 1972 – Man, West Virginia. A slag-pile dam collapses under the pressure of torrential rains flooding 17-miles of valley, and killing more than 118 people.

The number of deaths stood at 60 Sunday as cleanup operations entered their second day today in the Buffalo Creek area of Logan County. Three-hundred residents are still missing in the wake of a flash flood that caused the dam to collapse. More than four -hundred National Guard have been called up to assist in the search for those missing. The water surged as much as fifteen feet above the banks of the Buffalo Creek when the dam broke. Four-thousand people are homeless and many have only the clothes they are wearing.

June 9–10, 1972 – Rapid City, South Dakota. Two-hundred and thirty-seven people die in a flash flood. There is $160 million dollars in damage.

June 14–23, 1972 – Hurricane Agnes. Northwest Florida to New York. A rare June hurricane makes landfall on the Florida Panhandle and then moves northeast as a tropical storm. The worst damage occurs along a path from central Maryland through central Pennsylvania to the southern Finger Lakes region of New York bringing heavy rainfall, causing widespread flash floods, and **killing 129 people**. Railroad damage is so extensive it contributed to the creation of Conrail. The rainfall produced by Agnes makes this storm more than twice as destructive as any previous hurricane in the history of the United States and remains the worst natural disaster ever to strike Pennsylvania. Damages are estimated at over $2.3 billion and 50 people were killed in Pennsylvania.

July 14–26, 1972 – New York City. A 14 day heat-wave kills 891 people.

December 22, 1972 – Managua, Nicaragua. A major earthquake destroys the capital city of Managua, killing up to 6,000 people and causing an estimated one billion dollars in structural damage. Fifteen square kilometers of Managua's city center are reduced to rubble. The world, moved by the holiday devastation, donates aid on an unprecedented scale, but President **Somoza diverts almost everything to his family and friends.** President Somoza's ultimate response to this natural disaster contributed to the fundamental loss of confidence in his regime.

Man vs. Man / Wars:

Assassinated – Uganda. Ben Kiwanuka, Democratic Party leader, first Prime Minister of Uganda and Chief Justice at the time of his death. Kiwanuka had angered Idi Amin, **the "Butcher of Uganda,"** by releasing a European, for lack of evidence, on the ridiculous charge of stealing a telephone directory from a hotel. Amin then had Kiwanuka held in the local jail where he was tortured.

Chief Justice Kiwanuka was told by Amin to draft a letter claiming he was kidnapped by Tanzania-based Ugandan exiles and members of the Tanzania People Defence Forces, but that gallant soldiers of the Uganda National Army had rescued him. Kiwanuka refused and was tortured again for days while Amin tried to force him to sign the document. When Kiwanuka was taken to Amin and again refused to sign. "Amin was this time angered and he pulled out a pistol and shot him three times," says his son Maurice Kagimu Kiwanuka.

1972 – Representative Cornelius Gallagher (D-New Jersey), **is indicted** on federal income tax evasion, perjury, and conspiracy charges. On December 12, 1972 he pleads guilty to evading $78,000 in income taxes. He rambled on and on before the judge at his sentencing for an hour and 17 minutes, almost lapsing into incoherence, except perhaps to those thoroughly familiar with the minute details of his case. He pleaded for mercy without ever admitting his guilt and he again denounced those who had brought him to his present crisis. "I appeal to this court for leniency in sentence and ask for an opportunity to put my life back together without being put in an institution," he said. He begged the judge for a "second chance" and, removing his glasses, turned toward his wife and four daughters seated in the rear of the tiny courtroom, his voice choking on a sob as he concluded, "I ask . . . that I be allowed a period of redemption and renewal." The judge was not impressed and said his review of the record showed that a "custodial sentence" was indicated. He sentenced Gallagher to two years in prison and fined him $10,000. The sentence was relatively light even though the fine was the maximum possible. He also found the congressman in contempt of court for a letter he had written in violation of a court order and fined him an additional $500.

Life Magazine tied Congressman Neil Gallagher to Cosa Nostra figure, Joe Zicarelli in 1968.

January 26, 1972 – A Bomb explodes on a Yugoslav plane killing all but one passenger.

September 5, 1972 – Palestinian terrorists seize 11 athletes in the **Olympic Village** in **Munich, Germany.** The rescue plan failed and a bloody firefight between the Germans and Palestinians followed leaving 11 Israeli athletes, 5 terrorists and a German policeman dead. A joint Mossad, IDF operation in Beirut assassinated the head of Fatah's intelligence arm, the head of the PLO's Western Sector, which controlled PLO action inside Israel, and the PLO spokesman.

After 20 years they finally assassinate PLO's head of intelligence in Paris. The remaining terrorist is still in hiding from Israeli authorities.

November 10, 1972 –Three men successfully hijack a Southern Airways DC-9 from Birmingham, Alabama and force it to fly to various U.S. locations. While on the ground at McCoy Air Force Base, Orlando, the FBI shoots out the tires and the hijackers force pilot William Haas to take off. The plane finally lands on a (partially) foam-covered runway in Havana with a $2 million ransom and 10 parachutes.

In Cuba one hijacker is sentenced to 20 years, one to 15 years. When they are returned to the United States to face further charges the incident leads to a brief treaty between the U.S. and Cuba to extradite hijackers

1972 – Israeli commandos storm a hijacked Belgian Sabena aircraft at Ben Gurion airport, **Israel.** Four **Palestinian Black September terrorists** on board the aircraft are killed and the hostages freed. One passenger and five Israeli soldiers were killed.

1972 – The Popular Front for the Liberation of Palestine and **Japanese Red Army** terrorists open fire in the passenger terminal of Lod Airport, Israel. The terrorists kill 26 civilians and seventy-eight people are wounded.

1972 – British Honduras. Guatemala again masses troops along the border, and this time, the British send the aircraft carrier Ark Royal and several thousand troops to prevent an invasion. British Honduras also provides excellent training facilities in tropical warfare for the British army.

April 27, 1972 – Burundi genocide. Tutsi, Hutu. A rebellion led by some **Hutu** members of the gendarmerie breaks out in the lakeside towns of Rumonge and Nyanza-Lac and declare the "Martyazo Republic". Countless atrocities are reported by eyewitnesses, and the armed **Hutu insurgents proceeded to kill every Tutsi in sight**, as well as the Hutus that refused to join the rebellion. It is estimated that during this initial Hutu outbreak, anywhere from **800 to 1,200 people are killed.**

President Michel Micombero (Tutsi) proclaims martial law and systematically proceeds to **slaughter Hutus en masse using lists** of targets including the Hutu educated, the elite and former military. Once this has been completed, the Tutsi-controlled army moved onto the larger civilian populations. The Tutsi-controlled government authorities originally estimated that roughly 15,000 had been killed while Hutu opponents claimed that the number was actually far closer to 300,000. Today, estimates put the figure between 80,000 to 210,000 killed. Several hundred thousand are estimated to have fled the genocide into **Zaire, Rwanda, and Tanzania.**

Since independence, Burundi has suffered several cycles of violence and crimes which could be determined as genocide. The first two cycles of violence took place in 1972 and 1987. Both cycles were a reaction of the government to rebel activity. The third cycle is currently in progress in 2009.

August 10, 1972 – Algerian police seal off the **Black Panther Party** headquarters of Algiers and put those inside under house arrest. They confiscate **one million dollars** in ransom money from five African Americans who hijacked a Delta Air Lines plane to Algeria. **Eldridge Cleaver** demands that the money be returned and that the hostages be allowed to take refuge somewhere else.

February 17-28, 1972 – China. President Nixon visits the People's Republic of China.

1972 – Ecuador. General Guillermo Rodriguez Lara, with help from the military, deposes the elected government of President Jose Maria Velasco Ibarra in a coup. Soon after, Texaco's first barrel of oil is paraded through **Quito, Ecuador.**

January 30, 1972 – "Bloody Sunday" massacre in Ireland. Members of the 1st Battalion of the British Parachute Regiment shoot **twenty-seven** unarmed **civil rights protesters** during a **Northern Ireland Civil Rights Association March** in Bogside outside the city walls of Derry, Northern Ireland. Thirteen people, including seven teenagers, die immediately. Five people were shot in the back. Two protesters were injured after being run over by army vehicles. Many witnesses, including bystanders and journalists, testify that all those shot were unarmed.

Immediately following the deaths, two investigations cleared the soldiers of blame and the shooting was described as bordering on the reckless. The Saville Inquiry, established in 1998 to reexamine the events, is expected to report in 2009.

Bloody Sunday will remain significant because it was carried out by the army in full view of the public and the press.

Political violence increases dramatically in Northern Ireland during 1970 to 1972 when close to 500 people die as a result of various conflicts.

1972 – Lithuanian Students Revolt. Seventeen-thousand **Lithuanians** stand up to Party Chief **Brezhnev** and petition **Kurt Waldheim of the United Nations** asking for enforcement of Soviet constitutional guarantees of **freedom of religion.** The Lithuanians seek an interpretation of Soviet constitutional liberties that the Russian, Jewish, Baltic and Ukrainian liberals defend in the Soviet Union. They stand up to a country that answers with soldiers, weapons and tanks.

1972 – Madagascar. Student protests in Antananarivo. In May there is a general strike involving the nation's 100,000 secondary-level students focusing on three principal issues: 1) ending the cultural cooperation agreements with France, 2) replacing educational programs designed for schools in France and taught by French teachers with programs emphasizing Malagasy life and culture taught by Malagasy instructors, 3) and increasing access for economically underprivileged youth to secondary-level institutions.

On May 13 the Republican Security Force **shoots some of the demonstrators** killing 34 people and injuring close to 150. A state of national emergency is declared and the government loses control, effectively ending the First Republic. What is left is turned over to the National Army under the command of General Gabriel Ramanantsoa, a politically conservative. The Army has remained neutral during the crisis and this turn of events is welcomed by all sides.

The new military government breaks ties with the west and looks to the Soviet Union and other communist countries for assistance. The French military is forced out of the country and French businesses are nationalized.

August 16, 1972 – The Moroccan Air Force attempts to shoot down a Boeing 727 carrying **King Hassan II.** The attempt fails and the coup leaders are arrested. General Mohammad Oufkir is shot to death for the attack. In 2000 a letter is produced that implicates Abderrahmane Youssoufi, the Prime Minister from 1998-2002, as a coconspirator with Oufkir in the failed coup.

1972-1973 – Egypt. Anwar Sadat. Throughout 1972, and for much of 1973, Anwar Sadat, President of Egypt, threatens war with Israel unless the United States forces Israel to accept his interpretation of Resolution 242: total Israeli withdrawal from territories taken in 1967.

September 21, 1972 – Philippines. Due to rising lawlessness and the threat of a Communist insurgency, **President Ferdinand Marcos** declares **martial law** on September 21, 1972. Marcos, ruling by decree, curtails freedom of the press and other civil liberties, closes down Congress and the media, and orders the arrest of opposition leaders and militant activists, including his staunchest critics, Senators Benigno Aquino, Jr., Jovito Salonga and Jose Diokno. As crime rates dramatically drop after a curfew is imposed the idea of martial law is initially well received. Marcos' political opponents flee the country while Marcos changes the constitution from a presidential government to a parliamentary government to allow himself to stay in power beyond what had been previously legal. In effect he is consolidating power so he can begin to siphon every last bit of wealth from the Philippines.

Along with martial law the economy during the 1970s recovers and grows, with budgetary and trade surpluses. The Gross National Product rose from P55 billion in 1972 to P193 billion in 1980. Tourism rose, contributing to the economy's growth. However, Marcos, his cronies and his wife, Imelda Romualdez-Marcos, willfully engaged in rampant corruption. It was no exaggeration when **Imelda Marcos is said to have declared in an interview that her family owns practically everything in the Philippines.**

1972 – Philippines. Moro Rebellion. The Philippines has a long history of Moro insurgent movements dating back to Spanish rule. Partisan political violence, divided along religious lines, is rampant on **Mindanao** Island and the Sulu Archipelago by the summer. When martial law is declared in September all civilians are ordered to surrender their guns but the Moros have traditionally considered the right to carry arms a part of their religious heritage and are suspicious of the government's intentions toward them. With Muslim backers in Libya and Malaysia they will field a force of 30,000 troops within two years and 50,000 people will be killed up to 1976 when talks begin.

October 17, 1972 – South Korea. Park Chung Hee declares **martial law** and installs a repressive authoritarian regime, with a new constitution that will give him total control of the government. **Park Chung Hee** will be assassinated by his lifelong friend Kim Jae Kyu, the head of the KCIA, in 7 years.

1953-1972 – Sudan. The United Kingdom and Egypt finalize an agreement providing for Sudanese self-government and self-determination. The transitional period toward independence began with the inauguration of the first parliament in 1954. With the consent of the British and Egyptian Governments, Sudan achieved independence on January 1, 1956, under a provisional constitution and the United States was among the first foreign powers to recognize the new state.

The Arab-led Khartoum government broke all of its promises to southerners to create a federal system, which led to a mutiny by southern army officers and touched off seventeen years of civil war (1955-1972). In the early period of the war, hundreds of northern bureaucrats, teachers, and other officials, serving in the south were massacred.

1972

January 1972 – Vietnam. President Nixon announces the 7th withdrawal of troops, bringing 70,000 more soldiers home by May 1. The troop level is now **69,000.**

March 30, 1972 – Vietnam. North Vietnamese forces launch the largest attacks in four years across the demilitarized zone. The U.S. responds on April 15 with the resumption of bombing raids against **Hanoi** and **Haiphong** after a four-year lull.

April 26, 1972 – Vietnam. Twenty thousand more soldiers are withdrawn.

April 27, 1972 – Vietnam. The Paris Peace talks resume.

May 8, 1972 – Vietnam. President Nixon announces he has ordered **the mining** of major **North Vietnamese ports**, as well as other measures, to prevent the flow of arms and material to the communist forces that invaded South Vietnam in March. Foreign ships in North Vietnamese ports are given three days to leave before the mines are activated, and the U.S. Navy begins to search or seize ships. The Allied forces will also begin bombing rail lines from China and take whatever other measures are necessary to stop the flow of military supplies. Nixon warns that these actions will stop only when all U.S. prisoners of war are returned and an internationally supervised cease-fire is initiated. If these conditions are met, the United States will "stop all acts of force throughout Indochina and proceed with the complete withdrawal of all forces within four months." At this time the North Vietnamese are wining in the battlefield and could care less.

The Nguyen Hue Offensive begins on March 30 with a massive invasion of South Vietnam. The North Vietnamese use almost their entire army in a three pronged attack. Four North Vietnamese divisions attack directly across the Demilitarized Zone into Quang Tri province and also attack 60 miles north of Saigon at An Loc in Binh Long Province and at Kontum in the Central Highlands. The North Vietnamese send out 500 tanks, 150,000 regular troops, and thousands of Viet Cong, supported by heavy rocket and artillery fire.

The U.S. is withdrawing troops and trying to get them safely out of Vietnam. The American public and politicians are so disgusted with the war they no longer trust the elected government to do what they have been promising. The announcement about

North Vietnamese harbors being mined leads to a new wave of antiwar demonstrations across the United States that result in violent clashes with police and **1,800 arrests on college campuses** in cities from Boston to San Jose, California. Police use wooden bullets and tear gas in Berkeley; **three police officers are shot** in Madison, Wisconsin; and **715 National Guardsmen are activated** to quell violence in Minneapolis. The American people have had enough.

June 1972 – Vietnam. Nixon announced the withdrawal of 10,000 more troops by September. **August 27, 1972 – Vietnam. Nixon announced** the withdrawal of 12,000 more troops.

August 1972 – Vietnam. The last U.S. combat troops leave Vietnam. The last American combat unit was a task force from the 3d Bn, 21st Inf Regt and battery B, 3d Bn, 82d Field Artillery Regt which had been stationed in Da nang These were the last U.S. ground combat units in Vietnam.

October 1972 – Vietnam. The Supreme Court was steadfast in refusing to rule on the constitutionality of American involvement in Vietnam. As late as October 1972, the court voted 7-2 to decline to hear a case in which taxpayers challenged the use of foreign aid funds to finance American operations in Vietnam (Sarnoff vs. Schultz) Justices Douglas and Brennan disagreed with the courts' hands-off attitude since the Constitution specifically gives Congress the power to declare war, they said, and thus "impliedly bars its exercise by the executive branch."

October 1972 – Vietnam. When President Nixon's National Security Advisor, Henry Kissinger, concludes a **secret peace agreement** with North Vietnam's Le Duc Tho, South Vietnamese President Thieu demands major alterations to the document. In response, the North Vietnamese publish the details of the agreement and stall the negotiations.

Feeling that Hanoi has attempted to embarrass him and to force them back to the table, **Nixon ordered the bombing of Hanoi and Haiphong** in late December 1972 with Operation Linebacker II, the so-called **"Christmas Bombing" of Hanoi.** From December 18-30, waves of American B-52s drop nearly forty thousand tons of bombs on the mostly evacuated city. Kissinger and the Nixon administration defend the bombing as essential but much of the world and the U.S. are outraged. Nixon and Kissinger are rightly accused of acting out of revenge and frustration as the French embassy and many residential neighborhoods are destroyed. The peace talks resume in Paris three weeks later.

October 27, 1972 – Vietnam. President Nixon "pocket vetoed" the Veteran's Health Care Expansion Act of 1972. The health care act would have authorized $85 million in fiscal year 1973 for expanding health care services for veterans and their dependents. **The U.S. had money for another forty thousand tons of bombs but not $85 million for our soldiers, most of them honorable, dedicated, patriots.**

1972 – North-South Yemen War. The Soviet Union, People's Republic of China, Cuba, and radical **Palestinians**, all major communist powers, assist in building the **People's Democratic Republic of Yemen** (South Yemen), armed forces. Strong support from Moscow results in Soviet naval forces gaining access to naval facilities in South Yemen.

March 25, 1972 – Salvadoran Military Youth Coup. Party spokesmen began to push the issue of full agrarian reform, including credit and technical assistance, as a major platform plank for the 1972 Presidential elections. The thinking of the **Christian Democrats** is both practical and idealistic. **Agrarian reform** is not just a popular rallying point; it is also seen as a way to establish a new class of small-to-medium-sized landholders who would presumably demonstrate some loyalty to those that helped them become landowners.

Poll watchers for UNO claimed that the final tally nationwide was 327,000 for Duarte and 318,000 for Molina. Molina's government demands a recount and then wins by 100,000 votes. The election fraud is so blatant that a group of young army officers, led by **Colonel Benjamin Mejia**, launch a coup on March 25. They want to establish a "revolutionary junta," with Duarte as President but they only have minimum support within the Officer Corps and loyalist forces regain control of San Salvador by early evening. Duarte is found hiding in the Venezuelan embassy and is dragged out by security forces amidst blows from rifle butts. He was interrogated and beaten before fleeing to Venezuela.

1973

The Oldest Boomer is 27 years old.

Cost of the Average House: $35,500	
Median Family Income: $10,500	**Minimum Wage:** $1.60/ hr
Gallon of Milk: $1.35	**Gallon Gasoline:** 39 cents
New Car: **MG MGB Roadster:** $3,320 **Dodge Dart Sport 340:** $2,853 **Jaguar Series III E Type V12** **Convertible:** $8,470 Honda Civic :$2,150	**Average Monthly Rent:** $175 **21" Table Model** **Color TV:** $340 **Bread:** 29 cents/ lb loaf **Ice Cream:** 59 cents/ half gallon **GE Dishwasher:** $219
Unemployment Rate: 4.9%-5.0%-4.9%	**The first Love stamp** is issued. **First-class Stamp:** 8 cents

21 cents buying power in 1973 **= $1.00 in 2008.**
In 1973 what cost us 21 cents to purchase now costs us $1.00 in 2008.

Movies: "American Graffiti," "Mean Streets," "The Sting," "Cries and Whispers," "The Exorcist," "A Touch of Class," "Last Tango in Paris."

Broadway: "A Little Night Music," "The Rocky Horror Show," London. "National Lampoon's Lemmings," revue.

TV: Marcia Brady's Broken Nose. John Dean Testifies before the Senate Watergate Committee. "The Battle of the Sexes," tennis, Billie Jean King and Bobby Riggs. "The Young and the Restless," "Barnaby Jones," "Kojak," "Schoolhouse Rock," "Star Trek, Animated". "The Addams Family, Animated". "The $10,000 Pyramid," "Dean Martin Celebrity Roast," "Police Story," "World Series of Poker," "Concentration."

Music: "The Harder They Come," "American Graffiti," Three Dog Night, "Shambala." Elton John, "Candle in the Wind," Wings, "Live and Let Die." "Summer Jam at Watkins Glen," rock festival attended by 600,000.

Helen Reddy, "Delta Dawn" & "Leave Me Alone, (Ruby Red Dress)." Bachman-Turner Overdrive, "Let It Ride." Bruce Springsteen, "Blinded By the Light." Olivia Newton John, "Let Me Be There." Roberta Flack, "Killing Me Softly With His Song." Barry White, "I'm Gonna Love You Just a Little More Baby." John Lennon, "Mind Games." Allman Brothers Band, "Ramblin' Man." John Denver, "Rocky Mountain High." Deep Purple, "Smoke on the Water." Jim Croce, "Time in a Bottle" & "Bad Bad Leroy Brown." The Moody Blues, "I'm Just a Singer, In a Rock and Roll Band." Vicki Lawrence, "The Night the Lights Went Out in Georgia." Kenny Loggins & Jim Messina, "Your Mama Don't Dance." Tony Orlando & Dawn, "Tie a Yellow Ribbon 'round the Old Oak Tree." "Goodbye Yellow Brick Road" & "Crocodile Rock." Marvin Gaye, "Let's Get It On." Gregg Allman, "Midnight Rider." The Rolling Stones, "Doo Doo Doo Doo Doo, Heartbreaker." Gary Glitter, "I'm The Leader Of The Gang, I Am." Bette Midler, "Boogie Woogie Bugle Boy." Stevie Wonder, "Superstition" & "You Are the Sunshine of My Life." Alice Cooper, "No More Mr. Nice Guy" & "The Sweet The Ballroom Blitz." Cheech and Chong, "Basketball Jones." The Doobie Brothers, "China Grove."

Deaths: Bruce Lee, Eddie Rickenbacker, Bobby Darin, David Ben-Gurion.

President: Richard M. Nixon (R) Quaker; vetoes 43/ 7 overrides

Vice President: Spiro T. Agnew (R) Episcopalian
Vice President: Gerald R. Ford (R) Episcopalian

House: D-242 ; R-192

Senate: 93rd Congress (1973-1975) Majority Party: Democrat (56 seats) Minority Party: Republican (42 seats) Other Parties: 1 Conservative; 1 Independent Total Seats: 100

Federal Debt: $458.14 billion or 33 % of the GDP

Consumer Price Index CPI-U (1982 Base of 100): 44.40

GDP: $1,382.7 billion	**Inflation Rate:** 6.16%
Dow Jones: 1,051.70 (01-11)/ 893.96 (06-01)	**S&P Price Index:** 97.55/-17.37%

Prime Rate: 6.25% (02-27/ 10.00% (09-18)	**Average Home Mortgage Rate:** 7.44/ 8.82%
1 oz Gold: $97.81	**1oz of Silver:** $4.60

Average Monthly S.S. Benefits Paid: $161 / month

Federal Debt: $458,141,605,312.09

Federal Deficit: $14.9 billion dollars

Defense Spending: $92.83 billion	**Interest Spending:** $17.35 billion
Health Care Spending: $17.41billion	**Pensions Spending:** $51.13 billion
Welfare Spending: $16.78 billion	**Education Spending:** $13.71 billion
Transportation Spending: $9.07 billion	**Misc. Other Spending:** $15.18 billion
Protection Spending: $2.17 billion	**Total Government Spending:** $245.71 billion

% of GDP that goes towards just the interest payment: 1.33%

$1.00 = 2.040 Yuan, China NPC	**$1.00 =** 270.89 Yen, Japan
$1.00 = 3.73 Saudi Arabian Riyal. After the devaluation of the Dollar, the gold content of the Saudi Arabian Riyal remains unchanged.	**$1.00 =** 68.175 Iranian Rial. After the devaluation of the Dollar, the gold content of the Rial remains unchanged.
U.S. Population: 211,939,000	**World Population:** 3,938,708,588
U.S. Birth Rate: 3,136,965	**U.S. Abortions:** 615,831—744,600
U.S. Homicide Rate: 9.7/ 100,000 population	**U.S. Violent Crime:** 417.4/ 100,000 population

Annual Average Domestic Crude Oil Prices:
$4.75 / barrel, $22.80 (2007 adjusted)

1973

Oil:

January 1973 – The Shah of Iran announces that the 1954 operating agreement between a consortium of oil companies and Iran will not be renewed when it expires in 1979. The consortium was formed in 1954 as a means to settle a dispute between a new ministry in Iran and the Anglo-Iranian Oil Company (AIOC). The consortium included Standard Oil of New Jersey, Standard Oil of California, SOCONY-Vacuum, the Texas Company, Gulf, Royal Dutch-Shell, the Compagnie Francaise de Petroles, and the AIOC. In March the Shah of Iran and Consortium members agree to nationalize all assets immediately in return for an assured 20-year supply of Iranian oil.

1973 – Saudi Arabia. The Abu Jiffan, Maharah, Qirdi , and El Haba oil fields are discovered.

June 1973 – Libya nationalizes the Bunker Hunt concession and in September Libya nationalizes 51 percent of nine other companies' concessions: Esso, Libya/Sirte, Mobil, Royal Dutch Shell, Gelensberg, Texaco, SoCal, Libyan-American (ARCO), and Grace.

Libya is the first of a long line of oil producing countries to dictate terms to the West. Major oil companies controlled oil prices from the end of World War II and this is the end as control shifts very rapidly to the Middle East. Libya is OPEC's eighth largest producer in 2003 as oil is discovered in one out of every two wells drilled.

June 1973 – Nigeria acquires a 35 percent participation in Shell-BP concession.

1973 – Oil crisis. The oil crisis starts on October 15, when the members of **Organization of Arab Petroleum Exporting Countries** (OAPEC), consisting of the Arab members of **OPEC plus Egypt and Syria,** proclaim an **oil embargo** "in response to the **U.S.** decision to re-supply the **Israeli military** during the Yom Kippur war."

OAPEC declared it would no longer ship oil to the United States and other countries if they supported Israel in the conflict and agreed to use their leverage to force an increase in world oil prices. This will in effect stabilize their incomes after several years of falling prices following the end of Bretton Woods, as well as the recent failure of negotiations with the "Seven Sisters" earlier in the month.

The rise in oil prices and the stock market crash will be considered the first event since the Great Depression to have a persistent economic effect.

October 6, 1973 – Syria and Egypt launch a military attack on **Israel** starting the **Yom Kippur War.** The U.S. failed in its attempt to secretly fly planes into Israel at night. The U.S. planes arrived in the morning and were greeted by TV cameras. Panic begins in the West, as oil prices soar.

October 16, 1973 – OPEC announced a decision to raise the posted price of oil by 70%, to $5.11 a barrel. The West can not continue to increase its energy use 5% annually, pay low oil prices, and still sell inflation-priced goods to the petroleum producers in the Third World. This was stressed by the Shah of Iran, whose nation is the world's second-largest exporter of oil and the closest ally of the United States in the Middle East. "Of course the world price of oil is going to rise," the Shah told the New York Times in 1973. "Certainly! And how . . . ; You Western nations increased the price of wheat you sell us by 300%, and the same for sugar and cement . . . ; You buy our crude oil and sell it back to us, refined as petrochemicals, at a hundred times the price you've paid to us . . . ; It's only fair that, from now on, you should pay more for oil. Let's say ten times more." The Arab countries begin using oil as a weapon and many feel this is the beginning of an undeclared war.

October 17, 1973 – Arab states place an oil embargo on the U.S. as a punishment for its decision to resupply Israel during the Yom Kippur War. The embargo is quickly extended to Western Europe and Japan. The Arab states will continue to cut production over time in five percent increments until their economic and political objectives are met.

October 19, 1973 – President Nixon asks Congress to appropriate $2.2billion in emergency aid to Israel, including $1.5 billion in out-right grants. **Libya** immediately announces a total oil embargo of all oil shipments to the **United States**. **Saudi Arabia** and the other Arab states quickly join the embargo on October 20.

The Netherlands supplied arms to Israel and allowed the Americans to use Dutch airfields for supply runs to Israel so they are also included in the Arab oil embargo. Oil prices are increased but the demand stays the same until oil prices surge from $3 a barrel to $12. The world economies answer with various recessions and high inflation that will continue into the 1980's.

1973 – Nixon and Kissinger secretly contemplate seizing oil fields.

1973 – The Alaska Pipeline is approved by Congressional vote exempting it from Federal law.

1973 – In response to high oil prices, **Car Free Sundays** are organized in many European countries.

December 22, 1973 – OPEC. Gulf Six decides to raise the posted price of marker crude from $5.12 to $11.65 per barrel effective January 1, 1974.

1973 – Higher Oil Prices are traditionally followed by recessions (1973, 1981, 1990, and 2000). Higher prices of a necessity such as oil absorb consumer dollars that would have been spent on something else. This lowers corporate profits, increases costs and lowers demand. The end result is inflation and higher interest rates chasing fewer dollars.

1973-1974 – People will wait for an hour or more on gasoline lines that stretch for miles. You can only buy gas on alternate days, depending upon whether their license plate ended with an odd or even number. The federal government even prints gas-rationing coupons, although they are never used. The oil crisis is widespread and affects most consumers.

Major News:

January 22, 1973 – Roe vs. Wade. The Supreme Court rules, 7-2 that states may not ban **abortions** during the **first 3 months of pregnancy** and may only regulate, but may not ban, abortions during the second trimester.

1972-1973 – Woodward & Bernstein. Reporters Robert **Woodward** and Carl **Bernstein**, investigated the **Watergate break-in** and first cracked the Watergate scandal for the *Washington Post.*

January 1973 – There is a cease fire in Vietnam between North Vietnam and the United States.

January 27, 1973 – U.S. involvement in the Vietnam War ends on January 27. Four-party **Vietnam peace pacts** are signed in Paris and North Vietnam releases some 590 U.S. prisoners by April 1. The last U.S. troops leave March 29. **More than 58,000 U.S. service personnel were killed** in action during the war. The fighting continues until April 30, **1975 when South Vietnam surrenders** to the communist North Vietnamese forces.

January 27, 1973 – The end of the military **draft** is announced.

January 1973 – Five of seven defendants in the **Watergate** break-in trial plead guilty January 11 and January 15. Two others are convicted on January 30.

January 1973 – Former Nixon aides **G. Gordon Liddy** and **James W. McCord Jr.** are **convicted** of conspiracy, burglary and wiretapping in the Watergate incident and five other men plead guilty. Liddy led the group of five men who broke into the DNC and took his orders from the Nixon administration. He admitted to supervising the break-in from another hotel across the street and was convicted of conspiracy, burglary and illegal wiretapping. For his part in the crime **G. Gordon Liddy** is sentenced to 20 years in prison and ordered to pay $40,000 in fines. President Jimmy Carter will commute Liddy's sentence to eight years, "in the interest of equity and fairness. . ." He will serve a total of four-and-a-half years.

    James W. McCord Jr. writes a letter to Judge Sirica charging the Nixon White House with conducting a cover-up to conceal its connection with the break-in and then pressuring the defendants to remain silent. This is a direct tie to the Nixon White House. McCord is convicted on multiple counts of conspiracy, burglary and wiretapping and serves two months of a one-to-five-year prison term.

    Jeb Stuart Magruder then changed his previous testimony and said he committed perjury at the insistence of **Attorney General John N. Mitchell** and John Dean.

Magruder was the only direct participant in the scandal to confirm that **President Nixon** had specific foreknowledge of the Watergate break-in, and that Nixon actually directed Mitchell to proceed with the break-in. **Magruder** will serve only seven months in a prison near Allenwood, Pennsylvania.

John Dean, White House Counsel to President Richard Nixon, and master manipulator of the cover up according to the **FBI,** was convicted of multiple felonies as a result of Watergate. He will be a key witness for the prosecution in exchange for a reduction in his sentence. Dean will serve 127 days for taking part in the cover-up.

In 1975 white house advisors H.R. Haldeman, John Ehrlichman, and Attorney General John Mitchell will be convicted of conspiracy, obstruction of justice, and perjury. They are sentenced to prison. President Richard Nixon, fearing impeachment, will resign

February 1973 – The Senate votes (77-0) to establish a Select Committee on Presidential Campaign Activities. The Committee is to be chaired by **Senator Sam Ervin** (D-NC).

February 27, 1973 – Wounded Knee, SD was the site where 350 Sioux Indian men women and children were massacred by U.S. troops on December 29, 1890.

The town of Wounded Knee, South Dakota is seized by followers of the **American Indian Movement.** The occupiers control the town for 71 days while the **United States Marshals Service** and other law enforcement agencies cordon off the town while the two sides sporadically shoot at each other for most of the three months. The military had the use of fifteen armored personal carriers, grenade launchers, flares, and 133,000 rounds of ammunition at a cost of over $500,000. A journalist at the scene described "sniper fire from federal helicopters, bullets dancing around in the dirt and sounds of shooting from both sides all over town." On May 5 there is an agreement to disarm and the siege ends three days later. The town is then evacuated after 71 days of occupation and the government takes control of the village.

April 1973 – The FBI establishes the "Special Target Information Development" program and sends undercover agents to penetrate the Weather Underground.

April 30, 1973 – Nixon's top White House staffers, **H.R. Haldeman** and **John Ehrlichman,** and **Attorney General Richard Kleindienst** resign amid charges of White House efforts to obstruct justice in the Watergate case. White House counsel **John Dean** is fired.

May 21, 1973 – **Senator Fulbright** warns of War in the Middle East, an Oil Embargo, and Future Terrorism.

May 18, 1973 – **The Senate Watergate Committee** begins its nationally televised hearings. Attorney General-designate **Elliot Richardson** taps former solicitor general **Archibald Cox** as the Justice Department's special prosecutor for Watergate.

June 3, 1973 – **John Dean** has told **Watergate** investigators that he discussed the Watergate cover-up with **President Nixon** at least 35 times.

June 13, 1973 – **Watergate prosecutors** find a memo addressed to **John Ehrlichman** describing in detail the plans to burglarize the office of **Pentagon Papers** defendant **Daniel Ellsberg's psychiatrist.**

June 25, 1973 – **John Dean,** former Nixon counsel, tells the Senate hearings that Nixon, his staff and campaign aides, and the Justice Department had conspired to cover up **Watergate** facts.

July 1, 1973 – **DEA. The Drug Enforcement Administration** is established. It proposes the creation of a single federal agency to enforce the federal drug laws as well as consolidate and coordinate the government's drug control activities. Congress agrees and the Bureau of Narcotics and Dangerous Drugs, the Office of Drug Abuse Law Enforcement, and other Federal offices merge together to create the DEA.

July 13, 1973 – **Alexander Butterfield**, former presidential appointments secretary, reveals in congressional testimony that since 1971 **Nixon had recorded all conversations and telephone calls** in his offices.

   July 17: The Senate Watergate Committee asks President Nixon for the tapes concerning the Watergate investigation. **July 23**: President Nixon refuses to release the tapes. **August 7**: White House lawyers tell Judge Sirica that the courts have no power to force Mr. Nixon to release the tapes. **August 29**: Judge Sirica orders the President to produce the tapes for his examination, so that he can decide whether to give them to the grand jury. The White House announces that the President will not comply with the order. **August 30**: President Nixon decides to appeal to the Court of Appeals for the District of Columbia. **October 12**: The Court of Appeals rules that President Nixon must turn over the tapes to Judge Sirica. **October 19**: President Nixon announces that he will not hand over the tapes to Judge Sirica. **October 23**: President Nixon agrees to surrender the Watergate tapes to Judge Sirica. **November 26**: The seven existing Watergate tapes and other material are handed over by President Nixon to Judge Sirica, along with the **"missing 18 1/2 minutes."**

July 18, 1973 – Nixon reportedly orders the **White House taping system** to be disconnected.

1973 – The Saudi oil embargo results in gas lines in the United States.

August 14, 1973 – The U.S. officially stops the bombing in **Cambodia** at midnight August 14 in accord with a June congressional action.

September 1973 – The United States helps overthrow the government in Chile.

October 10, 1973 – Vice President Spiro Agnew resigns and pleads no contest to a charge of tax evasion (accepting bribes) on payments made to him by contractors while he was Governor of Maryland.

Agnew was under investigation by the United States Attorney's office in Baltimore, Maryland, on charges of **extortion, tax fraud, bribery, and conspiracy.** In October, he was formally charged with **having accepted bribes** totaling more than $100,000, while holding office as Baltimore County Executive, **Governor of Maryland, and Vice President of the United States**. On October 10, 1973, Agnew is allowed to plead no contest to a single charge that he had failed to report $29,500 of income received in 1967, with the condition that he resign the office of Vice President. **Agnew is the only Vice President in U.S. history** to resign because of criminal charges. Ten years after leaving office, in January 1983, Agnew paid the state of Maryland nearly $270,000 as a result of a civil suit that stemmed from the bribery allegations.

October 12, 1973 – Gerald R. Ford, becomes the **first appointed Vice President** under the 25th Amendment and is sworn in on December 6.

October 17, 1973 – OPEC declares an oil Embargo against Oil Exports to the U.S. and the Netherlands.

October 20, 1973 – The "Saturday Night Massacre." October 20, President Nixon orders Attorney General **Elliot Richardson** to fire **Watergate special prosecutor Archibald Cox,** who had sought the handover of Nixon's subpoenaed White House tapes. Richardson refuses to comply and resigns. Deputy Attorney General **William Ruckelshaus** refuses and is fired. Solicitor General **Robert Bork,** as acting attorney general, then fired Cox and abolishes the office of the special prosecutor. **Leon Jaworski** is named on November 1, by the Nixon administration to succeed Cox. Pressure to **impeach President Nixon** mounts in Congress.

November 7, 1973 – Congress overrides President Richard Nixon's veto of the **war powers** bill, which curbed the President's power to commit forces to hostilities abroad without congressional approval. Congress claims the right to restrict the use of American forces in combat when a state of war does not exist.

November 17, 1973 – Nixon declares, **"I am not a crook,"** maintaining his innocence in the Watergate case.

December 7, 1973 – The White House can't explain an **18 ½-minute gap** in one of the subpoenaed tapes. Chief of Staff **Alexander Haig** says one theory is **that "some sinister force"** erased the segment.

1973 – Symbionese Liberation Army, SLA is a multi-racial militant group with the broad slogan, "Death to the fascist insect that preys upon the life of the people." The group is founded in Berkeley by Donald DeFreeze, who escaped from San Quentin

1973

Prison and changed his name to Cinque Mtume. Their 1973 **assassination** of the Oakland superintendent of schools, Marcus Foster, brings them to national attention.

Civil Rights Movement:

1973 – The American Psychiatric Association removes **homosexuality** from its official list of mental disorders.

May 29, 1973 – Tom Bradley wins the mayoral election and becomes the first African-American Mayor of Los Angeles. He will be reelected four times and hold on to the Mayor's office for 20 years.

1973 – Marion Wright Edelman creates the **Children's Defense Fund.**

October 16, 1973 – Maynard Jackson wins the election in Atlanta and becomes the first African-American Mayor of a major Southern city.

November 6, 1973 – Coleman Young is elected the first black Mayor of Detroit, Michigan.

1973 – The National Black Feminist Organization is established by Elizabeth Holmes Norton.

Women's Movement:

1973 – Battered women's shelters open in Tucson, Arizona and St. Paul, Minnesota.

1973 – The Supreme Court holds that sex-segregated help wanted ads are illegal.

1973 – Puerto Rican women hold their first women's conference.

1973 – San Francisco, California. Margo St. James organizes Call Off Your Old Tired Ethics (**COYOTE**) to improve working conditions for **prostitutes.**

1973 – Antifeminist **Phyllis Schlafl**y attacks the Equal Rights Amendment in her newsletter and forms the "**STOP ERA**" organization. What once looked like it was on its way to easy ratification has now run into fierce opposition.

1973 – "**Playgirl**" arrives on news stands for women.

1973 – As a result of Roe vs. Wade, the Supreme Court establishes **a woman's right** to safe and legal abortion, overriding the anti-abortion laws of many states. This leads to an increase in abortions. The number of legal abortions in the U.S. from 1973 until 2005 is **45 million!** This is now very big business and decisions are profit based.

1973 – A woman looked and dressed like a woman again. It is the year of the "Great Gatsby" and the "Jazz Age" look. Fabrics, soft-flowing and liquid, illustrate the fashion revolution. Hemlines range from just above the knee to 3 or 4 in. below. Hairstyles are shorter, smoother, have movement, and are always feminine.

Popular Culture:

1973 – In Miller vs. California the Court lays down a three-part test to determine what material is **obscene**. The government can outlaw material based on the following standard: "whether the work, taken as a whole, lacks serious literary, artistic, political, or scientific value."

1973 – The Heroin Trafficking Act increases the penalties for heroin distribution.

1973 –*Playboy* **Magazine.** *Playboy's* **downfall** began in 1973 and continues today. Did *Playboy Magazine* help or hurt the Women's Movement over the last sixty years? **Hugh Hefner** says that he started Playboy for urbane, sophisticated men who enjoyed sex and liked to look at beautiful women. Although the magazine claims to be classy it is about men leering at women's passive bodies. And today's Playboy has a **Hooters**-like personality, with unpleasant "heh-heh-heh" snickering about women's bodies from readers who write in and staff members who reply. The cartoons appear dated and juvenile. **Sheila Gibbons** said, "It's like expecting to meet **James Bond** and finding yourself introduced to **Beavis and Butthead.**"

1973 – Endangered Species Act of 1973 protects environmental assets.

1973 – Drug Enforcement Administration (DEA) regroups the Bureau of Narcotics and Dangerous Drugs into DEA.

Mid-1970's – Saigon falls. The heroin epidemic subsides. The search for a new source of raw opium yields Mexico's Sierra Madre. "Mexican Mud" will temporarily replace "China White" heroin until 1978. **Repeat:** Saigon falls. The heroin epidemic subsides.

1973 – George Carlin's "Seven dirty words" results in a court slap-on-the-hand for Pacifica Radio.

1973 – Burger King, **"Have it your way,"** BBDO.

1973 – "Today the pits, tomorrow the wrinkles." Sunsweet Prunes, Freberg.

Business / Technology:

1973 – Equity Funding Case. Computer Data Fraud. The computer problems began just before the close of the financial year **in 1964 when** an annual report needed to be printed but the final figures simply could not be pulled from the mainframe. When the head of data processing told the president the bad news he was told to simply make up the bottom line to show about $10 million in profits and calculate the other figures so it would come out that way.

    By early 1973 there are over 64,000 phony transactions with a face value of two billion dollars, $25 million in counterfeit bonds, and $100 million in missing assets. All of the **earnings are completely fabricated.** The Securities and Exchange Commission is supposed to monitor publicly traded companies. Why didn't they have a clue? Various state insurance departments responsible for monitoring the activities of insurance companies were never even suspicious. And where were the auditors? Did they rubber stamp the books? Two billion dollars in fraud and no one could find anything wrong? It finally took an irate computer operator who had to work overtime to sound the alarm at Equity. Rumors spread throughout Wall Street and the insurance industry. Within days, the Securities and Exchange Commission had informed the California Insurance Department that they'd received information about the ultimate form of data manipulation. Tapes were being erased. The officers of the company were arrested, tried and sentenced to prison.

1973 – Biotech Industry / Genetic Engineering. Stanley Cohen, Paul Berg and Herbert Boyer make one of the first genetic engineering experiments. A major breakthrough in genetic engineering occurs with the first successful gene splicing (recombinant DNA) when they slip a gene from an African clawed toad into a bacterium. The transplanted gene starts producing protein inside the bacterium, proving that simple organisms could be called upon to become protein "factories." The discovery is recombinant DNA, the first time the stuff of life is taken from its natural place and artificially inserted into another piece of DNA. The biotech industry is born.

1973 – Computer Kit. Scelbi-8H. For $575 you get a computer kit with a microprocessor.

May 14, 1973 – Skylab, the first U.S. space station, is launched

1973 – IBM ships its first read/write **floppy disk** drive as a part of the 3740 Data Entry System.

1973 – The Cell phone is invented by **Martin Cooper** while he is working for Motorola.

1973 – Xerox sets up a LAN (local area network) called **Ethernet, while** a computer in England and another in Norway connect to **ARPANET.**

1973 – Before 1973 the U.S. had farm support that paid farmers to take corn off of the market. These were loans, not direct payments. During the Nixon administration food prices moved higher for a lot of reasons having to do with the Russian grain deal and the cost of energy. This drives the cost of hamburger, steak, grains, and butter sky high and people are in the streets protesting. The sudden rise in beef prices trigger a housewives' boycott of beef and Nixon sends Earl Butz to drive down the cost of food.

Earl encourages farmers to plant from fence-row to fence-row, and they change the subsidy system. Now, instead of taking food off the market to keep prices high and **loaning farmers** money so they can keep their corn off the market, Earl and Nixon just write a check. This encourages farmers to produce more and more corn. The American food system is in 2010 built on the abundance of corn, an abundance perpetuated by a subsidy system that pays farmers to maximize production.

Cows did not evolve to eat corn, but we feed them corn because it's so cheap and we need to get rid of it. It also makes them grow quickly. One of the side effects is that it also causes disease and a lot of the cattle in 2010 would die of disease (in 18 months) if they were not killed first (in 12 months) so that you could eat them.

Finance:

January 1, 1973 – EEC. The United Kingdom, Ireland, and Denmark enter the European Economic Community.

February 13, 1973 – President Nixon raises the **official gold price** in the United States from $38.00 an ounce to $42.22 an ounce. The dollar is devalued and the two-tier gold price is terminated.

April 1973 – Federal Express begins its operations with a fleet of 14 Falcon jets. In 1977, following air cargo deregulation Federal Express expanded by adding 727s and DC-10s to its fleet. In 1989 Federal Express purchased Flying Tigers Lines and integrated its fleet and operations into the Federal Express fleet.

Frederick W. Smith Founder, Federal Express in 1998. "By the early '70s when I'd gotten out of the service it was very clear that this new society was coming in earnest. And so, at that point I said, "What the hell, let's try to put it together." And that's how FedEx came to be. And then from that point forward, the requirements for this type of system were so profound and so big, really for the next 25 years to this date we've simply been running just to keep up with the requirements. And that's what led to the hundreds of planes and the thousands of trucks. I wish it was something that I could say I was so smart. It was just like Pogo the Possum said, "If you want to be a great leader, find a big parade and run in front of it." And that's what we've been doing for the last quarter century."

May-June 1973 – Black and Scholes introduce their options pricing model in the "Journal of Political Economy." Fischer Black and **Myron Scholes** of the **University of Chicago** devise a pricing model that establishes a standard by which options can be priced. Their methodology has paved the way for economic valuations in many areas.

Until Black-Scholes, traders and investors have been pretty much guessing. The model figures out a way to measure the volatility of the underlying instrument and its erosion of value over time. Black-Scholes adds enough credibility to pricing to make options, and later more complex derivatives, legitimate, liquid instruments for all sorts of institutional investors, ranging from **Goldman Sachs** to Nick Leeson.

1973 – Oil Embargo. Oil prices soar from $2.90 to $11.65 per barrel.

1973 – Price Controls. In reaction to the Arab Oil Embargo Congress passes laws that tried to protect consumers from gasoline shortages and high prices. The price controls of the Emergency Petroleum Allocation Act are generally considered a failure, and are later repealed.

Books:

1973 – **"Burr,"** the best-selling historical novel by **Gore Vidal.**

1973 – **Erica Jong** shocks people with her language in the **"Fear of Flying."**

1973 – **"Gravity's Rainbow."** Thomas Pynchon.

1973 – Kurt Vonnegut. **"Breakfast of Champions."**

1973 – **"Sybil."** Flora Rheta Schreiber.

TV:

1973 – Tennis. Billie Jean King and Bobby Riggs. After defeating Margaret Court in a tennis match, male chauvinist Bobby Riggs declares that men are superior to women, and calls Billie Jean King to a **Battle of the Sexes** tennis match, in which King easily defeats Riggs, leading to the celebration of feminists everywhere. The **"Battle of the Sexes"** remains **the most watched tennis match in the history of the world.**

January 14, 1973 – Elvis Presley's "Aloha From Hawaii" television special is seen around the world by more than **1 billion viewers.**

1973 – Jim Bakker, Televangelist. Jim Bakker, a prominent televangelist with his wife, Tammy Faye, develop the **PTL Club** ("Praise the Lord" or "People That Love") into a **multimillion-dollar television ministry** composed of a cable network and a real estate venture known as **Heritage USA.**

Bakker is credited with originating the **"700 Club"** talk-show format and is the first host. Bakker is also credited with creating the most successful on-air fund-raising shows, the proceeds of which establish **CBN** as a well-financed entity. Bakker left CBN in November 1972 to join **Paul Crouch at the Trinity Broadcasting System** (TBS), where he started the "Praise the Lord Show."

Bakker resigned as president of TBS in 1973 to develop PTL. His interpretation of Pentecostalism has been described as the **"gospel of prosperity"** because he claims material prosperity is a sign of God's love. Tammy Faye is an advocate for the right of Christian women to dress as they please without being censored by their congregations.

1973 – Johnny Carson." The Tonight Show." In the era of gasoline shortages, Johnny Carson jokes about an imminent **shortage of toilet paper**. Viewers panic and go on a hoarding spree, emptying store shelves and forcing Carson to publicly apologize the next night.

1973 – TV's "Maude" has an abortion and Catholic leaders are outraged.

1973 – Reality TV. PBS viewers watch while dysfunctional **"An American Family"** actually disintegrates. The show is twelve episodes long, edited down from about 300 hours of footage, and chronicles the experiences of a nuclear family, **the Louds of Santa Barbara, California,** during a period of time when parents Bill and Pat Loud separated and Pat filed for divorce. In 2002, "An American Family" was listed at #32 on "TV Guide's 50 Greatest TV Shows of All Time" list.

Sports:

June 9, 1973 – Secretariat wins the Belmont Stakes June 9, in record time and is the first **Triple Crown** winner **since Citation** in 1948. After wining the Belmont Stakes by 31 lengths some observers quipped that the only horse race this year was the four horses racing for second place. This third jewel of the Triple Crown is the coronation of Secretariat as the greatest race horse of all time.

1973 – Bobby Riggs vs. Billie Jean King. Billie Jean King beat Bobby Riggs in three straight sets after he challenged her to a match where he boasted of his superior male attributes. Both Riggs and King made a lot of money and everyone had fun.

Music:

July 28, 1973 – Summer Jam. Watkins Glen, New York. Larger than Woodstock by a hundred thousand people! **600,000 Rock fans** attend the concert at the Watkins Glen Grand Prix Raceway and like Woodstock; people are covered with mud after a drenching thunderstorm.

Many historians claim that the Watkins Glen event was the largest gathering of people in the history of the United States. This means that on July 28, one out of every 350 people living in America is at the New York state racetrack. Since most are from the Northeast, and the average age of those present is seventeen to twenty-four, close to one out of every three young people from Boston to New York are at the festival.

January 9, 1973 – Mick Jagger's request for a Japanese visa is rejected on account of a 1969 drug bust, putting an abrupt end to **The Rolling Stones'** plans to perform in Japan during their forthcoming tour of Hawaii, Australia and New Zealand.

January 14, 1973 – Grateful Dead bassist Phil Lesh is arrested for **drug possession** in California.

1973

March 8, 1973 – Paul McCartney is fined $240 after **pleading guilty** to charges of growing marijuana outside his Scottish farm.

1973 – Reggae music spreads out from Jamaica.

Natural Disasters:

April 17, 1973 – Bangladesh. Dhaka Tornado. In one of the worst tornado tragedies to hit Bangladesh, **681 people are killed.** Balurchar village is completely leveled and according to the Prime Minister not a single dwelling is traceable. Almost all houses are leveled in the eight villages along the Kaliganga River. Uprooted trees are crisscrossed and bodies are strewn all around. An unofficial death toll is 1,037. There were two funnels that merged together to form one large tornado that flattened almost everything in its zigzag path. One survivor said, It turned and came after us. It chased us down.

Man vs. Man / Wars:

1965-1973 – Vietnam War. An accurate estimate is 2,800,000 people died as a result of the Conflict in Vietnam. And 300,000 people died as a result of the incursion into Cambodia.

Assassinated – Portuguese Guinea / Guinea-Bissau. Am'lcar Cabral is assassinated by the **Portuguese secret police** in April.

It will never be known exactly how many of the 13 million human lives were bought and sold by the Portuguese in Cacheu, one of the largest slave markets **along the Guinea coast.** They thought of the coastline all the way up to southern Senegal, as their own special territory. Four and one-half percent of these human beings went to North America. **Thirty-seven percent of all slaves** imported from Africa were bound for the **Brazilian colonies.** Most of the slave trade ended in the 1830s although even in 2010 women and children are traded as **sex slaves** in many parts of the world. The forcible prostitution of girls, boys and women, is a $32-billion global industry in 2008. **The UN Office on Drugs and Crime** estimates that on any given day, 2.5 million people throughout the world are victims of the crime, which thrives at hallmark events such as the **Olympics or the FIFA World Cup.**

Assassinated – Ambassador to Sudan. The U.S. Ambassador to Sudan, Cleo A. Noel and other diplomats are assassinated at the Saudi Arabian Embassy in Khartoum by members of the **Black September** organization on March 2.

Assassinated – Bermuda. Sir Richard Sharples, Governor of Bermuda. The British Governor and his assistant have been assassinated in Bermuda, a British-dependent territory in the North Atlantic. Sir Richard Sharples and his aide-de-camp Captain Hugh Sayers, 26, were killed as they strolled in the grounds of the Government House on Saturday evening. It was the night of the annual police ball and the Governor's residence in Hamilton, the island's only town was unguarded save for a lone guard. He heard gun shots and ran to help but was too late. In spite of road blocks set up immediately after the incident the killer escaped. The deaths of the two men come six months to the day after the island's **British police chief, George Duckett, was shot dead**. Mr. Duckett's killer is still at large.

July 8, 1973 – Iraq. The Chief of Internal Security, Nadhim Kzar, is **executed** along with 35 others, after reports of a coup attempt.

Assassinated – Spain. Luis Carrero Blanco. In June 1973 he was appointed Prime Minister. In December 20, he is **assassinated** by ETA, the Basque nationalist organization.

July 5, 1973 – Representative J. Irving Whalley (R- Pennsylvania) is **indicted** on charges of mail fraud, obstruction of justice, payroll abuse, and threatening a federal witness. Whalley **pleads guilty** and receives a three-year suspended sentence and an $11,000 fine.

July 12, 1973 – Representative Bertram L. Podell (D-New York) is **indicted** on conspiracy, bribery, and perjury charges. In October 1974, Representative Podell pleads guilty to conspiracy and conflict of interest for accepting $41,350 in fees and campaign contributions from a small Florida airline to obtain a Bahamas route.

1973

Podell is fined $5,000 and serves four months in jail before he is disbarred. Under a rules change, he is reinstated as a lawyer by the appellate division of the New York State Supreme Court in 1980 and returned to a real estate-law practice.

1973 – The Candy Man. The Houston Mass Murders, as the case was later called, became one of the most **horrific series of murders** in U.S. history. Dean Corll is a 33-year-old electrician living in Houston, Texas, who with two teen accomplices is responsible for **kidnapping, torturing, raping and murdering** at least 27 young boys in Houston during the early 1970s. On August 8, 1973, Henley shot and killed Corll at his home.

While police are interviewing Henley about the shooting and searching Corll's home for evidence, a bizarre and brutal story of torture, rape and murder begins to unfold. Henley slowly begins to tell police about his relationship with Corll and explains how he was paid $200 or more "per head" by Corll to lure young boys to his house. Some of the boys were childhood friends of Henley and were easily persuaded to go to a "party" where there would be **free alcohol and drugs**. Once inside Dean Corll's home they became victims and were tortured, raped and murdered.

1973 – Edward Kemper III. The Coed Butcher. Kemper **murdered six hitchhiking college co-eds, resembling his mother**, in the Santa Cruz area of California, between May 1972 and February 1973. The murders usually occurred after a fight with his mother with each murder becoming more bizarre and brutal. Kemper took his victims to a desolate area where he killed them by shooting, stabbing, and later by smothering them. He brought the corpses back to his apartment where they were dissected and he had sex with the body parts before he ate them so they could "be a part" of him. Kemper dumped the remains in the California hills. He would later admit that he got a kick out of going to his psychiatric appointments with the head of a 15-year-old victim in the trunk.

1973 – A Black September suicide squad attacks the passenger terminals at Athens airport, Greece, killing three civilians and injuring fifty-five.

March 1, 1973 – Ten Diplomats are taken hostage from the Saudi Arabian Embassy in Khartoum, Sudan. After President Richard Nixon states that he will not negotiate with terrorists, and demanded that "no concessions" would be made, the three Western hostages were killed.

1973 – Palestinian terrorists bomb a Pan Am office at Fiumicino Airport in Rome, Italy. Thirty-two people are killed and 50 are injured. The terrorist then take seven Italian policemen hostage and hijack an aircraft to Athens, Greece. After killing one of the hostages, they flew to **Kuwait** where they surrendered.

1960-1973 – More than 500 incidents of air piracy have been reported around the globe over the past 70 years, and about two-thirds of them happened from 1960 to 1973.

July 18, 1973 – Afghan Military Coup. The coup forces Afghanistan's King Mohammad Zahir Shah from the throne and brought his cousin Sardar Mohammad Daoud Khan briefly to power. The 40-year reign of King Mohammad Zahir Shah can be describes as a nostalgic era of **peace and prosperity** compared to the troubled decades that followed.

The Afghan King had gone to Britain for medical treatment in the summer of 1973 when the events leading to Daoud Khan's coup began unfolding. On July 17, while Zahir Shah and his family were on a reported stopover visit in Italy, army commander Lieutenant General Mohammad Daoud Khan seized control in Kabul. Daoud Khan declared Afghanistan a republic, calling the coup a "national and progressive revolution," and then declared himself President. For millions of Afghans, Daoud Khan's coup marked the end of the last relatively peaceful and prosperous period of their lives. For the remainder of the 20th century, Afghanistan will suffer through **unstable governments**, **bloody coups**, and, after the **Soviet invasion** in late 1979, more than three decades of war.

1973-1977 – Southern Pakistan's Baluchistan region. Balochistan Insurgency. The tribal chiefs fear they will lose their control if the province develops economically. Grievances held by the Baluch stem from their poor economic condition while successive federal governments exploit their resources. Natural gas deposits were found in the Balochistan Sui area in 1953 and are necessary for all of the provinces of Pakistan for both industrial and domestic usage. The Baloch nationalists have had their nomadic lifestyle frustrated since the 1800's when national borders divided what they consider their land between **Iran, Afghanistan, and British India. They now want Soviet help to break free from Pakistan and establish their own country.** The Baluch nationalists also want a lot more money in natural gas royalties.

The insurgency is put down quickly by the **Pakistan Army** with the help of **Huey-Cobra helicopter gunships,** provided by Iran and flown by Iranian pilots.

1973-1997 – Bangladesh. Jumma Insurgency. The tribal insurgency in the remote **Chittagong Hill Tracts** will continue for at least forty more years. In the 1960s thousands of Jumma people were displaced when the Kaptai hydroelectric dam flooded one tenth of the **Chittagong Hill Tracts** and 40 percent of its arable land. Thousands fled to India's eastern states of Arunachal Pradesh, Mizoram, and Tripura.

The Bangladesh government intervenes in 1973 and its military occupation is soon responsible for many human rights abuses, including arbitrary arrests and murders, arson, rape, forced evictions, and the occupation of tribal lands. Hundreds of thousands of Bengali Muslims from the crowded delta region are relocated to the Chittagong Hill Tracts, often, on Jumma-owned land.

September 11, 1973 – Chile. The Chilean coup d'état of 1973. On September 11, the government of **President Salvador Allende** is overthrown by the military in a coup d'état with the support of the CIA. The coup occurs two months after a first attempt failed and a month after the Chamber of Deputies, with an Opposition majority, condemned President Allende's breaches of the Constitution. After the coup firefighters carried the body of Allende out of the bombed presidential palace and the door he came though was sealed, lest it become a shrine to the deposed President.

A military junta took control of the government with a plan to rotate power between the armed forces. The head of the army had other plans and never relinquished control. Instead **General Augusto Pinochet assumed power** and established a military government that ruled until 1990. Many say Pinochet undertook a coup against a rising dictatorship in order to restore democracy and law. General Augusto Pinochet will be arrested in London on October 16, 1998 on an extradition warrant **to bring Pinochet to trial in Spain** for human rights abuses under his dictatorship.

Because of CIA covert intervention in Chile, and the repressive character of General Pinochet's rule, the coup became the most notorious military takeover in the annals of Latin American history. Revelations that **President Richard Nixon had ordered the CIA** to "make the economy scream" in Chile to "prevent Allende from coming to power or to unseat him," prompted a major scandal in the mid-1970s, and a major investigation by the **U.S. Senate**. Henry Kissinger later was said to have told Nixon, We didn't do it, I mean we helped them. –created the conditions as great as possible. nsarchive.org

1973 – Ethiopia. The Oromo Rebellion in Ethiopia will continue through 2010 with no end in sight. The Oromo Liberation Front says it represents the 30 million Oromo people smack in the middle of Ethiopia and they want their own country.

November 26, 1973 – Greek Military Coup. Greek **dictator George Papadopoulos** is toppled by a military coup led by General Demetrios Ioannides and is replaced by General Phaidon Gizikis. "The day after the fall of Papadopoulos government**, calm returns.** The Curfew is lifted throughout Greece. Gizikis chooses a new cabinet."

October 6, 1973 – Israel. On the holiest day in the Jewish calendar, Egypt and Syria begin a coordinated surprise attack against Israeli forces occupying the Syrian Golan Heights and the Egyptian Sinai Peninsula. On the Golan Heights, approximately **180 Israeli tanks** faced an onslaught of **1,400 Syrian tanks.** Along the Suez Canal, **436 Israeli defenders** were attacked by **80,000 Egyptians**. At least **nine Arab states**, including four non-Middle Eastern nations, actively aided the Egyptian-Syrian war effort. **Saudi Arabia** and **Kuwait** committed both soldiers and supplies to the battle. A Saudi brigade of approximately 3,000 troops was dispatched to Syria, where it participated in fighting along the approaches to Damascus. Also, violating Paris's ban on the transfer of French-made weapons, **Libya** sent Mirage fighters to Egypt. **From 1971-1973, President Muammar Qaddafi** gave Cairo more than $1 billion in aid to rearm Egypt and to pay the Soviets for weapons delivered. Other North African countries responded to Arab and Soviet calls to aid the frontline states. **Algeria** sent three aircraft squadrons of fighters and bombers, an armored brigade and 150 tanks.

Approximately 1,000-2,000 **Tunisian soldiers** were positioned in the Nile Delta. **Sudan** stationed 3,500 troops in southern Egypt, and **Morocco** sent three brigades to the front lines, including 2,500 men to Syria. Lebanese radar units were used by Syrian air defense forces. Lebanon also allowed Palestinian terrorists to shell Israeli civilian settlements from Lebanese territory. **Palestinians** fought on the Southern Front with the Egyptians and Kuwaitis.

Jordan's King Hussein finally sent two of his best units, the 40th and 60th Armored Brigades, to Syria, where they took up positions in the south defending the main Amman-Damascus route and attacking Israeli positions along the Kuneitra-Sassa road. Three Jordanian artillery batteries also participated in the assault, carried out by nearly 100 tanks.

Israel was on the defensive for the first two days of fighting while the reserves were mobilized. As they continually repulse the invaders they carry the war deep into Syria and Egypt. The U.S. is working towards an immediate ceasefire while the Soviet Union is resupplying the Arab states by both sea and air. As a result, the United States belatedly begins its own airlift to Israel. Two weeks later, Egypt is saved from a disastrous defeat by the UN Security Council, which had failed to act while the tide was in the Arabs' favor.

On October 22, the Security Council adopted Resolution 338 calling for "all parties to the present fighting to cease all firing and terminate all military activity immediately." The vote came on the day that Israeli forces cut off and isolated the Egyptian Third Army and were in a position to destroy it. Despite the Israel Defense Forces' ultimate success on the battlefield, the war was considered a diplomatic failure. A total of 2,688 soldiers were killed and 7,250 were wounded. Approximately 5,000 Egyptian soldiers and 3,000 Syrian soldiers were killed.

1973 – Rwandan Coup. Juvenal Habyarimana, a **Hutu,** claims the government is ineffective and riddled with favoritism. He stages a coup and will remain President until 1994. After the **Burundi genocide** of 1972, there were many Hutu refugees which created widespread social unrest. President Juvenal Habyarimana installs his own political party into government and Rwanda enjoys relative economic prosperity during the early part of his regime.

October 13, 1973 – Thai Students & Workers Revolt. More than 250,000 people gather in Bangkok to protest against the military government for a more democratic constitution and genuine elections. The movement is led by students and workers which are closely allied with Washington. On October 14, troops open fire on the demonstrators, **killing seventy-five**, and occupy the campus of Thammasat University. King Bhumibol takes a direct role in dealing with the crisis, forcing Prime Minister General Thanom to resign. Then in consultation with student leaders, the King appoints the rector of Thammasat University, Sanya Dharmasakti, as interim Prime Minister, with instructions to draft a new constitution. Prime Minister Sanya **gave full credit to the student movement** for bringing down the military dictatorship. A new military coup will be staged in 1976 and over 5,000 students will go into the jungles of the Thai north and far south to join the still powerful Communist (CPT)-led insurgency. That insurgency was crushed in the 1980s.

January 8, 1973 – Vietnam. The final stage of peace talks begin. They will lead to the signing of a Vietnam cease fire on January 27.

January 15, 1973 – After pressuring South Vietnam to accept the peace deal, Nixon announced the end of offensive operations against North Vietnam. The Paris Peace Accords ending the conflict are signed January 27, 1973, and are followed by the withdrawal of the remaining American troops. The terms of the accords call for a complete ceasefire in South Vietnam, allow North Vietnamese forces to retain the territory they had captured, a complete release of U.S. prisoners of war, and called for both sides to find a political solution to the conflict. As an enticement to Thieu, Nixon offered U.S. airpower to enforce the peace terms.

The war exacted a huge human cost in terms of fatalities, including the 3 to 4 million Vietnamese people from both sides that were killed. There were 1.5 to 2 million Laotian and Cambodians killed. There are **58,260 names on the Vietnam Veterans Memorial Wall.** This number can change every Memorial Day if the Department of Veterans Affairs receives additional information.

January 23, 1973 – Vietnam. President Nixon announces an agreement "to end the war and bring peace with honor in Vietnam and S.E. Asia."

1973

January 27, 1973 – Vietnam. The official end of the Vietnam War. Between January 27, and March 29, 1973, a total of 587 military and civilian prisoners were released by the North Vietnamese, and during that same period, 23,500 U.S. troops were withdrawn from South Vietnam.

March 29, 11973 – Vietnam. Sixty-seven more U.S. P.O.W.'s are freed in **Hanoi.** The same day, the U.S. withdraws its remaining 2,500 troops from South Vietnam. This date also marked the actual end of military involvement in Vietnam.

May 10, 1973 – Vietnam. Due to continued bombing of Laos and Cambodia, the House votes (219-188) for the first time to cut-off Indochina funds.

May 31, 1973 – Vietnam. The Senate takes strong action **prohibiting** the use of any funds appropriated by Congress to be used for combat activities in Laos or Cambodia.

November 7, 1973 – Vietnam. War Powers Act. Congress deals President Nixon a stunning setback when it votes to override his veto of legislation limiting Presidential powers to commit U.S. forces abroad without congressional approval. Congress, with the Vietnam War and the showdown over continued bombing in Cambodia behind it, was anxious to reassert its role in the conduct of the country's foreign affairs. A cease-fire agreement is reached in Paris. The last American combat troops leave Vietnam.

1974

The Oldest Boomer is 28 years old.

Cost of the Average House: $38,900	
Median Family Income: $11,100	**Minimum Wage:** $2.00/ hr **Average Hourly Wage:** $4.42
Gallon of Milk: $1.59	**Gallon Gasoline:** 55 cents
New Car: **Alfa Romeo GTV:** $5,750 **BMW 3.0CSL:** $12,250 **Pontiac Trans Am:** $4,708	**Pepsi Cola:** 88 cents/6-12oz cans **Cigarettes:** 50 cents/ pack **Rosen Hotels and Resorts in Orlando, Florida:** $9.99 a night
Unemployment Rate: 5.1%-5.4%-7.2%	**First-class Stamp:** 10 cents

23 cents buying power in 1974 = **$1.00 in 2008.**
In 1974 what cost us 23 cents to purchase now costs us $1.00 in 2008.

Movies: "Chinatown," "The Godfather Part II," "The Conversation," "Blazing Saddles," "Lenny," "The Towering Inferno."

Broadway: "Liza Minnelli," concert. "Lorelei." "Sammy Davis on Broadway," concert. "Over Here!" "Fashion."

TV: "The Rumble in the Jungle," boxing with Muhammad Ali & George Foreman. The Oscar Streaker. Hank Aaron Breaks Ruth's Record. Nixon Waves Farewell as he leaves the White House after resigning. "Good Times," "Happy Days," "Little House on the Prairie." "Kolchak: The Night Stalker," "Chico and the Man," "Land of the Lost," "Movin' On," "Paper Moon," "Rhoda," "The Rockford Files," "Tony Orlando and Dawn," "Valley of the Dinosaurs, Animated," "The Six Million Dollar Man."

Music: "Chinatown," Jerry Goldsmith. The California Jam rock festival with 200,000 fans. Terry Jacks, "Seasons in the Sun." Paul McCartney & Wings, "Band on the Run." Jim Croce, "I'll Have to Say I Love You in a Song." Lulu, "The Man Who Sold the World." Joni Mitchell, "Help Me." Alvin Stardust,

"Jealous Mind." Bachman, Turner Overdrive, "You Ain't Seen Nothin' Yet." Hues Corporation, "Rock The Boat." Lynyrd Skynyrd, "Sweet Home Alabama." Bobby Vinton, "My Melody of Love." Harry Chapin, "Cat's in the Cradle." Steve Miller Band, "The Joker." Eric Clapton, "I Shot the Sheriff." Cat Stevens, "Oh Very Young." David Bowie, "Rebel Rebel." Steely Dan, "Rikki Don't Lose That Number." The Rolling Stones, "Ain't Too Proud to Beg." Elton John, "Don't Let the Sun go Down on Me." George McCrae, "Rock Your Baby." Carly Simon, "Haven't Got Time for the Pain." Olivia Newton-John, "I Honestly Love You." ABBA, "Waterloo" & "Honey, Honey." The Doobie Brothers, "Black Water."

Deaths: Christine Chubbuck, Louise Auchincloss Boyer, Chet Huntley.

President: Richard M. Nixon (R) Quaker; vetoes 43/ 7 overrides
President: Gerald R. Ford (R) Episcopalian; vetoes 66/12

Vice President: Gerald R. Ford (R) Episcopalian
Vice President: Nelson A. Rockefeller (R) Baptist

House: D-242 ; R-192

Senate: 93rd Congress (1973-1975) Majority Party: Democrat (56 seats) Minority Party: Republican (42 seats) Other Parties: 1 Conservative; 1 Independent Total Seats: 100

Federal Debt: $475.06 billion or 32 % of the GDP

Consumer Price Index CPI-U (1982 Base of 100): 49.30

GDP: $1,500.0 billion	**Inflation Rate:** 11.03%
Dow Jones: 873. (January)/ 577.60 (12-06)	**S&P Price Index:** 68.56/-29.72%
Prime Rate: 8.75% (02-25)/ 12.00% (07-05)	**Average Home Mortgage Rate:** 8.41/ 9.98%
1 oz Gold: $159.74	**1oz of Silver:** $4.71

Monthly S.S. benefits paid: maximum $140 - average $88 / month

Federal Debt: $475,059,815,731.55

Federal Deficit: $6.1 billion dollars

Defense Spending: $98.43 billion	**Interest Spending:** $21.45 billion
Health Care Spending: $20.37 billion	**Pensions Spending:** $59.40 billion
Welfare Spending: $20.18 billion	**Education Spending:** $13.47 billion
Transportation Spending: $9.17 billion	**Misc. Other Spending:** $14.15 billion
Protection Spending: $2.50 billion	**Total Government Spending:** $269.36 billion

% of GDP that goes towards just the interest payment: 1.49%

$1.00 = 1.840 Yuan, China NPC. The Rate is pegged to 15 currencies that are undisclosed and change daily.

$1.00 = 291.53 Yen, Japan	**$1.00 =** 67.50/ 67.75 Iranian Rial
U.S. Population: 213,898,000	**World Population:** 4,014,598,416
U.S. Birth Rate: 3,159,958	**U.S. Abortions:** 763,476—898,600
U.S. Homicide Rate: 10.1/ 100,000 population	**U.S. Violent Crime:** 461.1/ 100,000 population

Annual Average Domestic Crude Oil Prices:
$9.35 / barrel, $40.67 (2007 adjusted)

Oil:

January 29, 1974 – Kuwait announces a 60 percent government participation in the **BP-Gulf** concession and **Qatar** follows on February 20. In 1973 Qatar took a 25% stake in the onshore concessions of QPC and the offshore concessions of Shell Company-Qatar. Early in 1974, the year of Qatar General Petroleum Corporation's formation, the state increased its share in both companies to 60%. In 1976 it will take it all.

1974

March 18, 1974 – All Arab oil ministers except Libya, announce the end of the embargo against the **United States**.

1971-1974 – Oil price increases. In the years after 1971, OPEC was slow to readjust prices to reflect the depreciation that took place after the **U.S. stopped pegging the dollar to gold** under the Bretton Woods Accord. From 1947-1967 the price of oil in U.S. dollars rose by less than two percent per year. Oil prices are now extremely unstable. OPEC has not been able to update prices quickly enough to keep pace with market conditions and oil revenue lags behind for several years. The **substantial price increases** of 1973-1974 bring their income to a more accurate market level in terms of other commodities such as gold. The ability to control crude oil prices has passed from the United States to OPEC.

1974 – Oil Prices. The quadrupling of oil prices that result from the Arab oil embargo sends inflation soaring, throwing the U.S. and much of the West into a gas-line-laden recession. Huge Detroit gas guzzlers are no longer in demand and President Nixon enacts a national **55 mph nationwide speed limit** to reduce oil consumption.

March 18, 1974 – The Arab oil embargo ends.

1974 – The Hughes Glomar Explorer, built for the CIA, lifts a Soviet submarine K–129 from an 11,000 ft depth.

    In 1997, the ship was taken to Cascade General for modifications that converted her to a dynamically-positioned deep sea drilling ship, capable of drilling in waters of 7,500 feet and, with some modification, up to 11,500 feet, which is 2,000 feet deeper than any other existing rig. The conversion cost over $180 million and was completed during the first quarter of 1998.

May 18, 1974 – Nigeria announces a 55 percent government participation in all concessions.

November 1974 – Industrialized nations create the **International Energy Agency**, a Paris-based intergovernmental organization established under the umbrella of the

Organization for Economic Co-operation and Development in the wake of the oil crisis. The IEA is initially **dedicated to responding to physical disruptions in the supply of oil,** as well as serving as an information source on statistics about the international oil market and other energy sectors.

In 2009 the IEA acts as a policy advisor to its **28 member countries**, but also works with many countries outside of its membership, especially China, India and Russia. The Agency's mandate has broadened to focus on the "3Es" of sound energy policy: energy security, economic development, and environmental protection. The latter has focused on mitigating climate change. The IEA has a broad role in promoting alternate energy sources, including renewable energy, rational energy policies, and multinational energy technology co-operation. IEA member countries are required to maintain total oil stock levels equivalent to at least 90 days of the previous year's net imports. At the end of June 2007, IEA member countries held a combined stockpile of almost 4.1 billion barrels of oil.

1974 – Energy Reorganization Act. In response to changing needs in the mid 1970's, the **Atomic Energy Commission** is abolished and the Energy Reorganization Act of **1974 creates two new agencies**: the **Nuclear Regulatory Commission** to regulate the nuclear power industry and the **Energy Research and Development Administration** to manage the nuclear weapon, naval reactor, and energy development programs. The Department of Energy Organization Act combines the federal government's agencies and programs into a single agency. **The Department of Energy**, activated on October 1, 1977, assumed the responsibilities of the Federal Energy Administration, the Energy Research and Development Administration, the Federal Power Commission, and parts and programs of several other agencies.

1974 – OPEC now has the pricing power so Western companies start to hunt for oil outside the Middle East. Soon more oil is being produced from the **North Sea** than from many OPEC countries.

1974 – Vietnam Oil in excess of 1 billion barrels is discovered in Vietnam's Bach Ho field. Over fifty years of oil exploration preceded this discovery. Vietnam has 600 million barrels of proven oil reserves, according to data in 2005 from *Oil and Gas Journal,* but that total is likely to increase as exploration continues. President Johnson was financed by big oil and raised troop strength in Vietnam from 15,000 to over 550,000.

Major News:

February 1974 – Patty Hearst Kidnapping. Patricia Hearst, the granddaughter of publishing magnate **William Randolph Hearst**, is a college student in **Berkeley, California** when she is kidnapped by a neo-revolutionary group calling themselves the **Symbionese Liberation Army** (SLA). Hearst will later testify that she is kept in a closet for two months and brainwashed while the SLA tries to obtain its ransom demands. The Hearst family agreed to the initial demands, which included the distribution of **millions of dollars worth of food**, but negotiations reached a stalemate. Soon after the ransom demands were halted the security camera of the Sunset District branch of Hibernia Bank in San Francisco shows Patricia Hearst holding an assault rifle as members of the Symbionese Liberation Army carry out a midday robbery. She is said to have taken the name "Tania" and the SLA claims she has joined the revolution. Hearst is now on the FBI's Ten Most Wanted List.

When the SLA trades gunfire with the Los Angeles police in May 1974, six of the radicals die when a teargas grenade set the house on fire. Patty Hearst escapes with **Bill and Emily Harris.** Hearst is on the lam for about a year until she is arrested in 1975 and convicted of bank robbery. She is sentenced to seven years in prison. In 1979 her sentence is commuted by President Jimmy Carter.

March 1, 1974 – The **Watergate grand jury** indicts seven Nixon officials and aides for a variety of crimes committed as a part of the Watergate conspiracy, including perjury and conspiring to pay "hush money" to the convicted Watergate burglars. The indicted White House officials are former top Nixon aides **John Ehrlichman, H. R. Haldeman,** and **Charles Colson**; former assistant attorney general **Robert Mardian**; and Haldeman's former assistant **Gordon Strachan**. The former Nixon campaign officials are former campaign chairman **John Mitchell** and former campaign lawyer **Kenneth Parkinson**. The charges against Colson will be dropped after he pleads guilty to obstruction of justice in the Ellsberg case. **President Richard Nixon** is named by the Grand Jury as an unindicted co-conspirator.

April 30, 1974 – The White House releases more than **1,200 pages of edited transcripts** of the **Nixon tapes** to the House Judiciary Committee, but the committee insists that the tapes themselves must be turned over.

May 15, 1974 – Ma'alot massacre. Around 100 pupils between 14 and 16 years old were asleep in the school when the **Palestinian terrorists** stormed it early this morning. **The Israeli government** agreed to release 26 political prisoners but the Palestinians broke off talks when they failed to receive a codeword from their terrorist group in Damascus. As Israeli troops raided the school to free the **children,** the teenagers were reportedly attacked with hand grenades by the Palestinians. Seventy children were injured; eighteen children and the three Palestinians were killed.

June 3, 1974 – Charles W. Colson pleads guilty to the charges concerning Daniel Ellsberg. Colson claims he was following instructions from President Nixon.

July 13, 1974 – Watergate. The Senate Select Committee, under the chairmanship of **Senator Sam J. Ervin**, has been conducting an intensive investigation of the Watergate affair and they release their final **2,217 page** report in three volumes. The investigation and hearings took 18-months and were described as the most intensive congressional inquiry into alleged White House corruption in U.S. history. The Senate Committee held 52 days of televised public sessions, at which testimony was taken from 62 witnesses. More than 1,000 people were interviewed. The printed record of the Committee's hearings and exhibits covered nearly 6,000 pages in 18 volumes, with further volumes of previously undisclosed evidence and of executive sessions with witnesses.

When the committee's unanimous report is released it describes Watergate as one of America's most tragic breaches of public trust, followed by corruption, fraud and abuse of official power. The Senate Select Committee made some 35 specific recommendations calling for major reforms designed to prevent any recurrence of such a national scandal as Watergate.

July 24, 1974 – The Supreme Court rules unanimously that President Nixon must turn over the **tape recordings** of **64 White House conversations**, rejecting the President's claims of executive privilege.

1974

July 27, 1974 – The Judiciary Committee approved **Article I** of an impeachment resolution. The vote was 27 to 11. This is the first of three articles of impeachment, charging obstruction of justice.

July 29, 1974 – The Judiciary Committee approved **Article II** by a vote of 28 to 10. The charge was systematic abuse of power and violations of citizens' constitutional rights. The 1969-1971 wiretapping program is included.

August 8, 1974 – Richard M. Nixon addresses the nation and resigns.

August 9, 1974 – *The Washington Post* reports: **Richard Milhous Nixon announced last night that he will resign** as the 37th President of the United States at noon today. **Vice President Gerald R. Ford** of Michigan will take the oath as the new President at noon to complete the remaining 2 1/2 years of Mr. Nixon's term.

After two years of bitter public debate over the Watergate scandals, President Nixon bowed to pressures from the public and leaders of his party to become the **first President in American history to resign.**

"By taking this action," he said in a subdued yet dramatic television address from the Oval Office, "I hope that I will have hastened the start of the process of healing which is so desperately needed in America."

Vice President Ford, who spoke a short time later in front of his Alexandria home, announced that Secretary of State Henry A. Kissinger will remain in his Cabinet. Ford praised Mr. Nixon's sacrifice for the country and called it "one of the saddest incidents that I've every witnessed."

Mr. Nixon said he decided he must resign when he concluded that he no longer had "a strong enough political base in the Congress" to make it possible for him to complete his term of office.

August 19, 1974 – The House vote on the impeachment of President Richard M. Nixon was set for this date.

September 8, 1974 – President Gerald Ford pardons former President Richard Nixon of all charges related to the Watergate case.

Richard Nixon receives a highly controversial pardon from President Gerald Ford. Some charge that the pardon is part of an agreement reached with Ford when Nixon left office; others, including the *New York Times*, simply called the move unwise and unjust. Ford, who announced the pardon on live television on September 8, 1974, called the Nixon family's situation "an American tragedy in which we all have played a part." He added: "It could go on and on and on, or someone must write the end to it. I have concluded that only I can do that, and if I can, I must." Ford, however, may have also written his own end, politically speaking. Many believe the Nixon pardon was the reason he lost the 1976 election to **Georgia Governor Jimmy Carter.**

Civil Rights Movement:

1974 – South Carolina. Under pressure from the federal courts, the S.C. General Assembly rewrites election laws to end the at-large election of legislators from counties and create single member districts. This enables an additional ten African-Americans to be elected to the South Carolina House.

1974 – Southwest Voter Registration Education Project. The first major Latino voter registration organization begins and will register more than two million Latino voters in the first 20 years.

June 21, 1974 – U.S. District Judge W. Arthur Garrity initiates a busing program, involving several thousand students, designed to **desegregate** the public schools of Boston, Massachusetts. Judge Garrity orders busing of African American students to predominantly white schools in order to achieve racial integration of public schools. Most schools integrated quietly. In South Boston, however, protestors stoned buses, shouted racial epithets, and hurled eggs and rotten tomatoes.

July 1, 1974 – The largest single gift to date from a black organization is the $132,000 given by Links, Inc., to the United Negro College Fund.

1974 – African-American voter registration nearly equals that of whites and will remain within a few percentage points of the white figures.

1974

November 5, 1974 – George Brown and Mervyn Dymally are elected Lieutenant Governors of Colorado and California respectively. They are the first African Americans to hold these posts in the 20th century.

Women's Movement:

1974 – The Equal Credit Opportunity Act prohibits discrimination in consumer credit practices on the basis of sex, race, marital status, religion, national origin, age, or receipt of public assistance.

1974 – In Corning Glass Works vs. Brennan, the U.S. Supreme Court rules that employers cannot justify **paying women lower wages** because that is what they traditionally received under the "going market rate." A wage differential occurring "simply because men would not work at the low rates paid women" is unacceptable**.**

1974 – First Lady Betty Ford moves to the front of the feminist movement as she talks candidly about her pro-choice views and feminist stances. A moderate Republican, Mrs. Ford actively lobbies state legislatures to ratify the ERA, earning the ire of conservative who dub her "No Lady." She called the Supreme Court decision in **Roe vs. Wade "a great, great decision."**

1974 – Mexican-American Women's National Association is formed as a Latina feminist organization.

1974 – Over a thousand colleges are now offering **women's studies courses**, with eighty having full programs, and 230 women's centers on college campuses provide support services for female students.

1974 – Helen Thomas, after covering Washington for thirty years, is finally named White House reporter.

1974 – Elaine Noble becomes the first openly homosexual candidate elected to a state legislature. She is elected in Massachusetts.

1974 – **The Coalition of Labor Union Women,** a nonprofit, nonpartisan organization of trade union women affiliated with the AFL-CIO, is founded.

1974 – **MANA, the Mexican-American Women's National Association** is created.

Popular Culture:

1974 – **The U.S. government supports birth control clinics.** Just 15 years after President Eisenhower declared that birth control is not the government's business; **the government supports birth control clinics** in 2,379 of the nation's 3,099 counties. Of all the methods dispensed, the Pill is most popular.

1974 – **You can only buy gasoline** on either an **"odd" day** or an **"even" day** under a rationing system based on auto license plate numbers.

1974 – **The board-game "Dungeons & Dragons,"** is created by Gary Gygax and Dave Arnesen. It introduces multi-player role play and as of 2006, Dungeons & Dragons remains the **best-known and best-selling role-playing game,** with an estimated 20 million people having played. It has earned more than $1 billion in book and equipment sales. Dungeons & Dragons is also known for other D&D-branded products, references in popular culture and some of the controversies that have surrounded it, particularly a moral panic in the 1980s linking it to **Satanism and suicide.**

1974 – **Drug Abuse Treatment and Control Amendments** extends the 1972 act which established federally funded programs for prevention and treatment.

1974 – **Hustler Strip Clubs.** In an effort to promote a chain of strip clubs, **Larry Flynt** starts the *Hustler Club Newsletter* as an inexpensive way to promote the club's various dancers. Its popularity grew, and in 1974 he published the first issue of the magazine, *Hustler.* Flynt's sleazy publication set many new lows in the field of porn.

1974 – **CB radio** is a nationwide craze in the U.S. when it permits people a short-distance radio band for personal communication. Following the 1973 oil crisis, the

1974

U.S. government imposes a nationwide **55 mph speed limit,** and fuel shortages and rationing are widespread. CB radio is often used to locate service stations with a supply of gasoline, to notify other drivers of speed traps, and to organize blockades and convoys in a 1974 strike protesting the new speed limit and other trucking regulations.

1974 – **Intelligence Officer 2nd Lt. Hiroo Onada** emerged from the jungle of Lubang Island, Philippines, with his .25 caliber rifle, 500 rounds of ammunition and several hand grenades. He surrendered 29 years after Japan's formal surrender, and 15 years after being declared legally dead in Japan. He did not know WWII was over.

1974 – **Philippe Petit**, a French high wire artist, captures the world's attention when he successfully walks across a high wire **between New York's Twin Towers.**

1974 – **"Two all-beef patties,** special sauce, lettuce, cheese, pickles, onions, on a sesame-seed bun." McDonald's.

1974 – **Miller Lite beer,** "Tastes great, less filling." McCann-Erickson.

Business / Technology:

1974 – **India tests its first nuclear bomb**, developed from a supposedly peaceful nuclear power program.

1974 – **Atari.** The $439 Altair kit inspires many computer hobbyists.

1974 – **Aspartame** is the subject of public controversy regarding its safety. Some studies recommend further investigation into any possible connection between aspartame and diseases such as brain tumors, brain lesions, and lymphoma. These studies, combined with allegations of conflicts of interest in the approval process are refuted by an official U.S. governmental inquiry, but remain the focus of vocal activism and conspiracy theories.

    Although the FDA refused to license aspartame for eight years, Aspartame has been found to be safe for human consumption by more than ninety countries worldwide. In 1999 Jon Henkel reported that the U.S. Food and Drug Administration scientists believe that the safety of aspartame is "clear cut" and "one of the most thoroughly tested and studied food additives the agency has ever approved." As of 2008, however, concerns still exist among some scientists over aspartame's role in certain mental disorders, compromised learning, and emotional functioning, although other scientists are not concerned. **By 2009 Aspartame** is present in over 5,000 food items. Reactions among large-scale consumers of aspartame in, for instance, diet soda, can mimic conditions such as **multiple sclerosis, depression, diabetes, lymphoma, arthritis, Alzheimer's disease, panic attacks, epilepsy/seizures, Parkinson's disease and hypothyroidism.** The phrase **"Aspartame Disease"** is now known to cover a range of many pathological conditions that mimic more serious diseases and two-thirds of all patients improve after Aspartame is removed from their diet. **"Sweetpoison,"** by Dr. Janet Starr Hull, is a book exposing aspartame dangers.

1974 – Bar Codes. Universal Product Code (UPC). For the first time UPC's are scanned at a retail checkout. The first item is a 10-pack of Wrigley's Juicy Fruit chewing gum.

1974 – Rosen Hotels and Resorts. A more simple way of doing business. **Ethics, Trust, and a moral compass in 1974.** When Harris Rosen purchases his first hotel, the Quality Inn on International Drive in Orlando, the oil embargo is at its height and the tourism industry is struggling. To book business for the hotel on which he'd spent his entire $20,000 life savings, Rosen had to hitchhike to the Northeast to meet with tour bus operators. Once there, he met prospective clients in bars and pubs often negotiating contracts on cocktail napkins. "I would ask 'What rate do they want to stay with us?' and they would say 9 dollars, or 8 or 7; I would write that rate down and the name of the company on a cocktail napkin, sign my name, and that was the contract. **We shook hands and that was it,"** recalled Rosen. Often, his new clients felt so sorry for him, having no money and no transportation, they would drive him to their competitors for his next appointment. After seeing much of New England, securing new contracts all along the way, Rosen returned home thrilled and excited to have completed his mission with enough business to sustain the hotel for the first year.

1974

Finance:

January 21, 1974 – All operations of the **United States Customs Service** in New York City are located in the World Trade Center.

March 1, 1974 – The Bureau of Government Financial Operations is created.

1974 – Oil Prices. OPEC. In 1972 the price of crude oil was about **$3.00 per barrel** and by the end of 1974 the price of oil had quadrupled to over $12.00 per barrel. **While Arab nations curtailed oil production** by 5 million barrels per day, 1 million barrels per day was made up by increased production in other countries. The net loss of 4 million barrels of oil per day extended through March of 1974 and represented 7 percent of the free world production.

1974 – President Nixon announces a fiscal budget of 304,400,000,000 dollars.

1974 – The United States is in the midst of a **bear market** when **OPEC** institutes an oil embargo. Over the next nine months the Standard & Poor's 500 dropped a further 40 percent.

December 6, 1974 – The DOW closes at a **12-year low** of 577.60, ending the worst bear market since the 1930's.

July 12, 1974 – The Congressional Budget and Impoundment Control Act is enacted. Congress is not required to vote on a Presidential proposal and has ignored most Presidential requests. In response, some have called for a line item veto to strengthen the President's rescission power and force Congress to vote on the disputed funds. The Act is passed in response to Congressional feelings that President Nixon is abusing his ability to impound the funding of programs he opposed. This effectively removed the historical Presidential power of impoundment.

September 23, 1974 – An inspection is completed verifying the **gold** holdings at the **Fort Knox Bullion Depository.** The inspection by Members of Congress on September 23, 1974, of U.S. gold stocks stored at the Fort Knox (Kentucky) Bullion

Depository marks a unique departure from the long standing and rigidly enforced policy of absolutely no visitors, Mrs. Mary Brooks, Director of the Mint, announced today.

The Fort Knox inspection visit of several congressmen and news people on September 23 is still the source of more questions than answers. It is the first time any average citizen had been allowed inside the Fort Knox bullion depository in memory. However, no experts on gold were allowed, no assays were run, and some of the witnesses complained that they were only allowed to look at the gold through small peepholes, and a few added that the color of the gold seemed to be wrong.

2009 – Fort Knox Gold. "It has been several decades since the gold in Fort Knox was independently audited or properly accounted for," said **Ron Paul,** the Texas Congressman and former Republican presidential candidate, in an e-mail interview with *The Times.* "The American people deserve to know the truth." Ron Paul has so far attracted 21 co-sponsors for a Bill to conduct an independent audit of the Federal Reserve System, including its claims to Fort Knox gold, but an organization named the Gold Anti-Trust Action Committee (GATA) is taking a different approach. It has hired the Virginia law firm William J.Olson, PC, to test President Obama's promise to bring "an unprecedented level of openness" to the Government and next month it will file several Freedom of Information requests for a full disclosure of U.S. gold ownership and trading activities.

If there is still gold in Fort Knox there should be no problem with taking a look. And if the gold has been stolen by one of our fearless leaders . . .

December 31, 1974 – The limitation on **gold ownership** in the U.S. is repealed after **President Gerald Ford** signs a bill legalizing private ownership of gold coins, bars and certificates by an act of Congress which went into effect December 31. Gold will jump to $850 an ounce by 1981. Much of the Fort Knox gold was sold for $35 an ounce just before Nixon closed the gold window.

1974 – A New York periodical publishes an article claiming that the **Rockefeller family** is manipulating the **Federal Reserve** for the purpose of selling off **Fort Knox gold** at bargain basement prices to anonymous European speculators. Three days after the publication of this story, its anonymous source, long time secretary to Nelson Rockefeller, **Louise Auchincloss Boyer, mysteriously fell to her death** from the window of her ten storey apartment in New York.

Economists continually try and sell the public the idea that recessions or depressions are a natural part of what they call the "business cycle". This is simply not the case. Recessions and depressions only occur because the **Central Bankers manipulate** the money supply, to ensure more and more is in their hands and less and less is in the hands of the people.

1974 – **Even President Nixon** (1969 to 1974, when he resigned in disgrace) only had one year when he raised the debt more than 6%, 1971. His average was 5% for the six years he was in office and President Nixon faced an opposition Congress controlled by Democrats during his time in office.

Books:

1974 – **"Carrie"** is the first of **Stephen King**'s blockbuster gothic novels.

1974 – Robert Pasig's oddly titled novel, **"Zen and the Art of Motorcycle Maintenance."**

1974 – **"**My Life as a Man." **Philip Roth**.

TV:

1974 – **The Senate Select Committee**, under the chairmanship of **Senator Sam J. Ervin** holds 52 days of televised public sessions, at which testimony is taken from 62 witnesses. Over 1,000 people are interviewed.

1974 – **President Nixon** resigns as 110 million viewers watch on TV.

1974 – **One hundred Los Angeles police officers** mount an assault on a home at 1466 54th Street, a place determined to be an **SLA hideout.** The event is broadcast live.

Police ordered the home's occupants to "Come on out. Hands up." Gunfire answered and the heavily armed SLA members succeeded in pinning down the police for a time. After tear gas grenades are used a fire started inside the house and quickly burned out of control. In the end, six SLA members died in the assault. **Patty Hearst escaped** with John and Emily Harris.

Sports:

October 30, 1974 – The Rumble in the Jungle. Muhammad Ali defeats George Foreman in Kinshasa, Zaire to regain the world heavyweight championship. In one of the biggest upsets in boxing history, Ali regained his title on October 30, by defeating champion George Foreman in their bout in Kinshasa, Zaire. Hyped as **"The Rumble in the Jungle,"** the fight was promoted by Don King.

Almost no one, not even Ali's long-time supporter Howard Cosell, gave the former champion a chance of winning. Ali's tactic of leaning on the ropes, covering up, and absorbing ineffective body shots was later termed **"The Rope-A-Dope."**

By the end of the seventh round, Foreman was exhausted. In the eighth round, Ali dropped Foreman with a combination at center ring and Foreman failed to make the count. Against the odds, Ali had regained the title. Many years later, Foreman would become champ again at age 45. Muhammad Ali (Foreman's best friend at the time) did not attend the title bout. When asked why, he said "I would deviate attention from George. It was his moment, not mine."

April 8, 1974 – Hank Aaron of the Atlanta Braves hits his 715th career home run to break Babe Ruth's record. At 9:07 p.m., in front of 53,775 and a national television audience, in his second at-bat but on his first swing of the evening, Aaron shatters the record that had stood for 39 years.

Music:

February 12, 1974 – New York's legendary rock club, **The Bottom Line** opens in Greenwich Village.

1974 – Punk rock music emerges in Britain, with themes of nihilism, anarchy. Patti Smith releases her debut recording, which many consider to be the first punk rock single, **"Hey Joe."**

1974

April 25, 1974 – Pam Morrison, Jim Morrison's widow, is found dead in her Hollywood, California apartment from an apparent heroin overdose.

March 12, 1974 – John Lennon is involved in an altercation with a photographer outside the **Troubadour club** in Los Angeles, California. Lennon and friend Harry Nilsson had been heckling comedian Tommy Smothers and were forced to leave.

1974 – Dino Martin, singer and son of Dean Martin, is **arrested on suspicion** of possession and sale of two machine guns.

1974 – New Bands. Cheap Trick, Japan, The Nits, The Ramones, Talking Heads, The Stranglers and Van Halen. "Angel and the Snake," changed the name in 1975 to Blondie.

Natural Disasters:

April 3-4, 1974 – Super Tornado Outbreak. A series of 148 twisters within 16 hours comprised the deadly "Super Tornado Outbreak" that struck 13 states in the East, South, and Midwest. Before it was over, 330 died and 5,484 were injured in a path of damage extending more than 2,500 miles.

April 26, 1974 – A Landslide strikes Huancavelica Province, Peru, killing close to 300 people.

September14-19, 1974 – Honduras. "Fifi" strikes the northern part of the country leaving 8,000 dead and 100,000 homeless.

December 25, 1974 – Darwin, Australia. A cyclone almost destroys the entire city. Fifty people are reported dead.

1974 – Bangladesh famine. Possibly over a million people die in the **Bangladesh famine of July 1974- January 1975.** The causes are generally thought to be a combination of natural disasters including cyclones, droughts and floods in the early 1970's, combined with various local and internationally influenced socio-political factors which followed the **Bangladesh Liberation War** in 1971. The official records claim 26,000 people were killed, however, various sources claim about 1,000,000 people died as a result. When we say "people" we are referring to mothers and daughters, fathers and sons, babies and the elderly. They all had things to do, places to go and people to see. Most of these people just wanted to live out their lives with their families in peace.

1974-2003 – Floods and droughts show the fastest rate of increase relative to geological disasters and windstorms. The number of reported natural disasters has increased steadily, from almost 100 in 1974 to a little more than 400 in 2003.

Man vs. Man / Wars:

Assassinated – Germany. Gunter von Drenkmann, Berlin Chief Justice. Drenkmann is shot at his home when he opens the back door for a delivery man and several other people jump from the bushes and overpower him. He was shot three times and died in the hospital a short while later.

October, 2, Stuttgart. Andreas Baader, Ulrike Meinhof, Gudrun Ensslin, Jan-Carl Raspe, and Holger Meins, are indicted for dozens of crimes, including murder. Baader is transferred to join Ensslin in Stammheim prison. Meinhof is still on trial in Berlin. Holger Meins is too weak to be moved due to his hunger strike and stays in his Wittlich jail cell. All of the prisoners continue their hunger strikes and prison officials strap Ensslin and Meins to tables, open their mouths with pry-bars, and force feeding tubes down their throats. **November 10, Berlin.** Holger Meins now weighs less than 100 pounds and lays dying in his Wittlich cell. When Holger Meins dies at 5:00pm demonstrations take place in Frankfurt, Cologne, Hamburg, Berlin, and Stuttgart. Many people consider Meins' death to be murder by the government and side with the terrorists while there are those that still want the terrorists stopped by any means necessary.

1974 – A Korean resident of Japan visiting Seoul kills **Park Chung Hee** 's wife in another unsuccessful presidential assassination attempt.

1974

February 22, 1974 – Sam Byck, an unemployed former tire salesman, boards a plane at BWI Airport in Maryland, armed with a handgun. He intends to hijack the plane and to crash it into the White House in hopes of killing President Richard Nixon. Byck shot the pilot, copilot and then ordered a passenger to fly the plane. The plane stayed on the ground and police stormed it and fired four shots through the thick window of the aircraft door wounding Byck. Sam Byck committed suicide before police could gain entry.

April 11, 1974 – The Kiryat Shmona Massacre. Three members of the **Popular Front for the Liberation of Palestine,** General Command, cross the Israeli border from Lebanon. They enter an apartment building in the town of Kiryat Shmona and murder all eighteen residents there, including nine children.

September 8, 1974 – Athens, Greece. TWA Flight 841 crashes when a bomb explodes in the cargo hold. All 88 passengers are killed. The **Palestinian group** more commonly known as the **Abu Nidal Organization** may have been responsible.

November 23, 1974 – A British aircraft is hijacked at Dubai, UAE, by **Palestinian Rejectionist Front terrorists.** The aircraft is flown to Tunisia where a German passenger is killed.

December 14, 1974 – Robin Harrison charters a plane by phone. On arrival at the airport office in Tampa, he points gun at the pilot of a Piper Seneca and demands a flight to Cuba.

1974 – Cyprus. The Turkish invasion of Cyprus, launched on July 20, is a Turkish military operation in response to a Greek military coup in Cyprus staged by the Cypriot National Guard led by Nikos Sampson. Sampson deposed the Cypriot **President and Archbishop Makarios III,** with the intention of annexing the island to Greece. The Turkish invasion takes place in two stages and ends in August 1974, when Turkish troops occupy over a third of the island's territory. They establish the de facto Turkish Republic of Northern Cyprus that only Turkey recognizes even though both the United States and NATO supported the idea of a Turkish military intervention. During the military operation 4,500-6,000 Greeks are killed and 2,000 to 3,000 people are missing and presumed dead.

1974 – Ethiopian Civil War. In early 1974, Ethiopia enters a period of profound political, economic, and social change, frequently accompanied by violence. The government has failed to bring about significant economic and political reforms over the previous fourteen years and is seen as corrupt. There is also a famine that affects many provinces.

The **Eritrean rebellion** is a dispute over government policy toward Eritrea between the **Eritrean Liberation Front** and the **Eritrean People's Liberation Front.** The government decides on a military solution and within a year there will be over 10,000 members of the EPLF in the field. More than 250,000 people will die in the 31-year-long war, aggravated by drought and famine.

1962-1974 – Guinea-Bissau. War of Independence. Guinea-Bissau, a Portuguese colony, began an armed rebellion beginning in 1956. Independence was unilaterally declared on September 24, 1973, and recognition became universal following the 1974 socialist-inspired military coup in Portugal when Portuguese armed forces, frustrated and tired of fighting colonial wars, staged a coup d'état and deposed Prime Minister Marcelo Caetano.

January 1974 – Northern Ireland. The Troubles. Brian Faulkner was narrowly deposed as Unionist Party leader by his own party and replaced by Harry West. A UK general election in February 1974 gave the anti-Sunningdale unionists the opportunity to test unionist opinion with the slogan "Dublin is only a Sunningdale away". The result galvanized their opposition: they won 11 of the 12 seats, winning 58% of the vote with most of the rest going to nationalists and pro-Sunningdale unionists.

Not content the twenty thousand members of the Ulster Defense Association and the Protestant workers, who formed the Ulster Workers' Council, organize a general strike. All essential services including water and electricity are cut off. Businesses are closed, the pro-Sunningdale unionists resigned from the power-sharing government and the new regime collapsed.

1974

1974 – Korea. From the mid-1970s to the early 1980s, most **North Korean infiltration** of South Korea is conducted by heavily armed reconnaissance teams. Most of these teams are **intercepted and neutralized** by South Korean security forces.

December 31, 1974 – Madagascar Coup. The Ramanantsoa military regime could not resolve rising economic and ethnic problems, and narrowly survived an attempted coup d'état on December 31. The fact that the coup was led by several côtier officers against a Merina military leader underscored the growing Merina/côtier polarization in the military.

1974-1975 – Mali-Upper Volta War. The Republic of Mali is at war with Upper Volta / Burkina Faso, over a border area. This war occurs right after a devastating drought that lasted from 1968 to 1974. Current opinion is that between 50,000 and 100,000 people died as a result of the drought.

1974 – Paraguay. Genocide. The Ache Indians began the 20th Century with 10,000 people. The population had dropped to 2,000 by 1968 after another series of massacres killed 900 more Ache. The **Paraguayan Roman Catholic Church protested in 1972,** against the massacre of Indians in Paraguay. More protests followed from Paraguayan intellectuals which led to the removal of a few of the government leaders in charge of Ache policy.

In 1973 people realized the Indian situation had not changed when it was made know the **Ache Indians** were still being used as slave labor. Aché tribes are systematically raided with the intention of killing the men, and capturing women and children. The Aché children are then sold openly in the region.

Between 1971 and 1978 at least ten different contact and extraction events of forest-dwelling Northern Aché will take place. Over 130 people will die of respiratory ailments within two years of relocation and 68 members of tribes that flee into the forest will die.

Inhabiting a shrinking pocket of rainforest in Paraguay's Eastern Canindeyu Region, the Ache are one of South America's last hunter-gatherer societies and they are in imminent danger of cultural extinction. There is at least one tribe left in 2008. They are still considered expendable and in the way of "progress".

1975

The Oldest Boomer is 29 years old.

Cost of the Average House: $42,600	
Median Family Income: $11,800 (CPS)	**Minimum Wage:** $2.10/ hr **Average Hourly Wage:** $4.83
Gallon of Milk: $1.59	**Gallon Gasoline:** 57 cents
New Car: **Chevrolet Caprice:** $4,819 **Ford Mustang II:** $4,105 **Triumph TR7:** $5,105 **Corvette Convertible:** $6,810 base Auxiliary Hardtop +$267	**Kellogg's Corn Flakes:** 45 cents/ 12oz **Six Digit electronic calculator that can add, subtract, multiply, and divide:** $13.79 **Large Pizza with Sausage:** $4.00 **Bottle of Beer:** 45 cents
Unemployment Rate: 8.1%-9.0%-8.2%	**First-class Stamp:** 13 cents

25 cents buying power in 1975 = **$1.00 in 2008.**
In 1975 what cost us 25 cents to purchase now costs us $1.00 in 2008.

Movies: "One Flew Over the Cuckoo's Nest," "Jaws," "Nashville," "Dog Day Afternoon," "Barry Lyndon," "Funny Lady."

Broadway: "The Wiz," "Shenandoah," "A Chorus Line," "Rocky Horror Picture Show," "Me & Bessie."

TV: The Fall of Saigon televised LIVE! The Mary Tyler Moore Show, "Chuckles Bites the Dust." "Gunsmoke," the last show. MASH, "The Death of Henry Blake." "The Jeffersons." "Welcome Back, Kotter," with John Travolota as Vinnie Babarino. "Saturday Night Live," "Good Morning America," "Wheel of Fortune," "Barney Miller," "The Blue Knight," "Cher," "Baretta," "John Hagee Ministries," "Starsky & Hutch," "Ryan's Hope," "One Day at a Time," "When Things Were Rotten."

Music: "The Rocky Horror Picture Show," Richard O'Brien. "Jaws," John Williams. "Tommy," Pete Townshend. "Nashville." KC & The Sunshine Band, "That's the Way, I Like It." The Carpenters, "Please Mr. Postman." Bay City Rollers, "Bye Bye Baby, Baby, Goodbye." Mud, "Lonely This Christmas." Styx, "Lady." KISS, "Rock and Roll All Nite." Earth, Wind & Fire, "Sing a Song." Telly Savalas, "If." The Captain & Tennille, "Love Will Keep Us Together." The Sweet, "Fox on the Run." America, "Sister Golden Hair." Barry Manilow, "Could It Be Magic." Frankie Valli, "Our Day Will Come." Linda Ronstadt, "When Will I Be Loved." Joe Cocker, "You Are So Beautiful." Eric Clapton, "Knockin' on Heaven's Door." Manfred Mann's Earth Band, "Spirit in the Night." Bob Dylan, "Tangled Up in Blue." The Outlaws, "There Goes Another Love Song." Gladys Knight and the Pips, "The Way We Were." Queen, "Bohemian Rhapsody." Rod Stewart, "Sailing." Tammy Wynette, "Stand By Your Man." Bee Gees, "Jive Talkin." Freddy Fender, "Before The Next Teardrop Falls." Barry Manilow, "Mandy." Neil Sedaka, "Laughter in the Rain." Alice Cooper, "Department of Youth." Pink Floyd, "Have a Cigar." The Jackson 5, "I Am Love." Lynyrd Skynyrd, "Saturday Night Special." Art Garfunkel, "I Only Have Eyes For You." Olivia Newton-John, "Have You Never Been Mellow." ABBA, "SOS" & "Mamma Mia." Frankie Valli & the Four Seasons, "My Eyes Adored You." LaBelle, "Lady Marmalade." Helen Reddy, "Ain't No Way to Treat a Lady." John Denver, "Thank God I'm a Country Boy." Elton John, "Lucy in the Sky with Diamonds." Linda Ronstadt, "You're No Good." Bruce Springsteen, "Born to Run." C. W. McCall, "Convoy."

Deaths: Moe Howard, Larry Fine, Pete Ham, Kip Siegel.

President: Gerald R. Ford (R) Episcopalian; vetoes 66/ 12 overrides

Vice President: Nelson A. Rockefeller (R) Baptist

House: D-291 ; R-144

Senate: 94th Congress (1975-1977) Majority Party: Democrat (60 seats) Minority Party: Republican (38 seats) Other Parties: 1 Conservative; 1 Independent Total Seats: 100

Federal Debt: $533.19 billion or 33 % of the GDP

Consumer Price Index CPI-U (1982 Base of 100): 53.80

GDP: $1,638.3 billion	**Inflation Rate:** 9.20%
Dow Jones: 877.42 (07-01)/ 580. (January)	**S&P Price Index:** 90.19/31.55%
Prime Rate: 10.25% (01-01)/ 7.00% (06-09)	**Average Home Mortgage Rate:** 8.82/9.43%
1 oz Gold: $161.49	**1oz of Silver:** $4.58

Average Monthly S.S. Benefits Paid: $196 / month.
COLAs were first paid in 1975 as a result of a 1972 law. Prior to this, benefits were increased irregularly by special acts of Congress.

Federal Debt: $533,189,000,000

Federal Deficit: $53.2 billion dollars

Defense Spending: $110.19 billion	**Interest Spending:** $23.25 billion
Health Care Spending: $25.81 billion	**Pensions Spending:** $71.41 billion
Welfare Spending: $32.25 billion	**Education Spending:** $17.06 billion
Transportation Spending: $10.92 billion	**Misc. Other Spending:** $27.79 billion
Protection Spending: $3.03 billion	**Total Government Spending:** $332.33 billion

% of GDP that goes towards just the interest payment: 1.49%

$1.00 = 1.970 Yuan, China NPC	**$1.00 =** 296.79 Yen, Japan

$1.00 = 3.530 Saudi Arabia Riyal. Exchange rates for the Saudi Arabia Riyal are maintained on the basis of existing parity in terms of the **SDR**. **Special Drawing Rights,** SDRs, have the ISO 4217 currency code XDR.

$1.00 = 67.50/ 67.75 Iranian Rial. The Rial's is no longer pegged to the dollar but linked to the **SDR** at an exchange value of Rls82.2425 per SDR.

U.S. Population: 215,981,000	World Population: 4,088,224,047
U.S. Birth Rate: 3,144,198	U.S. Abortions: 854,853—1,034,200
U.S. Homicide Rate: 9.9/ 100,000 population	U.S. Violent Crime: 487.8/ 100,000 population
Annual Average Domestic Crude Oil Prices: $12.21 / barrel, $48.71 (2007 adjusted)	

Oil:

1975 – Ivory Coast. The West African country of Ivory Coast (Côte d'Ivoire) is known more as an oil refining country than an oil producing country. It does not have vast offshore oil fields. Its recoverable oil reserves have been estimated at 100 million barrels. Its oil producing fields are Lion and Panther and the national oil company, **Petroci,** is established in 1975.

April 7-15, 1975 – A preliminary meeting is held in Paris on the world economic crisis between oil-exporting (**Algeria, Saudi Arabia, Iran, Venezuela**), oil-importing (**European countries, U.S., Japan**), and non-oil Third World countries (**India, Brazil, Zaire**). Talks collapse after nations fail to decide whether the agenda should focus on oil/energy issues or have a broader economic scope.

1975 – The Energy Policy and Conservation Act is passed by Congress. The Act hopes to increase oil production by giving price incentives. This act also creates the **Strategic Petroleum Reserve** (SPR), and requires an increase in the fuel efficiency (miles per gallon) of automobiles.

1975 – North Sea Oil. As exploration and investment move further north, it becomes clear that there is a lot more oil out there that has not been discovered. In 1975 a small entrepreneurial American company, Hamilton Brothers working in the Argyle field, brings the first British oil ashore. This is followed very soon by BP in the massive **Forties field** and drilling in the North Sea begins to produce a lot of North Sea Oil.

October 28, 1975 – Venezuela nationalizes the Oil Industry. Venezuela and foreign oil companies agree on nationalization to begin on January 1, 1976.

December 1, 1975 – Kuwait and Gulf and British Petroleum agree on terms of nationalization.

December 9, 1975 – Iraq completes nationalization by taking over the BP, CFP, and Shell shares of the Basrah Petroleum Company.

Major News:

January 1, 1975 – John Ehrlichman is convicted of conspiracy, obstruction of justice, perjury and other charges, along with ex-presidential advisers **John N. Mitchell** and **H. R. Haldeman**. All three men are sentenced to between two and a half and eight years in prison. In 1977, the sentences are commuted to one to four years. Unlike his co-defendants, Ehrlichman voluntarily entered prison before his appeals were exhausted. He was released from the **Federal Correctional Institution,** Safford, after serving a total of 18 months. Having been convicted of a felony, he was disbarred from the practice of law. Haldeman served 18 months. Mitchell served 19 months.

January 29, 1975 – The Weathermen take credit for the **bombing of the United States Department of State Building** saying it was "in response to escalation in Vietnam." Their founding document called for a **"white fighting force"** to be allied with the **"Black Liberation Movement"** and other radical movements to achieve "the destruction of U.S. imperialism and achieve a classless world: world communism." The **Weathermen** had largely disintegrated shortly after the U.S. reached a peace accord in Vietnam in 1973, which saw the general decline of the New Left.

April 21, 1975 – A bitter, tearful President Thieu resigns during a 90 minute rambling TV speech to the people of **South Vietnam**. Thieu reads from the letter sent by Nixon in 1972 pledging "severe retaliatory action" if South Vietnam was threatened. Thieu condemns the Paris Peace Accords, Henry Kissinger and the U.S. "The United States has not respected its promises. It is inhumane. It is untrustworthy. It is irresponsible." He is then ushered into exile in Taiwan, aided by the CIA.

April 23, 1975 – 100,000 NVA soldiers advance on Saigon which is now overflowing with refugees. On this same day, President Ford gives a speech at **Tulane University** stating the conflict in **Vietnam** is "a war that is finished as far as America is concerned."

April 27, 1975 – Saigon is encircled. 30,000 South Vietnamese soldiers are inside the city but are leaderless. The NVA fire rockets into downtown civilian areas as the city erupts into chaos and widespread looting.

April 28, 1975 – 'Neutralist' General Duong Van "Big" Minh becomes the new President of South Vietnam and appeals for a cease-fire. His appeal is ignored.

April 29, 1975 – The NVA shell Tan Son Nhut air base in Saigon, killing two U.S. Marines at the compound gate. Conditions then deteriorate as South Vietnamese civilians loot the air base. **President Ford** now orders Operation Frequent Wind, the **helicopter evacuation of 7,000 Americans and South Vietnamese** from Saigon, which begins with the radio broadcast of the song "White Christmas" as a pre-arraigned code signal.

At Tan Son Nhut, frantic civilians begin swarming the helicopters. The evacuation is then shifted to the walled-in American embassy, which is secured by U.S. Marines in full combat gear. But the scene there also deteriorates, as thousands of civilians attempt to get into the compound.

Three U.S. aircraft carriers stand by off the coast of Vietnam to handle incoming Americans and South Vietnamese refugees. Many South Vietnamese pilots also land on the carriers, flying American-made helicopters which are then pushed overboard to make room for more arrivals. **Filmed footage of the $250,000 choppers being tossed into the sea** becomes an enduring image of the war's end. It is all watched by millions of Americans on TV.

April 30, 1975 – At 8:35 a.m., the last Americans, ten Marines from the embassy, depart Saigon, concluding the United States presence in Vietnam. North Vietnamese troops pour into Saigon and encounter little resistance. By 11 a.m., the red and blue Viet Cong flag flies from the Presidential Palace. President Minh broadcasts a message of unconditional surrender. **The war is over.**

May 12, 1975 – The U.S. merchant ship Mayaguez and its crew of 39 are **seized** by Cambodian forces in the Gulf of Siam. In a rescue operation, U.S. Marines attacked Tang Island, while planes bombed the air base. Cambodia surrendered the ship and crew.

May 16, 1975 – Congress votes $405 million for **South Vietnam refugees** and 140,000 are flown to the U.S.

June 10, 1975 – Illegal CIA operations are described by a panel headed by Vice President **Rockefeller.** The headlines read: **"Huge C.I.A. Operation Reported in U.S. against Antiwar Forces, Other dissidents In Nixon Years."** For over fifteen years, the CIA, with assistance from numerous government agencies, conducted a massive illegal domestic covert operation called **Operation CHAOS.** It was one of the largest and most pervasive domestic surveillance programs in the history of the U.S. The CIA spied on thousands of U.S. citizens throughout the duration of CHAOS and went to great lengths to conceal this operation from the public while every President from **Eisenhower** to **Nixon** exploited CHAOS for his own political ends. Over 300,000 illegal files are said to exist.

June 1975 – A covert CIA mind-control and chemical interrogation research program run by the **Office of Scientific Intelligence** began in the early 1950s, continuing at least through the late 1960s, and it used United States citizens as its test subjects. The project **MK-ULTRA** involved the clandestine use of many types of drugs, as well as other methods, to manipulate individual mental states and to alter brain function. Project MK-ULTRA is first brought to wide public attention in 1975 by the U.S. Congress, through investigations by the **Church Committee,** and by a presidential commission known as the **Rockefeller Commission.** Investigative efforts were hampered by the fact that **CIA Director Richard Helms** ordered all MK-

1975

ULTRA files destroyed in 1973. The Church Committee and Rockefeller Commission investigations relied on the sworn testimony of direct participants and on the relatively small number of documents that survived Helms' destruction order.

July 30, 1975 – Jimmy Hoffa disappears. Jimmy Hoffa reportedly tries to reconcile with mobster associates, possibly **Anthony Provenzano** and **Anthony Giacalone** or **Russell Bufalino,** in his attempts to regain his position as President of the **Teamsters Union.** He is last seen leaving for a meeting at the Red Fox restaurant in Bloomfield Hills, Michigan. His last known contact is a phone call to his wife at 2:15 pm.

Despite the massive manhunt by federal authorities, the fate of Jimmy Hoffa has eluded authorities. According to Ralph Picardo, the convict who fingered the conspirators, Hoffa's body was put in a 55-gallon steel drum and carted away in a Gateway Transportation truck. Picardo said he didn't know where it was taken. He may be **buried at Giants Stadium entombed in concrete at Section 107,** near the end zone.

Civil Rights Movement:

1975 – Senator Strom Thurmond votes for an extension of the Voting Rights Act, his first pro-civil rights vote. After his death it was revealed that Thurmond and a black maid, **Carrie Butler,** had a daughter whom Thurmond never publicly acknowledged.

1975 – Atlanta, Georgia. The Morehouse School of Medicine becomes the only black medical school established in the United States in the 20th Century. The first dean and President of Morehouse School of Medicine is Dr. Louis Sullivan who later becomes the U.S. Surgeon General.

1975 – Wallace D. Muhammad assumes control of the **Nation of Islam** after the death of his father, Elijah Muhammad. He changes the organization's direction and its name to the **World Community of al-Islam.**

1975 – General Daniel "Chappie" James of the Air Force becomes the first African American four star general.

Women's Movement:

1975 – Contraception. The Dalkon Shield, an intrauterine contraceptive device. As many as 200,000 American women testified they were injured by the Dalkon shield and filed claims against the **A.H. Robins Company.** The shield had been sold to an estimated 2.5 million women, from 1970-1974.

Two-hundred and thirty-five thousand women may have suffered injuries, most of which involved life-threatening pelvic infections. Many cases were severe enough to cause hospitalization, permanent infertility, complete hysterectomy, and/or chronic pelvic pain. There were over 200 documented cases of a rare, potentially lethal type of infected miscarriage called spontaneous septic abortion and at least twenty women died of complications associated with the Dalkon Shield.

To stop the number of lawsuits and contain its liability, A. H. Robins will file for Chapter 11 bankruptcy protection in 1985. As debt reorganization and not liquidation, the injured women lost their right to go to court, and a trust fund was set up for compensation. This limited the amount of the company's liability and placed the injured women in line with all of the other creditors. Limiting the liability made the company more attractive to potential buyers and in 1989, Robins was purchased by American Home Products. The company's stock, much of it owned by the Robins family, quadrupled in value.

The few who gave birth to babies with cerebral palsy won $2 million awards, but the majority received only $725 or less.

1975 – Taylor vs. Louisiana makes it illegal to exclude women from juries.

1975 – The U.N. sponsors the First International Conference on Women in Mexico City.

1975 – Women in Vietnam. The military, which prided itself on the records it kept in Vietnam, counting the enemy number of weapons captured, for instance, cannot to this day say with certainty how many women served. The army that sent them never bothered to count them. The estimate most frequently given is that a total of 7,500 served in the military in Vietnam.

1975

1975 – For the first time, federal employees' salaries can be garnished for child support and alimony.

1975 – The National Right to Life organized to stop women from obtaining abortions.

1975 – Phyllis Schlafly organizes her Eagle Forum as an alternative to "women's lib." The forum favors support of **school prayer**, **law and order**, and a **strong national defense.** It opposes busing, federally funded child care, and **abortion.**

1975 – Tish Sommers, chair of **NOW's Older Women Task Force,** coins the phrase **"displaced homemaker."**

1975 – Susan Brownmiller's "Against Our Will" on the ubiquity of rape is published. She later becomes one of *TIME's* "Women of the Year."

1975 – NOW sponsors "Alice Doesn't" Day, and asks women across the country to go on strike for one day.

1975 – Joanne Little, who was **raped by a guard while in jail,** is acquitted of murdering her offender. The case establishes a precedent for killing as self-defense against rape.

1975 – In New York City the first women's bank opens.

1975 – The United States Military opens its military academies to **women.**

1975 – *TIME* magazine declares: "Feminism has transcended the feminist movement. In 1975 the women's drive penetrated every layer of society, matured beyond ideology to a new status of general, and sometimes unconscious, acceptance." The *Time* **Person of the Year award** goes to American Women, celebrating the successes of the feminist movement.

1975 – Elizabeth Ann Seton is canonized, making her the first American-born saint.

Popular Culture:

1968-1975 – Thirty American diplomats and other U.S. Officials in foreign countries were kidnapped.

1975 – Atari releases the home version of **Pong**, one of the earliest arcade video games.

1975 – Venera 9 sends pictures of the surface of **Venus**. Although during this period, **Soviet and U.S. space programs** have limited official interaction, they inherently influence each other. Upon reviewing NASA plans for the Viking mission, scheduled for launch in 1975, Soviet scientists realized that at the present level of funding and the state of the Soviet technology, it would be difficult if not impossible to match the scale and ambition of the U.S. project. Rather then duplicating NASA efforts, the IKI's leadership made a controversial decision to abandon immediate plans for Mars exploration and jump-start a series of missions to Venus, known in the USSR as "Venera."

1975 – Los Angeles. The first computer store sells assembled computers.

1975 – U.S. television networks agree to set a "family hour" free of **sex and violence**.

1975 – Citizens band (CB) radio service is available for public use.

1975 – Social Security. COLAs. Congress changes the law to implement automatic, annual **cost-of-living adjustments** (COLAs). Benefit increases are based on inflation. When prices increase, benefits increase. That helps ensure seniors maintain purchasing power for goods and services.

1975 – The Netherlands licenses the sale of **cannabis** (Marijuana) in coffee shops.

1975 – Pet Rocks. The first Pet Rocks are ordinary gray stones bought at a builder's supply store and marketed as if they were live pets. The fad lasts about six months, ending with the Christmas season in December 1975. During its short run, the Pet Rock made Gary Dahl a multi-millionaire. The pet rock sold for $3.95 and estimates state Dahl sold over 5 million of his pet rocks in a six month period. His production costs were estimated at less than a buck and his profit at $3/ rock. With these totals Dahl earned over 15 million dollars during a six month period in 1975 which would be estimated at $56,000,000 in 2007.

1975 – The National Association of Bilingual Education is founded.

December 8, 1975 – *Newsweek's* December 8 cover story, **"Why Johnny Can't Write,"** heats up the debate about national literacy and the back-to-the-basics movement.

1975 – American Express, **"Do you know me?"** Ogilvy & Mather.

1975 – BMW, **"The ultimate driving machine."** Ammirati & Puris.

1975 – Xerox, "It's a miracle." Needham, Harper & Steers.

1975 – Jell-O, Bill Cosby with kids. Young & Rubicam.

Business / Technology:

January 1975 – The January edition of **Popular Electronics** featured the **Altair 8800** computer kit, based on Intel´s 8080 microprocessor, on its cover. The machine comes with 256 bytes of memory, expandable to 64K, and sells for $297, or $395 with a case.

1975 – Bill Gates and Paul Allen start a company they call **Micro-Soft.**

May 1, 1975 – Wall Street's fixed commissions end.

Finance:

February 3, 1975 – President Ford announces a deficit of fifty-one billion five hundred million dollars.

September 12, 1975 – The Federal Law Enforcement Training Center Facility in Glynco, Georgia, is dedicated.

1975 – Edith Roosevelt, the grand-daughter of President Theodore Roosevelt questions the actions of the government in a March 1975 edition of the *New Hampshire Sunday News*, in which she stated, **"Allegations of missing gold from our Fort Knox vaults** are being widely discussed in European financial circles. But what is puzzling is that the Administration is not hastening to demonstrate conclusively that there is no cause for concern over our gold treasure, if indeed it is in a position to do so." The United States government still did not undertake an audit of the gold in Fort Knox to quell this speculation.

1975 – The U.S. Treasury begins **public sales of gold stocks.**

Books:

1975 – "Ragtime." E. L. Doctorow.

1975 – Judith Rossner. **"Looking for Mr. Goodbar."**

1975 – "Why Survive? Being Old In America." Robert Neil Butler.

1975 – "Rumble Fish." S.E. Hinton.

1975 – "The Choirboys." **Joseph Wambaugh.**

1975 – "The Bankers." Martin Mayer. Describes banking at the cusp of deregulation.

TV:

1975 – HBO's **"Thrilla' In Manila,"** nationwide broadcast by satellite, begins the pay cable boom. **HBO** broadcasts the heavyweight boxing championship match between **Muhammad Ali** and **Joe Frazier** live from the Philippines. The "Thrilla in Manila" marks the first time satellites are used to deliver regularly scheduled programming and link together previously isolated cable systems. HBO's bold move helps create the modern cable business, now the largest single segment of the entertainment industry. In 1999 U.S. consumers will spend close to $40 billion on cable.

1975 – "Another World" is the first American soap opera to begin a one hour format.

1975 – The first black owned television station, WGPR, begins broadcasting in Detroit.

Sports:

1975 – Lee Elder, is the first black player at the **Masters golf tournament.**

1975 – Carlton Fisk's 12th-inning shot in Game 6 of the 1975 World Series. Fisk is best known for "waving fair" his game-winning home run in the 12th inning of Game 6 of the 1975 World Series, one of the greatest moments in **World Series history.**

October 1, 1975 – Muhammad Ali fights Joe Frazier for the third time. The bout is promoted as the **"Thrilla in Manila"** by Don King, who has ascended to prominence following the Ali-Foreman fight. The anticipation is enormous for this final clash between two great heavyweights. Ali believed Frazier was "over the hill" by that point. Ali's frequent insults, slurs and demeaning poems increased the anticipation and excitement for the fight, but also enraged a determined Frazier. Regarding the fight, Ali famously remarked, **"It will be a killa... and a chilla... and a thrilla... when I get the gorilla in Manila."**
 The fight lasted **14 grueling rounds** in temperatures approaching 100 degrees Fahrenheit. Ali won many of the early rounds, but Frazier staged a comeback in the middle rounds, while Ali lay on the ropes. By the late rounds, Ali had reasserted control and the fight is stopped when Frazier is unable to answer the bell for the 15th and final round because his eyes are swollen closed. Frazier's trainer, Eddie Futch, refused to allow Frazier to continue. Ali, in one of the toughest fights of his entire career, was quoted as saying, "It was the closest thing to death that I could feel."

October 12, 1975 – Frank Robinson becomes the first black Major League Baseball manager when he takes over the **Cleveland Indians.**

December 23, 1975 – It was called the Reserve Clause, but it was really indentured servitude. A paragraph in each player's contract allowed a baseball team to keep a player indefinitely until he was sold, traded or released. It was part of baseball's antitrust exemption and allowed the team to renew his contract the following year even if the player refused to sign. The Reserve Clause finally came to an end on December 23.

1975 – Arthur Ashe becomes the first African American to wins the British Men's Singles at **Wimbledon.**

1975 – Japan. Junko Tabei becomes the first woman to reach the summit of **Mt. Everest.**

Music:

January 6, 1975 – Approximately **1,000 Led Zeppelin fans** cause an estimated $30,000 in damage to the lobby of the **Boston Garden.** The fans had been waiting for tickets to go on sale for Led Zeppelin's February 4 concert when they reportedly broke chairs and doors and caused other damage to the building. Boston Mayor Kevin White cancels the upcoming show.

March 2, 1975 – Los Angeles Police make a routine traffic stop that turns out to be **Paul McCartney** and his wife Linda. **Linda McCartney is arrested** for having six to eight ounces of marijuana in her pocketbook.

April 24, 1975 – Pete Ham, founder of the group **Badfinger,** is found hanged in his London garage. His death is ruled a suicide.

Natural Disasters:

February 4, 1975 – Haicheng, China. A powerful 7.0 magnitude quake hits on schedule. Seismologists sent out warnings about this earthquake the day before and ordered evacuations. This was the first successful earthquake prediction in history and the successful prediction saved many lives. In the days leading up to the event cats and other animals were thought to have acted strangely and there are some that claim this aided in the prediction of the earthquake. The validity and accuracy of these reports is questionable as "It was the foreshock sequence that gave Chinese officials the solid prediction." Although over 2,000 people are killed, authorities estimate that over 150,000 fatalities could have occurred without the evacuation.

June 30, 1975 – Norris Junction, Yellowstone National Park, Wyoming. A 6.1 magnitude earthquake, the largest earthquake in Yellowstone Caldera since the 1959 Hebgen Lake event, is absorbed by the Park without damage or harm to people.

August 1975 – China. Super Typhoon Nina contributes to the Banqiao Dam failure. A one-in-two-thousand year flood occurs, and pours more than a year's rainfall into 24 hours. Communications to the dam were largely lost as buildings collapsed under the heavy rain and pulled down power and phone lines. The sluice gates were not able to handle the overflow of water and as the water crested at the Banqiao Dam, the dam itself failed. This led to the failure of 62 more dams downriver.

The runoff of Banqiao Dam was 13,000 cubic meters per second input vs. 78,800 cubic meters per second output, and 701 million tons of water was released in 6 hours, while 1,670 million tons of water was released in 5.5 hours at upriver Shimantan Dam, and 15.738 billion tons of water was released in total. According to the Hydrology Department of Henan Province, approximately 26,000 people died from flooding and another 145,000 died during subsequent epidemics and famine. In addition, about 5,960,000 buildings collapsed, and 11 million residents were affected.

August 1, 1975 – Oroville, California. A magnitude 6.1 earthquake shakes the **Sacramento Valley**. Earthquakes of this magnitude are not unusual in California and occur, on the average, every 3 to 4 years. However, such events are relatively rare in the foothills of the Sierra Nevada, and the Oroville earthquake might have been, triggered by water loads due to Lake Oroville being recently finished and then filled in 1968.

November 29, 1975 – Hawaii. A Tsunami is triggered by sudden, violent ground motion associated with a magnitude 7.2 earthquake on November 29. Waves reach 6 to 14 m above sea level on the southeastern coast of the **Big Island** and generally less than 4 m elsewhere on the island. The tsunami kills two people and causes property damage of about $1.4 million.

December 7, 1975 – Lubmin nuclear power plant. An electrician wanted to show his apprentice how to bridge electrical circuits. As an example he decided to intentionally short-circuit one of the windings of the Unit 1 pumps by developing an arc following the edge of a wiring loom. This started a fire in the main trough and destroyed the current supply and the control lines of 5 main coolant pumps (a single unit has 6 pumps). The fire was brought under control quickly and the pumps were temporarily repaired averting a disaster since emergency procedures were followed immediately. After this near disaster, fire protection was substantially strengthened and separate electrical lines for each pump were introduced.

1975 – Zimbabwe. Marburg haemorrhagic fever is a severe and highly fatal disease caused by a virus from the same family as the one that causes **Ebola** haemorrhagic fever. Viewed under electron microscopy, the viruses show particles shaped like elongated filaments, sometimes coiled into strange shapes that give the Filoviridae family its name. These viruses are among the most virulent pathogens known to infect humans and they kill one out of three. Between 1998-2005 there will be a few outbreaks with over 150 deaths each in **Congo, Angola, and Uganda.**

Man vs. Man / Wars:

Assassinated – President of Bangladesh, Mujibur Rahman. On March 26, 1971 Sheikh Mujibur announced the Declaration of Independence of **East Pakistan** and announced the establishment of the sovereign **People's Republic of Bangladesh**. He was then arrested and held for nine months. During this time he is tried by the military and sentenced to death by Rahimuddin Khan.

Guerrilla war between government forces and Bengali nationalists aided by India turns into an **all out war** between the **Pakistan Army and Bangladesh-India Joint Forces** which leads to the establishment of Bangladesh. **Mujibur Rahman** is set free and assumes the office of provisional President, and later Prime Minister. Mujibur struggled to address the challenges of intense poverty, unemployment, and rampant corruption. He immediately bans other political parties and declares himself President for life. In less than seven months **Mujibur Rahman and his family are assassinated by a group of army officers.**

Assassinated – British Isles, Ross McWhirter co-author of the Guinness Book of Records and far right wing political activist is assassinated by the **Provisional Irish Republican Army.**

Assassinated – President of Chad, François Tombalbaye. As the drought worsens throughout Africa people are forced to "volunteer" in a major effort to increase cotton production. With his support in the south diminished, Tombalbaye lashed out at the army, making arbitrary promotions and demotions. Finally, on April 13, 1975, after some of the country's leading **officers had been arrested** for involvement in an alleged coup, a group of soldiers killed Tombalbaye and installed General Félix Malloum as President.

Assassinated – President of Madagascar, Richard Ratsimandrava is killed just 6 days after taking power in military coup. His assassination begins a civil war.

Assassinated – Saudi Arabia. In 1975, **King Faisal** is assassinated by a nephew, who was executed after an extensive investigation concluded that he acted alone. Faisal was succeeded by his half-brother **Khalid** as King and Prime Minister. Their half-brother Prince Fahd was named Crown Prince and First Deputy Prime Minister. King Khalid empowered Crown Prince Fahd to oversee many aspects of the government's international and domestic affairs as economic development continued rapidly and the kingdom assumed a more influential role in regional politics and international finance.

September 5, 1975 – Lynette "Squeaky" Fromme attempts to assassinate **President Ford.** Fromme went to Sacramento's Capitol Park dressed in a nun-like red robe. She had a Colt.45 automatic pistol loaded with four rounds that she pointed at Ford. Secret Service agents immediately restrained Fromme, and while she was being handcuffed, she managed to say a few sentences to the news cameras, emphasizing that the gun did not "go off."

Fromme told her attorney she targeted Ford because she wanted to get attention for a new trial for Charles Manson. She refused to cooperate with her own defense and after a long trial she was convicted of the attempted assassination of the President and was sentenced to life in prison.

Lynette "Squeaky" Fromme is released from a federal prison in Texas on August 14, 2009. Fromme, 60, had previously completed her sentence for the assassination attempt in July 2008, but was ordered to serve additional time for a 1987 prison escape.

September 22, 1975 – Sara Jane Moore attempts to assassinate **U.S. President Gerald Ford** outside the St. Francis Hotel in San Francisco, just seventeen days after Lynette "Squeaky" Fromme had also tried to kill the President. Moore was about 40 feet away from President Ford when she fired a single shot at him with a .38 caliber revolver. That bullet missed the President because a bystander, Oliver Sipple, grabbed Moore's arm and then pulled her to the ground, using his hand to keep the pistol from firing a second time. Sipple said at the time: "I saw [her gun] pointed out there and I grabbed for it. I lunged and grabbed the woman's arm and the gun went off." The single shot which Moore did fire from her .38 caliber revolver ricocheted off the entrance to the hotel, slightly injuring a bystander.

February 19, 1975 – Representative George Hansen (R-Idaho) **is indicted** for violating campaign spending laws. He pleads guilty.

June 11, 1975 – Representative Wendell Wyatt (R-Oregon) is brought up **on charges of violating campaign spending laws.** Although he was not formally indicted, he pleads guilty.

May 6, 1975 – Representative Andrew J. Hinshaw, (R-California), **is indicted** by a California grand jury for soliciting a bribe, accepting bribes, embezzlement and misappropriation of funds. Hinshaw accepted money and equipment from a stereo company to influence his official conduct. A jury found that he had solicited and received a $1,000 contribution in exchange for favors while he was assessor of Orange County. Hinshaw was sentenced to 1 to 14 years in prison.

1975

January 24, 1975 – New York City. A bomb set off in historic **Fraunces Tavern** kills 4 people and injures more than 50 others. The **Puerto Rican nationalist group** (FALN) claimed responsibility, and police tied 13 other bombings to the group.

January 19, 1975 – Paris, France. Arab terrorists attack **Orly airport** and take 10 hostages from a bathroom. The French provided the terrorists with a plane to fly them to safety in **Baghdad, Iraq.**

September 30, 1975 – A Hungarian airplane explodes killing all 64 persons on board.

December 21, 1975 – Carlos "The Jackal" holds 11 oil ministers and 59 civilians hostage during an OPEC meeting in Vienna, Austria. On December 22 the rebels and forty-two hostages are given an airliner and flown to Algiers.

Carlos is said to have received between 20 and 40 million dollars that he kept for his personal use, unknown to the other **terrorists** from the **Popular Front for the Liberation of Palestine** that were with him. He later flew to Libya, Yugoslavia, and Baghdad. He settled in Damascus for awhile and then relocated to Khartoum, the capitol of Sudan. On August 14, 1994, Carlos' "personal bodyguards" burst into his room while he slept, drugged him, and handed him over to the French authorities. He was tried for the murder of two French policemen and sentenced to life in prison.

1961-1975 – Angola. After 14 years of war, Portugal finally grants independence to Angola. It has been estimated that 80,000 people were killed from 1961-1975 during the Angolan war of Independence. Then without a break the **Angolan Civil War** begins in 1975 after the end of the war for independence from Portugal.

1975 – Guatemala vs. Belize Border Conflict. The conflict has its roots in the 1859 Aycinena-Wyke Agreement between Guatemala and Great Britain. Guatemala insisted the agreement ceded the territory conditionally to Great Britain, and Great Britain insists that, since it already owned the territory, the agreement merely fixed the boundaries. The unresolved territorial dispute will still not be settled in 2009.

1970-April 17, 1975 – Cambodia. Surrender to the Khmer Rouge. Premier Lon Nol took over the government from Prince Norodom Sihanouk in a March 1970 coup, and on December 17, 1972 Lon Nol's troops were locked in a desperate battle with the communists. **The communist Khmer Rouge** and their **North Vietnamese allies** were trying to encircle the capital city of Phnom Penh in the face of weakened Cambodian resistance and antigovernment demonstrations against the Lon Nol regime broke out inside the capital. The government banned all protests and political meetings by authorizing police searches of private homes.

Lon Nol managed to retain control of the government despite the unrest in Phnom Penh and a series of major military defeats, largely because of U.S. support. The balance of power tilted against Lon Nol after the Paris Peace Accords in January 1973 were signed. American forces were withdrawn from Southeast Asia, and Lon Nol's forces soon found themselves fighting alone against the communists.

The last U.S. airstrikes flown in support of Cambodian forces were in August 1973. Lon Nol and his forces fought on, but without American support they were no match for the Khmer Rouge and North Vietnamese communists.

On **April 17, 1975**, Lon Nol's greatly depleted forces **surrendered to the Khmer Rouge.** During the five years of war, approximately 10 percent of Cambodia's 7 million people died.

The victorious Khmer Rouge, under the leadership of Pol Pot, emptied the cities and forced millions of Cambodians into forced labor camps, murdered hundreds of thousands of real or imagined opponents, and caused hundreds of thousands of deaths from exhaustion, hunger, and disease.

1975-1979 – Cambodia. Kampuchean Killing Fields. The mass graves of up to 2 million people who perished during the "**killing fields**" rule of Pol Pot in 1975-1979 were uncovered in 1995-1996.

In 1985, Pol Pot officially retired but remained the effective head of the Khmer Rouge, which continued its guerrilla actions against the government in Phnom Penh. In 1997, after an internal power struggle ousted him from his leadership position he was put on trial and sentenced to life imprisonment by a "people's tribunal, " in a "show trial." Pol Pot later declared in an interview, "My conscience is clear." Many in the international community hoped that his captors would extradite him to stand trial for his crimes against humanity, but he died of apparently natural causes while under house arrest in 1998.

1975

December 25, 1975 – **Equatorial Guinea**, officially the **Republic of Equatorial Guinea**. Dictator **Francisco Macías Nguema, has 150 alleged coup plotters executed** to the sound of a band playing Mary Hopkin's tune **"Those Were the Days"** in the national stadium.

March 1974-1975 – **Iraqi Kurd Uprising. Kurds led by Mullah Mustafa Barzani with help from the C.I.A. vs. Iraq.** In March 1974, the KDP rebels against **Saddam Hussein**, sparking a full-scale war in 1975. The Kurds were easily defeated and thirteen-thousand Kurds fled to Iran. In March 1975 tens of thousands of villagers from the Barzani tribes are forcibly removed from their homes and relocated to barren sites in the desert south of Iraq, where they had to rebuild their lives without any form of assistance.

April 13, 1975 – **Lebanese Civil War.** The spark that ignites the war occurs in Beirut on April 13, when gunmen kill four **Phalangists** during an attempt on **Pierre Jumayyil's** life. Perhaps believing the assassins to have been Palestinian, the Phalangists retaliated later that day by attacking a bus carrying Palestinian passengers and killing about twenty-six of the occupants. The next day fighting breaks out, with Phalangists pitted against Palestinian militiamen, thought by some observers to be from the **Popular Front for the Liberation of Palestine.** Most people stay inside their homes as the street fighting they are witnessing is the beginning of a war that will devastate the city and divide the country.

1953-1975 – **Laos. The Laotian Civil War** is an internal fight between the **Communist Pathet Lao** and the **Royal Lao Government** in which both the political rightists and leftists receive external support for a proxy war from the global Cold War superpowers. The fighting in Laos involves the **North Vietnamese Army, American, Thai,** and **South Vietnamese forces** directly and through irregular proxies in a battle for control over the **Laotian Panhandle.** The North Vietnamese Army occupied the Laotian Panhandle as part of the Ho Chi Minh Trail.

    After the withdrawal of U.S. forces from Vietnam, a ceasefire between the Pathet Lao and the government led to a new coalition government. North Vietnam never withdrew from Laos and the Pathet Lao was controlled by the North Vietnamese. In

April 1975, after the fall of South Vietnam, the Pathet Lao with the backing of North Vietnam and China took control of Laos with little resistance. On December 2, 1975, the King was forced to abdicate his throne and the **Lao People's Democratic Republic** was established.

On May 15, 1997, the U.S. officially acknowledged its role in the Secret War, erecting a memorial in honor of American and Hmong contributions to U.S. air and ground combat efforts during the conflict. **The Laos Memorial** is located on the grounds of the Arlington National Cemetery between the John F. Kennedy Eternal Flame and the Tomb of the Unknown Soldier. It is estimated that over 120,000 people died as a result of the conflict.

November 6, 1975 – Morocco occupied Western Sahara. **King Hassan** dispatches 350,000 unarmed Moroccans on a "Green March" to the former Spanish Sahara. This began a long war with the **Polisario Front guerrilla group, tribal Bedouin** who sought independence.

1961-1975 – Mozambique. The **Mozambican War of Independence** officially started on September 25, 1964, and ended with a cease fire on September 8, 1974, resulting in a negotiated independence in 1975. It is estimated that 63,500 people were killed.

1975 – East Timor. After centuries of Portuguese colonial rule in East Timor, a 1974 coup in Portugal led to decolonization among its former colonies, creating instability in East Timor. A small scale civil war begins in 1975 and the Indonesian military looks on with increasing interest.

March 9, 1975 – Vietnam. A major offensive begins against South Vietnam with an attack on Ban Me Thuot in the Central Highlands. South Vietnam fell in 55 days.

April 17, 1975 – Vietnam. The Cambodian government surrenders to Khmer Rouge forces.

April 29, 1975 – Vietnam. The last American soldier killed in Vietnam (the first was July 8, 1959). The official American presence in Saigon ends when the last

1975

Americans are evacuated by helicopter from the U.S. Embassy roof. Within hours the Saigon government surrenders to the VC.

Vietnam – There are 58,260 Americans listed on the Vietnam Memorial wall. Approximately 1,200 of these are listed as missing (MIA's, POW's, and others). According to the Vietnamese government, 1,100,000 Vietnam People's Army and National Front for the Liberation of Vietnam military personnel and 2,000,000 Vietnamese civilians on both sides died in the conflict. Estimates of civilian deaths caused by American bombing in Operation Rolling Thunder range from 52,000 to 182,000. Most researchers of war history put the civilian toll close to 4 million people.

1976

The Oldest Boomer is 30 years old.

Cost of the Average House: $48,000	
Median Family Income: $12,690	**Minimum Wage:** $2.30/ hr **Average Hourly Wage:** $5.22
Sugar: 24 cents/ lb	**Gallon Gasoline:** 61 cents
New Car: **Ford, Pinto:** $2,895 **Lotus Elite:** $15,406 **Chrysler Volare:** $3,220	**Hershey Bar:** 15 cents/ 1.2 oz **Bacon:** $1.59/ lb **Movie Ticket:** $2.15 **Coffee:** $1.60/ lb
Unemployment Rate: 7.9%-7.4%-7.8%	**First-class Stamp:** 13 cents

26 cents buying power in 1976 **= $1in 2008.**
In 1976 what cost us 26 cents to purchase now costs us $1.00 in 2008.

Movies: "Taxi Driver," "Rocky," "All the President's Men," "Network," "Bound for Glory."

Broadway: "Shirley MacLaine," revue. "Debbie Reynolds Show," revue. "You're Arms Too Short to Box With God."

TV: John Belushi's Samurai Deli. Nadia's Perfect 10. "Laverne & Shirley," "The Muppet Show," "Alice," "The Gong Show," "The Captain and Tennille," "Quincy, M.E." "Charlie's Angels," "Family Feud," "The Bionic Woman,""Mr. T. and Tina," "Baa Baa Black Sheep," "The Gong Show," "Mary Hartman, Mary Hartman," "Donny and Marie," "The Scooby Doo Show."

Music: "Taxi Driver," Bernard Herrmann. ABBA," Dancing Queen," "Fernando" & "Money, Money, Money." Paul Simon, "50 Ways to Leave Your Lover." Brotherhood of Man, "Save Your Kisses for Me." Rick Dees & His Cast Of Idiots, "Disco Duck." Dr. Hook, "A Little Bit More." Frank Zappa, "Disco Boy." Captain & Tennille, "Lonely Night, Angel Face" &

"Muskrat Love." Led Zeppelin, "Candy Store Rock." Donna Summer, "Love To Love You Baby." Rod Stewart, "Tonight's The Night." Wild Cherry, "Play That Funky Music." Sex Pistols, "Anarchy in the U.K." Stevie Wonder, "I Wish." Aerosmith, "Last Child." Elton John, "Pinball Wizard." Tina Charles, "I Love To Love, But My Baby Just Loves To Dance." Barry White, "Don't Make Me Wait Too Long." The Carpenters, "I Need to Be In Love" & "There's a Kind of Hush, All Over the World." Leo Sayer, "You Make Me Feel Like Dancing." Barry Manilow, "I Write The Songs." Diana Ross, "Do You Know Where You're Going To." Elton John, "Bennie And The Jets." Chicago, "If You Leave Me Now." KC & The Sunshine Band-"Shake, Shake, Shake, Shake Your Booty." Peter Frampton, "Do You Feel Like We Do." Paul McCartney & Wings, "Silly Love Songs." Aerosmith, "Back in the Saddle." Lou Rawls, "You'll Never Find Another Love Like Mine." Bellamy Brothers, "Let Your Love Flow." Dion, "Born to Be With You." Marvin Gaye, "I Want You." Elton John & Kiki Dee, "Don't Go Breaking My Heart." Gordon Lightfoot, "The Wreck of the Edmund Fitzgerald."

Deaths: Robbie McIntosh, Phyllis Browne, Richard J. Daley.

President: Gerald R. Ford (R) Episcopalian; vetoes 66/ 12 overrides

Vice President: Nelson A. Rockefeller (R) Baptist

House: D-291 ; R-144

Senate: 94th Congress (1975-1977) Majority Party: Democrat (60 seats) Minority Party: Republican (38 seats) Other Parties: 1 Conservative; 1 Independent Total Seats: 100

Federal Debt: $620.43 billion or 34 % of the GDP

GDP: $1,825.3 billion	**Inflation Rate:** 5.75%
Dow Jones: 994.84 (07-01)/ 875.0 (January)	**S&P Price Index:** 107.46/ 19.15%
Prime Rate: 7.00% (01-12)/ 6.25% (12-13)	**Average Home Mortgage Rate:** 8.73/9.02%
1 oz Gold: $125.32	**1oz of Silver:** $4.62

Federal Debt: $620,433,000,000

Federal Deficit: $73.7 billion dollars	
Defense Spending: $114.47 billion	**Interest Spending:** $26.73 billion
Health Care Spending: $31.57 billion	**Pensions Spending:** $80.91 billion
Welfare Spending: $42.07 billion	**Education Spending:** $19.95 billion
Transportation Spending: $13.74 billion	**Misc. Other Spending:** $28.91 billion
Protection Spending: $3.43 billion	**Total Government Spending:** $371.79 billion
% of GDP that goes towards just the interest payment: 1.54%	
$1.00 = 1.880 Yuan, China NPC	**$1.00 =** 296.38 Yen, Japan
$1.00 = 3.530 Saudi Arabia Riyal	**$1.00 =** 70.630 Iranian Rial
U.S. Population: 218,086,000	**World Population:** 4,160,391,803
U.S. Birth Rate: 3,167,788	**U.S. Abortions:** 988,267—1,179,300
U.S. Homicide Rate: 9.0/ 100,000 population	**U.S. Violent Crime:** 467.8/ 100,000 population
Annual Average Domestic Crude Oil Prices: $13.10 / barrel, $49.46 (2007 adjusted)	

Oil:

1976 – Iran acquires 25 % of the **West German steel giant Krupp.**

1976 – Mexico. Huge offshore oil reserves are discovered and the Cantarell field becomes the mainstay of **Mexico's** oil production. **Cantarell Complex** is the largest oil field in Mexico and one of the largest in the world. It is discovered in 1976 by a fisherman, Rudesindo Cantarell.

1976

April–May, 1976 – The Lebanese civil war causes a drop in **Iraq** exports through trans-Lebanon pipelines to the Mediterranean.

December 15, 1976 – The Oil tanker Argo Merchant runs aground on the **Nantucket Shoals.** The 641-foot oil tanker Argo Merchant, en route to Boston from Venezuela with 7.6 million gallons of home heating oil, runs aground on Nantucket Shoals 25 miles southeast of Nantucket. Six days later, after the crew is evacuated, the vessel succumbs to the high winds and heavy seas of the North Atlantic in winter and breaks apart. None of the oil had been offloaded due to high seas. The disaster that follows is the **worst ship-borne oil spill** in American history, exceeded only by the Exxon Valdex in Alaska 13 years later. The effects of the accident would have been far worse had northwesterly winds not pushed the oil away from Cape Cod and prime fishing grounds.

Major News:

March 31, 1976 – In a "right to die" case, the New Jersey Supreme Court on March 31, allows comatose **Karen Ann Quinlan** to be removed from her respirator. She survives in a coma for nine years, until her death from pneumonia in 1985.

July 2, 1976 – The Supreme Court reinstates the **death penalty,** subject to conditions. On June 29, 1972, in Furman vs. Georgia, the Supreme Court had ruled that capital punishment as it was currently practiced was cruel and unusual. The death penalty is now back on the books.

July 4, 1976 – The Bicentennial of the **United States** is celebrated throughout the nation. Its **200th anniversary of independence** is celebrated July 4, with festivals, parades, and New York City's **Operation Sail,** a gathering of **tall ships** from around the world.

July 21-24, 1976 – "Legionnaire's disease" kills 29 people who attend an American Legion convention in Philadelphia. In 1977 a bacterium is discovered as the cause.

August 18, 1976 – Two U.S. officers on a routine mission near the DMZ in South Korea are slain by **North Korean soldiers.** North Korea stated "regret," on August 21.

1976 – A U.S. Senate committee chaired by Senator Frank Church, **The United States Senate Select Committee to Study Governmental Operations with Respect to Intelligence Activities,** revealed the **FBI's illegal activities** and many agents were investigated.

Former **FBI Associate Director W. Mark Felt** publicly states he ordered break-ins and the agents were merely obeying orders and should not be punished for it. He also claims acting director **L. Patrick Gray** also authorized the break-ins, but Gray denied this. Felt said on the CBS television program *Face the Nation* that he would probably be a "scapegoat" for the Bureau's work. "I think this is justified and I'd do it again tomorrow," he said on the program. While admitting the break-ins were "extralegal," he justified it as protecting the "greater good."

Mark Felt and Edward Miller, the highest-ranking convicted criminals in the FBI, are found guilty in 1978 of breaking into Vietnam protesters' homes and offices without warrants **during the Nixon presidency.** They had been trying to keep the FBI and Nixon informed of activities that they considered to be undertaken by hostile foreign powers and collaborators. The jury returned guilty verdicts on November 6, 1980. Felt was fined $5,000 and Miller was fined $3,500 although they could have been sent to prison for up to ten years. Overstepping his own Justice Department, **President Ronald Reagan pardoned the two men** in the midst of their appeals, after three years of prosecution proceedings.

1976 – Mark Felt revealed himself in 2005 as the whistleblower known as **Deep Throat.**

Civil Rights Movement:

1976 – College and **university enrollment for African American students** rises sharply from 282,000 in 1966 to 1,062,000 in 1976.

1976 – Negro History Week becomes **Black History Month.**

1976

1976 – Matthew J. Perry becomes a federal judge with the support of **Senator Strom Thurmond.** Perry had been chief counsel for the **South Carolina -NAACP** for twenty years, helping in key cases like the integration of Clemson.

Women's Movement:

1976 – Congresswoman **Barbara Jordan** of Texas, the first black woman elected to the U.S. Congress from the former Confederate States of America who received widespread recognition as a key member of the House Judiciary Committee during President Nixon's impeachment now delivers the **keynote address** to the **Democratic National Convention.** She is the first black and first woman to address the convention as a keynote speaker, famously declaring that what was different and special about that night was that "I, Barbara Jordan, am a keynote speaker." She was a truly eloquent speaker with a tremendous grasp of the English language.

1976 – The first marital rape law is enacted in Nebraska, making it illegal for a husband to rape his wife.

1976 – Sarah Caldwell becomes the first woman to conduct at **New York's Metropolitan Opera House.**

1976 – The United States Naval Academy at Annapolis admits women for the first time in June. Janie L. Mines becomes the first African American women cadet to enter. She graduates in 1980.

1976 – ERAmerica is launched to promote the ratification of the Equal Rights Amendment.

1976 – Many professional and women's organizations decide to **boycott those states** that have not passed the ERA and to hold their conferences elsewhere. The pressure is on states to ratify the amendment before the 1979 deadline.

1976 – The Organization of Pan Asian American Women forms for women of Asian and Pacific American Islander descent.

1976 – *Redbook* magazine polls its readers about **sexual harassment,** and 90% of young women view the situation as serious.

1976 – A bill that defines a "person" as "a human being" from the moment of fertilization is signed by Louisiana's Governor.

Popular Culture:

1976 – **Both the House and Senate pass the Hyde Amendment,** which prohibits the use of federal Medicaid money for **abortions.**

1976 – **The Supreme Court** agrees with **General Electric** that the company's failure to cover **pregnancy-related disability** is not discriminatory.

1976 – **The pinnacle of the Leisure Suit.** Leisure suits were the attire to be seen in at the disco until this fashion was "out" in 1979. **The Full-Cleveland:** a leisure suit combined with a white belt and white dress shoes, was second.

1976 – **The Court** finds, in Buckley vs. Valeo, that **campaign donations** are a form of symbolic speech protected by the 1st Amendment, a decision that greatly complicates campaign finance regulation.

1976 – **Lonnie Frisbee** is an American closeted **gay Pentecostal evangelist** and self-described "seeing prophet" and mystic in the late 1960s and 1970s that despite his **"hippie"** appearance had notable success as a minister and evangelist. Frisbee is a key figure in the **Jesus Movement** and is involved in the rise of two worldwide denominations, **Calvary Chapel** and the **Vineyard Movement.** Both churches later disowned him because of his **active homosexuality** removing him first from leadership positions then, ultimately, firing him. He eventually dies from AIDS in 1993.

April 1976 – **The Video Game "Breakout"** is released by **Atari.** Its design got a little help from **Steve Wozniak and Steve Jobs**, but the original design was by **Nolan Bushnell.**

1976

Bushnell told the designers at Atari that he would pay anyone who could reduce the number of ICs the game used. At $100/ IC removed Steve Jobs, a low paid technician at Atari, took up the challenge. He started work on a new design but soon found himself in over his head and asked his friend, Steve Wozniak for help. Woz, who liked to hang out at Atari and play-test the new games as they rolled off the assembly lines, agreed. Woz and Jobs worked on the game day and night. Woz worked at **Hewlett-Packard** as his day job, and then stayed up almost all night working on the games redesign. Finally Woz **reduced the design down to 42 Ics.** Jobs received a $5,000 bonus, told Woz it was only $700 and gave Steve Wozniak his '50%'. . . $350. When Woz finds out years later it does nothing to strengthen their relationship and may have led to Steve Wozniak quitting Apple.

Steve Wozniak's design was so brilliant and minimized that no one could figure out how to get it into production so the game just sat on the shelf at Atari until it was redesigned for production with about 100 ICs.

There were 11,000 units produced in an upright cabinet with side-art of the word **"Breakout"** in red letters, being smashed in by a ball.

1976 – **"Death Race 98"** raises public complaints about **video games.**

1976 – **The New Jersey State Legislature** passes legislation **legalizing casinos** in the shore town of **Atlantic City** beginning in 1978. After signing the bill into law, Governor Brendan Byrne declares "The mob is not welcome in New Jersey!" referring to the Mafia's influence at casinos in Nevada.

During the heady days of the 1920's when Atlantic City was the holiday destination for the rich and famous, organized crime flourished. **Meyer Lansky, Lucky Luciano, Dutch Schultz** and **Al Capone** all gathered in Atlantic City in an effort to suppress the gory turf war which threatened to topple the Mafia Empire. Aniello Dellacroce, moved his aides and muscle to Atlantic City in 1976. He was aiming for the number one position of boss of bosses, and realized the huge potential of the New Jersey domain.

The Mafia invested in bars and pizza joints and scouted out hotels for sale in the city and soon took over some of the service industries including the supply of linen to the growing number of casino-hotels and the distribution of liquor.

On May 26, 1978 the first casino, **Resorts International** opens. After the U.S. government made a deal with Lucky Luciano during WWII a long and secret association between the OSS, CIA, and the Mafia developed. Resorts International was originally incorporated in 1958 as **Mary Carter Paint Company** with ties to both the CIA and organized crime. The mob was now welcome in Atlantic City.

1976 – Small satellite dishes go into residential backyards. People are limited to TV signals that are more or less **"line-of-sight",** which meant a big tree in your neighbor's yard could block your signal. Cloud coverage, weather patterns, hills and tall buildings would also block peoples TV signals. Not everyone could receive equally. Whole towns in mountainous areas received more "snow" on their TV sets than programs. Small satellite dishes are still "line of sight" but a major improvement because unlike randomly placed TV towers with their low broadcast signal, there is only one source high in the sky to point your dish at.

1976 – Nuclear Weapons. The number of **designated targets** for U.S. nuclear weapons in the Single Integrated Operational Plan: **25,000** (1976), **16,000** (1986) and **2,500** (1995).

1976 – Viking II sends color photos from Mars.

1976 – California's **sodomy** law is repealed.

1976 – Columbia. Drug traffickers start out with modest goals. In the mid-1970s, marijuana traffickers in Colombia begin exporting small quantities of **cocaine** to the United States hidden in suitcases. Cocaine can be processed for $500/ kilo in jungle labs and can be sold on the streets of America for as much as **$10,000/ kilo.**

In 1988 it cost $2,000 per kilo to buy the coke from the cartel. You can easily bring into the U.S. 1,000 kilos at a time and sell it for $14,500/ kilo NY, and gross $14.5 million. The profits are higher at $26,000/ kilo Spain & Italy, with a gross of $104 million. All this for an upfront cost of $2 million. In the U.S. alone, between **$400 Billion and $500 Billion dollars/ year,** of drug money is being laundered in 1988. Additional info "The Infiltrator," Robert Mazur.

By 2009 a lot of the drugs enter the U.S. through Mexico. Now you understand why so many politicians do not want to close the border. So much money is available that Presidents, heads of countries, and lesser politicians are bought and sold daily.

Business / Technology:

Autumn 1974-1976 – Apple Computer. After returning from India, Steven Paul **"Steve" Jobs** is invited by Stephen Gary **"Steve" Wozniak** to join the **'Homebrew Computer Club',** held at Stanford Linear Accelerator Center, where electronic-enthusiasts met, sharing knowledge and helping each other with their self-made computers. While Woz just enjoys creating electronic devices, Jobs has an eye for the marketability of personal computers. Jobs persuades Wozniak to build a personal computer with him and Woz agrees, although in his eyes it is a "hobby, for-fun basis" and not for making money, as he later emphasizes.

1975 – Jobs and Wozniak begin working on the Apple I in Jobs' bedroom. Every two weeks, they present their latest improvements of their design to the members of the **Homebrew Computer Club.**

1976 – The **Apple I** design is finished. Originally, the two had intended to sell it to the other members of the Homebrew Computer Club, but **as an employee of HP, Wozniak** has to get a legal release from HP to produce electronic devices professionally. **They offer their low-cost PC to Hewlett Packard first,** but no one at HP is interested in it. After being turned down, Jobs insists on producing the Apple I on their own so he sells his old Volkswagen Bus and Wozniak sells his beloved programmable HP calculator. They pool about **$1,250** and begin producing the first **Apple I mainboards.**

Jobs asks a former colleague from **Atari, Ronald Wayne,** 41 year old draftsman at Atari, to join them in their startup. Jobs offers Wayne ten percent interest in the company and Wayne agrees, although he keeps his job at Atari and works at night for Apple I.

April 1st, 1976 – Apple Computer is founded by Steven Wozniak, Steven Jobs and Ron Wayne. Ron Wayne designs the first Apple logo.

Early April 1976 – The local computer store **"Byte Shop" orders 50 Apple I computers,** which are sold for **$666.66.** Jobs, Woz and Wayne face one major problem though: They don't have enough money to buy the parts for 50 Apple I computers, each costing over $100 to build so Jobs persuades a local part supplier to give them the parts on 30 days' net credit. The three assemble the Apple I at night in their garage and manage to deliver the ordered Apple I in ten days.

April 12th, 1976 – Ron Wayne resigns from Apple Computer, with a one-time payment of $800. He felt that the financial risk was too great especially since Woz may still be waiting on the legal release from HP.

May 5th, 1976 – HP grants Wozniak the permission for the Apple I.

2008 – Apple has about 35,000 employees worldwide and had worldwide annual sales of **$32.48 billion** in its fiscal year ending September 29, 2008.

1976 – Don Taylor makes the first round-the-world flight in a home-built airplane, a Thorp T-18.

1976 – The Cray-1 supercomputer contained about 200,000 gates, roughly the same as the Intel 386 of the 1980s. Its theoretical performance is roughly 160 MIPS. In 2009 the Intel Core i7 Extreme 965EE runs at 76,383 MIPS at 3.2 GHz.

Humans have about a hundred billion neurons, each of which has an average of a thousand connections to other neurons. Because all these connections can perform their computations at the same time, the brain can perform about a hundred trillion simultaneous computations. A hundred trillion computations being performed at the same time add up to about twenty million billion calculations per second.

1976 – Software. "Electric Pencil," is the first popular microcomputer word-processing program.

1976 – Battle of the Video Tapes. Betamax vs. VHS. Sony's Betamax and JVC's VHS battle for the home market. Sony will lose.

1976 – The Toxic Substances Control Act is signed into law by the U.S. Congress and directs the administrator of the **Environmental Protection Agency** (EPA) to establish testing procedures for **toxic chemicals,** publicize results of chemicals that prove to be dangerous, and to set guidelines for controlling toxic chemicals.

1976

July 20, 1976 – The Viking 1 space probe successfully lands on Mars. It will be followed by a second unmanned **Viking II** on the Utopia Plains on September 3. The first color photos of the surface of Mars are taken on these flights and sent back to Earth.

1976 – The SR-71 Blackbird reconnaissance aircraft breaks both a speed record, 2,193 mph over a 10/15- mile course, and an altitude-in-horizontal-flight record at 85,069 feet.

November 26, 1976 – Microsoft becomes a registered trademark, one year after its name for microcomputer software is first mentioned by Bill Gates to Paul Allen in a letter. By 1998, Gates was worth $59 billion; a year later, he was worth $85 billion. Gates is twice as wealthy as the second richest American, Microsoft co-founder Paul Allen, worth $40 billion (1998).

Finance:

1976 – National debt. Between uncontrolled inflation and **President Gerald Ford's** conservative bend, the debt increased 17% his first full year in office (1975), and 13% his second (1976). Ford's plan to impose a policy of price controls failed to bring government overspending and inflation under control. Ford faced an opposition Congress controlled by Democrats during his time in office.

February 11, 1976 – The last **public meeting** of the **U.S. Assay Commission** is held. For nearly two centuries, distinguished Americans assembled each year to examine random samples of United States coinage and see whether they conformed to legal requirements. This prestigious gathering, known as the U.S. Assay Commission, carried on a tradition which dates back centuries.

    In 1977 President Jimmy Carter, newly installed in the White House, will eliminate all public members from that year's assay panel. The U.S. Assay Commission met for the final time in 1980. The Assay Commission's function had come to be largely ceremonial.

1976 – Bill Clinton is elected Attorney General of Arkansas. Two Indonesian billionaires come to Arkansas, **Mochtar Riady and Liem Sioe Liong**, and both are close to **Suharto** who rules a military dictatorship in Indonesia for 32 years.

Riady is looking for an American bank to buy and finds **Jackson Stephens** with whom he forms Stephens Finance. Stephens will broker the arrival of **BCCI** to this country and steer BCCI's founder, **Hassan Abedi**, to **Bert Lance**. Riady's teen-age son is taken on as an intern by Stephens Inc. He later says he was "sponsored" by **Bill Clinton.** Hassan Abedi is a close associate of **Saudi Intelligence Minister Kamal Adham.** The Riadys are Chinese-Indonesian businessmen who, of all places, move to Arkansas in the late 1970's, despite holding billions of dollars of assets in Asia.

October, 1992, the Senate Foreign Relations Committee releases an 800-page report on the BCCI collapse. They call the BCCI scandal, "**the largest case of organized crime in history".** It represented an "international financial crime on a massive and global scale", that included 72 nations. Adding that and that the bank "systematically **bribed world leaders and political figures** throughout the world." The Senate report concluded that **among the provable charges** against BCCI are "BCCI's criminality, including fraud . . . **involving billions of dollars; money laundering in Europe, Africa, Asia, and the Americas;** BCCI's bribery of officials in most of those locations; its **support of terrorism, arms trafficking**, and the **sale of nuclear technologies;** its management of **prostitution;** its commission and facilitation of **income tax evasion, smuggling,** and **illegal immigration;** its **illicit purchases of banks and real estate;** and a panoply of financial crimes limited only by the imagination of its officers and customers."

Jackson Stephens relationship with BCCI's **Agha Hasan Abedi is not casual** and Jackson Stephens is frequently linked with America's super-secret **National Security Agency.** The Stephens financial empire's national headquarters of **"Jackson Stephen's Beverly Enterprises"** is at the edge of the same **Venice, Florida airport where the 911 terrorists** will be trained and furious government intelligence officials will accuse the NSA of destroying data pertinent to the Sept 11 probe, as reported in the *Boston Globe,* stating possible leads stemming from the September 11 attack weren't being followed because of NSA.

In response to the concerns over Jackson Stephens' involvement in BCCI, the **Ohio Attorney General** notes in a 1993 report, "Stephens' name has been linked to securities violations that allegedly occurred when the Bank of Commerce and Credit International (**BCCI**), a foreign bank dominated by Pakistani financier Agha Hasan Abedi, acquired stock and control over the Washington-based **First American Bank**."

In 1983 **Stephens and Riady** bought the **Hong Kong Chinese Bank** and the **Seng Heng Bank** in Macao. Stephens then invited Riady to invest in a Little Rock, Arkansas bank called **Worthen**. In 1991, Stephens joined BCCI investor **Mochtar Riady** in buying BCCI's former Hong Kong subsidiary from its liquidators. Moktar and his son James Riady, also own the **Lippo Bank** in Indonesia.

NEW YORK TIMES **February 5, 1992 LITTLE ROCK, Ark**. Two days before **Bill Clinton's** bitterly contested re-election in 1990; the Arkansas Governor grew concerned that his campaign was slipping. He placed calls to members of an influential Arkansas business group, asking them to raise $50,000 for his campaign, according to people involved in the effort. "He was somewhat in a panic," recalled Warren A. Stephens, one of those contacted by the Governor. Mr. Stephens is President and Chief Executive Officer of Stephens Inc., the investment banking flagship of the **Stephens family empire**, which has vast holdings in natural gas, finance and real estate. Published estimates of the family's wealth put it well **over $1 billion.**

1976 – BCCI. Faisal Islamic Bank of Egypt (FIBE) is founded in 1976, as part of the banking empire built by **Saudi Prince Mohammed al-Faisal.** Several of the founding members are leading members of the **Muslim Brotherhood**, including the **"Blind Sheikh," Sheikh Omar Abdul-Rahman.** The growth of **Islamic banking** directly funds the political growth of the Islamist movement. This gives **the Saudis control over poorer Islamic nations, like Egypt.** FIBE is also closely associated with the **infamous Bank of Credit and Commerce International (BCCI),** which will be implicated in the **illegal arms** and **narcotics** trades, and with the **funding of terrorist organizations** when it collapses in 1991.

BCCI. Intelligence agencies need a network of banks to help finance covert intelligence operations and **Saudi Intelligence Minister Kamal Adham** is given the task. **George H. W. Bush** as the head of the **CIA** helps and encourages Adham as he transforms a small **Pakistani merchant bank,** the Bank of Credit and Commerce International (**BCCI**), into **a world-wide money-laundering machine,** buying banks around the world to create the biggest clandestine money network in history. When **French customs** raid the **Paris BCCI branch** they will discover an account in former head of the CIA and then President, **George H.W. Bush's** name.

BCCI will solicit the business of every major terrorist, rebel, and underground organization in the world and the intelligence gained will be shared with "friends of BCCI." Time magazine will later describe BCCI as not just a bank, but also "a global intelligence operation and a **Mafia-like** enforcement squad. Operating primarily out of the bank's offices in Karachi, Pakistan, the 1,500-employee **black network** used sophisticated spy equipment and techniques, along with bribery, extortion, kidnapping and even, by some accounts, murder. The black network, so named by its own members, stops at almost nothing to further the bank's aims the world over." *TIME*, 7/22 1999

September 1 1976 – The Safari Club. Prince Turki al-Faisal, is head of **Saudi Intelligence** in 1979. In a 2002 speech in the U.S. he is quoted as saying, "In 1976, after the **Watergate** matters took place here, your intelligence community was literally tied up by Congress. It could not do anything. It could not send spies, it could not write reports, and it could not pay money. In order to compensate for that, a group of countries got together in the hope of fighting Communism and established what was called the **Safari Club.**" The Safari Club included **France, Egypt, Saudi Arabia, Morocco,** and **Iran.** The group created staff, and operational capability to manage and fund off-the-books covert operations mostly in Africa and the Mid-East.

There is reason to believe the Saudi Intelligence Minister Kamal Adham and then his nephew Prince Turki from 1979 onwards, fund off-the-books covert operations for the CIA. Rather than work with the Carter administration as the CIA is being reformed, Safari preferred to work with the **ex-CIA Director George Bush Sr.** It has been reported The Safari Club and rogue CIA play a major role in supporting the **Mujahideen in Afghanistan.** The Club is exposed after the Shah of Iran is removed from government in 1979 and seems to have disappeared or reinvented itself by 1982.

August 1976 – John Bogle launches the First Index Investment Trust. John Bogle founds Vanguard and the index fund movement. They buy index funds, which track the performance of a large selection of stocks usually grouped by market cap, and hold on to them for a long time as they appreciate over time. This theory is based in part on Bogle's own research. On August 31, the fund that becomes the mighty **Vanguard, VFINX**, starts with just $11 million in assets under management and can't even buy all of the **S&P 500** stocks until 1977. But it starts a revolution in investing; luring billions from investors concerned about the risks and costs of actively managed funds. $10,000 invested on 12/31/1976 would be worth VFINX: $215,402 (Vanguard S&P 500) 6/30/2009.

October 4, 1976 – The Tax Reform Act is signed into law.

December 14, 1976 – The first issue of **Treasury Bills** in book-entry form are sold.

1976 – The International Monetary Fund (IMF) begins a 5-year gold sales program which includes IMF auctions. Coupled with a lower inflation outlook this drives gold prices down.

1976 – The average American's personal income grew by 9.1% in 1976, well above the inflation rate, the Commerce Department reported Tuesday.

Books:

1976 – Alex Haley's search for his ancestors is published as "**Roots.**"

1976 – "Interview with the Vampire." Anne Rice.

1976 – "Trinity." Leon Uris.

TV:

1976 – The TV Family Hour. A U.S. Judge Rules the TV Family Hour constitutes federal censorship. The 7 to 8 p.m. hour was considered a safe haven for TV shows the whole family could watch. The TV industry was trying to voluntarily set standards and reform itself by insuring viewers that all 7 p.m. shows were acceptable to even **young audiences.** This proves to be unsuccessful after money speaks and the networks sit up and pay attention.

1976 – HBO is the first station to provide its programming to cable companies by satellite TV transmission. Due to the genius and curiosity of **one Stanford Professor** who built his own receiver dish and was able to see the transmissions that HBO was sending, the C-band dish was born. This same professor tried to pay HBO for his service and the payment was rejected. The professor then published a **How-To Book** on the C-band dish because by this time other companies were also beginning to transmit their programs to the cable companies via satellite without encryption. This is the beginning of **small dish antennas in residential backyards.**

Sports:

July 18, 1976 – Nadia Comaneci, the 14-year-old Romanian, **Montreal Summer Games** scores a perfect 10, the first in Olympic history.

Music:

January 7, 1976 – Kenneth Moss, a former record company executive, is sentenced to 120 days in the Los Angeles County Jail and four years probation for involuntary manslaughter in the 1974 drug induced death of **Average White Band** drummer **Robbie McIntosh.**

February 15, 1976 – Bette Midler bails seven members of her entourage out of jail after they are arrested on charges of cocaine and marijuana possession.

December 1, 1976 – The Sex Pistols achieve public notoriety as they unleash several 4-letter words live on Bill Grundy's TV show.

December 3, 1976 – Bob Marley and his manager Don Taylor are shot in an **assassination attempt** in Kingston, Jamaica.

Natural Disasters:

February 4, 1976 – Guatemala. An earthquake leaves over **23,000 people dead.**

1976

July 1976 – **Flash Flood**. A stationary rainstorm in the Rocky Mountains causes a flash flood of the **Big Thompson Canyon** that kills **145** people and causes more than $40 million dollars in damage, including the destruction of parts of highway 34.

July 28, 1976 – **The Great Tangshan Earthquake,** is believed to be responsible for more deaths than any other **earthquake in the 20th century.** The earthquake strikes near Tangshan in Hebei, People's Republic of China, an industrial city with approximately one million inhabitants. It shakes the area for about ten seconds early in the morning, while most people are still asleep. Close to 250,000 deaths are reported by the Chinese government, and 164,000 people are severely injured. Chinese sources list the quake at 7.8 to 8.2 on the Richter magnitude scale. It was followed by a major 7.8 magnitude aftershock some 16 hours later, increasing the death toll. The Beijing government turned down outside aid.

August 17, 1976 – **Mindanao, Philippines. An earthquake** and tidal wave leave up to 8,000 people dead or missing.

1976 – **The Ebola virus.** Between June and November, the Ebola virus infected 284 people in **Sudan,** causing 151 deaths. In the **Democratic Republic of the Congo,** there were 318 cases and 280 deaths in September and October. The disease spread by close personal contact and by use of contaminated needles and syringes in hospitals/clinics. This outbreak is the first recognition of the disease.

Man vs. Man / Wars:

Assassinated – British Isles. Christopher Ewart-Biggs, the British ambassador to Ireland is assassinated by the **Provisional Irish Republican Army** in Sandyford, Dublin. He was 55 when he was killed by a landmine planted by the IRA. Dublin launched a man-hunt involving 4,000 police and 2,000 soldiers. Thirteen suspected members of the IRA were arrested during raids as the British and Irish governments attempted to apprehend the killers. No one was ever convicted of the killings.

1976 – Chile. Exiled Chilean Foreign Minister Orlando Letelier is killed by a car-bomb in Washington, D.C.

January 11, 1976 – Rodriguez Lara is removed from office by the military. Poveda Burbano is the head of the military junta that overthrows the regime of **Ecuadorian President Guillermo Rodríguez Lara** in a bloodless coup on January 11. Burbano holds power until the return to civilian rule in 1979. Burbano is Vice Admiral of the navy at the time of the coup.

Assassinated – Nigeria. Murtala Ramat Mohammed, President of Nigeria is killed on February 13, 1976 in an abortive coup attempt led by Lt.Col Buka Suka Dimka, when his car is ambushed while en route to his office. Several top officers were accused of either planning or approving the coup attempt. He was succeeded by the Chief of Staff, Supreme HQ Olusegun Obasanjo.

1976 – Representative Henry J. Helstoski, (D-New Jersey), is **indicted** on 12 counts of bribery and conspiracy. He is accused of soliciting and obtaining bribes from resident aliens in exchange for facilitating legislation on their behalf. The case was dismissed after a court ruled that the "Speech or Debate" clause of the Constitution prohibited the use of legislative acts as evidence.

September 21, 1976 – Representative James F. Hastings (R-New York) is **indicted** for mail fraud and filing false vouchers. The indictment alleged that Hastings had received kickbacks from the salaries of three staffers over six years. He is convicted on December 17, 1976, on 28 counts and is jailed for 14 months.

June 12, 1976 – Representative Allan T. Howe (D-Utah) is **indicted** for soliciting sex acts for pay. Howe is convicted on July 23, 1976 and the verdict was upheld on appeal.

January 29, 1976 – Representative James R. Jones (D-Oklahoma) is **charged with** failing to report a cash campaign contribution. Although he was not formally indicted, he pleads guilty.

February 28, 1976 – President Ford issues Executive Order 11905, which limits the power of the **CIA,** the **NSA,** and **military intelligence** to engage in surveillance of

U.S. citizens. Perhaps its most well-known provision is a total **ban on "political assassinations"** by U.S. government personnel.

1976 – Terrorists attack **Istanbul airport,** Turkey, killing 4 civilians and injuring 20.

December 4, 1976 – Terrorists occupy the **Indonesian Embassy** in The Hague, Netherlands, killing one person.

December 14, 1976 – Beilen, Netherlands. A passenger train is hijacked by members of the RMS movement and the passengers are kept hostage. Three passengers are killed.

August 11, 1976 – Istanbul airport, Turkey. Popular Front for the Liberation of Palestine and **Japanese Red Army terrorists** attack a passenger terminal at Istanbul airport, Turkey, killing four civilians and injuring twenty.

1976 – A TWA aircraft en route from New York to Paris is hijacked by Croatian **terrorists,** seizing 93 hostages. The terrorists surrendered in Paris and released their hostages.

1976 – A New York policeman is killed by a bomb left by **terrorists** in a locker in **Grand Central Station.**

1976-1983 – Argentina's "Dirty War" refers to the state-sponsored violence against Argentine citizens from 1976 to 1983 carried out primarily by **Jorge Rafael Videla's military government.** Trade unionists were **targeted for assassination** as early as 1973.

After **Perón's death** in 1974, the government was left in the hands of his widow, **Isabel Martínez de Perón,** who signed a number of decrees empowering the military and the police to **"annihilate"** left-wing subversion. **Isabel Perón** was ousted in 1976. From 1976 until 1981, juntas led by **Jorge Rafael Videla's military government** and then by Roberto Viola and Leopoldo Galtieri, were responsible for the **illegal arrest, torture, killing or forced disappearance of thousands of people,** primarily trade-unionists, students and activists. Videla's dictatorship referred to its systematized persecution of the Argentine citizenry as the "National Reorganization Process". **Up to 30,000 people "disappeared"** during this time. Argentine security forces and **death squads** worked hand in hand with other South American dictatorships under the campaign called **Operation Condor. Operation Condor** involved assassination and intelligence operations officially implemented in 1975 by the governments in **Argentina, Chile, Uruguay, Paraguay, Bolivia, Brazil** and the **United States. Ecuador** and **Peru** became involved later on. More than 60,000 people are killed. An Argentine court would later condemn the Argentine government's crimes as crimes against humanity and **"genocide."**

1945-1976 – People's Republic of China. Mao Zedong dies September 1976. Chairman Mao is responsible for **3,000,000 people's deaths** by execution, mob or suicide during the suppression of counterrevolutionaries, 1950-1951. During the Three Anti Campaign in 1952-1953 Mao is responsible for 200,000 – 300,000 suicides. His "Great Leap forward" 1958-1961 killed at least 38,000,000 people from starvation and overwork as slave labor. 3,000,000 people died violent deaths as a direct result of Mao's Cultural Revolution during 1966-1976. Although the death tolls from the **Laogai Labor Camps** are not known it is estimated that **27,000,000 people died** as a direct result of forced labor in the camps from 1949-1976. These forced labor camps are still active in 2010 and are responsible for supplying many "low cost" products to major companies who are very much aware of the deaths they cause. The total number of deaths during the regime of Mao Zedong is about **70,000,000 people.** Seventy Million People!

October 1976 – China. The armed forces arrest **Jiang Qing, Mao's wife,** and her radical associates. They are called **The Gang of Four** to emphasize that they represent only a small group of radicals. In 1981 Jiang Qing and the other members of the Gang of Four are put on trial. Jiang Qing is sentenced to death but with a two year reprieve. The death sentence is never carried out. Jiang Qing commits suicide while in prison in 1991, thus bringing the **Cultural Revolution Era** to an end.

1976 – China. Laogai Camp Deaths. China's booming economy continues to increase through its use of slave labor or Laogai camps. **Laogai** means "reform through labor." It's a system of **prison factories and detention centers** set up by former **Chinese leader Mao Zedong** during the 1950's as a means to re-educate through labor and increase economic gain for the People's Republic of China. As of 1979, there were apparently only several thousand people being forced to work in the Laogai system. In 2009 it has become an enormous source of free labor and financial profit for the Chinese government.

Forced labor has become both a form a torture and a source of great profit for China. With the enormous amount of **free labor that comes from Laogai,** China has lured many overseas businesses into its profit-through-slave-labor system. With ridiculously cheap wholesale labor costs many cannot resist the bait and unknowingly come to support this illegal practice. According to estimates from the Laogai Research Foundation, **there are 6.8 million people incarcerated in China's 1,100 Laogai labor facilities,** although the actual number of detainees is uncertain. In "Mao: The Unknown Story," Jung Chang and Jon Halliday estimate that perhaps 27 million people died in prisons and labor camps during Mao Tse-tung's rule. And it did not end there.

For those incarcerated in these facilities, the reality they face is long hours of brutal treatment with little sleep or food to sustain themselves. Reports of 20-hour work days and violent oppression force some detainees to choose suicide instead of being beaten, starved, or worked to death according to a paper by Stephen D. Marshall, **"Chinese Laogai: a hidden role in 'Developing Tibet."** Others mutilate or injure themselves in an effort to avoid the work. Inmates who fall behind or refuse to work are shocked with electric batons, beaten, sexually assaulted, or thrown into solitary confinement. Common everyday products ranging from artificial Christmas trees, Christmas tree lights, bracelets, tools and foodstuffs, et cetera are among some of the products manufactured and exported from these facilities. According to a 1998 **House Committee on International Relations report,** companies who reportedly have or had products made in China's Laogai are . . . Many, many major **International, American and European companies knowingly deal** with middle men who in turn deal with the Laogai system in China.

July 4, 1976 – Israeli Raid on Entebbe. An Air France aircraft is hijacked by a joint **German Baader-Meinhof/ Popular Front for the Liberation of Palestine terrorist**

group and its crew is forced to fly to Entebbe airport in **Uganda.** Some two hundred and fifty-eight passengers and crew are held hostage and the terrorists threaten to kill the hostages if their demands for the release of prisoners are not met. All non–Israelis are released.

A counter-terrorism **hostage-rescue mission** is carried out by the Israel Defense Force at **Entebbe Airport in Uganda.** The covert Israeli plan takes into account the likelihood of armed **resistance from Ugandan military troops.**

AP **Israeli commandos have rescued 100 hostages**, mostly Israelis or Jews, held by pro-**Palestinian hijackers** at Entebbe airport in Uganda. At about 0100 local time (2200GMT), Ugandan soldiers and the hijackers were taken completely by surprise when three Hercules transport planes landed after a 2,500-mile trip from Israel. About 200 elite troops ran out and stormed the airport building. During a 35-minute battle, 20 Ugandan soldiers and all seven hijackers died along with three hostages and one commando.

1975-1990 – Lebanon erupts in civil war between Christians, Muslims, and Palestinians, resulting in an estimated 130,000 to 250,000 civilian deaths. Another one million people (one third of the population) were wounded, half of whom are left with lifetime disabilities.

April 13, 1976 – Morocco. Abdennaceur Bnouhachem's work as a left-wing **student activist** comes to an abrupt end when plainclothes officers corner him in the street and throw him into an unmarked van. He is tortured and spends 9 years in prison. Years later he will be awarded 1 million dirhams ($114,500) for his ordeal, but said the money will not erase his memories.

1971-1976 – Oman. SAS Secret War. From 1971-1976 the **SAS, British Special Air Service,** fought and won a guerilla war in the hills and deserts of southern Oman. The SAS fought in secrecy, saving the Omani regime and preventing Soviet-backed guerillas from seizing control of the Persian Gulf. They kept the operation so secret that the British Labour party was mostly unaware of what was happening until the 1974 election.

1976

October 1976 – Syria. Syrian troops enter Lebanon to stop the **Lebanese civil war**. In early 1976, the Lebanese civil war is going poorly for the Maronite Christians. Syria sends **40,000 troops** into Lebanon and quickly becomes embroiled in the Lebanese Civil War. This begins a 30 year Syrian occupation of Lebanon. Many crimes in Lebanon are associated with the Syrian forces and intelligence agencies, including the **assassinations** of Kamal Jumblat and Bachir Gemayel, which are usually connected to Syria or Syrian backed groups.

After more than a year and a half of devastation, relative calm returned to Lebanon. Although the exact cost of the war will never be known, the number of people killed may have approached 44,000, with about 180,000 wounded. Many thousands of others were displaced, left homeless, or had left the area. Much of the once-magnificent city of Beirut was reduced to rubble and the town was divided into Muslim and Christian sectors, separated by the so-called Green Line.

1976 – Thailand. Field Marshal **Thanom Kittikachorn** oversaw a decade of military rule in Thailand from 1963 to 1973, until public protests exploded into violence and forced him to step down. His return from exile in 1976 sparked protests which led to a massacre of demonstrators, followed by a military coup. Thousands of students were killed between 1973-1976 in Sanam Luang by the Governments of both Field Marshal **Sarit Thanarat** and Field Marshal **Thanom Kittikachorn.**

1976 – Zimbabwe. On November 11, 1965, the **conservative white-minority government** of **Rhodesia** declared its independence from **Britain**. The country resisted the demands of black Africans, and **Prime Minister Ian Smith** withstood British pressure, economic sanctions, and guerrilla attacks in his effort to uphold white supremacy. On March 1, 1970, Rhodesia formally proclaimed itself a republic. Heightened guerrilla war and a **withdrawal of South African military aid in 1976** marks the beginning of the collapse of Ian Smith's 11 years of resistance.

1977

The Oldest Boomer is 31 years old.

Cost of the Average House: $54,200	
Median Family Income: $13,570 **Accountant:** $12,000/ year **Chemical engineer:** $18,000/ year **Receptionist:** $140/ week	**Minimum Wage:** $2.30/ hr **Average Hourly Wage:** $5.68 **Typist-clerk:** $650/ month
Gallon of Milk: $1.69	**Gallon Gasoline:** 65 cents
New Car: **ToyotaCorolla:**2,870.00 **Buick Electra 225:** $7,033 **Ford Pinto Wagon:** $4,075 **Dodge Aspen:** $4,515	**Perdue Chicken:** 69 cents/ lb **Bacon:** 99 cents/ lb **Morton TV Dinner:** 39cents/10oz **Daily Newspaper:** 20 cents
Unemployment Rate: 7.5%-6.9%-6.4%	**First-class Stamp:** 13 cents

28 cents buying power in 1977 = **$1.00 in 2008.**
In 1977 what cost us 28 cents to purchase now costs us $1.00 in 2008.

Movies: "Star Wars," "Annie Hall," "Close Encounters of the Third Kind," "The Turning Point," "The Goodbye Girl," "Julia," "Saturday Night Fever," "Looking for Mr. Goodbar."

Broadway: "Side By Side By Sondheim," review. "Beatlemania," concert. "I Love My Wife."

TV: "CHiPs," "Three's Company," "Black Sheep Squadron," "The 700 Club," "Eight is Enough," "James at 15," "The New Mickey Mouse Club," "What's New, Mr. Magoo?" "The Love Boat," "Eight is Enough," "Tabitha," "Lou Grant," "Shields and Yarnell," "The Man From Atlantis." "Roots" draws 130 million viewers over 8 nights.

Music: "Saturday Night Fever," Bee Gees. "Star Wars," John Williams. Barbra Streisand, "Evergreen" the love theme from "A Star Is Born" & "My Heart Belongs to Me." Elvis Presley, "Way Down." Donna Summer, "I Feel

Love." Marvin Gaye, "Got to Give It Up." Julie Covington, "Don't Cry for Me Argentina." ABBA, "Knowing Me, Knowing You." Mary MacGregor, "Torn Between Two Lovers." Kenny Rogers, "Lucille." Barry Manilow, "Looks Like We Made It." The Eagles, "Hotel California." Linda Ronstadt, "Blue Bayou." Sex Pistols, "God Save the Queen." Thin Lizzy, "Dancing in the Moonlight." The Emotions, "Best Of My Love." Rod Stewart, "I Don't Want to Talk About It, The First Cut Is the Deepest." David Soul, "Don't Give Up On Us." The Manhattan Transfer, "Chanson D'Amour." Shaun Cassidy, "Da Do Ron Ron." Johnny Mathis, "When A Child Is Born." Hall & Oates, "Rich Girl." Ted Nugent, "Cat Scratch Fever." Kiss, "Christine Sixteen." AC/DC, "Dirty Deeds Done Dirt Cheap." Eric Clapton, "Lay Down Sally." Carly Simon, "Nobody Does It Better." Ian Dury, "Sex & Drugs & Rock & Roll." Queen, "Tie Your Mother Down." Cheap Trick, "I Want You to Want Me." Leo Sayer, "You Make Me Feel Like Dancing." Wings, "Mull of Kintyre." Andy Gibb, "I Just Want To Be Your Everything." Fleetwood Mac, "Dreams." Supertramp, "Give a Little Bit." The Jacksons, "Show You The Way To Go." Crystal Gayle, "Don't It Make My Brown Eyes Blue." Talking Heads, "Psycho Killer." Debby Boone, "You Light Up My Life." Stevie Wonder, "Sir Duke." Glen Campbell, "Southern Nights." Manfred Mann's Earth Band, "Blinded by the Light." The Carpenters, "All You Get from Love Is a Love Song." The Tubes, "White Punks on Dope." Rita Coolidge, "Your Love Has Lifted Me, Higher and Higher." Elvis Costello, "Alison."

Deaths: Elvis Presley, Tom Pryce, Jansen Van Vuuren.

President: James Earl Carter, Jr. (D) Southern Baptist; vetoes 31/ 2 overrides

Vice President: Walter F. Mondale (D) Methodist; Presbyterian

House: D-292 ; R-143

Senate: 95th Congress (1977-1979) Majority Party: Democrat (61 seats) Minority Party: Republican (38 seats) Other Parties: 1 Independent Total Seats: 100

Federal Debt: $698.84 billion or 34 % of the GDP

Consumer Price Index CPI-U (1982 Base of 100): 60.60

GDP: $2,030.9 billion	**Inflation Rate:** 6.50%

Dow Jones: 952.0 (January)/ 806.91 (11-01)

S&P Price Index: 95.10/-11.50%

Prime Rate: 6.50% (03-13)/ 7.75% (10-24)	**Average Home Mortgage Rate:** 8.67/8.96%
1 oz Gold: $148.31	**1oz of Silver:** $5.40

Federal Debt: $698,840,000,000

Federal Deficit: $53.7 billion dollars

Defense Spending: $121.62 billion	**Interest Spending:** $29.90 billion
Health Care Spending: $36.65 billion	**Pensions Spending:** $93.85 billion
Welfare Spending: $39.77 billion	**Education Spending:** $22.18 billion
Transportation Spending: $14.83 billion	**Misc. Other Spending:** $33.68 billion
Protection Spending: $3.70 billion	**Total Government Spending:** $409.22 billion

% of GDP that goes towards just the interest payment: 1.51%

$1.00 = 1.730 Yuan, China NPC	**$1.00 =** 267.80 Yen, Japan
$1.00 = 3.530 Saudi Arabia Riyal.	**$1.00 =** 70.480 Iranian Rial
U.S. Population: 220,289,000	**World Population:** 4,232,928,595
U.S. Birth Rate: 3,326,632	**U.S. Abortions:** 1,079,430—1,316,700
U.S. Homicide Rate: 9.1/ 100,000 population	**U.S. Violent Crime:** 475.9/ 100,000 population

Annual Average Domestic Crude Oil Prices:
$14.40 / barrel, $51.02 (2007 adjusted)

1977

Oil:

1977 – The Trans Alaskan pipeline opens.

1977 – President Carter gives a televised speech declaring that the energy crisis is the **"moral equivalent of war."**

1977 – Brazil announces the discovery of a huge offshore oil field that could contain between 5 to 8 billion barrels of oil, enough to expand the country's proven reserves by 40 to 50 percent.

1970-1977 – Peak Oil issues have been of secret concern to policy makers in the U.S. for a long time. Oil production in the U.S. peaked in 1970. This was arguably the most important economic event of the past half-century. Up until 1970 **America** was the world's foremost **oil producer** and for much of the twentieth century it was also the world's foremost **oil exporter. American oil won both World Wars** for the Allies and made the U.S. the world's richest and most powerful nation. Throughout most of this same period the **USSR** remained the world's second foremost oil-producing nation. The American oil peak signaled the end of an era and from this point on, the U.S. becomes increasingly dependent on imports. The Arab OPEC oil embargo of 1973, which sent the U.S. economy into a tailspin, brings this imbalance into the public focus. CIA analysts in 1977 understood the importance of oil and believed that a peak of petroleum production in the USSR would have similar or even graver consequences for that nation.

1977 – The United Arab Emirates University, the country's first university, opens in al-Ain. By 1998, 15,000 students will attend UAE University. **The Higher Colleges of Technology,** today with 10 campuses, opened in 1988, and provided an additional 10,000 students with advanced technical training. These universities, like other development projects, are funded by oil money.

1977 – The formation of the People's Republic of Angola of which Cabinda is a province, resulted in a hiatus in drilling operations until the concession is renegotiated in 1977. The Cabinda Gulf Oil Company (**CABGOC**) became the operator and a 49% partner with the Angolan state-owned oil company **SONANGOL.**

1977 – Libya. New discoveries were drilled in the Ghadamis sedimentary basin (400 kilometers southwest of Tripoli) in 1974 and in the offshore fields **northwest of Tripoli in 1977.**

October 1, 1977 – Department of Energy. In response to changing needs in the mid 1970's, the **Atomic Energy Commission** was abolished and the Energy Reorganization Act of 1974 created two new agencies: the **Nuclear Regulatory Commission** to regulate the nuclear power industry and the **Energy Research and Development Administration** to manage the nuclear weapon, naval reactor, and energy development programs. The Department of Energy Organization Act brought the federal government's agencies and programs into a single agency.

    The Department of Energy, activated on October 1, 1977, assumed the responsibilities of the Federal Energy Administration, the Energy Research and Development Administration, the Federal Power Commission, and parts of several other agencies.

1977 – President Jimmy Carter created for Cuba an **"Exclusive Economic Zone"** extending from the country's western tip to the north, virtually to Key West, Florida. This will allow **the Cuban government to hire the Chinese to drill** for oil 45 miles off the shores of Florida in 2006. At the same time Chevron announces the discovery of the giant Jack Field estimated to hold as much as 15 billion barrels of oil, in the Gulf of Mexico. This is enough to increase the U.S. proven reserves by 50%.

    Environmentalists in the U.S. have largely blocked offshore ultra-deep oil exploration in the U.S while the Chinese are allowed to drill for the Cubans 45 miles offshore.

Major News:

January 17, 1977 – Convicted murderer **Gary Gilmore** is executed by a Utah firing squad. This is the first instance of capital punishment in the U.S. since 1967. Gilmore gained international notoriety for demanding that his death sentence be fulfilled following two murders he committed in Utah.

February2, 1977 – A Natural gas shortage, caused by severe winter weather, leads Congress to approve an emergency federal allocation program.

1977 – Jimmy 'the Weasel' Fratianno becomes the highest level **Mafia** informer to date. The weasel believes there is a contract on his life and makes a deal with Federal prosecutors. As a known mob hit man and one time acting head of the Los Angeles Cosa Nostra he has a lot to sing about. He becomes the Justice Departments star witness for ten years and fingers notorious mob bosses Frank "Funzi" Tieri, Carmine "Junior" Persico, and the head of his own former crime family, the late Dominic Brooklier. As a paid informant Fratianno is sheltered by the federal witness protection program, which provides him with bodyguards, financial support and a series of phony identities. This will all come to an end in 1987 when the Feds release the weasel back into the wild.

January 21, 1977 – President Jimmy Carter pardons the majority of **Vietnam War draft evaders,** ten thousand in number.

March 1977 – Twelve African-American Muslim gunmen, take over three buildings in **Washington, DC** where they take 149 hostages and kill a radio journalist and a police officer. The hostage situation ends two days later.

July 13, 1977 – The New York City blackout results in massive looting and disorderly conduct during its twenty-five hour duration. There was also a large increase in New York's birthrate nine months after the blackout.

1977 – Son of Sam. The 44 Caliber Killer. David Berkowitz is a **serial killer** His crimes became legendary because of the bizarre content in the letters that he writes to the police and the media explaining his reasons for committing the attacks. With the police feeling the pressure to catch the killer, "Operation Omega" begins with over **two hundred detectives** working on finding the **Son of Sam** before he kills again.
  July 29, 1976, Donna Lauria (18) and Jody Valenti (19) are both shot as they sit

inside a car parked on the street outside Lauria's apartment in the Bronx. October 23, 1976, a couple are shot as they sit in a car in Queens. November 26, 1976, Donna DeMasi (16) and Joanne Lomino (18) are walking home from a movie theater in Queens when both are shot. January 30, 1977, 26-year-old Christine Freund and her fiancé John Diel are shot as they sit in a parked car. April 17, 1977, 18-year-old Valentina Suriani and her 20-year-old boyfriend Alexander Esau, are both shot. The killer leaves a letter at the scene, signed **"Son of Sam."** June 26, 1977, Judy Placido and Sal Lupu are shot while leaving a disco. July 31, 1977, Bobby Violante and Stacy Moskowitz are shot as they sit in a car parked at a lover's lane. Residents of New York are terrified.

A parking ticket for a yellow Ford Galaxie, which had been parked too close to a fire hydrant, leads to **Berkowitz** being arrested. His first words upon arrest were reported to be, **"You got me. What took you so long?"**

Berkowitz confessed to killing six people and wounding several others in New York City in the late 1970s. He stated that his obsession with the occult played a major role in the Son of Sam murders.

September 21, 1977 – Fifteen nations, including the **United States** and the **Soviet Union**, sign a **nuclear-proliferation pact**, slowing the spread of nuclear weapons around the world.

December 7, 1977 – **The FBI** releases 40,000 pages of previously secret files relating to the **assassination of President John F. Kennedy.**

Civil Rights Movement:

1977 – **The Seattle School Board** adopts a plan designed to eliminate racial imbalance in schools by fall 1979.

1976-1977 – **When Georgian Jimmy Carter** was elected President in 1976, he appointed more blacks to influential positions in the federal government than any President before him, and he seemed to have a deep personal commitment to racial equality. However, the economic situation deteriorated under his presidency. The **Congressional Black Caucus** labeled Carter's federal budget favoring military spending over domestic funding for social relief programs "an unmitigated disaster" for black people.

1977 – Martin Luther King, Jr. is posthumously awarded the **Presidential Medal of Freedom.**

1977 – About 300 disabled demonstrators paraded outside the **Department of Health, Education and Welfare** headquarters and crowded into the secretaries outer office Tuesday to demand enforcement of **civil-rights** laws for the handicapped.

Women's Movement:

1977 – New First Lady Rosalynn Smith Carter takes an active role in government, heading policy proposals and sitting in on cabinet meetings, as more women serve in White House staff positions and in the U.S. Cabinet than ever before.

1977 – The First National Women's Conference is held in Houston, Texas. **Twenty-thousand representatives,** women from all states, gather to pass a far-reaching National Plan of Action.

1977 – The National Association of **Cuban-American Women** is formed.

1977 – The National **Coalition Against Domestic Violence** is established.

1977 – Eleanor Smeal, President of **NOW,** demands that homemakers should have their own Social Security accounts.

1977 – The American Civil Liberties Union asks the **Rhode Island Supreme Court to allow women to use their own names,** rather than that of their husbands.

January 1977 – Patricia Harris is appointed by President Jimmy Carter to head the Department of Housing and Urban Development. She becomes the first African American woman to hold a cabinet position.

1977 – **The first women pilots** of the United States Air Force graduate.

Popular Culture:

1977 – **Vietnam Draft Dodgers. President Jimmy Carter** fulfilled a controversial campaign promise on his first day in the White House by issuing a pardon to those who avoided serving in the **Vietnam Conflict** by fleeing the U.S. or not registering. President Gerald Ford had earlier introduced a conditional amnesty, but Carter, hoping to heal the "war's" wounds, made no conditions. He did, however, exclude many groups of individuals from the pardon: deserters were not eligible, nor were soldiers who had received less-than-honorable discharges. Also not included were the civilians who had protested the war. Close to 10,000 people are pardoned.

February 1977 – First published in February, *Gambling Times* becomes America's first gambling magazine.

1977 – **After winning the post** of supervisor for the City of **San Francisco, Harvey Milk** becomes the nation's first openly gay elected official. Two years later he became a martyr when he was shot to death by a fellow city supervisor.

1977 – **Atari. Video Computer System game console.** Atari introduces a programmable home video game system in a cartridge.

1977 – **Andre Blay** begins **renting videotapes. Magnetic Video,** operating as **Video Club of America,** is the first company to provide theatrical motion pictures on home video.

Company founder Andre Blay convinced **Twentieth Century-Fox** to license 50 titles for sale directly to consumers. The cost of the license was $7.50 for each video sold, and Blay had to pay a $300,000 advance. Video Club of America marketed itself through a two-page ad in the November 26-December 2, 1977 edition of TV Guide and included both the Betamax and VHS formats of "Butch Cassidy And The Sundance Kid," "Hello, Dolly!," "M*A*S*H," "Patton," "The French Connection," "The King And I," and "The Sound Of Music." **Membership in the club is $10.00** and the price of the videos s $49.95 each. They are for home use only and thirteen thousand people respond to the ad. **Blay recoups his initial $300,000 investment in just two months.**

October 1977 – RCA begins selling the first **VCR** in the U.S. based on JVC's "vertical helical scan" (VHS) system. Manufactured by Matsushita and branded as "SelectaVision," the VBT200 retails for **$1,000.**

1977 – Polaroid, "It's so simple." Doyle Dane Bernbach.

Business / Technology:

1977 – Nintendo begins to sell computer games.

1977 – Magnetic resonance imaging, MRI, is invented by American scientist Raymond V. Damadian.

1977 – In Chicago, **AT&T** transmits telephone calls by **fiber optics.**

1977 – MCI ends the AT&T exclusivity for long distance phone service.

August 4, 1977 – The cabinet level **Energy Department** is created by Jimmy Carter.

October 1977 – The Atari 2600 is released and becomes one of the most influential video game machines. It ships with a "joystick," at a retail price of $249.
    Specs: **Media Type:** cartridges, cassettes via SuperCharger. **Processor:** 6507 (8-bit). **Processor Speed:** 1.19 MHz. **Screen RAM:** 128 bytes. **Screen Resolution:** 192 x 160. **Color Palette:** 16 colors, 4 max on-screen. **Sound:** 2 sound channels.

1977 – The Apple II microcomputer becomes an instant success when it is released and the included floppy disk drive leads to the writing of many software programs.

1977 – TRS-80. In the first month after its release, **Tandy Radio Shack's** first desktop computer, the TRS-80, sells 10,000 units its first month.

December 1977 – George Atkinson launches the first video rental store, a 600-square foot storefront on Wilshire Boulevard in Los Angeles. Atkinson was the proprietor of **Home Theater Systems**, a company that **rented Super 8 movies and projectors** for parties. He bought one Betamax and one VHS copy of each of the Magnetic Video titles through a third-party for $3.00 over cost. Atkinson announced the availability of the Fox titles for rent in a one-column-inch ad in the December 7, 1977 Los Angeles Times. He had previously advertised **"Video for Rent,"** although he didn't have any videos.

In order to raise capital, Atkinson charges $50 for an "annual membership," $100 for a "lifetime membership," which provides the opportunity to rent the videos for $10 a day. He is threatened with a lawsuit for renting the videos, but quickly discovers U.S. copyright law gives him the right to rent and resell videos he owns. There is a question whether Atkinson was actually the first person to open a video rental store. Some believe that Arthur Morowitz, who started renting videos from a storefront in New York's Times Square around the same time that Atkinson began renting videos, was the first.

Finance:

February 14, 1977 – The Annual Assay Commission is abolished. The Commission was created in **1792** to ensure that coins produced by the **Bureau of the Mint** contained the required equivalent value of gold and silver.

May 27, 1977 – **The Internal Revenue Service** begins a program to expedite resolution of problems taxpayers had with IRS after filing tax returns.

1977 –U.S. **Treasury gold sales** are temporarily suspended.

1977 – **Again this year the Gold in Fort Knox** is required to be audited. By 2009 a full independent audit of the Gold held at Fort Knox is still being requested. "It has been several decades since the gold in Fort Knox was independently audited or properly accounted for," said Ron Paul, the Texas Congressman and former Republican Presidential candidate, in an e-mail interview with *The Times.* "The American people deserve to know the truth."

1977

1977 – Apple Computer. Armas Clifford "Mike" Markkula Jr. is the American entrepreneur, angel investor, who provided early critical funding for Apple. He was introduced to Steve Jobs and Steve Wozniak when they were looking for funding to manufacture the Apple II personal computer, after having successfully sold some units of the first version of this computer, the Apple I. Markkula brought his business expertise along with $250,000. In the right place at the right time with more than enough money and expertise to bring it all together and make it happen. With this funding and his guidance, Apple ceased to be a partnership and was incorporated as a company.

Books:

1977 – Marilyn French, "The Women's Room."

1977 – "Song of Solomon," Toni Morrison.

TV:

1977 – National "Turn the TV Off Week" is a failure, viewers want their shows.

1977 – Thirty-seven million viewers tune in to see **Alex Haley's, "Roots VIII"** (finale). **Kunta Kinte** is taken into slavery in West Africa and his and his descendant's subsequent lives under American slavery.

1977 – "David Frost / Richard Nixon" interviews air in four 90 minute segments. Nixon received $600,000 and thought he could outperform Frost and redeem his image. Most of the viewers came away with the conviction he was a crook.

Sports:

August 17, 1978 – The first balloon, Double Eagle II, to cross the Atlantic Ocean comes to rest in Miserey, France, after one hundred and thirty-seven hours of flight from Presque Isle, Maine.

1977 – **Seattle Slew** wins the Triple Crown of Thoroughbred Racing, only the 10th horse to accomplish the feat.

Music:

1977 – **Disco music** becomes the rage. The film **"Saturday Night Fever,"** promoted disco-music beyond gays and blacks and launched disco fever around the world.

January 12, 1977 – Rolling Stones guitarist Keith Richards is fined 750 pounds for possession of cocaine which was found in his wrecked car on May 19, 1976. Richards was charged an additional 250 pounds for court costs and found "not guilty" of possession of LSD.

January 26, 1977 – Patti Smith falls off the stage while opening for **Bob Seger** in Tampa, Florida. Smith is rushed to the hospital for 22 stitches to close head lacerations. While recovering, Smith writes her fifth book of poetry, *Babel.*

1977 – **Fleetwood Mac**'s original lead guitarist, Peter Green, is committed to a mental hospital in England after firing a pistol at a delivery boy bringing him a royalty check.

1977 – **Alice Cooper** enters rehab for his alcoholism, after ten years of heavy drinking.

August 16, 1977 – Elvis Presley, age 42, the undisputed **King of Rock and Roll,** is found dead at his home **Graceland** in Memphis, Tennessee. He rose from humble circumstances to launch the rock and roll revolution with his commanding voice and charismatic stage presence. Elvis began his career in 1953 as one of the first performers of rockabilly, an up-tempo fusion of country and rhythm & blues with a strong back beat. His novel versions of existing songs, mixing "black" and "white" sounds, made him popular, and controversial, as did his uninhibited stage and television performances. Presley had a versatile voice and had unusually wide success encompassing many genres, including rock and roll, gospel, blues, country, ballads and pop. In the words of the historical marker that stands outside the house where he was born: **"Presley's career as a singer and entertainer redefined popular music."**

1977

August 17, 1977 – Florists Transworld Delivery (FTD) reported that in one day the number of orders for flowers to be delivered to Graceland for the funeral of Elvis Presley had surpassed the number for any other event in the company's history.

Natural Disasters:

January 28-29, 1977 – Blizzard of 1977, Buffalo, N.Y. The Blizzard of 1977 dumps about 7 inches of new snow on top of the 30-35 inches already on the ground. With winds gusting to 70 mph, drifts are as high as 30 feet. The death toll reaches 29 and seven western N.Y. counties are declared national disaster areas.

July 25, 31, 1977 – Typhoon, Thelma. A tropical disturbance east of the **Philippines** organized into a tropical depression on July 21 and then moved to the northwest. It grew into a tropical storm and then into a typhoon on the 22nd. Thelma passed northern Luzon and turned to the north, where it reached a peak intensity of 95 mph winds. The typhoon hit southern **Taiwan** on the 25th, crossed the island, and dissipated over southeastern **China** on the 26th. Though not a particularly strong storm, Thelma brought strong wind gusts and heavy rain, claiming more than 30 lives and bringing damage and destruction not seen to the island for over 80 years.

November 19, 1977 – Cyclone. Andhra Pradesh, India. A cyclone and tidal wave kills 20,000 people.

March 4, 1977 – Earthquake. Bucharest, Romania. A 7.5 magnitude earthquake that lasts 5 minutes devastates the Capitol and is responsible for over 1,500 people's deaths. More than 11,000 people are injured and 35,000 buildings are damaged.

1977 – AIDS. An estimated 26 million people received transfusions between 1977 and 1985, years when the **AIDS** epidemic exploded.

Man vs. Man / Wars:

Assassinated – Congo. Marien Ngouabi, President of Congo (Brazzaville). On March 16, 1977, President Ngouabi is assassinated. An 11-member Military

Committee of the Party (CMP) is named to head an interim government with Colonel Joachim Yhombi-Opango to serve as President of the Republic.

Assassinated – Germany. Siegfried Buback, **German Attorney General.**

Assassinated – Germany. Jurgen Ponto, **CEO Dresdner Bank.**

Assassinated – Germany. Hanns-Martin Schleyer, **President of the German Employers' Organization.**

Assassinated – Lebanon. While he is in the area of the Shouf Mountains **Kamal Jumblat** and his bodyguard are both shot and killed by four gunmen.

Lebanese politician, Kamal Jumblat the strongest Druze leader in Lebanon for years, had many supporters among the **Sunni Muslims** and was known as one of few politicians that opposed the Syrian influence over Lebanon. On March 16, 1977, Kamal Jumblat is assassinated by the pro-Syrian faction of the Lebanese Syrian Socialist Party, possibly in collaboration with Syrian secret service agents (Mukhabarat).

Assassinated – North Yemen. Ibrahim al-Hamadi, President of North Yemen is assassinated and Colonel Ahmed ibn Hussein al-Ghashmi, another member of the Military Command Council which Hamadi had set up, takes over. In 1978 Ghashmi is killed when a bomb explodes in a suitcase carried by an envoy from South Yemen.

1977 – Representative Richard T. Hanna (D-California) is **indicted** for conspiracy to defraud the government based on his dealings with Korean rice broker **Tongsun Park.** Hanna received more than $200,000 in bribes for his services. Hanna pleads guilty and is **sentenced** to 6 to 30 months in prison.

1977 – Representative Edward A. Garmatz (D-Maryland) is **indicted** for bribery and conspiracy following a two-year probe of corruption in the shipping industry. The indictment alleged that Garmatz had accepted up to $15,000 in 1972 from shipping companies for facilitating legislation beneficial to them while he chaired the Committee on **Merchant Marine and Fisheries**. Prosecutors dropped the case when it learned that a key witness had committed perjury and forgery. The federal courthouse in Baltimore was named for Garmatz.

1977 – Representative Richard A. Tonry (D-Louisiana) is **indicted** for receiving illegal campaign contributions, promising Federal patronage to contributors, obstructing justice, and conspiracy. He pleads guilty July 1, 1977 and is jailed for 6 months.

January 1, 1977 – F.E. Melov the U.S. ambassador to Lebanon, and **Robert O.Waring, the U.S. economic counselor,** are kidnapped and later killed in Beirut.

October 13, 1977 – Palestinian terrorists hijack Flight 181, a **Lufthansa Boeing 737** and order it to fly to a number of Middle East destinations over a period of four days. The terrorists kill the plane's pilot and the aircraft is stormed by German GSG9 counter-terrorist troops, assisted by two British Army Special Air Service soldiers, at the airport in **Mogadishu, Somalia.** All ninety hostages are rescued and three terrorists are killed.

1975-1977 – Federal Islamic Republic of the Comoros. The first Comorian government took power on July 6, 1975 led by Ahmed 'Abdallah. It unilaterally **declared independence from France and was overthrown within a month** on August 3, 1975 with the aid of foreign white mercenaries.

Prince Said Mohammed Jaffar created a National Executive Council that favored a more conciliatory policy toward Mayotte and France. In January 1976 a military coup replaced Jaffar with 'Ali Soilih. **Four unsuccessful coup attempts were launched** during Soilih's rule. Then on May 13, 1978, Soilih was overthrown and killed by mercenaries led by **Bob Denard**, whose previous exploits in **Zaire** and elsewhere made him infamous throughout Africa. Denard remained the true power and reinstalled the nation's first President, Ahmad 'Abdallah, who had been living in exile in Paris. Their government was close to right-wing elements in **France** and to South Africa, where the Comoros served as a conduit for supplies to the Renamo rebels in **Mozambique.** Soon after the coup, France agreed to restore economic and military aid, which had been suspended during the Soilih regime. Most African countries are not happy with the precedent set by the mercenaries removing the Soilih government and the Comoros are expelled from the OAU (Organization of African Unity).

1977 – The Ogaden War. Ethiopia vs. Somalia. The Ogaden war is one of the bloodiest wars ever fought in East Africa. This war starts on July 23, 1977 when **Somalia** invades **the Ogaden province of Ethiopia.** The Somalians quickly capture most of the Ogaden province but are defeated and thrown back to Somalia by a massive Soviet airlift of men, thousands of Cuban mechanized troops and large numbers of Soviet aircraft. The war showed Soviet airlift and power projection capabilities and Somalia never recovered militarily which led to the collapse of Somalia in the 1990s. The number of people killed is estimated at 15,000 civilians and 21,000 military from 1972-1980. On December 12, 1994 a major American newspaper reported 1,500,000 people had died from war, drought and forced resettlement.

February 1977 – Iraq. This marks the beginning of mass deportations **to Iran** of **Iraqi Shi'a.** The property of the Iraqi Shi'a is confiscated and their sons **"disappear."** It has been estimated that by early 1980, **200,000 Iraqis were deported** to Iran and stripped of nationality and property. Exact figures for how many "disappeared" and were killed is difficult to estimate.

1973-1977 – Pakistan. Zulfikar Ali Bhutto, the President of Pakistan continued his populist and socialist rhetoric, while the economy stagnated, largely as a result of the dislocation and uncertainty produced by Bhutto's frequently changing economic policies. **President Bhutto** proclaimed his own victory in the March 1977 national elections. The opposition screamed Fraud! And Bhutto responded by arresting the opposition leadership.

With increasing anti-government unrest, the army grew restive and on July 5, 1977, arrested Bhutto and declared martial law. Chief of Army Staff Gen. Muhammad Zia ul-Haq became Chief Martial Law Administrator and promised to hold new elections within 3 months. Zia postponed the elections when it became clear that Bhutto was still a formidable opponent and had him arrested and sentenced to death. Despite international appeals on his behalf, Bhutto was hanged on April 6, 1979. Zia assumed the Presidency and called for elections in November, but still afraid of losing, he banned all political activity. Upwards of 9,000 people died during the conflicts of 1973-1977.

1977 – Romania. Coal Miners Strike. A prolonged strike by coal miners in the Jiu Valley reaches a climax when the miners take the **Prime Minister captive** and hold him for two days in a mine shaft. On August 1, 1977, 35,000 Jiu miners gathered in the main yard of the Lupeni mine. They were protesting against a new decree which raised the age of retirement from 50 to 55 and reduced the miners' pensions.

"The 1977 strike was one of the most important protest movements against the communist regime, an explosion of discontent that had accumulated over many years", explained Volodea Macovei, spokesman for the miners' union, on the 20th anniversary of the strike. In his opinion the miners' anger had been provoked by the "deterioration of their standard of living, but more especially the political situation in the country which had become intolerable." **President Nicolae Ceausescu** came in person to negotiate, as the miners had demanded, and agreed to all their demands. Then as soon as the miners went back to work he ordered immediate reprisals.

March 8, 1977 – Zaire vs. Angola. Shaba I is a conflict between the neighboring states of **Zaire** and **Angola** and is a consequence of Zaire's support for the FNLA and UNITA factions in the **Angolan Civil War.** The conflict began on March 8, 1977 when about 2,000 members of the Front for the National Liberation of the Congo (FLNC), invaded Shaba province in southwestern Zaire, with the support of Angola's MPLA government and the possible involvement of **Cuban troops**. President Mobutu Sese Seko of Zaire appealed for outside support on April 2. The war ended when 1,500 Moroccan troops, airlifted into Zaire on April 10 by the French government, beat back the FNLC. The attack led to government reprisals, which led to the mass exodus of refugees as well as further political and economic instability within Zaire itself. The FLNC carried out a second invasion, **Shaba II,** the following year. **The UN European peace keepers were defeated and 50,000 soldiers and civilians were killed in the conflict.**

1978

The Oldest Boomer is 32 years old.

Cost of the Average House: $62,500	
Median Family Income: $15,060	**Minimum Wage:** $2.65/ hr **Average Hourly Wage:** $6.17
Tide Laundry Soap: $1.99 / 3lb	**Gallon Gasoline:** 67 cents
New Car: **Chevrolet Chevette:** $3,644 **Chevrolet Camaro Z28:** $6,326 **Dodge Magnum XE:** $5,509	**Hershey Bar:** 25 cents 1.2oz **Bing Cherries:** 69 cents/ lb **Apples:** 29 cents/ lb **Pocket Radio:** $2.99-$5.99
Unemployment Rate: 6.4%-5.9%-6.0%	**First-class Stamp:** 15 cents

30 cents buying power in 1978 = **$1.00 in 2008.**
In 1978 what cost us 30 cents to purchase now costs us $1.00 in 2008.

Movies: "The Deer Hunter," "Coming Home," "Heaven Can Wait," "Midnight Express," "An Unmarried Woman," "Superman," "The Wiz," "Sgt. Pepper's Lonely Hearts Club Band."

Broadway: "I'm Getting My Act Together." "Evita," London. "Timbuktu," "On The 20th Century," "Best Little Whorehouse In Texas."

TV: "Taxi," "WKRP in Cincinnati," "Diff'rent Strokes," "Incredible Hulk," "The Paper Chase," "Fantasy Island," "Mork & Mindy" with Robin Williams as Mork. 120 million watch the "Holocaust" drama on TV. "Dallas," The Blues Brothers make their first appearance on "Saturday Night Live."

Music: "Grease." "The Last Waltz," The Band. Nick Gilder, "Hot Child In The City." Player, "Baby Come Back." Rolling Stones, "Miss You." Barry Manilow, "Can't Smile Without You" & "Copacabana, At The Copa." Earth Wind and Fire, "Got To Get You Into My Life." Chaka Khan, "I'm Every Woman." Billy Joel, "Just The Way You Are." The Carpenters, "Sweet,

Sweet Smile." Crystal Gayle, "Talking In Your Sleep." Electric Light Orchestra, "Mr. Blue Sky." Black Sabbath, "Never Say Die." Eric Clapton, "Promises." Andy Gibb, "Love Is Thicker Than Water." Rod Stewart, "Do Ya Think I'm Sexy?" Dionne Warwick, "Déjà vu." Alice Cooper, "How You Gonna See Me Now." Waylon Jennings & Willie Nelson, "Mamas Don't Let Your Babies Grow Up to Be Cowboys." Bruce Springsteen, "Prove It All Night." Talking Heads, "Psycho Killer." Jefferson Starship, "Runaway." Van Halen, "Ain't Talkin' 'Bout Love" & "Runnin' With The Devil." Dolly Parton, "Here You Come Again." Meat Loaf, "Paradise By The Dashboard Light" & "Two Out Of Three Ain't Bad." Bee Gees, "Stayin' Alive" & "Night Fever." Barbra Streisand & Neil Diamond, "You Don't Bring Me Flowers." Johnny Mathis & Deniece Willams, "Too Much, Too Little, Too Late." ABBA, "Take A Chance On Me." Blondie, "Denis" & "Hanging On The Telephone." Kenny Rogers, "The Gambler." Elvis Costello and the Attractions, "I Don't Wanna Go To Chelsea." Bob Marley and the Wailers- "Is This Love?" Commodores, "Three Times A Lady." Boney M, "Rivers Of Babylon." Donna Summer, "MacArthur Park." John Travolta & Olivia Newton-John, "You're the One That I Want" & "Summer Nights." The Village People, "YMCA." Steve Martin, "King Tut."

Deaths: Georgi Markov, Janet Parker, Margaret Bowman, Janet Levy.

President: James Earl Carter, Jr. (D) Southern Baptist; vetoes 31/ 2 overrides

Vice President: Walter F. Mondale (D) Methodist; Presbyterian

House: D-292 ; R-143

Senate: 95th Congress (1977-1979) Majority Party: Democrat (61 seats) Minority Party: Republican (38 seats) Other Parties: 1 Independent Total Seats: 100

Federal Debt: $771.54 billion or 34 % of the GDP

Consumer Price Index CPI-U (1982 Base of 100): 65.20

GDP: $2,294.7 billion	**Inflation Rate:** 7.62%
Dow Jones: 879,33 (09-01)/ 743.33 (03-01)	**S&P Price Index:** 96.11/1.06%

Prime Rate: 8.00% (01-10)/ 11.75% (12-26)	**Average Home Mortgage Rate:** 9.02/10.35%
1 oz Gold: $193.55	**1oz of Silver:** $10.40
Federal Debt: $771,544,000,000	
Federal Deficit: $59.2 billion dollars	
Defense Spending: $130.94 billion	**Interest Spending:** $35.46 billion
Health Care Spending: $41.29 billion	**Pensions Spending:** $103.62 billion
Welfare Spending: $38.29 billion	**Education Spending:** $27.87 billion
Transportation Spending: $15.52 billion	**Misc. Other Spending:** $49.59 billion
Protection Spending: $3.92 billion	**Total Government Spending:** $458.75 billion
% of GDP that goes towards just the interest payment: 1.60%	
$1.00 = 1.580 Yuan, China NPC	**$1.00 =** 208.42 Yen, Japan
$1.00 = 3.485/ 3.295 Saudi Arabia Riyal.	**$1.00 =** 70.48 commercial 84.00 noncommercial, Iranian Rial
U.S. Population: 222,629,000	**World Population:** , 4,305,403,287
World AIDS Victims: Known Deaths in the U.S. this year— we are just beginning to even know there is a problem.	
U.S. Birth Rate: 3,333,279	**U.S. Abortions:** 1,157,776—1,409,600
U.S. Homicide Rate: 9.2/ 100,000 population	**U.S. Violent Crime:** 497.8/ 100,000 population
Annual Average Domestic Crude Oil Prices: $14.95 / barrel, $49.27 (2007 adjusted)	

1978

Oil:

1978 – The Energy Tax Act creates an **ethanol tax incentive,** expanding U.S. ethanol use and production. Ethanol production capacity is expanding rapidly and is currently expected to produce 12.9 billion gallons annually by 2009/2010. Corn used for ethanol production is expected to expand from 2.125 billion bushels or 20.0% of the annual corn production in 2006/2007 to 4.3 billion bushels during the 2009/2010 marketing year, or approximately 30.0% of the annual corn production. After milling the alcohol is removed the Steepwater Solubles that remain are reduced to the consistency of molasses and can be mixed with corn bran to produce a corn gluten feed for cattle.

1974 to 1978 – World crude oil prices are relatively flat ranging from $12.21 per barrel to $13.55 per barrel, and are in a period of moderate decline.

1978 – Exxon. "Public attitudes towards Exxon and the industry are quite negative," admitted Exxon's President during the company's 1978 shareholders meeting.

November 1978 – Iran. Oil production is cut from 6 million barrels per day to 1.5 million barrels per day when **37,000 production workers** at Iran's nationalized oil refineries go on strike. Many other foreign workers flee the country as the Shah of Iran's government begins to collapse.

1978 – Northern Yemen. The President of North Yemen and an envoy from South Yemen are killed when a bomb explodes in a briefcase. Ali Abdullah Saleh is the new President and embraces a Western-style market economy for Northern Yemen.

1978 – Southern Yemen. South Yemen President Rubayi Ali is deposed and executed. While Northern Yemen practices a market economy, Southern Yemen's economy is controlled by the state. Ali Abdullah Saleh will rule for two decades before being declared senile and removed from power.

March 16, 1978 – Amoco. The tanker **Amoco Cadiz,** carrying a load of 220,000 tons of crude oil (68.7 million gallons), approaches the western entrance of the English

Channel. The supertanker runs aground three miles off the coast of Brittany, spilling 1.6 million barrels of crude oil. This is the largest crude oil spill to date.

1978 – Sudan. Large amounts of oil are discovered in Bentiu, in southern Sudan. The oil becomes an important factor in the strife between the North and South. Over 2,000,000 people will die as a direct result of this struggle for wealth and power from 1956–2005.

Major News:

April 10, 1978 – Weather Underground Organization. The Attorney General in the new Carter administration, Griffin B. Bell, investigated, and on April 10, a federal grand jury charged Mark Felt **(the FBI's deputy director),** Edward S. Miller **(former FBI chief of domestic intelligence),** and L. Patrick Gray **(acting FBI director from May 1972 to April 1973),** with conspiracy to violate the constitutional rights of American citizens by searching their homes without warrants. **L. Patrick Gray's** case did not go to trial and was dropped by the government for lack of evidence.

The indictment charged Felt and the others did unlawfully, willfully, and knowingly combine, conspire, confederate, and agree together and with each other to injure and oppress citizens of the United States who were relatives and acquaintances of the Weatherman fugitives, in the free exercise and enjoyments of certain rights and privileges secured to them by the Constitution and the laws of the United States of America.

In 1980 Judge William Bryant announced the sentences of Mark Felt and Edward S. Miller, two **former top FBI agents convicted** on November 6, 1979, for their roles in approving illegal break-ins during the Nixon Administration. They were found to have conspired to violate citizens' Fourth Amendment rights to be free from unreasonable searches and seizures and could have been given ten years and $10,000 fines. They were not jailed and Felt was fined $5,000 and Miller $3,500. This ends a five year probe of the abuse of power by many FBI agents. **The FBI broke the law** when they approved **"black-bag jobs** that included illegal search and seizure, breaking and entering, and burglary while trying to gather evidence against the Weathermen. Even though the Weather Underground claimed they were responsible for dozens of Viet Nam-era bombings, the government agents had no right to break the law. Any evidence obtained illegally cannot be used and this allows the former Weathermen to turn themselves in and face minimal charges.

After thirty years of denying his involvement with reporters Bob Woodward and Carl Bernstein, **Mark Felt** revealed himself on May 31, 2005 to be the **Watergate scandal** whistleblower called **"Deep Throat."** The Watergate break-in eventually led to the 1974 resignation of **President Richard Nixon**. "I'm proud of everything that Deep Throat did," Felt, 92, told CNN's **"Larry King Live"** in 2006, his first public interview on the subject.

April 18, 1978 – The Senate votes, 68-32, to turn over the **Panama Canal** to Panama on December 31, 1999. A March 16th vote had given approval to a treaty guaranteeing the area's neutrality after the year 2000.

May 1978 – Unabomber. An unmailed package is found in a car park at the **University of Illinois,** Chicago, and brought to **Northwestern University** in Evanston because of its return address. The professor named on the package does not recall sending it and hands it over to security where it explodes while being opened.

From 1978 to 1995, **Unabomber, Theodore Kaczynski** sent 16 bombs to targets including universities and airlines, killing three people and injuring 23. Kaczynski sent a letter to *The New York Times* on April 24, 1995 and promised "to desist from terrorism" if the *Times* or *The Washington Post* published his manifesto. In his "Industrial Society and Its Future," also called the **"Unabomber Manifesto",** he argued that his bombings were extreme but necessary to attract attention to the erosion of human freedom necessitated by modern technologies requiring large-scale organization.

Kaczynski will be convicted in 1996. While in prison in 1998, according to journalist Stephen J. Dubner, Ted Kaczynski (Unabomber) says Timothy McVeigh (Oklahoma City Bombing) lent him one of the most interesting books he's read lately, **Tainting Evidence: Inside the Scandals at the FBI Crime Lab, by John F. Kelly and Phillip K. Wearne.** "I mean, I knew from my own experience that they were crooked and incompetent," Kaczynski says, shaking his head and laughing. "But according to this book, they're even worse than what I thought."

And the beat goes on . . .

June 6, 1978 – California. Californians approve **Proposition 13,** a constitutional state amendment slashing property taxes.

September 17, 1978 – The Camp David Accords. Egyptian President Anwar al-Sadat and Israeli Prime Minister Menachem Begin reach an accord on "framework for peace," after President Carter-mediated talks at **Camp David.** Anwar Sadat and Menachem Begin share the 1978 **Nobel Peace Prize.**

October 1978 – The California asbestos lawsuits begin. The only known cause of **malignant mesothelioma** is exposure to a carcinogenic mineral group called asbestos. Asbestos was commonly used in a number of industrial and commercial products, from floor tiles to toasters and hair dryers. **Asbestos** is an inexpensive, fire-resistant and flexible insulator and has been in wide use for 100 years.

Once the hazards of asbestos exposure were discovered, steps were taken to regulate its use. Asbestos was one of the first airborne contaminants to be included in the **Clean Air Act of 1970, because** occupational asbestos exposure was all too common. The **National Cancer Institute** estimates that 70 to 80 percent of all malignant mesothelioma cases are the result of occupational asbestos exposure. Mesothelioma lawsuits and subsequent investigations discovered that many asbestos manufacturers were aware of the hazards of exposure prior to regulation but instead of addressing the problem to safeguard employees, **they chose to hide the problem** in order to protect profits. The resulting occupational **health disaster has been labeled the worst in U.S. history.**

1978 – White water. Bill and Hillary Clinton. Arkansas Attorney General Bill Clinton and Hillary Clinton join with James B. and Susan McDougal to borrow $203,000 to buy 220 acres of land in Arkansas' Ozark Mountains. They soon form the **Whitewater Development Corp.,** intending to sell building lots and construct vacation homes. The partnership did poorly and was dissolved in 1992, leaving the Clintons reporting a net loss of more than $40,000. Hillary Clinton also worked as an attorney for a savings and loan company that James McDougal owned. Due in part to a series of fraudulent loans, McDougal's Madison Savings and Loan was one of many S & L's **that went bust at taxpayer expense** in the 1980s. Some Clinton associates clearly broke the law during the Arkansas years. The McDougals were both found guilty of fraud. Bill Clinton's successor as Arkansas Governor, Jim Guy Tucker, was also convicted and served time in prison for his role in the fraud. Susan McDougal later served time in prison for contempt of court for refusing to answer any questions relating to Whitewater, but was later **granted a pardon by President Bill Clinton.** Bill and Hillary Clinton were never charged.

December 13, 1978 – John Wayne Gacy, Jr. Killer Clown, Serial Killer. Most everyone who met Gacy liked him. He was charming, a good catholic and successful businessman. He operated a construction company, was active in the Jaycees and was a Democratic Party precinct captain. He also spent much of his free time hosting elaborate street parties for his friends and neighbors, serving in community groups and entertaining children as "Pogo the Clown". **John Wayne Gacy** was also a **serial killer.**

During the investigation of a missing 15 year old boy a search warrant for Gacy's house was obtained on December 13, 1978. When police entered the crawl space under Gacy's home they were discouraged by the rancid odor but believed it to be sewage, due in part because the dirt in the crawl space had been sprinkled with lime but appeared to be untouched.

Gacy was convicted and later executed for the rape and murder of 33 boys and young men between 1972 and his arrest in 1978. He drew a detailed map to the locations of 28 shallow graves under his house and garage and admitted to dumping five other victims into the Des Plaines River. He became notorious as the **"Killer Clown"** because of the many block parties he threw for his friends and neighbors, entertaining children in a clown suit and makeup.

1978 – Ted Bundy, Serial Killer. Bundy murdered numerous young women across the United States between 1974 and 1978. He eventually confessed to 30 murders, although the actual total of victims remains unknown. Estimates range from 29 to over 100 with the general estimate being 35. Typically, Bundy would bludgeon his victims and then strangle them to death. Most were also raped.

November 18, 1978 – Peoples Temple, Jonestown. The Peoples Temple Agricultural Project is a community in northwestern Guyana formed by a cult from

California, led by **Jim Jones**. Jim Jones assembled a large following of over 900 members in Indianapolis, Indiana during the 1950's. It was an interracial congregation, structured as an inter-racial mission for the sick, homeless and jobless, which was almost unheard of in Indiana in the late 1970's. When a government investigation began looking into his cures for cancer, heart disease and arthritis, he decided to move the group to Ukiah in Northern California where he preached the imminent end of the world in a nuclear war.

The magazine **New West** raised suspicions of illegal activities within the Temple during the mid 1970's and he moved some of the Temple membership to **Jonestown, Guyana where** they had leased almost 4,000 acres of dense jungle from the government. The Jonestown members established an agricultural cooperative, called the "Peoples Temple Agricultural Project," and farmed part of the land, raising animals for food, and assorted tropical fruits and vegetables.

Jones developed a belief called **Translation** in which he and his followers would all die together, then "Translate" to another planet for a life of bliss. Many people testified later that mass suicides were practiced with the followers pretending to drink poison and then falling to the ground.

Tim Stoen, the Temple attorney and right-hand man to Jones became disillusioned and left to form a group called *Concerned Relatives*. They claimed that Jonestown was being run like a concentration camp, and that people were being held against their will. These concerns motivated **Congressman Leo Ryan** to visit Jonestown in November 1978 for a personal inspection. At first, the visit went well. Later, on November 18, about 16 Temple members decided that they wanted to leave Jonestown with the visitors. This came as quite a blow to both Jones and the rest of the members. While Congressman Ryan and the others were waiting at Port Kiatuma airfield, heavily armed members of the Temple's security guards arrived and started shooting. **Congressman Ryan, three members of the press, and one person from Jonestown who wanted to leave, were killed. Eleven others were wounded.**

Fearing retribution, the project members discussed their options and reached a consensus to commit group suicide. Most of the dead appeared to have committed suicide by drinking a grape drink (perhaps Kool-Aid), laced with cyanide and a number of sedatives, including liquid Valium, Penegram and chloral hydrate. Other victims appear to have been murdered by poison injection. The Guyanese coroner said that hundreds of bodies showed needle marks, indicating foul play. Still other victims were shot. A very few fled into the jungle and survived. Nine hundred and eighteen people died; nine hundred and nine people died at the Jonestown site and nine people died at the airport. This is the largest mass suicide in American history.

Civil Rights Movement:

June 28, 1978 – The Supreme Court case, Regents of the University of California vs. Bakke holds that **affirmative action is acceptable but** strict quotas are not. This is to ensure that providing greater opportunities for minorities would not come at the expense of the rights of the majority. Medical school admission programs that allow for positions based on race are unconstitutional.

1978 – Seattle becomes the largest city in the United States to desegregate its schools without a court order. Nearly one-quarter of the school district's students are bused as part of the "Seattle Plan."

1978 – Louis Farrakhan breaks with the **World Community of al-Islam** and becomes the leader of the revived **Nation of Islam.**

Women's Movement:

1978 – The Oregon vs. Rideout decision leads to many states allowing prosecution for marital and cohabitation **rape.**

1978 – The Pregnancy Discrimination Act bans employment discrimination against pregnant women, stating a woman cannot be fired or denied a job or a promotion because she is or may become pregnant, nor can she be forced to take a pregnancy leave if she is willing and able to work.

1978 – The Equal Rights Amendment deadline arrives with the ERA still three states short of ratification. **Congresswoman Elizabeth Holtzman** leads a successful bill to extend the ERA's deadline to 1982.

1978 – For the first time in the history of the United States, more women than men enter college.

Popular Culture:

1978 – Free Love. Sexual Revolution. In the late seventies and early eighties new won sexual freedoms **are exploited by big business looking to capitalize** on a more open society. **Public pornography and hardcore pornography** usher in a significant loss of power from the values of a morality rooted in Christian traditions. This leads to the rise of permissive societies worldwide. Attitudes that not only accept but also promote sexual freedom to experiment in any way the person feels may be good, also begin to spread all over the world. This attitude is captured in the phrase **Free Love.**

1978 – The pill and the IUD are used by 36.9% of women aged 20-44 in 1978, and by 62.7% in 2000.

1978 – Point and Shoot Camera. From Japan's Konica, the point-and-shoot, autofocus camera changes the way we take pictures.

1978 – Alcohol and Drug Abuse Education and Treatment Amendments. The Department of Education now provides Drug and Highway Safety Prevention and Intervention Programs. The amendments also allow authorities to **seize drug traffickers' assets.**

1978 – The U.S. and Mexican governments find a means to eliminate the source of **raw opium** by spraying poppy fields in Mexico with **Agent Orange**. The eradication plan is termed a success as the amount of **"Mexican Mud"** in the U.S. drug market declines. In response to the decrease in availability of "Mexican Mud," another source of heroin is found in the Golden Crescent area, **Iran, Afghanistan and Pakistan, creating a dramatic upsurge** in the production and trade of illegal heroin.

1978 – Ecstasy. MDMA, starts being widely used as a recreational drug. As part of the amphetamine family it produces entactogenic, psychedelic, and stimulant effects. Iinitially called **"empathy,"** it becomes known as "ecstasy" and goes global.

1978

Despite harsh legal sentencing and widely publicized reports of neurotoxicity and fatalities associated with Ecstasy exposure, the prevalence of its use in the United States is increasing among young adults. It costs as little as 25 to 50 cents to manufacture an Ecstasy tablet but the street value of that same Ecstasy tablet is around $25. At "raves" it's common for "Ravers" to take an additional 1/2 or 1 tablet approximately 6 hours into the party. **Ecstasy** suppresses the need to eat, drink, or sleep, enabling users to endure two to three day parties.

In 2000 the **U.S. Drug Enforcement Agency** estimated that **750,000 tablets** of Ecstasy are used every weekend in New York and New Jersey alone. **Ecstasy culture** has surpassed the LSD-centered psychedelic movement of the 1960s, in both its longevity and number of users.

Business / Technology:

July 25, 1978 – Test Tube Baby. Louise Brown becomes the world's first test tube baby. Since then, more than three million babies have been born through **"In vitro fertilization."**

When Gilbert John Brown left Oldham General Hospital early one evening last week, he had no idea it was to be a special night. He and his wife Lesley, due to give birth in about nine days to the world's first baby conceived outside the human body, had spent a-quiet day together reading the papers and watching television. But shortly thereafter, rumors began to circulate that the baby would arrive soon. Reporters and photographers thronged the entrance to the maternity unit. At 10:45 p.m., John Brown was summoned back to the hospital. Soon after midnight, the announcement came: "Mrs. Brown has been safely delivered by caesarean section of a female child. The child's condition at birth was excellent. All examinations showed her to be quite normal." *TIME* August 7, 1978

1978 – Illinois Coal Miners Strike. The records of the Illinois Department of Mines and Minerals list more than 8,700 miners who died and 90,000 who were injured in Illinois mines between 1882, when statistics first were kept, and 1978. The unprecedented 110-day holdout in 1977-1978 reveals unexpected reservoirs of determination among union members. After **the longest strike in the union's**

history, Illinois miners barely ratified the second contract negotiated on their behalf in Washington. The strike revealed that union coal, although still important, is no longer vital to either the state's or the nation's economies.

1978 – AT&T tests a cell phone system in Chicago.

1978 – Hewlett-Packard begins development of the inkjet printer.

1978 – BBS, Bulletin Board Software lets computers communicate via **phone modems.**

1978 – Japan. Smaller, more fuel efficient automobiles now account for almost half of the U.S. auto market.

1978 – RCA introduces the **Selectavision** video disc.

May 1978 – First tests of cellular telephones. The **Bahrain Telephone Company, Batelco** external link, in May, began operating a commercial cellular telephone system. It probably marks the first time in the world that individuals started using what we think of as traditional, mobile cellular radio. The two cell system had 250 subscribers, 20 channels in the 400 MHz band to operate on, and used all **Matsushita equipment**. **Panasonic** is the name of Matsushita in the United States.

1978 – Intel offers a 16-bit microprocessor.

1978 – PBS goes to satellite for delivery, abandoning telephone lines.

1978 – The University of Phoenix, a for-profit university, is accredited. The **University of Phoenix** is accredited in 1978, and few think that it will amount to much without the benefit of a **Final Four**-bound athletic team or ivy-encrusted heritage. It becomes the nation's largest private university. And unlike its more traditional academic competition, it turns a profit.

1978 – Video Games. Atari's arcade game **Football** introduces video sports. **Space Invaders** one of the most influential video games of all times is released by Taito corp.

Space Invaders was so popular in Japan that it caused a yen shortage and more coins had to be minted.

Finance:

1978 – The U.S. Treasury resumes selling gold and Middle Eastern investors increase their gold purchases.

June 1978 – Iran and Saudi Arabia block efforts of **OPEC price** hawks to fix the price of OPEC oil in a currency more stable than the U.S. dollar. They say the world economy cannot support associated price increases and are accused by hawks of being U.S. agents.

September 1978 – The Shah of Iran puts Iran under military rule. Ayatolla Yahya Noori calls openly for attacks on the Jews. The Islamist struggle against the Shah of Iran includes anti-Semitism and Muslim leader, Ayatolla Yahya Noori is arrested in a crackdown of opposition groups. Anti-Semitism will remain as a focal point to rally the people behind a leader, any leader, until this role is taken over by the Kurds, and then the Shias, and then the Shiites, and then the Iraqi's, and then whoever the "leader" in Iran feels the need to eliminate.

1978 – The U.S. begins deregulating interstate airfares and schedules, enabling **Southwest Airlines** to fly outside of Texas.
     While other discount airlines rush to grow, often destroying themselves in the process, Southwest expands more cautiously, becoming the nation's dominant low-fare carrier by avoiding expensive mistakes. In 2008 Southwest will fly to 67 cities in 34 states, carry 102 million passengers and have a Net Income of $178 million.

1978 – BCCI. A group of foreign investors attempt to buy **First American Bankshares,** the biggest bank in the Washington, D.C., area. This group is fronted by **Kamal Adham,** the longtime **Saudi Intelligence Minister.** In 1981, the Federal Reserve asks the CIA for information about the investors, but the CIA holds back everything they know, including the obvious fact that Kamal Adham was the former

Saudi Intelligence Minister and as a result, the sale goes through in 1982. It turns out that Adham and his group were secretly acting on behalf of **the criminal Bank of Credit and Commerce International (BCCI),** and BCCI takes over the bank.

March 18, 1978 – Burt Lance. In a lawsuit filed March 18, 1978, the Securities and Exchange Commission charged Lance with violations of federal security laws, and **BCCI's** application to purchase Financial General Bankshares was denied. **Agha Hasan Abedi** then formed **Credit and Commerce American Holdings** (CCAH), Netherlands Antilles. On October 19, 1978, CCAH filed for approval with the Federal Reserve to purchase Financial General. This application was dismissed on February 16, 1979, but a new application was submitted later.

Clark Clifford served Presidents Truman, Kennedy, Johnson and Carter, serving as United States Secretary of Defense for Johnson. Clifford assured the Federal Reserve that BCCI would not control the American bank. Clifford and Altman soon became BCCI's principal American attorneys. The Federal Reserve finally approved the purchase on April 19, 1982, and BCCI renamed the bank **"First American"** three months later. **Clark Clifford** was made chairman and **Robert Altman** President. The head of Bank Supervision at the Federal Reserve when BCCI's purchase was approved was **Jack Ryan,** who later became head of the **Resolution Trust Corporation,** in which role he denied **Rep. James Leach**'s requests for documents related to Madison Guaranty, the **Whitewater** thrift.

Clifford and Altman were accused by prosecutors of lying to U.S. banking regulators so that BCCI could secretly acquire the First American Bank. Ten years later it was disclosed that Clark Clifford made about $6 million in profits from bank stock that he bought with an unsecured loan from BCCI. A New York grand jury handed up indictments, as did the Justice Department. Clifford's assets in New York, where he kept most of his investments, were frozen. **Clifford and his former law partner, Robert Altman, are indicted** in July 1992 on charges of fraud and accepting $40 million in bribes from the foreign-owned BCCI. Both were charged with concealing from federal regulators BCCI's secret ownership of First American Bankshares Inc.

Indictments against Clifford were set aside because of his failing health and he died in 1998 from natural causes at age 91. He was buried at Arlington National Cemetery, in Arlington, Virginia.

1978

December 20. 1978 – New York's Chemical Bank leads the move to raise the **prime interest rate** to a near-record 11.75%.

Books:

1978 – "The Stand," Stephen King.

1978 – Ken Follett, **"Eye of the Needle."**

1978 – "Chesapeake," James A. Michener.

1978 – John Irving, **"The World According to Garp."**

1978 – "War and Remembrance," Herman Wouk.

1978 – Graham Greene, **"The Human Factor."**

TV:

June 6, 1978 – "20/20" a TV news magazine debuts to scathing criticism. The *New York Times* described it as "dizzingly absurd" and the *Washington Post* denounced it as "the trashiest stab at candy cane journalism yet." In his autobiography "Roone: A Memoir," Arledge recalled that probably the most embarrassing part of that initial program was the **Claymation** segments featuring caricatures representing then-President Jimmy Carter singing "Georgia on My Mind" and Walter Cronkite closing the show intoning, "That's the way it was." ABC fires the anchors and producer.

January 15 – The Super Bowl is played, and broadcast, at night for the first time, on CBS. It is the first Super Bowl played inside a domed stadium. Dallas Cowboys defeat the Denver Broncos. 27/ 10

1978 – "Holocaust" won the Emmy for Outstanding Limited Series. The nine hour TV miniseries wins both acclaim and criticism for its portrayal of Nazi Germany during WWII.

Sports:

February 1978 – Muhammad Ali looses the heavyweight title to 1976 Olympics Champion **Leon Spinks.**

September 15, 1978 – Muhammad Ali fights a **rematch** in the New Orleans Louisiana Superdome against **Leon Spinks** for the **WBA version of the Heavyweight title**, winning it for a record third time. After this victory Ali retired on June 27, 1979, but returned in 1980 to face then current champion Larry Holmes in an attempt to win a heavyweight title an unprecedented four times. Angelo Dundee refused to let Ali come out for the 11th round, in what became Ali's only loss by anything other than a decision.

Music:

1978 – The Bee Gees dominate the singles and album charts as **Saturday Night Fever** becomes a cultural phenomenon. At one point, the album was selling 1 million copies per week.

September 1978 – Alice Cooper is released from rehab. He releases the album **"From the Inside,"** which tells of his stay in the rehab centre.

Natural Disasters:

1978 – AIDS. Gay men in the U.S. and Sweden, and heterosexuals in Tanzania and Haiti begin showing signs of what will later be called AIDS.

February 6-8, 1978 – Eastern U.S. "Blizzard of 1978." The blizzard batters the East Coast, particularly the Northeast. Fifty-four people are killed and there is over $1 billion in property damage. Snowfall ranges from 2-4 feet in New England. This came on top of nearly 2 feet of snow already on the ground from an earlier storm.

September 16, 1978 – Earthquake. Tabas, Yazd Province, Iran. A 7.8 magnitude earthquake strikes Tabas. Approximately 26,000 people are killed. The worst damage is to the town Tabas, a city of 30,000 people, located in central Iran. Tabas is completely flattened and forty villages within a 30 mile radius are damaged. Nine thousand people out of the thirteen thousand population are killed, leaving only 4,000 people living in the town.

October 27, 1978 – Philippines. Typhoon Rita. Over 400 people are killed. Typhoon Rita came ashore on Luzon and stayed a typhoon the entire time it moved across the Philippines. Rita emerged into the South China Sea as a minimal typhoon and then decayed slowly and dissipated as a depression near the coast of Vietnam.

Man vs. Man / Wars:

Assassinated – Afghanistan. Sardar Mohammed Daoud Khan, the President of Afghanistan is killed in a communist coup on April 28, 1978.

In July 1973 Sardar Daoud Khan overthrew his cousin King Mohammad Zahir, and abolished the monarchy in Afghanistan. He then proclaimed himself the President of the Republic of Afghanistan. Sardar Daoud Khan was a strong supporter of **Pashtunistan,** and worked towards reform and modernization. He encouraged the abandonment of the veil by Afghan women, and their participation in the building of a progressive and modern Afghanistan.

After he is assassinated in 1978 Marxists take power in Kabul.

Assassinated – Comoro Islands. Ali Soilih, President of Comoros is assassinated on May 29, 1978. Soilih emphasized the central role of young people in the revolution to break the hold of traditional values and French influence on Comorian life. He lowered the voting age to fourteen and mobilized Comorian youth into a special revolutionary militia, **Moissy,** which, particularly in the villages, launched violent attacks on conservative elders not unlike the **Red Guards.**

Soilih, described himself as a devout Muslim, and advocated a secular state with limitations on the privileges of the muftis, or Muslim jurists who interpret Islamic law. These reforms are perceived as attacks on Comorian traditions and combine with a deepening economic crisis to erode support for his government. Several attempts were made on Soilih's life, and in a referendum held in October 1977, only 55 percent of the voters support a new constitution proposed by his government. Attacks by Soilih's youth militia, the Moissy, on real and imagined political opponents escalated. Raids on mosques were common and a number of refugees fled to Mahoré.

The eruption of the Kartala volcano in April 1977 and the influx of refugees from Madagascar following a massacre of Comorians make the government's situation even worse. Popular support dwindled to such a level that when a **mercenary force of fifty,** consisting largely of former French paratroopers, landed at Itsandra Beach north of the capital on May 12, 1978 **the regular armed forces offered no resistance.**

The mercenaries were led by French-born **Bob Denard** (an alias for Gilbert Bourgeaud, also known as Said Mustapha M'Hadjou) a veteran of wars of revolution, counterrevolution, and separatism from Indochina to Biafra. Denard had also played a role in the 1975 coup that had enabled Soilih to come to power.

Most Comorians supported the coup and were happy to be free of Soilih's ineffective and repressive regime. The deposed head of state was killed under mysterious circumstances on May 29, 1978. The official explanation was that he had attempted to escape.

Assassinated – British Isles. Georgi Markov,a Bulgarian dissident. London, England. In one of the most **notorious acts of assassination** carried out during the **Cold War,** Bulgarian dissident Georgi Markov is **killed by a** ricin **poison dart** fired from an umbrella. Markov, a **communist defector** working for the *BBC World Service,* left his office at Bush House in London on September 11 and walked across Waterloo Bridge to take the train home. As he waited at the bus stop he felt a sharp jab in his thigh and saw a man picking up an umbrella. He developed a high temperature and died in four days.

An autopsy, conducted with the help of scientists from the UK government's germ warfare centre, established that Markov had been killed by a tiny pellet containing a 0.2 milligram dose of the poison ricin. It is believed that the operation was supported by the technical staff of the **Soviet KGB** and seems to have involved many senior members of the **Bulgarian secret police.**

Assassinated – North Yemen. Ahmad al-Ghashmi, the President of North Yemen and an envoy from South Yemen are killed when a bomb explodes in a briefcase carried by the envoy. Colonel Ali Abdullah Saleh takes over as President of North

Yemen and on August 10, orders the execution of 30 officers on the charge of conspiracy to topple his regime. He will survive several assassination and coup attempts.

In the aftermath of Ghashmi's death, the **South Yemen President Rubayi Ali is deposed and executed.** Two days later the three political parties of South Yemen agree to merge and form a 'Marxist–Leninist vanguard party', the Yemen Socialist Party. Abdul Fattah Ismail becomes its Secretary General. In December 1978 Ismail is appointed head of state but four months later he resigns and goes into exile in the Soviet Union. He is succeeded by Ali Nasser Muhammad and **Civil war breaks out** between North Yemen and South Yemen.

October 24, 1978 – Representative Joshua Eilberg (D- Pennsylvania) is **indicted** for illegally accepting $100,000 in legal fees for helping a Philadelphia hospital receive a $14.5 million grant. Eilberg pleads guilty and is sentenced to five years' probation and fined $10,000. He pleads guilty on February 24, 1979.

May 27, 1978 – Representative Herbert Burke (R-Florida) is **charged** with intoxication, resisting arrest, and influencing a witness. He **pleads guilty** on September 26, 1978.

1978 – Representative Daniel J. Flood (D- Pennsylvania) is **indicted** on three counts of perjury and bribery for taking $60,000 in bribes and using his influence as chairman of an appropriations subcommittee for political favors. His jury trial ends in a mistrial. Flood **pleads guilty** to defrauding the government and receives one year's probation.

September 5, 1978 – Representative Frank M. Clark (D- Pennsylvania) is **indicted** on 13 counts of mail fraud, perjury and income tax evasion following a two-year **FBI investigation.** Clark **pleads guilty** to mail fraud and income tax evasion and is sentenced to two years in prison and fined $11,000.

October 7, 1978 – Representative Charles C. Diggs Jr. (D-Michigan) is **charged** with 35 counts of mail fraud, and perjury. First chairman of the Congressional Black

Caucus, Charles Diggs Jr. is charged in March 1978 with taking kickbacks from staff whose salaries he raised. He is convicted, October 7, on eleven counts of mail fraud and filing false payroll forms. **While awaiting sentencing he is re-elected.** Diggs is sentenced to three years in prison. He resigns from the United States House of Representatives and serves 14 months of a three-year sentence for mail fraud.

Diggs was **the first African-American elected to Congress from Michigan.**

November 27, 1978 – "Twinkie defense." Harvey Milk, one of the first openly gay elected officials in California, and **Mayor George Moscone** are shot to death by **Dan White,** another city supervisor who had recently resigned and wanted his job back.

At White's murder trial, **his attorneys successfully argued** that his judgment had been impaired by a prolonged period of clinical depression, one symptom of which was the former health enthusiast's consumption of junk food. The attorneys' argument, mischaracterized as the claim that junk food had caused White's diminished capacity, was derided as the **"Twinkie defense"** by the satirist Paul Krassner while reporting on the trial for the San Francisco Bay Guardian. Dan White is convicted of voluntary manslaughter and this sparks the **"White Night Riot."** The rioters are responsible for hundreds of thousands of dollars in property damage to City Hall and the surrounding area.

March 11, 1978 – Gail Rubin, the niece of U.S. Senator Ribicoff, is among 38 people shot to death by terrorists on a beach near Tel Aviv.

June 2, 1978 – A bomb kills 2 people at the Commonwealth Heads of Government Meeting in Sydney Australia.

1978 – An El Al stewardess is killed when the crew bus is ambushed by **Popular Front for the Liberation of Palestine terrorists** outside the Europa Hotel, London, England.

1978 – An Air Florida flight from Key West to Miami, is hijacked by seven Cubans and flown to Cuba, where they release their hostages and are taken into custody. Six more U.S. aircraft are hijacked to Cuba over the next month. All the passengers were released unharmed.

1978

1978 – Two people are injured in a bomb explosion on an American Airlines flight in the United States. The so-called **Unabomber** is held responsible for the incident.

1978 – Three passengers are killed when Cubans hijack an aircraft in Peru and demand to be flown to the United States

1978 – Cyprus. An aircraft is hijacked at Larnaca airport by Arab terrorists who had just murdered a leading Egyptian publisher at a nearby hotel. After being refused permission to land at a number of Arab capitals the hijackers returned to Larnaca. Egyptian commandos attack the plane which results in a gun battle with Cypriot troops. Fifteen Egyptian troops, seven Cypriot soldiers and a German cameraman are killed.

1978 – The President of United Airlines is injured by a bomb in Chicago that is blamed on the **Unabomber.**

1978 – Four Iranian hijackers are killed when Turkish security forces storm a hijacked Turkish Airlines aircraft after it landed in eastern Turkey. The terrorists killed one of the 155 hostages.

1978 – Afghanistan Civil War. Civil War begins in Afghanistan. Afghanistan has experienced civil war since the late 1970's and unlike conflicts which principally derive from deep seated hostility among their constituent religious, ethnic and linguistic communities, Afghanistan's war has largely been the product of external influences. In the 1980s the Soviet Union and the United States will chose Afghanistan as a battleground in their global competition. From 1978-2009, 1,500,000 to 2,000,000 people will be killed.

1971-1978 – Bolivia. Military Coup. Hugo Banzer is overthrown by General Juan Pereda in July. Pereda had made statements that he would call for new elections within a reasonable span of time but the general feeling is that he will try to retain power. General Juan Pereda is then overthrown by democratically-oriented officers under General David Padilla. They then set a firm date for a new vote.

Human rights groups claim that during Banzer's 1971-1978 dictatorship several thousand Bolivians sought asylum in foreign countries, **3,000 political opponents were arrested, 200 were killed, and many more were tortured.** Many others simply disappeared. Among the victims of the regime are Colonel Andrés Selich, Banzer's first Minister of the Interior and co-conspirator in the August 1971 coup. Selich was accused of plotting to overthrow Banzer and died from a beating while in custody. Two others that were seen as a threat were murdered under suspicious circumstances while in exile in 1976: General Joanquin Zenteno Anaya and, President Juan José Torres.

1978 – Cambodia. Kampuchean Intervention. Border clashes with Vietnam led to Kampuchea cutting off diplomatic relations with its neighbor in late 1977. The **Vietnamese,** who stepped up their border attacks, encouraged Kampuchean rebels to overthrow the **Pol Pot** regime. In late 1978, about **200,000 Vietnamese troops invaded** and occupied Kampuchea, whose capital, Phnom Penh, fell on January 9, 1979. The Vietnamese do not withdraw until 1989.

May 4, 1978 – Cassinga Massacre. A Namibian refugee camp in southern Angola. At daybreak on May 4, **South African planes flew over Cassinga.** Claudia Ushona, who was then a sixteen-year old refugee living in the camp, recalls; "We were gathered outside to salute the flag when we saw white things falling from the sky. We thought it was our President Sam Nujoma, President of SWAPO, sending us candy. We were eager to see him. We said, 'The President is coming! And he is bringing us candy!' We were living in a refugee camp, we were all dreaming of the candy the President would bring us. But they were bombs."

   After the bombs, came the paratroopers. This was the massacre of Cassinga, **more than 600 Namibians, mostly women and children were slaughtered** by the soldiers of Apartheid. A United Nations delegation that visited Cassinga a few days later reported: "What the South Africans did was criminal in legal terms and savage in moral terms. It reminds us of the darkest moments in modern history."

1978 – Iran. Islamic revolution. The Shah's policies alienate the clergy and his authoritarian rule leads to riots, strikes and mass demonstrations. Muslim fundamentalists seeking to establish a Muslim state are continually trying to undermine the Shah's rule. Martial law is imposed and the Shah's police kill hundreds of protestors in Qom, Tabriz, and elsewhere. Mass demonstrations are ruthlessly crushed but people are persistent. The Shah is exiled and Ayatollah Khomeini returns to Iran.

1978 – Israeli Invasion of Lebanon. The Palestine Liberation Organization (PLO) had engaged in **cross-border attacks on Israel** from southern Lebanon as far back as 1968, and the area became a significant base following the arrival of the PLO leadership and its **Fatah** brigade after their 1971 expulsion from Jordan. Israel's invasion of Lebanon in 1978 failed to stop the Palestinian attacks.

On March 11, 1978, a raiding party of Palestinian militants floating on two rubber boats from Lebanon broke through Israeli defenses and landed on the Israeli coast in broad daylight. The Palestine Liberation organization militants attacked civilians, hijacked a bus and a car, drove down to the outskirts of Tel Aviv, and battled Israeli forces. By day's end 37 Israelis, most of them civilian, and the 9 Palestinian militants were dead.

Barely two days later, the night of March 14, 1978, approximately **25,000 Israeli soldiers cross the Lebanese border in Operation Litani** not 20 miles from the Israeli border. Israeli Defense Minister Ezer Weizman said the invasion was designed to "clean up once and for all terrorist concentrations in southern Lebanon." But there were no such terrorist "concentrations." There were bands of Palestinian gunmen and militants spread throughout Lebanon and this was the fault of the government in Lebanon, which had allowed them to be armed.

1978 – Italy. Red Brigades, Terrorists. Italy has a history of politically motivated extremist groups. The most notorious was the Bologna-based, **Marxist-Leninist Red Brigades** formed in the 1970s by student protesters dedicating themselves to an armed struggle against the capitalist state. The Red Brigades created such fear during the 1970s and early 1980s that the period is known in Italy as the **Years of Lead,** referring to the vast number of bullets fired.

1978 – Lebanese Civil War. Relations between **Lebanon** and **Syria** deteriorate even further when fighting occurs between the ADF and the Lebanese Army in East Beirut in February, followed by a massive ADF bombardment of Christian sectors of Beirut in July. **Lebanese President Sarkis** resigned in protest against the latter action but was persuaded to reconsider. Syrian bombardments of East Beirut ended in October 1978 as a result of a UN Security Council cease-fire resolution that **indirectly implicated Syria as a party to the Lebanese Civil War.** To strengthen its influence over the Sarkis government, Syria threatened several times, in late 1978 and early 1979, to withdraw its forces from Lebanon. After a relatively cordial meeting between Presidents Sarkis and Assad in Damascus in May 1979, Syria stated that the ADF, which by then had become a totally Syrian force, would "remain in Lebanon as long as the Arab interests so require."

1978 – Madagascar. More than 1,000 people are killed in race riots in Majunga city in the northwest.

August 22, 1978 – Sandinista Revolution, Nicaragua. Nicaragua went from being controlled by the right–wing Somoza dictatorship to being controlled by left–wing revolutionaries. On August 22, twenty–four Sandinista guerillas take control of the government in a coup and then pass a reform constitution guaranteeing human rights. This was a good start but the economy was still falling and the newly imposed **embargo by the U.S. was not helping.**

After promising free elections the Sandinistas set up a ruling Junta made up of five top Sandinista officials including **Daniel Ortega.** This Junta then quickly aligned itself with the **Soviet Union** and **Cuba.** As they receive more and more financial and military aid from these countries they move further away from the west and are seen as a potential threat by the U.S.

1978 – The Ogaden War is a conventional conflict between **Somalia** and **Ethiopia** in 1977 and 1978 over the Ogaden region of Ethiopia. The Soviet Union switched from supplying aid to Somalia and started supporting Ethiopia, which had previously been backed by the United States; this led to the U.S. to start supporting Somalia. The war ended when Somali forces retreated back across the border and a truce was declared.

1978 – Somalia. Majeerteen officers are the primary organizers of an unsuccessful **coup in April**, following the army's humiliating defeat in the Ogaden War. An estimated 500 rebel soldiers are killed in fighting with forces loyal to **Siad Barre,** and

subsequently **seventeen officers, all but one of them Majeerteen, are executed.**
Several colonels suspected of plotting the coup escaped, and fled abroad. One of them,
Yusuf Ahmad, will play a major role in forming the Somali Salvation Front, the first
opposition movement dedicated to the overthrow of the Siad Barre regime by force.

**1978 – Turkey. Centered in East and Southeast Anatolia and Northern Iraq the
Turkey-Kurdistan Workers' Party conflict** is between the Republic of Turkey and
the militant ethnic separatist **Kurdish guerrilla group.**

Less than fifty students and former university students meet secretly in southeast
Turkey and plan a war for an independent Kurdish state. The young men and women
do not see any reason they should fail. The Turkish military had hundreds of
thousands of soldiers, Turkey is a NATO member, and there is no reason the newly
formed PKK (Kurdistan Workers Party) should be successful, but it is successful. The
PKK will become the dominant party with a guerrilla force of 15,000 and a civilian
military force in Turkey of more than 50,000. They will also have active backing in
Europe of over 15,000.

The war inside Turkey will leave close to 40,000 people dead, result in human
rights abuses on both sides, and draw in neighboring **Iran, Iraq, and Syria,** as they all
seek to use the PKK for their own purposes.

1978 – Uganda. Uganadan-Tanzanian War. Some units of Uganda's armed forces
mutiny, following dissatisfaction with **President Idi Amin,** and flee across the
Tanzanian border to join with the **National Liberation Front.** Amin accused
Tanzanian President Julius Nyerere of waging war against Uganda and invaded
Tanzania where he formally annexed a section of the Kagera Region on November 1.

1978 – Zaire. Shaba II. During the first Shaba invasion the FLNC launched an
invasion of Zaire. The second Shaba invasion is an infiltration of Zaire when FLNC
battalions enter through northern Zambia, a sparsely populated area made up of the
same ethnic groups as the FLNC. The invaders combine forces and focus on
economically important Kolwezi. As the FLNC threatened the disruption of mining
operations and the lives of Europeans, 700 French and 1,700 Belgian soldiers
supported by the U.S. air force ended the attack and routed the invaders.

1979

The Oldest Boomer is 33 years old.

Cost of the Average House: $71,800	
Median Family Income: $16,530 **File clerk, Bank Teller:** $130/ wk **Engineer:** $375/ wk	**Minimum Wage:** $2.90/ hr **Average Hourly Wage:** $6.70 **Legal secretary:** $160/ wk
Gallon of Milk: $1.59	**Gallon Gasoline:** 75 cents – $1.08
New Car: **AMC Pacer:** $3,100 **Pontiac Sunbird:** $4,274 **Toyota Corolla:** $3,698	**Loaf of Bread:** 29 cents **Tuna:** 69 cents/ can **Bacon:** 99 cents/ lb **Computer, TRS-80, 4KB:** $499
Unemployment Rate: 5.9%-5.6%-6.0%	**First-class Stamp:** 15 cents

34 cents buying power in 1979 = **$1.00 in 2008.**
In 1979 what cost us 34 cents to purchase now costs us $1.00 in 2008.

Movies: "All That Jazz," "Apocalypse Now," "Breaking Away," "Norma Rae," "Kramer vs. Kramer," "The Black Stallion."

Broadway: "They're Playing Our Song," "I Remember Mama." "Tommy," London. "Sugar Babies," revue. "Sweeney Todd."

TV: "The Dukes of Hazzard," "The Facts of Life," "Knots Landing," "B.J. and the Bear," "The Ropers," "60 Minutes," "Archie Bunker's Place," "Benson," "The Bad News Bears," "Dance Fever," "Eischied," "Hart to Hart," "Real People," "Trapper John, M.D.," "Hello, Larry," "Solid Gold."

Music: "Manhattan," George Gershwin. Kiss, "I Was Made For Lovin' You." The Jacksons, "Shake Your Body, Down to the Ground." Sex Pistols, "Friggin' in the Riggin." Buggles, "Video Killed the Radio Star." Sister Sledge, "He's the Greatest Dancer." Anne Murray, "I Just Fall in Love Again." The Sugarhill Gang, "Rapper's Delight." Donna Summer's, "Bad Girls." The Police, "Message in a Bottle." Marianne Faithfull, "The Ballad Of

Lucy Jordan." Tom Petty & the Heartbreakers, "Don't Do Me Like That." Rod Stewart, "Do Ya Think I'm Sexy." M, "Pop Muzik." Billy Joel, "Big Shot." The Dead Kennedys, "California Über Alles." ABBA, "Does Your Mother Know" & "Gimme! Gimme! Gimme!-A Man After Midnight." The Stranglers, "Duchess." The Specials AKA, "Gangsters." Blondie, "Heart of Glass" & "Sunday Girl." Dr. Hook, "When You're in Love with a Beautiful Woman." Barbra Streisand & Donna Summer, "No More Tears, Enough is Enough." Doobie Brothers, "What a Fool Believes." Gali Atari, "Hallelujah." Art Garfunkel, "Bright Eyes." Michael Jackson, "Don't Stop 'Til You Get Enough." The Knack, "My Sharona." Judas Priest, "Take On the World." Herb Alpert, "Rise." Gloria Gaynor, "I Will Survive." Donna Summer, "Hot Stuff." Peaches & Herb, "Reunited." Cliff Richard, "We Don't Talk Anymore." David Bowie, "Boys Keep Swinging." Supertramp, "Goodbye Stranger." AC/DC, "Highway to Hell." Dr. Feelgood, "Milk and Alcohol." Pink Floyd, "Another Brick in the Wall." Robert Palmer, "Bad Case of Loving You, Doctor Doctor." Charlie Daniels Band, "The Devil Went Down to Georgia." GQ, "Disco Nights." Village People, "Go West" & "In the Navy." Rupert Holmes, "Escape, Piña Colada." Vic Godard and Subway. "Sect Ambition."

Deaths: Robert Williams, Darla Hood, Ted Cassidy, Mary Pickford.

President: James Earl Carter, Jr. (D) Southern Baptist; vetoes 31/ 2 overrides

Vice President: Walter F. Mondale (D) Methodist; Presbyterian

House: D-277 ; R-158

Senate: 96th Congress (1979-1981) Majority Party: Democrat (58 seats) Minority Party: Republican (41 seats) Other Parties: 1 Independent Total Seats: 100

Federal Debt: $826.52 billion or 32 % of the GDP

Consumer Price Index CPI-U (1982 Base of 100): 72.60

GDP: $2,563.3 billion	**Inflation Rate:** 11.22%
Dow Jones: 872.95 (10-01)/ 815.84 (03-01)	**S&P Price Index:** 107.94/12.31%

Prime Rate: 11.50% (06-19)/ 15.25% (12-07)	**Average Home Mortgage Rate:** 10.39/12.90%
1 oz Gold: $307.50	**1oz of Silver:** $25.00

Average Monthly S.S. Benefits Paid: $180.55 / month

Federal Debt: $826,519,000,000

Federal Deficit: $40.7 billion dollars

Defense Spending: $143.72 billion	**Interest Spending:** $42.63 billion
Health Care Spending: $46.99 billion	**Pensions Spending:** $116.91 billion
Welfare Spending: $39.33 billion	**Education Spending:** $31.52 billion
Transportation Spending: $18.08 billion	**Misc. Other Spending:** $48.13 billion
Protection Spending: $4.29 billion	**Total Government Spending:** $504.03 billion

% of GDP that goes towards just the interest payment: 1.70%

$1.00 = 1.500 Yuan, China NPC	**$1.00 =** 219.02 Yen, Japan
$1.00 = 3.295 / 3.365 Saudi Arabia Riyal.	**$1.00 =** Iranian Rial Preferential Rate: 78.00 Unofficial Rate: 105.00 Resident Travel Rate: 87.74
U.S. Population: 225,106,000	**World Population:** 4,380,776,827

In the late 1970s, **the top one percent of the U.S. population** held 13 percent of the wealth; in 1995 it held 38 percent.

China's "Planned" Birth Policy begins.

World AIDS Victims: Known Deaths in the U.S. this year, we are just beginning to even know there is a problem.

U.S. Birth Rate: 3,494,398

1979

U.S. Abortions: 1,251,921–1,497,700	
U.S. Homicide Rate: 10.0/ 100,000 population	**U.S. Violent Crime:** 548.9/ 100,000 population
Annual Average Domestic Crude Oil Prices: $25.10 / barrel, $73.60 (2007 adjusted)	

Oil:

1970-1979 – The cost of oil rose 200% from 1970 – 1979. Forty–five percent of U.S. oil is now imported. **American oil company profits rose 150%** and they invested their profits by buying up the coal companies, natural gas companies and even solar power companies. They are motivated by controlling energy supplies, energy prices, and power within government. By 1979 the largest coal companies are also oil companies. The **cost of imported oil rose** from $2.9 billion in 1970 to $49.5 billion in 1979. Natural gas and electric rates rose 99% from 1973 – 1977.

After the Iranian revolution in 1979 oil prices increase another 36% in one month. The major U.S. (American?) oil companies withhold supplies to deliberately drive up their profits and put independent producers and distributors out of business.

In April 1979 the Carter administration begins a phased deregulation of oil prices which increases the price of oil **from $15.85 a barrel to $39.50 a barrel in 12 months.**

January February 1979 – Prime Minister Shapour Bakhtiar suggests to the Shah of Iran, Muhammad Reza Pahlavi, that it would be better if both he and his wife left the country. **The Shah of Iran is in exile.** Iran is in a revolution. The followers of Ayatollah Khomeini come to power.

Second quarter of 1979 – OPEC members are in a price increase free-for-all when Saudi Arabia cuts production, and Western influence over Mid-East oil shrinks even further. **Ayatollah Khomeini** takes real control of the government in **Iran** after the fall of the Shah, and feels he can raise prices at will. Infighting and the need to control also brings out **Iraqi leader Saddam Hussein** when he sees an opportunity to either take control of Iran's oil industry or destroy it. The **Iran-Iraq War** will be fought for eight years, until both sides realize they can not win and quit for the time being.

March 28, 1979 – The Three Mile Island nuclear accident is a partial core meltdown in which the mechanical failures are compounded by the plant managers' lack of training. A loss of coolant precipitated **the largest accident in U.S. nuclear power history.** Metropolitan Edison is concerned enough to suggest emergency evacuation of the area over the next five days, but by this time the reactor is brought under control.

A popular movie called **"The China Syndrome,"** concerning an accident at a nuclear reactor was released just 12 days earlier. The movie along with the anti nuclear power statements made by political and social activists, virtually halts nuclear power plant construction in the United States making the U.S. even more dependent on imported oil.

Spring 1979 – There is a gasoline shortage and a world oil glut. The U.S. once again has long lines of cars waiting at the pumps for gas.

March 26, 1979 – OPEC increases prices 14.5 percent effective on April 1. **Crude oil is raised to $14.56 per barrel.** November 4, **Iran takes western hostages.** November 12, **President Jimmy Carter** orders cessation of Iranian imports to the United States. November 15, **Iran cancels all contracts with U.S. oil companies.** December 13, Saudi Arabia raises the **crude price to $24 per barrel.**

April 1979 – The United States begins **deregulation** of oil prices.

April 11, 1979 – President Carter says he'll work with Congress or do the job himself as long as the results meet his demand: America's oil companies must use half of any new profits from decontrolled oil prices to search for more oil or gas. **Congress has already given frosty receptions to Carter's request for a 50 percent tax on "windfall profits"** expected to flow from the phased oil decontrol he's ordered to begin June 1. Instead of spending the exorbitant profits on new oil and gas exploration, the oil companies are allowed to buy up major sections of the energy market in the U.S. This leaves oil companies even more powerful and wealthy.

1979

July 15, 1979 – President Jimmy Carter to the Nation. What I have to say to you now about energy is simple and vitally important.

Point one: I am tonight setting a clear goal for the energy policy of the United States. **Beginning this moment, this nation will never use more foreign oil than we did in 1977 . . .never.** From now on, every new addition to our demand for energy will be met from our own production and our own conservation. The generation-long growth in our dependence on foreign oil will be stopped dead in its tracks right now and then reversed as we move through the 1980s, for I am tonight setting the further goal of cutting our dependence on foreign oil by one-half by the end of the next decade -- a saving of over 4 1/2 million barrels of imported oil per day.

   Point two: To ensure that we meet these targets, I will use my presidential authority to set import quotas. I'm announcing tonight that for 1979 and 1980, I will forbid the entry into this country of one drop of foreign oil more than these goals allow. These quotas will ensure a reduction in imports even below the ambitious levels we set at the recent Tokyo summit.

   Point three: To give us energy security, I am asking for the most massive peacetime commitment of funds and resources in our nation's history to develop America's own alternative sources of fuel, from coal, from oil shale, from plant products for gasohol, from unconventional gas, from the sun.

...In closing, let me say this: I will do my best, but I will not do it alone. Let your voice be heard. Whenever you have a chance, say something good about our country. With God's help and for the sake of our nation, it is time for us to join hands in America. Let us commit ourselves together to a rebirth of the American spirit. Working together with our common faith we cannot fail.

   Thank you and good night.

March 26, 1979 – Camp David Accords. Washington, D.C. Israeli Prime Minister **Menachem Begin** and Egyptian President **Anwar Sadat.** A peace agreement is signed between **Egypt and Israel.** The treaties, which began with the Camp David Accords, call for a complete Israeli withdrawal from Sinai. In return, Egypt will recognize Israel and maintain full diplomatic relations with her. In addition, the Sinai is to be demilitarized, with the **United States** providing troops to monitor its continuing demilitarization. **President Carter's involvement is instrumental** in bringing about the agreement.

1979 – Mobil's top five executives took home a total of more than $10 million. That's more than $2 million per executive in a single year! In 1979 this is considered a lot of money. The average two–income family earns $315 a week.

Major News:

January 1, 1979 – The U.S. establishes diplomatic ties with **mainland China** for the first time since the Communist takeover in 1949.

January 19, 1979 – Former Attorney General John Mitchell, the last of 25 persons still jailed for crimes relating to the **Watergate scandal**, is released.

May 25, 1979 – An American Airlines DC-10 jetliner crashes after takeoff from Chicago, killing 275 persons.

June 18, 1979 – SALT II negotiations began in November 1972. A major breakthrough occurred at the Vladivostok meeting in November 1974, between **President Ford and General Secretary Brezhnev.** At this meeting, the sides agreed to a basic framework for the SALT II agreement.

The completed SALT II agreement is **signed by President Carter and General Secretary Brezhnev in Vienna on June 18.** President Carter transmitted it to the Senate on June 22 for its advice and consent on ratification.

On January 3, 1980, **President Carter** requested the Senate majority leader delay consideration of the **Treaty on the Senate floor in view of the Soviet invasion of Afghanistan.** In May 1982, **President Reagan** stated he would do nothing to undercut the SALT agreements as long as the Soviet Union showed equal restraint and the Soviet Union agreed to abide by the unratified Treaty. Then President Reagan declared that the Soviet Union had violated its political commitment to observe the SALT II Treaty in 1984 and 1985, and on May 26, 1986, President Reagan stated that ". . . the United States must base decisions regarding its strategic force structure on the nature and magnitude of the threat posed by Soviet strategic forces and not on standards contained in the SALT structure . . . "

July 15, 1979 – President Jimmy Carter speaks of a national **"crisis of confidence"** and outlines a proposed 10-year $140 billion dollar program to **reduce U.S. dependence on foreign oil.**

October 1, 1979 – Panama takes control of the Canal Zone. Under a 1903 treaty Panama granted to the U.S. the Panama Canal Zone and the rights to build and operate a canal. The U.S. has governed the Canal Zone since construction began. Facing enormous obstacles, George Washington Goethals directed the construction from 1907, and the canal opened on Aug. 15, 1914. The canal enabled ships traveling between the Atlantic and the Pacific Ocean to cut costs by avoiding the lengthy circumnavigation of South America.

From 1979 to 1999 the canal itself was under joint U.S.-Panamanian control. Following the application of the Panama Canal Treaty with Panama in 1979 the office of the Governor of the Canal Zone ceased to exist; the Seal of the Canal Zone and the flag of the Governor became obsolete.

November 4, 1979 – The Iranian hostage crisis is a diplomatic crisis between Iran and the United States when **53 Americans are held hostage for 444 days** from November 4, 1979 to January 20, 1981, after a group of Islamist students and militants took over the American embassy in support of the Iranian Revolution. They demand that the former Shah, Muhammad Reza Pahlavi, who is undergoing medical treatment in New York City, return to Iran to stand trial. Beset by advanced cancer, the Shah left Iran in January 1979 to begin a life in exile. He lived in Egypt, Morocco, the Bahamas, and Mexico before going to the United States for treatment of lymphatic cancer. His arrival in New York City led to the Iranian takeover of the American Embassy in Tehran.

Civil Rights Movement:

1979 – The Nobel Prize in Economics goes to **Sir Arthur Lewis** of Princeton University. He is the first black person to win the award in a category other than peace.

1979 – Frank E. Petersen, Jr. becomes the first African American to earn the rank of General in the United States Marines.

Women's Movement:

September 1979 – Hazel W. Johnson becomes the first African American woman to be promoted to the rank of General in the United States Army.

Popular Culture:

1979 – Presidential Directive 59 states U.S. policy is **to win** a six month long **nuclear war.**

1970-1979 – The 1970's is a terrible time for the United States. We had government corruption and a President so close to impeachment that he chose to resign instead. There are **high taxes, inflation and even gasoline shortages**, while (American?) oil companies make record profits by starving the supply to drive up the price of oil and food. The government gave up in **Vietnam, Laos, Cambodia, Angola, Ethiopia, and Nicaragua,** which was probably a good thing because the politicians have no understanding of what they are doing or any real purpose. (Unless the real purpose is to drive the U.S. into a Global Government. Then it all makes some sense.) They continue to try to "change" the basic nature of cultures while the culture they are trying to change takes the money and mocks the U.S. for being so naive. The U.S. is pushed around by the oil cartel, gives up the Panama Canal, and stands silent on the world scene for too long, impotent and confused. Carter provided no real answers and the American people no longer had any confidence in their President.

1979

November 1979 – Atari 400 and 800 model game computers. The names originally referred to the amount of memory, **4 KB RAM in the 400 and 8 KB in the 800, but** by the time they were released the prices on RAM had started to fall, so the machines were instead both released with 8 KB. As memory prices continued to fall Atari eventually supplied the machines fully expanded to 48 KB, using up all the slots.

1979 – USENET begins. USENET is invented as a means for providing mail and file transfers using a communications standard known as UUCP. **Duke University** and the **University of North Carolina** at Chapel Hill, graduate students Tom Truscott, Jim Ellis, and Steve Bellovin, develop it as a joint project.

1979 – ABSCAM. The Federal Bureau of Investigation conducts a sting operation in which agents pretend to be wealthy **Arab sheiks** seeking investment opportunities in the United States. A **Senator** and **six Congressmen** are videotaped accepting **bribes** from these agents in return for political favors. The scandal comes to be known as **ABSCAM,** after the bogus Abdul Enterprise Company. The investigation ultimately led to the conviction of a United States Senator, five members of the House of Representatives, one member of the New Jersey State Senate, members of the Philadelphia City Council, and an inspector for the Immigration and Naturalization Service.

1979 – Since 1975, there has been an increase in the incarceration rate for **white collar criminals.**

July 12, 1979 – Organized crime figure Carmine Galante is gunned down in a New York City café. Carmine Galante was the boss of the Bonanno crime family. He was feared by everyone and ordered many executions while he spent time in prison. No one knows how many people he personally murdered.

On July 12, Galante decided to eat at Joe and Mary's Restaurant in the Bushwick section of Brooklyn. The owner, Galante's cousin, was leaving for Italy soon and Galante stopped in to visit. The others at Galante's table left one at a time until he was seated alone finishing his meal when three masked men came out of the kitchen area, walked quickly up to the table and emptied both barrels of a shotgun into him. No dessert tonight for Carmine.

1979 – This year bank robberies in the U.S. hit an all-time high. Federal and state officials made arrests in 69 percent of the 11,000 bank robberies reported to the **Federal Bureau of Investigation** in 1978 and 1979, but they made arrests in only 17 percent of all robberies. Bank robberies accounted for only 1.3 percent of all robberies reported.

1979 – CompuServe comes online. CompuServe was established in 1969 by Jeffrey Wilkins to computerize his father-in-law's insurance company. In 1977, he expanded into computer time-sharing services and through its pioneering efforts in videotex technology.

CompuServe introduced an online service, the **CompuServe Information Service in 1979.** This network initially represented an extension of its core business. Starting the information service was as simple as offering existing hardware to about 1,200 nighttime users in its first year. The following year, in exchange for $20 million, CompuServe became a wholly owned subsidiary of H&R Block, Inc., which provided the financial support to foster CompuServe's rapid growth through expansion as well as research and development.

At its height, the service boasted of having over half a million users simultaneously on line. In the end **WorldCom** bought CompuServe from **H&R Block** with WorldCom stock. H&R Block received WorldCom stock which it resold immediately for $1.2 billion. WorldCom then retained the CompuServe Network Services Division, sold its online service to **America Online,** and received AOL's network division, ANS.

1979 – The first Multi-User Domain, MUD1, goes on-line. Two students at the **University of Essex,** write a program that allows many people to play against each other on-line. It immediately becomes popular with college students as a means of adventure gaming and for socializing.

1979 – A Michigan man became the first human to be killed by a robot when he was struck by a robotic arm at a casting plant in Michigan on January 25, 1979.

1979

1979 – Asteroids, a video arcade game is released by **Atari Inc.** It is one of the most popular and influential games of the **Golden Age of Arcade Games.** Asteroids uses vector graphics and a two-dimensional view that wraps around in both screen axes. The player controls a spaceship in an asteroid field which is intermittently traversed by flying saucers. The object of the game is to shoot and destroy asteroids and saucers while not colliding with either, or being hit by the saucers' counter-fire. The game then publicly records the initials of high scorers.

1979 – The Sony Walkman tape player starts a fad. According to Sony, "In 1979, an empire in personal portable entertainment was created with the ingenious foresight of Sony Founder and Chief Advisor, the late Masaru Ibuka, and Sony Founder and Honorary Chairman Akio Morita. It began with the invention of the first cassette Walkman TPS-L2 that forever changed the way consumers listen to music."

Business / Technology:

1930-1980 – Smoking Deaths.
1930-1959 –11,000,000 deaths due to smoking
1960s – 9,000,000 deaths due to smoking
1970s – 13,000,000 deaths due to smoking

1979 – The coal miners of Illinois (the UMW's District 12) numbered 19,660 down from its peak of some 100,000 in the 1920's but still a sizable presence in the state since the UMW mines about 96 percent of the coal dug in Illinois.

1979 – Harvard MBA candidate Daniel Bricklin and programmer Robert Frankston developed **VisiCalc,** the spreadsheet program that made a business machine out of the personal computer, for the **Apple II.**

1979 – Canada tests Telidon videotex. From the late 1970s to mid-1980s, **Videotex** is one of the earliest implementations of "end-user information systems," and delivers pages of text to a user which is usually displayed on a television. Videotex can also be used to refer to the Internet, bulletin board systems, online service providers or even the arrival/departure displays at an airport. A more limited definition would be a two–way information service as opposed to a one way information service. However, unlike the modern Internet, all traditional videotex services were highly centralized.

1979 – WordStar, an early, successful word processing program is released. **WordStar,** a word processor application, published by MicroPro International, was originally developed for CP/M in 1978. It was the most feature-rich and easy-to-use word processor available for this operating system, and became a de facto standard. In 1981 WordStar version 2.26 was bundled with **the Osborne 1 portable computer.** Notably, WordStar was the last commercial word processor supporting the CP/M operating system. The 3.0 version of WordStar for DOS was released in April 1982.

August 29, 1979 – Great Britain performs a nuclear test at the U.S. Nevada Test Site.

November 1, 1979 – The Federal government announces a **$1.5 billion dollar loan-**guarantee plan to aid the ailing **Chrysler Corporation.**

Finance:

August 1979 – Paul Volcker becomes Chairman of the Federal Reserve in August as **President Jimmy Carter** is fighting to rein in the inflation caused by the oil price increases 1973 and 1978. Volcker leads the Fed until 1987, often using tactics that are unpopular, like rapid increases in interest rates. Criticized at the time for causing a recession, Mr. Volcker is later praised for the effectiveness of his efforts.

August 27, 1979 – The Taxpayer Ombudsman position is established in the Internal Revenue Service to serve as taxpayers' advocate in resolving problems.

1976-2006 – BCCI. Pakistan's economy is on the brink of collapse. Pakistan owes large debts to international organizations such as the **World Bank** and the **International Monetary Fund** (IMF), but does not have the money to pay off its loans. The BCCI bank comes up with a scheme that it will use often. It simply deposits money into Pakistan's State Bank for 90 days so the bank can get the IMF's OK to increase the lending limits for commercial banks. As banks are able to loan more money the Pakistani economy begins to perform better. After the 90 days BCCI takes the money back and moves it for the original drug cartels. BCCI helps Pakistan's State Bank numerous times in subsequent years to avoid financial limitations placed on Pakistan.

BCCI will continue to use this policy of "holding" large amounts of money for clients that include major drug traffickers and money launderers. The money would be on the books for a yearly or quarterly audit and then go back into a transfer that would further launder the money. Although money launderers are not required to allow BCCI to hold $5 million or $10 million for a few months, it was greatly appreciated by the bank.

Books:

1979 – "Sophie's Choice," William Styron.

1979 – Douglas Adams, **"The Hitchhiker's Guide to the Galaxy."**

1979 – John le Carré, "Smiley's People."

TV:

1979 – The Daytona 500 is the first stock car race to be televised live nationally from start to finish, **"flag-to-flag coverage,"** CBS said.

February 11, 1979 – Forty-three million viewers watch **"Elvis!"** on ABC, a made for TV movie starring Kurt Russell as Elvis.

Music:

1979 – Rap music goes beyond the streets of New York.

1979 – Disco reigns supreme with several #1 hits from The Bee Gees and Donna Summer this year.

December 3, 1979 – **In Cincinnati, Ohio,** a stampede for seats at Riverfront Coliseum during a **Who concert** kills 11 fans (band members were not made aware of the deaths until after the show).

Natural Disasters:

March 28, 1979 – Three Mile Island, near Harrisburg, Pennsylvania. One of two reactors loses its coolant, which causes overheating and a partial meltdown of its uranium core. Some radioactive water and gases are released. **This is the worst accident in U.S. nuclear-reactor history.**

March 1979 – Avalanche. Lahaul Valley, India. Over 200 people are killed.

April 10, 1979 – Tornadoes. Eleven tornadoes in northern Texas and southern Oklahoma are responsible for the deaths of 59 people.

April 15, 1979 – Earthquake. Herceg Novi, Dubrovnik, Montenegro, Croatia. A 5.6 magnitude earthquake strikes, killing over 100 people.

August 6, 1979 – Coyote Lake, Santa Clara County, California. A 5.7 magnitude **earthquake** strikes.

August 30-September 7, 1979 – Hurricane David. Caribbean/ Eastern United States. Hurricane David formed near Cape Verde off the African coast in the eastern Atlantic Ocean. It devastates the island of Dominica, and then the Dominican Republic.
   Roseau, the Capital of the small island of Dominica is devastated by winds up to 150 mph. Thirty-seven people die and 60,000 lose their homes. Nearly 75 percent of the entire population is affected. Banana and citrus crops, essential to the island's economy, are wiped out.
   Santo Domingo and the **Dominican Republic** are hit the following day as hurricane David is now a Category 5 storm with 175 mph sustained winds, gusts over 200 mph, and waves as high as 20 to 30 feet. Mudslides kill nearly 1,200 people.
   In Padre Las Casas more than 400 people tied themselves together as they attempted to climb to higher ground. They did not make it. A dike broke releasing a

flood of water and they were all washed away. On September 1, David hit the Bahamas and, two days later, caused $60 million damage in Florida. From there, the hurricane moved up the coastline of the United States. Charleston, South Carolina, took a heavy hit and the storm caused flooding from Virginia to New York. On September 7 it was finally over. Over 1,500 people were killed.

August 29 - September 15, 1979 – Hurricane Fredrick. The State of Alabama suffers its worst natural disaster when Hurricane Frederic comes ashore. Alabama had not seen a storm of Frederic's intensity since 1916 and thousands suffer unprecedented damage.

During 1950-2000 only two hurricanes have made landfall along the Gulf coast with stronger winds than hurricane Frederic: **Hurricane Camille** in 1969 and **Hurricane Carla in** 1961. Hurricane Frederic causes $2.3 billion in damage and is the most costly hurricane in American history up to this time.

October 15, 1979 – Earthquake. Imperial Valley, California A 6.4 magnitude earthquake strikes. Damage from the earthquake, estimated to be $30,000,000 is most evident in residential areas of southern Imperial County and northeastern Baja California. Agriculture suffers greatly as there are many lateral slope failures along irrigation canals resulting in crop damage from insufficient irrigation.

December 12, 1979 – Tsunamis. San Juan, Colombia. Over 250 people are killed by drowning when a tsunami sweeps over the area destroying all the homes. The wave was probably generated by an earthquake.

Man vs. Man / Wars:

Assassinated – Afghanistan. Adolph Dubs, the U.S. ambassador to Afghanistan. On February 14, four Afghans kidnap U.S. Ambassador Adolph Dubs in Kabul and demanded the release of various "religious figures." When Afghan police storm the hotel room where he is being held, Dubs is killed, along with four terrorists.

Assassinated – Afghanistan. Nur Mohammad Taraki, President and Prime Minister. At the beginning of September 1979 Taraki traveled to Havana for a summit conference of nonaligned nations. Returning via Moscow, he was believed to have been advised by **Soviet President Leonid Brezhnev** to eliminate **Hafizullah Amin,** because the Soviets felt his anti-Islamic policy was aggravating the political situation in Afghanistan. Taraki's attempt to have Amin assassinated failed, and Amin seized power on September 14, 1979. Amin ordered the commander of the palace guard to have Taraki executed. Taraki reportedly was suffocated with a pillow over his head.

Assassinated – Afghanistan. President Hafizullah Amin. Many Afghans held Hafizullah Amin responsible for the Taraki regime's harshest measures and the Soviets are worried that their huge investment in Afghanistan might be jeopardized so they increase the number of their advisers. Amin became the target of several failed assassination attempts in early and mid-December 1979.

   The Soviets began their **invasion of Afghanistan** on December 25, 1979. Within two days, they secured Kabul, deploying a special Soviet assault unit against Darulaman Palace, where elements of the Afghan army loyal to Amin put up a fierce, but brief resistance. **President Hafizullah Amin** is killed at the palace and Babrak Karmal, the exiled leader of the Parcham faction of the PDPA is installed by the Soviets as Afghanistan's new head of government.

Assassinated – British Isles. Airey Neave, a Conservative British politician, is killed by a car bomb as he exits the Palace of Westminster. The **Irish National Liberation Army** claims responsibility.

Assassinated – British Isles. Lord Mountbatten of Burma, the Admiral of the Fleet, and last Viceroy of India. The IRA **assassinated** Lord Mountbatten of Burma and, on the same day, **ambushed a party of British soldiers, killing 18 of them.** The assassination of Lord Mountbatten is widely condemned.

Assassinated – South Korea. Park Chung Hee, President of South Korea. After Park Chung Hee's removal of popular opposition leader Kim Young Sam from the National Assembly, Korea erupts with severe riots and demonstrations. **Park Chung Hee** is assassinated by his lifelong friend Kim Jae Kyu, the head of the KCIA.

1979

July 19, 1979 – Nicaragua. The Somoza Regime. The Sandinista revolution marched to victory on July 19, and Somoza fled the country. **Anastasio Somoza Debayle** was assassinated shortly afterwards in Paraguay. His U.S. backed dictatorship, hiding behind fraudulent elections and puppet governments, allowed Somoza to amass landholdings equal in size to all of El Salvador. The Sandinistas inherited a country in shambles. Poverty, homelessness, illiteracy and staggeringly inadequate health care were just a few of the widespread problems. Some 50,000 people had been killed in the revolutionary struggle and 150,000 people were made refugees.

Executed – Pakistan. Former Prime Minister Zulfikar Ali Bhutto is hanged after a controversial trial.

Bhutto ordered new elections in 1977 to obtain a popular mandate because the public was turning against his regime. His party won by a large majority and the opposition charged him with electoral fraud and seized the government on July 5, 1977. Mohammad Zia-ul-Haq, the army chief of staff, took control and had Bhutto imprisoned and then sentenced to death on the charge of having ordered the assassination of a political opponent in 1974. After an appeal to a higher court, **Bhutto was hanged,** despite appeals for clemency from several world leaders. His daughter Benazir Bhutto also served twice as Prime Minister; she was assassinated on December 27, 2007.

May 5, 1979 – Attempted Assassination. President Jimmy Carter. Two minutes before Carter is about to speak at the civic center mall in Los Angeles, Raymond Lee Harvey is arrested carrying a pistol. He later tells authorities that he and another man, Osvaldo Ortiz, were hired to create a diversion so that Mexican hit men armed with sniper rifles could kill Carter. Charges against him are dismissed for lack of evidence.

1979 – President Carter, Ronald Reagan. Robert Parry reported in "Reagan & Guatemala's Death Files" that in the late 1970s, when Carter's human rights coordinator, Pat Derian, criticized the Argentine military for its dirty war, with tens of thousands of disappearances, tortures and murders, political commentator **Ronald Reagan joshed** that she should walk a mile in the moccasins of the Argentine generals before criticizing them. Ronald Reagan found virtually every anticommunist action justified, no matter how brutal.

Guatemala is one of the world's most violent societies. The total Guatemalan death toll from 1956 – 1996 during its civil war is close to 200,000 people. Most were civilians. There is no historical evidence that President Reagan was ever bothered by the bloodbath that occurred during his presidency.

An August, 1996, series in the *San Jose Mercury News* by reporter Gary Webb **linked the origins of crack cocaine in California to the contras**, a guerrilla force backed by the Reagan administration that attacked Nicaragua's Sandinista government during the 1980s. Webb's series, "The Dark Alliance," has been the subject of intense media debate, and has focused attention on a foreign policy drug scandal that leaves many questions unanswered.

January 16, 1979 – Representative Michael O. Myers (D- Pennsylvania) is **charged** with disorderly conduct, bribery, and conspiracy. On May 5, 1980 he pleads no contest.

Arlington. Representative Michael O. Myers, (D-Pennsylvania) received **a six-month suspended sentence** in return for his no contest plea to a charge of disorderly conduct in connection with a hotel bar brawl.

The Philadelphia Democrat had been charged with **assault and battery against a plainclothes security guard** and a **female cashier** at an Arlington hotel earlier this year.

But the charge was reduced under a plea bargain agreement in General District Court here Tuesday.

Myers' cousin, John L. Sullivan, also pleaded no contest and received the same suspended sentence from Judge Jospeh Gwaltney.

Because both defendants were first time offenders, Gwaltney said, they won't have to go to jail if "they keep their records clean" for the next six months.

Arlington County police testified during the non-jury trial that Myers, Sullivan, and unnamed companions dragged security guard Michael Loper into a hotel elevator and kicked and punched him.

Kimberly Ervin, **a female cashier, who was working part time, was beaten** when she went to Loper's aid, according to the testimony.

1979

July 29, 1979 – Terrorists bomb two railway stations in Madrid, killing 7 people.

November 4, 1979 – Terrorists seize the U.S. Embassy in Tehran and take 66 American diplomats hostage. Thirteen are freed, but the remaining 53 are held for 444 days until their release on January 20, 1981, at the inauguration of President Ronald Reagan.

Washington Post June 16, 1991. While golfing last weekend in the company of President Bush, the former President Ronald Reagan denied he had done anything to delay a hostage release before the 1980 election, but he also suggested that others in his 1980 presidential campaign may have dickered about the hostages' fate with officials of Ayatollah Khomeini's regime.

December 1979 – The Soviet Union vs. Afghanistan. The **Afghanistan War,** 1979-1988, is a nine-year conflict involving Soviet forces supporting the Marxist People's Democratic Party of Afghanistan (PDPA) government, against the Islamist mujahideen resistance. The PDPA government is also supported by **India,** while the mujahideen found support from a variety of sources including the **United States, Saudi Arabia, Pakistan** and other Muslim nations in the context of the Cold War. This conflict is concurrent to the **1979 Iranian Revolution** and the **Iran–Iraq War.** The Soviet Union did not militarily defeat the Afghan guerrillas. An estimated 15,000 Soviet soldiers are killed and 35,000 wounded.

1979 – Cambodia. Pol Pot, is the leader of the Cambodian communist movement known as the **Khmer Rouge** and is **Prime Minister of Democratic Kampuchea** from 1976–1979. During his time in power, Pol Pot imposed a version of agrarian collectivization, forcing city dwellers to relocate to the countryside to work in collective farms and forced labor projects, toward a goal of **"restarting civilization" in "Year Zero".** The combined effects **of slave labor, malnutrition, poor medical care, and executions resulted in the deaths of an estimated 1,700,000 to 2,500,000 people,** approximately 21% of the Cambodian population.

After the invasion of Cambodia by Vietnam in the Cambodian–Vietnamese War in 1979, Pol Pot fled into the jungles of southwest Cambodia and the Khmer Rouge government collapsed. Total deaths of people, men women and children, from several regimes in the years 1970-1980 is close to **4 million people.**

September 20, 1979 – Central African Republic. In the Central African Republic Jean-Bedel Bokassa is toppled in a **French-backed coup** when 700 French paratroopers take control of Bangui while Bokassa is away on a state visit to **Libya. France** made an embarrassing mistake in supporting Jean Bodel Bokassa, whose "coronation" in 1977 cost 10 million pounds, mostly paid by France. He arrived in a coach drawn by horses flown in from Europe, wore a flowing scarlet robe trimmed with ermine, sat on a throne under a great eagle, and like Napoleon, his great hero, he crowned himself. He had 9 wives and 54 children. He also had a cookie jar of diamonds in his office from which he would take some to hand to visitors as a gift. In 1979, he was said to have ordered the killing of over 100 school children following a protest over expensive uniforms owned by one of the wives. He ended up in jail in 1993.

1979 – China, Vietnam. Sino-Vietnamese War 1979. The Third Indochina War was a brief but bloody border war fought in 1979 between the People's Republic of China (PRC) and the Socialist Republic of Vietnam. The PRC launched the offensive in response to Vietnam's invasion and occupation of Cambodia, and Vietnamese raids into Chinese territory near the border. A PRC force of about 200,000, supported by 200 tanks from the People's Liberation Army (PLA) entered northern Vietnam.

   PRC troops withdrew about a month later. Both sides claimed victory and Vietnamese troops remained in Cambodia until 1989. The number of casualties is disputed, with some Western sources putting PLA losses at more than 25,000 killed throughout the month long war. According to Chinese democracy activist Wei Jingsheng only 9,000 Chinese troops had been killed and more than 10,000 wounded. An estimated 6,954 PLA soldiers were killed and 14,800 were wounded.

October 15, 1979 – El Salvador. Guerrilla war begins throughout the country **launching a 12-year civil war.** A cycle of violence takes hold as **rightist vigilante death squads kill thousands of people.** The poorly trained Salvadoran Armed Forces also engaged in repression and indiscriminate killings.

   When the Sandinistas overthrow Somoza in a coup they supply large amounts of military supplies and weapons to five **Salvadoran guerrilla groups.** This allowed Salvadoran military officers and civilian leaders to oust General Carlos Humberto Romero's government in Salvador in a coup and **Jose Napoleon Duarte** leads a civil-military Revolutionary Government Junta until the1982 elections. The military government initiated a land reform program and nationalized the banks and the marketing of coffee and sugar. Political parties were allowed to function again and on March 28 1982 Salvadorans elected a new constituent assembly and authority was peacefully transferred to Alvaro Magana the provisional President.

Communists groups demanded ever greater collectivism and launched a military campaign against the Duarte government which resulted in the Salvadoran Civil War from 1980–1992. Over 75,000 people will be killed during this civil war.

June 4, 1979 – Ghana. Lieutenant Jerry Rawlings leads a coup that deposes the Akuffo government in Ghana. A small group of disgruntled officers, led by Flight Lieutenant Jerry John Rawlings and several junior officers and corporals in the Air Force, try unsuccessfully to stage a coup. During his court martial Rawlings justified his action by claiming that official corruption had eroded public confidence in the government and had tarnished the image of the armed forces. He also charged that the local economy had been taken over by Syrian and Lebanese businessmen living in Ghana.

On June 3, a group of junior officers and enlisted personnel staged a successful coup, freed Rawlings, and then formed the Armed Forces Revolutionary Council to rule the country. Elections are held on June 18, but the AFRC retained power until September 24, when President Hilla Limann and the People's National Party assumed control of the government. In order to eliminate the opposition to the new government the AFRC begins eliminating members of the senior ranks of the armed forces. **Eight officers are executed and one hundred and fifty–five officers,** former officials, and wealthy businessmen are sentenced to prison. Back taxes are collected under threat of imprisonment and assets are seized from those that have embezzled or stolen money from the state.

March 13, 1979 – Grenada. On March 13, while Eric Gairy is out of the country, the NJM stage a **bloodless coup,** proclaim a People's Revolutionary Government and name Maurice Bishop, as Prime Minister. The new government holds to socialist ideals and moves to restore the nations devastated economy.

Prime Minister Maurice Bishop is killed during a military coup in 1983.

1979-2010 – India. The Tripura Rebellion in Northeast India is embroiled in a separatist rebellion as several rebel groups fight for independence.

1979 – Iran. Iranian Mujahadeen Khalq Guerrilla War. After the Iranian Revolution in 1979 topples the government of the Shah, the **Mujahadeen–e–Khalq** soon begin a **bloody guerrilla war** against the new Islamic government. They are the largest and most militant group opposed to the Islamic Republic of Iran. The Mujahadeen–e–Khalq are based in Iran and conduct assassinations, guerrilla operations, and terrorist raids in Iran. When the revolution overthrows the Shah, leadership is taken by the fundamentalist mullahs.

Saddam Hussein wants to take over or destroy the oil fields in Iran. This Iraq–Iran war will last nine years with no clear winner. Iraq will be left with a foreign debt of $80 billion and 1,000,000 people dead.

July 16, 1979 – Iraq. President Al-Bakr resigns and is succeeded by Vice-President **Saddam Hussein.** One of his first measures is to forcibly remove **a million Kurds** under his "arabisation" plan. The Kurds rose up and Saddam was only able to put down the revolt **with the help of the U.S.** and 150,000 **Turkish soldiers** which **NATO** had sent to Iraq. **Egypt, Sudan** and **Yemen** also sent troops.

Iraqi Military Intelligence Chief, Saddam Hussein, takes over as President of the Ba'th regime. He then sets about eliminating any and all people or groups of people he feels may become a threat. He executes them, one at a time or in mass. The Communist Party of Iraq is outlawed and Saddam purges the ranks of his own Ba'th party. Hundreds of top ranking Ba'thists and army officers are executed. Between 20,000 and 30,000 people are arrested from 1979-1981 and thousands of people are detained or disappear. Many people were simply executed.

1964-1979 – Southern Rhodesia. The Rhodesian Bush War also known as the **Zimbabwe War of Liberation** or the **Second Chimurenga**, is a civil war in Rhodesia, which lasted from July 1964 to 1979. The Rhodesian government under **Ian Smith**

and Zimbabwe-Rhodesian government under **Abel Muzorewa** fought against **Robert Mugabe's** Zimbabwe African National Union and **Joshua Nkomo's** Zimbabwe African People's Union. When the formerly British colony of Southern Rhodesia declared itself independent on November 11, 1965, it changed its name to Rhodesia, while the British continued to refer to it as Southern Rhodesia. The country returns to colonial status from 1979–1980.

1979 – Nicaragua. Sandinistas overthrow the **U.S.-backed Somoza dynasty's** 44 year dictatorship in **Nicaragua.** This family ruled the country in a harsh and unscrupulous way for more than four decades. The dynasty was overthrown after the **National Sandinista Revolution,** which took place when people from all sectors, workers, businessmen, peasants, students, and guerrillas, joined forces and finally defeated the Somoza dynasty and the National Guard.

Daniel Ortega of the Sandinista National Liberation Front of Nicaragua (FSLN) was one of those who led the revolution that overthrew the 43-year dictatorship of the Somoza family. During the decade of Sandinista rule **President Ronald Reagan's government** invested millions of dollars to undermine and destroy the new Nicaraguan state. A counter-revolutionary army, the Contras, waged a well financed war that left 50,000 people dead. The Contras will also be linked to cocaine trafficking in the U.S. along with the CIA.

1978-1979 – Uganda. The Uganda-Tanzania War led to the overthrow of **Idi Amin's** dictatorship. Most authorities do not know Idi Amin was born on May 17, 1928. Amin's close associates are few in number and he is facing increasing dissent from within Uganda. In early October 1978, dissident troops ambush Idi Amin at the presidential lodge in Kampala, but he escapes with his family in a helicopter.

When the Vice President, General Mustafa Adrisi, is injured in a suspicious car accident, troops loyal to the Vice President mutiny and Amin sends troops against all of them. This forces the Vice President and his loyal troops to flee into Tanzania where they are joined by the Tanzania-based anti-Amin exiles.

Idi Amin then declared war against Tanzania, and sent troops to invade and annex part of the Kagera region of Tanzania, which he claimed belonged to Uganda.

Libya's Muammar al-Gaddafi sends 2,500 troops to aid Amin, equipped with T-54 and T-55 tanks, BTR APCs, BM-21 Katyusha MRLs, artillery, MiG-21s, and a Tu-22 bomber. While Gaddafi's troops are moving closer and then occupying the front lines, Amin's troops are filling supply trucks with plundered loot and heading in the opposite direction.

The Tanzanian army easily defeated the **Ugandan and Libyan troops forcing** Amin to flee to Libya and then to Saudi Arabia. The Libyan forces retreated to Jinja and then returned to Libya through Kenya and Ethiopia, while the Tanzanian army remained in Uganda to maintain peace until new elections could be held.

Idi Amin, as the dictator and President of Uganda from 1971-1979, was responsible for the deaths of close to 200,000 people. Many sources list a higher figure but according to people who were there and lived through it the numbers were lower than 200,000 people killed.

1979 – Yemeni Civil War. North Yemen and South Yemen. President Ghashmi of North Yemen had assumed power when his predecessor President Ibrahim al Hamdi, was assassinated. President Gashmi served for eight months before he was assassinated in 1978 leading to a new war between the two Yemens.

The Arab League arranged a ceasefire in 1979, and for the second time the two countries agreed to unite. This time definite progress is made so that by 1983 a joint Yemen council was meeting at six-monthly intervals, and in March 1984 a joint committee on foreign policy sat for the first time in Aden.

December 11, 1979 – Great Britain grants independence to Zimbabwe (Rhodesia).

1980

The Oldest Boomer is 34 years old.

Cost of the Average House: $76,400	
Median Family Income: $17,700	**Minimum Wage:** $3.10/ hr **Average Hourly Wage:** $7.27
Gallon of Milk: $2.16	**Gallon Gasoline:** $1.25
New Car: **Buick Regal:** $6,119 **Camaro Z28:** Dash $7,263 **Pontiac Sunbird:** $5,164	**Coca-Cola:** $0.99/ 1 liter **Ground Beef:** $1.85/ lb **Loaf of Bread:** 50 cents **Flour:** 21 cents/ lb
Unemployment Rate: 6.3%-7.8%-7.2%	**First-class Stamp:** 15 cents

38 cents buying power in 1980 = **$1.00 in 2008.**
In 1980 what cost us 38 cents to purchase now costs us $1.00 in 2008.

Movies: "The Empire Strikes Back," "Raging Bull," "The Elephant Man," "Tess," "Ordinary People," "Coal Miner's Daughter," "Private Benjamin."

Broadway: "Grease" closes its run of 3,388 performances. "A Day in Hollywood, A Night In The Ukraine," "Really Rosie," off Broadway. "42nd Street."

TV: "Who Shot J.R.?" episode of "Dallas." "The Miracle on Ice," "Bosom Buddies," with Tom Hanks as Kip Wilson. "Magnum P.I.," "Pink Lady and Jeff," "Heathcliff and Marmaduke Show". "Barbara Mandrell and the Mandrell Sisters," "David Letterman Show," "Fonz and the Happy Days Gang, Animated," "Flo," "It's a Living," "I'm a Big Girl Now," "The John Davidson Show," "Richie Rich," "Solid Gold," "This Old House," "That's Incredible!" "The Tim Conway Show," "Zola Levitt."

Music: "The Long Riders," Ry Cooder. Blondie, 'Call Me" & "Atomic." Kelly Marie, "Feels Like I'm in Love." Odyssey, "Use It Up and Wear It Out." Michael Jackson, "Rock with You." The Police, "Don't Stand So Close to Me." Bob Seger and the Silver Bullet Band, "Against The Wind." Pete

Townshend, "Rough Boys." Bob Dylan, "Man Gave Names to All the Animals," Grace Jones, "Private Life." Ramones, "Do You Remember Rock And Roll Radio?" Queen, ""Crazy Little Thing Called Love" & "Another One Bites the Dust." The Jam, "Going Underground," "The Dreams Of Children." Air Supply, "Lost in Love." Billy Joel, "It's Still Rock and Roll to Me." The Grateful Dead, "Alabama Getaway." Judas Priest, "Living After Midnight." ABBA, "The Winner Takes It All." Pretenders, "Brass in Pocket." Detroit Spinners, "Working My Way Back to You." Lipps Inc, "Funkytown." Diana Ross, "Upside Down." Kenny Rogers, 'Coward of the County." Olivia Newton-John, "Magic." Olivia Newton-John & Electric Light Orchestra, "Xanadu." Boz Scaggs, "Look What You've Done to Me." The Soft Boys, "Old Pervert" & "I Wanna Destroy You." The Captain & Tennille, "Do That to Me One More Time." The Whispers, "And the Beat Goes On." Bob Marley and the Wailers, "Blackman Redemption," "Buffalo Soldier" & "Chant Down Babylon." Kenny Rogers, "Lady." Dead Kennedys, "Kill the Poor." Barbra Streisand, "Woman in Love." Plasmatics, "Butcher Baby-Tight Black Pants." Kool & the Gang, "Celebration." The Mash, "Suicide Is Painless." David Bowie, "Ashes To Ashes." Steely Dan, "Babylon Sisters." Christopher Cross, "Sailing." Frank Zappa, "I Don't Wanna Get Drafted." The Only Ones, "Why Don't You Kill Yourself." Ian Dury and the Blockheads, The Psychedelic Furs, Bruce Springsteen, "Out in the Street." "Imitation of Christ." "I Want To Be Straight." Bonnie Raitt, "You're Gonna Get What's Coming."

Deaths: Larry Williams, David Johnston, Jesse Curry, Dr. John Holbrook.

President: James Earl Carter, Jr. (D) Southern Baptist; vetoes 31/ 2 overrides

Vice President: Walter F. Mondale (D) Methodist; Presbyterian

House: D-277 ; R-158

Senate: 96th Congress (1979-1981) Majority Party: Democrat (58 seats) Minority Party: Republican (41 seats) Other Parties: 1 Independent Total Seats: 100

Federal Debt: $907.70 billion or 33 % of the GDP

Consumer Price Index CPI-U (1982 Base of 100): 82.40

GDP: $2,789.5 billion	**Inflation Rate:** 13.58%
Dow Jones: 969.45 (12-01) / 759.13 (04-21)	**S&P Price Index:** 135.76/ 25.77%
Prime Rate: 15.75% (02-19)/ 11.00% (07-25)/ 21.50% (12-19)	**Average Home Mortgage Rate:** 12.88/ 16.33%
1 oz Gold: $612.56	**1oz of Silver:** $48.70

Average Monthly S.S. Benefits Paid: $321 / month

Federal Debt: $907,701,000,000

Federal Deficit: $73.8 billion dollars

Defense Spending: $167.88 billion	**Interest Spending:** $52.53 billion
Health Care Spending: $55.26 billion	**Pensions Spending:** $134.40 billion
Welfare Spending: $54.86 billion	**Education Spending:** $33.22 billion
Transportation Spending: $21.33 billion	**Misc. Other Spending:** $53.43 billion
Protection Spending: $4.70 billion	**Total Government Spending:** $590.94 billion

% of GDP that goes towards just the interest payment: 1.93%

$1.00 = 1.530 Yuan, China NPC	**$1.00 =** 226.63 Yen, Japan

$1.00 =Iranian Rial
Preferential Rate: 82.00; Unofficial Rate: 115.00

U.S. Population: 227,726,000	**World Population:** 4,456,705,217

World AIDS Victims: Known Deaths in the U.S. this year are 31; this includes all known cases through 1981.

U.S. Birth Rate: 3,612,258	**U.S. Abortions:** 1,297,606—1,553,900

1980

U.S. Homicide Rate: 10.7/ 100,000 population	U.S. Violent Crime: 596.6/ 100,000 population
Annual Average Domestic Crude Oil Prices: $37.42 / barrel, $97.68 (2007 adjusted)	

Oil:

1980 – The 1980s oil glut is a surplus of crude oil caused by falling demand following the 1973 and 1979 energy crises. The world price of oil peaks at $37.42 and then moves lower for six years. Energy conservation due to high prices and slowing economic activity is partially responsible for the oil glut. OPEC countries are cheating each other by producing more than they are saying in order to gain more economic power.

President Jimmy Carter signed an executive order in 1979 that will remove market controls by October 1981, when oil prices will be allowed to float and those in the market are now maneuvering to get richer.

September 1985 – Saudi Arabia tries to gain market share by increasing production, creating a huge surplus that angers many of their colleagues in OPEC. High-cost oil production facilities become less profitable and even unprofitable. The U.S. imported 28 percent of its oil in 1982 and 1983, down from 46.5 percent in 1977, due to lower consumption. Reliance on Middle East sources dwindle even further as **Britain, Mexico, Nigeria** and **Norway** join **Canada** as American suppliers.

March 10, 1982 – Imported crude oil from Libya is banned in the United States.

January 1980 – The Carter Doctrine threatens nuclear war over the Persian Gulf oil fields. President Carter issued the Carter Doctrine, which declared that any interference with U.S. oil interests in the Persian Gulf would be considered an attack on the vital interests of the United States.

"Let our position be absolutely clear: An attempt by any outside force to gain control of the Persian Gulf region will be regarded as an assault on the vital interests of the United States of America, and such an assault will be repelled by any means necessary, including military force." President Jimmy Carter.

February 1980 – The U.S. Rapid Deployment Joint Task Force is created, in what turns out to be a controversial and bitterly contested decision, RDJTF focuses on the Middle East. In his Fiscal Year 1981 annual report, Secretary of Defense Harold Brown announced, "the President and I believe the prospect of renewed turbulence in the Middle East, the Caribbean, and elsewhere, and the possibility of new demands on our non-nuclear posture, require additional precautionary actions. As a consequence, we will accelerate our efforts to improve the capabilities of our **Rapid Deployment Forces.**"

The Department of Defense will create as many as five additional 'light' Army divisions, but without adding any significant manpower to the Army. The Department of Defense budget will allocate $59 billion for the RDF in 1985, with $47 billion going to the Persian Gulf or Southwest Asia.

September 22, 1980 – The Iran-Iraq war begins. Iraq attacks Iran in an attempt to seize the oil rich provinces in western Iran for its own use. The United States encouraged Saddam Hussein to attack Iran.

October 1980 – October Surprise is a **deal between the Ronald Reagan / George H.W. Bush campaign** and the **Iranian government** to delay the release of the U.S. Embassy hostages until after the Presidential election. In 1980, the death of the Shah on July 27th and the invasion of Iran by Iraq in September made the Iranians more receptive to resolving the hostage crisis. The hostages were released on the very day of Reagan's inauguration, twenty minutes after his inaugural address.

1980 – Iran. Following the Iraqi invasion of Iran, oil production in Iran nearly stopped, and Iraq's oil production was severely cut. After 1980, oil prices began a six-year decline that culminated with a 46 percent price drop in 1986. This was due to reduced demand and over-production, and caused OPEC to lose its unity. By November the combined production of both Iran and Iraq was only a million barrels per day which is 6.5 million barrels per day less than a year before. As a consequence worldwide crude oil production is 10 percent lower than in 1979. **Oil exporters** such as **Mexico, Nigeria,** and **Venezuela** expanded. The U.S. and Europe use more oil from **Prudhoe Bay** and the **North Sea.**

1980 – Iraq. Because of the 1973 crisis in the Middle East, the defeat of the U.S. in Vietnam and the world economic slump of 1974-1975, western countries were incapable of intervening in Iraq. The sharp increase in oil prices which ensued had a dramatic effect on the country.

In the previous 20 years profits from oil had steadily increased four-fold reaching the modest figure of $572 million. Now these profits shot up dramatically reaching $26.5 billion by 1980. More than $59 billion flowed from the energy producing states to the Federal Treasury from 1980–1984 due to the Crude Oil Windfall Profits Tax.

1978-1980 – Texas. When West Texas intermediate crude oil **increased 250 percent** between 1978 and 1980, the oil-producing areas of **Texas, Oklahoma, Louisiana, Colorado, Wyoming, and Alaska** began experiencing an economic boom and population inflows.

1980s – Libya. Most Libyans enjoy educational opportunities, health care, and housing that are among the best in Africa and the Middle East due to the oil revenues.

1980 – Turkey uses half its export earnings to pay for oil and has a military coup in 1980. The military rules for the next three years through the National Security Council, before democracy is restored.

1980 – The National Academy of Sciences calls leaded gasoline the greatest source of atmospheric lead pollution.

1980 – Gasohol. The National Security Act of 1980 mandates all gasoline be blended with a minimum of 10 percent grain alcohol, termed "gasohol." This was subsequently scuttled by the Reagan Administration. Gasohol or ethanol from corn mixed with gasoline, it is basically the same thing.

1980 – During the 1970's the CIA grew fat and lazy. President Carter is changing policy toward Israel and the mid-east due to false data suggesting the Soviets need oil and are planning to invade the Middle East. Oil man George Bush was the director of **the CIA** when the oil fraud began with the Carter administration. Bush begins in 1976 as soon as they know Carter will win the election and before Carter can remove Bush as Director in 1976. The oil companies were a big retirement area for ex-CIA staff and there were so many it was easy to fake data in the mid 1970's.

The American people are angry the U.S. is being jerked around by a few desert states and embrace President Carter's oil conservation policies. Prices fall and the "Global" oil companies try to sell the idea that there is plenty of oil but they cannot afford to drill for it unless price controls are lifted.

Major News:

January 4, 1980 – President Carter announces economic sanctions, and an embargo on the sale of grain and high technology, **against the Soviet Union** in response to the **Soviet invasion of Afghanistan.**

February 2, 1980 – Abscam. The FBI's undercover bribery investigation implicates a U.S. senator, seven members of the House, and 31 other public officials.

April 24, 1980 – The U.S. rescue mission of hostages in Iran is aborted. Eight American military helicopters with the secret mission to rescue 52 American hostages held by Islamist students at the U.S. embassy in Tehran is aborted when one of the choppers slams into a fuel transport setting both aircraft on fire. Eight servicemen are killed and the mission is over. President Carter is humiliated with another sign of his weakness and is certain to have a very difficult reelection campaign.

November 4, 1980 – In a sweeping victory, Ronald Reagan (R) defeats incumbent President Jimmy Carter. Republicans also gain control of the Senate. The victory in the Electoral College, 489 to 49, as well as an 8 million vote margin in the popular vote over Carter ensured a mandate for the new president. Reagan never carries out his pledge to reduce the federal role in education by eliminating the Department of Education. The hostages in Iran are released 20 minutes after Reagan is sworn in due to a secret deal struck with the Iranian government. Hold the hostages a little longer or just not release them a little sooner? Is there a difference?

1980

December 8, 1980 – Former Beatle John Lennon is shot to death by Mark David Chapman in New York City. **John Lennon**, 40, was shot several times as he entered the Dakota, his luxury apartment building on Manhattan's Upper West Side, opposite Central Park. As he lay semiconscious, hemorrhaging from four bullets in his back, Mark David Chapman stood quietly a few yards away leafing through the pages of J.D. Salinger's novel, "Catcher in the Rye." John Lennon was placed into a police car and rushed to St Luke's-Roosevelt Hospital Center, where he died.

Several years after going to prison **Chapman gave this account in a BBC interview.** "He walked past me and then I heard in my head, 'Do it, do it, do it,' over and over again, saying 'Do it, do it, do it,' like that." "I don't remember aiming. I must have done, but I don't remember drawing a bead or whatever you call it. And I just pulled the trigger steady five times." Chapman described his feeling at the time of the shooting as "no emotion, no anger dead silence in the brain." There has always been speculation that **Chapman had been programmed as an assassin,** carrying out someone else's command. The book "Who Killed John Lennon," by Fenton Bresler, points to the CIA.

1980 – The Titanic wreckage is found. Although there are differing accounts of who actually found the wreckage, it is found in 1980.

1980 – The Gang of Four. China's notorious Gang of Four and six other high-ranking officials are put on trial. The most celebrated defendant is **Jiang Qing,** 67, the widow of **Mao Tse-tung,** who, along with her allies in the Gang of Four, led Mao's reckless and violent Cultural Revolution from 1966 to 1976. They were arrested four years ago, shortly after Mao's death in 1976. Also on trial are a group of senior military officials who allegedly plotted with the late Defense Minister Lin Biao to assassinate Mao in 1971 and seize supreme power for themselves. They were found guilty of treason and their sentences ranged from death to 20 years in prison.

Civil Rights Movement:

May 17-18, 1980 – Liberty City riots. Arthur McDuffie Riots. Liberty City is named for the Liberty Square Housing Project built in the late 1930s for Miami's low-income

African-Americans, the second of its kind in the South at the time.

Black leaders tried to calm Miami's "Liberty City" section, after police officers were acquitted for killing an unarmed black man. Two nights of looting, burning and shooting left 19 known dead and hundreds injured in the worst racial violence in the nation since the Detroit riot in 1967. Two-hundred riot-equipped state policemen and other state lawmen are already on duty when Florida Governor Robert Graham orders another 2,500 National Guardsmen to Miami increasing the guard troops to 3,600. In Washington, **President Jimmy Carter** dispatched Attorney General Benjamin Civiletti to Miami. The attorney general told the President the Justice Department will convene a federal grand jury to consider whether there are civil-rights grounds to prosecute four former white policemen acquitted in the beating death of a black insurance agent.

October 10, 1980 – President Carter signs legislation establishing **Boston African American National Historic Site,** which includes the oldest Black Church in America and other historic sites of the Black Heritage Trail in Boston, Massachusetts.

1980 – Census of 1980. The U.S. population: 226,545,805.
Black population: 26,495,025 (11.8%). White population: 188,371,622

Women's Movement:

1980 – Ronald Reagan. For the first time since the passage of the ERA, **an anti-ERA President is elected.** Ronald W. Reagan.

1980 – The Equal Employment Opportunity Commission issues a set of guidelines detailing prohibited **sexual behavior** that applies to all federal agencies and to private businesses with 15 or more employees.

1980's – Feminist Movement. American society is becoming more conservative politically and the feminist movement experiences a backlash within its ranks from anti-feminist detractors. The Feminist Movement has been thought of as mostly white, upper middle-class with little or no real understanding of the concerns of poor, African-American, and Hispanic women. Liberal feminists focus on the rights of women as individuals while radical feminists align themselves with revolutionary groups, viewing women as a disenfranchised class of citizens. Lesbians were a driving force in the early feminist movement but now have more in common with the gay liberation movement. **President Ronald Reagan** makes his opposition to the ERA public and religious and mainstream conservative groups attack Roe vs. Wade.

Popular Culture:

1980 – Ten Commandments. U.S. Supreme Court ruling, Stone vs. Graham. The Court said posting of the Ten Commandments in the nation's schools is unconstitutional.

February 27, 1980 – Bogota, Colombia. **Dominican Republic Embassy Siege.** Seventeen guerrillas dressed in the warm-up clothes of joggers storm the embassy compound, and hold 60 people, including 14 ambassadors, for 61 days. Then, after demanding $50 million dollars and the release of 311 jailed comrades, they eventually lower their demands to $2.5 million dollars and the release of twelve prisoners. They were finally paid the $2.5 million dollars and were flown out of the country to Cuba with the approval of Fidel Castro.

April 15-October 31, 1980 – Mariel Boatlift. The Mariel Boatlift brings 125,000 undocumented Cuban migrants to South Florida from Port of Mariel, Cuba. This is accomplished by a flotilla of mostly U.S. vessels **in violation of U.S. law.**
   Cuban Premier Fidel Castro removed Cuban guards from the **Peruvian embassy** in Havana on April 4, and two days later 10,000 Cubans sought asylum in the embassy. The U.S. appeared to be taken by surprise.
   Two weeks later Fidel Castro allowed anyone wanting to leave Cuba free access to do so from the port of Mariel, and immediately every available boat and then anything that can float began carrying Cubans the 90 miles to south Florida. When Cubans and others heard that the port of Mariel was an open Port, appeals were made for all available boats to volunteer and assist the fleeing refugees. The exodus was organized by Cuban-Americans with the agreement of Cuban Prime Minister Fidel Castro and hundreds of small boats, mostly pleasure craft of varying size left Miami in

groups for the trip to Cuba and the return to Miami. As the boats arrived in Cuba, Fidel emptied the Cuban prisons and mental institutions and these people were added to the exodus. The Carter administration again suffered from the decisions it made with regard to how they handled the mass exodus and documentation, when this became public knowledge. Was it just coincidence that Miami became the major drug entry point to the U.S.?

1980 – By 1940, the Federal Bureau of Prisons had grown to 24 facilities with 24,360 inmates. Except for a few fluctuations, the number of inmates did not change significantly between 1940 and 1980, when the population was 24,252.

From **1980 to 1989,** the inmate population more than doubled, from just over 24,000 to almost 58,000. As of June 2003, there were about 34,000 **employees** in the Bureau. The total population of **prisons** and jails in the **United States** neared the 2.1 million mark in June 2003, according to the Bureau of Justice Statistics.

1980 – Brook Shields whispers, "You know what comes between me and my Calvins? Nothing." The ad is banned from many outlets.

1980 – The Drug Abuse Prevention, Treatment, and Rehabilitation Amendments extend prevention education and treatment programs.

1973 – Jim Bakker. Televangelists, Jim and Tammy Faye Baker have built and manage the very profitable Heritage USA theme park in Fort Mill, South Carolina, (south of Charlotte). It is the third most successful theme park in the U.S. and includes a satellite system to distribute their PTL network 24 hours a day across the country. Viewers exceed twelve million, and contributions requested 24/7 from viewers are estimated to exceed $1 million a week.

Although the Bakers state proceeds go to expanding the theme park and the mission of PTL, Jim and Tammy Faye also take conspicuous consumption to a new level for a non-profit organization **as they hustle the "prosperity message."** In Jim's 1996 book he will admit the first time he read the Bible all the way through was in prison and came to the conclusion his "prosperity message did not line up with the tenor of Scripture."

1980

1980 – Rubik's Cube, a 3-D mechanical puzzle invented in 1974 by Hungarian sculptor and professor of architecture **Ernő Rubik** becomes one of the most popular toys ever. Originally called the "Magic Cube," it won the German Game of the Year special award for Best Puzzle. After being licensed to Ideal Toys for production Rubik's Cube went on to sell over 350,000,000 cubes worldwide by December 2008.

1980 – Abortion. RU-486, the abortion pill is released in France. **RU-486** uses two powerful synthetic hormones with the generic names of mifepristone and misoprostol to chemically induce abortions in women five-to-nine weeks pregnant.

1980 – Broderbund is founded by brothers Doug and Gary Carlston to market the games Doug has created. Their first games are **Galactic Empire, Galactic Trader** and **Galactic Revolution.** They continued to have success with popular games such as **Myst** in 1993 and **Riven** in 1997.

1980 – Post-It Notes, first used exclusively at 3M headquarters in 1977, are now introduced nationally in the United States. Lee Iacocca and other Fortune 500 CEOs write to say how much they love the product.

1980 – Richard Pryor gets badly burned trying to freebase cocaine. Procedures for crack and freebase cocaine are based on the fact that while cocaine hydrochloride, regular cocaine, requires a high temperature to ignite, base cocaine requires a much lower temperature to ignite. This makes it ideal for smoking.

September 9, 1980 – The Plowshares Eight. The Plowshares peace movement against the modern arms race is founded on the Biblical ethic of beating swords into plowshares. **Philip Francis Berrigan**, WWII veteran, former Roman Catholic priest, his brother **Reverend Daniel Berrigan,** and six others begin the **Plowshares Movement** when they enter the **General Electric Nuclear Missile Re-entry Division** in King of Prussia, Pennsylvania. They hammer on two nose cones, pour blood on documents and offer prayers for peace before they are arrested and initially charged with over ten different felony and misdemeanor counts. On April 10, 1990, after nearly ten years of trials and appeals, the Plowshares Eight were re-sentenced and paroled in consideration of time already served in prison.

Two decades later **Philip Francis Berrigan** was still at it, though the world had largely stopped paying attention. In his final clash in December 1999, he and three other Plowshare activists broke into an Air National Guard base near Baltimore and attacked two A-10 warplanes with blood and hammers to protest the military's use of depleted uranium in armor-piercing shells. He was imprisoned for the act and remained behind bars until December 14, 2001.

Philip Francis Berrigan at the age of 77 missed the 2001 premiere of a documentary film about his role in Catonsville. He was in an Ohio prison on charges of interference with a weapons system. "There are times when I'd like to just sit back in my rocking chair, but I'm going to fight all the way and hopefully die with my boots on," Berrigan told Reuters in a May 2001 interview at a federal prison in Ohio."

Philip Francis Berrigan died late on Friday, December 6, 2002, at Jonah House, his communal living facility for pacifists in West Baltimore, after being diagnosed with liver and kidney cancer in October. He stopped chemotherapy after one treatment and received last rites at a November 30 ceremony officiated by the Rev. Daniel Berrigan.

1980 – Isuzu, "Lying Joe Isuzu." Della Famina, Travisano & Partners.

Business / Technology:

1980 – The Supreme Court allows gene patenting. For the first time **"Life Forms"** are allowed to be patented by the U.S. court. Prior to 1980, life forms were considered a part of nature and were not patentable. Diamond vs. Chakrabarty changed this with the 5 to 4 U.S. Supreme Court decision that genetically engineered (modified) bacteria are patentable because they do not occur naturally in nature. In this case, Chakrabarty had modified a bacterium to create an oil-dissolving bioengineered microbe. This leads the way for the large chemical companies to patent other life forms, such as seeds.

And "Away we go!!" July 2, 2009, gene patenting is still being bitterly fought in the courts. Myriad Genetics owns, human genes, and a recent lawsuit challenges this right. Currently over three million genome-related patent applications have been filed. U.S. patent applications are confidential until a patent is issued, so determining which sequences are the subject of patent applications is impossible. Patents for stem cells from monkeys and other organisms already have been issued. Therefore, based on past court rulings, **human embryonic stem cells are patentable. July 2009** - Calls for more proof have greeted claims that **human sperm** have been created in the lab for the first time. If further tests show that the lab-grown sperm are indeed identical to the natural kind, they might be patentable. This will unleash a whole new market for **"Designer Children."**

1980 – It is widely reported that Japan has surpassed the U.S. as the world's largest automaker.

August 1980 – Solidarity. Poland has massive strikes. Solidarity, the first free trades union within the communist bloc, is the also the first step in the eventual dissolution of the **Soviet Union.**

The birth of the **Solidarity** trades union, a massive social movement, with more than 10 million members, begins when Polish workers, led by **Lech Walesa,** strike the Gdansk shipyards. The government soon agreed to demands made by the newly-formed union to both legalize unions, as well as affirm the right to strike. In the course of the strike it is decided to make demands of a political nature and the 21 demands made by the Strike Committee in August 1980 in Gdansk, lead to the creation of the union when the striking workers demanded: 1) Free trades unions will be established, 2) Censorship is abolished, and 3) Political prisoners are released.

The independent free trades union Solidarity is active for more than a year until December 1981, when martial law is declared in Poland. The Soviet Union forced Poland to outlaw Solidarity or face possible invasion, but it was too late. The Solidarity movement had already eroded the dominance of the Communist Party. In ten years it will win the presidency.

September 22, 1980 – Toxic Shock Syndrome. Procter and Gamble Co. announce a recall of its Rely brand tampons when federal studies conclude their use increases chances of toxic shock syndrome.

1980 – Insulin. The genetic engineering of insulin begins clinical trials.

1980 – FAX Machine Standards. The CCITT Group 3 recommendation for facsimile machines is adopted. Although the FAX machine is an improvement it is not until an international FAX standard allowing various FAX machines to communicate with each other that business really speeds up. Now for the first time one Fax machine can talk to any other Fax machine in the world. **Fax is FAST** until email and then faxing seems to take forever.

1980 – Voyager 1 sends back images of **Saturn and its moons,** one billion miles away. Flying 40,000 miles above the planet's clouds, Voyager 1 makes its closest approach to Saturn and takes stunning images of the gem of the solar system and its rings, showing that the rings are far more complex than ever imagined. The spacecraft also studies Saturn's largest moon, Titan, finding a thick atmosphere from which a rain of organic molecules likely forms lakes on the moon's cold surface.

1980 – Sony introduces the consumer camcorder.

1980 – Intelsat V relays 12,000 phone calls, 2 color TV channels.

April 26, 1980 – Great Britain performs a **nuclear test** at the U.S. Nevada Test Site. **October 24, 1980 – Great Britain** performs a **nuclear test** at the Nevada Test Site. **December 17, 1980 – Great Britain** performs a **nuclear test** at the Nevada Test Site.

1980 – The IBM 3380 1 gigabyte disk drive is the size of a refrigerator and sells for $40,000. **The average PC hard drive** holds 10 MB by 1984.

May 22, 1980 – Pac-Man is the best-selling coin-operated game in history. In the game's first year, over 100,000 Pac-Man machines are made and sold around the world. **Namco** estimates that the original Pac-Man arcade title has been played more than **ten billion times**. Namco's total Pac-Man revenues have reached $100 million. The original Pac-Man arcade title took eight people fifteen months to complete. Four worked on the hardware, four worked on the software.

1980 – VCR. Only 1% of U.S. homes have VCRs.

1980 – In France, a holographic film shows a gull flying.

1980

1980 – Addressable cable TV converters pinpoint individual homes enabling billing.

Finance:

January 7, 1980 – The government bails out Chrysler Corporation. President **Jimmy Carter** signs the Chrysler Loan Guarantee Act, offering the troubled automaker $1.5 billion in federal support. Did it work? The Chrysler Corporation Loan Guarantee Act of 1979 required creditors to make certain "concessions" which allows Chrysler to pay off more than $600 million in debts at just 30 cents on the dollar. They also are allowed to convert nearly $700 million in debts into a special class of preferred stock that pays no dividends and is unredeemable for several years. It has been estimated Chrysler cut its white collar work force by 20,000 and laid off 42,000 of its hourly workers.

1980 – The IMF completes a 5-year gold sales program. Negative political events in Iran, Afghanistan, and elsewhere propel the price of gold to an historic high of **$850 per ounce** on January 21.

1980 – Fort Knox Gold. Firestone, LTD, a Swiss corporation, sets up a string of dummy corporations to purchase **Fort Knox Gold** and keep it in Switzerland, never to return to the U.S. An article titled **"U.S. Charges Firestone In Illegal Gold Trading"** in the *New York Times* and an article titled **"Firestone Trial Opens On Gold Chances Today"** in the *Richmond Times Dispatch* on October 14, 1980 gives a great deal of information. Some were prosecuted, found guilty and sent to prison.

1980 – Usury Laws. Each U.S. state has its own statute which dictates how much interest can be charged before it is considered usurious or unlawful. If a lender charges above the lawful interest rate, a court will not allow the lender to sue to recover the debt because the interest rate was illegal anyway. In a lot of States the maximum interest rate is **10%** and it is common to charge much less. Usury laws are tied to fundamentalist religious beliefs, and before 1980, credit cards were subject to usury laws that generally capped interest rates in all 50 states.

The **U.S. Supreme Court held unanimously in 1978** that the **National Banking**

Act of 1863 allowed nationally-chartered banks to charge the legal rate of interest allowed by the state where it had its headquarters. States such as **South Dakota** and **Delaware** removed their interest rate caps after the ruling, and banks flocked there so they could charge higher rates.

Congress passes the Depository Institutions Deregulation and Monetary Control Act **exempting** federally chartered savings banks, installment plan sellers and chartered loan companies **from state usury limits, in 1980.** This in effect ends all state and local usury laws.

Under the act the **Federal Reserve Bank can** simply print tens of billions of dollars of U.S. debt, repayable to the Federal Reserve with interest by you, the taxpayer, to buy the worthless bonds of dictatorial regimes which is called "monetizing foreign debt." This effectively props up these dictatorial regimes in other nations.

So, up until 1980 there were consumer protections in place that limited banks from robbing the gullible. In 2008 the average bank interest rate is around 28%, along with a barrage of fees. The Supreme Court ruled in 1996 that credit card fees were "interest" charges, again subject to state law where the bank is headquartered. That basically gave banks freedom to expand and raise credit card fees as much as they want. Bankers love this and increase the late fee from an average of $10 to $40 within 3 years.

1980 – FDIC Bailout, First Pennsylvania. Established in 1782 as one of the first U.S. private banks, First Pennsylvania was among many banks in the 1970s made insolvent by high deposit interest rates that outstripped earnings from lower-yielding assets. It was the first large-scale bailout by the FDIC, which provided a $325 million five-year subordinated note that allowed First Pennsylvania to sell off government securities and reduce its interest drain. The FDIC made its money back, without interest.

1977-1980 – President Carter tries to control government spending. By March 24, inflation and interest rates, are both over 18%, and are so far beyond anything that Americans have experienced in peacetime that most Americans are afraid it may get worse. This fear affects the U.S. financial markets.

President Carter is thrown out of office after one term for numerous policies that are deemed failures including the Mariel boatlift, the Iranian Hostage Crisis and the decisions required to cut spending and deal with the energy crisis. There is a total lack of trust in his abilities as President.

1980 – S&L crisis. An S&L association is a financial institution in the United States that accepts savings deposits and makes mortgage loans. Massive failures of savings and loan associations begin in 1980 and by 1989, close to 1,000 S&L's are shut down. Under the **Carter Administration the United States Congress** allowed S&L's to make consumer loans of up to 20 percent of their assets, issue credit cards, accept negotiable order of withdrawal accounts from individuals and nonprofit organizations, and invest up to 20 percent of their assets in commercial real estate loans.

The **ultimate cost of the S&L crisis is estimated to be around $160 billion, about $125 billion** of which is directly paid for by the U.S. government (**U.S. taxpayer**) either directly or through charges on their savings and loan accounts. One of the most important contributors to the problem is deposit brokerage, while unabashed **corruption** is believed to be responsible for at least 25% of the total S&L loss.

Rodney Stich says the S&L crisis may be just another CIA scam in his 1994 book **"Defrauding America."** After Congress cut back on CIA funding the CIA needed money. There is reason to believe they took advantage of the new laws that deregulated thrifts/savings and loans, and set up scams to steal billions of dollars from our government for their covert operations. **George H.W. Bush** is said to be linked at this same time to **BCCI** and the **Safari Club.** Also **Charles Keating,** the biggest name of the scandal, is thought to have had extensive CIA ties.

1980 – Brazil. The beginning of Hyperinflation. Political liberalization and the declining world economy contributed to Brazil's economic and social problems. In 1978 and 1980, huge strikes took place in the industrial ring around São Paulo as protesters claimed wage increases indexed to inflation were not acceptable. Union leaders and politicians are arrested for violation of national security laws, the International Monetary Fund imposes a painful austerity program, and Brazil is required to hold down wages to fight inflation. Catholic Priests who become a voice for rural peasants seizing unused private land are expelled from the country and the government is forced to institute land reform.

Chronic inflation turns into hyperinflation due to the expansion of the money supply. **The government financed** its operation and its development projects, **not out of taxes or borrowing funds,** but **by simply creating money.**

In 1980 the consumer price index is 4. It doubles in 1981 and doubles again in 1982. It more than doubles again in 1983 and then triples in 1984. It roughly, triples again every year for three years and then jumps seven times in 1989 to 328,113.

The CPI jumps to 100,000,000 in 1990, 500,000,000 in 1991, and 5,600,000,000 in 1992. In 1995 it is 4,104,400,000,000! From 1980 when the IMF price level series began to 1995 the price level increased by a factor of 1.0 trillion.

Hyperinflation. **What had cost 1.0 Real in 1980 cost 1.0 trillion Reais in 1997!**

Books:

1980 – Marshall Clinard's book, "Corporate Crime," reveals that between 1975 and 1976 the country's 582 largest corporations had violated the law a total of 1,553 times.

1980 – "Midnight's Children," **Salman Rushdie.** An example of postcolonial literature.

1980 – "**Housekeeping,**" Marilynne Robinson.

TV:

November 21, 1980 – Who Shot JR? From the TV show "**Dallas," the episode "Who Shot J.R.?** draws more viewers than any other show in TV history up to this point. It was estimated that 83,000,000 people watched the episode.

1980 – Robert L. Johnson begins the BET, Black Entertainment Television, out of Washington, D.C.

February 1, 1980 – The soap opera Love of Life airs its last episode, after twenty-nine years on the air.

1980 – "The David Letterman Show" debuts as a morning show but is soon canceled.

1980

Sports:

1980 – World Series. The Philadelphia Phillies of the National League end 97 years of frustration by defeating the American League champion Kansas City Royals.

January 20, 1980 – President Carter announces that U.S. athletes will not attend the **Summer Olympics in Moscow** unless the Soviet Union withdraws from **Afghanistan.** The U.S. Olympic Committee votes on April 12, against U.S. participation in the Moscow Summer Olympics.

February 13, 1980 – The opening ceremonies of the 1980 Winter Olympics Games are held in **Lake Placid, New York.** One of the most thrilling moments include the **"Miracle on Ice"** when a team of **U.S. amateur ice hockey players** defeat the vaunted Soviet Union professional all-star team in the semi-final game, then win the gold medal over Finland. U.S. speed skater Eric Heiden also concluded one of the most amazing feats in sports history when he **won all five speed skating medals** from the sprint at 500 meters to the marathon 10,000 meter event.

February 22, 1980 – The "Miracle on Ice" is the nickname given to the February 22 medal-round men's ice hockey game during the 1980 Olympic Winter Games, in which a team of amateur and collegiate players from the United States, led by coach Herb Brooks, defeat the hockey team from the Soviet Union, 4–3. The Soviet team is considered to be the best international hockey team in the world. The explosion of cheers was deafening, and most of the 10,000 fans squeezed into the 8,500-seat arena began a chant of **"USA! USA!"** that never slowed for the final 10 minutes. The U.S. team won the gold medal two days later, rallying from a 2-1 deficit after two periods to beat Finland 4-2.

April 21, 1980 – Rosie Ruiz, banned from the major marathons, became a synonym for cheating. On April 21, the clock read 2 hours, 31, minutes, 56 seconds, the third-fastest marathon ever by a woman and a record by a woman in this race when the 26-year-old New Yorker came nowhere to claim the victory in the **Boston Marathon.**
   Nobody believes Rosie Ruiz ever tried to win the race, never mind set a world

record, but once they hustled her into the news conference for a bizarre string of non-answers there was no turning back. It was already too late and Rosie was on her way into the history books as one of the greatest frauds in sports.

Rosie has never stopped insisting she ran the race, even though no one saw Rosie at any of the checkpoints and witnesses later say she ran out of the crowd and onto the course less than a mile from the finish line.

Running off of the course and then back on at the last mile never should have worked. Today it would be much more difficult because runners have computerized chips on their shoes and electronically monitored stops on the race course, to track them and record their starting and finishing times.

July 5 1980 – Bjorn Borg wins his fifth consecutive **Wimbledon** men's singles championship, sending a cross-court backhand shot out of **John McEnroe's** reach for the 1-6, 7-5, 6-3, 6-7 (16-18), 8-6 triumph 3hrs and 53 minutes. This five-set match is often cited as the best Wimbledon final ever played. Having lost the opening set 6-1 to an all-out McEnroe assault, Borg took the next two 7-5, 6-3 and had two Championship points at 5-4 in the fourth. But McEnroe averted disaster and went on to level the match in Wimbledon's most memorable 34-point tiebreaker, which he won 18-16.

August 20, 1980 – Reinhold Messner makes the first solo ascent of Everest without supplemental oxygen. Messner reached the summit of the mountain solo for the first time, without supplementary oxygen or support, on the more difficult Northwest route via the North Col to the North Face and the Great Couloir. He climbed for three days entirely alone from his base camp at 6,500 meters (21,300 ft).

Music:

1980 – Disco is dying and going down fast as the year begins with a strong disco backlash, which causes the majority of musicians to abandon the use of acoustic and analog instruments in an attempt to distance themselves from anything related to disco.

1980

January 16, 1980 – Paul McCartney is arrested in Tokyo for possession of a half pound of marijuana forcing the remaining part of McCartney's tour to be canceled.

January 25, 1980 – Paul McCartney is released from a Japanese jail and is kicked out of the country by Japanese authorities.

February 19, 1980 – Bon Scott, lead singer of **AC/DC,** dies in London. Common folklore cites pulmonary aspiration of vomit as the cause of his death, but the official cause is listed as "Acute alcohol poisoning" and "Death by Misadventure."

March 19, 1980 – Elvis Presley's autopsy is subpoenaed during the trial of Dr. George Nichopoulos, who will later be found guilty of overprescribing drugs to Presley, **Jerry Lee Lewis** and other clients.

November 21, 1980 – The Eagles' Don Henley is arrested when **cocaine, Quaaludes,** and **marijuana** are found in his hotel room after a nude 16 year-old prostitute had drug-related seizures. Henley is also subsequently charged with contributing to the delinquency of a minor.

December 4, 1980 – Led Zeppelin disbands following the **death** of drummer John Bonham.

December 7, 1980 – Darby Crash, leader of seminal L.A. punk band **The Germs** dies of a **heroin** overdose in a suicide pact.

December 8, 1980 – John Lennon is shot dead outside of his apartment building in New York City. There are reported links to the CIA.

Natural Disasters:

January 24, 1980 – Livermore, California. A 5.8 magnitude earthquake causes light damage and no deaths.

May 18, 1980 – Mt. St. Helens. The 1980 eruption of Mt. St. Helens is the most studied volcanic eruption of the twentieth century. Dormant since 1857, the Mt. St. Helens volcano, in Washington State, erupts on May 18, May 25, and June 12, killing fifty-seven people and bringing economic devastation to the area with losses near $3 billion. The blast is estimated to have a power five hundred times greater than the Hiroshima atomic bomb.

U.S., volcanologists were keenly aware of the potential danger and the **U.S. Geological Survey** established a base of operations in Vancouver to monitor the volcano months before the eruption.

David Johnston, a geological survey volcanologist, is camping on Coldwater Ridge, only a few miles north of Mt. St. Helens, when the eruption occurs. At 8:32 a.m., Johnston radioed the USGS base and exclaimed "Vancouver, Vancouver, this is it!" The ensuing volcanic blast devastated the northern flank of the volcano, **killing Johnston.**

A large portion of the rock wall on the north side of the mountain fell, followed by a lateral blast of rock, stone, and poisonous gas that carried debris over 17 miles. The surrounding forest is flattened and most of it is buried. The disaster wiped out substantial populations of elk, deer, bear, and coyote, and destroyed 230 sq mi of vegetation. A volcanic plume rose 80,000 ft into the air, blanketing a large area of the NW United States with volcanic ash. The summit of Mt. St. Helens was replaced by a horseshoe-shaped crater 2,460 feet deep.

May 25-27, 1980 – Mammoth Lakes, California. Three earthquakes hit the area on May 25, at magnitudes 5.8, 6.1, and 5.9. A 6.0 quake hits on May 27.

June-September 1980 – Heat Wave, Southern U.S. An estimated 10,000 people are killed during the summer in a long heat wave and drought. Damages total about $20 billion.

August 4-11, 1980 – Hurricane Allen. Caribbean/Texas. Hurricane Allen is the strongest hurricane of the 1980 Atlantic hurricane season. It is one of the strongest hurricanes in recorded history and one of the few hurricanes to reach Category 5 status on three separate occasions. Allen is the second of only two hurricanes in the recorded history of the Atlantic basin to achieve sustained winds of 190 mph. Hurricane Allen causes $2.6 billion dollars in damage and kills at least 271 people.

August-September 1980 – Landslides. Following heavy and continuous rain on August 27 and September 3-4, landslides in Darjeeling, India kill 250 people.

October 10, 1980 – Algeria. The El Asnam earthquake. A 6.5 magnitude earthquake strikes killing 2,500 people and injuring more than 7,000.

November 8, 1980 – Gorda Plate, California, west of Eureka. A 7.2 magnitude quake hits.

November 23, 1980 – Irpinia, Southern Italy. A 6.8 magnitude earthquake hits the village of Conza, killing 2,914 people, injuring more than 10,000 and leaving 300,000 homeless.

Man vs. Man / Wars:

Assassinated – Liberia. William R. Tolbert, Jr., **President of Liberia** is executed in a military coup on April 12. Tolbert was overthrown by military mutineers **led by Samuel Kanyon Doe** who then took over the country. Within two weeks more than a dozen officials of Tolberts' regime, mostly of Americo-Liberian descent, are put on trial in a kangaroo court and sentenced to death. They were not allowed to a defense and had no right to appeal. They are publicly executed. Samuel Doe personally killed President Tolbert during the coup.

Under President Doe, Liberian ports are opened to Canadian, Chinese and European ships. This generates substantial investment from foreign shipping firms and earns Liberia a reputation as a tax haven.

The U.S. will cut off aid to President Doe's government in the late 1980's when accusations of human rights abuses, mismanagement and rampant corruption become common knowledge. On September 9, 1990, deposed Liberian strongman Samuel Kanyon Doe is tortured and executed in Monrovia by the members of the coup that overthrew him. It is all gruesomely filmed.

March 1980 – El Salvador. Archbishop Oscar Romero is assassinated in March.

1978-1980 – Abscam is the FBI's operational name for its 1980 **"Arab Scam" sting.** The sting uses **FBI agents** posing as two fictitious sheiks seeking to bribe local, state and federal officials. Seven members of Congress will wish they had just said, No.

An FBI agent masquerading as "Sheik Kambir Abdul Rahman" and other agents masquerading as his American employees said they had millions of dollars in a Chase Manhattan bank account that they wished to invest in an American titanium mine, **New Jersey casinos** and East Coast port facilities. They also wanted to bribe various local, state and federal officials in order to facilitate and protect their investments. Another FBI agent played sheik Yasser Habib, who claimed he was going to flee from his country and sought asylum in the U.S. for himself and his wealth. The sting lasted 23 months, involved 100 agents and cost $800,000. Nineteen people, including seven members of Congress and at least one Senator were eventually convicted in the Abscam case in 1980 and 1981.

1980 – Representative Richard Kelly (R-Florida) is **indicted** for bribery, conspiracy and violation of the Travel Act in **ABSCAM.** Kelly was filmed stuffing $25,000 into his suit and asking the "sheik's men" if it showed. He is convicted in 1981, but his motion for dismissal of the indictment was granted on the grounds that the government violated due process in its investigation.

1980 – Representative Michael Myers (D-Pennsylvania) is **indicted** for taking a bribe. Another $50,000 **ABSCAM** bribe-taker Meyers is indicted for bribery, conspiracy and violation of the Travel Act. He is sentenced to three years in prison and fined $20,000. The House voted to expel him with a vote of 376/30. Meyers became the first sitting member of the U.S. House of Representatives to be expelled since the Civil War.

October 30, 1980 – Senator Harrison 'Pete' Williams (D-New Jersey) is **indicted** on charges of conspiracy to defraud the government, bribery, receiving unlawful gratuity & illegal compensation, inter-state travel to commit bribery & aid racketeering

On May 1, 1981, Senator Williams is **convicted** in ABSCAM of bribery, receiving an unlawful gratuity, receiving illegal compensation, interstate travel to commit

bribery, and interstate travel to aid racketeering. Williams agreed to a scheme involving receipt of a loan and stock certificates from "Arab businessmen" for a titanium mine in return for political favors. He is sentenced to **three years in prison** and will be the first Senator to actually serve time in prison in 80 years.

June 18, 1980 – Representative John M. Murphy (D-New York) is **indicted** on charges of influence-peddling, accepting outside money to perform official duties, aiding racketeering receipt of unlawful gratuity, bribery. He was filmed taking a $50,000 bribe in ABSCAM. On December 3, he is **convicted** of conspiracy to demand and accept money to influence the performance of his official duties, acceptance of outside compensation for the performance of his official duties, and receiving an unlawful gratuity. He is sentenced to three years in prison and fined $20,000.

1980 – Representative Frank Thompson Jr. (D-New Jersey) is **indicted** on charges of influence-peddling, accepting outside money to perform official duties, aiding racketeering receipt of unlawful gratuity, and bribery. After 13 terms in which he built a reputation as a powerful advocate of liberal causes in the House of Representatives, he is **convicted** in December 1980. Several charges are dismissed. He subsequently served two years of a three-year prison sentence.

July 1980 – Representative John W. Jenrette Jr. (D- South Carolina) is **indicted** on bribery, conspiracy, and violating the Travel Act. He accepted $50,000 from undercover FBI agent posing as Middle Eastern businessman (ABSCAM). He is **convicted** on October 7, 1980, on all counts and sentenced to two years in prison.

May 1980 – Representative Raymond R. Lederer (D- Pennsylvania) is **indicted** on influence-peddling, bribery, conspiracy, accepting illegal gratuity, aiding racketeering, He is **convicted** January 1, 1981 and sentenced to three years in prison and fined $20,000. Lederer served ten months in Allenwood Prison. Raymond Lederer had served in the same seat that had been occupied by both his father and older brother and then filled by his sister-in-law. The family business.

1980 – Colombia, Peru, Ecuador. Serial Killer. Pedro López is a Colombian-born confessed serial killer, accused of killing more than 300 women across South America. López became known as the **"Monster of the Andes"** in 1980 when he led police to the graves of 53 of his victims in **Ecuador,** all girls between nine and twelve years old. In 1983 he was found guilty of murdering 110 young girls in Ecuador alone and confessed to a further 240 murders of missing girls in neighboring **Peru** and **Colombia.**

September 13, 1980 – A Delta Air Lines flight from New Orleans, bound for Atlanta, is hijacked. The pilot flies to Havana where the hijackers are taken from the plane and the flight, with 81 passengers, continues to Atlanta, Georgia.

May 5, 1980 – Iranian Embassy, London, England. Iranian terrorists take over the Iranian Embassy in London, holding 26 hostages, 2 of whom die on May 5th after being tortured. The siege ends when **British SAS commandos and police** storm the building. Five Iranian gunmen are killed and one is arrested. Nineteen hostages are set free but one died and two were injured in the cross-fire. Much of the Embassy was destroyed by fire as millions of people watched the rescue live on television when all programming was interrupted to show the real-life drama unfold.

1980 – The Iran-Iraq War.Saddam Hussein launches war against Iran over oil rights and control of the Shatt al Arab waterway, an essential resource providing water and transportation that runs along the border of both countries. Half a million Iraqi and Iranian soldiers and civilians died in the eight year war. Many more were injured and in the end, nothing changed very much.

The War was fought much like WWI, including large scale trench warfare, manned machine-gun posts, bayonet charges, and Iraq's extensive use of chemical weapons.

In February 2003, The National Security Archive at George Washington University published a series of declassified U.S. documents detailing the **U.S. and Saddam Hussein** in the early 1980's. The documents show that while the Reagan administration is supporting Saddam Hussein he invades Iraq, wants to develop nuclear weapons, harbors known terrorists in Bagdad, murders his own citizens, and uses chemical weapons on Iranians. The Reagan administrations' response is to send Donald Rumsfeld to shake Saddam's hand and support him with U.S. "intelligence."

1980

Reports on Iraqi chemical weapons use are concurrent with the **Reagan administration's decision to support Iraq,** and decision directives signed by President Reagan reveal the specific U.S. priorities for the region are preserving access to oil, expanding U.S. ability to project military power in the region, and protecting local allies from internal and external threats.

1980 – Chad. A series of four international conferences held first under Nigerian and then Organization of African Unity sponsorship attempted to bring the Chadian factions together. None of the parties trusted each other and the intense rivalry between Former Prime Minister Hissein Habré and President Goukouni insured failure.

In 1980 **former Prime Minister Hissein Habré's guerrilla forces** have been at war with **President Goukouni's National Army** in the Chad Capital for almost one year when **Libya sends 15,000 troops** at the request of President Goukouni. By the end of 1980 the Libyian troops have control of the Capital and Former Prime Minister Hissein Habré, flees to Sudan, vowing to resume the guerrilla war.

Economic assistance from Libya never materializes, Qaddafi is suspected of helping both sides in the war, and Libya is still trying to retake land that it lost to Chad over 100 years ago. President Goukouni tells the Libyian troops to leave the country and seeks help from the OAU and France.

From 1979 to 1982, Chad will experience unprecedented change and spiraling violence. Southerners finally lost control of what remained of the Chadian government, while civil conflicts became significantly more internationalized.

January 31, 1980 – Guatemala. Spanish Embassy Deaths. The Church, which had supported earlier **dictatorships,** began to defend Indians and workers against random executions and genocide. A group of K'iche' and Ixil Indians made their way to Guatemala City to denounce the kidnapping and murder of nine peasants from the municipality of Uspantán, El Quiché. To the government of **Lucas García,** this is an act of rebellion. Protesters were denied a hearing in Congress and **their legal adviser was assassinated** outside of police headquarters. Protestors then took hostages and barricaded themselves inside the ambassador's office of the Spanish Embassy to gain media attention that will allow them to inform the rest of the world.

President Lucas García, police chief Germán Chupina Barahona, and Minister of the Interior Donaldo Alvarez Ruíz decided to use force to clear the Embassy. The police charged, hurling incendiary devices and Molotov cocktails starting an explosive inferno that trapped the protestors and their captives. Screams could be heard but the police refused to unblock the doors or allow firemen to put out the blaze. Thirty-nine people were **burned alive** including protesters and hostages. Then things got worse. The Guatemalan **government continued killing people it felt may be a threat.** They killed unionists, students, intellectuals or anyone else who continued to participate in the mass opposition movement. The killing increased in 1980 and 1981. There were 18,000 people killed in 1982 alone and people were kidnapped on the city's streets with alarming frequency. The protests continued and hardly a day went by when the newspapers did not report on a political disappearance or the appearance of a mutilated corpse in the metropolitan area.

2009 – A U.N.-backed truth commission found that about 200,000 people were killed and more than 40,000 disappeared during Guatemala's 36-year Civil War that ended in 1996. The killings peaked in the mid-1980s. Many of the victims were ethnic Mayans.

1980 – Guinea-Bissau. A Military coup led by Joao Bernardo Viera deposed President Luis Cabral of the Republic of Guinea-Bissau. Viera will be President on and off until he is killed in 2009. President Viera worked with the Colombian cartels that took advantage of the country's feeble law-and-order institutions.**Guinea-Bissau,** one of the world's poorest states, becomes a major cocaine **smuggling route** to Europe.

1980 – India. Assam Rebellion. The United Liberation Front of Assam was formed in April 1979 in response to an influx of non-Assamese from Bangladesh and parts of North East India. This movement seeks to evict those "foreigners" and seek greater autonomy from the Indian government.

1980 – Iraq. Thousands of people opposed to the Ba'th regime are detained, and hundreds of Communist militants "disappeared" or were killed. After Iraq's Ba'th government ordered the Iraqi military to attack Iran in September 1980, the surviving Communist Party of Iraq leaders decided to retreat into Iraqi Kurdistan and form an alliance with Kurdish nationalist activists in Iraq. In 1981, the Communist Party of Iraq then expressed its support for the overthrow of the Ba'th regime.

1980 – Jamaica. Political Culture of Violence. Michael Manley is the **Prime Minister** when Jamaica experiences a significant escalation of its **political culture of violence.** A bloody struggle which began before the 1976 election between Manley's People's National Party and Edward Seaga's Jamaica Labour Party finally ends when Seaga is installed as Prime Minister in 1980. Close to 800 Jamaicans are killed as armed gangs from both parties roam the urban areas in search of "votes."

August 1980 – Libya. Libyan Army Revolt. Col. Moammar Qadhafi quickly suppresses an unsuccessful army revolt and several hundred people are killed. After the French-led plan ends in disaster the head of the French secret service, Colonel Alain de Gaigneronde de Marolles, resigns.

1980 – The Maldives Coup is an attempt by a group of Maldivians, led by Abdullah Luthufi and assisted by about 80 armed mercenaries of a Sri Lankan secessionist organization, to overthrow the government of the island republic of Maldives. The coup is foiled after Indian forces are invited by the Maldivian government to intervene.

1980 – Morocco vs. the Sahrawi rebel movement. Working for the independence of Western Sahara from Morocco, the Algeria-backed Polisario Front proclaimed the Sahrawi Arab Democratic Republic on February 27, 1976, and waged a guerrilla war against both Morocco and Mauritania. In 1978 the Mauritania government was removed in a coup d'état led by war-weary military officers who agreed to a cease fire.

    King Hassan II of Morocco immediately claimed the area of Western Sahara evacuated by the Mauritania government and began building a huge sand wall to keep the Polisario troops back. The Moroccan Wall is home to an army roughly the same size as the entire Sahrawi population and encloses the economically useful parts of Western Sahara. Although neither side could now "win" the continued artillery strikes and sniping attacks by the guerrillas strains Morocco economically and politically. From 1975-1980 over 7,000 people are killed.

December 1980 – Nigeria. Maitatsine Rioting. Followers of the Maitatsine, a quasi-Muslim fringe group sparked religious riots in Kano. The disturbance in Kano is responsible for the deaths of 4,177 people, from December 18-29.

1980 – Peruvian Civil War. Peru returns to civilian rule with the re-election of Fernando Belaunde as President, and the **Shining Path** guerrillas begin an armed struggle. In 2000 the Peruvian human rights ombudsman's office says **4,000 people have "disappeared"** since 1980 in war against left-wing rebels.

1980-1981 – Poland. Solidarity Movement. Strikes occur in the summer of 1980 in Poland, leading to the establishment of independent trade unions and extensions of civic freedoms. The strikes in Poland show there are ways non-violent protests can be effectively employed for a deep transformation of a political system.

May 17, 1980 – South Korea. Gwangju Uprising. A civil uprising against military rulers takes place in the southwestern city of Gwangju. It is the start of a ten-day bloody conflict between soldiers and citizens.

Former **President Park Chung-hee** was **assassinated** in October of 1979, ending his 18 years of dictatorial rule and for a very short time there was hope for democracy. **General Chun Doo-hwan** launched a military coup in December 1979 and took power. Many campus rallies and violent street clashes between students and the police followed, as hopes for democratization quickly faded away.

General Chun declares martial law on May 17, and students in Gwangju protest against the closing of the Chonnam National University. The armed forces block the University in a violent response that unifies people in massive rallies around the entire city until additional troops are dispatched to Gwangju where they brutally suppress the protesters. More than 200 people are killed, 400 people are missing and thousands are wounded.

February 25, 1980 – Surinam. Military Coup. After the government's refusal to sanction trade union activity within the armed forces, **the elected government is overthrown** by 16 noncommissioned officers. The military-dominated government then suspends the constitution, dissolves the legislature, and forms a regime which rules by decree. Although a civilian occupies the Presidency, **Desi Bouterse and the**

military actually rule the country. The coup is welcomed by most of the population and after the new Cabinet proclaimed that Suriname would return to democracy in two years, the Dutch government agreed to finance an emergency development program.

As the government is pressured to return to civilian rule in 1982, they respond by arresting and executing 15 prominent opposition leaders, including journalists, lawyers, and trade union leaders.

March 23, 2009 - **The Committee for the Remembrance of Victims in Surinam** is to investigate whether it is possible to bring the Netherlands before the International Court of Justice. Speaking on Dutch radio, the committee's chairman Romeo Hoost said the charges would concern the Dutch role in the coup staged in Surinam by Desi Bouterse in 1980. The then Dutch ambassador to the former Dutch colony, Max Vegelin van Claerbergen, confirmed last week in a history program on public NPS television that the chief of the Dutch military mission Colonel Hans Valk was the brains behind the coup.

1980 1998 – Syria has nearly 2 million Kurds in residence and backs the PKK, when its leader Abdullah Ocalan, retreats across the border into Syria. Damascus allows safe haven and trains **Turkey's PKK terrorists** as the PKK wage an armed guerrilla battle against Turkey with the aim of creating a Kurdish state. They concentrate their activities in the **Bekaa Valley,** a central **Lebanese region** controlled until recently by Syria. Here, the rebel army not only trained in terrorist tactics, but also **cultivated** and sold **opium** to fund its operations. The Bekaa Valley is an incredibly beautiful land known for its wheat, barley, vegetables, citrus, grapes, apples, apricots, sugar beet, tobacco, olives, and poppies (heroin). The Bekaa Valley has a long history of drug cultivation and sales going back to Roman times.

1980 – Turkey. The violence from 1980-2000 started with the massacre of the leader of the Communist Party of Turkey Mustafa Suphia and his 14 comrades on **January 29, 1921.** What followed were massacres in Nasturi in **1924** and Seyh Sait in **1925.** The number of people who were executed by the Independence Courts is unclear. In Turkey, massacres such as the ones in Agri in **1926** and Dersim in **1938** became more common. **The March 12, 1971, Junta** is remembered as the terror years when the army generals hunted the revolutionaries and the forces that opposed it.

As the death toll increases the parliament is afraid to act. General Kenan Evren, head of the general staff and also chief of Counter-Guerrilla, takes power in a military coup d'état. General Evren names a new National Security Council, dissolves the parliament and the government. According a widely believed story in Turkey, he and his team of force commanders were named "our boys" in the CIA headquarters. After the coup U.S.-support was acknowledged by the CIA Ankara station Chief Paul Henze. After the government was overthrown, Henze is said to have cabled Washington, saying, "our boys have done it."

Thousands of people are imprisoned after the coup, as the leaders try to consolidate power and remove any opposition. Intellectuals are arrested along with hundreds of the "Grey Wolves," although many are later released in exchange for their fighting against the PKK guerrilla activities. The PKK will still be active in Turkey in 2010.

1980 – Uganda. West Nile Terror. When the rival Democratic Party was declared the victor, Obote's loyal troops **"recounted" the votes** in Obote's favor. Obote became the President of Uganda and resumed his corrupt patronage system while the people of the Buganda heartland turn to open rebellion.

An August 12, 1980 secret memo from Obote urged party members to remember "…how much the Baganda hate me personally," further proposing that "the Baganda especially should be intimidated" for "There was no way their cooperation can be solicited," and further stating how he was "…. at pains to propose that if necessary leaders of other parties should be eliminated." The **Commission of Inquiry into the Violation of Human Rights** carries the testimony of a witness who quotes Obote as having warned the people of Soroti as to the fate of those that resist, stating, "I warn you people of Soroti, if you behave like a certain tribe you know very well, I shall not hesitate at all, I will send my boys to destroy both you and your property. I repeat; I will send my boys to destroy both your lives and property. I say this for God and my country... A good Muganda is a dead one."

Colonel Museveni, immediately declared his troops to be the **National Resistance Army** and fight Obote all during his rule. It has been estimated that approximately 100,000 people died as a result of fighting between Obote's **Uganda National Liberation Army** and the guerillas **National Resistance Army**.

1980

1980 – U.S. Grain Sales. The U.S. suspends grain sales to the Soviet Union in response to their support of the **war in Afghanistan.** In 1980 U.S. grain and farm products are still among the best in the world, but by 1999 U.S companies trying to force genetically engineered food on the rest of the world meet resistance even in countries that are desperate for food.

1999 - **In Africa, a group of nations, led by Ethiopia,** are developing draft legislation that would make it illegal to export Genetically Engineered (GE) foods or crops to their countries without prior country approval, according to an article in Nature magazine August 5, 1999. This prior consent law would force GE exporters to carry out human safety, environmental, and socioeconomic studies. This initiative has drawn opposition from biotechnology corporations and grain-exporting nations, **led by the U.S.,** who consider so-called **Biosafety Protocols a restraint of trade.**

While people in the U.S. are forced to eat Genetically Engineered foods because they are hidden in most processed foods, the rest of the world is moving away from Genetically Engineered foods associated with many U.S. grains and farm products. Even the poorest of the nations are now passing regulations to stop the import of GE products. U.S. grain used to be one of the finest products in the world. And the U.S. government which should be protecting the people, leads the charge against labeling GE foods.

1980 – United States. CIA. Cocaine. In August 1996 the now-notorious series on crack cocaine in the San Jose Mercury News, by Gary Webb made the case that the CIA, through the actions of several drug-dealing Nicaraguan contras it had funded, was involved in the introduction of crack into Los Angeles during the 1980s.

1944-May 4, 1980 – Yugoslavia, Tito's Regime. During WWII in Yugoslavia the Nazis, Chetniks, Croatian Ustashi, and the communist Partisans and successor Tito regime committed massive democide. The Croatians alone may have murdered some 655,000 people, the greater majority being Serbs. The Tito regime itself killed in cold blood some 500,000 people, mainly collaborators, anti-communists, rival guerrillas, Ustasha and critics. And after the war the Tito regime probably killed even more people, including the rich, landlords, bourgeoisie, clerics, and in the later 1940s, even pro-Soviet communists.

In 1942 tens of thousands of Serbian villagers were deported to Jasenovac Concentration Camp from the Kozara mountain area in Bosnia. Most of the men were killed at Jasenovac, but women were sent to forced labor in Germany. Children were taken from their mothers and either killed or dispersed to Catholic orphanages.

Jasenovac concentration camp was a complex of five smaller camps spread over 93 square miles on the banks of the Sava River. There was a camp for children and a women's camp. Jasenovac was one of the most brutal of the concentration camps during the Holocaust. The Nazi puppet regime that ruled Croatia from 1941 to 1945 imprisoned hundreds of thousands of Serbs, Jews, Gypsies and opponents in Jasenovac and other camps

On March 16, 1944, Nazi SS Maj. Gen. Ernest Fik reported to Berlin that the Ustasha had killed between 600,000 and 700,000 concentration camp inmates "the Balkan way," implying extreme cruelty. Six months after the liberation of Belgrade, Yugoslavia's capital, by Soviet troops in September 1944, Jasenovac continued to function as a death camp. On April 22, 1945, withdrawing Ustasha troops blew up the barracks, torture chambers and other remnants of their monstrous death factory and killed the remaining 1,100 inmates, throwing their corpses into the Sava River. After the war, **Tito allowed the creation of the Jasenovac memorial grounds** but never went there himself.

Secret prisons including Goli Otok (men's prison), and Sveti Grgur (women's prison), **were kept in use until 1988 and 1980,** respectively. The civilian population was terrified of being sent to either one.

President Josip Tito dies in 1980 but the "second Yugoslavia," a socialist federation that he started will go on until 1992 when The **Socialist Federal Republic of Yugoslavia** was formally dissolved during the **Yugoslav wars** as the independent states **of Slovenia, Croatia, Republic of Macedonia** and **Bosnia** and **Herzegovina** separated from it with more deaths and innocent people being killed.

1980-1987 – Zimbabwe. Rebellion. Zimbabwe, formerly Southern Rhodesia, gains independence from a large white settler population after years of hostilities.

The first British explorers, colonists, and missionaries arrived in the 1850s, and the massive influx of foreigners led to the establishment of the territory Rhodesia, named after Cecil Rhodes of the British South Africa Company. In 1923, European settlers voted to become the self-governing British colony of Southern Rhodesia. After a brief federation with Northern Rhodesia, now Zambia, and Nyasaland, now Malawi, after WWII, Southern Rhodesia, also known as Rhodesia, chose to remain a colony when its two partners voted for independence in 1963.

The white minority in the face of war, economic sanctions, and international pressure, finally consented to hold multiracial elections in 1980, and **Robert Mugabe** won a landslide victory. The country achieved independence on April 17, 1980, under the name **Zimbabwe.**

BOOMERS: HOW WE CHANGED THE WORLD continues in **Volume 2, 1981-2010.** We're not done yet.

For those of you born between 1981-2010 What kind of world did YOU inherit? I will let you in on a secret. The world gets much better . . . and much worse.

Purchase it soon at Amazon.com or your local bookstore.

Visit our website and help use improve the content of *Your Story*.
While we cannot acknowledge all emails, we appreciate your input concerning data corrections and will try to look into all of your suggestions.

www.AlfordPress.com   **e-mail us at . . . . Boomers@AlfordPress.com** Thank you for your time.

Alford Plea – Under the law in the United States, the Alford Plea is a guilty plea in criminal court where the defendant admits that sufficient evidence exists to most likely sway a judge or jury that the defendant is guilty beyond a reasonable doubt. However, the defendant does not admit the act and still asserts innocence.
In other words: The defendant says it sure looks like he is guilty. All the evidence says he is guilty, but there must be some mistake because he still says he is innocent.
BOOMERS How We Changed The World.

www.ingramcontent.com/pod-product-compliance
Lightning Source LLC
Chambersburg PA
CBHW080808280326
41926CB00090B/4107